# KEEPING FAITH

# KEEPING FAITH

## The History of The Royal British Legion

## BRIAN HARDING

*If ye break faith with us who die*
*We shall not sleep, though poppies grow*
*In Flanders' Fields.*

From 'In Flanders Fields', John McCrae, 1915

Leo Cooper

First published in Great Britain in 2001 by
LEO COOPER
an imprint of Pen & Sword Books
Church Street
Barnsley, South Yorkshire S70 2AS

Copyright © The Royal British Legion 2001

A CIP record of this book is available from the British Library

ISBN 085052 826 7

Printed by

CPI UK

To the Members of the Legion
and the many devoted Poppy Appeal workers
who, remembering past sacrifice, have
kept faith

# Contents

## PART III – 1971-2001 – A NATIONAL INSTITUTION

# Preface

For eighty years the Legion has advanced on a broad front. Its activities have ranged from making poppies to discussions with Hitler and from running convalescent homes to resettling young men leaving the services. It has fought for changes in Parliamentary legislation and clothed penniless ex-officers. Its work has been, and remains, local, national and international. Such diversity has indicated the layout of this book. Each principal function is dealt with separately over the same period of time. The first twenty-five years start with the Legion's beginnings in the aftermath of the First World War; the next quarter century is heralded by the arrival of the welfare state, and the final period begins with the grant of the Royal title in 1971.

The principal sources have been contemporary documents. The Legion's Annual Report is the main authority. The minutes of the National (Executive) Council provide a useful and sometimes revealing insight, while the Legion magazine under its various titles enlivens the scene as well as containing much other useful material. These three complement each other, but it is still necessary to read between the lines on occasion; I have found my time on the Legion staff useful in this respect.

I am indebted to the Secretary General, Ian Townsend, and those at Legion headquarters and in the field for their assistance, as well as to the staffs of the Officers' Association and the Women's Section. In particular I would like to thank Jonathan Powell and George McGilvery for their support for the project and for unearthing the source documents, a task that should not be underestimated. I am especially grateful for the help of the gallant team who comprised the advisory panel: Dennis Cadman, Colonel Jimmy Hughes, Dame Mary Bridges, Captain Patrick Mitford-Slade, Michael Day and Lieutenant Colonel John Franklin; they undertook the chore of reading the draft and their observations and suggestions have been invaluable. Not least must I thank the Officers and Council of the Legion who entrusted me with this task and who have supported me throughout.

Lastly my thanks are due to my wife, whose contribution has been decidedly practical: by urging me on to the tennis court at the end of each day's work she has kept me fit enough to finish the task.

Cothill, Oxfordshire.                                             BCMH
June 2001

# Abbreviations

Where less common abbreviations are used in the text they are first preceded by the full title. But the following list may assist the reader:

| | |
|---|---|
| ATS | Auxiliary Territorial Service |
| BCEL | British Commonwealth Ex-Services League |
| BESL | British Empire Services League |
| CEAC | *Confederation Européenne des Anciens Combattants* |
| CFO | County Field Officer |
| CIP | *Comité Internationale Permanente* |
| COBSEO | Confederation of British Service and Ex-service Organizations |
| FEPOW | Far Eastern Prisoner of War |
| FIDAC | *Fédération Interalliée des Anciens Combattants* |
| GS | General Secretary |
| ICEO | International Committee of European Organizations |
| MOD | Ministry of Defence |
| NEC | National Executive Council |
| NUX | National Union of Ex-servicemen |
| OA | Officers' Association |
| RAFA | Royal Air Forces Association |
| RSL | Returned Services League (of Australia) |
| SG | Secretary General |
| SSAFA | The Soldiers, Sailors, Airmen and Families Association |
| TA | Territorial Army |
| TSRO | Tri-Services Resettlement Organization |
| UNC | Union Nationale des Combattants |
| VAD | Voluntary Aid Detachment |
| VdK | *Verband deutscher Kriegsbeschädigten* |
| WRAC | Women's Royal Army Corps |
| WRNS | Women's Royal Naval Service |
| WVF | World Veterans Federation |

## Use of upper case

In order to avoid confusion upper case has been used in the following instances:

| | | |
|---|---|---|
| Area | signifies | a Legion Area |
| County | " | a Legion County |
| Conference | " | The Legion's Annual Conference |

# PART I

## 1921–1945

# THE FIGHT FOR JUSTICE

# CHAPTER 1

## The Forming of the Legion

# *In Unity Lies Strength*[1]

### At the Cenotaph

As the hands of Big Ben crept towards nine o' clock on the morning of Sunday 15 May 1921 the rain beat down on nearby Whitehall where a group of several hundred men had defied the weather to gather around the Cenotaph. Six months earlier great crowds had assembled there when the procession taking the coffin of the Unknown Warrior of the Great War to Westminster Abbey had paused for the memorial's unveiling. But now the wet pavements held few onlookers.

On the strike of the hour four men stepped forward. Each carried a laurel wreath and together they laid them at the base of the Cenotaph, stepping back for a moment before inclining their heads. When the last chime had died away four buglers of the Grenadier Guards sounded the Last Post and when those echoes too were silent the men rejoined their comrades.

Thus was an accord solemnly sealed. It was the agreement to found the British Legion.

★      ★      ★

What did the actions of the four symbolize? The answer lay at the centre of each wreath; not the badge of a ship or regiment, but the device of an ex-service organization. Placed side by side at the Cenotaph, they represented the union of four associations formed during and immediately after the Great War. Each had agreed to set aside its own interests so that all might benefit.

And what were these associations? They embodied a new approach to the plight of the ex-serviceman. Earlier wars, and their often appalling consequences – not only for those who had fought in them but for their families – had led to the formation of organizations such as the Soldiers' and Sailors' Families Association and the Royal Patriotic Fund. But these had been founded by concerned individuals in the spirit of Victorian philanthropy. The new Great War associations were different. These were the men themselves, joined together in a spirit of self-help based on their wartime comradeship. Yet, there was also to be an element of philanthropy present.

### The Great War

The Great War of 1914-18 was unlike any previous war. It involved the whole nation. As the continental powers poured more and more men into the field so Britain found itself for the first time raising an army of millions. The 'contemptible' little British regular army, having conducted its heroic fighting retreat to Mons, was relieved by Kitchener's New Armies raised from volunteers whose patriotism 'matched the hour' and later, when the artillery and machine guns of the Western Front and the Dardanelles had taken their toll, there was conscription.

Such rapid expansion was matched by huge numbers of casualties. In the four years of war more than two million homes would be affected by disablement or death. In the early years, the authorities, whose resources also had to be rapidly augmented, were by no means on top of the situation. There was muddle. There were mistakes and delays in paying widows' pensions, in assessing the effects of wounds or illness and in awarding pensions to the incapacitated. Those affected included the families, many of whom had no other form of income once the service pay book had been withdrawn. Afer two years of war, with more and more suffering and no end in sight, there was a reaction.

## The first of the new movements

The *National Association of Discharged Sailors and Soldiers*, formed at Blackburn in 1916, was unique. It cut across the traditional service and regimental boundaries, owing no allegiance to anyone except those it intended to assist – the ex-servicemen and their families. And, since it presumably saw its purpose on behalf of the ex-servicemen as reflecting what the trade unions and their political arm – the Labour Party – sought to achieve for the workers, the new Association looked to these organizations for support. It formed links with both.

The next year, 1917, saw an intensification of the war. The offensive which became known as First and Second Ypres was intended to turn the German flank. But all the factors favoured the defence and the attacks slithered to a halt in the muddy confusion of Passchendale, with appalling casualties.

The need for fresh manpower was now paramount. The Military Service Act of 1917 involved recalling to duty those discharged soldiers or sailors who were in civil employment. The argument was that if they were fit enough for civilian jobs they could equally well be employed by the military in an administrative post, thus releasing someone else for the front line. There was undeniably some logic to the idea, but those men affected by the Act saw it as a gross injustice. They had 'done their bit' – and many had been discharged as a direct result of a wound. They subscribed, not unreasonably, to the view that there were many others who should be called to the colours before them.

The issue was taken up by Liberal MPs and the Act was modified. But in the process a further ex-service organization came into being: the *National Federation of Discharged and Demobilized Sailors and Soldiers*. The Federation had strong roots in central and east London, but it also covered Scotland, Ireland and Wales, no doubt making use of its Liberal Party connections.

There were now therefore two 'national' organizations in being. Both had overt political links and, it must be presumed, were regarded by the political parties concerned as likely to form a useful extension of their support base after the war. And both were 'membership' organizations, composed of people who had banded together with the intention of helping themselves and others in the same situation. In this they were unlike the conventional charity.

Their differences were not only geographical and political (the one northern and Labour, the other London-based and Liberal): the Association admitted officers, whereas the Federation only took those officers who had been commissioned from the ranks, known as 'ranker officers'. This anti-officer attitude in the Federation may have reflected the politicians' misunderstanding of relationships in the armed services; but whatever the cause it was to persist into the Legion era and surface from time to time.

## The reaction – a third force

The existence of two politically inclined national ex-service organizations and the force of the campaign against the Military Service Act undoubtedly gave the authorities food for thought. The revolution which had broken out in Russia in March 1917 was based on war-weariness and had made use of disaffected servicemen. Political groupings of former soldiers and sailors raised at the very least the spectre of instability when the vast armies returned home.

The response by some of those at the heart of the nation's affairs – whom we would now term 'the Establishment' – was to form a third group. Although this further body was not officially sponsored by the government, it clearly had their tacit approval. No less a worthy than the Secretary of State for War presided over the inaugural meeting, albeit in a private capacity. The main movers were two MPs, both former colonels, and the launch included a letter to every Lord Lieutenant.

In such circumstances it is perhaps surprising that this third element, entitled the *Comrades of The Great War*, received its fair measure of support from the rank and file. But this was a non-political organization and even in a citizen army there were many who preferred to follow their traditional leaders. Furthermore, it was promoted to the troops in France by the charismatic Captain Towse, a blinded VC of the Boer War and a national hero, who became Chairman.

Thus, despite its paternalistic overtones, the new organization flourished. It certainly had ample resources; among its sponsors were the Duke of Westminster and three newspaper magnates (Lords Rothermere and Northcliffe, and Major Gavin Astor whose family owned *The Times*). If nothing else, the Comrades seemed assured of a good press.

By the end of 1917, therefore, the war had spawned three ex-service organizations: the first two – the Association and the Federation – were a response to the problems faced by discharged soldiers and sailors, but their political connections had provoked a reaction which resulted in a third organization    the Comrades – with no party affiliations but nevertheless with powerful patronage. Each of the bodies had distinctive roots and there was little love lost between them; sadly such divisions were hardly likely to improve the cause of the ex-serviceman and his family.

## The prospect of unity

Possibly because it was the least strong of the three, the Association began to think in terms of unity in 1918. But there were still many in the Federation and Comrades who thought that amalgamation was neither desirable nor practicable, among them no doubt some office-holders who feared a diminution of their own status. All the signs were that unity  would be a stony path to tread – and so it proved.

The process was one of evolution, but it owed much to the vision and determination of two individuals whose backgrounds could not have been more different. Field Marshal Earl Haig had been the resolute British commander in France and was acclaimed a national hero when victory came in November 1918. Mr TF Lister's wartime profile was somewhat lower; he had not even risen from the ranks before being wounded and discharged in 1916; but he was President of the Federation and, while Haig's prestige would underwrite the unity concept, Lister's negotiating skills would prove vital in overcoming the antipathy between the factions. In a sense Haig, although he would simply have regarded it as his duty, represented the element of philanthropy, while Lister embodied the self-help principle.

The story of the fusion of these independent bodies into one great national organization is not straightforward, nor are the events themselves a simple progression. But three phases can be identified: the first comprised outside attempts to impose unity, which were rejected; the second represented a shift in attitude brought on by events elsewhere; the third and final phase was an initiative to exploit this new mood.

## The First Phase – external attempts

In the summer of 1918, with the the war still in progress, a retired officer – a Major Jellicorse – persuaded a distinguished general, Sir Horace Smith-Dorrien (who, interestingly, had been removed from command of the Second Army in France for baulking at what he believed to be unnecessary casualties) to chair a meeting of the leaders of the three organizations in order to explore the idea of unity. The meeting took place, but there was little common ground.

With the arrival of peace there was a further attempt, this time at the behest of the three service departments – the Admiralty, the War Office and the newly formed Air Ministry. During the war a considerable amount of money had been accumulated in canteen profits. The service authorites wished to use the money for benevolent work and in February 1919 they sought the help of the ex-service organizations. The idea seems to have been to involve the three bodies in an officially sponsored 'Empire Services League', a move which would also bring them 'on side' with the authorities. This time General Sir Ian Hamilton, who had commanded the ill-fated Dardenelles operations, presided. But even Hamilton's lively personality did not win them over; although the Comrades were prepared to go along with the idea, the other two declined, no doubt sensing that such an involvement would conflict with their political connections.

Winston Churchill, the new Secretary of State for War, then came on the scene. Changing the tactics, he engineered a move to bring the Comrades and the Federation together, perhaps thinking that they had more in common with each other than with the trade union-connected Association, which was anyway the weakest of the three. If so, he miscalculated; again there was no accord.

Thus ended the first phase. All direct attempts to secure the objective of unity had failed. It would seem that each organization, including the Comrades, resented any move from outside, and particularly by government, to impose unity.

## The demobilization muddle

There were nonetheless good reasons for the official interest in ex-service matters at this time. Against a background of the upheavals in Russia following the Bolshevik Revolution and the dissolution of the Kaiser's Germany into near-chaos, with returning regiments about to form workers' and soldiers' councils, the government's own demobilization plans were not going well. To help re-start the economy, demobilization had been based on giving priority to the 'key men' to return to industry. Since the key men were designated by the employers the scheme was not only open to abuse but took no account of other circumstances such as length of service. It was a recipe for disorder. There were mutinies both in France and at home and armed and insubordinate soldiers descended on Whitehall. The government promptly changed the basis of demobilization, increased service pay and took other measures to defuse the situation. But the mood of the citizen army had changed: the exultation of the Armistice had been followed by anger at the muddle over the discharge arrangements and was now succeeded by grievances on return to civil life. Where was the 'land fit for heroes'? There was a housing shortage and the trade unions, strengthened by easy victories over government in wartime disputes, were unsympathetic to the employment needs of the returning soldiers and sailors. And in the civil service the vacancies left by the men who had gone to the front, as well as many of the posts in the new ministries, had been filled by women.

There was some apprehension in official circles that a disaffected army of ex-servicemen might take a lead from events in Russia and Germany, particularly as yet another organization had been formed, this time strongly left-wing – the *National Union of Ex-servicemen*. The NUX, as it was known, was born out of the turbulence associated with the original demobilization scheme. But the three original bodies, the Association, the Federation and the Comrades, had refused to climb aboard this particular bandwagon. On the contrary they contributed stability, doing their best to counteract revolutionary propaganda and giving an early glimpse of that sense of national responsibility which would temper the Legion's activities.

## The Second Phase – a change of attitude

Despite their shared outlook on such matters, as the first anniversary of the Armistice approached, the three principal ex-service bodies were no closer to unity. But now they would receive a nudge in that direction from a new quarter. The Empire Services League idea had come to naught, but the wartime canteen profits of some £7 million still needed a charitable home. The authorities therefore set up the United Services Fund under General Lord Byng. A British officer, Byng had commanded the Canadian Corps that in 1917 had at last captured Vimy Ridge – a feat that had heartened the whole army and set church bells ringing in Britain and Canada. The fund was popularly known as 'Byng's Millions'.

The USF, however, still needed help. If the three principal ex-service organizations would not merge their identities in order to help adminster the fund, at least they might be prepared to act in concert. In October 1919 Byng brought them together once more. The conference was noteworthy in three respects. First the sensitivities over status: before the discussion proper began much time was spent in establishing that the Association was still regarded as an independent body since Lord Byng had (correctly as it happens) been informed that it was 'negotiating' with the Comrades. Second the dominance in the discussions of the clear-sighted and reasonable Mr Lister who led the Federation team. Thirdly, that despite their differences, the three organizations reached an agreement as to how they would assist in ensuring the proper use of the funds. Apart from Lister's influence, this successful outcome owed much not only to General Byng's tact in handling the delegates but to his foresight in insisting that the USF would not be under government control. Appreciating that those attending the conference were particularly sensitive on this point, Lord Byng made it clear that he had only agreed to be chairman on that understanding.

The conference set up a United Services Fund field structure, dividing the country into areas, counties and districts. Although in some parts of the country only one of the ex-service organizations was represented, there were plenty of instances where the rivals found themselves working together (along with others) on USF committees in pursuit of a common purpose. And that purpose was at the core of their very existence – to administer relief to the ex-service community. Thus were the seeds of unity sown.

## Fall in the officers

Meanwhile there were the officers. Their plight will only be briefly summarized; it is set out in more detail at Chapter 8. But the action now to be taken would set in train the events which would lead to unity.

In the period immediately following the Great War the situation of former officers could be as desperate as that of any section of the community. The enormous expansion of the army, coupled with the high casualty rates among junior officers on the Western Front, had necessitated commissioning all levels of society. But the authorities had been slow to recognize the social changes in the officer corps. If their attitude towards returning soldiers was lukewarm it ignored returning officers. They would be left to fend for themselves. Hence the disgraceful spectacle, viewed by one of his former men, of an officer wearing the ribbon of the Military Cross standing in the gutter trying to sell matches and shoelaces.[2]

At this point Haig enters the stage. Up to now he had remained in the wings. But he had not been inactive: his testimony before a Commons Select Commission had brought war and war widows' pensions up to a reasonable level and his concern for the welfare of ex-servicemen and their families had impressed itself not only on the government but also on the veterans' associations. Here was the man to lead them. But, knowing the propensity of politicians to exploit disunity, Haig was not prepared to take on the task unless the associations came together. The way ahead, therefore, was to create a strong national organization, but the initiative would have to come from the bodies themselves. Nevertheless it was Haig's next move that would result in that initiative being taken.

The divisions among the men were echoed in the officers' situation. A number of organizations existed to assist officers and their widows and here Haig could become directly involved. His solution was to combine them into one body, the *Officers' Association*, on the back of a national appeal in 1920 which raised a much-needed three-quarters of a million pounds. The other organizations could have been jealous of the instant success of this move; but in fact their reaction was wholly positive. It was indeed something of a revelation; already losing membership and short of funds, they saw the effect on the public consciousness of a national movement under the guidance of a distinguished figure. This was surely the way ahead: national unity would ensure national support.

Thus two external events – the common involvement in the United Services Fund and the example set by the new Officers' Association – had focused minds on unity. The scene was set for the final phase.

## The Third Phase – the Federation initiative

The torch that Haig's action had lit was now taken up by the Federation, whose president, it will be remembered, was Mr Lister. At their annual conference in May 1920 they voted for unity, albeit by a narrow margin. This led, first, to a discussion the following month between the Federation and the Comrades, and then to the Federation inviting the other organizations to a conference. The meeting took place at the Royal United Services Institute in London in August 1920 and was the high point on the road to unity. It was attended not only by representatives of the Federation, the Association and the Comrades but also by those of the Officers' Association and the National Union of Ex-servicemen. Since the NUX was strongly left-wing in character the other representatives must have viewed it warily, particularly as it had poached a number of their members, but in the event it made little contribution to the discussion.

The conference was chaired by Lister and, although delegates included senior officers, among them some generals, he dominated the meeting, setting out the principles on which a unified ex-service organization would be based: firstly no political alliances; secondly that unity meant total integration – not simply an alliance of the four existing bodies, but their dissolution and replacement by a completely new structure. The latter stipulation cannot have been an easy pill for many of the delegates to swallow. They were proud of their organizations and most had been with them from the start. But the chairman's clarity of purpose, reasoned argument and determined yet tactful approach won through: when it came to the vote all supported unity, except for one Federation representative, and the NUX delegates who abstained and took no further part in the proceedings, no doubt reluctant to abandon their political links. Their organization then faded into obscurity.

The leaders had made their decision; even so it needed to be ratified by the grass roots of each of the four organizations concerned. But this was done with a speed that would be astonishing even with to-day's communications. A constitution was drafted in a week,* approved at a further conference and then circulated to all of the branches. After discussion at branch level each organization called a meeting of branch delegates to decide whether or not to support the proposals. By December 1920, just four months after Lister had tabled his proposals, he had his answer: the rank and file agreed in principle.

That month there was another conference of the leaders; they formed a Unity Committee comprising six representatives of each body. With no slackening of momentum, the committee was given six months to achieve its goal: it would be dissolved on 30 June 1921. Its first task was to propose the name of the new body; no less than forty-nine suggestions had been made including 'Warriors Guild', 'Imperial Federation of Comrades' and 'British Empire Services League'. But the Federation's suggestion of 'British Legion' carried the day.

The only distraction to the process was the discovery that the Officers' Association, although outwardly committed to unification, had continued to seek its own Royal Charter. This, it appeared, was to protect its funds, since they had been donated specifically for the benefit of former officers. To that extent it might well be acting properly and in the interests of its beneficiaries; the mistake was not to tell the others.

It aroused a suspicion and resentment that would resurface.

* By J.R. Griffin, then General Secretary of the Federation, and it was to form the basis of the Legion's Royal Charter.

## Unity

The curtain now rose on the final act. Each organization had individually agreed to unity; now the rank and file needed to approve the constitution of the new body. This time however their delegates spoke not under their old colours but as the representatives of all ex-servicemen in their locality, meaning that where there were two or more of the old associations in the same place they had first to meet together to elect one representative.

On this basis seven hundred delegates met for the Unity Conference on Saturday 14 May 1921 at the Queen's Hall in London, a large concert hall in Langham Place, close to the future site of the BBC's Broadcasting House. It was the Whitsun weekend, no doubt chosen to allow the maximum number of delegates to attend. Ever since, the Whit weekend* has continued in the Legion's calendar as the time of the Annual Conference and the Queen's Hall was a regular venue until it was destroyed in the Second World War; a hotel now stands on the site.

The result, after all the Unity Committee's work, was a foregone conclusion. The draft constitution was approved and the Prince of Wales elected as the Legion's Patron. Four national officers were then elected: Earl Haig as President, Mr Lister as Chairman, Colonel Crosfield as Vice Chairman and Major Brunel Cohen, MP, as Treasurer. For the first year the Unity Committee would constitute the National Executive Council, which was thus representative of the former organizations.

It is worth noting that the Patron was elected – subsequent Patrons, as reigning sovereigns, would grant their patronage – and that the election of the President was contested, the unsuccessful candidate being a Member of Parliament, Colin Coote (later Editor of the *Daily Telegraph*) who was defeated by 658 votes to 49 by the absent Field Marshal,† an indication of Haig's standing among his former comrades. The democratic nature of the new body was demonstrated by the motion to approve the constitution: it was proposed by an ex 'other rank' and seconded by a former general. At nine o' clock the following morning, at the Cenotaph, the shrine to their dead comrades, the ex-servicemen sealed their agreement.

The Legion had been born. But who did this fledgling really represent? What were its aims? And how did it propose to achieve them?

---

*Now renamed the Spring Bank Holiday.

†Haig was en route to South Africa to found the British Empire Services League – see page 141.

# CHAPTER 2

## THE LEGION AND THE NATION 1921-1945

# *The Years of Struggle*

### 1921 – 1925

### Born into hard times

The Legion's basic purpose was straightforward: to care for those who had suffered as a result of service in the armed forces in the Great War, whether through their own service or through that of a husband, father or son.

The suffering took many forms. It might be the effect of a wound on a man's ability to earn a living and support his family or a war widow's struggle to give her children an education. But even those who had come through the war unscathed were vulnerable to the employment situation in the country. As a result of the war Britain's economic position had declined. The switch of industry to war products meant that those countries formerly dependent on British goods had turned to other suppliers or had become manufacturers themselves and the clock could not be turned back. After a very short post-war boom the slump came in 1921, just as the Legion began, and in a short time unemployment reached the two million mark. Lloyd George's wartime coalition was still in office but its policy of simply letting events take their course[1] led to its replacement by

*Unemployment – an ex-serviceman tries to make a living with a dancing dog and a gramophone. A street scene after the Great War.*

a Conservative government that year. Their policies also failed and a general election at the beginning of 1924 resulted in the country's first Labour administration. It lasted ten months and in October 1924 the Conservatives were back under Stanley Baldwin. Not only the economic state of the country but the resulting political turbulence were to exacerbate the difficulties that the Legion faced.

In this unpromising situation the Legion was assuming responsibilities towards perhaps twenty million people. Over six million men had served in the war, 725,000 never to return. Of those who came back nearly one and three-quarter million had suffered a disability of some kind, of whom half were permanently disabled.[2] To this figure had to be added those who depended on those six million – the wives and the children, the widows and the orphans, as well as the parents who had lost sons in the war, on whom they were often financially dependent.

Thus, when the Legion's leaders looked around them in July 1921, not only did they see a gigantic task but one made infinitely more difficult by the clouds of economic depression that lay thick overhead. Furthermore their purpose was not confined to looking after those who had suffered in the recent war; the National Executive Council's programme,[3] set out at their first meeting, sought to prevent further sacrifice by reminding the nation of the human cost of war. More than this, they intended to work actively for peace, a perhaps unusual aim in an ex-service movement, but very much representative of the feelings of all those who had fought in the Great War. This policy would bring the organization into the international arena in the years that followed.

### Early days

An active campaign to secure justice and to prevent war was all very well, but the immediate need was to help those who had fought and their families, most of all the widows and orphans. Government provision was inadequate and often denied through ill-framed rules. In this situation the Legion required both organization and money.

Within the overall structure the network of branches gradually developed, enabling the Legion to bring relief to those in need, while the rising membership lent the organization strength in its dealings with the government of the day. But it was not as strong as it would have wished. Far from every ex-serviceman being a Legion member, some four years after its formation only one in every twenty-five veterans had joined and in 1926, the year of the General Strike, the numbers acually went down; but happily for the Legion's campaigning it was more than once assumed by the press that its membership was of the order of a million, even at a time when it might have been less than a quarter of that figure.

The remarkable success of the first Poppy Day in November 1921, described at page 122, provided the money for the relief which was so desperately needed while the symbol itself struck a chord with the public which has lasted ever since. There were some early campaigning* successes, the most important of which was to pressurize the government into keeping war disability pensions rates at their existing level despite a fall in living costs. Other endeavours were less successful: despite enormous efforts the Legion could not persuade successive governments to remove patently unfair restrictions in the pensions rules, although it was able to reduce their impact. Nevertheless in its early years the organization showed a remarkable vigour in getting to grips with the problems of the time, urged on by its membership who had no hesitation in expressing their views at the annual conference; they saw too many appalling situations at first hand.

---

* The Legion's principal campaigns are set out at Table C on page 434.

## A brush with politics

On the eve of the first General Election after its formation, that of 15 November 1922 which followed the collapse of Lloyd George's post-war coalition, Legion headquarters wrote to every branch emphasizing that, although the organization was strictly non party-political, branches should nevertheless find out the views of parliamentary candidates on ex-service matters and make them known to their members so that they might be taken into account when voting. The letter was accompanied by a questionnaire prepared by the National Executive Council containing thirteen issues to be put to the candidate. After the branch had digested the replies, they were to be forwarded to headquarters to be filed for future reference.[4]

On the face of it the exercise was a good one. It exploited the Legion's organization and focused prospective MPs on ex-service issues (and on the Legion itself), all without departing from the Legion's strict non party-political stance. Furthermore those elected could be held to account. Nor did it affect members' political freedom: as the National Chairman pointed out at an Area conference, 'Every member of the Legion has a perfect right to follow the dictates of his conscience on political question (as long as he is not) speaking on behalf of any branch of the British Legion.'[5]

A policy which rested on a Legion member, when casting his vote, simply taking into account a candidate's view on ex-service matters, was reasonably straightforward. However, the chairman then ventured into deeper waters. Referring to the questionnaire, he stated that it was within a branch's right actively to support a candidate who had shown support for the Legion's policies as opposed to one whose replies were unfavourable or who had declined to answer. Put into practice, this had the inevitable result: the Legion was subsequently accused in the press of playing party politics. In fact the external damage was limited; the main danger was the divisions that might have been created within the organization.

To some extent this attempt to exercise the power of the ex-service vote was understandable: the Legion was faced with an immense task and desperately needed support at Westminster. But it had come perilously close to political entanglement in direct contravention of its own constitution. Moreover, any expectation that a signed set of responses would assure the Legion of a member's support was misplaced. The party whips would see to that.

Neither the questionnaire nor the advice to branches to back particular candidates were repeated and from then on the Legion kept scrupulously clear of political involvement. Before long this policy was to earn approbation.

## Reaction to the Legion's work

Whatever the Legion's level of political sophistication, by the mid-1920s it was beginning to make some practical progress. 'The Legion may congratulate itself on what it has achieved' stated *The Times* in a report on the 1924 Annual Conference, and 'with even more satisfaction . . . look back on the concessions which it has won from Government Departments', going on to say that 'it was a real asset to the country as a whole' and contrasting the Legion's example as an organization 'drawn from men of all ranks' with those who promoted 'class war as the only war that matters'. The sentiments were echoed in the provincial press and a number of papers laid particular emphasis on the Legion's non-political stance.[6] Further testimony as to its political independence came from a former Prime Minister. Replying to a query from a Legion branch chairman,

Mr Ramsay MacDonald, the leader of the Labour party, noted that any friction between party members and those of the Legion arose from 'local mishandling', and went on to assert that 'so far as my own personal experience has gone, I am glad to say that I have always received from the Legion and its officials the most friendly consideration, and I have found them to be anxious to observe with strict rectitude the declarations of the Legion that it is independent of all political parties and allows its members the fullest freedom to choose their politics in accordance with their own reason and conscience'.[7] The sentiments may have been a touch ponderous, but they were no less genuine.

Not all, however, held the same views. Some perceived it as an organization to hold the ex-servicemen together in the event of a national emergency. A delegate told the 1924 conference that a local union secretary had accused the Legion as being 'nothing more or less than Haig's White Guards', a reference to those who had attempted to overturn the Bolshevik revolution in Russia. This may have been the old antipathy between the ex-service and union interests re-surfacing but it was sufficiently serious for the Legion's National Executive Council to investigate this anti-Legion 'subversive propaganda' and devise means of combatting it,[8] although in the event the problem seems simply to have gone away by itself.

Often the Legion's greatest critics were the members themselves. Delegates at the 1923 Annual Conference reflected the general frustration at the employment situation: 'not sufficient push', 'too much education, not enough action'; the leadership needed 'more force, more spirit and more manhood'. It showed a fundamental difference over tactics that in many ways reflected the Legion's mixed parentage: philanthropy and self-help. Which would get the best results – persuasion or confrontation? The arguments would continue.

Not one delegate would, however, have taken issue with the Legion's support for national remembrance for the dead of the war.

## The Legion's role in Remembrance

The Armistice that ended the Great War took effect at eleven o'clock on 11 November 1918. Eight months later, in July 1919, there was a Peace Day march through London, for which a temporary structure – a cenotaph or 'empty tomb', identical to the present day Cenotaph – was erected in Whitehall. But, as the first anniversary of the Armistice approached, there was no sign of any official commemoration being planned for 11 November.

On 4 November the cabinet received a letter from Sir Percy Fitzpatrick, a distinguished South African whose son had been killed in France in 1917. The letter suggested that the Armistice anniversary be commemorated by a silence, on the lines of the three-minute silence that had been observed at noon each day in Cape Town during the war, in memory of the dead.[9] The cabinet agreed and King George V issued a personal request which appeared in the press on 7 November. In it he asked that 'at . . . the eleventh hour of the eleventh day of the eleventh month, there may be for a brief space of two minutes, a complete suspension of all our normal activities'.

And so there was. In London and the cities maroons signalled the silence, in the villages it was marked by the church clock or bells. Everywhere the silence was kept, 'even the cynics were on their feet and uncovered' *The Times* reported. Almost by instinct the crowds in London were drawn to the Cenotaph and a way had to be cleared for an

*The meaning of Remembrance.*

*(Left) The King places his wreath at the Cenotaph, Whitehall, London, November 1924.*

*(Above) A war orphan lays the Legion wreath at Bottisham War Memorial near Cambridge, the same year.*

equerry to lay the King's wreath.

It was all very informal on that first anniversary of the war's end. But the Comrades of the Great War held a service at the Cenotaph at one o'clock, led by their band through Horse Guards and down Whitehall, although at least one observer saw it as a 'sad and pathetic procession . . . largely a pilgrimage of the maimed, the halt and the blind . . . some still wearing the familiar hospital blue'. [10]

The next year, 1920, the Cenotaph in its permanent form was unveiled by the King on 11 November at eleven o'clock, the ceremony being included in the funeral procession of the Unknown Warrior to Westminster Abbey, and it was followed by a two-minute silence. Thus, by the time of the Legion's formation in 1921, the tradition of an annual two-minute pause in memory of the dead had been established. But it was not as yet enclosed in any formal national commemoration.

Since it was one of the Legion's aims to ensure that the nation did not forget the human cost of war, the National Executive Council instructed the General Secretary to find out what the government's intentions were for the following 11 November – and to register the Legion's intention to 'hold such function as may be subsequently determined' at the Cenotaph between the hours of twelve and two on that day. In August 1921 Mr Lister, the National Chairman, noted: 'I think the Legion will touch the popular imagination in its desire for a National Day of Commemoration' and at its meeting in September the Council resolved 'That November 11th be the date adopted by the British Legion as Remembrance Day' and, further, that a letter be sent to the Prime Minister proposing that that day be adopted as the National Day of Remembrance.[11] To what extent the Legion's letter influenced the government's plans is not recorded, but when told that there would be an official ceremony in Whitehall on that day the Council asked that the Legion be represented. In the meantime the Legion had adopted the poppy as a symbol of Remembrance* and was urging everyone to wear one on 11 November.[12] But it was also concerned with events outside London and suggested to Legion branches that a wreath of poppies be placed on all local War Memorials.[13] On the day itself 'a party representative of all ranks of the Legion' assembled in Wellington Barracks and, headed by the band of the Scots Guards playing 'The Boys of the Old Brigade', marched to Whitehall. Before the two-minute silence wreaths were laid on behalf of the Royal Family and by the Prime Minister and government representatives, many already including Flanders poppies.[14] After the silence, the turn came for the Legion to pay its tribute with 'an immense wreath of laurel leaves and poppies' and bearing the inscription 'The Legion of the living salutes the Legion of the dead. "We will not break faith with ye"'.† From 1922 onwards the ceremony at the Cenotaph followed the same lines, except that the King himself was present and laid a wreath while the Legion wreath was normally laid by the President.

The day was known to the public as 'Armistice Day', but Legion members were told that their Council had decided that it should 'for all time, be regarded as Remembrance Day'. There is no evidence of any approach to government for this particular name to be adopted; it seems simply to have to have been a Legion practice which spread.[15] However, a 1924 Legion Conference proposal that a national Remembrance Sunday should follow Remembrance Day[16] was formally put to religious leaders by Earl Haig. It was well received and after the Second World War would replace Remembrance Day itself.

As early as 1923 the Legion became concerned at attempts 'in certain quarters' to limit the scope of the observances. This was probably officialdom reflecting on the fact that some five years had elapsed since the end of the war. The Legion has no such doubts – the dead must be honoured in a fitting way and the nation must remember the human cost of war – and it made its views known. There is little doubt that the nation felt the same, for the ceremonies that marked those early Remembrance Days have endured over the succeeding three-quarters of a century.[17] For many the expression of Remembrance lies not so much in Whitehall as in the town squares and on the village greens where the names of the fallen are faithfully recorded. Here the local men saluted their fallen comrades and the widows and mothers grieved. Here too was the heart of the Legion and the ceremonies had their individual character: at Higham in Kent the wreaths were placed by mothers of sons lost in the war. Throughout the country Legion branches, large and small, led the people in remembering the dead.[18] They have done so ever since.

# 1926 – 1930

## The General Strike – and the General Secretary

Britain's relentless industrial decline continued into the second half of the decade, not helped by the General Strike of May 1926, triggered by a marked drop in coal exports the previous year. The miners were supported by the manufacturing and transport industries and the government used troops, backed by volunteers, to maintain essential services.

Such was the speed of events that the Legion's reaction to the strike had to be decided by its General Purposes Committee. It was no easy matter to determine: although the

---

* The origin of the poppy as a symbol of Remembrance is described in Chapter 5.

† It is not recorded who laid the Legion wreath on this occasion; Earl Haig was at Westminster Abbey to hand over for safekeeping the Union Jack that had flown at Ypres. It was probably the Chairman, but it may have been the General Secretary.

14

strike had been called by the trade unions which were linked to the Labour Party, some smelt revolution in the air and the Legion might well have a duty to the country to assist in maintaining the constitution. The decision was that it would remain neutral in the dispute, but if the situation deteriorated into a breakdown of law and order then members should 'support such steps as are taken to ensure the interests of the community'; in other words to resist anarchy.

Feeling perhaps that this needed greater definition, a few days later, at the height of the strike, the General Secretary issued a press statement. In somewhat high-flown language this spoke of the Legion's loyalty and of the principles of peace and justice for which it stood; the punch came in the last line – the Legion called on ex-servicemen to 'come forward once more and offer their services in any way that might be needed by the authorities'. The statement might not have attracted much interest – the press too had been affected by the strike – had an unidentified individual not taken it upon himself to re-publish the General Secretary's statement in the form of a leaflet addressed to 'all workers' and bearing the ambiguous heading 'additional guarantees'.

Although the leaflet was distributed only in parts of Greater London it came to the notice of Legion branches and, as was no doubt intended, some saw it as the Legion taking sides in the dispute without even consulting the membership, while the upright Colonel Heath's involvement gave the affair an added zest.

Stoke Newington and South Paddington branches, each of which claimed to have lost substantial numbers of members as a result of the leaflet, led the attack. The Legion's Annual Conference took place a few days later, enabling an emergency resolution to be tabled. Delegates from other parts of the country were, however, suspicious: who had issued the leaflet, they wished to know, and what was the real motive? By and large branches had supported the line that had been taken in the wording of the press release. After all the Legion could hardly do other than support law and order.

With some skilful handling of the debate on these lines by Lister, the motion of censure was overwhelmingly defeated. The incident, however, served to underline the need for the very greatest caution in how the Legion approached any issue which might provide the opportunity for mischief-makers to divide it through its members' political allegiances.[19]

Legion neutrality did not prevent many branches, particularly those in the mining areas of Wales and the North-East giving practical help to those suffering as a result of the strike: soup kitchens were organized and food provided for the wives and families, branches running concerts and social events to find the money.[20] Although the General Strike was soon ended by the government's firm measures, the miners, whose grievances had brought about the situation, remained out for a further six months.

It was not a happy time for the great majority of people in Great Britain, adding to the privations of those already suffering as a result of the Great War. But it contributed to a major change in social legislation in 1929 with the passing of the Local Government Act which transferred the responsibility for administering Poor Law relief from Boards of Guardians to County Councils, a change which the Legion welcomed and would seek to exploit on behalf of the ex-service community.

## The first Festival

In 1925 the *Legion Journal* had noted the change in attitude towards Armistice Day over the seven years that had elapsed since the war had ended: rather than an opportunity for uncontrolled rejoicing it had become a solemn and thoughtful occasion with a common urge among the people to observe the two-minute silence in memory of the dead. It was perhaps fortunate that the Legion's policy of trying to make 11 November a public holiday did not succeed; it might well have produced the very opposite effect to that intended.

In 1927 the authorities decided that the ex-service community should be more fully represented at the Cenotaph and Legion headquarters was asked to organize the whole of the ex-service parade. And, following a successful broadcast of the Legion's Whitsun parade at the Cenotaph earlier that year, the BBC was allowed to broadcast the event.[20] Meanwhile the *Daily Express* had approached the Legion with a suggestion that there should be an evening function: a rally of ex-service men and women in the Albert Hall, again broadcast by the BBC. The National Executive Council agreed and the rally took place; not surprisingly the number of applications to attend much exceeded capacity and the directors of the newspaper decided that attendance should be limited to those who had actually served in the war areas.

11 November 1927 was therefore a memorable occasion. The ex-service contingent at the Cenotaph numbered 2,000, ten times the figure in previous years. At the Legion's suggestion it also included ex-service women for the first time and, following the practice established the previous year, the ex-service contingent marched at the head of the whole parade. At the Albert Hall that evening the flags of the Grand Fleet – some of them in tatters – hung from the roof, while the Union Jack which had flown over the Menin Gate at Ypres was over the royal box. The hall was packed with bemedalled veterans each wearing a Flanders poppy, their faces barely visible through the haze of tobacco smoke. When the Prince of Wales, accompanied among others by Mr Winston Churchill, entered the ten thousand present rose and cheered him repeatedly, following with 'For he's a jolly good fellow'. At the end of this impromptu overture the band of the Grenadier Guards struck up the first of the old wartime songs, the veterans singing themselve hoarse by the time the final tune, 'Tipperary', had been reached. A two-minute silence, begun and ended by cavalry trumpets sounding the Last Post and Reveille, was followed by a speech from the Prince: 'We must,' he said, 'think and speak of peace.' Led by the Prince the whole audience then left the Albert Hall and marched to the Cenotaph by the light of torches, the immense column being joined at Knightsbridge by a further throng of ex-servicemen who had listened to the proceedings in Hyde Park, and along the route to Whitehall by members of the public. At the Cenotaph itself the torches formed a huge ring around the wreath-encircled memorial in a final act of Remembrance.[21]

Inspiring though these events were, the Legion's officers had been much concerned at the heir to the throne's safety as the crowds pressed in on him during the march. The following year the arrangements were taken out of the newspaper's hands. The march would not be repeated and the Legion's General Secretary took on the organization. The scene was set by a wartime dugout erected in front of the stage with a sandbag-lined 'trench' leading up to it along the centre of the hall. For the first time the King and Queen were present and as soon as they had taken their places the lights dimmed and khaki-clad battalions marched along the trench into the dugout to the accompaniment of the choruses of the old songs. Then came the service: the chaplains and choristers entered the dimmed hall and the Legion standard was carried through the arena, followed by the flags of the dominions borne by Chelsea Pensioners. 'Abide With Me' was followed by the Last Post and Reveille before the audience filed out into the rainswept streets.

Nor was the Festival the only tradition to arise out of that tenth anniversary of the ending of the Great War. At Westminster a Field of Remembrance was established by the

*At the end of the march from the Albert Hall in 1927; a ring of torches surrounds the Cenotaph. The first Legion-organized Festival of Remembrance: as the old songs were sung khaki-clad battalions marched up the sand-bagged 'trench' and into the dug-outs.*

simple act of members of the public buying poppies from disabled men and placing them in the ground, most with a message attached.[22] (See page 132.)

## Death of Earl Haig

Earl Haig, the Legion's first President and one of the founders of the organization, died on 29 January 1928. His death, at the comparatively early age of sixty-seven, was unexpected – he had inspected a Boy Scout troop named in his honour the day before –

17

and it created a shock wave which went not only through the Legion but through the nation as a whole. Haig was a national hero, his popular reputation as yet untarnished by criticism of his strategies on the Western Front. Within the Legion the feelings amounted almost to veneration; indeed as Haig's effective co-founder of the organization, Lister, remarked, 'The Legion has lost a President but found a patron saint.'

Lister meant it. Haig's dedication to the Legion had been total: a reserved man with no pretentions as a public speaker but so obviously sincere that his words invariably created a deep impression, he travelled the country tirelessly to support the body whose creation he had overseen and in which he fervently believed. Wherever he went he was feted not only by Legion members, most of whom had been under his command at one time, but by the civic authorities who had helped find the enormous drafts of manpower for Haig's armies.

Contrary to his latter day image, Haig was very conscious of the sacrifices of the war; but his overriding characteristic was his sense of duty. It was his duty to defeat the foe; equally, once the battles had been won it was his duty as their former commander-in-chief to look after the men's interests. It was as simple as that. As the *Daily Telegraph* put it, 'He did not deem the account to be closed on the day of victory.'

The Legion was much involved in Haig's funeral, providing guards for the Field Marshal's lying-in-state, lining the funeral route and furnishing a Guard of Honour at Waterloo station for their late President's final journey to his native Scotland.[23] All was done with a standard of discipline and bearing which, as General Sir Ian Hamilton noted, 'impressed the people'. He also remarked on the comparison with the events of 1919, when those same men had exchanged blows with the police they now stood alongside in a state event; he believed that there could be no greater tribute to the man who brought this about.[24] But it was not only in London that Haig was remembered. Nearly every branch of the Legion held a memorial service for their late chief: in Yorkshire 'in Cathedral, Parish or Village Church the passing of the great leader was reverently observed by record numbers of Legionaires'. In Cardiff the Cathedral was filled to 'the uttermost corner' and loud-speakers had to be installed on the outside for the large crowd. In the mining valleys to the north of the city, in a village such as tiny Tir Phil, every member was present at a parade in the Field Marshal's memory.[25] Moreover the Legion would hold an annual service in Haig's memory for another fifty years.

## The 'Exhortation'

The 1929 Remembrance Festival saw massed Legion Standards carried on to the platform of the Albert Hall for the first time, although the Legion must have found it a costly innovation as, on the entry into the hall, a number of the gas jet globes were 'wiped off' their perches. Another, and particularly moving, tradition was begun with the descent of over one million poppies at the sounding of the Last Post – one for every life lost in the war. It is recorded too that on this occasion Laurence Binyon's words,

> *They shall grow not old, as we that are left grow old:*
> *Age shall not weary them, nor the years condemn.*
> *At the going down of the sun and in the morning*
> *We will remember them*

were spoken. They had been written as one of a collection of poems published just after the Great War, entitled *The Four Years*.* Binyon, who was Keeper of Oriental Prints at the British Museum, had not himself served in the war, but his words evoked such feelings that they were instinctively adopted as the spoken memorial of those who fell. In the Legion they became known as the 'Exhortation' and in 1930 the National Executive Council decided that they would be spoken at the beginning of each full Council meeting.[26] This practice spread through the Legion so that the words became the preamble to any formal meeting whether in the NEC's council chamber or in a humble branch committee room, serving as a poignant reminder of the Legion's purpose.

In 1930 another threat to Remembrance was perceived when the government instructed ambassadors no longer to place wreaths on local war memorials. When questions in Parliament to the Prime Minister produced an unsatisfactory response, the National Executive Council immediately passed a resolution that there should be 'no diminution of respect for our fallen comrades', a view echoed by the Archbishop of Canterbury and church leaders – except for the Bishop of Ripon who said that he would welcome the end of the observance. In response the Prince of Wales told the Legion that it was their duty to see to it that 'this memory never fades'. The same day the leading article in *The Times* expressed the hope that 'centuries hence there might still be on 11 November those two minutes which are the only time now set apart for universal silence and universal prayer'. The size of the crowds around the Cenotaph, however, provided an even more emphatic statement of the public view.[27]

## The Bridgeman Committee

The Legion's take-over of the Albert Hall Remembrance Festival had strained its relations with the *Express* newspapers. On 5 January 1930 the *Sunday Express* attacked the Legion over the use of its funds, alleging that the elected officers were paid salaries disguised as subsistence allowances and that trading activities were being mismanaged. The charges followed the NEC's summary dismissal of the Metropolitan Area Organizing Secretary after loss of funds in the Area.

The Legion President, now Earl Jellicoe, wrote to the editor of the newspaper pointing out that the Legion's accounts were not only subject to audit and scrutinized by the London County Council but their wide distribution included the press. After rebutting each point in detail Jellicoe asked that the letter should have the same publicity as the original article. The paper, however, merely printed excerpts while continuing to level criticisms at the Legion, intending no doubt to keep a good story running. One was particularly irritating: included in 'the excessive administrative costs' was the expenditure on poppy manufacture. As the Legion's Chairman angrily pointed out in a letter to branches there were certainly cheaper ways of getting poppies but the Poppy Factory gave work to 275 seriously disabled ex-servicemen, who would otherwise be unemployed. No one in the Legion would contemplate putting disabled ex-servicemen back on to the streets in order to save costs.

Many branches responded by passing resolutions of confidence in the National Executive Council. But matters were not allowed to rest there: the President invited Lord Bridgeman, assisted by experts, to conduct an impartial investigation into the Legion's administration. Bridgeman was a former Home Secretary and First Lord of the Admiralty and a highly respected public figure. The Inquiry was conducted quickly but thoroughly and in a little over three months the report was in Lord Jellicoe's hands. It expressed confidence in the Legion's staff before going on to make a number of useful but hardly

---

* Binyon said later that they had been written on a clifftop at Polscath in Cornwall, just after the retreat from Mons. The poem was set to music some time afterwards by both Sir Edward Elgar and Dr Cyril Rootham of Cambridge.[28]

How the
London Press received the Bridgeman Report.

*The verdict of the inquiry into the* Sunday Express *attack.*

earth-shattering recommendations.*

One of these was that the Legion's administration needed an overhaul. That was true enough and if the paper's attack achieved nothing else it at least spurred action in that quarter. And, in the end, by exonerating the Legion from the charges which had been levelled against it by the *Sunday Express*, it had provided the organization with some useful, if unexpected, publicity. In London the newspaper sellers' boards shouted the news: 'British Legion Vindicated', 'British Legion OK – Official', even (the *Daily Herald*) 'British Legion Sensation'. On the inside pages the comments were more prosaic but no less satisfactory: *The Times* editorial noted that it was 'highly satisfactory that the honour and credit of the British Legion have been vindicated', the *Daily Telegraph* stated that 'the public, whose confidence in the Legion has never been shaken, will heartily welcome (the Inquiry's) judicial decision', while the *Daily News* observed that the Legion 'emerges from its severe ordeal . . . without a stain on its character'.

But the *Sunday Express* did not find space even to mention the outcome of the inquiry.[29]

## 1931 – 1935

### The great depression

The Wall Street crash of 1929 had coincided with the election of a Labour government, once more under Ramsay MacDonald, but with a small majority. It was an inauspicious time to win power. The tidal wave generated in Wall Street swept around the world; in Germany the effect was so to sharpen political differences that they developed into extremism; as for Britain it created yet more damage to the remnants of overseas markets, further deepening unemployment at home. By 1931 the Ramsay MacDonald government had become convinced that it could not cope and a further General Election that year resulted in a coalition National government, but still led by MacDonald.

In order to strengthen exports the government devalued the pound, at the same time putting up taxes and cutting expenditure; this last measure involved pay cuts for the Armed Forces, resulting in the mutiny in the Fleet at Invergordon. It was not the least of the government's troubles: there was an international flight from sterling and nearly a quarter of the workforce was now unemployed. But the electorate continued to keep closed ranks and in 1935 once more returned a National government, by which time the economy was beginning to show signs of an upturn, assisted by the beginnings of a re-armament programme. This time the coalition was led by the Conservative Stanley Baldwin, now, however, an ageing man.

* Detailed under the relevant chapters.

A decade after its formation therefore the Legion's task was, if anything, more difficult. Those who had fought in the Great War were now in their mid-thirties; many of the men who had been employed lost their jobs, while the situation for those permanently out of work was even more depressing as cohorts of young people entered the marketplace. Nor did cuts in government expenditure help the Legion to correct the injustices which still afflicted the ex-service community. Yet it rose to the challenge and the success of the Legion's employment campaign in the early and mid-1930s must rank among the greatest of all its achievements (see page 101.)

### Calls for a more militant approach

Government economies might not make campaigning any easier, but this did not abate internal criticism over the Legion's tactics on ex-service issues. Some members felt that the approach was altogether too gentlemanly, suggesting that the leadership were themselves too involved with the 'establishment'. This feeling had expressed itself in resolutions at the Annual Conference every year since 1925, when the Council had been urged to adopt a more 'militant' policy on pensions matters. Nor was it confined to the rank and file: in Metropolitan Area the severest critics of the lack of progress on some issues were the Area President, General Sir Ian Hamilton, and the Chairman, Admiral Sir Henry Bruce.

This feeling was reflected in the *Legion Journal*. One outcome of the Bridgeman Inquiry had been to relieve the General Secretary's burden by appointing an editor. Following the rejection in early 1933 by the Minister of Pensions of a Legion submission on disabled war pensioners, the *Journal* sharply criticized the Ministry's record in two successive issues. In addition to pointing out that in nearly 60 per cent of the cases sent to appeal the Ministry's ruling had been overturned the magazine condemned their attitude to the war disabled, alleging that 'everything was wrung from unwilling hands' and 'the Ministry had failed in its trust'. The press picked up these comments and the Minister, Major Tryon, was forced to make a statement in the House of Commons in which he not only said that these statements were untrue but that the Legion's leaders knew them to be untrue.

The *Journal* article had been approved by Major Brunel Cohen, the Honorary Treasurer and a long-time campaigner on behalf of the war-disabled; he was himself confined to a wheel-chair as a result of the war. Both he and the Chairman appeared in front of the President, now General Maurice, who told them that the *Journal's* remarks were 'receiving strong criticism in influential quarters'. Ten days later, in the course of an address to the Women's Section Annual Conference, Major Cohen expressed his regret at the remarks; and at the subsequent Conference Dinner where Major Tryon was guest of honour, Colonel Crosfield, a past Legion Chairman, made a further apology which the Minister, at the outset of a lengthy speech, gracefully accepted.

These speeches were, however, fully reported in the *Legion Journal* and many Legion members, among them Admiral Bruce, disapproved of the retraction. The Legion's Annual Conference, which fell at that precise juncture, gave them the opportunity to make their feelings known. In a debate which the Chairman had some difficulty in controlling delegates unanimously approved a motion calling on the NEC to refute the Minister's statement in Parliament that the *Journal* allegations were untrue; in other words the delegates, to a man, believed that the criticism was entirely justified and that no apology should have been made.

It was of course impossible for the Legion's leaders to comply with the resolution; they could hardly withdraw the apology. But a line had to be drawn under the affair and the closing speeches were so worded as to leave no doubt that the matter was not to be reopened. Since they were delivered by the ever-popular Prince of Wales and the respected President there was no argument. In any case they contained sufficiently vigorous expressions of determination to right the injustices in the pensions system to receive applause from the audience. Nevertheless the message was clear: the tactics would not change. The fault lay with the editor of the *Journal* for letting his pen get the better of him and the immediate action was to devise a means of exercising stricter control over his activities.[30]

What the delegates said to each other about this sidelining of their resolution as they streamed away can only be left to the imagination. The problem did not, however, disappear with them and again it was a journalist who stirred the pot. One of the newest-formed Metropolitan Branches was the Fleet Street Branch. In October 1933 an article in the *Legion Journal* by a member of the Branch Council expressed the view that the Legion had got it wrong from the outset: it should not be non-party-political; it should have put up candidates for Parliament, held demonstrations in Hyde Park and marched on the House of Commons. It would then have had a membership of three million rather than three hundred thousand which, as Ministers had often pointed out, was hardly representative of the five million who had returned from the war. The American Legion had adopted just such an approach – and won far better treatment as a result.

These views were reflected in a resolution at the Metropolitan Area Conference the following March, once again calling for a more aggressive NEC policy. And following the dismissal of the Legion Journal's editor (see page 61) *Reynolds Illustrated News* attacked the Legion in May 1934, claiming that, because it lacked an 'active policy', the Legion had been 'going downhill for a long time'. The *Sunday Dispatch* joined the hue and cry shortly before Annual Conference by suggesting that the award of a knighthood to the British Legion's Chairman was in exchange for not having pressed the case for pension reform too strongly. But the *Dispatch* had gone too far and their attack backfired. Colonel John Brown, the Chairman, was a distinguished and popular figure and the gross personal insult served merely to close the ranks of delegates at the Conference; a resolution of confidence in the National Executive Council was carried with only two dissenters among over a thousand delegates. The press attacks did, however, score one significant hit: for the first time in the Legion's history there was no Royal Prince present at Annual Conference, Prince George (later to be Duke of Kent) declining his invitation because of the hubbub.[31]

The outcome of all this was a clarification of Legion policy: in early 1935 a circular to branches stated that 'the Legion remains independent of party politics. But it must not be interpreted as precluding the Legion from active and responsible participation in the affairs of the nation and in everything that affects the wellbeing of ex-servicemen.' Thus the criticism was acknowledged. But events would show whether it also implied a change to a more aggressive policy.[32]

## Attacks on Haig and Jellicoe

To add to its problems at this time, the Legion had to endure assaults on those national figures with whom it had been proud to be identified. In 1934 extracts from the memoirs of the war-time Prime Minister, Lloyd George, were published in national newspapers. There had already been some criticism of Haig by Liddell Hart (see page 47) but Lloyd

George's book was effectively to destroy his reputation in the eyes of future generations. Despite having supported Haig's strategies, the politician now sought to shift on to him all responsibility for the loss of life. Conveniently for Lloyd George, Haig was dead and unable to defend himself; coming at a time when yet another war seemed possible, perhaps involving even greater sacrifice, the book made a great impression.

The Legion rallied to Haig's support. Branches around the country passed resolutions deploring Lloyd George's vilification of their 'beloved leader', while in London military experts lined up to justify Haig's policy of maintaining the pressure until the Germans broke and to deplore the book's personal attacks on him.

Nor did Jellicoe escape Lloyd George's caustic pen: as with Haig, his character was demeaned in the process of examining his strategies. But Jellicoe had to live with the harsh criticism until his death in November 1935.

In the following months Legion meetings around the country deplored Lloyd George's action. But, although there was no effect on the Poppy Appeal, or on any other activity, the association with Haig no longer gave the Legion only lustre; their late president was now a figure of controversy.[33]

## White poppies – a sad irony

Whatever the view of the wartime leadership, Remembrance continued to exercise strong feelings all over the country. In 1932 the Legion suggested that at the Cenotaph ceremony the troops should be replaced by ex-servicemen, widows and orphans. This idea is supposed to have originated with the Prince of Wales; but the government felt that change might be unwise. In the Irish Free State the service in Phoenix Park in Dublin continued to be attended by thousands and in places such as Tipperary and Tralee embraced both the Roman Catholic and Protestant communities.[34] But in Dublin in 1933 a gang of youths attacked a British Legion party marching away from the parade and threw its standard into the River Liffey; one of the Legion members gallantly dived in the river and, despite being carried away by a strong current, was rescued still grasping the standard. Thereafter, however, the ex-servicemen dispersed after the parade instead of marching home.

1934 saw a new symbol on sale: the white poppy. The sellers were members of the Women's Co-operative Guild, which had been founded in 1933. Unlike the Legion's red poppies they were not sold to raise funds for benevolent purposes but to signify belief in 'the sacred cause of Justice and the freedom of the World' – the words inscribed on the Tomb of the Unknown Warrior. The Legion was more than a little puzzled since this was the cause of those who had fought and suffered in the war and for whom it sought the nation's remembrance and support through the red poppy. However, the Peace Pledge Union, formed the same year, also adopted the white poppy and it continued to be on sale in November each year, the contrast in colour suggesting that the Legion's red poppy was in some way a glorification of war – a sad irony in view of the origins of the 'Flanders Poppy' and the Legion's firm belief that the way to peace lay through the remembrance of past sacrifice, which that poppy symbolized.[35]

## 'An absolute triumph'

By now the Festival of Remembrance at the Albert Hall had become an instittution. It was not easy to gain admittance: priority went to those who had served overseas and it was estimated that, although 8,000 passed through the doors, ten times that number applied. There was always a royal presence and King George liked to take part in the choruses to the old songs, while pictures of the war were flashed on to a huge screen. 'Take me back to dear old Blighty' received the most encores and whichever wag called out 'Are we downhearted?' it got the same inevitable, roof-raising response.

The Prince of Wales on several occasions – the last time as King in 1936, uttered the Exhortation 'They shall grow not old', a poignant moment with a picture of a cluster of wooden crosses in the Flanders mud on the screen. The falling poppies too stirred deep emotions, but not it would seem in everyone present: a report in the *Sunday Express* in 1932 said that the Legion should never hold another festival since the ex-servicemen had grown middle-aged, adding that 'they snowed poppy petals, made by those who are half-alive, on to the living in memory of the dead'. The remarks could hardly have caused greater offence, but, the newspaper – no friend of the Legion in the past – did not apologize. It was in any case a singular misjudgement. The idea had caught the imagination of both the public and the ex-servicemen and Remembrance Festivals on similar lines were held from Northumberland to the Channel Islands, and even in Nairobi. In 1934 Mr C.B. Cochran, the noted impresario, who had attended many of the Albert Hall festivals, said, 'I do not know who staged it . . . but it is an absolute triumph of organization and presentation'. Told that it was designed, organised and directed by the General Secretary, Colonel Heath, Cochran remarked, 'You have got me absolutely beat.'[36]

### The Legion and the threat of war

The Festival remembered past sacrifices. But now there were indications that new ones might be called for. By the mid-1930s Hitler was embarked on the expansionist policies that he believed would return Germany to its rightful position in Europe. In this atmospere of impending Armageddon the Legion found itself in an anomalous position; it worked actively for peace through its contacts with similar organizations in other countries, believing that if ex-servicemen opposed war then the politicians would be dissuaded; yet it was regarded by some, because of its make-up, as a 'militaristic' body which should be banned in the interests of peace. Such people saw the Legion's parades and standards, its insistence on keeping Armistice Day in the national calendar and its commemoration of the dead of the Great War by the wearing of poppies as glorifying war; indeed it was this mis-reading of the Legion's purposes that seems to have led to the introduction of the white poppy.

But if there was one thing on which nearly every Legion member of the time was agreed it was the pursuit of peace, to which end the organization was to stretch its credibility to the utmost in 1935 by making direct contact with Hitler himself; the full story is told in chapter 6. It was not, however, peace at any price – and here the Legion differed fundamentally from the white poppy sellers – through total disarmament. The Legion's attitude towards disarmament followed that of the government: there should be arms reductions, but not to the point where national security was threatened.

Individual Legion members held their own views on Hitler. When a wreath was laid on his behalf at the Cenotaph in 1933 it was quickly removed by a Legion member, Captain Sears. Sir Ian Hamilton was of the view that 'the truce of the Cenotaph' had been breached by Sears' action. But the general feeling was that Sears was right and, although the matter was reported to the National Executive Council, they took no action. That same year a new Legion branch formed in east London; composed entirely of Jewish ex-servicemen, it was called the Maccabean Branch, established its headquarters in the Whitechapel Road and in the first six months enrolled six hundred members.[37]

# 1936 – 1940

## The Abdication

A few months after his Silver Jubilee in May 1935, for which the Legion had organized some 10,000 ex-servicemen to line the route of the royal carriage drive through Hyde Park, King George V died. He was succeeded by his son, Edward VIII, who as Prince of Wales had been closely associated with the Legion since it had elected him the first Patron in 1921. There was much delight when the new King agreed to continue as Patron, turning to profound shock at his decision in December 1936 to abdicate. The relationship between the Legion and its Patron had been particularly intimate* and he was idolized by the members. Following the abdication the Legion's President wrote to the Duke of Windsor, as Edward was now styled, 'Members of the British Legion have watched with heavy hearts and deep anxiety . . . the crisis which has led to your abdication . . . You honoured us by treating us as your comrades.' In his reply, which he had typed himself on a portable typewriter from a castle in Austria, the Duke said that he was 'very touched' by the letter and went on, 'Will you please express to all my old comrades, my deep appreciation of their devotion and support. . . just now.'

King George VI, who succeeded his brother, consented to become the new Patron, while the Queen remained as President of the Women's Section, a post which she had held since 1924. It would seem that the King, a perceptive man, recognized the Legion's sense of loss, for he appears to have gone out of his way to include the organization in his visits around the country.[38]

## Into another war

As the war-clouds gathered in the mid-1930s the Legion shared with the country in general its strong desire to preserve the peace. The efforts of its Chairman to use the ex-service connections with Germany to prevent war, and in particular the assembly at short notice of a Legion Volunteer Police Force to keep order in the disputed areas of

SCHLOSS ENZESFELD
A. D. TRIESTING

20th, December, 1936.

*My dear General*

I am very touched by the letter you have written me on behalf of the British Legion. Will you please express to all my old comrades, my deep appreciation of their devotion and support in the past, and for their kind thoughts of me just now

Will you please also assure them, that any service I may have rendered to them as their Patron has been my privilege, and that I can be of some service to them again, is my sincere hope.

My best wishes to you all for a happy Christmas,, and may the New Year be a successful one for the Legion.

*Yours very sincerely*
*Edward*

*'To all my old comrades' – the Duke of Windsor's response to the Legion President's letter, following the abdication.*

*The Prince once said 'I feel more at home with the Legion than anywhere else.'[39]

*Ulster Legionaries parade in 1937 for the new King, who was particularly struck by the turn-out.*

26

Czechoslovakia (see page 160), were recognized with a knighthood. But when, in 1938, it seemed that war was inevitable the Legion's President wrote to the Prime Minister placing the organization at the government's disposal. In the meantime Legion Counties and branches helped organize military units and set up civil defence measures. They led the way in the formation of Air Raid Precautions (ARP) and were involved in the Home Defence Companies guarding local installations and in the more mobile National Defence Companies: Northern Ireland Area raised a National Defence Company and had them on duty in seven days. They helped with the expansion of the Territorial Army and there was Legion representation on many TA Associations. Much of this work fell on Legion Counties since both civil defence and the TA were organized at county level.

There was however some disappointment that the Legion structure as a whole was not utilized. 'I feel that the failure to give the Legion a definite job to do is a ridiculous anomaly,' the Legion's Chairman said, suggesting that it could be used, for example, to look after public services such as water or electricity.

On 31 August 1939, on the eve of Hitler's invasion of Poland, the Legion's President, Sir Frederick Maurice, made a broadcast to Germany as 'an English front-line soldier speaking to German front-line soldiers' which left the hearers in no doubt about who would be responsible for the outbreak of war. The broadcast was presumably intended to strengthen the ultimatum by dispelling any thought of lack of British ex-service support for hostilities.[40]

<br>

## 1941 – 1945

### The Second World War

The Legion, in the expression of the times, 'carried on' in the war. But, with the huge expansion in the armed forces giving rise to large numbers of dependent relatives, as well as those discharged for one reason or another swelling the ex-service ranks, its task rapidly grew. Inevitably the bulk of the work fell on the branches, some of which, to add to their difficulties, were operating in areas which were under heavy air attack. The seriousness of the situation did not distract the organization from its responsibilities. Its experts quickly brought to light the shortcomings in the war disability pensions provisions; they compared poorly with those that applied to First World War men. The government was forced to set up an Advisory Committee, on which the Legion was represented; even so, it took until 1943 and much Legion pressure to put matters right.

The Legion was much involved with the Home Guard, created in 1940 when the danger of invasion became apparent. Legionaries 'picked up their muskets' and it was estimated that by the end of that year nearly half of the volunteers were from the Legion. In the Legion's North Western Area the Chairman, a retired Lieutenant General, was asked to form a Zone of twenty-seven battalions. He did so, working from the Area Office and using the Area staff to assist him. Elsewhere there was a request from a firm on important war work to provide gun teams for the anti-aircraft defence of the factory. The local Legion branches found the men and it was later claimed that an attacking aircraft had been destroyed. Early in the war the War Office asked the Legion to open a Soldiers' Correspondence Department to oversee the exchange of letters between the public and serving men – a 'pen pals' scheme – the Legion's task being not only to manage the scheme but to ensure that the soldiers received no 'subversive' letters. But, although twenty-five thousand civilians wished to write, only a hundred soldiers were willing to respond and the scheme was dropped after six months.[41]

There had been some concern at the start of the war that the Legion would encounter financial difficulties, partly because of the increased demand for its services and partly because wartime conditions would affect fundraising. In fact its position greatly improved. Despite taking place at the peak of the bombing, the 1940 Poppy Day was a great success, as were succeeding wartime collections. Moreover, expenditure reduced as staff left for the war and wartime restrictions cut overheads, so that substantial reserves were accumulated. And despite the smaller staff and wartime demands, at the request of the Lord Mayor of London the Legion was able to organize a successful flag day for air raid victims.

Like many another wartime coming-of-age, the Legion's 21st birthday in 1942 was a muted occasion, without parades or bands. But a broadcast illustrated the Legion's work, in a series of sketches punctuated by a girl's voice: 'Will you buy a poppy, please'. The same year, on Remembrance Day, the BBC broadcast 'We Shall Remember Them', a series of discussions between individuals about the Legion's activities. This was all direct propaganda for the Legion, and there were other opportunities: in 1943 the National President broadcast on the Six o'clock News, a programme which at that time was heard by almost the whole nation as well as the forces overseas, telling servicemen how the Legion could help them. It would seem that in some ways the organization was being treated as part of the national war effort, which indeed it could claim to be. It had its effect on publicity: in 1943 press cuttings were up by 50 per cent, while scarce national newspaper space was given to articles by Legion leaders on post-war matters. There were features too in forces' newspapers, but some provoked adverse reactions: a letter in the 8th Army newspaper *Crusader* commented that the Legion's main interest was 'quiet and pleasant boozing places', while another correspondent said that young men and women were unlikely to have much use for it if all it could do was to give them charity.

Undoubtedly the Legion was concerned with its image at this time. The Second World War could revitalize the organization; in the early 1930s it had been worried about its future once the First World War veterans began to fade away. But there was also the possibility that the new generation would see the Legion as outmoded and have other ideas, perhaps even forming their own organization. It certainly needed to identify with them and in 1943 public relations consultants were appointed.[42]

## A boundary crossed?

In 1940 the National Executive Council had decided that it would be improper for it to negotiate on allowances for the families of those serving in the armed forces or to use Legion funds to assist them. It was solely an ex-service organization and indeed a body already existed to help servicemen's families – the Soldiers, Sailors and Airmen's Families Association. But the Legion would help in other ways and would monitor the allowance schemes in order to ensure that the machinery worked. The exception was where the men concerned were ex-servicemen recalled to the colours. Here the Legion felt it retained a responsibility to the families, who would in any case look to it for help on any service-connected matter, as they had been accustomed to do before the war. There was some discussion with SSAFA and a joint policy was agreed.

The fact that a large number of those in the forces were also ex-servicemen led the Legion into negotiations with the authorities over such matters as proficiency pay for previous service, in which it was successful. But a boundary had been crossed: the Legion was now involved with conditions of service in HM Forces, albeit to a limited extent. In 1941, however, the Council went a stage further and considered actively involving the Legion in negotiations with the government over service pay and allowances and there was a proposal to this effect* at the 1942 Annual Conference. The proposal was, however, rejected by Conference as a contravention of the Legion policy of non-interference with the forces. It was the closest the Legion had yet come to attempting to set itself up as the 'Forces Union', a course which would have led it into uncharted waters. But the following year it took up the case of a soldier undergoing detention who died after being struck by camp staff, instructing counsel for the inquest. The regimental sergeant major and a non-commissioned officer were sent to trial for manslaughter and subsequently there was a Government Commission into Army Detention Camps. Strictly speaking the Legion could claim to be acting on behalf of the family of an ex-serviceman; but, insofar as it affected the discipline of the armed forces, it was yet another step in a new direction.[43]

Even after the 1942 Conference decision there were some who continued to think that the Legion should act as an intermediary in this way: a writer to the *Legion Journal* in 1945 suggested that the Legion should be the link between the government and the armed forces and work to improve service conditions; all it needed was 'courage and vision'.[44]

## Post-war planning

As early as 1940 the Legion had appointed a Planning Committee to study demobilization and resettlement, conscious, as the *Legion Journal* succinctly put it, of the 'shambles' which had followed the Great War.[45] The committee's Chairman, Lister, could not have been better qualified for the task, having been the Legion's first Chairman when the organization had been heavily involved with the consequences of the government's mistakes. The study was wide-ranging, from the problems of the war-disabled to the post-war situation of women. It also approached the whole matter from the point of view of what was best for the nation as a whole, rather than representing only the ex-service outlook, a sign of the Legion's maturity.[46] Despite starting their work in the dark days of 1940 and 1941, like the vast majority of their countrymen the committee never entertained any doubts as to the war's outcome. By 1942 the government was being urged to introduce legislation for the reinstatement of servicemen in their previous jobs and to provide for training where this was not possible,[47] and the Legion's detailed demobilization plans were being explained to Annual Conference.[48] But the Legion would still not involve itself in party politics; ex-service issues were above party and it would most certainly stand aside if there were any attempt to form an ex-service party after the war.[49]

The Legion had been wise to get ahead on these matters. As the war drew to a close resettlement became the dominant issue, the most difficult problem being the priority for demobilization, bearing in mind not only the need for an army of occupation for Germany but for more men to fight what seemed likely to be a protracted war with Japan. But a government White Paper published in September 1944 contained many of the Legion's recommendations in a scheme which was both simple to understand and straightforward in execution. In November of that year a Legion team spent two hours with the Ministers of Reconstruction and Labour and National Service discussing the problems of those leaving the armed forces.[50]

*Although it referred to those with previous service; the Council perhaps had second thoughts about representing all servicemen.

### The Second World War and Remembrance

With the outbreak of war in 1939 the parade service at the Cenotaph was suspended, although wreaths were laid informally and the two-minute silence observed, several hundred people ignoring an air raid alert in 1940 to pay their silent tribute. The BBC, however, broadcast on each Remembrance Sunday in the war years from 1941 onwards a 'British Legion Service of Remembrance' from various churches around the country and Legion branches continued to organize church parades, with local contingents of the armed forces often taking part.

Now the question arose as to the future form of Remembrance. 11 November was strictly a First World War anniversary. The Second World War finally ended with victory over Japan in August 1945. There was much discussion between the Legion's leaders, senior churchmen and the Home Secretary over whether there should be a separate day for each war or whether they should be combined. If there was to be one single day, should it be in November or August? And of particular concern to the Legion was the question of Poppy Day, virtually its sole source of income.

The Legion had long recognized the practical advantages of Sunday as the day of commemoration and the Council took a joint position with the churches: a single Remembrance Day should be held on the Sunday immediately before 11 November and both the two-minute silence and the official ceremony at the Cenotaph should take place on that day.[51]

The government agreed and as it happened 11 November 1945 anyway fell on a Sunday. There was once again a parade and service at the Cenotaph with the King present; both he and Princess Elizabeth laid wreaths and the Legion organized the parade of 1,500 ex-service men and women. As a counterpoint to these sombre events a hundred Legion standards had been paraded two days earlier at the Lord Mayor of London's Show, their elderly bearers now 'a trifle ragged' in their marching but sustained by calls from the crowd of 'go to it, Pop'.[52]

The Festival of Remembrance had been suspended in 1939. Somewhat surprisingly, and no doubt as a contribution to wartime morale, it was resumed in 1943. Colonel Heath having retired, the pre-war organizer of the Aldershot Tattoo was recruited and for the first time there was an afternoon performance open to the public on payment, as well as the evening performance for members, who must have been disappointed that the Royal Family attended in the afternoon. Those taking part included an RAF bomber crew who came straight from their operations centre to the arena in full flying kit. The next year, 1944, saw the men who had taken part in the Arnhem operation earlier that year represented and the community singing was led by the new organizer, Squadron Leader Ralph Reader, who repeated his performance in 1945, 'turning the great occasion into a family party' as *Reynolds News* reported it. This time, perhaps because Princess Margaret was now fifteen, the Royal Family were present in the evening and the proceedings were broadcast by Richard Dimbleby. There were Festivals elsewhere too in the wartime and immediate post-war years, notably in Brussels in 1944.[53]

### Dawn of a new era

The Legion's wartime efforts on their behalf, and particularly its contribution to the demobilization plans and post-war rehabilitation, might have been enough to secure the allegiance of a new generation of ex-service men and women. But the organization was leaving nothing to chance. There was a concentrated public relations campaign with

*The Legion appeals to a new generation of ex-servicemen – a Second World War*
*poster. As well as offering help, the text was intended to encourage recruiting.*

posters on railway stations and even a forces essay competition on how the Legion could help the young men and women to realize their post-war ambitions. The outcome was the Legion's greatest ever increase in membership. And it was more highly regarded than ever before, being regularly consulted by government departments and by other charities. Headquarters' benevolent work rose to five times the pre-war level, but, thanks to the highly successful wartime Poppy Days and forced economies, the coffers were full.

Urgent matters such as disability pensions apart, the Legion had withheld campaigning during the war. With peace its policies were promoted vigorously. The re-establishment of family life was of major importance and at the top of the Legion's list were homes for the returning servicemen; but priority in training and employment followed closely, with particular attention to the disabled. All of these, together with more opportunities for ex-servicemen's education, including a ladder to university, and a chance for women to enter new occupations, were included in the Legion's policy statement to candidates at the 1945 General Election. But on this occasion there was no questionnaire; it would have been easily answered and as easily forgotten. There was a new realism: in the employment field old antagonisms were being set aside and there was now close liaison between the Legion and the TUC.

★     ★     ★

To those who had fought the war, and had survived, it was the dawn of a new era. At last Germany had been finally vanquished and there was the chance for peace and prosperity. This time the ex-serviceman would reap his proper rewards. Or, at least that was the expectation, and the Legion, now with renewed strength, was resolved to make it happen.[54]

# CHAPTER 3

## STRUCTURE 1921-1945
# *Building the Foundations*

### 1921–1925

**The first Council**

The newly-formed Legion faced an uncertain world in 1921 and good leadership would be crucial. By luck or circumstance the Unity Conference made the right choices. T.F. Lister, elected Chairman 'by acclamation'[1], was the obvious candidate: he had initiated the unity process and had dominated the subsequent meetings. But the other officers were scarcely less important. Lieutenant Colonel George Crosfield, the Vice Chairman, who had led the Comrades in the unity negotiations, was a one-legged veteran of both the South African War and the Great War. The Treasurer was even more severely disabled, having lost both legs in the war: the son of a Liverpool Alderman who had founded Lewis's stores, Major J. Brunel Cohen had joined for active service in 1914 and on leaving the Army became MP for Liverpool (Fairfield). On his first entry into Parliament he made a fighting speech on behalf of ex-servicemen and was to campaign vigorously in the Commons for the Legion and its causes.[2]

The first National Executive Council was already a working body, having been constituted from the Unity Committee which had been formed some five months earlier and would remain in being until the next conference twelve months hence.[3] Half of its twenty-four members were former commissioned officers, including two major generals, but Lister, the former gunner, was very much in charge. The Legion's

*The men who created the Legion: Field Marshal Earl Haig and Mr T.F. Lister.*

President, Field Marshal Earl Haig, was also entitled to attend Council meetings, but if Lister was in any way disconcerted by his presence it did not happen too often. Haig came to only three meetings in his seven and a half years in office, clearly finding lengthy discussion in committee not to his taste.* Furthermore his home was in the Scottish borders.

At the end of the first year a new Council was elected. The four constituent organizations were now part of history; instead, each of the eleven Legion Areas was represented by two members who held office for a year, giving a total Council of twenty-

*But he had a 100 per cent attendance record as Chairman of the Benevolent Committee.[4]

33

six, including the four national officers. They needed their wits about them; there was much to be done.[5]

## The staff

The Council made the decisions, but to put them into effect they needed staff support. The first meeting of the Council in July 1921 interviewed twelve applicants for the post of General Secretary from the 435 who had sought the job. Following a ballot, Colonel E.C. Heath DSO became the first General Secretary of the British Legion.

Heath had been a regular soldier and an infantryman, commanding a battalion of the Sherwood Foresters at the outbreak of the war, and was awarded his DSO following the Third Battle of Ypres. But it was his intellectual ability that made him a clear choice for the post: before the war he had tutored officers for promotion examinations and, following the Armistice, he was placed in charge of education in the Rhine Army – a task which he performed with 'conspicuous success'.[6]

There was no shortage of talent for the rest of the headquarters staff. The general secretaries of three constituent organizations were available together with their staffs. One of the three was outstanding: J.R. Griffin had worked for the Federation on being invalided from the Army in 1917 and by 1920 was General Secretary of that organization. He had also played a key role in unification, acting as Honorary Secretary to the Joint Conference on Unity from August 1920 to December 1920, drafting the Legion's constitution and generally acting as Lister's right-hand man. His ability certainly qualified him to be the General Secretary of the new organization, but he was very young for such responsibility. Moreover, the appointment would have been seen as giving too much emphasis to the former Federation, since Lister had been the Federation President. The Council therefore appointed Griffin Assistant Secretary, balancing his knowledge and youthful enthusiasm against Colonel Heath's maturity and wider background.

The other two former general secretaries were also absorbed into the new headquarters. The organization was functional, except for ex-officer matters, all of which came under the Officers' Benevolent Department, constituted from the Officers' Association. Fundraising was a vital function and the Legion had been able to inherit a going concern; the Officers' Association handed over their fundraising section which became the Appeals Department. (See Chapter 8 for officer benevolence and Chapter 5 for fundraising).

With so many experienced staff the headquarters was off to a flying start. Indeed for Comrades staff the transition was particularly smooth as the Legion took over the lease of their premises at 26 Eccleston Square, London, SW1, an imposing five-storey early Victorian building on the corner of a quiet square near Victoria station. It could not, however, accommodate everyone; the Officers' Benevolent Department remained at 48 Grosvenor Square while the Appeals Department continued to occupy premises at 1 Regent Street in London's West End. This hardly helped staff cohesion, but attempts to provide a larger headquarters came to naught because of lack of funds.

## The strategy

The Legion's strategy, agreed at the first Council meeting after its formation, rested on three aims. The first of these, which it termed its 'domestic object', was to establish its own power base. This would rest on a strong and well-organized membership, not only to carry out its work but to exert political pressure. As Lister put it, 'Just causes unaccompanied by the pressure of numerical strength pursue a slow and tortuous path ... the power of the Legion will depend on the strength of its branches.' This had indeed been a primary reason for unification and with an ex-service population of over six million the opportunities were immense.

From a firm domestic base the Legion could undertake its 'national objects' and 'Imperial objects'. The national objects were principally to protect ex-service interests through preference in employment and to guard the pension rights of the disabled, the widows and other dependants. The 'Imperial objects' mainly concerned the maintenance of peace, for further conflict would only make the Legion's task more difficult. It aimed to ensure that the nation remembered the folly and waste of war through an annual day of commemoration.

But it is necessary to return to the first of these aims. Having decided that a strong membership organization was essential to its other objects, how did the Legion set about achieving it and what success did it have?[7]

## Areas and counties

The branches of the 'old' organizations did not automatically become part of the Legion. Each had to decide to transfer their allegiance and in some cases rivals needed to amalgamate. It all took time. The network also needed to be expanded, not only to build up the strength of the organization but to ensure that no ex-serviceman or widow lacked access to a Legion branch, bearing in mind that life was still lived very much on a local level in the 1920s. This implied a regional support structure.

The country was accordingly divided into Areas. Ten were formed in England: East Anglia, East Midland, Home Counties, Metropolitan, North Eastern, North Western, South Eastern, South Western, West Midland and Yorkshire. Wales formed a further Area and a subsequent decision of the Wales Area Conference, meeting in Shrewsbury, divided the principality into three sub-areas: North, Mid and South Wales. Initially the branches in each Area simply elected an Area Council. But in 1922 this was changed: each Area was to hold an annual conference; the officers and committee elected for that conference constituted the Area Council until the next Area Conference.[8]

The Legion's constitution permitted Area Councils to delegate some of their responsibilities to Counties or Districts and South Eastern Area decided at an early stage to operate principally on a County basis.[9] Other Areas encouraged their counties to set up their own Councils soon after they themselves had formed: in October 1921 West Midland Area was already setting up County Councils and South West Area had taken a decision to do so. Metropolitan Area, however, cut across county boundaries and so formed 'Group Areas'. These were not necessarily on a territorial basis; one Group Area took in all the civil service branches in the London ministries, including the War Office, Air Ministry and Ministry of Labour branches.

There were therefore four levels from branch to national headquarters and at the Legion's first Annual Conference it was suggested that there should be 'a County system pure and simple'. The NEC opposed the idea and it was defeated.[10]

## Ireland comes in

The Legion's formation coincided with the peak of the troubles in Ireland, which brought about the country's division in 1922 into the Irish Free State and Northern Ireland. But Irishmen from both sides of the new border had fought in the war and those south of the border were no less entitled to the Legion's help than any other part of the ex-service community; indeed because of the situation in Ireland their needs were often greater than most. The Comrades of the Great War were represented in both North and South, but it proved impractical to hold an 'all-Ireland' meeting. While the North therefore became a self-governing part of the Legion in 1922, the South decided to form a separate organization – the Legion of Irish Ex-Servicemen.[11]

Nevertheless Legion headquarters in London went to some lengths to maintain close relations with Dublin, as did Belfast and, following much hard work by the General Secretary, Colonel Heath, both North and South Ireland became Areas of the Legion in January 1925, with representation on the National Executive Council and paid Area Organizers and staff.[12] Colonel Heath was present at the Engineers Hall in Dublin on 17 January 1925 when the Annual Conference of Irish Ex-Servicemen carried the Resolution of Incorporation.

## But Scotland is independent

In Scotland events had taken a different turn. In London it had been assumed that the Unity agreement extended north of the border since both the Comrades and the Federation had branches there. But on 18 June 1921, barely two weeks before the Legion's official formation, a meeting in Edinburgh established the Legion in Scotland.[13] At first the National Executive Council took this to be a grouping within the overall Legion structure. By September 1921, however, it seemed that they might be mistaken; the situation was 'not satisfactory' and Colonel Heath was instructed to visit Scotland. Heath seems to have had some success and, following his report, £200 was granted to Scotland to organize a Scottish Area on the condition that the annual Affiliation Fee of 1/6 per member was paid to Legion Headquarters.[14]

Now the difficulty arose: Scotland was not prepared to pay Affiliation Fees to headquarters in London and in November 1921 the General Secretary again went to Scotland, this time in the company of a Scotsman, Earl Haig. In speeches at Aberdeen and Edinburgh Haig stressed the need for unity, pointing out that politicians play one organization off against another. A united Legion would 'speak with one mighty voice'.[15] The General Secretary of the Legion in Scotland accompanied them, but confined his remarks to the Legion's work in Scotland.

A year later, in November 1922, Haig returned to Scotland, this time in the presence of the Prince of Wales. Again he emphasized the need for one powerful body if the ex-service community was to make a proper impact.[16] But it was too late; a separate Legion in Scotland was now in existence, with its own Council, headquarters and staff in Edinburgh. All the Legion's big guns had been fired to no effect and, for the moment at any rate, the NEC had to accept the fact of Scottish independence.

## An early reorganization

As the Legion's work developed, the field staff grew. Area Organizers had been appointed as early as October 1921, but fundraising needed seven Area Appeals Organizers. Concern over unemployment led to the appointment in four Areas of Area Employment Secretaries, while the need for proper representation at Pensions Appeals Tribunals meant that all eleven Areas appointed an Appellant's Representative. Finally the Area Councils themselves appointed Area Secretaries. These officials all worked virtually independently and in particular the 'double harness' of an Area Organizer and Area

Secretary, each without authority over the other, caused confusion. The system had developed in a piecemeal way and it was plainly inefficient.

In 1923 there was a wholesale administrative reorganization, led by the Chairman, Lister. Each Area would in future have a single Organizing Secretary responsible for all aspects of the Legion's work, supported by a small staff. The seven Appeals Organizers would be reduced to two; their duties would in future be to inspect and advise. Furthermore the Area staff would report to the General Secretary and to make the point they would be paid direct by headquarters, instead of through their Area Treasurers.

Inevitably some Area Councils resisted the change, but in the end they came round. It had been a much-needed overhaul and, as well as making economies, a clear management chain had been established. The cohesion of the area staff was further assured by the first Area Organizers' conference in October 1924.[17]

## The Big Push

By the end of 1921 there were nearly 1,500 branches.[18] While most had come across from the original organizations, others had formed as 'Legion' branches. Nevertheless the National Executive Council saw the need to boost membership in early 1922 with a 'propaganda and membership' campaign inaugurated with a mass meeting at the Central Hall Westminster in March, chaired by Earl Haig. Using a familiar expression from the Great War the campaign was entitled the 'Big Push' and was concentrated into a single week, based on public meetings at Area, County and Branch level. A trophy was presented by the National President (The Haig Cup) for award to the branch which had the best membership and the most activity.

Branches were advised that, whilst their activities should be based on public meetings, there were many other ways in which to publicize the movement: Legion displays in shops; articles in the local press; addresses to cinema and music hall audiences (the latter surely calling for an intrepid speaker); and original activities such as a torchlight procession with recruiting banners.[19]

National Officers, Council members and headquarters staff were all mobilized to speak. Churches were asked to mention the Legion – or to pray for it. At least one did: the Vicar of Denstone gave an eloquent appeal on the Legion's behalf.[20] An editorial in the *Journal* suggested that every member recruit one new member. In North Western Area over 300 meetings were held in the seven days of the campaign, fifty concerts and carnivals took place and some sixty branches organized house-to-house canvasses. In the East Midland Area a meeting at Derby attracted an audience of 2,000, whilst in Kent Hythe Branch doubled their membership, recruiting 544 out of the 600 ex-servicemen in the town. A rural branch, Ashampstead in Berkshire, managed to enrol every single ex-serviceman in the district by personal canvass on foot or by bicycle.[21]

These were the times, before the advent of television or radio, when people went to public meetings as a matter of course. Although it is difficult to judge the results of the 'push' since the Legion was anyway expanding at this time, the scale of the interest was remarkable and, as well as giving impetus to membership, it brought the organization into the public eye.

During the first six months of 1922 the branch total increased from 1,500 to over 1,800. This greatly helped the Legion's work; the branch was the principal point of contact between the Legion and those it sought to assist and its role as the 'eyes and ears' of the organization was particularly important when it came to helping the widows and orphans of those who had died in the service of their country. Some of the widows were reticent about their plight and, on hearing of a case, the branch needed to act with tact and discretion.[22]

In addition to the benevolent work which was its principal reason for existence (and which is described in Chapter 4) the branch had other functions: it helped with the Poppy Appeal and it ensured that annual Remembrance was properly observed in the local community – a matter on which the Legion laid great stress. The social side too was important. As an organization which depended on its members to do its work, to provide its income and to provide it with a powerful national lobby, it needed to attract people. But there was more to it than that. Very strong bonds of comradeship had been forged in the war and much had been endured because of those bonds. While some injuries were clearly visible, others – those that would now be described as 'stress-related' – were not. The company of those who had undergone the same experience sometimes helped. And in the hard times following the war there was the need for mutual support and encouragement, preferably over a pint of beer.

Some recreational activities were of the more healthy variety: football teams, athletic competitions and boxing evenings. The formation of military bands was encouraged and on 30 September 1922 these activities were brought together in a sports rally at the Crystal Palace which was attended by the Prince of Wales and supported by six Legion bands. Whilst the athletic events were largely confined to London and the South, in the football final Gosforth from Northumberland defeated the local side Hackney by six goals to nil to become the first winners of the Maurice Cup.

Meetings of ex-servicemen in town halls were not the only way of expanding: in 1924 Sheffield Branch was making regular broadcasts about the Legion through the Sheffield Relay Station and had formed an orchestra to supplement its band. Grimsby Branch paraded their band through the streets in June 1925, followed by three motor lorries carrying bemedalled men in uniform sitting alongside their comrades in 'civvies' under a 'Labour Exchange' slogan to illustrate the Legion's work in employment. By 1925 the total number of branches had grown to over 2,600.[23]

## Problems with clubs

If a Legion branch wanted to provide social facilities for its members it formed a club, often with financial help from the United Services Fund. Since the fund was derived from wartime canteen profits this was a not inappropriate use of the money. But the club had to be registered with the Registrar of Friendly Societies, under whose rules it was controlled by its members – in effect self-governing. This meant that a Legion branch had no statutory control over its club even though it had been formed by branch members. It was also an usatisfactory situation for the organization as a whole: the clubs were seen by the general public as part of the Legion and any shortcomings would be laid at its door; yet it had no authority in the matter.

The problem went beyond that: there were a number of clubs that been set up by groups of ex-servicemen, often with the assistance of a grant from the USF, which owed no allegiance either to the Legion or to any other ex-service organization; yet it was widely assumed by the public that the Legion, as the national body for ex-servicemen, was responsible for their activities.

The National Executive Council, in consultation with USF representatives, decided to look for a solution. The British Legion Clubs Affiliation Scheme, launched in December

1922 sought to regulate all ex-service clubs on a voluntary basis, in return providing them with expert advice and assistance. The scheme was free for Legion clubs but the rest had to pay; thus non-Legion clubs might be induced to save money by coming into the Legion's fold.[24]

Clubs nevertheless made money and a little earlier, in October 1921, the NEC had attempted to recoup some of their adminstrative expenditure by forming a 'Legion Trading Corporation' to supply branches and clubs with all manner of goods, including liquor. The idea was good: the Legion would have a percentage of the profits, whilst the branches could take shares in the company, which was free to trade outside the Legion;[25] but most clubs had agreements with local suppliers, often breweries which had given them loans, and the venture did not succeed.

The Legion's concerns over clubs were not misplaced. In 1922 the Chief Registrar of Friendly Societies severely criticized some ex-service clubs for inefficient control. A further report in late 1923 was even more critical. It pointed out that 'some clubs have come to an end after raids by the police for drinking and gambling after hours; others after seizure of their effects by the Excise authorities for non-payment of the Intoxicating Liquor Tax. In many cases the greatest difficulty was experienced in obtaining the names of the officers of the club visited.'[26] The report of course did not apply specifically to Legion clubs, but there is little doubt that some at least of the criticism applied – and in any case in the public mind all ex-service institutions would be tarred with the same brush. There was a need for further action.

In February 1924 therefore the National Executive Council, once again in consultation with the United Services Fund, set up a joint advisory committee to consider the problem. The outcome was the appointment of two inspectors to visit and advise ex-servicemen's clubs, one sponsored by each organization. By the end of 1925 the Clubs Inspectors had visited nearly 500 of the 4,000 clubs which had received USF grants. The situation was not as bad as it might be: less than 16 per cent of those visited were in a 'clearly unsatisfactory' condition. This was of course the overall appraisal; whether those clubs attached to Legion branches were better run than the rest was not stated.[27]

These problems must be seen in context. The great majority of the Legion's clubs, as the Inspectors' reports indicate, were on the whole well run and many of them had excellent facilities, whether provided by a local benefactor, assisted by the USF or obtained purely through the efforts of the members themselves. Westhoughton clubhouse, near Bolton, stood in its own grounds and was approached by a drive of ninety yards in length. 'Trees have been freely planted, and the grounds laid out as ornamental gardens, with rustic seats, arches and a summer hut.' All this had been provided at the expense of the firm of the Club President. Another benefactor, Mr Djunjibhoy Bomanji of Windsor and Bombay, gave Windsor Branch their headquarters and clubhouse. Opened by Earl Haig, the building contained a concert hall, a billiard room with four tables, two lounge bars, a reading room and a library. It was valued at £5,000, a considerable sum in those days.[28]

Other clubhouses were more modest. At Plumpton and East Chittington in Sussex the whole of the work of building the club premises was carried out voluntarily by the ex-servicemen, to a value of £175. A further £200 was needed to get the club started and the members lent the money by purchasing bonds of ten shillings each (about £10 at today's prices), on which they received 6 per cent interest. In Exeter the ex-servicemen of Heavitree and Wonford used a USF grant of £425 to purchase the materials for a brick and stone building which they constructed entirely by their own efforts and which was

*Farnsfield members built their own club; the impressive building at Windsor was provided by a benefactor.*

valued at £1,300. After such exertions it is good to note that it was also well run: a visiting Clubs Inspector reported on it in the highest possible terms.

The Legion hierarchy was keen that clubs should be used for the self-improvement of members and not just for recreational purposes. Following the example of Ramsgate, which accumulated a wide range of books on all topics for its members, clubs were urged to set up their own libraries. In opening the Peterborough Club at Thorpe Lawn (set up with a substantial loan from the USF), General Lord Horne urged the committee to arrange lectures on citizenship matters to qualify ex-servicemen to play a leading part on their local parish and district councils. The serious note was somewhat offset by the opening ceremony: Lord Horne was required to cut his way into the new clubhouse through barbed wire.[29]

The members themselves favoured 'Dug-Out' nights which attempted to reproduce some of the atmosphere of the trenches. The room was converted with the aid of military paraphernalia and lit by candles stuck into bottles. Whether or not it was the intention such events sometimes provided a form of therapy for those still suffering from the effects of life in the front line. A visitor to a Dug-Out night at the Legion Club in Crewe in 1924 noted that after the meal had been eaten with jack knives and the song 'Apres la Guerre' rendered 'in gallant fashion' the participants 'as though forced to do so' related their experiences – some amusing – others tragic. He found it a moving and memorable occasion.[30]

### Every level of society

Legion members at this time came from all levels of society, reflecting the changes wrought by the Great War. Former officers, some very senior and distinguished, worked in committees on equal terms with those who had served in the ranks. The honorary treasurer of Wales Area Council was Major General Lord Treowen, the secretary Mr Jones. Local exceptions applied, particularly where the Legion branch was a former branch of the Federation which had originally barred officers. It is remarkable how many senior officers, no doubt influenced by Haig's example, were prepared to play their part in the Legion's activities at that time; nevertheless some felt that that the officer corps should be involved to an even greater extent.

Membership was not exclusively ex-service, although those wishing to qualify as *Ordinary Members* needed to have served at least seven days in one of the armed forces of the crown or certain auxiliary forces. Almost from the start they included women, following a resolution at the Legion's first annual conference in 1922. But conscientious objectors, who might have qualified by service in, for instance, the Red Cross, were barred.

Those who had not themselves served, including women, could join the Legion as *Honorary Members* provided that they supported its aims. This meant that an ex-serviceman's wife or other relative could follow him into the Legion. Curiously, those who were still in the armed forces were only entitled to honorary membership. But Honorary Members could not vote or hold office.

Nor did the Honorary Members pay any fees. But all other Legion members were required to pay a minimum annual subscription which was initially set at 2s 6d (worth about £4 today) as well as an entrance fee of one shilling (£1.50). The subscription was paid to the branch which was required to pass on an 'affiliation fee' of 1s 6d for each of their members to headquarters. Needless to say it was not unusual for headquarters to experience difficulty in collecting affiliation fees: seven branches were expelled in 1923 for failing to pay their fees. The amount of the affiliation fee was often the subject of a debate at the Annual Conference and in 1924 an attempt to reduce the amount from 1s 6d to 1s was defeated, the matter having been left to the delegates to decide without NEC involvement. Strong opposition to any reduction came from the Oulton Broad Branch who said that if agricultural workers could afford the fee then anyone could.[31]

The membership, of course, largely comprised those who had served in the Great War. But any ex-serviceman was eligible and in 1921 at least two Crimean War veterans were Legion members: one, Philip Parker, a member of Slinfold Branch in Sussex, who was born in 1831, had served at the battles of Alma and Sebastopol before being wounded at Inkerman, after which he was tended in hospital by Florence Nightingale.[32]

Such veterans apart, the membership in the 1920s was young to middle-aged, reflecting the intense demands that the war had made on the nation's manhood. Some joined simply to ensure that they received any war pensions benefits to which they might be entitled.* Many were of course attracted by the social opportunities that the Legion provided, epecially in the hard times of the 1920s. Some looked to the Legion simply as a form of trade union that would protect their interests, particularly as far as jobs were concerned. Others were genuinely concerned about the plight of fellow ex-servicemen and determined to help: such men were active not only on the Employment and Relief committees of their local branch and in the Poppy Appeal but also organised activities: concerts, whist drives, dances, football, athletics and indoor games, as well as the parties and outings for war orphans and their mothers that were a feature of branch life at the time.

Members often paraded with their own branch band. There was no shortage of either musicians or instruments – the infantry had marched to the front in the Great War to the tunes of their regimental band. The Legion held an annual band contest under the adjudication of its Director of Music, Lieutenant Colonel Mackenzie Rogan, a leading figure in military music and the winning band became the Headquarters Band for the next twelve months, receiving £25 for six performances. The scheme, however, proved difficult to operate and in 1925 the Lewisham Band became, for the time being, the 'Headquarters London Band'.[33]

Increasingly seen on parade was the Legion standard, bearing a broad gold band on a blue field with the Union Flag in one corner. It was designed by the General Secretary, Colonel Heath* and first seen in public in June 1922 at the Crystal Palace Sports Rally.

*And left when they had got it, according to a memoir by Major General Maurice.[34]

41

It was paraded as a national standard at the Annual Conference Cenotaph service on Whit Sunday 1924 and the first branch to receive a standard is recorded as Wadhurst and Tidebrook. By the end of 1928 about one in three Legion branches possessed standards; the others no doubt simply did not have the resources in those depressed times.[35]

By 1925 total membership had reached 180,000, assisted by the acquisition of clubs and their development. Even so only one man in every thirty who had returned from the war had joined the Legion.

### The first Conferences

The Legion's first Annual Conference was held over the Whitsun weekend in May 1922, twelve months after the Unity Conference that had brought the organization into being. It met in the Cannon Street Hotel, assembling on Whit Sunday and dispersing on the Tuesday. The opening speech from Earl Haig had two strands: wars could be prevented if ex-servicemen throughout the world banded together; and the Legion's object was the betterment of the people as a whole. It reflected the confidence felt by the Legion at this time. As the representative of those who had brought peace to the world through their sacrifice, it would ensure that they would have their say in the future.

The Chairman and the Treasurer also gave their reports and the *Legion Journal* reported that though one or two points were 'freely criticized' there was 'complete satisfaction with the work accomplished'. The delegates, many wearing wing collars above

*Delegates listen attentively at the Legion's first Conference at the Cannon Street Hotel, London, Whitsuntide 1922.*

*The meaning of Heath's design is unrecorded. But the blue used for background apparently signifies loyalty and fidelity, while the gold band has been interpreted as 'tried by fire'.

their dark suits and sitting upright on their hard cane chairs, listened intently. But they greeted with gusto the unanimous re-election of Earl Haig as President and Mr Lister as Chairman, singing 'For He's a Jolly Good Fellow' in response to each announcement.[36]

A parade then took place on the Horse Guards. Some members wore long rows of medals, others, like their Chairman, just two Great War awards, or even none at all if their war service had not taken them overseas. Legion officers were in morning dress and top hats, while the rank and file wore country tweeds and bowlers or cloth caps and tightly buttoned suits; but all stood stiffly to attention as Prince Henry, later to be Duke of Gloucester, and Earl Haig inspected the ranks. The parade was followed by a service at the Cenotaph attended by large crowds and reminiscent of Armistice Day.

On the second and third days Conference dealt with the motions that had been submitted, the most far-reaching of which was the proposal to admit ex-servicewomen as Ordinary Members; this was passed unanimously but not before it had been first pointed out that women did not wish to enter into club life. Many of the resolutions dealt with employment: there were complaints about the number of women in work that could be done by men – especially those who had no family to support and spent their wages on dresses 'with which wives could not compete' – and the unhelpful attitude of the trade unions to ex-servicemen. A resolution sought government action to make occupation of empty houses compulsory, to force landlords to provide bathrooms and to erect blocks of flats.[37]

It had been a good-natured and lively first Conference: the delegates had entered fully into the spirit, approving popular and sensible policies without debate, making their views clear on critical issues, bringing any time-wasting discussion to an end with loud cries of 'progress', bursting into song when the occasion moved them and even insisting on a speech from a reluctant Lady Haig when she presented the Haig Cup for recruiting to the joint winners, Portsmouth and Forest Town.[38]

This first Conference established the pattern. The Whitsun timing enabled those in work to attend without loss of pay; delegates travelled on the Saturday and Conference assembled on the Sunday. On Whit Sunday afternoon at five o' clock there was a parade and service, followed in the evening by a dinner for delegates. The conference continued on the Whit Monday and ended on the Tuesday, although the voting figures indicate that by the end of Conference the number of delegates had halved: in 1924, of the original 450 who had attended the opening only 260 were present at the end to decide on the next venue; clearly many delegates had to return on the Monday.

In subsequent years Conference continued to meet in London (see Table B at page 431). Not only was it convenient to the organizers but there could be a parade and service at the Cenotaph in Whitehall. Except for the first occasion, the venue was the Queen's Hall. The proceedings opened with a presidential address. Earl Haig was always received very warmly by the delegates, who seem genuinely to have held him in great affection as well as respect as a strong leader in the dark days of the war. A distaste for party politics was strongly evident in his remarks and he constantly stressed the need for the Legion to avoid any involvement: 'even if the smallest branch is swept into the party machine the good name of the British Legion will become tarnished'. He was not above the populist touch, remarking at the 1924 Conference that he found too many foreign waiters about and much preferred to be looked after by ex-servicemen; he had even seen girls employed as grooms, which was undoubtedly the work of men. Such remarks, reflecting as they did the views of his audience, were received with loud cheers.[39]

Either the Legion's Patron, the Prince of Wales, or another royal prince attended, gave

*Members from all levels of society. At the Whit Sunday parade at the Legion's first Conference in 1922, heavily bemedalled former senior officers stand shoulder to shoulder with Great War men to be inspected by Prince Henry (later Duke of Gloucester) accompanied by Earl Haig.*

an address and took part in the parade and service. On many occasions the Prince of Wales's arrival on the platform was greeted with such enthusiasm that even he was startled. He nevertheless seemed to enjoy the atmosphere of Conference, relaxed, smoking and clearly amused at the raillery.

The Prince's first speech in 1923 included sentiments that would attract much publicity on a similar occasion twelve years later: there was a reference to comradeship, hinting that it might be extended to the 'other side'.[40] Whatever his audience made of this, his words were punctuated with cheers and applause and at the end they sang 'For he's a jolly good fellow'. But comradeship was to be a frequent theme of the Prince and on many subsequent occasions he was to address delegates as his 'comrades'.*

The parades on Sunday afternoons were impressive: the royal visitor and the President led the Legion's senior officers down Whitehall to the Cenotaph; prominent among them in an electric wheel chair was the Legion's Treasurer, Major Brunel Cohen MP. Behind a band the delegates followed their standards down Whitehall. As the writer Alec Waugh noted, this army of clerks, tradesmen and solicitors variously attired, some in silk hats and morning coats, others in caps and bowlers and threadbare suits was a reminder that it was

---

*As did other speakers in the inter-war years, notably General Maurice when President. It may have reflected the special bond felt by that generation.

a civilian army that had maintained the strain of battle for four years.[41] A few years later, in 1927, the *Daily Express* remarked with some surprise that when the marchers removed their hats 'there was not one head that could be called young . . . grey heads in hundreds and many bald heads. . . carried on shoulders that are bowed by time. The soldiers of the war are growing old.'

Despite the outward appearance of military restraint, in the conference hall itself few holds were barred. Early in his presidency, in 1922, Haig became ill at ease when a speaker attacked the NEC in a speech which 'made up in venom what it lacked in substance' and suggested to the Chairman, Lister, that the delegate be stopped. Lister, however, responded that the man should be heard out since Conference would be just as sick of him. He was right: the floor made its feelings clear in no uncertain terms when the delegate sat down. Haig was immensely pleased at this outcome and thereafter had much confidence in the good sense of Conference. But the episode is revealing about both men.

Women delegates, if thin on the ground, made their views known: a resolution at the 1924 Conference that Legion assistance should be available only to members was opposed by Dame Florence Simson of Bracknell who pointed out that the money came from the pockets of the public who would think badly of the Legion if they kept relief away from other ex-servicemen. The cheers that greeted her remarks suggest that, apart from their common sense, they may well have constituted the first contribution by a woman delegate to Conference.[42]

The 1925 Annual Conference saw the presentation of the Legion's Royal Charter; it had taken nearly four years and comparisons must have inevitably been made with the comparatively swift way in which the Officers' Association had obtained their Charter in less than eighteen months. But the Legion itself was a more complex organization and the Charter covered a wide range of activities from the objects to the management of branches. The possession of a Royal Charter gave the Legion a formal status and endowed it with authority in every aspect of its work. But the very fact that it was so comprehensive also meant that much of the minutiae of the running of the organization was 'set in concrete' and that, as the organisation developed, any changes would also have to go through the entire Royal assent process.

In making the Charter presentation the Duke of Connaught remarked on the Legion's 'steadying influence'. Both the words and the fact of the Charter itself indicate how firmly the Legion had placed itself on the side of authority.[43]

## The Journal

In an organization as large and as widespread as the Legion internal communication was vital. Branches were given guidance in a monthly Circular issued by the General Secretary, but members, and others, could buy *British Legion*,* published monthly from July 1921. It cost 3d (worth about 40 pence today) per month, was distributed through branches but was also on sale in bookstalls.

The magazine had its roots in one of the organizations that preceded the Legion, but it nonetheless had a somewhat turbulent start. The first editor had edited the *Comrades Journal* but left his new post after two months. After two further editors had also left in quick succession it was decided in March 1923 that the General Secretary should add the task of Editor to his other duties. The vital circulation battle was conducted by Captain Simson, a member of the NEC, who managed to raise the sales from 12,000 per month in 1921 to 70-80,000 per month in 1923, enabling the magazine to pay its way, for the

---

*The magazine's title would change from time to time – although it always included the word 'Legion' – and for simplicity it will be referred to as the *Legion Journal* or *Journal* – the name commonly used whatever the current title.

moment at least.

The NEC had itself approved the arresting cover: a standing lion in silhouette surmounting the title '*British Legion*'. The first issue included good wishes from distinguished individuals including the Prime Minister Mr Lloyd George and, perhaps the most striking, from 'an ordinary tommy': 'may the British Legion live long and prosper – otherwise God knows what will be the fate of the ex-serviceman in five years time! The Legion is our only hope.' There were contributions from well-known literary figures: Arthur Conan Doyle, Thomas Hardy and Rudyard Kipling (who had himself lost a son in the Great War). It advertised itself as 'The Journal for all ex-servicemen' and, through its public sales, provided publicity for the Legion.

The magazine covered the issues of the day, such as the work of the League of Nations, as well as ex-service matters and the editorial was frequently critical of government policies. But branch reports were encouraged and Scotland had its own page up to March 1923, by which time its separate situation in the Legion was acknowledged.

'On the Lost Trail' was a poignant feature, dealing with missing relatives:

'. . . reported missing on Passchendale Ridge October 30 1917 . . . mother would be glad of any information';

'. . . taken prisoner of war and reported dead twice . . . in each case number and name were wrong . . . any information gladly received'.

Some entries reflected a grim humour: a captain who had lost his right leg offered single boots and shoes size 9 to anyone who had a missing left leg.

In 1925 the price was reduced from 3d to 2d a copy and this led to increased circulation.

## 1926 – 1930

### Jellicoe becomes President

When the National Executive Council met in special session, a few days after the shock announcement of the death of Earl Haig on 29 January 1928 their first act, after recording their 'profound grief', was to invite Admiral of the Fleet Earl Jellicoe to be President.

Jellicoe was the obvious choice. A Vice President of the Legion since 1926, he had the national stature to take Haig's place. In the public mind he was for ever associated with the command of the Grand Fleet since the outbreak of the war and, although the only serious encounter with the enemy at the Battle of Jutland in 1916 was inconclusive, he had at least preserved that fleet so that naval supremacy was maintained, ensuring Germany's ultimate downfall. He had too something in common with the soldiers who formed the vast bulk of Legion members: as a young officer he had fought on land, leading a bayonet charge in the Boxer Rebellion and taking part with the Naval Brigade in the battle of Tel-el-Kebir. And, having been Governor General of New Zealand, he had some knowledge of politicians – a useful accessory for a Legion President.

It was perhaps this political sense as well as an innate modesty that guided Lord Jellicoe's response to the NEC's invitation: he would accept only if the Legion branches gave their approval at the Area Conferences then about to be held. The issue was in little doubt and a few months later delegates at the Annual Conference formally elected him to the post.

Like his predecessor, Jellicoe was no mere figurehead: he was an active and well-informed leader, insisting on being briefed by the staff (for whom, as he often said, he had a high regard) before going out to see for himself what was happening. His tours were exhausting. On one visit to the north of England he went to six major cities in ten days, with innumerable calls on Legion branches and clubs, everywhere received with Legion guards of honour and large crowds.

Of small stature, he was also humble. He travelled third class on trains to save Legion expenses and wrote all letters in his own hand, sticking on the stamps himself. Even when seriously ill, he refused to incur the cost of a secretary. Yet he was a personal friend of King George V.[44]

The National Executive Council wished to remember Haig in a practical way with a scheme for a Memorial Home. (See page 94). The government for its part decided on an equestrian statue, but the project did not have an easy ride. The Legion's views appeared in a letter sent by the General Secretary to *The Times*: 'The proposed statue bears little resemblance to the man it is supposed to represent . . . the horse is like nothing Lord Haig ever rode.' Comments from other quarters were even sharper, but a Legion delegation to the Ministry of Works achieved nothing. The statue was eventually unveiled in 1937, the Legion providing a Guard of Honour.

But even more contentious memorials were in the offing. In June 1930 the *Legion Journal* reviewed a book by a Captain B.H. Liddell Hart entitled *The Real War*. It was dedicated 'To John Brown and the Legion' (Colonel John Brown had just been elected Legion Chairman) but, although the *Journal* review skated delicately around these aspects, the book contained references to Earl Haig that were hardly flattering. Liddell Hart was a respected military thinker and historian and the fact that the criticisms were balanced not only by an acknowledgement of the daunting task that Haig faced but of the resolve that he brought to it did not cloud the judgement: there were chinks in the armour. It was not to be the last criticism of its kind.

## Legion Chairman – a demanding post

Shortly before Haig's death Lister had relinquished the office of Chairman and was made CBE. It was no less than he deserved: not only had he been instrumental in forming the Legion but, under his chairmanship, it had developed into a respected national institution. His successor, Colonel Crosfield, had also been one of the founders of the ex-service movement; a territorial, he won a DSO in France and, despite losing a leg, managed to return to the front in 1918 with the RAF. After the Armistice he devoted himself to the welfare of ex-servicemen in Manchester before becoming the Legion's Vice Chairman for its first year. It cannot have been easy to take over from a highly successful founder-Chairman, but Crosfield proved equal to the task: at his first Annual Conference as Chairman he dealt with some of the more difficult delegates 'right vigorously', according to an observer. Crosfield handed over in 1930 to another territorial soldier, Colonel John Brown. Brown was one of the Legion's 'characters': the territorial brigade which he commanded was universally known as 'John Brown's Brigade' and his election to the post of Chairman was greeted by the Conference delegates bursting into a version of 'John Brown's Body'.

The post of Legion Chairman was demanding. Not only did he need to be involved in day-to-day decisions as the head of a nation-wide organization with an enormous range of interests but he was expected to make himself available to attend Legion gatherings across the country. Invitations ranged from large Area rallies to events at small country branches: he was 'their' Chairman and they had no compunction in asking for him to be present. The greatest challenge was, however, the Annual Conference which needed not only skilful management of up to one thousand delegates, many with very strongly-held points of view, but at times the ability to take firm action with those whose enthusiasm exceeded their sense of propriety. A suggestion to National Executive Council in April 1927 that the position 'should carry a salary commensurate with the status of the Legion' was nonetheless rejected.[45]

## Negotiations with Scotland

Although responsibility for Scotland would have taxed the Chairman even more, the situation there continued to rankle with the National Executive Council, some members feeling that the Scots should not be allowed to use 'British Legion' in their title, and in early 1927 they despatched the Assistant Secretary, Griffin, to Edinburgh. He got a friendly reception from the Scottish Executive who agreed to consider a union with the British Legion. Negotiations were opened and after further discussions a memorandum was put before the Legion's NEC in December 1927. In effect Scotland would have the status of an Area and even pay branch Affiliation Fees to London, a sticking point in the past. There were in return some financial advantages for Scotland and the path to ultimate unity seemed rosy. The NEC clearly decided not to force the pace this time and 'conversations' continued throughout 1928. However, the following year the negotiations broke down; although the terms offered included an undertaking that Scottish funds would not be touched, the Scottish Legion had insisted on an amendment to this effect in the Legion's Charter. The NEC had taken the view that delegates would not agree.[46]*

It was a sad ending to high hopes. With the Legion now well established in the rest of the British Isles a reconciliation with Scotland would have ensured even greater unity at a time when ex-servicemen and their families faced continuing hardship as the economic situation worsened. But neither side seemed prepared to 'go the extra yard'.

## Better communications

If communications with Scotland had temporarily lapsed, south of the border they improved with the introduction of motor cars into Areas in 1928 to enable them to visit their branches.[47] Wales had already attempted to solve the problem by wireless, in 1926 arranging through the BBC a ten-minute broadcast to their members by the Organizing Secretary with branches setting up loudspeakers in their clubs.[48] Despite the new technology the more traditional methods of 'closing the communication gap' remained. Most Areas had now formed Counties and in 1929 one Area Chairman drew a parallel between the County Regiment and the Legion County. 'It might be described as the key to the permanence of the Legion's existence. For where a County organization exists, branches, quite unconsciously perhaps, become infected with the County spirit.'[49] But such was the growth in the Legion in the late 1920s that, even at County level, it was not easy to keep contact with branches, particularly in the more rural parts. Dorset was one County that had attempted to solve the problem as early as 1925 by arranging conferences of groups of branches. These produced 'increased efficiency, and development of local organization'. By 1926 Group conferences were being held in the whole of the South Western and Home Counties Areas.[50] Communication with the military improved in 1928 when the dedication of the Sandhurst Branch standard was marked by a parade of Berkshire and Surrey branches at the Royal Military College. The 350 Legion members paraded with the cadets before being inspected by the

---

*This seems a strange conclusion after such promising progress and it may be that the NEC's real concern was that the financial concessions given to Scotland might be demanded by the other Areas.

Commandant of the RMC, finally marching off between the lines of cadets, who 'gave the ex-servicemen a rousing cheer'. The success of the occasion prompted a combined church parade the following year and in 1930 South Eastern Area made it an Area Rally with over 2,000 members parading behind sixty-eight standards; so large was the gathering, which again included the cadets, that the Sandhurst parade ground was barely adequate. After the parade the Commandant expressed the hope that it would become an annual event, so great was his belief in 'the advantage to the cadets of having the Legion movement brought to their notice in so striking a manner'.[51]

### Life in the branches

The late 1920s saw the number of branches expand from 2,600 to over 3,500. The Legion's activities, relieving hardship at local level and campaigning nationally to change legislation, had made it known in almost every household. And, despite the steady growth of the cinema and wireless as popular entertainment, its social activities, providing the simple pleasures of a regular get-together and an occasional outing, were still the highlights of many families' existences, while the clubs provided further inducement to swell the membership.

Headquarters played their part. A 'trackless train' – a road vehicle in the form of a railway engine and carrying Legion posters – toured parts of the country in 1926, attracting large crowds.[52] Of more enduring value was the policy of giving special attention to the branches in the more thickly populated and industrialized districts in order to ensure that the Legion's work was effective where it was most needed;[53] although not the main intent, it stimulated membership. Another Legion practice involved short-term losses but had long-term benefits. Termed 'stabilization', it closed down

*The Legion sought constantly to expand. The slide shown to cinema audiences in the 1920s had a straightforward message. For Legion Week, 1931, in Laindon, Essex, set up a 'recruiting office'; note the 'Peace' slogan in the window.*

49

unsatisfactory branches until they could be brought back into the fold under a new team. But the stick was accompanied by the carrot. The Haig Cup for 'outstanding excellence' was shared between two branches each year, one large and one small, the cup being held by each for six months with the branch sometimes being accorded little short of a civic reception in their local town or borough, so highly was the honour esteemed. Greater efficiency was also the aim of a one week training school for branch chairmen and secretaries at Llandudno in the summer of 1926.[54] New branches were not always based on a town or village. Working communities also came together under the Legion standard. At the first meeting of the City of London Branch in May 1928 such was the interest that city men were observed to be marshalled into queues to enter the Mansion House by the police. The agenda was based on a timed 'slot' for each speaker after 'zero hour'. Since the speakers included not only Lord Jellicoe, the Legion's President, but also the Lord Mayor and at least one MP – and city men were no respecters of rank – the 'count-down' afforded the audience a certain amount of fun. The branch would have full-time staff since it could not be run by the members without affecting their businesses.[55]

December 1930 saw the closure of what had been one of the Legion's most thriving branches. The Rhineland Branch of the Legion was formed in Cologne in 1921 to look after the interests of the demobilized ex-servicemen who had remained in Germany with the army to work in a civilian capacity such as clerks or barrack wardens. The branch moved to Wiesbaden with the headquarters of the British Army of the Rhine, but when the decision was taken to evacuate Germany it ceased to exist.[56] The best branches played a full part in the life of their local community. Of a practical nature was Luton's purchase in the winter of 1923/24 of a bullock which they cut into joints to distribute to the families of the unemployed. More symbolic was Fulham's involvement in the borough's 'Civic Week' in February 1927, parading its band and over 500 members at a religious service at Stamford Bridge football ground. Less formality attended Earl Jellicoe's opening of Birkenhead Branch's two-day bazaar in 1928 when the Legion's President was invited to meet 'Madamoiselle from Armentières'. He commented that the mayor, who had fought in France, might know her well, although he himself had always wanted to make her acquaintance.[57] A more frequent 'character' at Legion events was 'Old Bill'* – the walrus-moustached 'old sweat' of the Great War, invented by the cartoonist Bruce Bairnsfather and remarkably accurately portrayed by Legion members. The emphasis was, however, on helping the needy members of the ex-service community. In 1929 Bethnal Green Branch gave 300 children of poor ex-servicemen in the borough the best dinner many of them had seen for a long time, consisting of 'roast beef, Yorkshire pudding, vegetables, Christmas pudding and custard'. At the long tables the small faces beamed.[58] In Birmingham by 1927 Windmill Street's free canteen for ex-servicemen had served 300,000 meals. A colour sergeant who held the DCM and MM would have been buried in a pauper's grave had not the North Lambeth Branch alerted the authorities and obtained a military funeral with a volley and the sounding of 'The Last Post'.

'Dug-out parties' remained popular. Shortly before Christmas 1926 Nottingham members were directed to 'Hell Fire Corner', from which signs led to the 'Rest Billets' in a barn where the bully beef and biscuits were accompanied by 'Plum and Apple and Sergeant Major's tea in which the spoon will stand upright'. The party was the idea of the Branch President, and Legion Vice Chairman, Colonel John Brown.

---

*The police nickname of 'Old Bill' is supposed to have derived from this character, because many ex-servicemen joined the police.

*A Legion children's party at Bethnal Green. Some of the children would have been war orphans and the branch noted that 'it was the best dinner many of them had seen for a long time, roast beef and Yorkshire pudding'.*

## A Clubs 'Federation'?

More regular, if less imaginative, entertainment was supplied by the clubs. But, despite all the efforts of the Clubs Inspectors, some continued to be poorly run. Either they were financially mismanaged or they broke the law by selling drink outside their licencing hours, or both. And whether or not they were Legion clubs, the Legion generally got the blame.[59]

The officials of the United Services Fund now took the view that the clubs themselves had to enforce control and in late 1928 they called a conference of club representatives with a view to forming a self-governing 'Federation of Ex-service Clubs'. The idea appealed to the delegates, but it ran counter to the Legion's strategy of trying to bring all ex-service clubs into the Legion, which, although obviously a calculated risk, could expand Legion influence, and the Council refused to support the idea. There were further discussions, but they stalled over the fundamental point of disagreement: a 'Federation' would put ultimate control in the hands of the clubs themselves, whereas the Legion wanted to retain its influence over clubs through its Affiliation Scheme. The difference could not be resolved and the USF initative failed.[60]

## The 'Spring Offensive'

As the number of branches increased in the second half of the decade, so too did their size. This combination of factors resulted in an overall membership growth from 180,000 at the end of 1925 to nearly 300,000 by the end of 1930. The increase was partly a natural expansion based on the twin factors of continuing economic depression and the Legion's growing reputation, and partly active recruiting. And in 1926 the Army League was absorbed into the Legion, some 50,000 pre-1914 regulars who had rejoined the colours in the war.[61]

The 1927 campaign was known as the 'Spring offensive'. Launched with an 'order of the day' from Earl Haig – a letter to the press – it was branch-led, based on personal canvass of ex-servicemen in the area using the slogan 'over the top and the best of luck' with medals awarded to the most successful.[62]

Nor were the armed forces forgotten. Those at home might encounter the Legion's activities, but at the time a substantial part of the Army served in India and headquarters liaised with units there to get details of those due for discharge. The Legion needed an influx of younger men; its increasing age was reflected in the ending of the annual football competition in 1926 and by the opening in 1930 of the first British Legion golf course, set up by Westhoughton Branch near Wigan. The same year an article in the *Legion Journal*, 'Keeping Fit At Forty', suggested that Legion branches should set up gymnasia.

## Legion Scouts

In 1926 the Boy Scouts Association asked the Legion, as an organization well known in the development of the will to peace' to help to find men to act as scoutmasters. After discussion it was decided that the Legion should form its own Scout troops from among the sons and brothers of ex-service men and women. The Scout movement's founder, General Baden Powell, backed the enterprise with a message to the effect that he wanted the Old Legion to lead out the Young Legion, not to learn fighting but to ensure peace. With that message ringing in their ears, the Legion's leaders set the standard: no branch could become involved without the specific sanction of headquarters, while articles in the Legion Journal gave expert advice on how to run a Scout troop or a pack of Wolf Cubs. The strict control, coupled with the lack of resources in many Legion branches, seems to have limited the number of Legion Scout troops and Cub packs and the chief importance perhaps lies in the Boy Scout movement's recognition of the Legion as an instrument for peace. Earl Haig's personal interest was underlined when the Scout troop formed by the Poppy Factory was given the title 20th Richmond (Earl Haig's Own). His inspection of the troop on 28 January 1928 was his last public engagement before his death the following day.[63]

## Conference leaves London

The 1928 Conference was the first to be held outside London. The decision, taken at the previous year's conference, was not altogether popular with the organizers. The arrangements for London were well-rehearsed and the service at the Cenotaph was by now a national institution, sealed by a BBC broadcast. The General Secretary was clearly upset, comparing the 'dignified setting' of the Queen's Hall in London with the 'garish ornament' of the Futurist Cinema in Scarborough.[64] But Conference had made its choice and Scarborough it was to be.

For the Memorial Service the Prince of Wales himself led the long uphill march from the Esplanade Gardens to the war memorial at Oliver's Mount, while the rear ranks, trudging along safely out of earshot, broke into an irreverent 'Tipperary'. More formality was evident in London where the customary Legion Whit Sunday service at the Cenotaph took place despite the absence of the Legion's leaders and huge crowds watched as the Duke of York headed the procession down Whitehall.[65]

But Scarborough had changed the pattern and Conference thereafter alternated between London and the provinces, the 1930 Annual Conference taking place in Cardiff where the presence of the Prince of Wales led to such dense crowds outside the Empire Theatre that the police had to request delegates to remain behind when the Prince left, to the accompaniment of Conference singing 'God Bless the Prince of Wales'. Three hundred Legion Standards were paraded in the grounds of Cardiff Castle and some 10,000 Legion members then followed the prince to the National War Memorial. But at the parade at the Cenotaph that year an observer, General Sir Hugh Jeudwine, commented on the 'absence of officers or ex-officers, and especially of officers or ex-officers of the Regular Army, particularly those of comparatively high rank. Why don't they come?'[66]

## A 'patriotic duty'

The decision to reduce the price of the Journal from 3d to 2d had increased circulation, but not enough. At the old price it had been self-supporting, but it now became a cost liability, the first problem confronting the new full-time editor, C.H. Turner, when he took over the magazine from the General Secretary in July 1930 following the Bridgeman Report (see page 19).[67] Nonetheless the *Journal*, which was on sale to the public, augmented press and wireless reports to give the Legion some useful publicity. But in the late 1920s the film industry began to come into its own with cinemas opening in almost every town, an opportunity the Legion was not slow to exploit. The film 'Remembrance', released in November 1927, had a story line intended to show how the Legion was able to help two comrades who had suffered as a result of the war, as well as the orphaned children of a third. A 'love interest' sought to enliven the somewhat ingenuous plot, but perhaps the chief attraction was a cameo appearance by the Prince of Wales at a Legion dug-out party. The marketing was straightforward, Legion members being instructed to 'demand' that the manager of their local cinema book the film as a 'patriotic duty.' Whatever effect this may have had, the film seems to have enjoyed reasonable success and continued on the circuit throughout 1928.[68]

# 1931 – 1935

## Maurice becomes President

Earl Jellicoe fell ill in 1931 and resigned the presidency at Whitsun the following year. The Legion was sorry to see him go; it had been no easy task to take over Haig's role but the diminutive Admiral of the Fleet had worked hard at the job. His straighforward manner had endeared him to Legion members and such was their reluctance to lose touch that Jellicoe was made Vice Patron on resigning the Presidency. In this capacity his last duty was to name an engine 'British Legion' at Euston station. Shaking hands with the driver, a former sergeant, he apologized for his 'bloody finger' which he had cut while breaking a bottle of wine over the nameplate, adding 'I'm sorry'. 'That's all right, sir,' was the driver's response, 'it's a good old army word.' Eight days later, on 20 November 1935, Jellicoe died at the age of seventy-six.

Sir Frederick Maurice, Jellicoe's successor, had ended the war as a major general, having been forced to resign as Director of Military Operations at the War Office after revealing inaccurate ministerial statements. Compared with the two previous presidents he was an obscure man holding relatively low rank. Why therefore was one of the famous

*Jellicoe's last duty; the Legion's much-loved President and Vice Patron names a railway engine; a few days later Jellicoe died.*

wartime military commanders, still public figures, not approached? The answer was given by Maurice himself: the duties entailed almost daily attendance at headquarters, frequent travelling in England, Ireland and Wales, and sometimes to the overseas Dominions, with endless speech-making. The wartime commanders, most now near seventy, were too old.

Maurice himself was sixty-one. What he lacked in fame he made up in qualifications: he had begun his connection with the Legion as General Manager of the Officers' Association, whom he had represented on the Legion's first National Executive Council. On leaving the OA a year later to become a university principal, he was co-opted by the NEC and was a key figure in resolving the 1925 dispute with the Officers' Department. In 1930 Maurice was briefly Treasurer in succession to Major Brunel Cohen. As Legion President he would hold that office for fourteen years, steering the organization through some memorable times.[69]

### Fetherston-Godley's quick progress

The Legion would have liked their Chairman, Colonel John Brown, to have stayed longer in office. His decision in 1934, after four years, not to stand again caused some surprise, and not a little regret among the rank-and-file to whom his blunt but warm personality meant as much as his ability. But his high level of commitment to the Legion affected his business as an architect in his native Northampton. There was some consolation when Brown was knighted in 1934, the award recognizing not only his services to the Legion but also to the Territorial Army.

Brown was succeeded by his Vice Chairman, Major Fetherston-Godley. Fetherston-Godley had only left the army in 1925 but had made quick progress in the Legion, moving from county chairman to Legion Chairman in eight years. In sharp contrast to the small, terrier-like figure of Brown, the new Chairman was tall, urbane, and a great lover of country sports.

Major Brunel Cohen had been the Legion's Treasurer for ten years when he handed over the books to General Maurice in 1930 to become Vice Chairman. One of the Legion's great figures, he would have been a natural choice for Chairman had he wished. But he did not wish, believing that without legs he could not carry out the duties properly, although he always made light of his injuries, maintaining that 'I am normal except when it is necessary for me to walk.' Instead, after two years as Vice Chairman, he made way for Fetherston-Godley in 1932, taking back the Treasurer's post which became vacant on Maurice's elevation to President. Thus Fetherston-Godley had just two years in which to prepare for the Chairman's role. He was to need every moment of it.[70]

The General Secretary himself received a much-deserved reward in 1935 when he was appointed a Commander of the Royal Victorian Order in the Jubilee Honours List. Not only had Colonel Heath been responsible for the ex-service arrangements at the

Cenotaph each year since 1921 but his inspiration and organizing flair had made the Festival of Remembrance a deeply moving as well as popular event. And in the Jubilee Year itself he undertook the arrangements for the ex-service and youth element of the Hyde Park Review. The Legion had good reason to be proud of its chief of staff: he presented an austere, almost martinet, appearance with an immaculate turn-out, but he was nevertheless a man of imagination as well as ability.[71]

## Unity with Scotland 'cannot be rushed'

The breakdown of the negotiations in the late 1920s did not end the Scottish problem as far as some Legion members were concerned. Three resolutions at the 1932 Annual Conference attempted finally to resolve the issue: they sought to bring the Scots into the fold as an Area, otherwise Scotland should lose the privilege of using the British Legion name and badge.

But by now the Legion's leadership in London had come to live with the situation; there were more important battles to fight. In Scotland there was no desire to change and in any case the clan feeling was strong, particularly in the north. Unfortunately some of the feelings were equally strong in Portsmouth where the debate was taking place and there was every chance that the motion would succeed. As the resolutions stood they could have done irreparable damage to the relationship.

With the debate about to be closed, General Sir Ian Hamilton came to his feet. Although he was at the conference as the President of Metropolitan Area, he was also President of the British Legion in Scotland. He spoke forcibly. Accepting that the Royal Charter undeniably gave the Conference jurisdiction over the whole of Great Britain – 'I have read the bally thing over and over again' – even so Scotland was entitled to special consideration and unity could not be rushed; the Prince of Wales had reached the same conclusion before addressing the last Scottish conference in Inverness. But, Hamilton said, the real reason was the money. In Scotland the Poppy Appeal collection did not go to the Legion; it went to two independent committees of trusted citizens with financial and legal experience. If that system were to be changed the public would not give the same support to the Appeal: 'Nothing will get it out of the heads of the old ladies of Scotland that men who have worked at business and money-making all their lives are more likely to manage it thriftily than admirals and generals or even sergeant-majors.'

Hamilton's argument won the day. A substitute resolution expressed 'earnest hope' for the unity of the two Legions, trusting in the meantime that 'the closest possible relationship will be fostered'. Sir Ian went off to Dunfermline to tell the Scottish conference of the close shave and there the matter rested. But neither the high road of confrontation nor the low road of developing friendly relationships was to lead to unity; the Legion in Scotland had enjoyed its independence for too long by now to change.[72]

## The 'green-eyed monster'

Sir Ian Hamilton's personality would also colour another argument. Although South Eastern Area shared a building with Metropolitan Area in Upper Belgrave Street within a mile of Legion headquarters, this did not prevent a storm over Metropolitan Area's boundaries. These extended to a fifteen-mile radius of Charing Cross but in early 1934 Metropolitan's South Eastern and Home Counties neighbours jointly proposed that the boundaries be re-drawn to restrict the Area to the County and City of London. Nothing could have been more calculated to arouse the ire of the Metropolitan Area's formidable

*A formidable duo led Metropolitan Area between the Wars; General Sir Ian Hamilton and Admiral Sir Henry Bruce, however, found time to relax at an Area sports day in 1937.*

leaders, General Hamilton and Admiral Bruce; the suggestion would cut the number of branches in the Area by more than half, and they had not even been consulted. At the Area Conference the General, never lost for a pithy phrase, called the proposal 'the green-eyed monster of jealousy', going on to suggest that South East Area might at least have walked down the stairs to the Metropolitan Chairman's office with their ideas: 'That would have been the proper thing to do, but if you take a good look at the Admiral you'll see why they didn't do it!' At this Metropolitan anger grew and almost every branch was represented at the Legion's Annual Conference at Weston-super-Mare. The outcome was inevitable. Although the intention was apparently simply to get the whole of the Legion on to a county footing for the benefit of men who had served in the same county regiment, it was seen as Metropolitan's neighbours coveting the growing London suburbs and, to cries of 'Up the Met', the proposal was overwhelmingly defeated. But the incident serves to show how the Legion could be riven by internal faction, consuming energies that would be better spent on other matters.

Metropolitan Area was nonethelesss content to take a leaf out of the South Eastern Area's book by holding a joint parade service with the Gentleman Cadets of the Royal Military Academy Woolwich in June 1934. 4,000 Legion members were present and the salute was taken by the Chief of the Imperial General Staff. Meanwhile South Eastern

Area continued their association with the next generation of the Army's leaders with their annual parade in September at the Royal Military College Sandhurst,* which had now become a tradition.

Rallies in general had become popular in the Legion. Some were huge: 24,000 attended the East Anglian Area rally at Chamberlin's Meadow in Norwich in July 1935. The many successful County rallies signalled a change in emphasis taking place in the structure of the Legion. As Counties became more prominent, so grouping of branches within counties developed. This administrative level was unofficial, and has remained so, receiving no financial support from Legion headquarters; but it seemed to fill a distinct need. A report on a meeting of the South West District of Gloucestershire in March 1931 stated that 'Branches get to know each other and are able to discuss problems and sift out possible resolutions for conferences', while Bedfordshire found in the same year that their Group meetings 'do good by removing that sense of isolation'. An Oxfordshire report in 1932 said that the group movement was 'putting new life into existing branches'.[73]

## Branch activities in the 1930s

Although the Group system helped, headquarters remained concerned that, with the growth in branch numbers – the total of some 3,500 in 1930 was to become over 4,000 by 1935 – they should get as much help as possible. In 1932 the NEC appointed three Headquarters Travelling Representatives; their task was to tour the country continuously to give branches advice and assistance. It was no doubt a two-way operation which enabled the Legion's management to get a shrewd idea of the effectiveness of some of the branches and the representatives must have had their work cut out to visit between them a thousand branches a year or about a quarter of the total, but the scheme was held to be a success; it of course paralleled the existing Clubs Inspectors operation.

In these difficult times most branches were very active. Children continued to have a special place in many branch agendas, particularly the orphans. In the summer of 1931 Stoke Newington Branch was able to provide two-week country holidays for 256 children with the help of country branches and in particular the Women's Sections of those branches. Half of the children had never before been on a holiday of any sort. Some of the parents were able to make a contribution, but for the majority, such was the poverty of their homes, the holiday had to be completely free. Many had no suitable clothes and the branch Women's Section spent months beforehand collecting and sorting out garments while no less than 145 pairs of shoes were provided by a private fund. The children returned laden with fruit, vegetables and flowers, one even carrying a sack of potatoes. There were no complaints of poor behaviour and some children were invited to stay for an extra week or two.

There were now twelve 'house' branches in Metropolitan Area. The House of Commons Branch had been formed in 1923 when Earl Haig overcame his dislike of politics long enough to address a gathering of MPs. The branch had the distinction of being re-formed with each General Election. If, as its chairman, Major Brunel Cohen, admitted, it sat a little uneasily in the non party-political Legion, it was at least able to promote the Legion's policies in Parliament as far as the party system would permit. Other house branches included Lloyds Bank and Thomas Cook's and such branches not only promoted the Legion and its work in their own ways but were also strong supporters of the Poppy Appeal. A new recruit in 1932 was the Fleet Street Branch. Having a press foot in its own camp was, however, to prove a mixed blessing to the Legion: a pithy article

---

*Woolwich trained officers for the Artillery, Engineers and Signals, Sandhurst the rest.

by a branch member in the Legion Journal in 1933 led to press attacks on the leadership the following year.[74] (See page 60).

### 'We that are left grow old'

Despite its steady growth, the Legion continued in the early 1930s to be very conscious of the fact that there were far more ex-servicemen outside the organization than in its ranks. Perhaps one in every fifteen of the surviving veterans of the Great War was a Legion member. Recruiting took precedence over everything else as a way of celebrating the tenth anniversary of the founding and 'Old Bill' appeared on the cover of the Legion Journal sporting a Legion badge with the message 'I've joined the British Legion. Have you?' It got such a favourable reaction that it was brought out as a recruiting poster with the additional slogan 'If yer knows a better badge – get it!' and reproduced as a postcard for sale at one shilling a dozen. But even 'Old Bill' was unable to achieve the sort of expansion that the Legion sought among his 1914-18 comrades, while some branches resolutely refused to allow post-war ex-servicemen to join.

*'Old Bill' joins the Legion; a recruiting postcard of 1934.*

Among those who did not join the Legion there were many who belonged to their Regimental or other Old Comrades' Association – their 'family' organization. A number of attempts had been made in the past to bring such organizations under the Legion's umbrella, but with little success. Now the attempts were revived, leading off with a call for a greater unity in the Duke of York's speech at the 1931 Annual Conference: 'I look forward to the day when all Old Comrades' Associations and similar bodies shall be part and parcel of one great organization working for the ex-serviceman'. This was followed at the 1933 Annual Conference with a resolution calling for action.

There was a favourable response from some of the organizations, including the Old Contemptibles' Association, but they wanted to retain their individual identity. The solution was to form them into their own Legion branches. This presented little problem – the Legion already accommodated 'house' branches – but the sticking point was the subscriptions. The Charter required branches to pay an affiliation fee for every member.

This meant that the old comrades would pay two subscriptions, one to their own association and another to be passed on to the Legion. Although one organization, the Machine Gun Corps Association, complied, the others were not happy, and once again the 'Legion umbrella' was folded up and put in the corner.[75]

Meanwhile attitudes on membership were polarizing. Despite the conservatism of some branches others sought change. At the 1932 Annual Conference the National Executive Council had been asked to take steps 'to secure the continuance of the Legion for all time' by opening up the membership. Someone expressed it in a line from Binyon's poem, familiar to all Legion members 'We that are left grow old'. It led to a debate that continued outside Conference. Some suggested that members' sons should be entitled to full membership at the age of twenty-one. A more common proposition was that membership should be open to those still serving in the Armed Forces, including the Territorial Army. But this met with the response that true comradeship could only be forged in war.

A sub-committee duly considered all these views, but decided not to seek changes in the membership qualifications. Instead salvation lay with recruiting more of those currently leaving the armed forces. In 1933 therefore the Legion distributed a pamphlet 'To all those leaving the Services – Navy, Army and Air Force – Join the British Legion' and the General Secretary visited service commands throughout the country to arrange Legion addresses.

Nevertheless the debate continued. A nineteen-year-old war orphan, in a forthright article in the *Journal* in September 1934, gave his view: 'If the new generation does not take up the work of the British Legion . . . The War Memorials will become mere blocks of stone. The poppy will become no more than the daisy. In short, you who are so fond of vaunting your loyalty to your fallen comrades will have broken your faith with them.' This brought an equally direct response from a Branch President representing the opposite camp: the Legion was formed to help the ex-servicemen of the Great War; its task performed, it should die with them.[76]

It is doubtful whether Lady Haig would have supported the notion that the organization her husband had so strongly believed in should simply wither away. Following Haig's death she had become a regular attender at Conference, often making a short informal address. Her sorrow in her bereavement had been intensified by distress at the attacks on her late husband's conduct of the war and she clearly found solace in the presence of those who still revered him. In 1934 she presented a bronze equestrian statuette of Earl Haig with the request that it be placed before the Chairman at each Annual Conference.

Concern with domestic issues gave way to wider and more dramatic events in the mid-1930s. The 1935 Conference was the occasion when the Prince of Wales gave his support to the notion of a Legion visit to Germany in an endeavour to 'stretch out the hand of friendship'. These few words were to have an effect on Anglo-German relations – and on both the Prince's and the Legion's place in history – that few present can have appreciated. The episode is described in detail at page 148.[77]

## A *Journal* crisis

Perhaps less newsworthy but still dramatic in its own way was the saga of the *Legion Journal*. At a price of 2d it made an annual loss of around £1,500, which was just about sustainable; but in 1931, despite having put the price back up to 3d in February, the deficit exceeded £3,000. A crisis point had been reached and the National Executive Council considered ceasing publication. In the worst year that the national press had faced, with many papers and journals closing because of the loss of advertising revenues in the face of the depression, the Council might well have been justified in closure; but instead they decided to carry on, appointing in December 1931 a new editor, C.E. Carroll. The need for a businesslike approach was apparent in the new editor's contract; Carroll's £750 salary would be augmented by a bonus of £150 in any year in which the magazine did not lose money.

The effect of the change was quickly evident: a sharper style and a more imaginative layout, together with a new breed of contributors, including the younger generation such as Randolph Churchill and Max Aitken, as well as an article from the famous T.E. Lawrence – Lawrence of Arabia – on his life as Aircraftsman Shaw. In early 1934 'Old Bill' became a regular cartoon, an article by his creator explaining that Old Bill was any one of a number of Birmingham men who served in the Royal Warwickshire Regiment. Area supplements were introduced, with an 'all-Ireland' section reflecting the good relations between the Legion formations north and south of the border.[78]

The magazine again appeared on the bookstalls of W.H. Smith and other newsagents with coloured covers depicting war actions and the circulation more than doubled; by 1935 the *Journal* was selling 113,000 copies every month.[79] In the light of this achievement it might be supposed that the Editor of the *Journal* was the hero of the hour and in an unassailable position; after all such great men of Fleet Street as Lord Rothermere had paid tribute to him in the pages of his magazine. But such was not the case as events were about to demonstrate.

The problem began with the Editor's perception of the magazine: he saw it as having its own point of view within the organization. Such an approach no doubt reflected Carroll's Fleet Street background but it did not accord with the Council's ideas; they regarded the *Journal* as the organ of Legion policy, under their control as the democratically-elected leaders of the movement.

At first a certain amount of editorial licence was tolerated. But the magazine's fierce attack on the Ministry of Pensions in 1933, leading to criticism of the Legion in Parliament (see page 21), embarrassed the leadership, although the *Journal's* line was supported by an emergency resolution at the Annual Conference that year, submitted by the Fleet Street Branch.

This resolution originated in a meeting called by the branch in *The Times* boardroom on the eve of Conference. It was attended by the editors of several national dailies as well as representatives of the National Union of Journalists and the Institute of Journalists and it unanimously passed a resolution calling for a free editorial policy for the *Legion Journal*, sending a copy of the resolution to the Prime Minister for good measure. Conference passed the resolution, which not only urged an inquiry into the Ministry of Pensions affair but sought 'complete freedom for the discussion in the *Journal* of all matters affecting ex-service men'. But delegates then accepted the National Chairman's announcement that a Journal Committee had been set up to oversee the magazine's policy in consultation with the editor.

The editor, however, largely ignored the committee. As the Chairman, Sir John Brown, subsequently told Conference, 'I have never met a man more difficult to work with.' There was more friction when the editor announced that he had instituted a fund to assist branches in deprived areas to be represented at the forthcoming Annual Conference; such a fund, according to the *Journal*, 'followed normal newspaper practice'. The General

Purposes Committee reacted by instructing the editor to publish in the following issue a prominent notice in the name of the NEC stating that no such fund existed and the announcement had been made 'without authority'. Unfortunately the Chairman appears not to have been informed of this rather heavy-handed response and when he ordered the notice to be withdrawn the editor was presented with a journalistic opportunity of which he took full advantage: he published both the notice and the withdrawal, together with quotations from letters from branches seeking financial help to be represented at Conference. It was, as he perhaps expected it to be, his parting shot; within a few days he was dismissed.[80]

There followed attacks on the Legion in the press. But the membership now closed ranks and the 1934 conference endorsed the dismissal. A new editor was only appointed after a policy review had decided that the magazine should be 'looked upon as a publication of propaganda for the Legion' subsidized if necessary by up to £1,000 annually. This reflected the actual situation since Carroll's departure, the magazine having once more made a loss. However, Major Verney's contract also made provision for a bonus if the *Journal* ran into profit.[81]

Under Verney the magazine's activities were less dramatic. In 1935 it introduced a 'British Legion Cubs' scheme, each month recounting the activities of 'Peter and the gang'. Members' children under fourteen or war orphans could form their own 'gangs', receiving a membership card and badge. It seems to have been intended as a low-key propaganda activity among the young: Peter and his friends had a poor opinion of politicians and those who had not joined up in the war, while performing good deeds for ex-servicemen; but it was more akin to the 'Ovaltinies' than a serious youth involvement and did not survive the war, ended by a paper shortage in 1941.[82]

A rather different audience had meanwhile been targetted in the Legion's first 'talkie'. 'Twenty Years After' gave the history of the Legion and its achievements, opening at the Manchester Hippodrome in October 1934, with a commentary by Mr J.R. Griffin and the epilogue spoken by the Prince of Wales. The Prince's popularity ensured the film's bookings at cinemas up and down the country, Legion branches once again putting pressure on the local management for good measure.[83]

## 1936 – 1940

### Into another war

In the Coronation Honours List of 1936 Major Fetherston-Godley became the first Legion Chairman to receive a knighthood for his work in that office. The distinction recognized his efforts to use the ex-service links with Germany, Austria and Italy to maintain peace; the full story is told in Chapter 6. Reflecting, as it did, the anti-war feelings of the majority of Legion members at the time, it was a popular award. A year later Colonel Sir John Brown, who had also been knighted while Chairman, but in his case for service to the Territorial Army as well as the Legion, became a Major General in the TA, while John Smedley Crooke, an NEC member who was a Birmingham MP and a doughty champion of the ex-service cause in Parliament, also received a knighthood. Such distinctions were an indication of the calibre of the National Executive Council. Yet in some ways it was not a truly representative body: of the thirty members of the Council in 1939 fully two-thirds were former officers, of whom six had held the rank of Brigadier or above. They had of course been democratically elected, but the proportion indicates not only how much the organization still looked to the traditional sources of leadership but also the extent to which such sources were prepared to provide it.[84]

On the outbreak of war on 3 September 1939 Fetherston-Godley was recalled to duty and John Brown was further elevated to Lieutenant General. A few days later, on 9 September, the NEC met under the Vice Chairman, Colonel Ashwanden. Anticipating grave difficulties in the management of the organisation under wartime conditions, the Council gave the power to a triumvirate – Ashwanden, the Treasurer, Brunel Cohen, and a former Chairman, Colonel Crosfield – to act together in an executive capacity to run the Legion.

That meeting took place at Cardigan House, Richmond Hill, which adjoined the Poppy Factory and which was to be the Legion's wartime headquarters (see below). But the NEC was able to meet regularly despite the emergency and, except on two occasions, every subsequent wartime meeting was held at the Great Western Royal Hotel, Paddington, although attendance sometimes fell to less than half.

In 1940 his active service commitments forced Fetherston-Godley to hand over the Chairmanship to Ashwanden. Although Fetherston-Godley will always be associated with the Legion's efforts in the 1930s to help Britain avoid war with Germany and in particular as the head of a Legion delegation which was received by Hitler, he was a strong reforming Chairman at a time when the Legion needed one. He believed in straight talking, not hesitating to tell delegates at an Area conference that they talked too much and did too little. He finished the war as a brigadier.

When Colonel Ashwanden took over as Chairman in May 1940 he had already been holding the reins for some nine months, overseeing the transition of the Legion to a war footing. A much less outgoing personality than his predecessor, he was nevertheless well-suited to the task: cautious, pragmatic and dependable. His task was to maintain the structure of the Legion intact whatever the stresses of war and to ensure that it was ready to deal with the problems that would undoubtedly come with the advent of peace. To him is due much of the credit for the Legion's post-war regeneration.[85]

It had been planned that Legion headquarters should leave central London in the event of war and in early September 1939 it moved to Cardigan House, a building that had been used to house disabled Poppy Factory workers and their families before new flats were built. But the move attracted strong criticism from at least one quarter: Metropolitan Area had chosen to stay in Upper Belgrave Street in London's centre and General Hamilton and Admiral Bruce were not slow to suggest that headquarters had been over-hasty, a comment strongly rejected by Fetherston-Godley, home on sick leave: 'Critics today would have been the first to complain if the Legion's benevolent records had gone up in smoke after a bombing raid.' In fact Cardigan House had several near-misses from bombing during the Battle of Britain while Haig House remained unscathed and was used as an American forces hostel later in the war. But, as the Legion's President pointed out to Conference in 1940, the Legion had simply followed government policy to move non-essential activities out of the centre of London.[86]

Accommodation was tight at Cardigan House, but mobilization had considerably reduced the staff, although not the workload. One person did not make the move to Richmond: Colonel Heath, the General Secretary since the Legion's inception, became seriously ill just before the outbreak of war and had to retire in September 1940. He was succeeded by J.R. Griffin, who had been at Heath's side for all of this time as Assistant and Organizing Secretary.[87]

### Areas cut to nine

In the run-up to the war there had been a number of changes in the Legion's field structure. As the Counties developed, economies were made at Area level. In 1935 East Anglia and Home Counties Areas amalgamated to form Eastern Area. The next year, as part of a Chairman's review, the NEC considered the wholesale abolition of Areas in favour of a county-based system; but that went too far and the compromise solution was further Area amalgamation. In 1937 South Western and South Eastern Areas were joined to form Southern Area, while Midlands Area was formed from the East and West Midlands. The amalgamation of Yorkshire and North Eastern Areas to form Northern Area took a little longer to achieve and was only completed in 1939. There were now only nine Areas in place of the original thirteen and such changes in an organization as deep-rooted as the Legion were not always easy. Well might the NEC thank the committee concerned for their 'tactful handling of Areas in connection with the negotiations'. But when the war came this increased emphasis on counties was to help the Legion to co-operate with the civil authorities since many of the government emergency schemes were also county-based.[88]

Not all counties were 'shires': Birmingham already had county status and Bristol Branch was elevated in 1937 after Gloucestershire abandoned their opposition and gave the new County a 'tenner' for good measure. Loyalties continued to be developed in annual rallies, as many as 9,000 Legion members attending the 1939 Essex rally at Clacton football ground. In June of the same year Surrey ran a tattoo at Wimbledon Stadium; the aim was to attract young people to play a part in the defence of the country and the highlight was an RAF raid.[89]

Meanwhile, after all the jousting with Scotland over the previous two decades, quiet diplomacy was at work. From March 1938 two representatives of the Scottish Council attended NEC meetings in London with a reciprocal arrangement north of the border. This led to a formal agreement, endorsed by the Scottish conference in 1939, for joint policies for national and international affairs, and in particular a joint approach to government over ex-service issues. It was not, perhaps, the end product that some desired, but it was an arrangement that was to be of great value in the war.[90]

### 'Were there no soldiers before 1914?'

With the increased County activity the number of branches continued to grow, until by 1939 there were nearly 4,500. A recruiting campaign in 1936 saw the introduction of the Jellicoe Cup and Shield for branch membership increase, as a memorial to the late President. But some branches still refused to recruit post-war men, suggesting that the public only supported the Legion because of its Great War associations. There was even a proposal at the East Midland Area Conference in 1936 that the Charter should be changed so that only Great War veterans were eligible for membership and benefits, interrupted by a very old soldier who 'demanded in a voice vibrant with indignation "Were there no soldiers before 1914? Was the British flag kept flying by perpetual motion?"' The debate also stirred up the Honorary Members who pointed out that many of them had joined to assist those who fought but they were often excluded from meetings. Did the Legion really want them?[91] But the discussion would be terminated abruptly in 1939.

The visit of members of the Canadian Legion in 1936, in Europe for the unveiling of the memorial on Vimy Ridge, sparked another debate. Some British Legion members were impressed by the fact that the Canadians all wore the same headgear – a beret with a maple leaf badge – an 'orderliness' which contrasted with the 'toppers, bowlers, straws, trilbys, caps and "no-hatters" seen on the ordinary British Legion Parades!' But others thought that a beret was undignified and might suggest a political organization. Gravesend, Northfleet and District Branch pointed out that they had worn a beret in Legion blue with gold tassel since 1933, although there was a difficulty: what to do with the ordinary hat during the parade?[92]

### 'The more we are together'

The Annual Conference in the Buxton Garden Pavilion in 1936 had greeted with almost unprecedented enthusiasm the decision of the new King, Edward VIII, to remain Legion Patron, a position that he had held as Prince of Wales since 1921. But the following year, back in the Queen's Hall in London, it was his brother, George VI, who held that office. On neither of those occasions was the Patron present; nor was there to be any royal representative at a Legion conference for many years.

There were, however, other visitors in those tense pre-war years. At Buxton the German Duke of Saxe-Coburg was present to express the hope that future generations would be spared the experience of war: it was not only his own wish but 'above all that of my Führer, Adolf Hitler' he concluded. At the Palace Theatre, Newcastle, in 1938 Major General Reinhard, described as the head of all German ex-servicemen, spoke of the common desire for peace. When he presented a silver rose-bowl as a reminder of this sentiment delegates rose spontaneously and sang ' The more we are together the happier we shall be', whereupon the General was so moved that he responded by giving the Nazi salute. But prior to Reinhard's speech the Legion's President had commended branches on their help with Air Raid Precautions work. At the 1939 Conference at the Queen's Hall there were no German visitors. Instead the cheering followed the President's words: 'If our country is attacked we are going to defend it to the last . . . if our friends are menaced we are going to stand by them.' And the following year, as delegates assembled in the same hall, some in uniform, German armour was thrusting through France and Belgium to the Channel ports and motions of urgency were being prepared to deal with the threat of enemy parachutists. It was the last Legion Conference to be held there; by Whitsun 1941 the Queen's Hall was a victim of the London blitz.[93]

## 1941- 45

### A new headquarters in Pall Mall

In 1943 Colonel Ashwanden handed over the Chairmanship to Brigadier General Fitzpatrick, another sound planner who had headed the committee which had persuaded the government to make changes in the war pensions scheme. His military background was also relevant: he had been the Army's Deputy Director of Personal Services and was well suited to lead the Legion into the era of post-war resettlement.[94] 1943 also saw the much-deserved award of a knighthood to the Legion's long-serving Treasurer, Major Brunel Cohen, who had started his duties in 1921 with a cheque for £200 handed to him by Lister with the cheerful remark, 'You can run the Legion on that.' At the investiture at Buckingham Palace the King was deeply stirred when Brunel Cohen was pushed towards him in a wheelchair.[95]

Concern over the need to ensure that the new generation of ex-service men and women came into the Legion, rather than perhaps start an organization of their own, was reflected in the public relations campaign as the war drew to an end. The importance with which the Legion regarded this project is shown by the fact that £100,000 of reserve funds were allocated to it. The aim, as the experts expressed it, was to create a desire on the part of serving men and women to join the Legion, but, they added, 'the commodity must look right'.[96]

To look right the Legion needed a suitable headquarters in central London. This would not only help the image but aid efficency by bringing the departments together, something which had been sought since the Bridgeman Committee report in 1930, and in late 1943 a search began. Towards the end of 1944 a building became available next to a bomb-damaged site in Pall Mall and the NEC unanimously decided to buy the leases on both, having to move quickly since there was another competitor. But, although its handsome Edwardian facade was disparagingly described in the *Journal* as 'somewhat ornamental', certainly in Fleet Street's view there was no better publicity for the Legion than a London centre like this. And for the staff, who were existing in bad and cramped conditions in Richmond, the move could not take place soon enough, the first of them occupying their new offices in March 1945 as soon as repairs were complete.[97]

### Working with Scotland

Nor did the Area staff have an easy time of it during the war. Those mobilized were not replaced and office expenditure was cut. The emergency added to the workload as branches faced new problems and, as demobilization plans were developed from 1943 onwards, the Areas ran training schools to prepare branch officials for the expansion of case work when the servicemen returned home. The wartime travel problems for Areas gave Counties even more responsibility towards their branches and the war years were something of a watershed in their development; in 1945 their adminstration was strengthened and in some cases their sub-divisions – Groups – were given financial help by the Council.[98]

The closer working arrangements with Scotland had been developed just in time for the war and there was Scottish representation on the committees set up to deal with both wartime and post-war problems. But something went wrong in 1943 when Scotland put forward a war pension proposal, which reached no less a personage than the Prime Minister, without consultation. This seems to have been solely an error in staffing as the Scots were quick to suggest a joint coordinating committee to avoid a recurrence. But the NEC, clearly feeling that this was an isolated incident, saw no need to change the existing arrangements. It says much for the improved spirit of mutual goodwill that the incident passed off so lightly.[99]

The war saw a reduction in the number of branches, thirty-one overseas branches being lost in 1940 due to enemy occupation, but not before Ostend Branch had distinguished itself by running, on the orders of the British Embassy, an evacuation centre at the port when the Germans invaded Belgium. Paris Branch kept its identity by re-establishing itself in London. There was a steady suspension of branches in England and Wales as some were in coastal areas which had to be evacuated and others found it impossible to keep going because of the loss of key officials. But altogether only around one hundred home branches, perhaps 2 per cent, were closed and from 1944 onwards there was some recovery, including new branches forming, and the final year of the war, 1945, saw an increase of 120 over the previous year.[100]

## Branches at war

Attitudes too had changed as a result of the war, or perhaps the First World War veterans saw their Second World War counterparts in a different light from the inter-war regulars: branches welcomed men serving in their areas and invited them to become Honorary Members, Westhoughton Branch in Lancashire having nearly 600 on their books in 1941. As men began to be discharged from active duty and joined the Legion, branches made positive efforts to involve them: in 1943 Stoke Newington Branch had duplicated all of their officers with ex-servicemen from the current war so that they could learn the ropes. By 1944 it was reported that there were large numbers of Second World War men on branch committees, in some cases holding office.[101]

The declaration of war had seen many Legion branches setting up collecting depots for comforts for the troops; most in demand were woollen garments made by wives and daughters of members from wool supplied by the Cambrian Factory. Others opened canteens and recreation centres for troops stationed in the district or organized concerts and dances. From June 1940, with the loss of much of the British Expeditionary Force at Dunkirk, there was involvement with prisoners of war who had not heard from their families. The Legion's Geneva Branch received the queries and passed them to Legion headquarters who referred them to the local branch to make inquiries. The Geneva Branch also organized an emergency scheme to send Red Cross food parcels to the prisoners when the collapse of France disrupted normal communications. Two other overseas branches, New York and the up-state Rochester, combined to raise funds to buy ambulances for Britain, while their ladies knitted woolen garments for despatch to the troops. Back at home Hornsey Branch made their contribution to morale with an event broadcast on both Forces and Overseas wavelengths – 'Sing with the Old Brigade'. Besides the old favourites it included the up-to-date ones such as 'Roll out the Barrel'.[102]

There was some social life, even if only an annual get-together. The heavy Legion involvement in the Home Guard sometimes helped: the annual supper of Wheelock Branch in North Western Area was provided from rabbits shot by the Home Guard as part of their marksmanship training. The clubs too played their part: Windmill Street Club in Birmingham continued a practice, started in 1924, of free meals to ex-servicemen – meat pie, a slice of bread and cocoa, serving over 100 people a day, including some discharged in the current war. But at the 1942 Annual Conference Southern Area asked that clubs that had made large profits in the war – as some would undeniably have done – should help the Benevolent Fund, resulting in a resolution that steps should be taken to 'co-ordinate' branch and club activities. It was the old chestnut: before the war, in 1938, the NEC had commissioned an investigation 'to go into the whole question of clubs', but there had been no positive outcome. The subject would reappear at the 1945 Conference when the NEC would again set up a committee to investigate. In the meantime the papers were speculating that ex-servicewomen would want equal rights in Legion clubs after the war. But this time there was an answer at hand: as private members' clubs it was a matter for them, not the Legion.[103]

As early as 1944 a new membership record was achieved. It brought one problem: shortage of metal meant that the new recruits had to wear a round celluloid button with the Legion badge overprinted; but it was exchangeable for a metal badge after the war.[104]

## The Victory Conference

Because of the 'blitzing' of the traditional London venue, the Queen's Hall, the 1941 Conference took place in the Cambridge Theatre with over 500 delegates, a remarkable figure under the circumstances. Equally remarkably, the usual parade and service was held at the Cenotaph. But the two successive Conferences, both held in London, in 1942 at the Wigmore Hall and the following year at the Porchester Hall in Bayswater, were even better attended, over 900 being present in 1943. Both of these conferences were concerned with post-war planning, the fact that they were taking place during some of darkest days of the war in no way affecting the delegates' view of the future. But in 1944, for the first time in the Legion's history, there was no Annual Conference. It was first postponed as the result of an urgent appeal by the Railways Executive – as it later turned out in order to keep the rails clear on the eve of the invasion of Europe – and then cancelled by the NEC.[105]

The 1945 Conference, held a few days after Victory in Europe had been celebrated, started at the Dominion Theatre and then moved on to the Central Hall, Westminster. There were over a thousand delegates – more than attended the Labour Party's Blackpool conference that same weekend – and the Second World War 'new boys' lost no time in queuing up at the microphone to speak; nor did they need any advice from the old hands on how to make their point. With over two hundred resolutions on the agenda (because of the cancellation of the 1944 conference) some were barely discussed. But it was nonetheless lively. Veteran attenders encamped themselves around the microphones and some speakers attempted to shout each other down.

Legion conferences could be robust and delegates did not always behave well. But there was an underlying good humour and a common sense that meant that whatever the emotions expressed – and there is no doubt that delegates sometimes had good cause to give vent to their feelings – in nearly every case there was a sensible outcome, as an experienced Chairman well knew.

The 1945 conference was certainly well-publicized: no less than 329 newspapers carried reports and the popular weekly *Illustrated* devoted its centre pages to a pictorial account.[106]

## The wartime Journal

In the war years the Legion Journal published regular articles such as 'grow more food' and reports on the Home Guard, of which 'Old Bill' was now a member. The paper shortage forced it to reduce to pocket size from 1942 onwards, a format that was to last eight years; despite the small size and rough wartime paper, it was popular, especially as the lack of space had forced a more pithy style together with eye-catching headlines, and the circulation for 1942 reached one million, a figure that would have been exceeded had paper rationing allowed. At the end of the war it featured advice on demobilization, with the Legion Chairman being taken through the entire 'demob' procedure and reporting that he could find nothing to criticize; the man could even telegraph home his time of arrival. By 1945, with some relaxation on the paper controls, the circulation had risen to 100,000 a month, twice the pre-war figure.[107]

★    ★    ★

At the end of the war the Legion's structure could hardly have been in a sounder state.

The framework had not only remained intact but it had developed with Counties coming into their own while the pre-war record number of branches was already exceeded. The old worries about its survival as a membership organization had been resolved with an influx of new blood. A new approach to public relations had put it firmly in the public eye, ensuring that its considerable wartime achievements were properly acknowledged. Financially it was in a strong position; the economies resulting from the pre-war overhaul of the administrative system had been augmented by wartime savings, while the public's generosity in the war years had replenished its coffers for benevolent work. Both the administration and the Legion's charitable activities would be carried out from new and commodious headquarters in the heart of London. Undoubtedly there would be many new and difficult challenges. But the Legion was surely well equipped for the task.

*The Legion points the way to bright new future. This poster sought to reinvigorate the membership from the new generation of ex-service men and women emerging from the Second World War.*

# CHAPTER 4

## WORK 1921–1945

# *'A Land Fit for Heroes'*

## 1921 – 1925

### The legacy of the Great War

Social attitudes in Britain were already changing when war broke out in 1914. Old Age Pensions (for over-seventies) had been introduced in 1908, followed by free medical treatment, sick pay and maternity benefits in 1911. In keeping with this trend the government did not neglect its wartime duties. It introduced the payment of pensions to war widows and to those men incapacitated by service. In previous wars no government had felt compelled to do more than pay those who were doing the fighting – and only for as long as they did so.

The war's principal social legacy was, however, unemployment. Following the Armistice in November 1918 some four million men were discharged from the armed forces; over one and a half million had already been discharged through wounds or sickness and nearly three-quarters of a million were dead.

The living returned to a highly developed industrial Britain which, for a short time, prospered and was able to absorb most of them back into the workforce. But, as noted in Chapter 2, the nation's economic position declined as pre-war markets could not be regained. This led to a fall in the domestic market as purchasing power diminished. By 1921 unemployment had risen to over two million, some 10 per cent of the workforce. It was not to fall below one million for the whole of the inter-war period.

Of the two million unemployed it was estimated that 600,000 were ex-servicemen. Many had had little opportunity to learn a trade before they left for war; they returned to the employment market with a row of campaign medals but with no civilian trade or profession. It was a problem that applied to all ranks; many officers had been on the verge of university or trying to make a start in one of the professions when they answered the call to arms. Such men were particularly disadvantaged; but the Legion believed that all those who had fought should have *preference* in employment and this was to be the cornerstone of its employment policy.

There was often less than a warm welcome to the returning soldier from his fellow workers, especially in the building trades where there was much hostility to the employment of ex-servicemen. The Minister of Labour himself noted that, particularly in the London area, attitudes had been 'so unfriendly in some cases that it had caused the ex-servicemen to throw the whole thing up'.[1] A former union official spoke in the House of Commons of the 'disgraceful conduct of the building trade unions towards the ex-soldiers'.[2] All this tended to make the Legion believe that the unions wanted to create an 'aristocracy of labour' composed of those who had spent the war in skilled employment presiding over a war-service generation of unskilled workers.[3]

Inevitably the former servicemen compared their situation with that of those who had remained in their civilian jobs. The coal miners and steel workers had clearly been essential to the war effort (and many had volunteered for service). But as the ex-servicemen looked in from the street to the warm and brightly-lit government offices, where the exempted civil servants went about their business, many felt bitter.

There was resentment too at the number of jobs held by women. Before the war a campaign had been fought for the emancipation of women. It was not a cause to which the average working man gave a great deal of thought, let alone support. But the war changed the employment landscape. Women were needed for work in the hugely expanded munitions industry. They also replaced men who had gone to the front: they took over their office stools, worked on the land, in munitions factories and even drove buses and trams. When the men returned they expected the women to move aside, making exceptions only for war widows and the wives of their unemployed comrades.

## The Legion's sword and shield

The Legion's response to the problem was twofold: to help those in distress because of unemployment and to tackle the problem at its root by assisting unemployed ex-servicemen to obtain employment.

The local Legion branches were directly involved. They could identify cases, assess the need and give whatever help they could, if necessary referring the problem back up the line for further assistance. Headquarters supported the work of the branches. But they also took the offensive by attempting to remove the cause of the misery. The analogy of a shield and a sword is appropriate both here and in the wider Legion context: while the shield gave protection to the vulnerable – all ex-servicemen and their families, not just Legion members – the sword attempted to change the circumstances which inflicted the misery.

*Legion soup kitchen run by the Crouch Hill Branch 1922. Supplies have just arrived; meanwhile, children with jugs await their turn.*

In general terms, while the Legion's leaders wielded the sword, the branches held the shields. They set up local Relief Committees which provided help in kind, through vouchers which were exchangeable for groceries, meat, bread, coal or other necessities, the branch paying the tradesman from its own Relief Fund, set up with a grant from headquarters and reimbursed on submission of the tradesman's receipts. It was a simple and effective system.[4] There was no doubt that this help was needed. In 1923 alone nearly a quarter of a million cases were given temporary relief by the Legion.[5] Although the unemployed might benefit from National Insurance, the allowance was a bare minimum, about a third of the average wage. Nor did it apply to certain groups such as agricultural workers and the self-employed, who had to rely on the locally-administered Poor Law. There were many cases of ex-servicemen whose families were saved from the workhouse (which was the 'indoor relief' function of the Poor Law, as opposed to 'outdoor relief' financial assistance) by the local Legion branch; even so some 35,000 ex-service family members were in Poor Law institutions in 1924.[6]

In Ireland the situation was even worse than in England and Wales. Here too there was unemployment, but any local relief, if it existed at all, was meagre and those who had served in the British Army had a low priority. The Legion therefore gave substantial help to the Irish branches from its general pool; nothing less would have been justified for those Irishmen who had fought so gallantly in the war.[7]

## Start-up loans

In keeping with its strategy, the Legion preferred to spend its money to promote employment and it set up a business loan scheme. Applications were first investigated by the branch. The branch recommendation could not be given lightly: it had to take account of prospects, local competition and anticipated income and expenditure; in other words a proper business plan was required. If approved the money was lent interest-free, but regular repayments were required. Local committees were urged to consult businessmen who could not only recommend whether a particular scheme should be supported but, if a grant was made, advise the ex-serviceman concerned on how to run his venture successfully.[8]

Although loans were limited to £25 (equivalent to perhaps £750 today) they helped ex-servicemen to set up businesses such as building and decorating, boot repair, window cleaning and toy making. One started as a grocer; a loan of £5 set him up and was repaid in half the time granted; a further loan of £20 enabled him to buy a horse and van and the business prospered.[9] The Central Relief Committee was cautious in making loans, especially in the early days: out of 2,000 applications received by August 1921 only 220 loans were made. Apart from a reluctance to

*A Legion loan enabled this business to be started in 1922.*

back 'possible losers' the funds available were limited and the continuing operation of the scheme depended on prompt repayments. An Auxiliary Company acted as a collecting agency[10] and appears to have had the desired effect, enabling the scheme to be extended to ex-service widows in July 1923. But branches often protested at the number of applications refused.

Another scheme provided much larger loans to back enterprises intended to give work to groups of ex-servicemen. Although such schemes also needed local branch support many appeared to be speculative ventures, but a number were supported. They included a shipbreaking scheme in Plymouth which employed nearly 100 men to break up six naval vessels which would otherwise have been sent to a German shipyard, a furniture-making enterprise in Wiltshire and a steeplejack business in Halifax employing twelve ex-servicemen.

## Finding jobs

The branches could also be useful with the sword. They preferred to get people into work rather than administer relief. They set up their own employment committees and formed alliances with local businesses in an effort to find openings. An Employment Department at headquarters supported this work and set up Employment Bureaux in those Areas where the need was judged to be the greatest – Metropolitan, East and West Midland and North Eastern, each with an Employment Secretary and clerk. The department's work did not, however, include ex-officers who were the responsibility of the Officers' Benevolent Department.

The Legion laid great stress on building up confidence with employers by finding the right man for the job. But it had to contend with allegations that the ex-serviceman had little wish for employment because war service had spoilt him; he was content, it was suggested, to exist on unemployment benefits and whatever else he could find. No doubt some might fall into this category, but it was an unworthy slur on the majority. There were also accusations that the Legion urged men to accept work at less than the going rate. These too were scurrilous, but reflected some of the attitudes prevailing in these difficult times.

As part of a staff reorganization in 1923 (see page 37) area bureaux were abolished and employment added to the Area Organizer's responsibilities; but the scheme depended on the branches and the local situation. The pattern of employment in the country was changing as heavy industry closed in the traditional manufacturing areas and new factories opened elsewhere, such as motor car manufacturing in Coventry, Luton and Oxford. In some branch localities there was simply no work to be had; others saw opportunities and, through an active Employment Committee with good local contacts, were able to find jobs. Ashford Branch in Kent was able to find no less than 180 members jobs in the course of a single year.[11] In 1923 the *Daily Express* reported the tribute by an employer to ex-servicemen recruited through a Legion branch: 'They polished off the job in the way you see things done in a first-class battleship.'

Such stories were momentary gleams of light in an otherwise grey landscape. The Legion's efforts, even including the business schemes assisted by loans from the Relief Fund, had only a marginal effect. The actual number of ex-servicemen finding work as a direct result of the Legion's efforts at national, area or even branch level was probably less than 10 per cent of the total ex-service unemployed of some 600,000. And there were even more ex-servicemen on the streets as a result of post-war cuts in the armed services, the so-called 'Geddes Axe'.

The Legion persisted in its efforts. In September 1924 there was a concentrated one-week 'National Work Drive' to obtain jobs for ex-servicemen, inaugurated with a BBC

'2LO' radio broadcast by Earl Haig. But there was little response: there were simply not the jobs to be had.

## A Legion plan for employment

To make real inroads on the ex-service unemployment situation the Legion knew that it had to intervene with government. It achieved an early success in 1921 by persuading the government that 75 per cent of those employed on relief works should be ex-service. These were government-backed schemes set up by local authorities to provide useful employment for those out of work. Initially the local authorities had discretion in the make-up of the work force; the Legion's intervention made the ex-service proportion compulsory and, under the NEC's watchful eye, was continued by successive governments. The branches were equally vigilant, ensuring that the local authorities played the game. At the end of 1924 some 100,000 men were employed on various relief works, but a Legion delegation to the Ministry of Labour in March 1925 was told that schemes to build motor arterial roads or improve the canal network had been turned down by the government as they were not paying propositions.[12]

Only action on a national scale by government could bring about any significant change in the overall employment situation. In order to influence public opinion in this direction, the National Executive Council circulated a manifesto in the autumn of 1923, advocating a national work scheme.

The scheme envisaged a politically independent National Employment Committee. Its task would be to devise projects which would both benefit the country and create employment. The Legion believed that there were many opportunities for such initiatives: a hydro-electric scheme using the Severn barrage, a canal from the Forth to the Clyde to shorten the voyage times on the growing Hamburg-New York route, a channel tunnel to promote trade with the continent and the introduction of light railways to open up the areas of the country which lacked transport, and thereby create new industries. It also proposed an expansion of the British film industry, pointing out that only 1 per cent of film production costs worldwide were spent in Britain.[13] The projects would be financed by a National Work Loan of at least £200 million, raised by public subscription with the interest met from the savings on unemployment pay.

These proposals were launched by the Legion's Chairman at a meeting in Chatham in September 1923, Mr Lister pointing out that £200 million represented less than one month's expenditure on the war. He referred to the unemployed as the 'Army of No Occupation', (a reference to the Army of Occupation then in Germany) reminding his audience that many of them were ex-servicemen under thirty years of age who had never had the chance to learn a trade. The Legion's branches became involved: members paraded the streets carrying billboards with posters advertising the manifesto in bold letters and the branches themselves passed resolutions which were sent to the Prime Minister.

But such ideas did not accord with the economic thinking of the times and would not be attempted until Roosevelt launched his 'New Deal' in the United States ten years later. The Prime Minister declined to receive a Legion deputation and the Legion's ambitious plan for national recovery came to naught.[14] As the *Legion Journal* noted in 1923:

> For two and a half years now thousands of ex-servicemen, and those who are dependent on them, have suffered intense privation and hardship through the lack

of opportunity to obtain a livelihood; great numbers of them are compelled, in order to keep body and soul together, to exist on the distasteful assistance provided by the poor law; hundreds have found it necessary to enter the workhouse . . . and there are thousands tramping the roads.

And the situation was to get worse rather than better.

### In the Legion's sights

If the problem could not be solved by bold measures the Legion would at least try to reduce it for the ex-serviceman. The antipathy to those civil servants who had remained at home has been noted, as have attitudes to women kept on after the war. The Unity Conference had resolved that as far as possible all female labour in government should be replaced with ex-servicemen, that all men who had entered government offices during the war and who had not served in the armed forces should similarly be replaced and that ex-servicemen be given preference in vacancies arising in local government offices.

These resolutions represented some very strong feelings. Continued employment of women was felt to deny a man the opportunity to support his family (which might at the time include his parents). The image was that of young girls frittering away their wages on clothes while the ex-serviceman was unable to feed his wife and children.

The Legion felt even more strongly about the return to their government posts of conscientious

*Post War unemployment: some of those in the Legion's sights for taking jobs away from ex-servicemen. A* Legion Journal *cartoon of 1921.*

objectors, men who had satisfied a tribunal that their conscience prevented them from taking part in conflict and had thereby been exempted from bearing arms. No matter that some at least of those exempted had voluntarily gone on to drive ambulances at the front or to work with the wounded. The Legion was not alone in its views. It was stated in Parliament in November 1921 that 99 per cent of the country objected to conscientious objectors being reinstated in their civil service jobs, which might otherwise have been filled by ex-servicemen.[15]

Aliens were also in the Legion's sights. Hotels and restaurants had resumed their pre-war practice of recruiting staff from the continent. Earl Haig himself wrote to all Army commanding officers to ensure that no military dinners were held at hotels or restaurants that employed foreign waiters,[16] while the Home Secretary assured the Legion that he was 'having the closest scrutiny made with a view to removal of all aliens who have come into this country improperly'.[17]

## Funding the relief

So far we have dealt with distress arising out of unemployment, of which there was certainly plenty. But the lives of ex-servicemen and their families could be made miserable for other reasons, the chief of which was sickness. Sometimes the dividing line might be blurred – poor diet arising from lack of work might well result in illness – but the relief was separately funded.

Those matters connected with *unemployment*, whether direct help to a family short of food or efforts to find the man a job, were funded by the *British Legion Relief Fund* which had been set up as soon as unity had been agreed.* The bulk of the money had come from an appeal by the Prince of Wales at the outbreak of the war. The *United Services Fund* provided principally for distress due to sickness. It did not apply to ex-RN: the Admiralty had decided to form the Royal Naval Benevolent Trust from its share of the wartime canteen profits. But with some £7 million at its disposal, at the outset the USF far exceeded the Relief Fund's £200,000.[18]

The United Services Fund was an independent body, but the Council of Management was chaired by Earl Haig, the Legion's President, and, of the twelve other Council members, nine were nominated by the Legion, the outcome of the conference chaired by Lord Byng (see pages 5–6). It had placed the USF administration in the hands of the organised ex-service bodies, which had then come together to form the Legion.

The USF had a further aim, the social welfare of ex-servicemen, and made grants to groups of former servicemen to set up clubs and institutes throughout the country, some under the auspices of organizations such as the Comrades, others standing alone. Many of these became Legion Clubs in due course and, in the expansion of the Legion after July 1921, more clubs were formed by Legion branches, using USF grants.

The United Services Fund had its own area network 'of Administrative Agents', corresponding to the Legion Areas, and this helped the two agencies to co-operate. At local level there were USF Benevolent Committees, involving local ex-service bodies, including the Legion.

The Legion's own welfare work was directed by the National Benevolent Committee, also chaired by Earl Haig. This most important committee not only oversaw the Legion's benevolent activities through the allocation of funds but was responsible for appeals and therefore also supervised all fundraising activity. Staff support was provided by the Relief Department, whose sections – Distress, Employment Schemes and Business Loans – represented the three aspects of the Legion's benevolent work, and the Appeals Department. However, in late 1923 the British Legion Relief Fund began to run out of money for its employment work and had to obtain a grant of £50,000 from the USF. The money was given under strict conditions, the USF insisting on representation on the Legion's Central Relief Committee, although in view of the heavy Legion involvement in the management of the United Services Fund this seems to have been a somewhat artificial arrangement.[19]

The Legion's Relief Fund continued to face increasing demand and by the end of 1925

*As the Unity Relief Fund.

expenditure had risen sharply. But the public response to the Poppy Appeal enabled the fund to continue its work.[20]

## The disabled

If the able-bodied ex-servicemen had problems with employment, so too did those who had suffered a disability as a result of war service. Disabled ex-servicemen were entitled to war pensions, although, as will be shown, the system was not without problems. But the majority were capable of some form of work and wanted to work; indeed, in many cases, work was a necessary part of the therapy to help overcome the psychological effect of the loss of one or more limbs or some other physical restriction.

The government recognized this need. There were two schemes to rehabilitate the disabled: one retrained those whose disability prevented them from resuming their pre-war occupation (or who had no pre-war occupation); the other was the King's Roll scheme to find them jobs.

The King's Roll scheme had shortcomings which were to give the Legion deep concern over the years. Introduced by Royal Proclamation in 1919, the concept was that firms prepared to answer the King's appeal should have their names entered on to the Roll and be allowed to carry a special design on their letterheads. The proportion of disabled men each employed would depend on the type of work, but once agreement had been reached the firm was expected to maintain that level. The status of being on the Roll, with its patriotic implications, were felt to be good for business.

The scheme was on the whole well supported. But in the autumn of 1921 there were still disabled men without jobs, a situation which the Legion was determined to change. Scrutiny of the Roll showed that 700 out of 900 Royal Warrant Holders were not on it. Nor were two-thirds of the local authorities in England and Wales.[21] The Legion pointed out that if each of these local authorities were to employ a small percentage

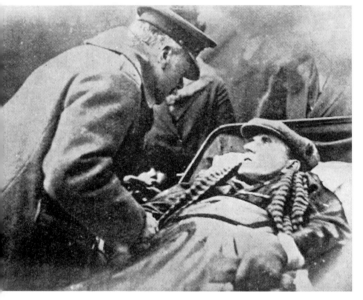

*Field Marshal Earl Haig with the disabled Sergeant Harper, Secretary of Attercliffe Branch, Sheffield, Yorkshire. In seven years Haig never missed a meeting of the Legion's Benevolent Committee, of which he was chairman and which provided the money to help men such as Harper.*

of disabled then the problem would be solved. It set the branches to work on their local authorities, providing Areas with a list of those not on the Roll.

This was not all. The Legion felt that the situation demanded that employers should be *compelled* to accept a proportion of disabled into their workforce, the numbers obviously depending on the type of work. Employers in Germany, Austria, France, Italy and Poland were either currently required to accept a proportion of war-disabled or were shortly about to be made to do so. The irony was of course that Germany and Austria were the defeated enemies.

A speech in the House of Commons in May 1922 by the Legion's General Treasurer

Brunel Cohen brought about a Select Committee,[22] to which the Legion gave evidence. It submitted that the voluntary scheme had failed and it put forward its own carefully worked-out plan for compulsory employment.[23] But the Select Committee's report, issued in September 1922, decided to give the voluntary scheme a further chance with more government publicity, until May 1923.[24]

The Legion was disappointed. It estimated that by now 100,000 ex-service disabled were unemployed and having to exist on a small pension, with their plight becoming more acute every month. The businessmen were not paying their debt to those disabled in defending their interests. The municipal authorities had ignored all approaches. In short the nation had forgotten the wartime sacrifices.[25]

May 1923 coincided with the Legion's Annual Conference. There was no doubt about the views of Conference: they considered the King's Roll scheme an abject failure.[26] The Legion's next move was to sponsor a private member's Bill for compulsory employment. Introduced in May 1924 by Mr D.P. Pielou MP, a member of the NEC who had been severely wounded in the war and who supported himself on crutches as he addressed the House, the Bill received strong support in the debate, but time could not be found to take it further. It would be another four years before Parliament discussed it again.[27]

A Legion campaign for free travel on buses and trams for those who had lost a leg in the war was a little more successful. This concession, operated by government decree in other countries which had taken part in the war, notably France, but in Britain it rested on the goodwill of the companies concerned. Nevertheless the scheme operated in some large towns such as Liverpool, Leicester and Northampton, although in the case of Leicester it was for Legion members only.[28]

In 1922 the Legion also succeeded in obtaining half-price travel on the railways for the war-blinded, a concession extended in 1923 to those blinded as a result of service prior to the Great War.[29]

### Shell shock victims

Among the disabled were the victims of what was then called 'shell shock', now known as 'post traumatic stress disorder'. The condition had come to be recognized during the Great War; every man had a reserve of courage to deal with danger but in some it was exhausted sooner than in others.

The Ministry of Pensions was responsible for such cases. Specialist treatment was available but there was a severe shortage of places, particularly in the immediate post-war years. Patients who recovered could resume their places in society. Those who had suffered more severe damage had to be certified insane and committed to public asylums, although they received special status.[30]

Among these unfortunates were some who, because of their inherent instability, should not have been in the armed forces in the first place. But the heavy demands on manpower, particularly in the latter part of the war, resulted in their being accepted for service.[31] By the end of 1921 the total number of ex-servicemen, both war-disabled and inherently unstable, in such asylums had risen to over 6,000. The Legion pressed for separate wards for ex-service patients, but the Ministry refused.[32]

Further Legion pressure won some concessions: visits by specialists to the ex-service patients and individual treatment for the 'more hopeful' cases. Sadly this type of patient was very much in the minority.

On the whole the Ministry fulfilled its obligations to the mentally-damaged ex-servicemen. But there were inevitably some shortcomings. Men awaiting or discharged from treatment were particularly vulnerable and the Legion and others offered a life-line to those who slipped through the official net.[33]

## War pensions

Harrowing though the 'shell shock' victims were, the majority of war cases were of death or physical injury. If a man died as a result of service then a regular weekly payment was made to his widow. In the case of an unmarried man a payment was also made to the parents; at the time many parents relied on their children for support.

A man discharged as a result of injury or illness went before a medical board. The Board assessed the extent of the disability and this determined the amount of the pension, which was paid weekly. However, the Board's assessment at the time of discharge could only be provisional: the man's condition might improve with treatment, especially in the case of an illness. On the other hand it might deteriorate. Within four years, therefore, a further Board reviewed the case and decided the *permanent* disability figure. This gave the Final Award.

Since a man's future well-being could depend on the final figure there was provision for an appeal against the Final Award. The Panel which heard this appeal was appointed by the Lord Chancellor; it consisted of two doctors and one disabled ex-serviceman. But the appeal had to be made within one year of the Final Award; otherwise it was at the ministry's discretion.

There were of course instances where a man might only become aware of a disability some time after his service. Conditions in the trenches could lead to rheumatism in later life; a disease contracted while serving in the East might have caused permanent intestinal injury not fully apparent on discharge. A claim could therefore be made at a later date, but only up to seven years after discharge.[34]

These limitations apart, the scheme was fair, reflecting the change in British attitudes towards social responsibilities and it is interesting to note that in 1921 there was no provision in America for government payments to disabled servicemen.[35]

The War Pensions scheme had been revised in 1921, with a considerable Legion input, principally through Brunel Cohen. There were nevertheless many matters of detail to be put right; but first the Legion would see how the revised scheme worked, based on the appraisals of the 450 local War Pensions Committees on which it was represented.

## The seven-year rule

The Legion's first concern was with the seven-year rule as it applied to widows. If her husband died as a result of a war wound or disability within seven years of the injury then the widow was entitled to a full widow's pension. But death after that time, even if it directly resulted from the man's war wounds, reduced the pension.

The Legion regarded this rule as quite unreasonable and even cruel. The seven-year limit was based on a medical view that after seven years the death must be due to other causes. But the Legion suspected that seven years was simply a bureaucratic yardstick. It could affect the mental state of a man who was 'lingering on', knowing that if he survived beyond seven years there would be no proper provision for his widow and children, who would then in all probability have to resort to Poor Law relief. It was the *cause* of death, not the date, which should determine the entitlement.[36]

Early in 1923 the Legion persuaded the government to *consider* applications where death took place beyond the seven-year point. It also got a change in the basis for calculating the seven years: it would start from the final removal from duty not the first, as had previously been the case. This was a most important concession: a man might have been wounded in 1914, recovered, received a further wound in 1917 and then been discharged. If he died as a result of the wounds by 1921 (seven years after 1914) then his widow received the pension. If he survived beyond that date she would have no entitlement, no matter what the effect of the second wound. The concession meant that the 'automatic' entitlement in the example given now extended to 1924.[37]

However, the Legion was by no means satisfied with these two concessions. The existence of a seven-year rule was in its view nonsensical. It continued to press the government very strongly, notably in a debate in June 1923 on the 'Minister of Pensions' salary', in which many MPs took a determined stand on the Legion's behalf. This brought about a further concession: any widow whose husband's death might be attributed to his war disability could apply for a widow's pension – at any time. But there was a qualification: at the time of his death he had to be receiving a minimum 40 per cent war disability pension.[38]

## The Legion petition

These were no mean achievements. But the Legion still had reservations. It was unhappy at the need for the disability pension qualification: through ignorance and human error – and even pride – there were cases where a man who died as a result of his war injuries had not drawn a pension. His wife and widow would be penalized.[39]

Nevertheless something had been done for the widows. But the same unreasonable time limit still applied to those men seeking a war disability pension; unless they submitted an application within seven years of their discharge, their claim, whatever the medical history, could not be considered. The Legion continued the fight. A deputation to the Ministry of Pensions in December 1924 failed to achieve any response from government and in May 1925 the National Executive Council resorted to a public petition, seeking one million signatures.[40]

The petition not only sought the removal of the seven-year rule, it also dealt with the question of Final Awards. These, as explained earlier, were intended to 'wind up' cases

*The 1925 Great Petition being loaded outside Legion headquarters at 26 Eccleston Square. It was to be presented to Parliament by Brunel Cohen who is supervising the loading from his wheelchair.*

either by granting a permanent pension or by making a lump sum grant in final payment. By these means the Pensions Register had been reduced from 900,000 to 600,000 over three years, over 250,000 men having been deleted by the payment of a final sum of from £7 to £100. As has been noted, any appeal had to be made within twelve months; but it was entirely up to the Ministry of Pensions as to whether the case was reopened, and in many instances they simply took no action. The Legion wanted all such cases to have the right of appeal before an independent Appeal Board at any time, provided that the man could produce medical evidence of his condition. As a result of incorrect Final Awards it believed that thousands of men were being forced to seek Legion help or go to the Poor Law Guardians for relief.[41]

The National Petition sought to right these two wrongs: to remove any time limit restriction on an application for a war pension or war widows pension and to provide the right to appeal to an independent tribunal over a Final Award. It did not quite reach its target of one million signatures; but the total of over 800,000 included not only MPs and Lord Mayors but the signatures of every one of the committees that assisted the Minister of Pensions to do his work, including those at the highest level. In numbers of signatures the petition was the largest since the Chartist Petition of 1848.[42]

But when the petition was presented in July 1925, having been brought to Parliament by lorry from 26 Ecclestone Square, the government made no response. So the Legion sent a deputation, led by the National Chairman. This time it got an answer: no concessions would be made – the seven-year rule would remain and the Ministry would continue to be the final arbitrators as to whether a case could be reopened more than twelve months after a Final Award. There was, however, one result. Lister's penetrating analysis of the operation of the Final Awards system clearly shook the Minister and, although there would be no right of appeal, more cases would be considered. But, as for the seven-year rule, it seemed that all the Legion's effort in organizing a national petition was wasted. The government was simply not prepared to listen.[43]

## A threat to pension rates

The petition did have one important outcome. There had been much concern in late 1922 when it became clear that the government intended to reduce War Pension rates because of the official fall in the cost of living. This might seem logical. If less money was needed because the cost of goods had fallen then the pension should be reduced. Had the opposite happened and the cost of living increased, the government would have been pressed to increase pensions.

There was, however, another aspect of the matter. The pension recognized that a man had made a  sacrifice for his country. Deprivation of a limb or blindness could not be assessed simply in terms of loss of earning power. To some extent the war pension acknowledged the nation's debt to an individual or to his family. Reducing the payment diminished that recognition. This was certainly the way that the Legion saw it and public sentiment was not far behind them. There was also an argument that if the disabled ex-serviceman's standard of living was higher than in 1914 (the basis of the comparison of costs) then that was what he had been promised for fighting the war.[44]

The National Chairman had led a delegation to the Ministry of Pensions in October 1922, arguing that two million pounds had already been saved from the pensions bill as many disabled had responded to treatment and had been re-assessed accordingly. Mr

Lister did not simply rely on the power of argument. He had informed the Minister that the Legion was prepared to wage war on the issue: any attempt to lower pensions would be met by an intensive press campaign to influence public opinion.[45]

A few days later, however, Lloyd George's post-war administration had collapsed and the new government agreed to maintain the existing pension rate until 1925. When, in early 1924, the Legion returned to the attack, asking for the existing rate to be taken as the minimum, the Minister's response was to defer a decision.[46] But, on the presentation of the National Petition to Parliament, he announced that the existing pension rate would continue until 1929. The petition had not of course been concerned with pension rates and the statement was no doubt timed to mollify the effect of its rejection. The Legion's National Executive Council welcomed the stabilizing of pensions until 1929, but it expressed its firm belief that the existing rates should be permanently stabilized.[47]

The Legion had also reacted to proposals in 1922 to merge the Ministry of Pensions with another department. In their view its work was specialized and a change would mean that the interests of three and a half million war pensioners would be subordinated. A strongly worded letter to the Prime Minster led to exchanges between the Legion and the government, the former making clear that it would organize opposition to the proposals if they were not abandoned. The government gave way and the Ministry would survive for a further thirty years.

## TB and Preston Hall

Another ministry – Health – dealt with one of the less obvious legacies of the war – Tuberculosis or TB. Sometimes called consumption, it is infectious and thrives in poor environmental conditions, particularly where there is overcrowding. There is little doubt that the circumstances of the war where men often lived in congested accommodation and, more especially, the conditions in the trenches, helped to spread the disease.

TB was a killer. Of 55,000 sufferers discharged from the service, 18,000 had died by mid-1922, often because they had returned to poor inner-city housing. The remedy was to treat them in special conditions in healthy surroundings, if possible accompanied by their families.[48] But once they showed improvement they needed to learn a trade suitable to their condition and to be able to practise it in the same healthy environment.

Two treatment centres, known as Village Settlements, had been set up – one by the Ministry of Health at Papworth in Cambridgeshire and another by a charity at Preston Hall near Maidstone in Kent, a country house used as a hospital during the war. But there was an urgent need for more facilities and, following Legion pressure, the government promised £20,000 in 1923 for the development of Papworth and Preston Hall.[49] Whilst welcoming the government's commitment, the Legion regarded £20,000 as merely a beginning: it would provide only twenty-five additional cottages at each of the two existing settlements, hardly bearing on the problem. There was then a change of government. The Legion seized the opportunity to re-present its case and seek a more realistic commitment. But the new government, although expressing much sympathy, was no more prepared to commit money to curing the disease than its predecessor.[50]

Events now took a new turn. The charity which had run Preston Hall since the war as an ex-service TB centre ran into financial difficulties and made the Legion's National Executive Council a free offer of the facilities. It was a gift that the Council needed to examine very closely: for one thing there was a heavy debt on the property to the government and for another the ongoing finance had to be considered. But after the

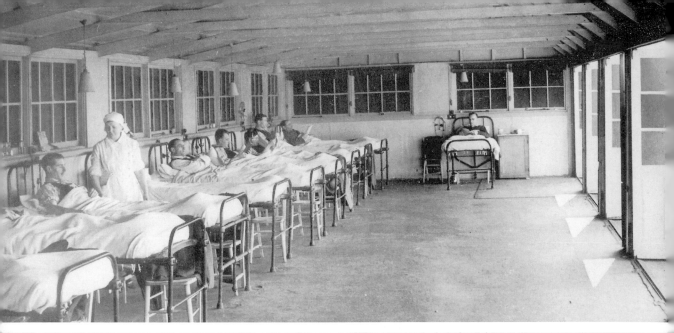

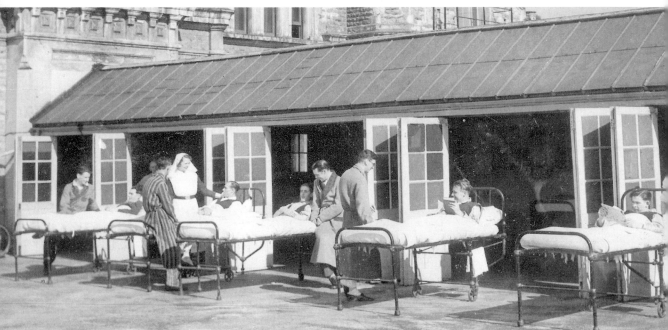

*TB treatment at Preston Hall, involved plenty of fresh air: patients were kept in open-air wards and exposed to sunlight whenever possible. Those who recovered could become settlers. They were then joined by their families and housed in cottages as shown.*

effective cancellation of the debt it decided to accept. An Honorary Director, Dr Varrier-Jones, the very eminent Medical Director of the Papworth Village Settlement, was appointed and the British Legion Settlement, as it was to be known, was established by a resolution of the National Executive Council on 24 January 1925 and handed over to the Legion on 1 April 1925.[51]

The Legion's new venture was not simply a TB sanatorium. The whole point of a 'settlement' was to enable the patient's family to share his life and, on his recovery, allow him to undertake work under conditions which would not bring about a relapse. The first consideration was therefore the type of patient: he, and his family, needed to be community-minded and prepared to regard the settlement as their future life and not just a temporary respite. Legion branches were asked only to recommend patients who met these criteria. The medical arrangements were nevertheless of the highest importance and the Legion brought the sanatorium up to date, adding new wards in which every patient had his own bell, bed light and headphones (provided by the Women's Section) to listen to the radio, updating the laboratory equipment, installing an X-Ray department and introducing artificial sunlight treatment and outdoor shelters where patients could have the benefit of fresh air.

The work aspect was also reviewed. It had previously been based on pig-breeding and horticulture, but these were now regarded as unsuitable occupations for TB patients. There was a small manufacturing business making prefabricated buildings: garages, bungalows, chicken houses, dog kennels and so on; but the machinery needed to be replaced. The Legion introduced a new enterprise, a printing press, at the then very considerable outlay of £5,000. The intention was that the Printing Department should meet the needs of both Legion headquarters and branches. It performed this task for some seventy-five years, a tribute to those who set up the venture.* In addition a Building Department was established to erect twenty-five cottages and to assist with some of the alterations and improvements.

By the end of 1925 there were ninety patients, as well as a 'village' community of sixty-nine former patients, fifty-two wives and 102 children. There was of course a Legion branch, to which a Women's Section was added towards the end of the year.[52] A visitor from a Northumberland branch to Preston Hall in late 1925, having left Aylesford station at one pm, 'tramped through orchard and fruity country' to the settlement. He found it a splendid mansion in a beautiful setting and was greatly impressed: everything humanly possible was being done to make the patients feel at home, those at work were content and keen to make the business pay and the houses were very comfortable. He returned to his branch with the message 'However much some people may criticise the Legion, it is doing great work at Preston Hall.'[53]

## Housing

One factor that contributed to the spread of TB was poor housing. But housing in general was one of the biggest problems in the years immediately following the Great War. The ex-servicemen felt particularly aggrieved: they had been promised 'houses fit for heroes' but they had returned from the war to find the situation worse than before. No house building had taken place during the war and the population had increased. Marriages made during the war, or immediately after, needed houses. A survey conducted by the Comrades, one of the Legion's predecessors, found that housing was the greatest of all the returning serviceman's problems – although this was before the recession took

---

*It finally closed in 2000, a victim of the widespread use of computers for printing.

hold and unemployment soared.

As always when faced with practical problems the Legion branches did what they could, in some cases giving up rooms in a branch headquarters to families in desperate need. But the problem was not just shortage of housing; it was also their condition. 180,000 homes, mainly in the industrial cities, had been declared unfit for human habitation, many lacking sanitation. The government response was, however, virtually non-existent: in the case of Leeds the share of the money allocated would have worked out at 2s 6d (12$\frac{1}{2}$ pence) per house to replace those condemned and 2s per house for those that could be repaired, while new housing provision for the whole country was limited to 176,000 – a hopelessly inadequate figure. Thousands of acres of land acquired for housing stood idle. It was, as a former Health Minister put it, 'an act of national dishonour to the armies of brave men who came from our poor streets in the war'.[54] In early 1924 the Legion proposed a National Housing Scheme, based on a continuous building programme over a number of years involving ex-servicemen in the labour force; but there was no response from on high.[55] Nor was the government prepared to give any priority in housing to the families of ex-servicemen. Mr Neville Chamberlain, the minister concerned, told Parliament in 1925 that he did not think it desirable to restrict the powers of local authorities in the control and management of housing; but, as a report in the *Legion Journal* noted, the local authorities were inclined to have their own priorities – 'kissing by favour' as the correspondent put it.[56]

### War orphans

Among the families suffering from poor housing there were many orphans. 330,000 British children had been made fatherless by the Great War, of whom 18,000 also lacked a mother. Most of these orphans were cared for by the other members of their families and had a reasonably normal and happy upbringing. But some 3,000 war orphans were in government care, about half of whom were placed in Poor Law institutions, locally-managed and by their nature often inhospitable places.

In a later age society would see the consignment of neglected war-orphaned children to Poor Law institutions as utterly heartless. At the time it was official policy. But it took the Legion and in particular the branches – who often made the care of local war orphans their special concern – to change the situation. The Legion – and no doubt others – pressurized the government to remove these children from the institutions and place them in homes more suited to children's needs such as Doctor Barnado's. By the end of 1923 the number of war-orphaned children in the care of the Poor Law had been reduced from 1,500 to 100.[57] There was especial heed over the transition of the war orphans into adulthood – a critical stage where the advice and guidance of a parent were lacking. In 1925 Legion headquarters established an advisory service for the 'after care' of war orphans, circulating information through Areas, Counties and branches and making use of the branches' close links with the local community to keep contact with the orphans and those who had charge of them.[58] For their part the branches did their best to brighten the young people's lives, organizing outings and events.[59]

### Visits to the graves

Most of the orphans' fathers lay in France. In that country the railways had granted half-fare concessions for relatives to visit war graves. The Legion was able to persuade the French railways to do the same for British pilgrims arriving at the channel ports; in

Britain the railway companies at first refused any concession, but eventually agreed a special group rate for not less than twelve relatives.

The Legion itself did not at first organize the visits, instead advising the relatives to join the Church Army-run pilgrimages. All the expenses had to be met by the pilgrims and the cost of the journey put it beyond the reach of many war widows and parents. Some funds had been provided by charitable organizations, but by 1923 they were used up, although the proceeds of a book describing a pilgrimage by King George V in 1922 were, at the King's wish, used to help with a pilgrimage to Arras in 1923.

For those who could not afford the journey there was one small consolation: the original wooden crosses that were replaced by headstones when the cemeteries were finally laid out could be claimed by the next of kin, through the Church Army. It was sometimes the practice for the cross to be presented to relatives at a church service arranged by the Legion branch.[60]

# 1926 – 1930

## Still no work

Addressing the 1926 Annual Conference, the Prince of Wales said, 'The most important of (the Legion's) several activities in the country is the finding of employment for individual ex-servicemen, and especially the disabled ex-servicemen (but) . . . employment is governed by economic factors over which the Legion has no control. The Legion . . . cannot create jobs out of nothing.'[61]

This was no more than the truth. But the Legion could – and did – make its views known: create more work by imaginative national schemes such as cheap electicity through hydro-electric projects and ensure that priority in assembling the workforce went to ex-servicemen. The country was in a state of economic siege and rather than wait for relief what was needed was a determined break-out. This thinking was not of course the Legion's alone, although others plainly would not attach so much importance to the place of the ex-serviceman. But whoever championed it, the difficulty was that the government of the day saw matters differently.

Nonetheless the Legion kept up its pressure for more home-grown action. A letter circulated to the press over the signatures of the national officers in early 1929 again sought a National Employment Committee and a national loan, pointing out that this was precisely what the next President of the United States was about to do. When the new government that year appointed an Employment Minister, the National Executive Council hastened to send a delegation, headed by the President. The Minister, Mr J.H. Thomas and his deputy, Sir Oswald Mosley, heard them out, expressed interest in their ideas and sympathy for the plight of ex-servicemen, promising that their points 'would receive careful attention'.

Projects such as a channel tunnel* would have brought not just work but a restoration of morale. For it was not just the material deprivation: as Earl Haig had remarked on many occasions, unemployment had sapped the pride of the generation who had fought the war, and a cartoon in the *Journal* summed the whole thing up: it showed a cloth-capped ex-serviceman in mid-ocean astride a jar of Bovril re-labelled 'Work', over the caption 'Prevents that sinking feeling!'[62]

---

*The April 1930 *Legion Journal*, however, wondered whether by the time it was completed all travel would be by air.

### Relief reorganized

There might be concern over the men's morale, but meanwhile unemployment continued to cause great distress to their families and relief measures were not helped by the split responsibility between the Legion's Relief Fund and the United Services Fund. Some cases fell betwen the two; in others help was duplicated. In 1926 Haig, as both Legion President and USF Chairman, improved matters by placing all relief in USF and Legion areas under one official – the former USF Area Administrative Agent – while at local level the two benevolent committees amalgamated, although this process took a little time. Nevertheless by 1928 the National Executive Council judged the new arrangement an 'unqualified success'.[63]

Although the two funds were now jointly administered in the field, they remained separate entities, the British Legion Relief Fund being maintained principally through the Poppy Appeal, while the United Services Fund drew on the interest from the wartime canteen profits. Relief Fund expenditure increased by 50 per cent in 1926 and 1927 because of the economic depression caused by the General Strike, and in 1928 the continuing situation in the North of England and in Wales made even heavier demands. But other factors contributed to the increase: the number of local committees was growing – the 2,200 committees in 1926 were to become more than 3,000 by the end of the decade – and the new co-ordination arrangements themselves created more activity. The result was that in 1929 and 1930 the Relief Fund did not have enough money to meet the demands on it and the local committees had to be told to curtail expenditure. This was not easy when so many needed help. But despite the constraints all were helped, regardless of whether or not they were members of the Legion – and some 85 per cent of beneficiaries were outside the organization.[64]

Some of the cases were harrowing: an ex-serviceman of sixty who suffered a stroke was not entitled to unemployment pay and his wife had to pawn her wedding ring and sewing machine to pay the rent and feed three children. Even so the bailiff was in the house when the local Legion branch arrived to provide relief and redeem the wife's possessions. A TB-afflicted war veteran was unable to work; since his wife was also ill and there were five children under eleven to support he could not pay the rent and the family was evicted; the Legion found the family other accommodation. An ex-serviceman living in the woods was found to be still suffering from spinal wounds and, not surprisingly, mentally ill. He would have died from exposure had the Legion not taken care of him. Some of the Boards of Guardians – those administering Poor Law Relief on behalf of local authorities – however, deducted the value of any Legion relief from their assistance. This, in the Legion's view, effectively neutralized the public recognition of the special circumstances of the ex-servicemen, demonstrated in their generosity towards the Poppy Appeal. A press statement to this effect was issued by the Legion in January 1928, but many of the Boards concerned remained unmoved.

They perhaps paid more attention to a letter sent to all Poor Law Authorities in September of that year asking that no ex-serviceman should be buried as a pauper – the Legion would meet the costs of the funeral.[65] Many branches would do more than that for a fellow ex-serviceman; they would provide the full honours whatever the circumstances of his death.

Some of the worst situations were in the Irish Free State. There great distress prevailed among the community which had volunteered to play their part in the war. A special report led to an appeal by Earl Haig in 1927 and funds being set aside for Irish ex-servicemen and their families.[66]

Committees themselves, even those at a lofty level, sometimes showed a human side: on Christmas Day 1926 the Legion's Central Relief Committee entertained 250 homeless ex-servicemen in London to dinner at Lyon's Corner House in Coventry Street, having already arranged their food and lodging over Christmas. Messrs Bass provided a barrel of their product and the party ended with a sing song, although whether this was intended by the Committee is unrecorded.[67]

## A Director of Employment is appointed

The war veterans standing aimlessly on street corners in London or elsewhere had little to sing about. The General Strike had effectively dashed all hopes of economic recovery and as the end of the decade approached the problem worsened. In 1928 the Legion appointed a national Director of Employment, Vice Admiral Payne, and, following a pilot scheme in Yorkshire Area, Area Employment Officers were reintroduced in the worst hit Areas. But the scheme was based on the branches; the Area Employment Officer persuaded those branches which had not already done so to form committees, assisted them in their work and put them in touch with employers with whom he had made the initial contact.

Despite therefore the fact that the industrial situation had become even worse in 1930 with unemployment figures throughout the country mounting by leaps and bounds, the Legion was able to find jobs that year for over 10,000 ex-servicemen. This figure must be seen in context: there were nearly two million unemployed, of whom more than 500,000 had fought in the war; for every man the Legion was able to place in employment another fifty of his former comrades remained in the dole queue.[68]

Meanwhile, in the absence of any other prospects, many ex-servicemen continued to try to start their own small businesses, making use of a Legion loan. Although 1926 was a bad year because of the effect of the strikes on local trade, towards the end of the decade around 3,500 bids were forwarded by local committees every year, of which one third were approved. Local committees were the key to the scheme: the

Ex-Service Man: "Well, that chap told me I was nearly there two or three miles back, let's hope it isn't far now."

*Nearly ten years after the war ended there was still great unemployment. A* Legion Journal *cartoon reflects the mood.*

good ones closely considered every application, taking particular note of any competition. They rejected any attempt to get a loan simply to exend a successful business, unless it would provide employment for more ex-servicemen; the object of the scheme was to get people into work, not to fund expansion. They also provided an after-care service, co-opting local businessmen. Repayments were made by instalment, usually by postal order, and in most cases were on time.[69] On the larger scale any venture with at least a reasonable chance of success would be considered by the Legion in these difficult times. A horse-haulage contractor was helped to expand his business so that he was able to employ four other ex-servicemen; thirteen fishermen in the south of Ireland, all of whom had served the Crown, were given a loan of £250 to buy boats, nets and gear for salmon fishing, selling the catches to the markets in London and Liverpool, while Haig's special appeal funded a furniture factory in Dublin employing thirty-two men, and a number of other concerns in the Free State.[70]

### A tweed factory in Wales

The Legion's activities brought in other benefactors. In 1918 a Mr Arthur Beckwith of Crickhowell had come to the conclusion that the hand-weaving of tweed would prove a suitable occupation for war-battered men and bought a factory among hills near Llanwrtyd Wells in Breconshire. Eight years later, in September 1926, he gave the factory to the Legion. The gift came complete with all the plant and machinery, included shops at Bath and Llandrindod Wells, and the Legion put up £500 to form a company and expand the business, which at the time employed eight disabled ex-servicemen and three boys, the sons of ex-servicemen. It would be known as the Cambrian Factory.

*The Cambrian Factory, set among rolling Welsh hills whose ups and downs would epitomise its fortunes.*

Despite a London launch and internal marketing, resulting in at least one large order, from the branch at Santiago in Chile, the early years were difficult and it was necessary to provide annual subsidies. However, the Legion's faith was to be justified; by 1932 the factory was self-supporting with the aid of a small government grant and was even able to expand.[71]

### Enter the motor car

Hand-weaving was a traditional craft but more modern opportunies were available to the enterprising. In June 1927 the Rochdale South Branch of the Legion noted that the number of motor cars in the town had increased to the extent that off-street parking was needed. A good relationship with the Town Council enabled the branch to get permission to make use of a large open space free of charge, erect a hut and employ two disabled men as full-time parking attendants.[72]

Meanwhile, across the Irish Channel motor vehicles were also making their presence felt and the British Legion Car Attendants (Belfast) Ltd began operations in March 1928 with seven disabled ex-servicemen; some eighteen months later the number had risen to forty with all of the city's car parks being run by the company, as well as those of nearby seaside resorts. In Cardiff and Swansea the local authorities themselves employed disabled ex-servicemen as car park attendants, but unlike the Legion schemes the men had to depend on motorists' gratuities for income.

By 1929 the Legion's Director of Employment was attempting to regulate the scheme. It had been given much publicity through the *Journal* following the Rochdale venture and brought to the notice of local authorities; but their schemes were mostly gratuities-only and, unlike Cardiff and Swansea, they did not reserve the work for disabled ex-servicemen. The Legion scheme required that there should be a fixed wage and proper benefits, with a uniform provided. But no Legion scheme could apply in London as all car parking was run by the Ministry of Transport and ex-servicemen competed with transport benevolent associations' nominees.[73]

*Belfast British Legion car attendants inspected by the President, General Maurice, 1932.*

The car, however, provided other opportunities in the metropolis. By the late 1920s the motor cab was a familiar sight on the streets of London. A number of servicemen had learnt to drive in the Great War and in 1928 the Metropolitan Area Chairman, Lieutenant General Sir Edward Bethune, a veteran of the Afghan and both Boer wars but nonetheless well abreast of the times, suggested a taxi driver training scheme. The National Executive Council provided the money, which covered both the tuition and maintainance of those involved, and 167 men began training. The biggest obstacle to most of them was the 'knowledge of London' examination set by Scotland Yard but about 100 men were able to find employment after the course and the training was repeated in 1929. Again it was successful and in 1930 the Council agreed that the scheme should continue for as long as there was a demand for trained taxi drivers. It was an expensive enterprise, taking the largest proportion of the money available for employment schemes, and after the trainees got jobs they were required to repay some of the cost. Nevertheless it provided work for seventy-five to a hundred men every year in difficult times and they were grateful. One successful graduate of the first scheme wrote 'after a month on the road I am earning a good living. I certainly hope to increase my income when I become more familiar with the "tricks of the trade".' But he did not explain himself further.[74]

### The Legion Training Centre

Such ventures provided openings for the few. Many more unemployed ex-servicemen were handicapped by their lack of a trade; whatever opportunities existed would go to those who had skills. Largely as a result of Legion pressure the government had, belatedly, set up four experimental training centres. The top age, however, was twenty-five, an astonishingly thoughtless decision since in 1926 anyone who had served in the war would

89

have been over-age. The Legion attempted to get this raised to thirty-five for ex-servicemen but had to settle for twenty-nine, meaning that those who had answered their country's call in 1914 at the age of eighteen were ineligible.[75]

In an attempt to help an even more deprived section – those who had been the mental casualties of the war but had recovered sufficiently to contemplate a return to work – the Legion set up in 1928 'The British Legion Training Centre (Wenvoe)' in a country house near Cardiff. The course did not teach a trade; it simply tried to prepare 'shell shock' victims to overcome the prejudice against anyone who had been in a mental institution, no matter for what reason. Unfortunately it did not succeed. Too many of the men were simply not up to permanent employment, whatever help they received.[76]

### Emigration: 'Its a great life, Colonel'

If there were few jobs to be had in Britain, for those who were of an adventurous frame of mind, or simply desperate, there was another solution: emigration. The dominions and some of the colonies wanted more British stock, particularly to develop the agriculture, and one of the objects of the British Empire Services League (see page 141) was to encourage 'Empire migration' by ex-servicemen. The Legion accordingly selected twenty-five families from urban areas to go to Canada; the men would be trained at one of the

*Emigrants on the Legion scheme about to depart for Canada in 1927. Those bidding them farewell include Crosfield and Lister, standing either side of the Assistant Secretary, Griffin (in spectacles), behind the two children on the left.*

four government centres in the rudiments of agriculture, while their wives learnt milking and poultry-keeping.* The Legion maintained the families and on completion of the training would also meet the cost of emigration and settlement. If the enterprise was successful it would be repeated.[77]

Twenty-one families successfully completed their training, nineteen sailing from Liverpool on a blustery day in April 1927. They did not lack clothing or necessities for the venture, Legion branches having seen to it that they left well-equipped. On the deck of the SS *Montrose* they posed for a farewell photograph, the faces of the men cheerful and determined under their cloth caps, the women, many clutching babies in their arms, perhaps a little more apprehensive. As the *Legion Journal* put it they were 'sailing away from poverty, hardship and despair, bred by constant unemployment' for 'a new life with hope and opportunity in front of them'. They certainly received a very warm welcome in their new land. On arrival in Quebec they were met by representatives of the Canadian Legion with gifts for the journey west and, for good measure, a Canadian Legion membership card and badge. When they settled in however they found it hard going: most lived on smallholdings but had to find other work to make ends meet, starting at four thirty am on their own farm, having to be at work some miles away by six am, and returning at eight pm to catch up at home. Nevertheless at least one emigrant believed it to be 'the finest opportunity any married man can have', concluding a letter to the Legion's Chairman 'It's a great life, Colonel'. For the wives it was an equal challenge: former shorthand typists found themselves left alone all day to milk the cows, feed the pigs, raise poultry and lift potatoes. A remarkably high proportion of the former town-dwellers stuck it out and were successful, fifteen out of the twenty-one families eventually living off their own farms.[78]

The venture led the Legion to undertake a further scheme for fifty, this time assisted by the Army who provided places at a vocational training centre in Wiltshire, which included the families, a Legion creche being established at the centre. This time forty-seven families made the journey, sailing from Southampton where the band of the Havant Branch 'played lively airs'. Again the Canadian Legion provided every assistance on arrival, but the size of the party made assimilation a slower process, a situation not helped by the poor harvest that summer. Two families returned and the National Executive Council sent Griffin, the Organizing and Assistant Secretary, out to Canada to investigate. He was sufficiently encouraged to recommend a further scheme.

At this stage the Council, wondering what to do with the Legion Training Centre at Wenvoe since the abandonment of the rehabilitation scheme, decided to use it to train families for overseas land settlement. By the summer of 1930 another thirty-one families had passed through the Centre and arrived in Canada. Although it was again a hard year the level of success remained reasonably high, twenty-five of the families finding a permanent living on the soil of Canada.[79]

The enterprise was summed up in an article in *'The Legionary'*, the publication of the Canadian Legion: 'The story of . . . these British Legion families in Canada is one of dogged determination, earnest effort and success, leavened by those failures which were due to no lack of trying on the part of the man and his wife, as well as failures which can be traced, sad to relate, to laziness, shiftlessness, or the unwillingness of one or the other to do their share.'[80]

Meanwhile the Legion went on assisting individual ex-servicemen and their families to find a new life overseas. Often a few pounds could lift a family from the despair of poverty at home to at least the chance of a brighter future – which was all that they asked. Six

---

*No men went unaccompanied; presumably the Legion did not want to risk having to look after a family left behind and subsequently abandoned when the husband found a new wife as well as a new life.

pounds enabled a former corporal of the King's Own Yorkshire Light Infantry to emigrate to Australia with his wife and nine children: it was for 'landing money' – given to the family on arrival to tide them over until the man found a job. He was one of over six hundred men helped to emigrate that year, 1927, together with four hundred wives and more than a thousand children. Around two-thirds of them went to Canada, one-third to Australia and New Zealand and a small number to South Africa. Most of the families came from the North East or Wales.[81] But the worldwide effect of the 1929 depression, following the failure of a 1928 scheme to resettle ex-service miners in Canada[82] and an unsuccessful venture in Australia, led the Legion to cut back on emigration and Wenvoe was finally sold in 1935.

## Disabled Men's Industries

Such schemes were hardly suited to the disabled. Some of these men had turned to making small articles, often assisted by Legion grants or loans. In early 1928 the National Executive Council set up a central selling agency, the British Legion Disabled Men's Industries (Sales) Ltd. A showroom was opened in London at 20 Buckingham Palace Road, the first clients' including the Legion's own Preston Hall Industries, and exhibitions were arranged at the Ideal Home Exhibition and the Chelsea Flower Show. By the end of September 1929 thirteen concerns employing disabled ex-servicemen were making use of the agency, which also promoted their goods to large stores in London and elsewhere, receiving in the process advice on marketability of the goods, which ranged from leather work to toys. A number of Legion branches also helped by selling articles at fetes and bazaars.

By 1930 turnover had doubled. The larger market place drove up sales, the agency was able to establish standards of quality and act as a guarantor of genuine disabled ex-service manufacture, while the industries themselves contributed by meeting to suggest ways of improving operations. All of this meant more work for over 1,500 men on the firms' books.[83]

## War pensions delays

Income from the work supplemented the war pension, which may, or may not, have been correctly assessed. There was provision for an appeal, if it was within the time limit. The Legion gave not only advice but free representation at such appeals. However, since 1926, which was the seven year 'closing date' for most War Pensions applications, the number of Legion representations before the Appeal Tribunals had fallen dramatically (see Chart B2 at page 446). The Legion's had a 60 per cent success rate in such appeals. This was not only a tribute to the advocacy but an indictment of the Ministry decisions in the original awards, making it all the more difficult for the Legion to accept that in those cases which fell outside the time limit or where the Final Award was challenged there should not be a similar right of appeal to an independent body.

There was, too, frustration at the bureaucratic delays and at some of the decisions reached: in one month, October 1926, the Legion dealt with no less than six refusals of war widows pensions without any explanation, even though in each instance their husband's death was due to a disability which the Ministry had already accepted was the result of war service. Within a few months an Appeal Tribunal had allowed every case, but in the meantime the widows had faced an uncertain future and endured added distress. It was this human aspect of the matter that gave the Legion the greatest concern, and the motivation to continue the battle to secure fair treatment for all of those whose lives had been blighted by the Great War.

Post-war servicemen were no less at risk, but in their case any compensation was a matter for the service ministry concerned – the Admiralty, War Office or Air Ministry. Here there was no right of appeal. The Legion saw no reason why the Appeals Tribunals should not be also used in their case and raised the matter with the deparments concerned in 1927. The answer they got was that Tribunals were only justified by 'the exceptional circumstances of the late war' together with the comment that 'the proposal can only have arisen from some misapprehension'.[84] In other words the Legion had been told to mind its own business, which as far as many people, and certainly those running the post-war armed services, were concerned, was to look after the veterans of the Great War. It was a misconception that was widely held and has continued in a general sense ever since, identifying the Legion only with the ex-service communities of the two World Wars.

Towards the end of the decade the cost of living again started to fall and the Legion was once more concerned that pension rates might be cut. A deputation was told in June 1928 that an announcement would be made in Parliament. When it came a month later it seemed encouraging: there would be no cuts in the rates if living costs fell; if on the other hand costs were to rise above the 1919 rate then pensions could be increased. The government, however, reserved its right to review the matter if there was a large increase in the numbers entitled to pensions. This proviso gave the Legion cause for concern: if there were to be a break-through on, for instance, the seven-year rule, would it be only at the expense of other pensioners? Nevertheless the Legion was able to reassure war pensioners that they would be unaffected by the fall in living costs.

## Preston Hall reconstruction

Also reassured by Legion action were the TB sufferers at Preston Hall. On taking over in 1925, the Legion had immediately begun a reconstruction programme: it brought the sanitorium up to date, reorganized the industries, extended the accommodation for families and built a village hall. The result was a new spirit among the 'settlers', due, as much as anything, to the industries being able to provide employment all the year round. Good sales of small buildings, a printing department that was increasingly being used within the Legion as well as outside and other ventures all led to a healthy trading situation. An informal visit from the Prince of Wales brought further cheer to the patients and their families, as well as an order for farm buildings. The only problem that year was the departure of Dr Varrier-Jones, the honorary Medical Director; he had found it impossible to run both Preston Hall and his other sanatorium at Papworth. But the principles that he had established in the treatment of the disease, particularly in the care of those who had made a recovery, were to endure.

The population of the 'village' – the permanent settlers cured of TB – grew: from under 200 men women and children at the start of 1926 it had doubled to nearly 400 at the end of 1927. The industries continued to prosper and the farm activities were renewed, Angora rabbits proving something of a money-spinner.

In January 1927 General Sir Ian Hamilton visited Preston Hall. He was impressed by the magnificent surroundings among which the 130 patients lived – 'a gorgeous mansion'. He noted that many of the men were former prisoners of war* and that as they improved they were, as he put it, 'hardened out' in shelters outside, at the same time learning a trade

---

*A FIDAC (see Chapter 6) report noted that one in four French Prisoners of War subsequently died of TB. [85]

before, if accepted for permanent residence, moving into a hostel if single or a cottage if married, where they were joined by their families. Their subsequent work not only paid for their own upkeep but met the running expenses of the whole enterprise (except for the treatment costs). By the end of 1928 the village population had grown to nearly 500, a new building department enabling additional cottages to be built by the direct labour of the settlers themselves. The same year saw a 'Council of Settlers' to advise the village management.

As the decade drew towards a close the number of more serious cases entering the sanatorium increased as some sufferers who had continued to work in order to provide for their families finally succumbed to the disease. Others had had a relapse after a premature discharge elsewhere for the same reasons, so that Preston Hall introduced an after-care scheme in early 1929 to assist discharged patients.

The social life of the village prospered: in addition to the Legion branch there was a Village Institute, a gardening society, a thrift club, a bowling club, Toc H, Boy Scouts and Girl Guides, while a village stores met essential needs. Nor was there any antipathy between the settlers and the patients; in fact the settlers made a voluntary contribution each week from their wages towards the needs of patients. In the five years since it had been founded Preston Hall had proved to be not only a medical, but also a social success.[86]

## The first Legion housing

But, while the Legion improved living conditions at Preston Hall, the country had done little to produce 'homes for heroes' or indeed for anyone else. Despite the politicians' wartime undertakings, ten years later less than 20,000 houses had been built, a staggeringly inadequate response to the problem. The ex-service housing problem was exacerbated by the Rent Acts. Only tenants renting houses before 1920 were protected, so that men returning from the war had to pay rents which could be nearly twice the amount paid by those who had stayed at home. Many of the cases coming to the Legion for help were families facing eviction because of inability to meet the rent.[87]

The Legion itself did not have the funds to engage in large-scale housing projects. But in 1927 it set aside £75,000 to build twelve houses in each Area for 'ex-servicemen advancing in years'. With the help of a government subsidy 146 families had been housed by 1930, the last twelve houses having been built in the Irish Free State only after some difficulty. All of the men concerned had been badly disabled in the war and one of those chosen wrote 'after being forced to spend five years of married life in one room, at the top of a large house, that one room unfurnished 8/- weekly – and now to think that we shall be in a house fit for a hero to live in'.[88]

The death of Earl Haig led the Council to press for a memorial of a practical nature related to his work. This resulted in an appeal to build Douglas Haig Memorial Homes, principally for war widows and the badly disabled. To assist occupants' employment they were sited on the outskirts of towns in groups of 12-20. But although the Legion had inspired the project and helped in many ways, including fundraising, it was a separate venture.[89]

## The 1928 Pilgimage

In the homes of the war widows, perhaps the only remembrance of a husband and father was the photograph over the fireplace; the grave was in a foreign land. Some had the wooden cross that had marked the resting place until it was replaced by a headstone, but that was the nearest that they had got to the graveside.

Following in the footsteps of the Church Army, Legion branches began to run their own pilgrimages; Hull was one branch that organized visits in both 1926 and 1927, leading to the unveiling of a City of Hull battlefield memorial at Oppy Wood near Arras where more of the men of Hull had fallen than on any other day in the war.[90] Legion headquarters organized its first pilgimage in 1927, the pilgrims being met by a band at Ostend and, after no little speech-making, proceeding by char-a-banc to Ypres, attending the Tyne Cot memorial inauguration on the way. There were visits to cemeteries and to battlefields, to the Cloth Hall and the Menin Gate, with receptions and speeches at every point, the pilgrims returning to Ostend each evening. It cost £5 a head, including eggs for breakfast.[91]

Plans for a 1928 pilgrimage on the same lines were overtaken by a request from the French authorities following the American Legion's 1927 Convention in Paris, when some twenty thousand participants had sailed the Atlantic to mark the anniversary of America's entry into the war. So impressed were the French that they wanted a similar British Legion visit. It was envisaged that ten thousand ex-servicemen from every part of the United Kingdom would return to the scenes of the great battles in France and Flanders and march through the Menin Gate in Ypres past Earl Haig – and it gave the NEC something to think about.

Major J.F. Harter was appointed to head a temporary department at headquarters. The tour was conducted by rail: trains of 500 pilgrims started from each Legion Area, further trains transporting the same groups from place to place on the far side of the Channel. Accommodation was the responsibility of French ex-servicemen and since there were not enough hotels most were 'billetted' in barracks, schools or private houses, each train party or 'battalion' under its Area Organizer being based on a particular town and split into five 'companies' of 100 under a 'company commander'. The Women's Section formed their own groups which included many visiting the graves of husbands, sons and brothers.

Major Harter did his job well. Recces established the best viewpoints and points of interest such as trench systems still in existence and the Imperial War Graves Commission agreed to provide some 200 gardeners to act as guides to the cemeteries. Meals were not difficult to arrange, but much serious thought had to be given to the problem of tea: it proved only possible to provide a real 'cuppa' at two locations, Beaucourt and Vimy, where about 100 volunteers of the women's party would operate urns borrowed from Messrs Lyons.

Such was the enterprise, but would it get a response from the rank and file? It did: by June all 10,000 places were filled and further demand brought the total to 11,000 pilgrims. The Legion staff were mobilized and the *Legion Journal* carried eight pages of detailed instructions ranging from maps of Ypres giving the routes for the march past to arrangements for the disposal of bottles – 'only in areas marked by yellow flags'.

The pilgimage was a remarkable success by any standards. As each party assembled a strong unit *esprit de corps* at once appeared; difficulties were overcome with a joke or a song. Following the visits to the battlefields the concentration at Ypres was achieved smoothly and the ramparts and causeway lined with Legion standards and the signs of the wartime Divisions. The pilgrims then marched through the Menin Gate to the Cloth Hall in front of which the Prince of Wales took the salute in place of Haig who had died six months before, Lady Haig bravely marching at the head of the Scottish Women's Section contingent.

## TRAIN PARTY T

| ARRIVE DEPART | PLACE. | TIME TABLE. | | MEALS. | PLACE WHERE PROVIDED. |
|---|---|---|---|---|---|
| d. | YORKSHIRE | | 5th August Sunday | Tea Supper | In Train On Boat |
| d. | HARWICH | 11. 0 p.m. | | | |
| a. | ZEEBRUGGE | 7. 0 a.m. | | Breakfast | On Boat |
| d. | ZEEBRUGGE | 11.10 a.m. | 6th August Monday | Lunch, Supper, Bed & Breakfast | In Billets in YPRES & POPERINGHE |
| a. | POPERINGHE | 1.20 p.m. | | | |
| a. | YPRES | 1.30 p.m. | | | |
| d. | YPRES | 7.15 a.m. | | Lunch & Tea | At BEAUCOURT STATION |
| d. | POPERINGHE | 7.35 a.m. | | | |
| a. | BEAUCOURT | 10.50 a.m. | 7th August Tuesday | Supper, Bed & Breakfast | In Billets in YPRES & POPERINGHE |
| d. | BEAUCOURT | 4.20 p.m. | | | |
| a. | POPERINGHE | 7.21 p.m. | | | |
| a. | YPRES | 7.40 p.m. | | | |
| | At YPRES | | 8th August Wednesday | Lunch & Tea Supper, Bed & Breakfast The POPERINGHE Party will have Lunch & Tea at The ABBATTOIR Party Assembly Place at YPRES, ABBATTOIR | In Billets in YPRES |
| d. | YPRES | 8.25 a.m. | | Lunch & Tea | At VIMY STATION |
| d. | POPERINGHE | 8.38 a.m. | 9th August Thursday | | |
| a. | VIMY | 10.35 a.m. | | | |
| d. | VIMY | 4.45 p.m. | | Supper | On Boat |
| a. | ZEEBRUGGE | 9. 0 p.m. | | | |
| d. | ZEEBRUGGE | 10. 0 p.m. | | | |
| a. | HARWICH | 5. 0 a.m. | 10th August Friday | Breakfast Lunch | On Boat In Train |
| a. | YORKSHIRE | | | | |

The POPERINGHE Party will proceed to YPRES by Char-a-banc on August 8th.

*Train Party T came from Yorkshire and each pilgrim had a docket holding this timetable, tickets and a billeting coupon.*

*The 1928 Pilgrimage. Arriving pilgrims proffer their billeting coupons naming their French host, who held a corresponding coupon listing his guests. 11,000 pilgrims were accommodated in this manner.*

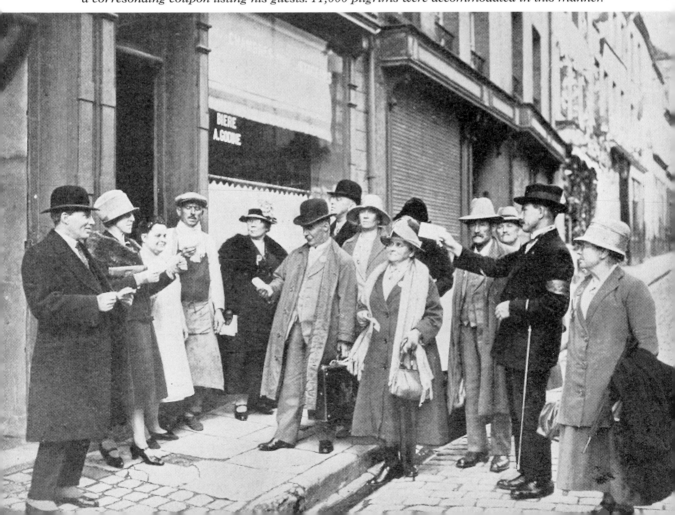

*The 1928 Pilgrimage. The pilgrims of No.4 Company, Party B, on their way to Vimy Ridge.*

*The 1928 Pilgrimage – pilgrims mass at the Menin Gate, Ypres for the service.*

It had been a thoroughly inspiring event, but the last word lay with the irrepressible General Sir Ian Hamilton, President of Metropolitan Area: in a BBC radio talk a few days later he noted that on arrival in Arras he found that his French hosts had allocated one small bed for the Area Chairman, General Sir Edward Bethune, and himself. 'I never expected a soft time but community sleeping was more than I had bargained for.' Needless to say the two generals got hold of another bed. The next day, on a part of the battlefield visit, 'the way was long and dusty and steep. The sun was hot. The pilgrims became weary despite the playing of an Irish piper at their head. Then it was that we espied . . . two tents flying the Union Jack and labelled "British Stout" and "English Cigarettes". We had triumphed!'[92]

Although the Prince of Wales, who had been greatly impressed with the 1928 pilgrimage, suggested that a national pilgrimage should become an annual event it was the Areas and Counties who were inspired to organize pilgimages in the following years. The Irish Free State Area organized its own pilgimage for the first time in 1930 and a number of contingents from Northern Ireland joined the party, finishing at Tyne Cot where a third of the 12,000 graves hold Irishmen.[93]

# 1931 – 1935

## Too old for work

The illustration on the cover of the December 1932 *Legion Journal* depicted the gallant stand of 'L' Battery of the Royal Horse Artillery at Néry in 1914. The following month a letter to the magazine noted that in the summer of 1932, eighteen years after the action, a survivor of the battery's stand had tramped the country with his wife and children from Yorkshire to Cornwall looking for work.

The ex-gunner was but one of some half a million survivors of the Great War still unemployed in the early 1930s. Their tragedy was that, having returned from the war to find all the jobs filled by others and lacking a trade other than the soldier's, any chance of work was now receding because of advancing years; often the upper age limit was 35, meaning that a man who had enlisted in 1916 at the age of eighteen was too old to be even considered. Small wonder that bitterness and despair reigned in this army of the damned as they trudged through a land that seemed to have forgotten them.

Not all had forgotten. The Legion still sought employment preference for ex-servicemen where they could; unfortunately they had little influence over most employers who, if they could not find a skilled man, preferred to train the rising generation. And even though the agreement giving three-quarters of the places on government-backed local authority short-term work schemes to ex-servicemen was maintained, there was a tendency among the authorities to seek to get the quota reduced.

The employment of women in work that could be done by men still aroused feelings of indignation, and not only among the men themselves: a lady complained in 1933 that the BBC was employing a woman announcer, thinking it 'most extraordinary and callous' when ex-servicemen were out of work and suggesting that the six o' clock news should be boycotted. The protest was backed by the Legion and the female announcer disappeared.[94]

## More changes in the organization of relief

In the face of this continuing demand it was decided to amalgamate the United Services relief with that of the Legion, in 1934 the USF effectively handing over to the Legion responsibility for administering their funds. There was now one single source of relief for ex-servicemen and their families, whatever the cause. But there was less money available, since the situation had also persuaded the USF to extend the life of their fund from 1939 to 1948.

As part of the reorganization the thirteen Legion Area offices gave up their relief function, which was transferred to five Regional Benevolent offices: three in England and one in Cardiff, while an office in Dublin covered both the North and South of Ireland. The activities themselves were re-scheduled into no less than seventeen schemes covering the whole welfare field from unemployment relief (Scheme A) to help for larger businesses employing ex-servicemen (Scheme Q). Each scheme had a specific level of authority: thus, while Scheme A could be operated by the local committee, only headquarters could authorize Scheme Q. It may have sounded bureaucratic but everyone knew what their responsibilities were – and it worked.[94] One problem remained. The funds, whether Legion or USF-based, were only intended for the relief of those who had served in the Great War. What about those who had served before or after the war? The Legion rank-and-file were firmly of the view that they were not entitled to money raised through the Poppy Appeal; it was after all the 'Flanders Poppy' that was sold and this view was upheld by a resolution at the 1933 Annual Conference. The effect of the decision was that such cases, however pressing, had be be referred to Region, which had access to non-Poppy Appeal monies.[95]

No doubt there were a number of post-war men among the unemployed and homeless ex-servicemen who once again appeared in the nooks and crevices of London's streets in the renewed slump of the early 1930s. But here at least no such distinctions applied; all were given refuge by the Legion's Homeless Office which provided not only meals and lodgings but clothing and boots, the last supplied from part-worn stocks provided by the Territorial Army and repaired by ex-servicemen. The office was situated at the same address as the Employment Department – 57 Palace Street – enabling some of those destitute to be found work, in which case the Homeless Office could provide tools and a travel warrant to reach the place of employment.[96]

## The Prince's Appeal

Rooted in the community, but with strong national and regional support, the Legion's relief network had become highly effective even before the 1934 restructuring. So much so that the Prince of Wales, deeply concerned with the wider problem of over two-and-a-half million people without jobs in Britain in 1931, believed that the Legion could help. Although outside the Legion's Charter, it was a call that could hardly be refused; in a sense the Legion was being conscripted for public assistance. Even so the leadership did not find it easy to define exactly what help was to be provided; the Prince himself was somewhat vague; his appeal merely said that 'Every branch should consider at once what service it can render to its own unemployed community.' The difficulty was of course that the branches already had their hands full with the problems of the ex-service families who were their proper charge.

But the branches did not let the Legion down. Quickest off the mark was South Battersea and Wandsworth who reopened their food depot at the London Regiment TA drill hall at Clapham Junction, supplying hot meals at 1½d. By April 1933 cheap or free meals were being provided by Legion-organized soup kitchens from Cornwall to Northumberland, while the unemployed were encouraged to help feed themselves through allotment schemes with loans of tools and free or subsidised seeds. Legion premises were opened as welfare centres with facilities and training provided for boot and shoe repairing and carpentry. Branches in the better-off areas collected clothing for distribution to the unemployed through their local Legion branch; others encouraged householders to 'spend for employment' through fence repairs or house painting. Brickhill in Buckinghamshire opened up a disused gravel pit while Carlisle added a parcel delivery service to its existing work schemes.

The Prince's Appeal continued throughout that year and the next, with many Legion branches working closely with local community organizations, sometimes establishing a community organization where none existed. Needless to say the Women's Section were heavily involved in much of the Legion response. From 1935, as the employment situation

*Battersea responds to the Prince's Appeal with a soup kitchen. Admiral Sir Henry Bruce, Metropolitan Area Chairman, and the Mayor hold the jugs.*

improved, the scheme faded away; but, although probably only a minority of the Legion's 4,000 branches were actively involved, it was an example of the Legion's organization being used to assist the community as a whole.[97]

## Employment success

Meanwhile the Legion had been steadily building up its employment service under Admiral Payne. By the end of 1931 there was a full-time Employment Officer in each Area and by 1935 some 2,100 Legion branches had formed Employment Committees.

In 1930 there had been 10,000 placements; in 1935 the Legion found employment for no less than 50,000 ex-servicmen. Included in these totals from 1932 onwards were some 3,000-4,000 post-war ex-regulars, the Admiralty and the War Office having sought the Legion's help in finding jobs for those leaving the service.

Against a general background of worsening unemployment in the early part of the period the figures show that the Legion's organisation was remarkably successful. It was also remarkably economic: the cost of each placement was 8/6d – about £16 at today's values – largely because much of the groundwork was done by the volunteer staff in the branches.

The best Branch Employment Committees, whose members were often hard-working men who somehow found the time to help others, followed the Director's policy of sifting out those with poor work records so that employers became accustomed to getting only good men from the Legion and would return for more of the same. This approach was firmly applied to Ireland where the task was even more difficult than in the other Areas: not only was there high unemployment in the Free State but the government gave no preference to former British servicemen, and private employers followed suit; yet the Legion's policy brought early success, the Dublin office filling 854 places in its first five months of operation. But another problem then arose: lack of proper nourishment had made the long-term unemployed physically incapable of taking on many tasks.

Often the work was short-term and Areas and branches had to be ready to act at a moment's notice. In 1933 the Metropolitan Office received a call from Gaumont British for 400 unemployed ex-servicemen to act as 'supers' – in two hours! Nonetheless the Area Office met the deadline and the men were put into khaki to form a battalion for a new film. The presence of the Area Chairman, Admiral Bruce, in the office at the time seems to have played no small part in promoting swift action.

In 1934 there was some improvement in trade and the task became a little easier; but the work of the Legion's employment service at a time of such economic depression must rank among its greatest achievements.[98]

The Legion's own employment schemes had taken on a different character by the early 1930s, reflecting the problem of the older man in getting a job as well as the lack of skills in those who had spent their formative years in the war: the work was increasingly low grade – car cleaning, tree felling, collection and disposal of waste and rags. And, as employers in general began to shed their older men in response to the economic situation, so the applications increased from middle-aged ex-servicemen for help in starting their own small businesses, often the implausible schemes of desperate men.

The depression seemed to have less effect on London's taxi trade and the Metropolitan Area Taxi Driver schools continued to thrive, although the average age was over forty by now since only Great War men were eligible for the scheme. There was a great camaraderie among the drivers and following two reunion dinners they formed their own

Legion branch in August 1933, based on the Chevrons Club in St George's Square, organizing the next year their first children's Christmas party. One successful trainee resolved that he would not charge his first fare wearing a Legion badge; by a singular coincidence the Legion's President hailed him to go to Haig House. But a rather more significant saving to the Legion was Ministry of Labour assistance with training expenses which brought down the annual £12,000 cost of the scheme to some £2,000.[99]

The motor trade in general seemed immune to the economic climate and the increase in cars prompted more and more Legion branches to persuade their local Councils to adopt the Legion-sponsored Car Parking Attendants scheme. It was not yet, however, a centrally-controlled organization: although the Legion regulated the scheme and provided start-up loans the initiative lay with the local Legion branch; the branch had to negotiate with the Watch Committee or local authority, arrange the contract, recruit the men and set up the company. By the end of 1935 the scheme operated in over fifty towns throughout the country and in 1938 Area companies began to be formed. In keeping with the Legion's belief in high standards the attendants were distinguished by their smart appearance, civility and attention to the motoring public; in particular the red caps of the Belfast attendants were as well known and respected by the city motorists as the uniforms of AA or RAC patrolmen.[100]

## A need for change

One man who had been successful in getting a job after the war was a London bus conductor by the name of Edward Howard. Howard had joined up in 1914. In 1917 he was severely gassed in France and evacuated to hospital. After treatment he was again in the thick of the fighting, but taken prisoner. Following the Armistice he went back to the buses, but his state of health was poor: as a result of the gassing he suffered from bronchitis, emphysema and a general weakness of the lungs. But he had to work; the Ministry of Pensions had disallowed his application for a war pension. It was a decision that cost him dear as the long hours on the buses combined with his condition to exhaust him and in 1931 he died from fibrosis of the lungs. However, before he died the Legion was able to get him a war pension on appeal and his widow, who had not only kept him going in his work but nursed him at the end of his days, was at least assured of a widow's pension. Or so she thought. But once again the Ministry declined to pay; it was more than seven years since her husband had been gassed. Once again the Legion took up the case – and failed. It did not give up; eventually, after much painstaking work by the Pensions Department, the Appeal Tribunal was persuaded to grant a pension to Edward Howard's widow.[101]

The fact was that Edward Howard might have survived if he had received better advice in the early days and his case was one of many that were studied by the new Chairman of the Legion's new National Pensions Committee, Captain G.E. Graves, when he took office in 1932. Giving up his two weeks' annual holiday for the purpose, he systematically went through the files at Legion Headquarters in order to identify why, despite all of the effort put in, so many cases still either failed or took such a long time to resolve. He came to the conclusion that sufficient expertise simply did not exist in the Legion's branches and Areas, a judgement which was reinforced when he was able to see the Area files of failed cases – another large-scale exercise. The outcome was a revised scheme with the branch sending the case direct to the experts at headquarters.

The new procedures were introduced on 1 October 1933, the Council simply ignoring the very considerable opposition within the Legion. There is no doubt that they were right to do so; whatever the Areas' wounded pride, more expertise was sorely needed; in the first year of operating the new scheme it was found that over 90 per cent of the cases referred to headquarters were incomplete. There are no before-and-after records to show the effect of the change, but in 1934 over 900 cases referred to headquarters were satisfactorily concluded and in the following year the figure had risen to more than 1,100.[102]

There was a further step forward in 1934. Hitherto, the decision of the Pensions Ministry's specialists had been regarded as final in any appeal where the medical evidence was disputed. But in 1934 the Minister agreed that if the Legion was able to show grounds why a further expert opinion should be obtained then the case would be referred to a nominee of the Royal Colleges of Physicians or Surgeons. This was a great concession and the Legion consolidated its position by making use of it only when advised to do so by its own specialist consultant.[103]

Even when a war pension had been awarded the battle was not over. Under the government's Unemployment Assistance Scheme of 1931 local authorities assessed the public assistance to those out of work. The Legion was anxious that no account should be taken of the disability pension but representations to government got the response that there was no reason to think that the authorities 'will not do justice to the claims of disabled men'. The Legion, with experience of the workings of such authorities, campaigned for legislation. After a long and hard-fought battle, which included giving evidence before the Royal Commission on Unemployment, it succeeded in 1934 in a change to the law so that in assessing the 'means' of disabled ex-servicemen the first twenty shillings of their pension would be ignored; this meant that most war disability pensioners would have no part of their pension included in the means test. Bearing in mind the necessity in those depressed times to keep the scheme solvent on the basis of 'real need', which was why a means test had been introduced, it was a remarkable achievement. And the important principle had been established that a war disability pension did not only compensate for reduction in earning capacity. But it was a point that would have to be made again – and again.[104]

### Another assault on the seven-year rule

Although constant pressure on successive governments had resulted in concessions to the seven-year rule, allowing the Legion to pursue cases outside the time limit to some effect, the official position was that any such concession was at the Minister's discretion, an unsatisfactory state of affairs since there was no right of appeal in a 'discretionary' case, should the Minister turn it down. The Legion's campaign to remove the time limit altogether continued and in 1931 the indefatigable Brunel Cohen introduced a bill in Parliament. The Legion's Treasurer did not pull his punches and after the bill had been accepted unopposed for a second reading Cabinet Ministers and ex-Ministers surrounded Cohen sitting in his wheelchair in the Lobby in an almost unprecedented scene, all congratulating him on his speech. With elder statesmen thus moved it seemed at last certain that the rule would be overturned.

But then things began to go wrong. There was no second reading because a few months later Parliament was dissolved over the national economic crisis. Brunel Cohen himself decided not to seek re-election and there was no opportunity to re-introduce the bill in the new Parliament. In December 1934, therefore, a Legion deputation, headed by the

*The Legion delegation outside Number 10, Downing Street, December 1934, led by the President, General Maurice (holding umbrella). It included the Chairman, Colonel John Brown, right, and the General Secretary, Colonel Heath, centre. But there was an unsatisfactory response from Ramsay MacDonald.*

National President, called on the Prime Minister. But they emerged only with a promise that the government would consider the matter. In January the answer came in a letter from Ramsay MacDonald. He rejected any idea of abolishing the seven-year limitation: it might lead to a 'vast number of claims, the majority of which would be without merit and unsupported by any evidence'.

Reluctantly the Council accepted the situation, putting the best face on it by pointing out that the administrative concessions that had been gained over the years had in fact achieved the same result by another means, particularly the Minister's agreement to accept expert medical opinion in disputed cases. They found further justification for this view in an examination of actual cases which revealed that in fact none of them would have had a different outcome if the seven-year limit had been removed, concluding that 'no useful purpose would be served by expending the Legion's energy on endeavouring to obtain legislation to achieve an object which had already been met'. In practical terms the Council was right. Nevertheless as an achievement it lacked spectacle: the Legion might have taken the fortress through the back entrance, but the seven-year banner still hung over the main gate.[105]

## Premature ageing

War Pensions were intended to compensate for death or disability. But by now another war-induced problem was beginning to be perceived: the premature ageing of some ex-service men and women as a result of their experiences, making them unfit for work. In 1931 the Prince of Wales suggested that the proceeds of the Legion Book (see page 131) should be used to set up a pension fund for such people and maintained by an annual grant from the Poppy Appeal. He pointed out that this could safely be done as permanent pensions would reduce the demand for temporary relief.

It is not clear to what extent the Legion's leaders had been consulted before the suggestion was made and it may be that it was simply dropped in their laps, one of the penalties of having an enthusiastic Royal Patron. If so it was accepted with good grace, including the annual charge on the Appeal proceeds. The Chairman read the Prince's letter to the 1931 Conference delegates who approved the proposal unanimously. In the following months the details were hammered out: the qualifying age was to be fifty and the pension was intended to bridge the gap between that age and the qualifying age for the Old Age Pension; branches would put forward recommendations, but Trustees appointed by the Prince would award the pensions, taking account of war service, health and means; the rate would be ten shillings a week, but reviewed annually. No one who was registered as fit for work would be eligible.

By 1935 some 1,500 pensions were in issue, allocated on an Area basis. Payment ceased when the pensioner received the state Old Age Pension; but for every recipient who passed the post to get his or her OAP three did not make it, an interesting commentary on the life expectancies of those involved and, if one were needed, a justification for the scheme. There was no shortage of deserving cases: a stoker who spent four and a half years at sea; a nursing sister with three years service, much of it overseas, now afflicted with deafness and at the end of her savings; a Lieutenant of infantry, a veteran of the Boer War wounded in the Great War. But they no doubt considered themselves to be the lucky ones; the number in need of such help at the time was probably ten times the capability of the fund.[106]

## Preston Hall expands

In 1934 the United Services Fund offered Douglas House at West Southborne in Bournemouth as an annexe to Preston Hall, increasing the capacity by 100. At the end of 1935 therefore the Legion was caring for 400 TB patients as well as nearly 600 settlers.

It might be thought that the community's children, many of whom had been born at Preston Hall, were at some risk of contracting the disease; although they lived among those who had been cured they were liable to encounter patients. In 1933 and 1934 stringent tests were carried out; they showed that of 350 children there was not a single case of TB and they in fact seemed to have developed an immunity.

Throughout the difficult years of the early 1930s the whole venture continued to be self-supporting: the contributions from the local authorities for their patients were augmented by the profits from the Village Industries employing the settlers, who also contributed by paying rent for their cottages out of their wages. As far as the Industries' success was concerned, it was simply good business management: the successful elements were developed, such as the printing press which numbered among its customers over half the Legion branches by the middle of the decade; the less successful changed their product lines, while a new café attached to the village store, catering for the many visitors as well as the settlers, also made a contribution.

At the same time Preston Hall retained its pre-eminence as a treatment centre for one of the most serious diseases of the time. Not surprisingly, many saw it as the jewel in the Legion's crown.[107]

### The war orphans grow up

Less fortunate than the children at Preston Hall were the war orphans. In the early 1930s nearly 50,000 orphans lost their government financial support every year as they reached the age of sixteen and, with the depression limiting work opportunities, the Legion's After-Care scheme was increasingly in demand. The local After-Care workers, acting as proxy fathers, advised the orphans and in many cases approached employers on their behalf for apprenticeships or other training, coming to headquarters for any financial assistance needed. Here again a principle was involved: no young person should be denied the chance of a fair start in life because of the death of the father in the war.

The Legion was particularly concerned with one category of orphan: those who were either physically or mentally impaired. It had persuaded the government to support them until they were 21 and in some cases beyond that age, and to provide work training suited to their needs. And in 1935, after repeated representations, it got a further concession: where no form of training would make the orphan self-sufficient then local authorities would provide support. The Legion had however less faith in the local authorities than the government and it continued not only to press its case for continuing the government payment in such cases but to keep a watchful eye on these unfortunates.[108]

### A Legion refuge in Ypres

Few orphans or widows were able to visit the grave of a father or husband. In most cases the cost – around £5 – was beyond their reach. But for those who had the money there was the opportunity to make a pilgrimage to France and Flanders. While there were no nationally organized pilgrimages in the early 1930s, headquarters assisted Areas, Counties and branches to organize visits to the graves and battlefields, as well as individuals. The branch pilgrimage was very much a community affair and they sometimes brought the branch band to play on the quayside at Dover or Harwich, entertain them on the ship and lead them up the cobbled streets of Arras or Ypres. It was too a community affair at the cemeteries, the rows of headstones, before which the pilgrims placed their wreaths of Flanders poppies, carrying the same county regiment badge.

In 1932 the Legion bought a house in the now rebuilt town of Ypres at 9, Route de Thorout, a narrow cobbled street just off the Grande Place. It was a small town house in the familiar Flemish style but it provided a place of rest for weary pilgrims and an information centre for those visiting the battlefields and cemeteries of the Ypres Salient. There were lounges and tea tables both indoors and in the garden and the Women's Section had had a hand in the arrangements, no doubt ensuring the quality of the much-sought cup of tea. Every type of wreath made at the Poppy Factory was on sale, as well as goods made by disabled men, while the Information Bureau could not only arrange the visits to the graves but book accommodation in Ypres. Despite the difficult time at which it opened it seems to have been well used and many pilgrims were moved to write of the courteous help and hospitality that they received at Haig House, Ypres.

Such visitors, and particularly the veterans, were familiar with the German 'pill boxes' that studded the battlefields. Not only were they monuments to the ingenuity of the foe but also to the valour of those who overcame them in battle. In 1933, however, the Belgian government decided that they should be demolished. Pressure by the Legion, in company with Toc H, the wartime all-ranks fellowship set up by an Army Padre, the Rev 'Tubby' Clayton, persuaded the Belgians that 180 of the most significant of these should remain and the Legion followed up by producing a small booklet *The Story of the Pill Boxes*.[109]

## 1936 – 1940

### Economic growth again

From the mid-1930s the recession began to ease as the worsening international situation led to a rearmament programme, regenerating industry and stimulating employment. It was perhaps ironic that it took the threat of war to achieve the self-stimulated growth in the economy that the Legion, and others, had long advocated.

Yet for many ex-servicemen it had all come too late. One of the Legion's greatest problems at this time was the advancing age of those who had fought in the Great War, which, combined with often inadequate diet and poor living conditions, led to chronic illness. Legion money now had to be used for an increasing number of veterans and their wives whose health had completely broken down, and there was some difficulty in meeting the demand. However, as the economic recovery took hold and the need for relief of distress caused by unemployment fell, more money was available for other cases. The local branches had to keep their eyes open: in one case a committee member discovered only by chance that a man and his wife had existed a whole week on eightpence, too proud to ask for help. In Sunderland in 1935 Vera Brittain found 'an ex-serviceman who had not been able to work since the war and who for the past nine years had lived with his semi-invalid wife and nine children in one moderate-sized room, indescribably filthy because the only way of cleaning it would have been to turn the sorry sticks of furniture into the streets for the neighbours to see'. [110] But many were without even a roof over their head: from its Homeless Office, now in Maiden Lane off the Strand, the Legion dealt with over 10,000 cases a year in London until the LCC finally took over the problem and the office closed in early 1939.[111]

Such cases demonstrated the unevenness of the recovery and the deprivation that still existed in too many parts of the country. In 1936 the Chairman of the Legion's Hertfordshire County had commented, 'How many know the conditions of homes where men have been out of work for six to eleven years? . . . 'How few care to think? . . . It has been the fate of too many splendid fellows who fought with you and me to exist and see their families existing on what amounts to twopence per meal for years.' A Legion Distressed Area Committee took control of the existing informal arrangements whereby branches in the South Eastern and Home Counties Areas had helped their less fortunate comrades with gifts of clothing and money. The distressed areas were defined and donor branches raised funds, while teams visited the Areas to determine the actual needs. Temporary work schemes were financed by the Legion ranging from allotment fencing to car park contruction, not only providing those involved with income but getting fit again for work men weakened by years of enforced idleness, while their sons and daughters were found jobs and supported by branches in other parts of the country. Legion Areas were twinned: South Western Area gave support to Wales, some sixty branches in 1936

*The Legion's Distressed Areas scheme: unemployed ex-servicemen being 'reconditioned' for work by levelling ground for sports pitches in the late 1930s.*

subscribing cash and another forty-four gifts in kind. The work schemes in particular were appreciated; one man given a month's work helping to construct a new road in a local park commented that 'it got our chins up a little higher. . . four weeks banishment of the Means Test and sixteen shillings more a week to support my wife and child, not forgetting dry feet thanks to a new pair of boots'. The schemes continued and as the threat of war drew closer the men thus 'reconditioned' for work were able to get employment in government-backed projects to build armaments factories and lay out airfields. As *The Times* noted, 'The real service the Legion renders is in the putting of men on their feet.' The Special Area scheme continued in the North East into 1939, until wartime direction of labour solved the problem.[112]

### 'The government does not understand'

In many other cases age continued to take its toll and in 1936 the Legion registered its concern for those suffering physical or mental disablement due to prolonged active service, referred to in Canada and elsewhere as 'burnt out veterans'. The Prince of Wales's initiative, the 'permanently incapacitated' scheme, provided some of them with a pension of ten shillings a week. Now a Legion committee investigated the scope of the problem, with a view to government action. It reported in 1938 that at least a hundred thousand ex-servicemen were physically unable to work and stated its belief that 'men who are suffering from the intangible results of war service, which it is not possible to connect medically with such service, should be able to obtain state assistance other than through the Poor Law'. But not all of the authorities that the committee had consulted agreed with the proposition that war was a cause of premature ageing and there was no hard evidence to support it.

A dialogue with the Prime Minister ensued, but his response was that there could be no distinction in this matter between ex-servicemen and the rest, and that the national social services which were replacing the Poor Law would be administered by local authorities 'on broad and humane lines'. The Legion's reaction was summed up by the National President: 'The government does not understand.' But it may be that on this

108

occasion the Legion itself did not appreciate the impossibility of getting the government to accept an argument which, whatever its merits, was based largely on perception.[113]

### The work extends in war

The outbreak of war in September 1939 brought much uncertainty over the future of the Legion's benevolent work. It was funded almost entirely by the Poppy Appeal, and there was some doubt whether the Appeal could take place in wartime and, if it was held, whether the public would be able to respond. At the same time there could be a vastly increased responsibility to a new generation of servicemen and women with even more pressure on resources. Restrictions were imposed on local committees and control placed in the hands of the Regional offices. Nevertheless, at their first wartime meeting, only a few days after hostilities had been declared, the National Executive Council, on their own authority,* determined that Legion relief would be extended to the ex-service of all wars, overriding any lingering thoughts that the Legion was purely a Great War charity.[114]

But the 1939 Poppy Appeal, held during the 'phoney war', set a new record (see page 137), and some of the early restrictions on the use of funds could be relaxed, for the moment at least. It was as well, for enemy air raids the following year made ex-service families homeless, while the damage to branch properties in the areas concerned hindered relief. Nevertheless, in the spirit of the times, the local committees 'carried on'. During the height of the London blitz, Brunel Cohen loaded his car with blankets sent to the Legion from America and, accompanied by the National Chairman and the Benevolent Secretary, set off for the East End. On arrival at a branch headquarters in the Barking Road they found the lady secretary to the local benevolent committee calmly doing her work under a large roof hole and surrounded by bomb debris. It was the first of many visits by the trio and such scenes were to be repeated.[115]

In such circumstances the local committees worked closely with the other agencies and they played a prominent part in setting up a new organization which exists to this day – the Citizens' Advice Bureaux – formed to advise people experiencing difficulties arising from the war. They also gave assistance to a new group to whom Legion help had been also extended immediately on the outbreak of war; these were those who maintained the nation's lifelines, the men of the Merchant Navy and, all too frequently during and after the Battle of the Atlantic, their widows and other dependants.[116]

### Employment in war

The Legion's employment work continued into the war with some 1,600 branches still involved in 1940 and finding work for those discharged unfit from the forces as well as the elderly, particularly in less strenuous war work such as fire watchers and caretakers. At the beginning of 1940 one branch, South Moor in Durham, was able to report that whereas three years before 97 per cent of ex-servicemen in the district were unemployed, by now the same percentage was employed.[117] But the Legion also ensured that the veterans' experience was put to good use in the current war: it got the bar on those in 'reserved occupations' removed so that they could join up and it found former warrant officers and NCOs for provost and administrative duties in the army and RAF.[118]

The need to concentrate on work directly supporting the war effort meant the suspension of the small business scheme in 1941, but the Cambrian Factory, which had steadily expanded its business pre-war, now found itself working overtime in order to meet the demand for knitting wool for comforts for the troops, putting it into profit but

---

*But endorsed by Conference the following year.

at the same time depriving it of its government subsidy.[119]

The car park attendants schemes had continued to develop in the late 1930s with Area involvement and by 1939 there was a chain of Legion Area companies covering the whole of England and Wales as well as Northern Ireland and the schemes operated in over fifty towns. But with the onset of war petrol rationing drastically reduced their activities and by 1940 most of the attendants had either been transferred to war work or were unemployed. The companies themselves remained in being, keeping a paternal eye on their former employees and, more practically, maintaining their life insurances.[120]

The Taxi School, previously supervised by Metropolitan Area, had been placed under national Legion direction in 1937 but remained at Hide Place, Westminster. Its Legion branch continued to thrive, not only assisting its members by keeping them up to date on new Acts and Bye-laws affecting their work but helping the London taxi driver community at large by getting the Legion to sponsor a private Bill in Parliament which got them full benefits under the Workmen's Compensation Act. In early 1938 the School formed a Legion unit for the London Ambulance Service from former trainees which, by the outbreak of war, was at a full strength of 250 and was used principally to lead emergency service convoys when the blitz came. The School itself, however, closed as a wartime measure in 1939.[121]

## The King's Roll enlarged

The coming of war also affected the King's Roll for the employment of disabled ex-servicemen. By 1939 more were being employed under the scheme than at any time since its inception. But it still did not include those who had suffered a disability in any conflict other than the Great War, the National Executive Council itself rejecting a suggestion from Scotland that it take in the rest. In 1939 all changed: the Roll was extended to cover all of those disabled, in whatever conflict, and jobs were available for most of them.[122] Meanwhile Disabled Men's Industries, which marketed the products of home workers or those operating under sheltered conditions, had had its ups and downs; in 1933 the shop in Buckingham Palace Road had been closed when modern designs and new technology began to affect the market. Traditional goods were back in favour in the Coronation year 1937, but thereafter sales levels were modest despite the high quality of the goods made, stylish leather handbags and wallets among them, and the level of sales support from Legion branches was often disappointing. Nevertheless work was provided for many who would otherwise be in enforced idleness.

For those unable to undertake any form of work due to premature ageing, or at least for 2,000 of them, there was ten shillings a week from the Prince of Wales's pension scheme until they were eligible for the state pension. Since, however, the scheme was funded partly out of capital the Legion had to top it up in order to maintain the level of awards. As the Prince himself, now the Duke of Windsor, was told on writing from Cap d'Antibes in 1939 to inquire about extending the fund, there was only enough money to keep the scheme going at its present level until 1971 when every Great War veteran would have received his Old Age Pension.[123]

## New attitudes to war pensions – and a new Warrant

In the late nineteen-thirties a number of post-war men had come to the Legion for help with pensions as a result of a wound or disability incurred in service, perhaps on the North West Frontier of India or in Palestine. In such cases the pensions were awarded by the War Office or one of the other service ministries and the Legion was now getting a sympathetic hearing from them, signifying that they no longer regarded it as an organisation devoted solely to veterans of the Great War, an important, if almost unnoticed, change in attitude.[124] It led to the Legion negotiating some improvements to the pensions rates in 1939, an involvement which would have been almost unthinkable to the service departments a few years before.

The outbreak of war in 1939 brought a new Pensions Warrant. Much had been learned from the experience of 1914-18, but not as much as the Legion thought should have been the case: in a number of respects the rules were inferior to those that applied to the earlier war. But this time the Legion was able to have its say. As well as using its organization to monitor the effects of the scheme, it was represented on the Ministry's Advisory Committee and was able to lead the way to some early reforms. Even so the new warrant remained unsatisfactory and in June 1940, mainly as a result of the four Legion representatives bringing their twenty years' experience to bear, the government issued a further Warrant with better rates and improved terms and conditions. But it was still inferior to the 1919 Warrant which applied to those who had fought in the Great War; the Legion's major concern was that the Ministry had refused to set up Independent Tribunals to hear Appeals against pension awards under the new warrant, on the grounds that it was impractical in wartime, although they had agreed the principle. The lines were drawn for yet another battle.[125]

## The war comes to Preston Hall

The Legion also had its concerns at Preston Hall. The patients now being admitted were often so advanced in years that even after successful treatment they would be unable to make their contribution to the settlement's economy, bearing in mind too that a TB sufferer was reckoned to have a physical age ten years beyond his time. Nor were the existing settlers getting any younger. The NEC struggled to find a solution, but in the event the new war was to resolve the issue, as it was to determine many other Legion problems arising out of its ageing dependency.[126]

The medical treatment itself continued to set the standard in its field with many overseas experts visiting to study its approach, particularly the use of surgery to cure the disease, and the hospital hosted postgraduate courses every three months. It even played its part in Anglo-German relations, hosting a visit from German ex-servicemen for which the lunch menu included 'fish from the sea that joins our lands'. The visitors must have been impressed by the atmosphere at Preston Hall which was free of petty rules and very relaxed, with the patients enjoying a good relationship with the staff and particularly the remarkable Matron, Miss Lee, 'mother of a family of more than a thousand people' as she was described by the Medical Director, the total including 150 at the annexe in Bournemouth. In 1939 one of the thousand was George Orwell who spent six months as a patient at Preston Hall where his brother-in-law was chief surgeon. The future author of *Nineteen Eighty-Four* may, or may not, have appreciated the television which had been provided for the use of patients by the Legion's Surrey County in 1938. [127]

Despite the ageing workforce the Industries continued to do well, although the production of decorated asbestos panels for 'the best houses in London' was in retrospect not perhaps the most suitable activity for a hospital settlement. But as war approached the building department took up large orders from the War Office and Territorial Army Associations and had to expand.

The situation in July 1939 also affected the hospital itself which was placed at the government's disposal in July of that year, with a 300-bed extension. No TB patient was forced to leave, although some went of their own accord. From then on there were two hospitals side by side, a 130-bed sanitorium for TB patients and a major 360-bed hospital for general casualties. The printing department disbanded and its staff were absorbed into other work, notably portable buildings, now at full stretch, but fancy goods continued, while in the village itself a Home Guard unit was formed in 1940 and other settlers joined Air Raid Precautions or the Auxiliary Fire Service.[128]

*Preston Hall at war: the Village Home Guard detachment parades. Some of the men would have been TB patients before becoming settlers.*

### Saving a standard

Despite the worsening international situation pilgrimages continued in the late 1930s, although mainly on a small scale and branch-organized. But the situation had become so grave by 1938 that the NEC turned down a Conference resolution for a national pilgrimage that year. Nevertheless Southern Area ran a tour in July 1939 while the last pre-war pilgimage was organized by Luton Branch for the August Bank Holiday weekend that year – six days at a cost of £5 7s 6d.[129]

The Legion's Annual Report is not noted for tongue-in-cheek entries but in 1939 it stated that 'members who may find themselves obliged to visit Belgium are assured of a warm welcome at Haig House'. No doubt this was so during the initial confrontation, but in the spring of 1940 the Legion standard, which had flown over Haig House since its inauguration, was hauled down as the Germans invaded Belgium, the manager and his wife just managing to get away before the town was occupied. Arriving at Dunkirk they handed their car over to a naval officer complete with Legion standard, very properly being given a receipt. An air attack a little later prompted the officer to take cover in the car, something he perhaps regretted when the windscreen was shot to pieces. Nevertheless he emerged with the standard and returned it to Legion headquarters in due course.[130]

# 1941 – 1945

## The work in war

During the long years of the Second World War the Legion's work intensified. Not only were the problems of its existing dependency increased by age and infirmity as well as by the effects of the war itself, but there was a new and growing body looking for help – the ex-service community of the current war. The Legion also wanted to assist as far as possible those men and women serving in the armed forces and their families, even if this stretched the bounds of its Charter. This last activity was in the main activated by a genuine desire to help the war effort in any way possible, but at the same time it recognized that the organization needed to identify with those on whom its future would depend.

One of the Legion's first wartime actions was to establish clothing depots in over a thousand locations near the big cities and other targets but away from the danger areas. Counties and Groups had organized the work and when air raids began in 1940 they set up flying columns, known as 'Legion Aid Parties', to reinforce and, if necessary, take over from the local committee should it become overwhelmed.[131]

It was not only the Legion relief organization in the United Kingdom that had to cope with enemy action. The island of Malta was subjected to almost continuous air attack in 1941 and 1942 and the Legion committee there had their premises destroyed no less than six times, each time salvaging their records and continuing their work. And even under enemy occupation the Channel Islands committee managed to carry on their relief activities.[132]

Meanwhile the routine welfare activities continued. Strangely the incidence of chronic illness declined during the war years, perhaps because wartime activity reinvigorated those jaded by years of enforced idleness and deprivation. But, as those years drew on, the local committees became more involved with the problems of a younger level of society as men and women were discharged from the forces for wounds or disability and a new generation of war widows sought the Legion's help. A woman whose husband had been killed in action had two children, one an invalid, and was unable to go back to work. With only £5 in the world her courage was strained to breaking point when the Legion secured her additional allowances, made a weekly grant for the children's upkeep and paid the doctor's bill. Like many another young victim of the war she simply did not know her entitlements and much of the work of the local committees at this time was to give advice to families. But there was often a need for temporary help while the official machine got into gear and sometimes widows had to be helped with food and coal following the husband's death and the cancellation of the weekly allotment from his pay.[133] By 1943 current war cases represented nearly a quarter of all the Legion's benevolent expenditure and by 1945 the proportion had risen to over a third.

In the South of Ireland poverty and suffering continued during the war, largely because of unemployment and despite large numbers of men crossing the Irish Channel to seek work or join the British forces. In 1943 the situation became so acute that the Benevolent Secretary made a visit and as a result the Legion's aid was increased by 50 per cent. Despite the war, there was also unemployment in the North and here too Legion expenditure rose.[134]

On 1 October 1944 Legion Branch Relief Committees became 'Service' Committees. This was more than just a change in title: the Service Committee was intended to cover all aspects of the Legion's work, including employment and pensions matters. These subjects were inter-related and the change enabled an individual seeking help to deal with one official or committee for all his or her needs. But the Council also stipulated that the committee should where possible include members from the women's services and the Merchant Navy.[135]

The new title was also used for the British Legion Service Offices which opened in London in the summer of 1944. Initially there were four, later extended to eight, manned full-time by members of wide experience and supervised by a committee drawn from the branches whose areas the office covered.[136] Another move the same year attempted to bridge the gap between Army and Legion welfare by the appointment of Legion Advisory Officers to visit those in hospital awaiting discharge and liaise with the branch near the service man's or woman's home so that there was no break in care.[137]

Some of those concerned would in due course benefit from the Legion's decision in 1943 to provide residential care for permanently incapacitated and disabled ex-service men and women. The original idea of a single 'country house' developed into regional homes for the aged and infirm. The first three were bought in 1945: Herrington Hall near Sunderland for the North of England, Doon House, Westgate-on-Sea to meet the needs of London and the South and in Northern Ireland a property at Helen's Bay in County Down. The same year the United Service Fund indicated that they would make over to the Legion their convalescent home, Byng House in Southport, although they stipulated that Great War men must have preference.[138]

Thoughts were turned to an institution of a different sort by a resolution at Gloucestershire County's conference in 1944, proposing a Legion College of Adult Education. After considering the idea the NEC decided to assess the need by sponsoring ex-service students at existing adult education centres and by asking Bristol University to run a summer course in 1945 specifically for the Legion, both schemes being intended to enable those who had taken advantage of the forces schemes to continue their education. They proved successful and the Legion decided to sponsor at least five hundred students in 1946.[139]

## Employment looks to the future

Education was linked to employment and the Legion had kept its Employment Department machinery active during the war in anticipation of the return of peace, although most labour was now directed by the government and only in Ireland was there serious unemployment, particularly in the South. On the mainland the work was much reduced with branches mainly helping to place those whose businesses had been closed by the war. But already in 1942, out of the 9,000 vacancies filled, 2,000 went to those who had been discharged in the current war; in 1945 this category accounted for more than half the total. In the early days many of those discharged from the forces had been sent home in uniform and with no money, so that employers were suspicious. The Legion got the instructions changed so that the men returned in civilian clothes and had their leave passes endorsed to show that they were free to take up civil employment.[140]

The importance of work on the land during the war produced a Legion scheme for training sons of ex-servicemen in agriculture. It was introduced in 1941 for youths between the ages of fourteen and seventeen and a half and, although the wages were low, the boys' physical condition was much improved by 'good food and fresh air'. Accommodation was in YMCA hostels and the scheme was financially supported by the Ministry of Agriculture. By 1945 of nearly 800 trained all but 125 had stayed on the land.[141]

Even younger than the aspiring farmworkers were some of the sons of deceased servicemen who, neat in their naval rig, formed the thirty-strong complement of the Training Ship *Stork*, moored in the Thames at Hammersmith and taken over by the Legion in 1942. The boys were prepared for careers in the Royal Navy and Merchant Navy and their naval discipline stood them in good stead when the ship was struck by incendiary bombs in 1944: called to Fire Stations, they promptly put out the blaze and the ship was saved.[142]

As the end of the war approached more thought was given to the resumption of normal employment. Already Rotary had been approached: with its local businessmen's clubs covering the country it had taken much interest in the Legion's employment work in the past and was willing to help. Advice was particularly needed when it came to reopening small local businesses. Special licences were needed and although the Legion got priority for ex-servicemen the attitude of Ministry of Labour local officials, locked into the straitjacket of wartime bureaucracy, was often less than helpful. One veteran, a qualified pharmacist, was refused permission to run a chemist's shop, which he had bought with a loan, because he had not been in business on his own account before the war. When the local Legion branch protested that this wartime regulation no longer applied, the local officials remained unmoved until the Ministry was persuaded to overrule them.[143]

The Legion itself managed to get a licence in 1945 to form British Legion Ex-service Industries to take over the Warminster furniture factory which had been started with the aid of a Legion loan in 1923. The recent war had brought the business to a halt, but, with a contract to make the new 'utility' furniture and no shortage of skills among the returning servicemen, there seemed to be a bright future.[144]

## Legion ventures in war and peace

The Warminster scheme joined the other Legion ventures to provide jobs for returning servicemen and women. But some would wish to strike out on their own and in 1945 the Legion resumed its small business loan scheme; there were many pitfalls and a monthly page of advice in the *Journal* carried many cautionary tales of those out to prey on the ex-servicemen's inexperience and occasional gullibility. Wide publicity was given to the scheme in 1945 when the *Daily Express* ran a serial on the progress of an ex-serviceman who had opened a shop with a Legion loan.[145]

Although the war years effectively closed down car parking activities, planning continued. In 1943, following a meeting of the chairmen, the existing Area companies were merged into the British Legion National Car Park Attendants Company, an organization which would, it was envisaged, complement the work of the AA and RAC, matching them in smartness and service to motorists. The change was timely: with the end of the war there was a great increase in the number of cars on the road and the number of active attendants, which had shrunk to twenty full-time in the war, rose to 160

115

in 1945, with the police using them to control parking on roads, an activity which the company intended to develop, foreshadowing the traffic warden schemes yet to come. It also planned to introduce a nationwide scale of charges and season tickets valid at any Legion-run car park in the country.[146]

The war had in no way limited the activities of the Cambrian Factory in Wales. Demand for wool for forces comforts exceeded supply and there were heavy orders for tweeds, which not only kept the wearer warm when fuel was short but represented good value for clothing coupons. Plans were made in 1941 to extend the factory and employ a further thirty disabled, but wartime difficulties prevented work starting until 1944 and the extension was only opened in 1945, together with a small hostel which was bought for housing trainees. Nevertheless the continuing profitability enabled the water-wheel, the pre-war power source, to be replaced by electricity in 1943.[147]

*Disabled of two wars: in 1943 the Queen visited a Legion exhibition of the work of disabled ex-servicemen; one of the two men making articles of Chinese lacquer was wounded in the First World War, the other in the Second.*

## At last – fair play for the disabled

Not only the Cambrian employees had been kept busy in the war; many other ex-service disabled had found employment. Peace might have brought another story, but a new government measure followed Lister's recommendations in a Legion report on the disabled. The Disabled Persons' (Employment) Act of 1944 placed on employers the obligation to include a quota of disabled on their staff, giving preference to ex-service disabled. At a stroke the old problems of the King's Roll were overcome; no longer would the Legion have to campaign to shame employers and particularly the local authorities into joining the Roll; its provisions were now in the statute book. Moreover the Legion was given a place among the employers and workers' representatives on the local advisory committees, Mr Bevin, the minister concerned, noting in Parliament that 'Within the meaning of the law the British Legion has been ruled by the umpires to be a workers' association', a definition that, whatever some of its leaders may have thought in private, the organisation did not dispute.[148]

## A change in pensions law

It will be remembered that, in response to Legion pressure, war pensions rates had been maintained between the wars when the official cost of living figure had fallen. This had an unexpected effect when the 1939 pensions warrant was issued; it was based on the cost of living in 1939, officially lower than in 1921. The result was that where a First World War disabled man was entitled to £3 a week, his Second World War counterpart received only £2. The Legion got the amount increased for the 1940 warrant, but it was still below the 1919 warrant figure, and the cost of living was rising, particularly rents. Further Legion pressure narrowed the gap in 1942 and eventually in 1943 the government matched the current war rates with those of the earlier war.[149]

The White Paper which announced these changes resolved most of the pensions problems that the Legion had been relentlessly pursuing since the 1939 warrant was issued. It included an undertaking to begin Appeals Tribunals later in 1943, the Legion having conducted its own investigation into the supply of doctors which the Ministry had claimed was the principal difficulty. But neither of these concessions, important though they were, was the most significant aspect of the 1943 White Paper: the breakthrough was the change in onus of proof in a claim for a War Pension; up to that point it had been necessary for the applicant to prove that his health had been impaired due to service; now it was the Ministry which had to prove that the disability had no connection with the service if they wished to dispute the claim.

There were other wording changes in favour of the applicant: 'directly due to service' became simply 'due to service' but it was the shift in the burden of proof that was the greatest change in pension law since the first warrant in 1916. Legion persistence over twenty years had paid off and it had good cause to congratulate itself, and the press, who, thanks to an efficent public relations campaign, had given good support.[150]

If the government, however, thought that it might hear no more from the Legion on pensions it was mistaken. There were still inequities, for example the denial of the married rate of pension where the serviceman had married *after* suffering his disability. Brunel Cohen cited the case of a legless airman who married the nurse who tended him in hospital: he was expected to take on family responsibilities with a single pension, his work prospects diminished by his disability and having to compete with men who had not fought. Such unfair rules, as Sir Ian Hamilton pointed out, did not apply in Canada, Australia or New Zealand.[151]

## Preston Hall at war

Well away from such arguments, Preston Hall tried to carry on as normal in the war. But its location in Kent meant that the General Hospital now adjoining the TB clinic took in many wounded in the Dunkirk evacuation, shortly to be followed by casualties from the Battle of Britain taking place in the skies overhead, including a number of German airmen. The TB wards themselves saw the arrival of serving patients, some of them ex-prisoners of war repatriated from Germany and by 1943 the staff were under some pressure, although the General Hospital had its own surgeons from Guy's Hospital in London. But the two institutions worked well together and serving patients at the hospital were employed in the grounds planting and harvesting vegetables while the wartime meat ration was augmented by rabbit and poultry from the farm.

As well as running the farm the settlement industries continued to be busy with government contracts for temporary buildings. But shortages of raw materials, which even if obtainable needed government permission, restricted other work.

Preston Hall dealt only with male TB patients, but women were no less susceptible to the disease and in 1943 the Legion acquired Nayland Hall near Colchester as an extension to Preston Hall; by 1944 100 tubercular ex-servicewomen were being treated. Meanwhile another outpost – Douglas House in Bournemouth – had become a treatment centre for elderly men and it soon achieved an important status. This was hardly surprising, given Preston Hall's reputation in the treatment of TB, a reputation which owed not a little to the quiet strength of the much-loved Matron, Miss Lee, and her death in 1945 was marked by a special tribute in *The Times*.[152]

$$\star \qquad \star \qquad \star$$

For twenty-five years the Legion had waged a campaign to get fair treatment for those whose lives had been afflicted by service in two wars. Meanwhile it had to sustain them as well as it could from its own resources. Gradually the action of the sword had relieved the pressure on the shield. Now, in a world free of war, it seemed the state would care for everyone. The Legion's world was about to change. Or was it?

# CHAPTER 5

FUNDRAISING 1921-1945

# *The Power of the Poppy*

1921 – 1925

## The need for money

In 1921 the Legion's campaigning on behalf of the widows, the ex-servicemen and their families had barely begun. In the meantime there was distress, often acute, and it seemed likely to grow. Whatever the government's response to the Legion's appeals for better legislation, money was urgently needed for immediate relief.

The unity discussions had included the question of funding the new organization. None of the participants had much to contribute – and indeed that was one of the reasons that had brought them together. All that was available was some £180,000 raised through earlier appeals by the Prince of Wales and Field Marshal Earl Haig, which, so pressing was the need, had been put to use without waiting for the unity negotiations to be formally concluded. Because of the terms under which most of the money had been donated it could only be used for one aspect of relief work, that of distress arising out of unemployment. But this was the major problem at the time anyway.[1]

£180,000 was a useful sum of money but it would hardly meet the needs of an organization which had a potential dependency of perhaps ten million ex-servicemen and dependants. A substantial fundraising capability was needed, and some ready money for administration. Both would be provided by the Officers' Association.

## The Officers' Association contribution

The Officers' Association fundraising operation was already established and had run a very successful public appeal to launch the Association. Now, as part of the unity agreement, the OA Appeals Department became the Legion's Appeals Department. In return the OA, having become the Officers' Benevolent Department of the Legion, would receive 5 per cent of the net proceeds of public appeals[2] and one third of all general donations and legacies. The share of donations and legacies recognized that the OA had handed over to the Legion the Great War Remembrance League, started by Earl Haig as a means of soliciting regular donations for benevolence.

The Officers' Association also gave the Legion £10,000 in cash. About a quarter of this sum represented the subscriptions of OA members being transferred to the Legion; the rest was a gift for administrative purposes.[3] Effectively this sum of money 'floated' the Legion as an organization. There would be no income from the members of the new body until their subscriptions could be collected; in the meantime there were office rents, staff salaries and other administrative expenses to be met.

It was a generous contribution by the officers, of which the most important element was a functioning appeals department. This was indeed a priceless gift.

## Legion funds

As well as being a charity the Legion was a membership organization. The membership was partly there to do the charitable work (including fundraising), partly to lend 'political weight' and partly for social reasons. The members made an annual contribution through their subscriptions to their branches, part of which – the Affiliation Fee – was sent to headquarters. Subscriptions were of necessity low and could do little more than assist the Legion to function as an organization – which of course included the cost of administering the membership. Nor was there any direct connection between Legion clubs and fundraising. Clubs were owned by their members and financially self-contained, existing solely for social activities. Some clubs contributed to Legion benevolence and many more provided fundraising facilities. But, in general, their purposes did not include Legion fundraising.

There were therefore two Legion accounts: a General Account to run the administration, with the members' subscriptions intended to provide the main source of income, and a Benevolent Account which made grants to charitable activities, such as the Relief Fund, and which depended on fundraising for its money supply.

## The Appeals Department

The Appeals Department did not at first exist only to fund benevolence. It was also tasked to raise monies for the 'general purposes' of the Legion, partly no doubt because the General Account at the time bore the cost of administering the charitable activities. In 1923 it ran a fundraising venture which provided nearly half the income of the General Account, and that account also received some of the Poppy Day receipts. At a later stage the administrative costs of charitable work would be transferred to the Benevolent Account and the Appeals Department would be identified solely with that side of the Legion.[4]

The National Benevolent Committee directed all appeals activities. The Appeals Department itself, partly because of its origins and partly because of accommodation problems, at first enjoyed a relatively independent existence, located in offices at 1, Regent Street in central London; moreover the salary of the Appeals Secretary, Captain A.G. Willcox, exceeded that of the General Secretary. Although this anomaly, unlikely to have been popular with the GS, was reversed in the 1923 administrative reorganization, it did not end there. When the salaries of headquarters staff were reviewed in March 1924 the NEC decided to pay Captain Willcox on the basis of his performance. But in May of the following year, no doubt as a result of the practical effect of this generous decision, the agreement was cancelled. South Eastern Area had also complained about the terms of the agreement, attracting press interest, and the rather unseemly debate dragged on until the issue was, for the moment, resolved, by reverting to a salary in 1926.[5]

The department at first had its own field staff of up to seven Area Appeals Organizers. But the 1923 reorganization reduced them to two, and they became advisers, with appeals added to the responsibilities of the eleven Legion Area Organizers. A little later, in 1924, the department moved to 26 Eccleston Square.[6]

Despite all these changes, the Appeals Department was performing well. Even before their official switch of allegiance to the Legion, Captain Willcox and his staff had organized in March 1921 a 'Warriors Day' appeal in which actors and entertainers gave performances free of charge at theatres and cinemas throughout the country, raising some £100,000. The first 'Legion' appeal was a few months later on 4 August 1921, the anniversary of the declaration of war; issued through letters to the press, it produced a further £10,400.[7] But the real test came with the first Poppy Appeal.

## Enter the poppy

The Poppy Appeal has become a national institution, but the Legion cannot claim the original idea. The inspiration came from across the Atlantic: a Canadian medical officer* serving in France had written a poem sitting on the step of the ambulance outside his dressing station on the banks of a canal during the Second Battle of Ypres in 1915.[8] He was Colonel John McCrae and he called his poem 'In Flanders Fields'. It begins:

> *In Flanders Fields the poppies blow*
> *Between the crosses, row on row*

and concludes with the stirring lines:

> *If ye break faith with us who die*
> *We shall not sleep, though poppies grow*
> *In Flanders Fields.*

The poem† was published anonymously in *Punch* magazine on 8 December 1915. It expressed so movingly what so many felt about a war which had descended from brave expectations into carnage, yet in which the high ideals of human endeavour were still represented, that it immediately attracted attention. McCrae died, of pneumonia, in France in January 1918 and among the many floral tributes was a wreath of artificial poppies, obtained by his fellow officers from Paris.[9]

Among those affected by the verses was a young American woman, Miss Moina Michael, whose wartime task was to train YMCA war workers. Receiving a gift of ten dollars, she used it to buy twenty-five artificial poppies from a department store in New York, which were then worn in memory of the dead at a conference of YMCA overseas workers in November 1918. This led Miss Michael to begin a campaign to make the poppy the symbol of remembrance and in September 1920 the American Legion adopted it as such at its annual Convention. Attending the convention was a French woman, Madame Anne Guerin, who had brought with her some artificial poppies to sell in support of her charity, a joint French-American organization seeking to help restore the areas in France devastated by the war. The poppies, made by the charity's widows and orphans, were widely worn in America on the following Armistice Day.[10]

It then occurred to Madame Guerin that her poppies could also be used for fundraising purposes in Britain. In August 1921 she called at Legion headquarters with some samples. Colonel Crosfield, the Legion's Vice Chairman, discussed the idea with the General Secretary and the outcome was that Sir Herbert Brown, the Chairman of the Appeals Department, went to Paris to investigate, reporting on his return that at least the suppliers were genuine.

This resolved part of the problem, but would people in Britain buy the poppy? Now

---

*McCrea had served with the artillery in the South African war and had wanted to go to France with the guns, but the medical authorities forbade it.

†McCrae had meanwhile made at least one other copy, which is why some versions substitute 'blow' for 'grow' in the first line.

that the Poppy Appeal is a national institution such caution may seem excessive. But few people in the street were familiar with McCrae's poem. Certainly they would not be surprised to know that the poppy grew in Flanders and had, with other wild flowers, proliferated in those areas where agriculture had been cut short by the guns; but there was nothing special about it and they did not associate it with the fallen of the Great War.

At the time, therefore, it was a venture not without risk: when and how should the poppies be sold? Would the public buy them? And, if so, in what quantity? Clearly the size of the order for the first consignment would be a guess. The Finance Committee, by its nature a prudent body, decided to order one and a half million. The General Secretary told the Appeals Chairman, 'For goodness sake order three million, whatever else you do.' In the end, according to the *Legion Journal* of December 1921, nine million were supplied.[11]

The timing of Madame Guerin's visit meant that the next suitable occasion for a poppy-linked appeal would be Armistice Day – 11 November 1921 – and this was the chosen date. It is quite possible that had Madame Guerin made her visit to Legion headquarters at a different time then another date would have been chosen, perhaps 4 August, the anniversary of the declaration of the war. But Armistice Day it was and the message from the Legion's President, Earl Haig, widely disseminated in November 1921, was very clear: everyone should wear a poppy each year on 11 November in memory of the fallen. Henceforward that was the date with which the poppy would always be associated – the bright red of the summer flower proclaiming its message of remembrance and hope amid the autumnal gloom.[12]

## The first Poppy Appeal

Haig's announcement attracted attention because of his enormous public prestige; for the same reason the appeal was advertised to the public as Field Marshal Earl Haig's Appeal,[13] hence the use of 'Haig Fund' as a title for the appeal and the letters 'HF' in the centre of the poppy. However the appeal was styled, the Legion's Appeals Department had just six weeks to organize the distribution and sale of several million poppies throughout the country and the collection of the proceeds. The headquarters staff were assisted by the Area Appeals Organizers, but they were new in post – their appointments had only been approved by the NEC on 3 September 1921. It was a sharp introduction to the Legion. But as *The Times* noted, the organisation of Poppy Day at the grass roots was very largely the work of women – Lady Mayoresses, the wives of council chairmen and the women workers at each local Legion branch. The Women's Section indeed provided an enthusiastic response: local sections formed committees and in central London the headquarters organized six depots for the sale of poppies, Westminster Hospital, railway stations and famous stores allowing their premises to be used.

On the day itself the first poppy was bought in London a few seconds after midnight. From that moment it was a sellers' market: the poppies were on sale at an official price of threepence but before breakfast single petals were selling in Smithfield Market for £5. All day long motor cars fetched poppies and crate after crate was emptied until supplies ran out. A message from Queen Mary brought sellers to Buckingham Palace, but hearing that poppies were in short supply she bought only two (the other no doubt for the King).[14] A basket of poppies auctioned at Christie's raised nearly £500. In London the public reaction had been staggering and the response in other cities and in the country generally had been no less astonishing. Even in Gibraltar, which held the Legion's first overseas branch, the Governor had to send the whole of his staff into the garden to gather red flowers when the poppies ran out; but they too quickly disappeared.[15]

It had all been a remarkable success, but one based on a structure which was largely independent of the Legion's own membership organization: Appeals Department worked through its Area Appeals Organizers to local committees which may have been based on Legion branches, or on branches of the Women's Section, or which may have had no allegiance to either. This was a pragmatic approach which made the best of local circumstances and which appears to have set the style for succeeding appeals: neither the local committees nor the poppy sellers* needed to have a formal connection with the Legion.

The proceeds of the appeal began to come in. By the end of November, only two weeks after the appeal, well over half (£65,000) of the final total of £106,000 had been received. There was of course some dispute over how the money was to be apportioned but it was eventually decided that, after expenses, 90 per cent of the money collected would go to the Benevolent Fund and the remaining 10 per cent to the general administration of the Legion.[16] Branches could bid for a refund of half of their local collection but they had to submit accounts to show how previous grants had been used and that they needed the money. [17]

## Poppy supplies

Inspired by the success of this first venture, the NEC's thoughts turned to future Poppy Appeals. Most of the cost of the original appeal had been the purchase of poppies, representing £21,000 out of a total outlay of £24,000.[18] Acting on the Council's instructions, the Appeals Department invested in the materials, including a standard centre† and invited application from any hospital or similar institution for their assembly.[19] They stipulated, however, that as many as possible should be made by disabled ex-servicemen.

One of the responses was from a Major George Howson who had launched the Disabled Society, principally for the improvement of artificial limbs. His proposal was accepted and he received a grant of £2,000 from the Legion's Relief Fund to set up a factory just off the Old Kent Road (282, St James's Road) in South East London. By August 1922 forty-one disabled ex-servicemen were being employed by the Society in making poppies, many of whom had previously been unemployed for a long time, some since being discharged from hospital. They worked a five-day week (at a time when the normal working week was five and a half or six days ) and were expected to produce 1,000 poppies a day each. All the men had either single or double amputations and some travelled from the furthest side of London for the work. But the *Legion Journal* described it as 'the cheeriest workshop in London', the men listening to a gramophone and singing as they made their poppies.[20]

Thirty million poppies were ordered for the 1922 appeal, a threefold increase on the original requirement. Contracts were let to other manufacturers as well as to the Disabled Society in order to meet this figure.[21] However, the following year the Legion was taken to task by the *Daily Herald* over the issue of the wages paid by contractors: although the Legion required them to employ ex-servicemen, some were using women at low rates. Henceforward a 'fair wages' clause was included in all contracts.[22]

*Poppies were 'sold' in the early days; charity legislation now requires them to be 'distributed in return for donations'.

†The initials 'HF' (Haig Fund) on the button in the centre of each poppy were mainly to ensure that no 'counterfeit' poppies were made and sold by individuals for private gain.

The Poppy Factory was at first managed by a joint committee of the Legion and the Disabled Society, under Major Howson's chairmanship,[23] but in early 1924 it became a non-profit-making company, still chaired by Howson, with the employment and welfare of its employees as its objects. The premises were moved from the Old Kent Road to Richmond Hill where a disused brewery donated by a well-wisher was converted into a factory and an adjoining estate purchased by the Legion to erect flats for the workers and their families, together with a club. Most of the work was completed by the end of 1925, funded by a grant of £30,000 from the Legion's Benevolent Fund. By now the original forty-one disabled employees had risen to 190 with well over another 300 on the waiting list. But by 1923, only a year after the factory had started, the National Executive Council had already recognized the dilemma it posed: should the profits be increased by using cheaper sources of supply or did the Legion's duty lie in providing employment for the disabled even if it added to the cost? There were strong feelings on the matter and the Council maintained the existing arrangement, disdaining more economic production methods (which in later years would indicate advanced machinery rather than cheaper forms of labour).[24]

By setting up their own arrangements for the manufacture of poppies the Legion had of course turned its back on Madame Guerin and the organization which had supplied

*The Prince of Wales made a number of visits to the Poppy Factory. On the left the workers give three cheers to the Prince and in the picture below they march past him. As his expressions suggest, he was much concerned at the plight of war-disabled men.*

not only the original idea but also the means of putting it into effect. The same thing was to happen in Canada, which had also been visited by the enterprising Frenchwoman, but which turned to the local 'Vetcraft Industries' to make the poppies from 1925 onwards.[25] There is no evidence of any protest from the original manufacturer, but at the time no legislation existed to prevent the Legion appropriating the idea from another country. In any case the National Executive Council had by now patented the poppy buttonhole in the United Kingdom.[26]

## But will it last?

On the eve of Remembrance Day 1922 in central London electric signboards at the tops of buildings in Piccadilly Circus and at the Elephant and Castle flashed 'EARL HAIG'S SPECIAL MESSAGE – BUY POPPIES FOR REMEMBRANCE SAKE'. The Legion was not only making use of the latest technology, it had also helped with its introduction. The inventor was a Canadian soldier who had worked out the idea in hospital. The last Canadian to be demobilized in this country, he obtained a loan from the British Legion Relief Fund, took on seventeen ex-servicemen and, trading as 'The Scintillating Sign Company', produced his signs.[27]

Despite the success of the 1921 Appeal, ordering 30 million poppies for the following year seemed to some to be hopelessly optimistic. There was not only the question of whether such a large number would be sold, but the handling and distribution problem had been tripled: the boxes of poppies would build a six-foot-high wall a foot thick and a mile long. Nevertheless the Appeals Department pressed on. A warehouse was acquired in London and Poppy Day committees were asked to approach local owners of lorries taking goods to the capital to request them to pick up a load of poppies for the return trip. Apart from the flashing signs in central London, the publicity drive included press material and a wide distribution of 'Flanders Poppy' posters which the local Poppy Day committees made good use of.

*The 'Electrical Newspaper' spells out Earl Haig's message at the Elephant and Castle.*

To the Legion's relief the second Poppy Day more than justified all the effort. The amount collected was nearly double the previous year – £204,000. Moreover, pro-rata, overheads were down: the 30 million poppies had cost £33,000 to make, whereas the Legion had spent £24,000 on the original consignment of 9 million; the decision to manufacture the poppies in UK had therefore been justified. Despite some problems over the collection of the proceeds, it had been very successful and the Poppy Appeal was now established as a major fund-raising event in the country.

Now the stock was widened. In 1923 four types of poppy were on offer: a large silk poppy, for which at least a shilling (equivalent to £1.50 at current values) was asked; half that amount was sought for a small silk version; a poppy made of lawn (cotton) required a donation of threepence (40 pence) and finally there was a card poppy for children at a penny. There was more advice too to the helpers in the field: committees were told to involve 'the principal civic authority' as well as the bank manager and the editor of the local paper. The best selling points should be mapped out and districts should liaise to prevent overlap. And it was suggested that branches should place a large wooden cross covered with moss on the War Memorial, to which people could fix poppies.[28]

The central organization had also developed: the Grosvenor Estate lent numbers 34 and 44 Lowndes Square in central London from September to November, one house being used as an office for the appeal while the other became the depot for packing and despatching poppies. Not only were the premises free of charge but electricity was supplied at reduced cost while the 100 voluntary workers staved off any pangs of hunger with cases of biscuits presented by a biscuit company, a practical gesture no doubt much welcomed by the night shift, working frantically in the last few weeks to cope with the despatch of late orders.[29]

A feature of the 1923 appeal was the loan of the London General omnibus 'Ole Bill'. This was an bus with a war record: it had carried the first troops (the 'Contemptibles') to the front in 1914. Now it was used to distribute supplies and, bedecked with poppies, it gave the Appeal much publicity,[30] as did the 3,000 lantern slides distributed to branches for their local cinema to show. That year too the 'official' Legion poppy was used as the basis of all the wreaths laid on Remembrance Day itself, by the King and other members of the Royal Family, by government departments, including the three service ministries, and by public corporations, while Legion poppy sprays appeared as table decorations in the majority of hotels, restaurants and clubs. The poppy could now be said to have become the national symbol of Remembrance.

As well as the ceremonies at the Cenotaph, 11 November 1923 saw an evening event at the Royal Albert Hall. An English composer, John Foulds, had written a 'World Requiem', 'a Cenotaph in sound', and the performing rights and the entire profits were donated to Legion benevolence. The Prince of Wales was present but, despite the accompanyment of a 1,000-strong choir, it is doubtful whether he enjoyed the evening. As *The Times* noted, it had a 'persistent monotone, representing grief and unhappiness' and it was not to add greatly to the Legion coffers.[31]

The real success of the appeal of course depended on the local committees. There were now nearly 2,500, double the figure for the 1921 appeal, by no means all comprised of Legion members; they included many people who simply wished to do something to help the nation 'remember'. The ranks of the poppy sellers – those who patiently stood in the open with their trays of poppies and collecting boxes – were also swelled by outsiders anxious to help. To many the Appeal provided an outlet for their feelings and in time some at least would see the poppy as a symbol in its own right, even to the extent that they would not necessarily connect it with the Legion.

The appeal was active overseas as well. Not only throughout the Empire but in places as far apart as Japan and Switzerland British communities supported the 'Flanders Poppy'. The Federated Malay States collected the enormous total of £3,500 and collections were held on ninety-seven liners at sea. British military garrisons ran their own collections and King's Regulations were changed in that year to allow sailors, soldiers and airmen to wear the poppy on their uniform on Remembrance Day.[32]

The success of the Appeal brought its own problems: poppy sellers were told to beware of handing over their collecting boxes to 'well-dressed people, often in motor cars'. But in 1924, whereas many of the hunts whose collections, known as 'caps', had more than doubled, some of the branches in the depressed areas found it difficult to match the previous year. They tried hard: Otley Branch organized a shop window poppy-dressing competition so that virtually every shop in the town was 'ablaze with poppies' and Leeds underlined the need for a 'big effort' by parading an elephant decked with poppies

*Legion branches often worked hard for the Poppy Appeal; in 1924 Wimbledon toured the district with a replica of the local war memorial on a goat cart, while Leeds' elephant sought a big effort.*

*From the start of the Poppy Appeal, women were much involved. A Seend (Morpeth) Branch group of collectors in the 1920s pose for a photograph before setting out on the rain-swept pavements.*

through the streets.[33] Nevertheless the collection increased overall, as the King was informed through a comprehensive report sent to his private secretary by the Appeals Secretary, His Majesty expressing 'much pleasure' at the results.[34]

Church collections were first donated to the Appeal in 1925 following Haig's request for the Sunday before 11 November each year to be observed as 'Remembrance Sunday'; hitherto the only services had been those on 11 November at memorials to the fallen. As well as providing the Appeal with additional income Remembrance was now in the churches' calendars. In all some £395,000 was raised that year, so that in the space of four years the collection had nearly quadrupled.[35]

## The Great War Remembrance League

On the eve of the first Poppy Appeal in 1921 the Legion's President had outlined a plan to provide Legion benevolence with a regular source of income. At that moment the success of the Poppy Appeal could not be foreseen, nor that it would become a fixture in the national calendar. Even so the appeal was only one day in the year and dependent on the public mood – and the weather. As the memories of the war faded so the giving might decline – paradoxically as the need was increasing.

Haig's ideas were based on defining the need in financial terms and endeavouring to meet that need by regular annual subscriptions, more or less guaranteed. It was a two-tier scheme: the *300th League* applied mainly to the business community, inviting them to contribute one day's profits a year (out of 300 working days) in recognition of those who fought and won the war and thereby allowed business to continue. *The Gratitude Fund* applied to the poorer section of the community. Cards would be distributed on which people could stick postage stamps – sixpence or threepence each week or fortnight. All would come under the *Great War Remembrance League*, already in use for legacies.[36]

The idea encountered problems at the outset. Lords Lieutenant, whose influence was particularly important as far as contributions from business communities were concerned, wanted 95 per cent of the money returned to the districts of origin and the scheme had therefore to proceed without their support. Legion Areas also wanted a share. But the principal difficulty was a decided lack of response from the business community who were either too concerned with the recession or simply ignored the appeal. By the end of 1925 the League had only managed, principally through generous donations from individuals, to raise some £43,000. It was much less than Haig had envisaged and under 5 per cent of the money generated by the Poppy Appeal over the same period.[37]

## Other fundraising

The League was not the only fundraising project that paled into insignificance alongside the charismatic Poppy Appeal. The Legion continued to run appeals on the anniversary of the outbreak of the Great War (4 August) and at Christmas. But again the results were negligible by comparison: the August appeal reached its highest point in 1925 but even so raised only £14,500; the Christmas Appeal by contrast had dwindled to a little over £2,500, probably because it followed so closely on the heels of 11 November. In 1925 the combined returns on these two events also represented only 5 per cent of the Poppy Appeal.

There were, however, other imaginative activities. Early in 1924 a prize draw was arranged for an album containing nearly 600 autographed contributions by contemporary world figures: Kings, Queens, Princes, Prime Ministers, statesmen and celebrities of every kind all made entries in their own hand. It was called the 'British Legion Album' and was valued at £25,000. Facsimile editions were sold by branches at five shillings each, the branch making a profit of one shilling. But although well supported in the press, the venture raised barely £2,000.

In 1925 there was a series of recitals by the world-famous Polish-born pianist (and one-time Prime Minister of Poland) Paderewski, who had given similar concerts in support of ex-servicemen in Paris and Brussels. Performances around the country and, in the presence of the Queen, at the Royal Albert Hall in London, raised over £5,000. Paderewski himself remained 'as poor as a church mouse', according to General Hamilton.[38] On a slightly different artistic plane the Prince of Wales made a gramophone record of a speech on 'sportsmanship' which realized some £1,500 for the Appeal.[39]

## 1926 – 1930

### The Poppy takes over

In the second half of the decade the Poppy Appeal proceeds rose steadily: from just under £400,000 in 1926 to a little over £600,000 in 1930. At a time of continuing economic depression, with no inflation – indeed the cost of living was falling – this was a remarkable growth and its effect in real terms is shown at Chart C1 at page 447. The reason for its success was not simply public concern for the victims of the war; the poppies themselves were more widely available as Appeal committees mushroomed in the towns and villages around the country. It is also to the credit of Captain Willcox and the Area organizers that they were able to harness and support that expansion so effectively. By the end of the decade the Poppy accounted for 96 per cent of the Legion's income for benevolent work and the Legion year was now based on the Appeal, having been changed in 1925, so that it began on 1 October. This enabled Poppy Day and its results to feature in the same twelve-month accounting period.

As the star of the show, the poppy, rose, so the other fundraising activities declined. The Christmas Appeal was now eclipsed by the November collection and by 1927 had sunk to barely a thousand pounds; it was discontinued after that year. The same year saw the last August 4th Appeal to mark the anniversary of the outbreak of the war in 1914; but it at least ended on a high note, raising twice the previous year's total, having been specifically targeted to raise funds for the ex-service community of the Irish Free State.

Legacies provided a useful but very variable source of income. But a campaign to breathe more life into the Great War Remembrance League by getting every contributor to introduce a friend had only limited success and towards the end of the decade it too began to go into decline: in 1927 it realized only £9,300 and in succeeding years receipts fell still further so that by 1930 the League contributed barely £6,000 a year, just 1 per cent of the total fundraising income.

As far as the Poppy Appeal itself was concerned a feature of these years was the support from overseas branches, Ceylon even raising enough money in 1926 to provide four additional flats for the workers at the Poppy Factory. Nor were the Appeal organizers slow to spot new openings: a Poppy Motor Mascot was introduced in 1930, at a cost of 2s 6d, a price which reflected the comparative affluence of motor car owners.* But the Legion's work needed everyone to give more and in 1927 the Patron, the Prince of Wales, made a broadcast appeal on the eve of Poppy Day; asking for a generous response he himself gave

*It would be £4.50 at today's values.

£100 for his poppy, as did the King and Queen. But some ordinary people were no less generous: an ex-schoolmistress sent her nest egg of six gold sovereigns in a case and a Southport schoolboy donated his pocket money after seeing disabled ex-servicemen at a service at the local war memorial.

The weather was often miserable in November, affecting takings; in Hull, where Poppy Day was bitterly cold in 1927 with frequent snow and sleet showers, the morale of the poppy sellers, who included the Lady Mayoress, was maintained by hot soup supplied by Messrs Heinz without charge. But spirits generally were raised by the new Patroness of the Poppy Appeal, Lady Haig who, even in the year immediately following her husband's death, was indefatigable in touring the country and meeting the local Appeal Committees. Although she had kept in the background when her husband was alive, she now came into her own; not only did she have the lustre of having been married to the man who was regarded by most people as a national hero but she had a charm all of her own and indeed an ease with people that her husband for all of his other qualities had perhaps lacked.

There were nonetheless some problems: the Bridgeman Committee (see page 19) had noted that the Poppy Appeal proceeds were rather less than the face value of the poppies supplied. This was mainly because of hoarding, some committees being under the impression that if poppies were returned disabled men at the Poppy Factory might lose their jobs. Furthermore poppies were frequently sold for less than the asking price, particularly in the poorer districts, where people did not like to be seen without a poppy on 11 November but were unable to pay the full amount. But there were certainly instances of theft of the takings: in an operation which extended over the whole country with committees and voluntary helpers at every level handling cash takings it would have been extraordinary if this had not been the case.[40]

Undoubtedly much of the credit for the Poppy Appeal's success was due to Captain Willcox. According to General Maurice he 'invented' Poppy Day.[41] He was an outstanding organizer, achieving results through quiet persuasion, an approach well suited to a voluntary and largely non-Legion structure. But such skills were in demand elsewhere and the NEC was plainly anxious to ensure that he stayed in place. In early 1926 he again became the highest paid member of staff with a salary four times that of his fellow department heads and, to head off trouble, the Council instructed the General Secretary to write to every Area Chairman about their decision. Since even he was paid considerably less,[42] the GS must have drafted the letter with mixed feelings. Perhaps at Colonel Heath's suggestion Willcox was then charged with generating more income for the General Fund while his departmental responsibilities increased when the Legion's new Publicity Officer was brought into Appeals in March 1929, the Department being renamed 'Appeals and Publicity'.[43]

## The Empire Fair and Ball

The Appeals Secretary's response to the General Fund task was a Legion Bazaar, which developed into an 'Empire Fair and Ball', held at the Albert Hall in May 1930. The fair took place over four days and combined the products of disabled men (which included 100 walking sticks made from the ancient roof beams of Westminster Hall by Preston Hall industries) and the work of local craftsmen with a wide variety of goods made commercially in the countries of the Empire. There were also individual donations – Legion members were asked to rummage through their cupboards for saleable items, as they would for their local church fete. For the occasion the arena of the Albert Hall was converted into an oriental bazaar with famous artists doing pavement work, fashion parades which included Cambrian Factory tweeds, and fencing displays by European experts, all to the background of recitals by well-known organists on the mighty organ. At the end of the final day swift action was needed to convert the arena into a dance floor for the ball. The Prince of Wales was present, ensuring an attendance of some 3,000 and at midnight there was a pageant to represent 'Britain and her Industries': Lady Scarsdale came as 'wool', leading triplets dressed as lambs, Lady Ashley 'made a slim and glittering figure as coal' while Mrs McCorquodale, representing shipping, wore a dress on the train of which floated an immense model of the White Star liner *Britannic*, presumably bringing the house down. The net profit of all this effort by the Legion's Appeals Department, assisted by the British Empire Services League, was £3,509, of which one third was given to the Women's Section in acknowledgement of their help. The balance was roughly equivalent to the Appeal Secretary's annual salary; but, as the Legion's Annual Report noted, the fair and ball were 'definitely popular and successful additions to the London Season and obtained much valuable publicity for the Legion'.[44]

The Prince of Wales himself was not short of ideas and, at his instigation, the 'Legion Book' was published in 1930. It was a collection of writings by eminent authors and reproductions of drawings and paintings by equally famous artists. The contributors included Arnold Bennett, Rudyard Kipling, Winston Churchill and P.G. Wodehouse, while the art work ranged from Augustus John to 'Snaffles'. It sold at one guinea and five guineas, depending on the binding, but one hundred copies were specially printed and bound in white pigskin for the Prince to present to generous donors; these were signed by each of the eighty contributors as well as by the Prince himself. The project enabled the Prince of Wales' Pension Fund to be formed (see page 105) with a nucleus of just under £90,000.[45]

### The Poppy Factory expands

1926-1930 were years of expansion for the Poppy Factory, following its move to Richmond. The growth was based on the success of the Poppy Appeal itself and the consequent demand for more poppies: from 16 million in 1925 manufacture had nearly doubled to 31 million by 1929, although it would seem that there was undoubtedly some over-ordering. The number of men employed to make the poppies grew steadily to around 270 by the end of the decade; all had at least a 75 per cent disability, meaning that most were without a limb, and the basic qualification for the waiting list for employment at the factory was an 80 per cent disability. When Countess Haig opened a new block of flats at the Poppy Factory in December 1928 there was a march past of 275 employees: in fact, as an account of the opening ceremony drily noted, the majority were wheeled past.

Lady Haig was a frequent visitor to the factory in her capacity as Patroness of the Appeal. Earl Haig's last public engagement, on the day before his death, had been at the factory to attend the inauguration of the troop of boy scouts which bore his name. All were children of men employed at the factory whose families lived in blocks of flats, steadily added to by the Legion until, by 1930, the maximum number allowed by local bye-laws had been reached. At that stage sixty-eight families lived on the estate, comprising a total colony of 330 people.

Paradoxically Earl Haig's death led to new marketing opportunities: because of the number of wreaths required for his funeral extra staff were taken on and, not wishing to dismiss any of them afterwards, the factory management looked for new openings. They found them in the manufacture of other artificial flowers and similar items and very shortly the factory was making the roses for the St George's Hospital appeal, devices for other flag days, favours for the supporters of Leicester City and Bolton Wanderers football clubs and rosettes in Legion colours for Legion branches, in addition to its basic product. There were now five versions of the poppy, from 2/6d to one penny and the poppies were also used to make table decorations, motor garlands and mascots. Much of the new trade was developed by the Women's Section who sought markets for the factory's skills and further publicity was provided in 1930 in a film, a 'talkie' about the factory's work in which Countess Haig herself featured.[46]

### The Field of Remembrance

Major Howson, the Poppy Factory's chairman, had conceived most of these new ideas and in 1928 he had a further thought. At Remembrance time he and his wife took a group of disabled men, a tray of poppies and a collecting tin to the grounds of St Margaret's, Westminster, close by the great Abbey where, gathered round an original wooden cross taken from the battlefield grave of an unknown British Soldier, some of the men pushed poppies into the ground. Passers-by stopped, asked questions and soon began to buy and plant their own poppies. The Field of Remembrance had been born.

The practice continued, supported by the church authorities, and it developed. In 1931 a disabled man at the factory made a small wooden cross with a poppy at the centre and this became the expression of personal remembrance, a simple message added before it was planted in the Westminster turf, or in due course in many other churchyards in

*The first Field of Remembrance in 1928. Poppies were simply pushed into the ground around an original battlefield cross, on a site close to Westminster Abbey. Each poppy had a message attached.*

cities, towns and villages throughout the land and overseas.[47]

So great was the public response that by 1934 the turf had to be divided up into ship, regimental and squadron plots with a map giving the locations where the personal crosses could be planted. Following Remembrance the crosses were cremated and the ashes taken to France to be scattered over the graves of the fallen.

# 1931 – 1935

## Support continues

Despite the economic decline of the early 1930s the Poppy Appeal continued to grow in real terms since people still paid the same for a poppy while living costs fell. Organizational support was undiminished: the number of committees stayed at around 4,000, while the estimated size of the army of mainly lady helpers had grown to over 300,000 by 1935, leading to the NEC's agreement in 1935 to a proposal for the formation of a 'League of Poppy Sellers'; the idea does not, however, appear to have been developed. The appeal continued to expand overseas, contributing a substantial 11 per cent of the total, as well as on the high seas with nearly 250 vessels taking collections. The annual distribution of some 40 million poppies included those despatched to permanent Poppy Committees in over forty foreign countries, as well as to the colonies.

The low overheads were a matter of pride: not only were the local organizers and sellers all volunteers but much of the publicity was free; there was powerful press support and some 2,000 national advertisers gave the appeal free space; similarly nearly a million Poppy Appeal posters were displayed gratis by the trade associations. Poppies were transported without charge by railway and motor transport companies and to overseas destinations by the steamship owners. All over the country premises for storage and distribution were made available at no cost, while in London the Grosvenor Estate continued to provide the Appeal Headquarters in Grosvenor Place almost rent free. All of this meant that the only significant expense was the cost of the poppies themselves, reducing the appeal's overheads to around 20 per cent of the gross receipts, and any profit made by the Poppy Factory's other enter-prises was used to defray the poppies' cost.

Poppies were increasingly being sold for planting in Fields of Remembrance, to embellish churches and in hotels and restaurants as table decorations over Armisticetide, while business houses bought them in increasing numbers to make window displays. And in 1933 Major Howson

*"Ole Bill', a London omnibus used in the Great War to take troops to the front, regularly supported the appeal in the 1920s and 1930s.*

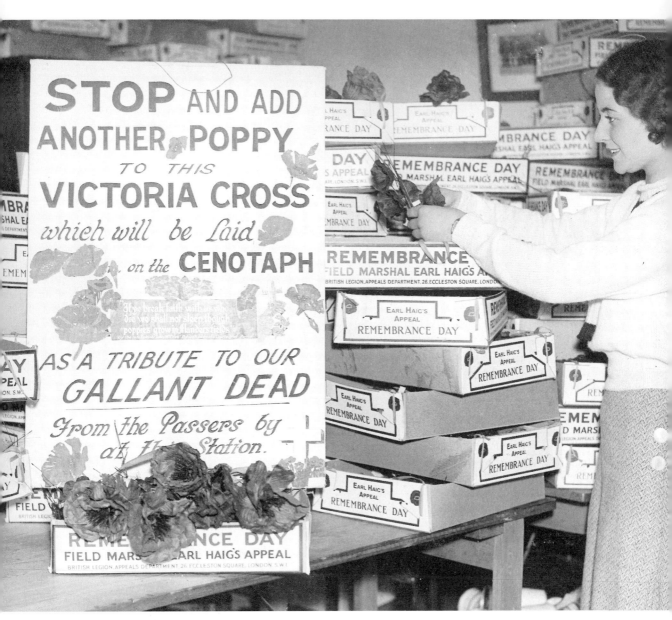

*Poppy Appeal preparations in 1933 included a poster apparently intended for a railway station, perhaps Victoria. Note the prominent reference to Earl Haig on the boxes of poppies.*

came up with yet another idea: his attention drawn to a framed war memorial in a village hall when a man inadvertently hung his hat on it, he invented a poppy that could be attached to memorial tablets in churches, schools, banks, railway stations and indeed anywhere such tablets were displayed. Known as the 'war memorial poppy', it had a medal ribbon streamer attached, thus making a proper use of surplus ribbon stocks.* Two-thirds of all the money raised went to the Relief Fund with the rest being given out in grants which included outside bodies such as St Dunstan's. A grant was also made to the Legion headquarters account for general administrative expenses: in the first eight

*Surplus campaign medal ribbons had been used for braces until a *Legion Journal* campaign stopped the practice.

years of the Legion's life this had been 10 per cent of the Poppy Appeal's net proceeds but had reduced to 6 per cent by 1931. It approximately matched the income from branch Affiliation Fees and these two sources met the cost of headquarters administration and Area expenses.[48]

## An investigation

There were no special fundraising activities over these years other than a 'British Legion Annual' at Christmas for children. Meanwhile the Great War Remembrance League continued to decline: the annual income had fallen below £5,000 by 1935, little effort seemingly put into it after the death of Earl Haig, its initiator. The apparent lack of growth in the Poppy Appeal may have been the reason for an investigation into the work of the Appeals Department in 1935 which not only came up with proposals for staff redundancies but included an attack on Captain Willcox's salary, this time envisaging a reduction that might have left the captain in straitened circumstances; but by a narrow margin the NEC voted to allow Willcox to retain his existing pay and he responded by offering to hand back 10 per cent. Some staff redundancies, however, went ahead.[49]  In retrospect it seems that the critics may not have appreciated the significance of the falling living costs which increased the appeal's value despite the marginally lower face-value takings.

Perhaps the staff might have been retained if the Council had taken up a scheme put forward also in 1935 by Foleshill Branch for the establishment of British Legion shops throughout the country. The idea, foreshadowing the charity shop so popular some fifty years later, was, however, turned down by the NEC as it was not their policy to compete with other shops on the marketplace.[50]

## More employment at the Poppy Factory

Such shops might perhaps have sold poppies at Remembrancetide, but in 1932 there was a shortage of poppies when a fire at the warehouse, now at York Road near King's Cross Station, destroyed half of the stock. This proved another turning point in the affairs of the Poppy Factory: in order to make up the losses it engaged on a temporary basis a hundred additional staff from its waiting list – all disabled ex-servicemen, many of whom had been without a job for years. But when the lost stock had been replaced, which took about a year, Howson was reluctant to dismiss the extra men and reduced the factory to a thirty-five-hour working week in order to retain them, so that by the end of 1933 he was employing 360 men in place of 265 two years earlier. It so happened that the factory moved into new premises on the same site in early 1933 so that not only was there room for them all but they were able to work in good conditions. The reduction in the working week seems to have been accomplished without complaint from the original workers and presumably a deal was struck over their pay. However, even after taking on the extra 100 there were still 300 disabled ex-servicemen on the factory's waiting list.

A decision by the Legion's NEC to return poppies damaged in storage to the factory for renovation, although it cost the warehouse thirty jobs, helped to provide the factory with more work. But there had also been an expansion in orders as the Appeal organizers looked more optimistically into the future with the easing of the recession. The range of commercial products was increased to include artificial flowers, badges, Christmas crackers and in 1935 a completely new line, jig-saw puzzles, an order for 10,000 being received from St George's Hospital for an appeal. The same year the factory made two

*Poppy Factory employees at work. In the top right hand picture the man with one arm is using the stump of the other to operate a press which stamps the poppies into shape. In the 1930s the Poppy Factory employed over 350 men; but there was still a long waiting list.*

136

million emblems and ten thousand collecting trays for the King's Jubilee Trust street collection, as well as half a million blue roses for the Cancer Appeal.

The community's social facilities now included the Remembrance Club and a bowling green with a pavilion. An annual garden competition was popular and since the judges were from Kew Gardens their decisions were not disputed. There were an endowment plan for the workers, with half the premiums paid by the factory, and hospital and other savings schemes. As the Home Secretary said on a visit, the Poppy Factory was 'one of the finest and most human war memorials there is in the country'.[51]

# 1936 – 1940

## War and the Appeal

From 1936 onwards Poppy Day takings steadily grew, the improved economy due to rearmament being reflected in the results, which were perhaps also influenced by the looming war. Each year's takings surpassed the last and the final peacetime collection in November 1938 exceeded £581,000. But, as war approached, the Legion's leaders became concerned about the Appeal. Would it be possible to take street collections with the towns and cities facing massive aerial bombardment? Would people give money under the stresses of wartime living? And what about all the other charities that might spring up in a war, stretching the public's generosity to the limit? Whatever the answers to these questions one thing was certain – there would be even greater demands on the Legion's benevolence.

In the event the 1939 Poppy Appeal was yet another record. Despite the conflicting demands of Civil Defence the organizers gave their time and the poppy sellers were out on the streets as usual, but this time able to tell donors that from now on their money would be used to assist the ex-service community of all wars, following the NEC's decision a few days after hostilities began.

One person able to play little part in the 1939 Appeal was Lady Haig. She had overtaxed herself in 1937 by a month's continuous travelling on the Appeal's behalf and her health never fully recovered. The same year the Legion's Conference had again become concerned about the white poppy, their sale at Remembrancetide being seen to menace the income from the Haig poppy. But it is doubtful if the white poppy was ever a serious threat in this way; it was simply that it implied a misinterpretation of the Legion's purpose that aroused resentment in some of the members. Certainly there were no white poppies in the city of Harar in Abyssinia, caught up in Mussolini's colonial war. Despite the fact that the city was threatened with destruction and the inhabitants with death, the British residents held their customary collection in 1936 and it was a record. It was a record too that year at Kilndown in Kent where the average of 1s 2d per head of population would be equivalent to over £2 today.[52]

The Legion's volunteer organization, by now perhaps the largest charity collecting network in the country, had been called into use for a new purpose in 1937 – the Coronation Emblem appeal. And it would certainly have been involved in a 'Warrior's Day' appeal in 1940, some twenty years after the first such appeal, intended to raise money not only for the Legion but for ex-service charities generally. But the project failed to gain support from SSAFA and others who felt that it might cut across their flag days.[53]

Another idea that year was more successful: a 'war chest' permanent collecting box placed in cafes, shops and pubs.[54]

## Death of Howson

A few days after Remembrance 1936, on 28 November, Major George Howson, the founder and chairman of the Poppy Factory, died. On his last journey to hospital he had been brought to the gates of his beloved factory and had led the men who gathered round him, many on crutches, in singing the old wartime songs. With his death at the early age of fifty they had lost one of their greatest friends – a remarkable man who had served in the thick of the fighting with the Hampshire Regiment, winning a Military Cross, and had then devoted himself to his disabled comrades. His funeral was conducted by his father, Archdeacon Howson, the coffin having been guarded day and night by the men of the Poppy Factory. He was commemorated at the factory by a 'Hall of Remembrance' in which were displayed plaques bearing the names of all those workers who had died while at the factory.[55]

Life had to go on at the factory and it continued to expand, by 1939 employing 400 workers who were now making many more wreaths than before, the poppy wreath having by now been accepted as the only proper wreath for military use, but the other lines included a growing trade in jig-saw puzzles, as well as luminous armbands for wartime blackouts. With the approach of war the factory formed an ARP scheme and, in 1938, assembled 36,000 gas masks for Richmond Borough.[56] But in late 1940 came another tragedy. An air raid killed four wives and four children of disabled workers when the factory's shelter suffered a direct hit, while several workers lost their lives the same night in their own homes. There were more names to be added to the plaques in the Memorial Hall.[57]

# 1941- 1945

## The poppy at war

Winston Churchill, now Prime Minister, sent a message to the Legion for Poppy Day 1940. Wishing the appeal every success he wrote, 'I have no doubt that this year, when the war has been brought into our own homes, the response will be more generous than ever.'

As it turned out, despite the fact that many of Britain's cities were under air attack on the day itself and some collecting boxes sent by train were found on arrival to have bullet holes in them, the public were certainly no less generous, the total collection equalling that of the year before. It said much for the devotion – and courage – of the poppy sellers. One overseas branch, Malaya, doubled its total collection; it was fitting – it

*These Poppy Factory workers had been switched to war work in 1943.*

would be the last collection for five cruel years.[58]

The next year, 1941, much to everyone's surprise, saw an increase of nearly 30 per cent, bringing the total collection to over three-quarters of a million pounds. It was again due to the determination of the gallant band of poppy sellers, nearly all women, no doubt reflecting the wartime spirit which had taken hold of the nation. It was fitting that in December of that year the Legion gave recognition to the efforts of those who had worked for the appeal since its inception twenty years before by the award of a Certificate. It was not recorded whether Sergeant Scarlett, Haig's batman and standard bearer in the Great War, received a certificate but he was a busy appeal worker at Haig House for many years.[59]

The Appeal proceeds rose each year for the rest of the war, a 'Remembrance Week' with whist drives and dances being held in 1943, and in 1944 the total exceeded one million pounds, despite more enemy action – this time flying bomb attacks on London and the Home Counties – as well at the rather more familiar hazard of bad weather. As before it was largely due to sheer hard work by poppy collectors such as a seventy-eight-year-old member of Sheffield Women's Section who had lost three sons in the Great War and who collected from dawn until she could no longer see the poppies. The BBC also played their part: that year there were no less than thirty mentions of the appeal, one by an MP who aptly described the Legion as an organization for helping lame dogs over stiles.[60]

Apart from the Poppy Annual, a collection of stories and jokes aimed mainly at those serving, there were no other forms of fundraising during these war years. But the income from legacies rose, reaching nearly £50,000 in 1945. Gratifying though this was, the Legion had little assured income and needed even more in the way of legacies, the Great War Remembrance League by now having virtually ceased to provide any input.[61]

### Problems at the factory

With the increased demand for poppies the Poppy Factory too was busy in the war. But it had problems: the shortage of raw materials first affected the output of 'other lines' and then the poppy itself, leading to a strike when the metal centre and stem of the poppy had to be replaced with other material and the men in the section concerned thought that they would earn less. The dispute was settled within twenty-four hours but, as the local press noted, it was sad to see such men out on the street. It led to the setting up of an Advisory Committee representative of all sections of the factory, chaired by the highly respected (and severely disabled) Brunel Cohen, the Legion's Treasurer.

Despite such difficulties the supply of poppies was able to keep up with demand, although there was some concern that the Poppy Warehouse, situated next to King's Cross station, was vulnerable to bombing and some of the stock was held elsewhere as a precaution. But the warehouse survived both the blitz and the later flying bomb attacks, its structure standing up to some near misses.[62]

It was as well that the poppy stocks survived. From early 1943 until July 1945 a large proportion of the factory's employees was switched to war work for the Ministry of Aircraft Production, assembling some ten million radio condensers in order to overcome a bottleneck in supply. The workforce was by now down to just over 300, as it had been decided not to replace those lost through death or illness until the war ended, to allow room for a new generation of disabled workers. This meant that more labour-efficient machinery had to be introduced for those remaining on poppy production, allowing a much higher output once the factory was back to normal; the question was, would the demand continue to increase when peace had been restored? In the meantime the tight little community in Richmond kept up their morale by continuing to hold their social events and raising money for a comforts fund for the sons and daughters away at the war.

Each November the factory staff ensured that up in Westminster, in the shadow of the Abbey, the Field of Remembrance with its tiny poppy-adorned crosses, continued all through the war, smaller than in peace but still providing the opportunity for individual remembrance.[63]

★      ★      ★

In August 1945 the post of Appeals Secretary was advertised. The retiring secretary, Captain Willcox, had much to reflect upon. The success of the Poppy Appeal had been phenomenal almost from the outset, the symbol and its link with 'Flanders fields' catching the public imagination, while the connection with the national act of Remembrance elevated it almost to an institution. The rest had depended on organization – and the remarkable army of helpers.

Yet that very success had meant that the Legion had become utterly dependent on the poppy. Now, in a new post-war world, the Legion's work was to be expanded. Would the poppy still be able to sustain it?

# CHAPTER 6

## INTERNATIONAL 1921-1945

# *The Desire for Peace*

### 1921 – 1925

### Attitudes to war

Those who had fought and survived the Great War felt that they were men set apart from their fellow citizens. They believed that their views should be taken into account if a new international crisis were to develop. It was this thinking that was to influence the Legion's objects and its actions when Europe began to drift into another war. It was not confined to the British veterans. Those who had fought as their allies were of the same mind, as indeed were many who had been on the opposite side. But for the moment there was no contact with the former foe. In another of its objects the Legion would co-operate with other ex-service organizations, not only in the Empire but in allied countries, and encourage exchanges and visits.[1] There were of course other reasons for such interchanges; but the idea of an international expression of ex-service views in times of tension gave an extra dimension to the role of the war veteran.

### The Legion's overseas links

In pursuit of the second of these objects the Legion became involved with two bodies.

*The Federation Interalliee des Anciens Combattants*, known as FIDAC, founded in November 1920 by Charles Bertrand, the General Secretary of the leading French ex-service organization – the *Union Nationale des Combattants*. FIDAC was a grouping of ex-service bodies of France, Great Britain, Belgium, the United States of America, Italy, Romania, Serbia and Czechoslovakia. It was, as the title proclaimed, an interallied grouping: no former enemies were admitted.

*The British Empire Services League* (BESL) founded by Earl Haig during his visit to South Africa in early 1921. It brought together the ex-service organizations of the Empire – unity was very much Haig's watchword – and among its objects was to promote and assist emigration of ex-servicemen to the Dominions and colonies.

In addition to these formal associations there were direct contacts between the Legion and the ex-service organizations of other nations, principally those of France and America. France had five veterans organisations totalling over a million members, of which the Union Nationale des Combattants (UNC) was the foremost. Relations between the Legion and the UNC were close, aided by the very active Legion branch in Paris.

Relations with the American Legion were equally cordial, tinged perhaps with envy; it was already in 1922 a powerful organization exerting considerable influence. It had preceded the British Legion by some two years, having been formed in Paris at a meeting of all ranks of the American Expeditionary Force in early 1919. By 1924 it had 11,000 branches and one million members. When unemployment became a problem in America in 1923 a 'Legion Employment Day' apparently got half a million men back to work[2] and was the inspiration for the British Legion's 'National Work Drive', which was somewhat less successful. (See page 72-73)

It has been noted that the Legion's objects included support for the work of the League of Nations. Here it did not see eye to eye with its French comrades. France regarded the activities of the League with a great deal of scepticism; indeed M Bertrand saw FIDAC itself as the principal movement for peace. At the FIDAC 1922 conference the member organizations, which included the Legion, adopted a set of principles aimed at maintaining peace and agreed to urge their respective governments, as conditions would permit, 'to entirely disarm and disband land, sea and air forces and destroy the implements of warfare'.[3]

These proposals, naive as they may seem, particularly in the light of subsequent events, indicate two things: firstly the ex-service organizations of the allied nations felt so passionately about peace that they were prepared to advocate total disarmament; secondly the veterans believed that they could influence their government's policy on matters of this sort.

**The occupation of the Ruhr**

No sooner had FIDAC passed their resolutions than an international crisis occurred. Strictly according to the terms of the Armistice Germany had failed to meet its reparations commitments to France, defaulting on timber and coal deliveries. This provided France with an excuse to occupy the Ruhr, taking Belgium with them, early in 1923. Great Britain did not support the action: the effect on her trade, at a time of worsening unemployment, could be catastrophic. From her point of view what was needed was not to ruin Germany but to restore her to trading partnership. The Legion backed the government's stance as they saw only too plainly the effect of unemployment on ex-servicemen. The French and Belgian veterans' organizations of course followed their own national line. FIDAC solidarity had fallen at the first hurdle.

At this precise juncture the League of Nations' International Labour Office called a meeting of ex-servicemen's oganizations to discuss, among other matters, the maintenance of peace. Since the Germans and Austrians were also invited, FIDAC banned its members from attending. This put the Legion in a dilemma. It was already involved with the ILO on employment of the disabled; talking to Germans could do no harm and might even help trade relations. But it did not wish to upset FIDAC. In the event, after insisting that all controversial matters be excluded, the Legion went to the meeting.[4] This episode illustrates the fundamental difference of attitude between the Legion and its French-influenced European counterparts: the Legion was prepared to do business with the former enemies if necessary.

In the meantime General Sir Ian Hamilton had become involved. Hamilton features several times in Legion history but he is chiefly remembered for his views on relations with the Germans. A Gordon Highlander, he had served with great distinction in the Boer War, a hero of the young war correspondent Winston Churchill. Paradoxically Churchill was to be the author of a plan which tarnished Hamilton's reputation: the Gallipoli landings of April 1915. In retirement Hamilton had become the first President of Metropolitan Area (and held the same office with the Legion in Scotland). With a lively turn of phrase and forthright approach, he was very active in the Legion and his tall, lanky presence, invariably in uniform and topped by his Highland Glengarry, enlivened many a gathering.

In December 1922, in the course of a tour of the north of England, Hamilton addressed crowded meetings of ex-servicemen, speaking of reconciliation with the former enemy: all that was needed was to hold out a hand to the two and a half million ex-enemy war veterans. 'It may be a very difficult thing for us to do but if we don't do it, it looks to me as if we are going to be in two camps.' The one chance of world peace 'lay on the ex-servicemen of all nations getting together and insisting on reconciliation'.[5] A few months later, in early 1923, standing for re-election as President of Metropolitan Area, in the course of a typically vigorous address, he again spoke of peace. The Legion should get together with its German and Austrian counterparts, with a view to holding out the hand of *camaraderie* to the millions of ex-enemy war veterans. He went on to suggest that these ex-enemies should be brought into FIDAC. The Ruhr crisis, which could develop into a reopening of the war, might, he believed, have been averted through action by ex-servicemen on both sides.[6]

It is possible that, in advocating such policies, Hamilton was testing the water on behalf of the Legion's leaders. If so, the only strong reaction was from those whom the war had left with only an implacable hatred of the enemy. It seemed that for the majority the argument did not lack force at a time when hundreds of thousands were enduring privation as a result of unemployment stemming, at least in part, from the loss of the German markets. Peace equated to prosperity in many people's minds, and if making friends with a defeated foe was the price then they were prepared to pay it. At any rate this theme was now to be taken up by the Legion's leadership.

## FIDAC and the 'ex-enemies'

Peace was certainly very much in the minds of delegates at the Legion's annual conference in May 1923, which had a strong international flavour: not only were the American Legion and the other allied ex-service organizations represented but the Secretary General of the League of Nations addressed Conference: 'I feel that there is an underlying resolve in the minds of Legion members that the terrible catastrophe of 1914 should never happen again'.[7] He was cheered by his audience.

A few months later, in September 1923, the annual FIDAC congress took place in Brussels. The Belgian hosts made it an occasion to be remembered: bands, a guard of honour, parades, banners, receptions and banquets all demonstrating the solidarity of the allies of the Great War, or at least the stamina of the delegates.[8] Those who survived all this cordiality managed some work, the principal problem for the British Legion delegation being of course the Ruhr question. The matter was debated hotly at first, but eventually an understanding was reached: FIDAC recognized both the additional distress to the British ex-service community caused by the breakdown in trade and the just demands of the French and Belgians for reparations. Unity had been restored.

Further conference resolutions renewed FIDAC's commitment to peace. But the tone of the resolutions reflected high ideals, suggesting a power and influence which FIDAC, despite all the ceremony which attended their meetings, simply did not possess[9] and at the 1924 congress in London the Legion attempted to bring matters down to earth: a draft resolution deleted the restriction on former enemies becoming members of FIDAC.[10] But, perhaps disconcerted by a letter from the 'Peace Alliance of German Ex-servicemen', hoping that it would be possible to 'advance together' under the motto 'No More War', the conference was cautious: first of all, each member organization should seek to find out the real feelings of the ex-service bodies in the former enemy countries concerning peace.[11]

In the event the matter was taken no further at the 1925 congress in Rome, where the delegates were received by the Italian Prime Minister, Benito Mussolini, jaw thrust forward as he listened impassively to the opening speeches under the marble busts in the hall of the Capitol of the Roman Emperors, perhaps ruminating on the state of Italian railway timetables following an unexpected delay to the delegates' arrival in Rome. The Legion's proposition was not even debated, congress merely stating that it would in future 'consecrate the greater part of its efforts to avoid the return of war', while noting the 'menace which military preparations in Germany make to the peace of the world'.[12]

The Legion could, however, console itself in the knowledge that the next FIDAC President would be Colonel Crosfield. It should provide the opportunity to move things forward.

## Peopling the Empire

Although it too was concerned at events in Europe, the British Empire Services League's principal interest was migration within the Empire. But even before the first of its biennial meetings, Earl Haig himself came close to creating a rift. Opening the Leverhulme Legion Club in Manchester in December 1922, he said that he could not encourage ex-servicemen to emigrate 'until the Governments of the Dominions set their house in order'. Not surprisingly these words upset the governments concerned, but Haig stood his ground; he had received letters from dissatisfied migrants. The first biennial conference of BESL, in London in July 1923, provided an opportunity to clear the air. Group migration would overcome the loneliness of the individual settler, while Haig, the League's Grand President, reminded delegates that emigration not only found work for Britain's unemployed but brought fresh blood to the Dominions and Colonies. On another topic a resolution at the conference advocated the formation of an English-speaking veterans association, bringing in the American Legion. But this interesting idea was not to be realized: the furthest the American Legion would go was to form a BESL liaison committee.

Lister, the Legion Chairman, took the chair at this first BESL conference and at the next biennial conference in Ottawa in 1925. It was again concerned with 'Empire migration'. As Lister noted, it 'was talked about almost to the exclusion of everything else. It was the topic at committee meetings on the outward-bound steamer, it dominated the conference.' It was not of course the simple matter that it might have seemed: most of the dominions and overseas territories were enduring their own economic difficulties and there were few jobs to be had. But, again quoting Lister, there was 'a genuine desire to assist in peopling the Empire with men of the British race' and the League decided to set up a department to act as a clearing house for the migration of ex-servicemen, not only from the British Isles but between the nations of the Empire.

To Earl Haig goes the credit for the most lasting achievement in Ottawa that year. At least eleven Canadian ex-service organizations were represented at the conference. When

Haig pointed out that in all parts of the Empire, except Canada, the veterans had achieved unity, it sparked off an immediate debate in the margins. Within two days the Canadian organizations had met and formed 'The Canadian Legion of the British Empire Services League'.[13]

# 1926 – 1930

## The depression affects migration

As the decade wore on, the League continued to be chiefly concerned with Empire migration by ex-servicemen and their families. In theory this meant movement between any member country. In practice it dealt almost exclusively with emigration from the United Kingdom to other parts of the Empire. BESL maintained a Migration Department at its offices in King Street, London, W1, which provided information to intending migrants, financial help in some cases, and, in the case of Legion members, a letter of introduction to the local branch of the ex-service organization in the new land, often ensuring practical help as well as a friendly welcome.

BESL gave much help to the Legion in its group migration schemes to Canada in 1927 and 1929 (see pages 90-91). But Canada was the only Empire country able to accept migrants on a large scale, and then only if properly trained and prepared. Australia could take only limited numbers and settlement in South Africa required considerable capital. All were suffering the effects of the world-wide depression and the League's endeavours to promote more trade between the countries of the Empire, creating demand and increasing the opportunities for population growth, had little practical effect. Nevertheless concern with the economic problems in the Irish Free State at the 1927 conference led to a resolution to provide ex-servicemen in Ireland with similar Empire settlement rights to their British comrades.

Like FIDAC, the League was mainly a forum for discussion; its members could only make things happen by exerting pressure on their own governments on their return from their meetings, and, as with FIDAC, government policies were usually swayed by other considerations. But BESL evoked the spirit of loyalty to the Empire and it inspired much pride, and some hope for the future, in those depressed times. Following the 1929 conference the Legion's Chairman, Colonel Crosfield, expressed the hope that on the twentieth anniversary of BESL's formation, in 1941, every Legion member would be able both to see and hear the conference at work: by that time 'television and broadcasting combined will have been so perfected that my wish will be realized'. It was not to be.[14]

Although the League's earlier idea of an English-speaking international ex-service organization had not taken root in the United States, there were still close ties between the British and American Legions. In 1927, following the American Legion annual convention in Paris, the National Commander's party came to Britain as the guests of the British Legion, disembarking to a guard of honour provided by Harwich Branch, and, on arrival at Liverpool Street Station, being met by another guard of honour some 400 strong supplied by Metropolitan Area. After a march to the Cenotaph behind a Guards band, lunch with the Prince of Wales and a banquet at the House of Lords hosted by the Prime Minister, the party could feel that their arrival had not passed unnoticed. The following days included a reception at Buckingham Palace and luncheon with the Lord Mayor of London at the Guildhall. At a time when the United States was pursuing an isolationist policy the honours accorded to their veterans indicate the value attached to America's intervention in the war.[15]

## National interests still prevail

In 1926 Germany was admitted to the League of Nations. The allied ex-service community, led by France, still had their faces firmly set against a similar admission to their organization but, under Crosfield's Presidency, the FIDAC Executive grudgingly agreed a Legion proposal to hold a meeting with the ex-enemy organizations. It took place at Luxembourg in 1927, but was nearly a disaster, the German and Austrian delegates expressing their resentment at the stiff terms of the 1919 peace treaty and attempting to alter a resolution calling for peaceful solutions to international problems.[16] But at a second conference the following year the Germans sent a different batch of representatives and everyone parted on good terms. In fact little had been achieved and there would be no more such meetings. The chief significance was that the British and German ex-service organizations had met. The encounters would encourage the Legion to take a slippery path.[17]

National interests continued to prevail at FIDAC annual conferences. There was no argument over resolutions on peace or education programmes to remind the rising generation of the devastion of war. But when, in 1929, the tricky question arose of the allied debts to the United States of America incurred during the war and European delegates pointed out that such debts increased the tax burden, contributed to unemployment and caused much bad feeling, the representatives of the American Legion resented any suggestion that they should try to influence public opinion in their country in order to get the charges reduced.

Some practical work was done at these meetings: ideas were exchanged over the treatment of the disabled, help arranged for visits to cemeteries by relatives of the fallen while the FIDAC Women's Auxiliary, chaired since its inception in 1925 by the Legion's Women's Section Chairman, Lady Edward Spencer Churchill, set up exchanges by groups of war orphans. And, no doubt, much goodwill was generated between individuals. But if the right hand sought to grasp the elusive dove of peace, the left held a glass of champagne. The host nations vied to outdo each other in hospitality: delegates were welcomed by bands and feted by Kings, Presidents and Prime Ministers. It was thus little wonder that a place on the national delegation was highly prized and in June 1926 the National Executive Council passed a resolution that half of the ten Legion representatives to each FIDAC Congress should be those who had been before and half should be those who had not.[18]

# 1931 – 1935

## Another Legion peace initiative

The front cover of the November 1933 *Legion Journal* carried a striking figure of a warrior standing astride a dead mother; her child, also dead, lies nearby. The warrior, clearly overcome by remorse, is casting aside his sword and unbuckling his armour. Beneath is the single word: 'Disarm'.

It may seem remarkable that the journal of an ex-service organization should parade such a sentiment, but by the early 1930s a harsh truth was dawning: the efforts of the League of Nations since 1919 to limit rearmament had failed. It was not for want of effort by the League. After all its chief function was to prevent war, but it was hamstrung by having only weak sanctions at its disposal and not only Germany but Japan, the USA and Russia were opposed to any system of international control of their armaments. And, as far as Europe was concerned, with an aggrieved Germany rearmament could only lead in one direction – that of war. It was a prospect that appalled those who had fought in the Great War as much as any of their fellow citizens; the difference was that the veterans still believed that it was within their power to prevent another such war.

The Legion had long supported the League. In late 1926 Lister, then Legion Chairman, had made a broadcast entitled 'The League and the Legion' in which he spoke of the Legion's desire to promote peace and its support for the League, referring to the efforts to persuade the other allied veterans associations to meet the German and Austrian ex-service representatives in pursuit of peace. Legion support demonstrated that the League of Nations was not, as some attempted to label it, a pacifist organization; if necessary the objective of peace might have to be achieved through war. He concluded, 'The Legion stands by the League.'[19]

Accordingly, since Legion-inspired efforts for peace seemed to have run out of steam after the 1928 conference in Luxembourg, the organization now tried the League of Nations route. In 1931 a resolution at the Legion's Annual Conference sought to place the views of ex-servicemen before the League's Assembly.

The approach still had be made through FIDAC, but the Executive Committee supported the initiative and called an international rally of ex-servicemen, to include Germany, Austria and Hungary. But when the rally took place at the League of Nations headquarters in Geneva in March 1933, despite the fact that the FIDAC President had made a personal visit to Berlin and had been well received, no German representative was present among the 10,000 ex-service delegates who adopted a resolution to maintain peace without recourse to force, with 'substantial, simultaneous and progressive disarmament'. Since the President's visit to Berlin there had been a new development: in January 1933 Hitler had come to power.

The resolution was duly presented to the World Disarmament Conference already in session at Geneva and the old soldiers went home. They might as well have stayed at home, for the conference itself achieved nothing, the crux of the problem of course being that no man trusted his neighbour. Certainly the British veterans were not prepared to go too far in their disarmament proposals. Time had moved on since FIDAC had adopted its 'total disarmament' stance in 1922. At the Legion's 1934 Annual Conference a resolution was passed stating that any national reduction in armaments should not be below that required to defend the Empire and nation, with a request that this view be passed to the Prime Minister. The Prime Minister duly replied that the resolution exactly reflected the government's position. But, having seen the futility of Geneva, 'less of a peace conference than a war of words', the Legion was now firmly of the view that, since the politicians were failing, the battle to preserve the peace had to be fought by those who understood the full horrors of war: the ex-servicemen.[20]

## Talking to the ex-enemy

Few knew more about the horrors of war than General Sir Ian Hamilton. Following his speeches in 1922 and 1923 on the theme of reconciliation, Hamilton had gone on to urge in 1924: 'Whilst Geneva talks of holding out a hand to the ex-enemy, let us Legionaries shake. The rest will follow.' For this the Metropolitan Area Council had sought to have him reprimanded*; but now the words were to be the basis of Legion policy. Hamilton

---

*Lister, as Legion Chairman, had simply 'sat on' the complaint, suggesting that Hamilton's utterances had leadership acceptance.

147

returned to his theme in early 1934 at the Metropolitan Area Conference. Having just returned from a visit to Germany to receive back the Gordons' drums lost in the war he told his audience that the British were better liked there than any other Allied nation. The General may have inferred too much from the remarks of his German hosts, but there is no doubt that the Legion as a whole believed that the goodwill to avoid war existed in Germany if it could only be tapped, and that the way to tap it was through contact between the ex-service organizations. It had asked a former German Minister of Defence to give his views in the *Legion Journal* in December 1932. General Groener wrote that, while Germany sought to achieve recognition of her rights as a nation, the German people 'does not dream of a war of revenge; its only wishes are for peace and quietness to put its own house in order'.

General Groener's article was written a month before Hitler took power and certainly at that stage it appeared to justify the policy that the Legion was still attempting to pursue through FIDAC. At the 1931 FIDAC congress in Prague the Legion delegates had extracted a resolution that 'the time had arrived to resume contact with the ex-service organizations of the ex-enemy countries', while another Legion-sponsored resolution at the 1933 conference in Casablanca took the matter a stage further by tasking FIDAC to 'consider the best means of organizing a permanent and still closer collaboration with ex-enemy ex-service organizations'. At the 1934 conference in London FIDAC appealed to ex-servicemen of former enemy countries 'to take part in efforts directed at any conflicts between peoples', the British Minister for War, Lord Hailsham, adding his own view at a luncheon that 'It is the soldier who is able to recognize better than anyone else the horrors and dangers of war.' Finally, at the 1935 conference in Brussels, the Legion sought to bring matters to a head by getting FIDAC to alter its name (but not its initials) by changing the 'I' from 'Interallied' to 'International', thus making the Germans, Austrians and Hungarians eligible for membership. But at this FIDAC baulked. It was a step too far; instead it decided to hold annual meetings for peace which would include the former enemy ex-service representatives, at the same time recognizing the right of every FIDAC organization to establish direct contact with ex-enemies. It was as well that FIDAC had endorsed direct contact, for it was the route that the Legion was now embarked on.[21]

### The 'hand of friendship'

Events were now about to unfold which would bring the Legion into the theatre of world politics and propel its Royal Patron to the centre of the stage. Its belief that a brotherhood linking the veterans of both sides could prevent the great powers from going to war again had not gone unnoticed by at least one observer. Joachim von Ribbentrop was in England as Hitler's unofficial ambassador and his special task was to try to promote an Anglo-German alliance. Friendly contact between veterans' groups would fit into the overall design and Ribbentrop made an approach through an intermediary to Colonel Crosfield, regarded as the Legion's foreign expert because of his long involvement with FIDAC. Crosfield sounded out Anthony Eden, who although his post was then Lord Privy Seal, was closely associated with foreign affairs. Eden saw no objections to Legion contact with a German veterans' group, but he warned that those taking part in the visits would be subject to propaganda. Neither the Legion nor Eden, however, had reckoned on the propaganda hazards of an involvement with Ribbentrop himself.

Some time in April or May of 1935 invitations were received for Legion delegations to visit the ex-service organizations of Austria and Germany in July. The matter was still being treated circumspectly: any discussion in the Legion's NEC went unrecorded and the first announcement of the visits was to be made at the Annual Conference in June. The President, General Sir Frederick Maurice had however taken the precaution of notifying the Foreign Office of the Legion's policy.* The reason for the secrecy appears to have been that the Legion's rank and file had not yet been consulted and the Annual Conference would provide the opportunity both to tell delegates and obtain their approval. However, the Legion's Patron would need to be told, particularly as he was due to address Conference that year, and General Maurice included the matter in his annual report to the Prince.

The Austrian visit was to be led by Brunel Cohen, the Honorary Treasurer; that to Germany by the Chairman, Major Fetherston-Godley. But it was of course the latter event which was likely to be the most controversial since Adolf Hitler had by now been in power for over two years and his activities were already causing consternation in Europe. Inevitably his power extended into the veterans' organizations: of the four in whose names the Legion's official invitation to Berlin was issued, two had the words 'National Socialist' (or Nazi) in their titles.

A month before the visits were due to take place, the Legion's Annual Conference assembled in London at its traditional venue, the Queen's Hall. As normal the proceedings opened with the President's address and in the course of his review of the Legion's work General Maurice referred to the recently-issued NEC policy statement which included suggestions that the Legion should enter into friendly relations with ex-service organizations of other countries, irrespective of the side on which they fought in the war. Noting that for a long time steps had been taken in that direction without any very positive result the President said, to the accompaniment of applause, that he believed that the time had come to go further. Such a step would not commit the Legion to the endorsement of the policy of any particular country and, to further applause, he went on to say:

> 'You may have noticed that on the same day last week when HRH our Patron received me to hear my report on the Legion's work he received before me the Vice-Bourgomeister of Vienna, while the Army has resumed the pre-war practice of the exchange of officers with the German Army. I see no reason why we should not follow these distinguished examples.'

The business of the conference was nearly concluded on the final day when His Royal Highness the Prince of Wales suddenly walked on to the platform unaccompanied and unannounced. On seeing him the 950 delegates interrupted the proceedings by bursting into spontaneous applause. There was further tumultuous applause when the Prince rose to make his address. He began by assuring his audience that he was not going to bring up any controversial matters and, after reviewing the year's activities, he moved to his conclusion, the future of the Legion. Having lent his support to the idea of opening the ranks to some of the younger generation, he then said:

> 'There is one point which your President, when I was speaking to him the other day, brought up, and which also commended itself to me, and that is that a deputation might go, or a visit might be paid by, representative members of the Legion to Germany at some future time. I feel that there could be no more suitable body or organization of men to stretch forth the hand of friendship to the Germans than we ex-servicemen, who fought them in the Great War, and have now forgotten all about that.'

*In a letter to Sir Robert Vansittart at the Foreign Office on 12 May 1935.

*'The Hand of Friendship' speech. The photograph seems to have been taken just after the Prince of Wales had endorsed the Legion plan to send a delegation to Germany. The Prince stands between Major Fetherston-Godley (right) and Colonel Ashwanden, while Colonel Heath is seated behind him.*

The Prince's words were accompanied by cheers at his first mention of a visit to Germany and at the end of the passage, when he declared that there was no more suitable body to 'stretch forth the hand of friendship', by a deafening cheer. There was further cheering moments later when he formally concluded his speech and sat down, and this was the only occasion on which the Legion's Patron stayed until the Conference formally ended with the singing of the National Anthem.

Up to that point, minutes from the end, it had been a normal Legion conference, largely concerned with domestic matters, and the press reporters who remained must have been looking at their watches and wondering how to give their editors a story. But now they had one; headlined 'Hand of Friendship to the Germans' the Prince of Wales's remarks were flashed around Europe and the world.

Even so the impact might not have been that remarkable but for the interpretation put on the episode by others and particularly by Ribbentrop. He liked to please his master and the tale lost nothing in the telling; it was portrayed not only as representing a change in British policy towards Germany but one initiated by the future King, who was now openly adopting a pro-German stance. In Germany the speech was hailed as a breakthrough in Anglo-German relations, overtaking the Anglo-French alliance that had preceded the Great War and which had governed British policy in Europe up to this point. And it helped to implant in Hitler's mind the idea that the Prince had significant political

150

influence, a misapprehension that was to persist.

The German reaction of course raised the temperature elsewhere. Although General Maurice had informed the British Foreign Office of the Legion's intention to open relations with ex-enemy organisations (see page 149), no one had anticipated this level of publicity. The French were particularly unhappy and in London a cabinet meeting concluded that either the Foreign Secretary or the Prime Minister should have been consulted before the Prince made his remarks, a view communicated to him by the King, who had already expressed his own displeasure to his son.

How did it all get out of hand? The idea that the Legion should make contact with its German and Austrian opposite numbers in the interests of preventing another war might seem naive in the face of the political realities in Germany at the time, but it was hardly outrageous. Nor was there any suggestion that the Legion accepted what was happening in Germany under Hitler; that much had been made very clear by General Maurice in his conference address. The visits themselves were simply the logical development of a policy which the Legion had openly pursued for some years and which was now about to be agreed by FIDAC, while Conference's reception of the proposal showed that was keenly supported by delegates representing hundreds of thousands of ex-servicemen whose loyalty to their country was unquestioned. Indeed it probably also reflected the views of the majority of the British population, who at the time would have backed almost any chance of avoiding another war.

It was the Prince's personal endorsement of the idea which had provoked the situation. So why did he allow himself to become involved? There are two reasons. In the first place he was himself inclined to the view that the Germans had been unfairly treated by the terms of the Versailles Treaty that had ended the war and that there was room for friendship and understanding. He was not alone in his opinion, but it was perhaps better expressed at private dinner parties than in public. In the second place he had been asked to commend the idea, but not, it would seem, by the Legion's President, although it had certainly been mentioned at his pre-conference meeting with the Prince. It has since been established that it was the Chairman, Major Fetherston-Godley, who specifically asked him to give his support, and he quite probably did so in an informal discussion on the Prince's arrival on the conference platform where the two were seated next to each other. If that was the case the Prince would have had little time to reflect on the wisdom of what he was about to say or to consult others.

One thing is, however, clear: the initiative to 'stretch forth the hand of friendship' to the Germans did not come from the Prince of Wales himself; whatever his private feelings, on this occasion he was merely backing a policy which the Legion had been pursuing for many years.[22]

## The visits to Germany and Austria

Such had been the publicity over their announcement that the visits themselves might have gone ahead almost as an anti-climax had it not been for the German propaganda machine which, as Eden had warned, could operate with ruthless efficiency. The first delegation to leave was that led by the Vice Chairman, Colonel Ashwanden, and the Honorary Treasurer, Major Brunel Cohen; the visit was principally to Vienna which, as the former capital of the Austro-Hungarian Empire, Germany's allies in the Great War, still had something of the aspect of an 'enemy' stronghold, despite the fact that that empire was now scattered to the four winds. Having first attended a national celebration

*Berlin welcomes the 1935 Legion delegation.*

in the neighbouring Czechoslovakia the delegation had a polite reception in Vienna, meeting the Austrian Chancellor and having some informal meetings with the heads of the veterans' organizations, who expressed their support for the Legion's attempts to promote contact between former foes. It was all, however, very low-key; the fact of the matter was that Austria no longer counted beside Germany, as would be all too graphically demonstrated two years hence when Hitler's troops simply marched into Austria without any resistance. The final part of the visit, to Budapest, now the capital of an independent Hungary, engendered somewhat more enthusiasm, the delegation, which had made the journey by river, being met at the quayside by a uniformed guard of honour several hundred strong and a band playing the British National Anthem. Again a visit to the Head of State and the Prime Minister were on the programme, together with discussions with their hosts, the Hungarian War Veterans' Union, with whom the visitors seemed to have struck an accord, perhaps because in addition to their friendliness they were a non-political organization. They wore uniform at all times and saluted one another

152

punctiliously. But Hungary too was eventually to fall under the sway of Hitler.

The spotlight was of course on the visit to Berlin and before the delegation left London the Legion's Chairman, who was leading it, called a press conference. Major Fetherston-Godley had something of the air of a great statesman about him and his briefing was in statesmanlike terms: he spoke of the link of the brotherhood of arms and the Legion's wish to use this as a basis of friendship between nations. The visits to ex-enemy countries, he said, were intended to form a foundation for international diplomacy. Accompanied by Colonel Crosfield, as well as a former naval attaché in Berlin and three others, the party set off on 13 July.

The welcome in the German capital was astonishing. Thousands of people packed the streets as a procession of motor cars headed by an open tourer, in the back of which sat Fetherston-Godley, took the party to the official reception at the Kaiserhof hotel. In the broiling sun they gave cheer after cheer, pressing so close on the passing cars that their arms, outstretched in stiff salute, almost grazed the corners of the windscreens. The reception itself was no less impressive, the arrival of the Union Jack being greeted by the British National Anthem. The visits to war cemeteries and memorials and the wreath-layings also took place against a backdrop of thousands of assembled citizens who, as the Legion delegation, accompanied by the German veterans, marched away, applauded and saluted them. Even a reception at Herr Ribbentrop's house in a small village in the Berlin suburbs brought hundreds of men, women and children who roared out a welcome to every arrival and were still waiting to cheer when the delegation left half an hour before midnight.

In his enigmatic way Hitler had given no indication as to whether he would meet the delegation. But two days after their arrival, quite unexpectedly, they were taken to the Chancellery and spent two hours with Hitler. He asked each of the six members of the Legion party in turn where they had fought and exchanged war memories, his interpreter afterwards noting that, but for the difference in language, it might have been a typical meeting of old comrades. Hitler ended by saying that in the interests of peace he attached a special value to collaboration between soldiers who had fought in the last war. Fetherston-Godley, according to Hitler's interpreter, responded to the effect that the

*Fetherston-Godley and Crosfield talk to Hitler at the* Reichschancellerie *in Berlin, July 1935.*

English had only once fought against the Germans and in the opinion of the British Legion this had been a mistake, a mistake that would not be repeated. When this was reported in the press Fetherston-Godley hotly denied making any such remark: all he had said was that the Legion stood for peace and would do all that it could to avoid war.

Perhaps even more remarkable than the summons to Hitler was a visit to the Dachau concentration camp. The Legion party was told that among its 1,500 inmates there were nearly a thousand political prisoners and they were allowed to visit the cells of those in solitary confinement. This they found a depressing experience due not only to the conditions but to the low types of humanity they found; but it has since been stated by a refugee that those seen were SS men acting as prisoners. As an end to a interesting day, they had a family supper with Himmler, the head of the SS, who lived nearby and who gave the impression of being an unassuming man, anxious to do his best for his country.

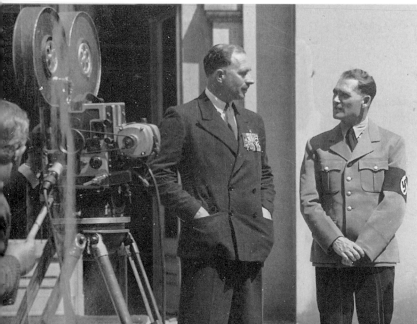

*The hosts ensured that the visit was well recorded. On the left, the Legion's Chairman is in conversation with Deputy Führer Rudolf Hess, while the gathering above in front of the* Reichschancellerie *conveys an impression of good fellowship.*

*The 1935 visit was efficiently stage managed by the Germans; here the Legion party is met by a Guard of Honour formed by the* **Sicherheitsdienst** *(the Nazi Security Service) while crowds throng the pavement.*

This, as he explained, included removing and segregating the leaders of subversive movements, there being no doubt that the healthy life of the camps in which they were confined would effect a cure in many cases.

There were also of course discussions with the leaders of the German ex-service organizations and everyone agreed that there must be more such exchanges; the next would be a visit of German ex-servicemen to the Legion. Meanwhile both countries would work on the French to bring their ex-servicemen into this happy union. Youth, including presumably the Hitler Youth, should be taught to understand what war meant and throughout the world veterans should work to prevent another war. And so, their mission accomplished, the British Legion delegation returned to their own country.

The Germans ensured that the visit was well recorded both on movie film and in photographs. In the shot of the party standing in a carefully arranged semicircle around Hitler in the sunshine outside the Reich Chancellery, Ribbentrop has the slightly detached air of a successful stage manager. He must indeed have seen the visit as a minor hit, perhaps the first in a series of increasingly lavish productions that might ultimately lead to his master's cherished Anglo-German alliance. But had the Legion simply been exploited? In fact both sides were working to the same end: no war between Britain and Germany; but as far as Hitler was concerned any understanding with Britain was only intended to allow him to pursue his ruthless expansionist policies unhindered. Four years

155

later, on the advice of the same Ribbentrop, he was to overplay his hand, as a result of which Britain would go to war. In the meantime the Legion initiative, by contributing, albeit unwittingly, to Hitler's illusion of British friendship, may in a small way have helped to create more time for Britain to prepare. By the same token it might have encouraged his aggressive behaviour. But the idea that goodwill between the veterans of a war fought twenty years before could stop any politician, maniac or otherwise, from using military force to achieve his current purposes was sadly misplaced and in this instance the German ex-servicemen were clearly as firmly under Nazi control as almost everything else in the country.

As a postscript to the visit there is an account by the interpreter attached to the party by the German hosts. He refers to Fetherston-Godley's radiant smile, always a gentleman and never departing from his theme of a world-wide understanding between all ex-servicemen. Colonel Crosfield talked very good German and was well-informed about Germany. The interpreter expressed regret that Sergeant Major Clive, the standard bearer and secretary of the party, was not allowed to take part in the meetings: he was evidently impressed by the Sergeant Major's soldierly bearing and attitude. But, whatever impressions the interpreter may have formed, the delegation had few illusions about their hosts. Suspecting the nature of the programme that had been arranged, they insisted on some changes to suit their own purposes. Nevertheless they returned convinced that Germany was not intending to go to war and indeed they were probably right – at that stage.

A few days later the leaders of the two delegations reported to a National Executive Council meeting and a Committee of Foreign Relations was established. It was also decided to invite representatives of the ex-enemy organizations to the next Legion Annual Conference, together with those of the French veterans' bodies, thus making the 'peace party' complete.

There had, however, already been at least two visits that year by German ex-servicemen: assistance given by Brighton Branch in finding the grave of a German prisoner of war led to a visit by a party of thirty-one members of the German Ex-Prisoners of War Association in June of 1935. Supported by the town it seems to have created genuine good feeling. But standing before the Cross of Sacrifice the Germans wore their swastika armbands and raised their arms in the Nazi salute. There was a return visit soon after, fifty Brighton members arriving in Cologne on 25 September. Here were shades of the Legion leaders' visit to Berlin in July: the factories had been closed and the streets were lined with ex-servicemen, while behind them, tightly packed, stood thousands of people. The triumphal progress continued with rallies and visits, speeches and dinners, singing and wreath-laying. Cologne Cathedral was specially floodlit for the visitors and at Bad Godesburg there was a message from Herr Hitler; but at the conference of their host association the Brighton members noticed that, although there were speeches, there was no debate.

Hornsey Branch assisted with a visit in June 1935, hosting thirteen German ex-servicemen who had fought against the British in France. There was a sensible flavour to the programme, the visitors arriving during a routine branch meeting and, after laying a wreath at the War Memorial, being entertained to tea before attending a service at the Muswell Hill Methodist Church, although it is not recorded whether it was floodlit for the occasion.

Not everyone was happy with the hand of friendship. Although Major Fetherston-Godley stressed that the Legion's initiative had been non-political, he acknowledged that many people thought that the meeting with Hitler held political significance. The former Senior Jewish Chaplain with the British Forces in France and a holder of the DSO, now Chaplain of the Legion's Maccabean Branch, made his views clear: writing in November of that year of the degradation and persecution of German Jewry, 12,000 of whom had died in the war, he went on to say, 'We Jews earnestly hope that the authorities of the Legion will make it perfectly plain to the ex-soldiers of Germany that, whilst justice and liberty are denied to the Jews of their country, the Legion must strongly disapprove of this policy.'[23]

## The recession hits the Empire

All this activity in Europe in search of peace dominated the Legion's external relations in the early 1930s. But a more immediate concern for the member countries of the British Empire Services League was the the world-wide rececession and it was the main topic at the biennial conferences. The 1929 meeting had attempted to promote Empire migration, but by the next conference in Ottawa in 1931 the recession and its effect on employment in countries such as Canada and Australia had made those proposals impossible. Their concern now was their own job situation which had suffered as a result of the down-turn in trade. Many ex-servicemen were among the workless and the objective was to restore that trade. There was much indignation about 'unmarked goods from foreign countries' and the the conference slogan became 'Empire Trade'. Unfortunately the situation was well beyond anything that mere slogans could achieve.

Trade, or the continuing lack of it, again dominated the proceedings at the 1933 Conference but the League was no more able to do anything about it than before. The greatest value came from the exchange of views over matters of common interest: as far as unemployment was concerned attention was drawn to the British Legion car park attendants scheme which provided an example of adapting to social change, although its application might have been limited in the Empire at the time. The next conference, which should have taken place in 1935, was brought forward to 1934 to coincide with the Melbourne Centenary celebrations. But by now there was a greater concern with events in central Europe and the Australian ex-service organization took advantage of the presence of delegates to hold a peace conference in their country in addition to the BESL conference. As noted elsewhere it was the supreme irony that unemployment would only be cured by the approach of the war which the Legion was striving to prevent.[24]

## 1936 – 1940

## Open season for goodwill visits

Returning the Legion leaders' visit to Germany in 1935, a German ex-service delegation arrived in England for a week's stay on 19 January 1936. Three days later they were on their way back. On the evening of the second day, after laying a wreath at the Cenotaph, arms raised stiffly before them in salute, they were entertained to dinner by the Legion's President at the Army and Navy Club. As the toast to the King was about to be proposed, General Maurice was handed a telegram. He read it out: 'The King's life is moving peacefully to its close.' There was a sudden hush; the President said, 'The King is dying, long live the King', and the toast was drunk. The German party made its departure the next morning.[25]

The President's reference to the succession, although not intended in that way, was significant. When the German party returned in October King Edward VIII was on the throne and it must have seemed to the Nazi leaders that events were moving their way. Well might the Duke of Saxe-Coburg, leading the visitors, assure the members of the NEC in his address to the Council that his Leader, Adolf Hitler, 'hated war from the bottom of his heart'. When the party were taken to see the Changing of the Guard the King heard of their presence and at the end of the ceremony he sent them an invitation to come into the palace, where he received them in person. It was no more than an act of courtesy, but, reported back to Berlin, it must have impressed the German leadership.[26]

A few months earlier the new King had sent a message to Sandon Hall in Staffordshire. There, the Earl of Harrowby, the Legion Patron for the county, was hosting a house party to support the Legion's objective of a brotherhood of veterans in the interests of peace and thirty-six ex-service representatives of both sides in the European theatre of operations in the Great War were present. They seem to have been given 'the English experience' – living in an ancestral home, enjoying walks with their host on his estate,

*The visiting season. Above: visiting German 'brownshirts' lay a wreath on Douglas, Isle of Man, War Memorial. Below: former German prisoners of war lay a wreath at Brighton in memory of their comrades who died in captivity.*

eating eggs and bacon for breakfast and sirloins of beef in country inns, entertained by mayors, feted by flag-waving villagers and townspeople and given the hand of friendship by ploughmen and factory hands. The King's message had expressed his interest and support for the venture, which no doubt generated much goodwill among those who took part.[27]

It was the visiting season from 1936 to 1938: French and German delegations visited South Wales at the invitation of Swansea Branch, while German ex-officers attended a dinner at Barry Branch. Thatcham Branch entertained three German visitors for a week and at a dinner at the Chequers Hotel in Newbury the Mayor assured the visitors that Germany was not really an enemy since nine-tenths of the men who fought did not know what they were fighting for. On the Isle of Man twenty brownshirts from a visiting tourist ship were moved to buy a wreath from the Douglas Branch and lay it at the War Memorial, performing the ceremony in their uniforms and jack-boots. Many other branches entertained German visitors in those years of Legion-led goodwill and the season culminated with a grand visit to London of no less than 800 German ex-servicemen in the summer of 1938 where the visitors paraded in the grounds of the Royal Hospital, Chelsea, their stiff black-uniformed and capped figures contrasting with the scarlet of the watching in-pensioners.[28]

There were of course many return visits: the Legion's leaders went on a tour of central Europe in the summer of 1937 and, although travelling only semi-officially, they were met by guards of honour and welcomed by Royalty; the National Chairman, Major Fetherston-Godley visited Rome where he told Mussolini that 'We who have fought alongside Italian soldiers deeply resent the imputations levelled against their courage.' Portsmouth Branch visited a German ex-naval reunion in Dusseldorf and shared recollections of the battle of Jutland, while Warrington Branch, on a visit to Germany in

*'Hitler is strong for peace,' was General Sir Ian Hamilton's conclusion after meeting the German Führer at the Berghof, Berchtesgaden. Hitler had sent an aircraft to pick up the General, who was on a tour to Germany with his Legion Area in September 1938.*

159

July 1936, sent Hitler a greetings telegram and were surprised to receive a telephone call from the Führer in response. A Metropolitan Area tour received a salute from a battery of guns at Bad Godesburg, while their leader, Sir Ian Hamilton, flew to Berchtesgaden in an aircraft sent by Hitler; the photograph of their conversation shows Hamilton animated, Hitler attentive and Sir Ian returned with the message, 'Hitler is strong for peace. It is up to the rest of Europe to give up its pin-pricks against Germany.' There were many other visits to Germany and all were met with full honours from their hosts, the efficiency of the reception arrangements being explained when it emerged that Hitler had appointed an official co-ordinator for the visits, no doubt with adequate financial support. There were of course costs on the Legion side but headquarters explained that no Legion funds were expended: all visits were financed by prominent Legionaries and 'other well-known men'.[29]

Fetherston-Godley was convinced of the value of such contacts. He told North Eastern Area in 1936, 'Hitherto, you have had the old communication of diplomatic channels hedged in by restrictions. We applied the ordinary common sense by which we run the Legion, and can now go to the other fellow over a glass of beer and tell him what we think without fear of the consequences. He can do the same with us.' But some remained unimpressed; the Manchester Jewish Ex-servicemen passed a resolution regretting the NEC's action in inviting a German delegation to the next Annual Conference and the National Chairman had a rough ride at a meeting in Bristol to which the members of the Polack Branch had invited Jewish ex-servicemen from all over the country. A letter to the *Legion Journal* clearly challenged the policy: 'We are deceiving ourselves and are foolish if we think that the expression of opinion of a handful of ex-servicemen can have any influence on those who . . . allow the expression of no views which run counter to their own policy.'[30]

Events would shortly bear out the *Journal* correspondent's view.

## Back to the Army again, Sergeant

In 1938, having already occupied the Rhineland and annexed Austria, Hitler decided to add Czechoslovakia to his conquests, on the pretext that some of its citizens were of German origin. Initially he sought the area adjoining the German border, the Sudetenland. The British government attempted to mediate, proposing a neutral force in the area while the matter was decided by plebiscite. Acting on a suggestion from the Legion President, Sir Frederick Maurice, to the Foreign Secretary, they turned to the British Legion.*

It was first necessary to obtain Hitler's agreement to the Legion's role. Accordingly Maurice flew to Berlin and saw Hitler on Sunday, 25 September 1938. Hitler supported the use of Legion members to oversee the plebiscite,† but they needed to be in place quickly as he wanted the plebiscite in November 'so that by Christmas true peace would reign'. Maurice placed this reply before the Prime Minister, Neville Chamberlain, and went off to oversee the Legion's preparations for this extraordinary duty, involving up to 10,000 men. Meanwhile, there was frantic diplomatic activity

---

*Foreign Office files leave no doubt that the suggestion originated with the Legion, who by now must have felt that they had good relations with the German leaders. The Prime Minister gave his consent but there were reservations in government circles: Duff Cooper at the Admiralty thought it unwise. 'The Legion is simply a collection of middle aged and elderly men . . . I am afraid the result would certainly be ludicrous and might possibly be disastrous.' Halifax, the Foreign Secretary, did not disagree, so that later suggestions that the idea to involve the Legion came from the Foreign Office are plainly mistaken.[31]

†According to Maurice's report to No 10 Downing Street, Hitler was at first 'in a difficult mood', having been warned by Ribbentrop that it was simply a delaying tactic by the British. But when all had been explained Hitler's attitude changed and the two got on well, ending with wartime reminiscences, always the Führer's favourite topic of conversation.[32]

but no clear instructions. Eventually, on 4 October, some ten days after the Legion had received the initial request, it was told that a force of 1,200 men would be required to sail on 8 October, the size having been reduced because the War Office was now sending six battalions of infantry.

At the outset the Legion had been told not to make any announcement to members but simply to prepare plans, which had involved the staff working twenty hours out of every twenty-four. Now they had just three days to put those plans into operation. Recruitment was no problem; from the moment the newspapers reported a Legion involvement members began to volunteer and within forty-eight hours the total had reached 17,000. As soon as the go-ahead was received each Area was given a quota to fill. Metropolitan Area had little difficulty in filling its quota of fifty, which included drivers from the Taxi School, all chosen following interview by an Area Council panel; in other Areas men were summoned by a telegram or telephone call: 'You are selected for the Volunteer Force, report Olympia tomorrow 3pm.'

At Olympia the men were kitted out: blue serge suit, striped Legion tie and blue peaked cap bearing the Legion badge mounted on a crowned star. For a weapon they were given a stout ash plant and for welfare gifts of chocolate and cigarettes, organized by the Women's Section Chairman, together with personal messages from the King and Queen. They were then addressed by the National President: 'You are going out as referees – take with you the British spirit of fair play', and by the Force Commander, Major Fetherston-Godley, their National Chairman. But they also learned that their departure was delayed: they would now sail on 12 October.

On Saturday, 8 October, there was a route march through London headed by the band of the Welsh Guards, the intervening day providing time to solve the problem of how to carry the ash plant on parade. But among the rank and file were a number of former senior officers, including some generals who, unused to ammunition boots, had a hard time of it. On the Sunday there was of course a Church Parade.

The Force embarked on two troopships at Tilbury on the 12th, the old soldiers climbing the gangways with haversack slung over one shoulder, water bottle over the other and kitbag on top of all, and sailed within the hour. They were now on their way and excitement rose. But, two hours later, they dropped anchor off Southend and there they stayed for three days 'for final orders', filling in the time, as so often they had done in the past, with lectures, PT and, no doubt, the traditional 'housey-housey'. But when the orders came, they were to turn back and disembark: it had been decided by an International Commission in Berlin that the German-Czech border would not now be decided by plebiscite. Three days later the British Legion Volunteer Police had been disbanded, having existed for just ten days.

As the Force members returned to their homes, each with a letter of thanks signed by the Foreign Secretary, Czechoslavakia was dismembered to satisfy Hitler. It was the final act in the policy of 'appeasement', shown to be utterly worthless when, six months later, the Nazis occupied the whole country.

Although it had been a wasted exercise, the Volunteer Police saga had revealed something of the spirit of the Legion, as well as its organizing ability. How the veterans would have fared, caught up in the action of Hitler's ruthless policies, is a matter of conjecture. In the words of at least one member of the force as he grasped his newly-issued ash-plant, 'he would fight like hell for peace' and a Christmas card that year caught the mood: a drawing of a be-medalled and monocled veteran energetically striding out, his ash-plant at the shoulder. Perhaps an inkling of the German view, but perhaps

*Men of the Legion Volunteer Force about to board the train taking them to Tilbury for embarkation. The Metropolitan Police supplied the caps and greatcoats, the War Office the kitbags, haversacks and water bottles. While morale was clearly high, so was the age of many volunteers.*

intended as a deliberate 'put down', was an invitation issued by the Duke of Saxe-Coburg as soon as the Legion had been told to stand down: he invited the whole Force to visit Germany, an invitation the National Chairman regretfully refused as the men were already dispersing. Meanwhile the Chairman himself was writing to his Area, County and Branch Chairmen to rebut complaints that the membership had not been consulted in the decision to assist the government.

It is said that when the Polish question arose in the summer of 1939, someone sent a telegram to Hitler which read: 'Czech Police send hearty greetings. What about Poland?' to which the reply was 'Danzig corridor draughtier than Olympia'. But the authenticity of the story is open to question not so much as having been told at a Volunteer Police re-union dinner, but on attributing a sense of humour to the Führer.[33]

## Another Legion intitiative – CIP

In the meantime Legion pressure had led to FIDAC agreeing to a new body being formed specifically to work for peace, although, since the Germans had to be included, FIDAC itself kept at arm's length. CIP – the Comité Internationale Permanente – was formed in Rome in 1936 with Colonel Crosfield as Secretary. In February of 1937 it met in Berlin. 'Above everything,' Hitler told the committee, 'there was the recognition that a new conflict would have catastrophic consequences for all nations.' It was what the delegates wanted to hear and after the speeches, which included contributions from Goering and Hess, they crowded around Hitler in informal conversation with him, Crosfield reporting afterwards that they were unanimous in declaring that 'they were proud and happy to give him their hands in the inner certainty that both he and they willed that the years of the war should never come again'. Hitler chatted with the delegates for some time and when he eventually left he was spontaneously applauded. Crosfield later told Warrington Branch, of which he was president, that he found Hitler simple and charming and that all Germany wanted was 'a square deal, not war'.

CIP Congresses were held in Paris in 1937 and London in 1938. The international situation continued to deteriorate as Hitler pressed his demands ever further, but in CIP, in the words of a *Journal* report, 'the spirit of good fellowship' was 'steadily dissipating the dangerous fogs of ignorance, mistrust and suspicion'. By the middle of 1938, however, some were seeing through the good fellowship, Crosfield acknowledging that 'Ex-servicemen working internationally cannot of themselves maintain peace and prevent war; no one but a rabid lunatic would make such a claim.'

*Colonel Crosfield, the Legion's foreign affairs expert and a fluent German speaker, was CIP Secretary. Here he meets Hermann Goering.*

FIDAC's disowned offspring had nonetheless sidelined the parent. There were FIDAC Congresses each year with speeches urging settlement of differences by peaceful means, but the same message might have been heard at gatherings of postmen or plumbers in the late 1930s. On 3 September 1939 all was at an end; neither the ex-servicemen nor anyone else had been able to prevent war.

With the outbreak of hostilities the American Legion withdrew in order not to offend against United States neutrality and the 1939 Congress was cancelled. FIDAC Executive meetings continued in Paris where the headquarters organized relief for distressed Polish and Czech comrades, the last meeting being held in March 1940. A few weeks later France was over-run and FIDAC's existence had come to an end.

As for CIP, some time after Czechoslavakia had been seized in early 1939, the Legion received notice of an Executive Committee meeting in the Black Forest. The reply not only made clear the Legion's response to the invitation but wrote the finale to all the effort that had been made to preserve the peace: 'So long as the German government ignored solemn pledges in the way that they had done, further meetings of this international body would be futile and misleading.' Indeed they would, and CIP too went into limbo.[34]

### The lights go out

Both the Canadian and Australian ex-service organizations had been represented at the CIP Congresses. Peace was on the agenda too at the 1937 British Empire Services League Conference in London and there was a pledge to support every effort to secure it, short of any danger to the Empire itelf. But the 1939 BESL Conference was postponed and Canada and the rest of the Empire joined Britain in its declaration of war.

For the moment, however, the United States were neutral. Even so, a few days after the war broke out two members of the NEC, Colonel Crosfield being one, attended the American Legion Convention in Chicago. They found that, although the vast majority of Americans were sympathetic to Britain's cause, they were anxious not to be drawn in to the conflict and Legion branches in the United States were forbidden from holding public functions lest they be accused of propaganda. All this would change by the end of 1941 with the Japanese attack on Pearl Harbor, and even before that an American Legion delegation would visit England in February 1941 to make contact with the British Legion and survey its war work. In the meantime, if Crosfield needed reminding that all his work in the cause of peace had been set at naught, it was provided by the zig-zags of the returning ship to avoid U-boat attack.[35]

In August 1939, despite the fast deteriorating international situation, the Legion visited Paris; barely four weeks later Europe would be plunged into five years of war. A thousand Legionaries disembarked at Calais, chanting 'Here we are again' to the bemusement of the waiting French officials, the Legion flag streaming from the vessel's masthead. There were visits to Versailles and Fontainebleau and a banquet in the Invalides but the high point was a march down the Champs-Elysées led by the band of the Coldstream Guards, to the Arc de Triomphe to relight the flame on the Unknown Warrior's Tomb. The falling rain did not in any way affect the bearing of the Legionaries as they swung down the broad avenue eight abreast to the old familiar tunes between the crowds of Parisians, whose tension at the threat of approaching war seemed to be relieved by their enthusiasm for the marchers. So high was the standard of marching that a French general remarked, 'If these are the veterans, what are the young men like?'

It was almost as if they realized – and perhaps some of them did – that it was the end of an era. The 'Old Guard' of the Legion, the Great War men, were marching together for the last time in a great parade. The war which they had hoped and tried to prevent was coming and would change everything, not least the Legion itself.[36]

★     ★     ★

In the coming months and years some of the Legion's leaders were to feel that they and their great organization might be open to criticism over their dealings with Hitler, now clearly revealed as the megalomaniac that he had always been. Their speeches in wartime made much of the Führer's duplicity. Yet, if they had cause to reproach themselves, so did the politicians and not only those of Great Britain. All had acted in what they thought were the best interests of their fellow-countrymen. During the Second World War there were some discussions over a new federation of Allied ex-service organizations, but nothing was decided. Nor would the Legion again find itself at the centre of international affairs.[37]

# CHAPTER 7

## WOMEN'S SECTION 1921-1945

# *They Also Serve*

### 1921 – 1925

**A time of change**

The Great War was a watershed in the changing role of women in British society. The campaign to win votes for women, begun by Mrs Pankhurst in 1903, had failed to achieve its object by 1914. With the outbreak of war it was abandoned and women devoted their energies to the war effort. As the men responded to the demands of the front, women replaced them in the factories and offices. New industries were set up to supply the armies and much of the work was done by women. They drove trams and worked as farm labourers. Many went to France and elsewhere as nurses or ambulance drivers, sometimes within range of the enemy guns. The Women's Royal Naval Service was formed, the Women's Auxiliary Army Corps and later the Women's Royal Air Force. Meanwhile millions of mothers and wives of servicemen carried on with their daily tasks, praying for the safe return of their menfolk.

After the war most of the women employed in the offices and factories and in other men's work' returned home. The nurses came back from overseas and the Women's services were disbanded, while the widows and bereaved mothers were left with their memories. But the social consequences of the upheaval were great. Not only were women over thirty given the vote in July 1918* but many of the changes wrought by the war would remain: more roles would be open to them and social conventions less restrictive.

**A difficult start**

Nonetheless in most matters the women followed the men. The ex-service organizations founded during the war – the Federation, the Association, the Comrades and the Officers' Association – had all formed women's groups. As the organizations themselves pursued the path to unity, so too the women's groups came together. Only three weeks after the Legion's own official start date a conference of women of three of the organizations (the Association's women's representatives did not attend) was held at Legion headquarters on 24 July 1921. A provisional committee was formed and bye-laws drawn up for approval by the Legion's NEC. The question of membership was discussed. As well as women who had themselves served in uniform, the women's auxiliaries and the nursing services of the armed forces, other wartime women's organizations including the Voluntary Aid Detachment (a wartime function of the St John Ambulance and Red Cross), and the Land Army, it was agreed that wives and widows, mothers, sisters and daughters of servicemen were eligible.[1]

In October 1921 Princess Mary agreed to become Patroness of the Section. She was the only daughter of King George V and Queen Mary and sister to the Prince of Wales, who a few months previously had become Patron of the Legion. Aged twenty-four, she

*It was not until 1928 that women were granted equal voting rights with men.

was, like her brother, a popular choice – 'winsome and charming' as the *Legion Journal* put it. As a former VAD she was anyway qualified in her own right for membership of the Section. The following year she married Viscount Lascelles, later Earl of Harewood, and in 1932 she was given the title Princess Royal.[2]

The first President of the Women's Section was Countess Haig, but in 1923 Princess Alice was elected. A granddaughter of Queen Victoria, she was married to the Earl of Athlone. She was active in the Section and a popular figure despite the fact that her brother, who had become Duke of Saxe-Coburg, had fought on the German side in the Great War and had been stripped of his British title in 1919. He was to feature in Legion history in the 1930s as a leader of German ex-servicemen. (See page 158.)

The first Chairman was Lady Robertson, wife of Field Marshal Sir William Robertson, wartime Chief of the Imperial General Staff, notable for having risen from private soldier to his high office.[3]

A Women's Section Secretary was appointed – Miss Miller – and work began.[4] As with the Legion itself the Section did not have to start from scratch: it was a matter of bringing together the activities of the women's groups of the Legion's predecessors. There was initially some confusion over the title of the Section. Described by the women themselves as the 'Women's Section', the Legion's National Executive Council resolutely referred to it as the 'Women's Auxiliary Section', the expression used in the bye-laws. However, in 1923 the bye-law was amended, 'Auxiliary' dropped and henceforward the only title in use was 'Women's Section'. The title applied both to the organization as a whole and at local level where a 'Women's Section branch' was attached to the Legion branch, or 'men's branch' as the women sometimes called it.

All was going well until the Legion took a decision which might have threatened the Section's very existence. At the first Legion Conference over Whitsun 1922 the men decided to admit as full Legion members women who had served in the auxiliary branches of the armed forces during the war. This was an enlightened step, but since one of the principal reasons for the Women's Section was to provide ex-servicewomen with a national organization it had a direct bearing on the constitution of the Women's Section, due to be discussed at the Section's own conference in July 1922. The conference had to be postponed. Nevertheless the decision was warmly welcomed by the women's services Old Comrades Associations and at least one organization, the Women's Auxiliary Army Corps, urged its members to join their local Legion branch forthwith.[5]

Following this decision the NEC ruled that the Women's Section was for 'women other than those eligible for Ordinary Membership of the Legion', although it gave the ex-servicewomen who were also war widows or the dependants of ex-servicemen the option as to which organization they joined. At the postponed Women's conference, however, it was decided that Ordinary Membership of the Section would include ex-servicewomen as well as women dependants (which included war widows) and it would seem that in the event there was rather more flexibility for ex-servicewomen than the men had intended: they could join either organization, or both.

Despite the Conference vote some Legion branches refused to admit women as Ordinary Members and even banned the forming of a Women's Section branch alongside their own. In early 1923 the *Legion Journal* had to remind everyone of the amended constitution and later that year the Legion's Area Organizers were called in to help the women's branches to organize. They were needed in order to overcome such attitudes which were 'sadly lacking in that spirit of mutual friendship and co-operation which is absolutely essential to the well-being of both sides of the organization' according to the

*Legion Journal* of May 1924. The following year it was necessary for Earl Haig to write to the chairman of every Legion branch urging support for the Women's Section. Even so a significant number of Legion branches still did not want the women in their organization, some members no doubt regarding their branch or club as a 'safe haven' away from their womenfolk. Not to be outdone, the women were sometimes able to form their own clubs, the Women's Section of Plymouth Branch opening their club as early as 1921.[6]

It is hardly surprising in the circumstances that in the first two years membership of the Section was small. Although they enthusiastically took part in the Legion's 'Big Push' for members in early 1922 there were only about six women to every hundred Legion men. Moreover there was yet another problem to be overcome before the Section could be said to be properly established. In the meantime it was to win its first laurels.

## Women and the Poppy

In November 1921, only a few months after both the Legion itself and the Section had come into existence, the first Poppy Appeal took place. The full story of the Appeal is told in Chapter 5, but it is perhaps worth reminding ourselves that it was a woman who conceived the idea of the poppy as a Remembrance symbol (Miss Moina Michael, an American) and another woman who suggested to the Legion the fund-raising possibilities (Mme Guerin, from France).

There were many uncertainties about that first Appeal, but the support of the Women's Section was never in doubt: they took up the idea with immediate and unbounded enthusiasm. Where there were Women's Section branches the local Appeals Committee invariably included members of the Section and some local Women's Sections formed their own committees. The President herself set up the appeal in Windsor and other local appeals were run by sections as far apart as Cardiff, Croydon and Billericay, whilst the headquarters section organized six depots in London for the storage of poppies. But it was in the actual sale of the poppies themselves that the women carried the day and in most areas stocks had been exhausted by noon. There is little doubt that the effect on the public of using women poppy sellers greatly helped sales. Simply by their work to promote this first Poppy Day the Women's Section of the Legion had fully justified their formation.[7]

From that moment on the Section was fully committed to the Appeal, its members working tirelessly on the myriad preparations and sometimes rising before dawn on the morning itself to sell poppies for long hours in bitter weather. Preparation was certainly the key: writing on the 'Women's Page' of the *Legion Journal* in November 1924 the Section Chairman urged women to canvass shopkeepers to display Poppy Day bills, to ask hotels and restaurants to use Flanders Poppies for table decorations and to 'be in evidence' as sellers on the day itself; the public was sympathetic, but 'it will not go out of its way to discover sellers of poppies'.[8]

The Poppy Appeal had certainly struck a chord with the public. But, as the Chairman had pointed out, the poppies had to be on the streets. Had it not been for the Section's unstinting support for the Appeal, the Legion's capacity to do its work would have been much curtailed. It is therefore all the more unfortunate that, soon after that first Appeal, there was a serious split between the Legion and its more than willing helpmeet.

## The Section leaderless

Although the Women's Section's organizing body was the Central Committee, overall control was firmly in the hands of the Legion's National Executive Council: in November 1921 the Council's grant to the Section (of £200) had been 'subject to a satisfactory report being furnished to them by the General Secretary on the question of the organization of the Women's Section and their agreement to a system of general supervision by the GS and the NEC'. But there was no Women's Section representation on the Council itself and this may have sown the seeds of the problem that now arose.[9]

It concerned the Section's Secretary, Miss Miller. In August 1922 the Council informed the Section's Chairman of their view that the Secretary was quite unable to carry out her duties. At their two subsequent meetings in October and December 1922, following advice from the General Secretary, the Council ruled that the Section was to become a department of Legion headquarters and that no separate funds would be maintained. The Section would be financed through the Legion's General Fund.[10]

In the course of this episode Lady Robertson and the entire Women's Section Central Committee resigned. There is no record of why they took this extreme step. It may be that they objected to the way in which the problem was handled, or that the Secretary's activities simply reflected their own attitudes over a contentious issue such as responsibility for women's issues. It would, however, seem likely that the NEC 'takeover' in December 1922 was the direct result of the Central Committee's resignation rather than the other way round, since the Council would hardly have thrust the Central Committee aside in this way.

Whatever the cause it was a defining moment in the history of the Section. It had been in existence barely eighteen months. The hierarchy was distinguished: a princess as Patroness, Countess Haig as President, the wife of the former Chief of the Imperial General Staff the Chairman, together with an experienced Committee drawn from the former organizations. It had already won its first battle honour through its unhesitating and wholehearted support for the Poppy Appeal. Some local Legion attitudes apart, it could hardly have had a more promising start; yet now it was leaderless. What was to be its future?

## An uneasy first conference

In these circumstances the first Women's Section Annual Conference assembled at Caxton Hall, Westminster on 7 April 1923 in a somewhat uncertain atmosphere. The arrangements had been made by the Legion's General Secretary and the Legion's Chairman, Mr Lister, presided; the situation demanded both his authority and his tact. Also on the platform were Princess Alice, due to be President,* and Lady Edward Spencer Churchill, who was a candidate for Chairman, whilst Mrs Heath, the wife of the Legion's General Secretary, acted as secretary.

It was a testing occasion even for Lister's diplomatic skills. The delegates were all well aware that their founding committee had resigned and, as well as apologizing for the delay in setting up the conference, he had to refer to 'differences of opinion', although these were 'in the past'. He was, however, careful to pay tribute to the work of those who had set up the Section and in a clear attempt to placate his audience he appealed to them to 'show the men the way to do their duty' if they found them 'not to be as zealous as they should'. He went on to stress that the role of the Section was not simply social and to support the Legion on Poppy Day; he hoped that they would help to solve the problems of women affected by the war, especially the widows, and he wanted them to be more knowledgeable about the relief available.

*It seems likely that Lady Haig resigned as President when the original Central Committee left.

*'You will not make a great organization of this unless you bring your women in.' Earl Haig greeting the new Central Committee of the Women's Section at the Legion Whitsun Parade in 1923. This committee had replaced the original body after the 1922 dispute.*

In the circumstances it was a good effort: the Legion's Chairman had asked the Women's Section to become more directly involved in the work of the organization, thereby demonstrating his confidence in them. It must have helped to repair the breach, although it tends to suggest that it was the Section's role in these matters that had brought about the disagreement in the first place.

The conference then got down to business. Princess Alice was elected President and, out of two candidates for Chairman, Lady Edward Spencer Churchill was chosen, together with a new Central Committee of sixteen, of whom only one had served on the original committee. It was a completely new management team under a Chairman with no previous experience of managing the Section's affairs. That, however, was to prove to be no obstacle to Lady Edward.*

Significantly, the conference resolved that the NEC should have guidance on matters affecting women: a Consultative Committee consisting of three NEC members and three Women's Section members would be established. The NEC subsequently appointed its Chairman, Vice Chairman and Treasurer as its representatives so that it must be inferred that the resolution did not come as a complete surprise to them and was probably a way

*She was Winston Churchill's great aunt by marriage.

169

of getting around the 'difference of opinion' that had arisen. The proceedings concluded with an address by Lord Haig.

The Women's Section was once again a going concern, in charge of its own destiny, at least up to a point.[11]

### A new impetus

Not only had there been a trauma in the relationships at the top but there were also widely-held misconceptions to be overcome at all levels in the Legion if the Women's Section was to be able to play its proper part in the organization. The task could hardly have been more daunting – but the hour had produced the man – or in this case the woman: under Lady Edward Spencer Churchill's vigorous leadership the Central Committee set to work to get matters on to a sound footing. Committee representatives travelled all over the country addressing Legion Area, County and Group meetings to persuade the men of the value of women's involvement in the Legion, a task that must by no means have been easy. A new Secretary, Miss Niven Gerds, was found, but lack of funds precluded Women's Section Area Organizers. A single Organizer therefore toured the whole country.[12]

The emphasis was on expansion and in 1924 Mr Lister appealed to Legion branches to form Women's Sections within three months, where they did not already exist. During the course of 1924 the number of branches in the Section increased from 165 to 251. By the end of the following year the figure was 419, including for the first time branches in Northern Ireland. Undoubtedly there was a fresh spirit abroad and Lady Edward seems to have had considerable influence with the Legion's leadership, enlisting the personal support of Earl Haig or Mr Lister when she needed it. When a trophy was needed to encourage efficiency in Women's Section branches Lister at first proposed to share the Haig Cup between men's and women's branches for six months each; but Earl Haig felt it expedient to present a new trophy for the Section.[13]

### A new partnership

In early 1924 Princess Alice had to resign as President when her husband, the Earl of Athlone, was appointed Governor General of South Africa. Her place was taken by the Duchess of York, then aged twenty-four, who was to become Queen Elizabeth when her husband ascended the throne as George VI following the abdication crisis.

The second Section Annual Conference in 1924 was a rather more relaxed occasion than the first. It took place at the Royal Society of Arts in London's Adelphi and Lady Edward was able to tell delegates that 'speaking generally' there was great harmony between Legion branches and the Women's Section. The Legion's Chairman, Mr Lister, echoed the spirit of co-operation when he said that 'Today no movement and no organization which had not got a strong Women's Section could hope to be thoroughly flourishing.' Unfortunately neither the Patroness, Princess Mary, nor the new President were able to be present; they would have heard businesslike discussions showing that the position of the Section within the Legion was now firmly established, no mere adjunct of the men's organization but an active participant in its work.[14]

The growth of the Section meant that the 1925 Conference needed larger premises: the King's Hall of the Holborn Restaurant in London. The Patroness, Princess Mary, attended the conference for the first time, facing an audience, resplendent in hats of every description gleaming under the light of an enormous chandelier, who gave her 'prolonged and rapturous applause'. This conference was much concerned with Legion policy matters affecting women, an indication of the new approach to the partnership between the Section and the Legion itself.[15]

Funding was always a topic, the Section having started life with a bare cupboard. The account was maintained by the Legion but the women were expected to be self-sufficient as far as possible. Yet the Section only received 3d per member per year in Affiliation Fees and with eight thousand members that represented an annual income of £100 per year in total. Theatre matinees, where the attendance of the Patroness could be guaranteed to fill seats, were a useful source of fundraising but did not solve the problem and in 1925 the Legion's Treasurer, Major Brunel Cohen, had to tell the Section that their budget did not balance: the NEC had had to make a grant of £1,000 and either affiliation fees would have to be increased or money raised in other ways. The 'ways and means' discussion which ensued brought the comment that 'it took them all their time to keep the men's section going'.[16]

### The Women's role

Far from being mesmerised by its domestic difficulties, the Section had been active from the start, in its first few weeks drawing up a maternity scheme for ex-servicewomen at Islington Maternity Home and seeking assistance from the United Services Fund for ex-servicewomen whose health had suffered as a result of the war. Even during the 'interregnum' it had run a stall at the Women's Exhibition at Olympia in July 1922 advertising the Legion's work for the welfare of the ex-service community.[17] It had also been concerned with women's issues in a wider context, helping to inaugurate the Consultative Committee of Women's Organizations in which over sixty women's organizations were involved and whose object was to promote the political, economic and social interests of women. Already, with over ten thousand members the Legion's Women's Section was one of the largest participants.

Now, with domestic problems behind it, the organization began to consider its role. There were fundamental issues to be resolved: clearly the women had a supportive task within the Legion itself and had already demonstrated their ability in that respect by the magnificent assistance given to the Poppy Appeal. But what was its function in relation to women and their sufferings as a result of the Great War? The care of dependants was at the heart of the Legion's own welfare operations and the direct responsibility of the Relief and Pensions Departments. Was the Section simply to provide support wherever and whenever the main organization called on it to do so? Or was it to take the lead in matters affecting women? There can be little doubt that these considerations must have exercised many of the Legion's leaders, as well as Lady Edward Spencer Churchill and her committee, and in many ways reflected the world outside where the emancipation of women was increasingly drawing them into the management of their own affairs.

Attitudes had a part to play. Much of the Legion, particularly at the grass roots level, wanted the women 'in their proper place'. Indeed, as we have seen, some did not want them at all. But the women had their views too and expressed them. At the top both the Legion's President and Chairman seem to have been sympathetic to the women's aspirations and in the event the Section began to develop its own initiatives on certain women's matters, Lady Edward delicately picking her way through the minefield of existing Legion policies.

171

The first concern, as with the Legion itself, was unemployment. As the post-war recession deepened, the number of women on the Unemployment Register, most of whom were dependants of ex-servicemen, rose. The industrial work which they had done in the war was closed to them since that would have put them in competition with the ex-servicemen themselves; instead government policy was to train women in domestic work. The Section pressed not only for more expenditure on such training but for other opportunities to be provided. As a result the Minister added nursing and office work to the programme and the Women's Section Organizer, visiting one centre in 1925, found that the trainees had 'a natural pleasure that comes to any average person, who, after a long spell of apparent failure, finds an outlet for energy and intelligence, and begins to acquire a market value in the world'.[18] Encouraged by such experiences, the Section would appoint its own Employment Officer in 1928.

Many war widows were driven out to work because the pension arrangements were inadequate. The fact that they were destitute because of their husbands' service to their country was seen by the Women's Section as 'a blot on our national honour'. Accordingly they drafted a Bill to put to Parliament which would provide for the maintenance of such families through a weekly pension. Although it failed to get a reading the government itself unexpectedly introduced a Bill in 1925 dealing with widows' pensions in general. Unfortunately the scheme did not cover the self-employed so that many widows did not qualify. The ladies stuck doggedly to their point: all ex-service widows and their children should be included and an amendment was tabled by the Legion's Vice Chairman, an MP. It failed by eighty-one votes, but it had been well supported by MPs from constituencies where the Women's Section had branches.[19]

Nor did the women hold back at local level in the relief of distress. Since the Section was a constituent part of the Legion they were not formally represented on the district United Service Fund committees, but they could, and did, fill some of the Legion's places. In the case of the Legion Relief Fund not only were Section members eligible to sit on local Legion Relief Committees but the fund's governing body, the Central Relief Committee, included two members of the Women's Section. All of this was of course eminently sensible since many of the cases appearing before the local USF benevolent committee either directly or indirectly involved women.[20]

Yet more involvement of the Section in welfare matters came with the introduction by the Ministry of Pensions in 1924 of War Pensions Advisory Councils. There were six such councils in England and Wales and their task was to advise on the working of the War Pensions scheme in the local area. Of the five Legion representatives on each, one was from the Women's Section, representing the widows and dependants.[21]

## 'Pearls without price'

At branch level members assisted with the functioning of the War Pensions scheme by giving out information, interviewing and helping with applications, and making investigations. But Women's Section branches found many other ways of giving practical help to the ex-service community. Swansea succeeded in moving ten families from the workhouse to Corporation housing, as well finding suitable homes for six orphans from the same workhouse. Hampstead, on behalf of the Mayor, ran a soup canteen for the unemployed, feeding nearly three hundred a day. Wooton-Under-Edge in 1924 managed to place fifteen women in employment as well as providing nurses and equipment for maternity cases and boots and clothing to distressed families. And an appeal to all branches provided the TB patients at the Legion's village settlement at Preston Hall with 'wireless' headphones.[22]

Women's Section branches were given advice on what activities to undertake. High among these were to assist ex-servicemen and dependants who were in need, making clothes and running crèches for the benefit of mothers who went out to work. Education was considered important: lectures on the Empire and questions arising out of the use of the vote (which, as noted, had only recently been granted to women). There was an inter-branch needlework competition with national finals calling for skills which ranged from a properly darned sock to embroidering a Legion Standard, and a singing competition for choirs. In 1925 competitions were expanded to include handicrafts and home produce. As the Women's Page of the *Legion Journal* noted such events not only brought members together in a common interest but made the family income go further: an accomplished housewife was 'a pearl without price to the harassed head of a household'. And of course such skills could be used to help relieve distress in others.[23]

1926 – 1930

## A time of growth

In his address to the Annual Conference of the British Legion in 1926 the Prince of Wales made special reference to 'those who have worked up the Women's Section of the Legion so magnificently. That Section has made a great advance this year.' 1926 was indeed a notable year of progress for the Section: an increase of over 100 branches meant there was now one to every five Legion branches and the total was over 500; and an Area structure had been introduced, conforming to the Legion's own Area boundaries, except that there were no Irish Areas since the Section did not have branches there.

There were thus to be eleven Women's Section Areas, each represented on the Central Committee. The development of the scheme, however, depended on money, still in short supply in the Section, and although the Affiliation Fee was to be increased from 3d to 4d this would not allow for the establishment of Area Councils or for the further division of the Area for organizational purposes. But the women were given more control over their finances with a further staff appointment, although the Legion's General Treasurer would still supervise.[24]

From 1927 the Area Conferences elected the Central Committee representatives. The same year the first Women's Section branches were formed in the Irish Free State; these seventeen new branches lost no time in setting up their own Area Conference so that by 1928 there were twelve Women's Section Area Conferences, most meeting on the same day and at the same place as the Legion Area Conference, so that, as well as simplifying the arrangements, the women could sit in on the men's meetings.

1927 also saw South West Area overcome the shortage of funds and form the first Area Council. By 1930 there were six Area Councils in being, but administration, or rather the cost of it, was a problem: the Council could not be paid for out of the one penny per member that was the Area's share of the increased Affiliation Fee; for an Area Council to be formed each branch had to find one pound a year. Most branches were nonetheless agreed that it was a help to have an Area Council; their local difficulties could be understood and represented to the distant headquarters in London, and they were able to obtain local help and advice, particularly if, as was usually the case, the Council based itself on the corresponding Legion Area headquarters. And since a county structure was also too costly it was decided to have an annual cycle of meetings within Areas based on large towns such as Birmingham and Portsmouth. The meetings passed out information and advice and more than two-thirds of the branches invited to each meeting actually turned up.

The enthusiasm generated by all this activity resulted in an astonishing growth: over the five years up to 1930 an average of nearly 150 new branches formed each year with, in the autumn of 1928, forty branches being formed in a single month. Well might the Section's unstoppable Chairman, Lady Edward Spencer Churchill, mark the occasion of the formation of the Section's 1,000th branch by giving a dinner party for the Central Committee in October 1929; needless to say, the menu came straight out of the Women's Section Cookery Book, *Popular Home, Dominion and Allied Dishes.* The Legion's National Executive Council, meanwhile, remained anxious for the women's welfare, in April 1928 deciding 'that a letter be addressed to the Central Committee of the Section indicating the inadvisability of meetings of branches of the Section being held in licensed premises whether club or otherwise'.[25]

## But who has the final say?

The Section's forward momentum was, however, to receive a check from an unexpected quarter. Although most of the initiative for the growth of the Section had come from the women themselves, Legion Presidents and Chairmen had given strong support, impressing on the 'men's' Areas, Counties and branches that there should be a Women's Section branch for every Legion branch and that they should do their utmost to bring this about. No doubt a number of Legion branches heeded the call, while others were still opposed; but there was male consensus in at least one respect: the relationship between the Legion branch and its Women's Section.

At the 1930 Annual Conference of the Legion the men passed a resolution to the effect that the NEC should clearly state that the Women's Section branches were under the jurisdiction of the Legion branches; in other words the men had the final say in their activities. This, equally clearly, was not the way the women saw it. The tensions started to build up. Following the conference therefore the joint Consultative Committee, set up in 1923 as a result of the difficulties between the NEC and the first Central Committee, was resurrected; as before, it was made up of the Chairman and two principal officers on each side. The discussions cannot have been altogether easy, but the outcome required the Women's Section branches to clear beforehand with the local Legion branch any activity involving the general public, or for it to be run as a joint enterprise, and there should be local Consultative Committees to prevent misunderstandings. This was not an easy pill to swallow; the women needed to raise money because of the state of their finances and the rule could curb their fundraising. There was a loss of esteem in having to seek approval for their own activities from the men at a time when women were beginning to make a little headway in improving their status. The Section was undoubtedly shaken by the episode and the slow growth the following year was ascribed to 'uncertainty', implying a certain loss of confidence.[26]

The pot was stirred further when the Legion's South Eastern Area Chairman expressed the view that Women's Section members should not be allowed to march with the Legion. His reasoning was that the Section was not in the main made up of those who had served but of civilian followers. These remarks reached the press and gave rise to some correspondence in the *Journal*. But the women themselves maintained a dignified silence.[27]

## The Annual Conferences

As the Section grew in size, the Annual Conference attendance increased from some 200 delegates in 1926 to nearly 500 in 1930. The general enthusiasm was reflected in the number of visitors – the 1930 conference attracted 1,500. Ever bigger halls were needed and the venue, always in central London, had constantly to be changed. Central Hall, Westminster, used in 1928 and 1929, was particularly convenient for the service at St Margaret's (see below) but the 1930 conference had to be held at the Kingsway Hall, some distance away at the far end of the Strand. There was always a Royal presence, normally the Patroness, the young Princess Mary, but in 1928 her place was taken by the Duchess of York, the President since 1924, making her first appearance at conference; she was introduced as 'the mother of the sweetest and most delightful baby' (the Princess Elizabeth, then aged two) and was 'heartily cheered'. The Royal involvement was confined to the presentation of awards and, unlike Legion conferences, there was no formal address. The Legion's Treasurer, Major Brunel Cohen, presented the accounts. Although the women were better at paying their annual branch Affiliation Fee than the men, it was a great deal smaller, the majority of members having little 'disposable income' and the finances continued to be precarious, depending to an extent on voluntary donations from branches. However, the decision to hand over to the Women's Section part of the profits of the 1930 Empire Fair and Ball (see pages 130-1) recognized their contribution to the the event and added a much-needed £1,000 to the funds.

Resolutions covered the whole range of Legion activity, the women having no inhibitions about giving the National Executive Council the benefit of their advice, especially where family matters or, a particular interest, such as the welfare of war orphans, was concerned. The 1928 conference heard some harrowing accounts of the situation in Southern Ireland and made a very clear recommendation to the NEC on this issue, while the interest in benevolent matters led to the introduction of a 'Half-Day School' at the 1930 Conference at which Legion experts spoke on welfare and pensions work.

The 1926 Conference saw the introduction of a special service at St Margaret's Westminster, during which new branch standards were consecrated, carried to the altar by their cloche-hatted bearers, some themselves be-medalled. It was a simple, dignified and moving occasion on which the women remembered the war dead: sons, husbands, fathers – and in some cases their own comrades, for nurses had perished at the front or been torpedoed at sea – and following the service wreaths were laid at the Tomb of the Unknown Warrior in the adjacent Abbey. As the number of conference delegates grew so too did the size of the congregation until in 1930 the church was packed to its limits and some thought was given to holding the service in the Abbey itself. By now a National Standard added to the dignity of the occasion, having been presented by Princess Mary in 1928.

Following the service there was a dinner for the conference delegates, also introduced in 1926. This was held at the Lyons Corner House in Coventry Street just off Leicester Square and was a popular event for those who could afford the five shillings cost, in 1928 some 600 people. It was an occasion not only for speech-making but also provided the opportunity for the winners of the Section singing competitions to show off their talents, after which the singing appears to have become more general. The speeches too tended to be light-hearted in tone, the Chairman, Lady Edward Spencer Churchill, concluding her address in 1929 with the exhortation:

'Plan for more than you can do and do it,
Bite off more than you can chew and chew it.
Hitch your wagon to a star,
Take your seat and there you are.
Go to it!'

The words of the popular song of the time might have been written for her.[28]

## Concern for young people

The branches were certainly prepared to 'go to it'. Their work at this time was highly practical. They provided clothes and boots for those taking up work, ensured that the families emigrating to Canada under the Legion group scheme (see pages 90–1) were properly equipped on departure and helped ex-servicewomen and dependants to get jobs, a difficult task at this time of rising unemployment when such office posts that came up were rapidly filled by the younger women leaving the training colleges. Domestic work was available but the need was for living-in staff, whereas most of the ex-service wives and widows could only leave their families for daytime working. For those less committed and seeking a new life the Section set up a Migration Hostel in Newcastle to train them for domestic posts in the Dominions.

There was much concern for young people. Women's Section members were co-opted onto the Legion's After-Care Advisory Committees for the war orphans, now reaching the age when they needed parental guidance. Guide companies were formed by some branches following an agreement with the Girl Guides Association. Others helped with the government employment schemes for adolescents, seeking accommodation for boys and girls from depressed areas who had been found work elsewhere. Most were away from their homes for the first time and the branches helped them to settle into their new surroundings, giving particular attention to the children of ex-service families.

By the end of the decade around a hundred branches each year had become involved too in a scheme to provide country holidays for children from the inner cities: the Women's Section branch at the 'sending' end made up the party of children, with those whose fathers were disabled or deceased being given priority, and the 'receiving' branch in the country or at the seaside provided the accommodation, usually free of charge, and organized the holiday. The cost was therefore limited to the rail fares and these were often met by a special fundraising effort or by donations from branches not directly involved.[29]

The growth of the Section and the generally buoyant mood among the women, at least until the issue of the men's 'final say' arose, undoubtedly contributed to the 50 per cent increase in the Poppy Appeal in the last five years of the decade; as ever they threw themselves into the work of helping to set up centres for the distribution of poppies and to organize teams of collectors to take their trays on to the streets and to make the house to house calls. They sometimes needed a sense of humour: calling at a distant farm one Section member was told 'not this year' by the farmer's wife; her immediate response was to ask, 'May I book you for next year?'[30]

The Section also needed to look to its own finances. The Legion's NEC continued to provide an annual subsidy, normally £1000, but the Women's Section headquarters had to find the rest, which was usually of the order of £500 – £1000, running ventures such as a 'monster whist drive' in the winter of 1927 – 1928 which showed a useful profit of £512 and the Cookbook venture of 1929 which, as well as giving some rather doubtful 'Empire' recipes, included popular 'allied' dishes; happily, whatever their battlefield performance, the allied nations knew their food and their recipes could compete with Walton-on-Thames' Green Tomato Chutney.[31]

# 1931 – 1935

## A common bond

The previous decade had ended with a dispute with the men over the control of the Section's activities. Nevertheless, whatever they might have said among themselves, and no doubt a great deal was said, there had been an agreement and the Section stuck to it. A positive outcome was the encouragement to form a Consultative Committee at every level in order to bring the men's and women's organizations closer together; however, while these certainly operated nationally and at Area level, they were probably rather less common in branches, although there was likely to have been more informal consultation than before.

Now the Section moved forward again. Over the next five years 400 new branches were formed, bringing the total to over 1,550, so that now there was one Women's Section branch to every two and a half Legion branches. The women were catching up and in parallel with the expansion more thought had to be given to the field organization. There were now thirteen Areas but lack of funding meant that only six had an Area Committee. The money was found after an attempt to run Legion and Women's Section Areas with joint committees had proved unsuccessful and Women's Area Committees were established in all Areas except Ireland by 1935. The Irish branches were, however, enthusiastic attenders at the informal meetings which headquarters continued to organize, with teams visiting various parts of the country to inform and advise branches.

An article in the *Legion Journal* in 1934 wondered why so many women, who had little else in common, had joined the Section. It decided that for women as well as men 1914 to 1918 had been nightmare years compared with the graciousness of an earlier time and that the experience of those years had forged a common bond that the Women's Section of the Legion, with its emphasis on helping those who had suffered as a result of that war, represented. In any case the women felt that in many ways they were better equipped than the men to deal with the distress that the war had left in its wake. But Lady Edward Spencer Churchill was by no means satisfied with the size of the membership: in 1935 she noted that the majority of women who had served in the war had not joined and that only one third of those women who sold poppies were members.

The Section now had more prominence. The Legion's Tenth Anniversary in 1931 had been strongly supported with the women much in evidence at the rallies around the country; at the largest, at Newmarket, they had been cheered by the men as they marched their standards across the ground; in November of the same year one of the eight ex-service columns at the Cenotaph was composed entirely of women, while in 1932 the

*By the 1930s the Women's Section was achieving more prominence. The picture shows the Standard Bearers arriving for the Annual Service at St Anne's Westminster in 1934.*

Women's Section standards were for the first time paraded at the Festival of Remembrance at the Albert Hall. During the summer of 1931 parties of American mothers who had lost sons in the War, known as the Gold Star Mothers of America, came to England. They were met by members of the Section, a party of twelve coloured women being especially touched by the kindness of their reception. The Women's Section ran its own Pilgrimage to the battlefields of France and Flanders in 1935, when the mothers and widows of the dead scattered ashes of the crosses from the Westminster Abbey Field of Remembrance on the graves of Vlamertinghe Military Cemetery.[32]

## From strength to strength

The 1934 Section Annual Conference was held for the first time at the Queen's Hall where the Legion itself held its Annual Conference when in London. The change underlined not only the growing strength of the Women's Section but also its motivation which in terms of conference attendance far exceeded that of the men: a comparison of the figures for the 1930s shows that the proportion of women's branches sending delegates was almost double that of the men's branches (see Tables B and E at pages 431 and 439). Apart from the change of hall, however, the pattern was now established: the conference began with the entry of the standards – 100 in 1931, over twice that number five years later – followed by the marching on of the Union Jack to the tune of 'Rule Britannia'. After the Tribute to the Fallen and the Exhortation the gathering sang Rudyard Kipling's 'Recessional' before getting down to business. The same evening delegates gathered with the standards at St Margaret's Westminster for a Service of Dedication, at the end of which the Central Committee moved across to the adjacent Abbey where a poppy wreath was laid at the Tomb of the Unknown Warrior. The mood changed for the next item, the Conference Dinner which, despite the inevitable speech-making, seems to have been a highly popular event since the attendance grew steadily each year, exceeding 1,000 by 1934. At the half-day school on the second day Legion experts spoke about benevolence, the Poppy Appeal or the work of FIDAC, although in 1932 the rather more controversial subject of 'Relationship between the British Legion and the Women's Section' was unflinchingly delivered by Mr Griffin, the Legion's Organizing and Assistant Secretary, his words being received 'with the greatest attention'.

In the spirit of the times there was an international flavour: leaders of sister organizations in Poland, Serbia, Czechoslovakia and France, all wartime allies, attended and addressed delegates; but Colonel Crosfield's suggestion at the half-day school in 1932 that, in the interest of world peace, the Section should get in touch with women's organizations in Germany and Austria does not seem to have been taken up. Lady Edward may have had her own views on the matter.

Of the two royal officers, in the 1920s the Patron, the Princess Royal, had been the more regular visitor to Conference. But in the early 1930s the Duchess of York, the President since 1924, was able to devote more time to the Section and attended four out of the five conferences in the period. She also made some changes: hitherto the Royal

*The Duchess of York, as Women's Section President, about to distribute awards at the 1933 Conference; she would hold this office into the next century. On the right is Lady Edward Spencer Churchill, the dynamic Chairman of the Section, who had rebuilt it after its early difficulties.*

*At five shillings a head Conference dinners were popular and here delegates and guests pose for the camera at Lyons' Corner House in 1934. Lady Edward Spencer Churchill is standing behind the microphone at the top table.*

visitor had merely presented the annual awards and her only words to delegates had been to express her thanks for their welcome; but the Duchess of York, beginning in 1931 with a brief address, was by 1935 comprehensively reviewing the work of the Section before presenting the trophies. No doubt the Section's Chairman had a hand in this but the President's interest in their activities was much appreciated by the delegates who were moved by the Duchess's 1935 speech to rise and sing 'Land of Hope and Glory' at the end.

Another office was added to the Section in 1935 when Lady Haig returned as Deputy

President. Her work with the Poppy Appeal, of which she was now Patroness, had brought her back into close contact with the Women's Section and in accepting the office she reminded the audience of Haig's words: 'You will not make a great organization of this unless you bring your women in.' The remark went down well.

At the same conference, congratulating Lady Edward Spencer Churchill on a recent honour, the Section's Vice Chairman had remarked that their Chairman was not only a CBE but the mother of the whole Section. The comment was apt: the Chairman had now been in office for twelve years and had overseen not only the rebirth of the Women's Section but its growth to maturity, encouraging its every step.[33]

## Burnham Hall

On the Sunday following the 1935 Conference about 300 delegates set off early in the morning to visit Burnham Hall near Hunstanton in Norfolk, driving through villages gay in red, white and blue for the following day's Royal Silver Jubilee celebrations. The hall had been given to the Legion in 1932 and passed on to the Women's Section for use as a training centre for women of the ex-service community. The Section's particular concern was for women who needed an income but found their previous work no longer available to them, often because they were now middle-aged. The only openings at the time were in domestic service and the aim was therefore to qualify such women in cooking, laundry, dressmaking and other domestic activities. In many cases their health had suffered as a result of anxiety or inadequate nourishment and it was first necessary to restore their vigour. When, however, Burnham Hall opened its doors in June 1933 it was found that the state of the women's health was even worse than had been anticipated, so that extra time had to be given to recuperation.

The following year forty-three women were in residence. The average training time was six months and the courses had been well planned: the majority found good residential posts on leaving, as cook-housekeepers or in similar work while those with children were able to use their new skills at daily employment or by working at home as dressmakers. By the time the delegates from the 1935 Conference made their visit, however, the character of the centre had changed somewhat: that year there were seventy-six residents but over a third were there purely for convalescence and the facilities had been extended to meet this need. Funding was already a problem. Although the Legion Benevolent Fund had made a grant each year and the Women's Section branches contributed through donations, it was a struggle to make ends meet and strict economy had to be exercised in administration. Nonetheless the visiting delegates found it a pleasant place, a 200 year-old mansion with spacious rooms, set in five acres of parkland.[34]

## The bleak mid-winter – and summer holidays

If the only vacancies for women were in domestic service, the situation for the men was hardly less grim. There were still some jobs to be had, but a problem for those starting work, or even attending an interview, was suitable clothing. Those still workless, and their families, were equally ill-clad, especially in winter; by some irony the areas hardest hit by unemployment were generally those with the bleakest climate. The Legion maintained a clothing store at the poppy warehouse near King's Cross Station and half of the supplies came from Women's Section branches. These were mainly cast-off garments, but in 1931, as the depression was reaching its height, the Section introduced a 'wardrobe scheme'. Branches joining the scheme undertook to supply a certain number of new garments each

*Women's Section Children's Holiday Schemes. Above: a group of children about to leave Paddington Station for Wenvoe, the Legion Training Centre, which the Section used for holiday schemes. Note the Legion flag on each carriage window; but presumably the 'smoking' signs gave the occupants no licence on this occasion.*
*Left: after a bathe at Barry Island, South Wales, the children look happy, although the young woman at the tailgate seems a little stressed.*

year based on the branch strength. The Section took over part of the warehouse and Metropolitan Area branches redistributed the clothing via Legion and Women's Section branches in needy areas. By 1933 over 300 branches were contributing to the scheme and two-thirds of the 30,000 items were new. Most of the donor branches were in East Anglian Area and the south of England but there were some in the North Eastern Area and Wales. The wardrobe scheme continued to grow and by 1935 fully one third of the Section's branches were actively involved.

Children were also clothed for the annual holiday scheme; indeed many of the children could not have gone on holiday without complete re-clothing and a set of spare garments. This scheme had grown with those branches not directly involved helping meet the expenses. The children came mainly from the inner-city branches and were hosted by those on the coast; but in the North East, in order to save travel costs, the Area Committee ran holiday camps while Burnham Hall and the Legion centre at Wenvoe in Wales also provided cheap accommodation. By 1935 some 1,500 childen were benefiting each year. Many returned home with gifts for their families:

flowers, fruit, eggs, even a live rabbit, complete with hutch. But the scheme needed much co-ordination by headquarters, who even ensured that each child was medically examined before leaving home to avoid any risk of infection being spread.[35]

## Soup canteens and sewing bees

As if these schemes were not enough, the branches had plenty of other activities. The Legion's National Executive Council may not have thought so: they passed a resolution in December 1932 urging the Women's Central Committee to turn the attention of their branches to pickling, jam making, fruit bottling and other rural pursuits 'likely to be advantageous to the families of men who through lack of opportunity elsewhere take up work on the land'. What the Central Committee made of this is not recorded but they responded strongly to the Prince of Wales's Appeal made at about the same time for the Legion to go beyond its ex-service boundaries and assist the unemployed generally (see pages 99–100). Branches set up centres where women could 'make and mend' clothes in a social atmosphere, provided canteens and collected money to supply needy families with coal, milk and groceries, as well as to buy seeds and tools for allotments; Newquay raised the money to rent a recreation hall for use by the unemployed men, supplying them with teas and clothing; Gerrards Cross Section helped the Legion branch to set up an allotment scheme and the soup kitchen organized by Slough Women's Section branch was visited by the Prince himself, who, on being invited to peel potatoes, somewhat to the ladies' surprise proved to be very competent.

The Prince's Appeal was a special challenge. But the average Section branch was anyway busy and its activities might have included opening a shop for a week to promote the sale of disabled men's goods, running an employment agency, organizing jointly with the Legion branch a village fair in aid of the branch building fund, setting up and running a sale at the town hall, collecting and issuing maternity sets, organizing a Christmas treat for the local children and perhaps a tea party and outing in the summer, running whist drives and dances to raise funds. Branches in the more prosperous areas would adopt a branch in a poorer region of the country, organize special fundraising events and send off monthly parcels. And no doubt some may have taken up the NEC's suggestion to make jam and bottle fruit, if they had not already thought of it.[36]

Over the period the Section managed to balance its accounts, although it was still dependent on an annual grant of £1,000 from the NEC. The growth in the number of branches, together with an increase in the individual member's annual affiliation fee from fourpence to sixpence, now gave it more income and strict economies were practised; although the high level of activity meant a great deal more work for the small staff the amount spent on salaries actually decreased a little. Prudence was the order of the day.[37]

# 1936 – 1940

## The approach of war

Writing in the *Legion Journal* in 1936, Vera Brittain was critical of women's attitudes to the prevention of war: 'The persecutions of Hitler in Germany, the aggressions of Mussolini in Abbysinia, leave her unmoved in comparison with the discovery of a new recipe for tomato salad.' Vera Brittain was perhaps a little too judgemental; in her case the Great War had been a defining experience and she was to become a convinced pacifist.

But the Legion Women's Section seemed less convinced than their male counterparts that the dictators could be diverted from their ambitions by ex-servicemen, or anyone else for that matter. They simply got on with their work.

The need to march in step with the Legion sometimes caused problems. When Legion Areas were reduced in the late 1930s from thirteen to nine, the Section had to conform; however, the Legion was only able to do this because it had by now developed a County structure. The Section had no choice but to institute County Committees, despite the extra cost; but the changes helped to promote still further expansion and by 1940 there were over 1,800 Women's Section branches, an increase of nearly 20 per cent in five years and approaching a ratio of one to every two men's branches.

One thing that both sides had in common was the feeling of dismay at the abdication in 1937 of King Edward VIII, so long and so closely associated with the Legion. But for the Women's Section the accession of a George VI brought about a curious situation. Their President, the Duchess of York, was now Queen and clearly 'outranked' their Patron, still the Princess Royal. But the Queen was quite content to carry on as President, despite her new role and her many new duties and, in effect, the Patron acted as her relief, attending an Annual Conference when the President could not be present.

With the approach of war the members began to be drawn towards what was then defined as 'national service'. They were encouraged to support the Women's Voluntary Services which had been inaugurated in 1938 to support Civil Defence and which linked up women's organizations with local authorities, and they did so either on an individual or a branch basis, nursing, cooking or looking after refugees. Other members joined the Land Army, the Red Cross, National Savings or one of the women's auxiliaries to the armed forces. But this generous response had an effect when the war came: so many officials were on war work that a number of branches had difficulty in carrying on. Nonetheless over a hundred branches were able to set up depots for the Central Hospital Supply Scheme, making garments and all manner of hospital supplies.

Financial stability was at last achieved in 1937 when the Affiliation Fees, paid by branches on the basis of their membership, were doubled from 6d a head to one shilling. The increases took time to work through the system but by 1938 its annual NEC grant of £1,000 could be used to fund a scheme of weekly allowances for widows. In 1940 the Legion's Treasurer, Brunel Cohen, was able to congratulate the Section on the 'really excellent' state of their finances, gallantly forbearing to mention that he had been urging them to pay a realistic subscription rate for more years than he or they cared to remember.[38]

## A tumult of cheering

The acceptance of a much greater Affiliation Fee was a sign of the Section's maturity. The women's interest and a pride in their organization was manifest in the Annual Conference attendance which by 1938 attracted nearly 1,000 delegates with twice that number of visitors. The Queen's Hall in Langham Place was now the regular venue and in every year in the period except 1937, the year of the Coronation, the standards were paraded at St Paul's Cathedral, an impressive and colourful background to the memorial service, a standard at the end of every row, 250 in all.

Only in the Coronation year was there no Royal presence. Conference that year took place in a London gay with bunting and the massive attendance the following year no doubt owed not a little to their President's attendance for the first time as their Queen.

The welcome given to her as she entered the conference hall was unprecedented even in an organization which showed as much loyalty to the Crown as the Legion: there was a tumult of cheering from every level of the packed assembly. The Queen then spent no less than an hour receiving purses which had been donated to the Burnham Hall fund, personally thanking and shaking hands with every purse bearer and pausing to examine the needlework on the purse. In this first purse presentation nearly £5,000 was raised; moreover the delegates had a tale to tell on returning to their branches.

In 1939 the proceedings concluded with a steamer trip through the Pool of London to Greenwich. It was to be a farewell to an era: the war would change many things, not least the skyline of London. But the following year, 1940, the conference still took place at the Queen's Hall and despite the fact that the war had been going more than six months over 600 branch delegates were present to hear the Queen remind them not to forget in the pressures of a new war those who still suffered as a result of the last. Nor did they: the resolutions dealt with the problems of that earlier generation, as well as calling attention to the anomalies in the new pensions warrant and regretting the need to cancel the children's holiday scheme.

The Annual Conference was always preceded by conferences at Area, and in time, County, level, and the same year, 1940, the delegates at the Wales Area Women's Section Conference in Cardiff were taken aback when, without warning, the doors of the City Hall opened and the Queen came in, followed by the King. The Queen walked to the platform, wished the stunned audience a successful conference and then left with the King the way she had come while the delegates struggled to their feet to sing the National Anthem. What officialdom made of this spur-of-the-moment change to the Royal programme is not recorded, but no doubt the King was a willing party to his wife's gesture towards the members of a movement with which she had increasingly identified over nearly two decades.[39]

## A diversity of work

The purses which had been donated towards Burnham Hall were much needed. Although set up to provide training in domestic work, it had in practice become a convalescent home for half the women who passed through its doors. The majority arrived under-nourished and debilitated from homes which had long endured the effects of unemployment. Some had a deformity and one even had to be fitted with an artificial limb before she could undertake any form of training. Nonetheless, of those who were able to complete the training, some got good residential posts such as cook-housekeeper or matron of a girls' hostel. In August 1939, however, it all came to an end when the trainees were sent home in order that the hall might be used as an evacuation centre for children. It was then leased for wartime purposes.[40]

From 1936 onwards the Section concerned itself with employment in a wider sense, establishing branch employment committees and placing several hundred women dependants of ex-servicemen in work each year. Since the Legion itself had a highly skilled employment service the Section worked very closely with Legion Area Employment Officers and it became in effect an extension of that service, by 1937 finding work for over 3,000 women and war orphans. As with the Legion its work was curtailed by the wartime direction of labour but even under wartime conditions it still managed to find some openings, particularly in domestic work.

Despite the improving economic conditions of the late 1930s as the nation re-armed, there remained desperate shortages of clothing in some areas and the Section's wardrobe scheme continued with over 600 branches involved by 1938, a quarter of the total, many garments being made by branch working parties. Some clothing went to the Legion's Employment Department for job seekers and some to the Officers' Benevolent Department for similar purposes. With the coming of war there was a reduction in the demand – some at least of the needy now had their clothing supplied by the War Office or one of the other service departments – and the work parties turned to making horse and mule bandages as well as supplies for hospital depots. But other clothing was stockpiled for use by those losing their homes and possessions in air raids. It would be needed.

No clothing was now needed for the childrens' holiday scheme. It was suspended in 1940, having flourished in its last few years with part of the cost met out of a welfare fund. The fund was established in 1937 after the Affiliation Fee increase that year enabled both the NEC annual grant and branch donations to be switched from administration to benevolence. Apart from contributing to the holidays it funded weekly allowances for widows. This was hardly a comprehensive scheme – by 1940 about fifty widows each received ten shillings a week – but at least that number of genuinely deprived women could be helped in their declining years. To qualify they had not only to be in need but incapable of earning any money because of ill-health or age and not entitled to any of the statutory allowances. That the scheme was necessary at all indicates the holes in the government's welfare provision at the time.[41]

Almost all of this work depended heavily on the branches. Like any other organization the Legion Women's Section had its share of 'sleepers'. But few such branches were tolerated for long; the level of commitment was too high and in the dark days to come this approach was to prove its worth.

## 1941 – 1945

### A tragic loss

In September 1941 Lady Edward Spencer Churchill died as a result of a car accident. The news came as an immense shock to the Section. Lady Edward had not only been Chairman for nearly twenty years but she had been its guiding light. Taking over in circumstances which threatened its continued existence, she had revitalized the Section, given it leadership and direction, and brought about an astonishing growth based on a strong sense of identity and purpose. Her obituary in *The Times* spoke of her 'organising genius and astonishing vitality' . . . 'a friend has gone who cannot be replaced'.

Lady Edward's replacement was indeed a difficult matter. The Vice Chairman, Mrs Harris, took over temporarily but did not seek the post. Instead, at the 1942 Annual Conference, after a contest with Lady Jellicoe, wife of the former Legion President, Lady Apsley was elected. A nurse in the Great War, a qualified pilot and a senior officer in the ATS despite being confined to a wheelchair as a result of a hunting accident, Lady Apsley was a woman of many parts: she had at one time gone to Australia with her husband to live as a poor migrant to find out what the conditions really were; and in 1943 she became an MP.[42]

Soon after Lady Apsley took office the objects of the Section were redefined. The first was to support the Legion in all its activities, the second the welfare of dependants, of both serving and ex-servicemen, and the third to serve the community. In peace this last might have been something of an 'also ran'; in war it was demanding. Already the Section had helped to recruit women for part-time war work and members were involved in the 'make and mend' campaign and the 'personal knitters' scheme; this last included responding to an urgent appeal for comforts for the Russian Army in the early Spring of 1942, still winter in front of Leningrad. Some branches helped Ordnance Depots repair Army clothing and made camouflage nets, while others provided hostels, club and canteen facilities for the forces, especially the womens' services and the men from overseas. Parcels of needlework and materials were sent to women's service detachments in remote areas and country branches were involved in preserving fruit and vegetables for the government's Preservation Centres.[43]

*During the Second World War Women's Section Branches provided canteen facilities for local forces. Here the branch chairman serves tea to the troops.*

An important wartime activity was to advise the dependants of those serving, some of whom were not only unaware of their official entitlements but, in the absence of their men, needed help on a whole range of matters normally outside their province, such as changing a tap washer or repairing a fuse; in such cases a good relationship with the men's branch worked wonders. The contacts sometimes resulted in an addition to the branch membership; but it was the combination of a growing service and ex-service community together with an involvement with that community that led to a 20 per cent growth by 1945 over the 1939 total; there were now over 2,100 branches.[44]

Even so a new Women's Section branch could only form where there was already a Legion branch and only if the men agreed. In 1943 the women asked that this rule be waived for the duration of the war. The Legion's NEC, however, refused as it might lead to friction. But, despite this strict control of the women's activities, there was good co-operation in the war years, in some cases new Legion branches asking that a Women's Section branch be formed simultaneously.[45]

Nor did the Council in any way try to differentiate between the wartime contribution of men and women. In considering the recommendations of the Planning Committee which had been set up under Mr Lister early in the war, on which the Women's Section had a sub-committee, the NEC recorded in September 1944 that the position of ex-service women was exactly the same as the men as far as Legion benefits and privileges were concerned and they would have the same resettlement facilities as the men.[46]

Meanwhile, as the size of the Section grew, the stronger financial position meant that field staff could be appointed and by 1945 all except one of the Women's Areas had a full-time Secretary, while grass roots efficency was improved in 1943 by summer schools involving the officers of 600 branches, in many cases accompanied by their designated successors from the new wartime generation. The number of County Committees too was growing and there were now more than thirty.[47]

Despite all the change that was in the air, as far as employment was concerned the emphasis was still on domestic service. A 'Home Service Corps' of ex-servicewomen was planned: they would be employed by the hour, day or week, wear a uniform and live in hostels, not unlike District Nurses. No doubt the idea had its merits but it smacked somewhat of the wartime existence that most young women were anxious to leave behind them and at least one critic thought that women would want something better in the new post-war world.[48]

In 1945 the Section suffered a further loss with the death of the Secretary, Miss Gerds. Associated with the ex-service movement since 1917, she had been appointed in 1922, following the dismissal of the original Secretary in the row with the NEC and had thereafter worked very closely with Lady Edward Spencer Churchill, sharing with her much of the credit for the Section's transformation. The Women's Section faced the uncertain future of the post-war world with a new team.[49]

## Business as usual

The Women's Section Conference in 1941 would long be remembered by the 380 delegates who braved the London blitz and wartime travel difficulties. It was to be the last appearance of Lady Edward Spencer Churchill before her death, and it would also be the last Section conference to be held in the familiar surroundings of the Queen's Hall – or any other meeting for that matter. A motion to hold the wartime conferences in the provinces was overwhelmingly defeated; if their President, living at Buckingham Palace, was prepared to defy the bombing, so were the delegates. But, as if to answer such presumption, a few days later the Queen's Hall was a ruin, destroyed in an air raid. At the conference itself the President received a welcome which, depite the reduced numbers, surpassed even her arrival at the 1938 conference; the enthusiasm and affection were almost unbounded. She stayed over an hour, speaking to, and getting a response from, each woman who received an award.

For the rest of the war the conferences were held at the Central Hall, Westminster, the 1943 Conference greeting the new Chairman, Lady Apsley, with great applause as she was wheeled on to the platform alongside Sir Brunel Cohen, also in a wheelchair, and perhaps showing something of their feelings for her; her husband had been killed in action a few months before. She wore Lady Edward's badge, presented to her by her predecessor's daughter, noting that it would be passed on to all who succeeded her.

In only one wartime year was the Queen not present, her place being taken in 1944 by the Princess Royal, and on each occasion she stayed for over an hour, spending more time at the stalls where the goods made by disabled men were sold, making many purchases. One year she bought a model destroyer made by a Dunkirk man and there was some discussion as to whether the guns were correctly mounted; the Queen ended the argument by saying, 'I'll take it home and ask the King – he'll know'. In 1945 she brought Princess Elizabeth, who was in ATS uniform, and presented her with a gold badge and Life Membership of the Section. Over 900 delegates were present on that occasion, the numbers having steadily risen during the war years, with the inclusion from 1943 onwards of many servicewomen who listened intently to the debates, in the later years taking part. A contentious issue in 1943 was the raising of money for outside organisations, some branches having collected more for other bodies than for the Legion, and even doing so in the Legion's name. The normally jovial Brunel Cohen, seems to have been fiercely critical on this occasion, and indeed it was misguided, although no doubt done with the best of intentions. But the Section itself was still financially very sound with handsome donations being given by many branches in the war years, building up the Welfare Fund.

Most of the activities that were traditionally associated with the Annual Conference were not possible in the war, but in 1945 the Section's standards were once again proudly massed on the steps of St Paul's for the resumption of the Annual Service. It was apt; the Section had come through the war with colours flying.[50]

## The work continues

Whatever the Legion Treasurer's view may have been later in the war, there had been no dispute in 1940 when Lady Edward Spencer Churchill suggested that branches raise funds for mobile canteens to provide meals for those made homeless by air attack. No time was wasted and in November of that year the first was presented to the London County Council; it was followed by many others, both in London and elswhere. But Lady Edward's death in 1941 led to an equally earnest endeavour to raise money for a suitable memorial. In the following years over £16,000 was raised, a measure of the Section's regard for their late Chairman, and in April 1944 the first Lady Edward Spencer Churchill Memorial Home was opened by the Princess Royal at Knaresborough in Yorkshire. Known as 'Queensmead',* it provided eighteen convalescents with up to four weeks' rest and change free of charge. Any ex-servicewoman or female dependant was eligible and branches made the recommendations, over 250 patients being admitted annually by 1945. Meanwhile 'Saxmundham' in Swanage had been bought as a second home to serve the south of the country. But there were difficulties over getting permission to carry out the repair work and for the moment one home had to suffice, with admission much in demand.[51]

The need for comforts for the forces, particularly knitted garments to augment issued clothing on some of the bleaker work, caused the pre-war 'wardrobe' scheme to become

---

* It was the name of Lady Edward Spencer Churchill's own home at Windsor.

189

a 'clothing and comforts' scheme. Clothes rationing severely affected contributions, but arrangements were made for materials to be supplied coupon-free to the branches as well as to relatives of those serving and more than a thousand branches became involved, the joint activity forging useful contacts with the relatives who could be helped in other ways. But by the end of the war, while knitting had continued unabated, the shortage of clothing meant that the wardrobe element had effectively come to an end.[52]

With more funding becoming available, the number of widows benefiting from the Allowance Scheme could gradually be increased and by 1945 there were over seventy beneficiaries receiving ten shillings a week, some particularly deserving cases getting a five shilling supplement.

These were the official schemes. But there were many other ways in which the branches of the Women's Section helped the serving and ex-service communities in the difficult days of the war. And when it finally came to an end there were some thoughtful touches such as in Cornwall where the Section ensured that every serving man who lived in an outlying district was met by a taxi when he returned home.[53]

★    ★    ★

From its uncertain beginnings the growth of the British Legion Women's Section in the 1920s and 1930s had been remarkable, so that by the outbreak of another war it was a thriving organization more than able to 'do its bit'. There had certainly been moments of friction with the Legion itself – the marriage had not been all perfect harmony – but the Section's loyalty had been unswerving. And, if the Legion might at times appear to be chauvinistic in its determination to ensure that it kept firm control over its helpmate, there could only be one national organization with one set of policies to represent the interests of the ex-service community, as the women's leaders well understood.

The Great War had brought change. So too had its successor. Many more woman had served with the armed forces in the second war than in the first. They had been more involved in the war itself, some even manning guns against air attack. Moreover the aspirations which had been voiced in those faraway days before August 1914 had not yet been satisfied and the Legion itself had insisted on equality of treatment for ex-servicewomen alongside men. A new aged dawned.

190

# CHAPTER 8

## OFFICER BENEVOLENCE 1921-1945

# *Distress has no Boundaries*

## 1921 – 1925

### The officer of the Great War

The enormous number of men needed to take up arms in the Great War led to a very rapid expansion of the officer corps, particularly in the army. A high sense of duty and patriotism led many young men to 'go for a commission' as soon as they left school at the age of eighteen, and in some cases even earlier if they could get away with it. They were joined by others who abandoned their place at university, or on the first rung of the ladder of their profession, to respond to the call. Pro rata the losses among officers were roughly double those of the men they led and the War Office had to dig deeper: warrant officers and NCOs, some of whom had completed a period of service with the regular army before 1914, were commissioned; private soldiers who showed qualities of leadership were, often after the briefest of selection boards, made second lieutenants, particularly towards the end of the war when the upper- and middle-class sources had dried up.[1]

As a result the officer corps was unlike that of any previous British Army. Up to 1914 officers had been expected to have at least some private income. The way of life could not be sustained on their pay alone. There were of course one or two exceptions: warrant officers commissioned into Quartermaster appointments somehow had to manage, but no one expected them to maintain the 'lifestyle' of a company officer. In short an officer was a gentleman; and a gentleman was expected to be able to support himself.

The perception that officers had independent means continued through and beyond the Great War. The government was obviously aware of the true situation, but found it convenient to ignore. After the war those who had served in the armed forces but could not find a job were given an 'out of work donation' with allowances for their wives and children. It was a forerunner of the Unemployment Benefit scheme but limited to ex-servicemen. Former officers were ineligible, even though many of them had lost all civilian prospects because of their war service.[2] It was this situation that brought about the spectacle of destitute ex-officers selling matches on the streets or playing a barrel organ in the West End of London with an eye open for the police.[3]

### Haig's solution – unity

The Officers' Benevolent Department of the Legion might be said to have its origins in a wooden hut at Victoria Station. The hut provided refreshments for officers arriving from the front and it was here in 1915 that Lady Haig, wife of Sir Douglas Haig, then commanding the First Army in France, helped with the cooking and learned of the problems that many officers and ex-officers faced.[4] She began to make it her special work, for few others seemed to realize their difficulties, and established a fund* to assist disabled officers. Her concern matched her husband's sympathies and at the end of the war Haig

*It was the basis of what was to become the Disabled Branch of the OA.

191

involved himself in the problem. His wife's initiative had been accompanied by others which helped former officers in various ways. All did excellent work. But it was not co-ordinated.

During the war three great ex-service movements had been formed – the Association, the Federation and the Comrades (see pages 2–3). Two of these admitted officers, but the problems with which they were concerned were in the main those of the other ranks. Something needed to be done specifically for the officers and in late 1919 Haig set to work on the existing officers' societies, persuading them to agree in principle to come together under one umbrella, while each continued their special function. A united front assured, Haig and the other wartime service chiefs, Admiral of the Fleet Earl Beatty and Air Marshal Sir Hugh Trenchard, asked the Lord Mayor of London to hold a meeting to establish a National Relief Fund for officers and their families, administered by an 'Officers' Association'.

The meeting took place at the Mansion House on 20 January 1920. The appeal which followed was nationally organized, well supported in the press and by the theatres, music halls and cinemas. It harnessed public emotion in much the same way as in a later age the South Atlantic Fund was to do. So effective was it that the new Officers' Association received over £600,000 in donations from the public alone in the first twelve months of its existence.[5]

The appeal's success gave the other major ex-service organizations food for thought. No doubt there was some irritation that the officers had stolen a march on them – the Comrades for one had been about to launch their own appeal – but it also showed what a unified, national approach could achieve, and, as noted in Chapter 1, it would influence them to come together to form the Legion.

The Officers' Association began work in February 1920 with a staff of about six. At first there was a rented office in Grosvenor Place in Victoria, but after a short while the Duke of Westminster offered premises at a peppercorn rent at No 48, Grosvenor Square, in the west end of London. Here the OA nucleus was augmented by the staff of the other organizations which had been brought into the Association and formed into branches such as Disablement, Families and Employment and Relief. Although the Association assisted all ex-officers regardless of whether they belonged to it or not, they were encouraged to become members. In the first few months over 10,000 did so, the number eventually rising to 26,000 and providing a useful income through subscriptions. Membership brought additional benefits such as the use of an officers' club in Bayswater in central London which provided temporary residence. 'Provincial Branches' were formed to assist in the work of the OA and after some twelve months there were over 100 in the United Kingdom, including two in Scotland, one in Wales and twenty-five overseas. Unlike the branches of the other ex-service organisations, however, the OA branches had no social purposes and a member of the Association did not have to belong to a branch.[6]

At first the Officers' Association had both a General Manager and a General Secretary. The General Manager was Major General Sir Frederick Maurice, a distinguished officer and a man of high principles. But in 1922 he left the Association to take up an academic post and the position of General Manager then lapsed, the General Secretary, another major general, Sir Harold Ruggles-Brise, becoming the OA's chief executive. General Maurice nevertheless continued to be very active in ex-service affairs and would ultimately be the Legion's President.[7] The General Secretary reported to an Executive Committee which included men distinguished in civil life and the organization was headed by three joint Presidents representing the three services, Admiral Beatty, Air Chief

Marshal Trenchard and of course Haig. Apart from Glasgow, Edinburgh and Paris, the field work was all done by volunteers; the two Scottish branches were, however, regarded as autonomous.[8]

## An uneasy start in the Legion

Soon after its formation the Officers' Association met with the other ex-service bodies for the discussions over unity. By December 1920 it was represented on the Unity Committee. But in the meantime the OA had petitioned for its own Royal Charter which it continued to seek during the course of the unity negotiations, but without telling the other organizations. When this was discovered, the others were, not surprisingly, upset: it seemed that the officers were playing a double game; while outwardly agreeing to integration they appeared at the same time to be secretly taking steps to preserve their own identity. Were they therefore serious participants in a unified organization?

In fact a number of those on the OA Executive Commmittee had been reluctant to see the Association swallowed up in the new body; but they bowed to Haig's views on unity. The strategy they had therefore adopted was as the others suspected: to come under the Legion banner but, even though this flouted the agreement, to maintain a distinct identity within the organization, safeguarded by their own Charter. It was not a course that would endear them to the rest; as Graham Wooton has observed, this approach 'undoubtedly clouded the relationship' during the Legion's first decade.[9] To make matters worse, the Charter* itself was granted on the very eve of the Legion's formation, 30 June 1921.

The next day the Officers' Association was retitled 'The Officers' Benevolent Department of the British Legion'. But it retained its own Council, General Secretary and staff, with offices in a separate location.

Well aware of the possible reaction by some at least of the Legion members, the General Manager, Sir Frederick Maurice, in the very first issue of the *Legion Journal*, sought to explain the Officers' position: the trusts and funds now incorporated into the Officers' Association had been donated specifically for the welfare of former officers and could not be used for any other purpose. If there was any suggestion that the Legion would apply these funds in other ways the trustees would withdraw them. Moreover the regulations for officers' pensions and allowances differed from those for other ranks and their interpretation required a specialized department.[10]

With these reassurances relations for a while were reasonably amicable. Indeed the Legion had every reason to be grateful to the officers for their financial help, without which it would have had a difficult time (see below). But the question of the separate Charter and the special status that it conferred still rankled. Matters came to a head in May 1925 with the grant of the Legion's own Charter, the National Executive Council declaring that it was 'convinced that the time has arrived when steps should be taken to abolish all means indicating that the Officers' Benevolent Department of the British Legion is a distinct organization' and it resolved to set up a committee to investigate.[11] The clear intention was to obtain the surrender of the Officers' Association Charter and it provoked a swift reaction. The Officers' Department sought legal advice, the burden of which was that surrender of its Officers' Association Charter might not be considered to be in the interests of the officers and could require an Act of Parliament.† But now the hounds were loose and the matter did not end there.

In the middle was General Sir Frederick Maurice. As a co-opted member of the Legion's National Executive Council he had been present at the May 1925 meeting; but,

*In the name of the Officers' Association.

†Because there was no provision in the Charter for its surrender.

193

although he had by now given up the General Manager's post, he was also Vice Chairman of the Officers' Department's Executive Committee. His first, somewhat unenviable, task was to present to the Executive Committee the report of the Legion committee, although by now this had been watered down. The effect of the recommendations, which were all backed by the NEC, would be to give the Legion greater control over the Officers' Department but leave it as a distinct activity, keeping its Charter. The name 'Officers' Association' would, however, be restricted to legal documents.[12]

Even these modified proposals were not well received by the Officers' Executive Committee and General Maurice, who was seen as having come from the enemy camp, had a rough ride. He was also mistrusted by some in the NEC because he had been involved in obtaining the OA Charter, the cause of the problem as they saw it. Maurice was therefore under fire from both sides and the result might well have been for him to quit the field.

But Maurice held his ground and he brought common sense to bear. Writing to the Officers' Department Treasurer he advised, 'If you . . . adopt the attitude that we are completely independent . . . there will be a row. . . What they require is a demonstration that we are an integral part of the Legion.'[13] The Executive Committee's response to the NEC proposals, when it came, was therefore measured: it expressed loyalty to the Council but insisted that it was bound by the terms of its Charter and could not therefore change any of its practices. And with this the NEC, its leaders no doubt also advised by Maurice, had to be content. Delegates to the 1926 Legion Annual Conference were not so reconciled: they passed a resolution that the OA Charter should be merged, together with the Charter of the United Services Fund, into the Legion's Charter. But the battle was already over and could not be refought.

None of this affected the work of the Officers' Department. The dispute was over control or, some might argue, about the Officers honouring the Unity agreement. But the outcome left the way open to more loosening of the ties. And it is possible that, had the Department been fully absorbed at this stage, in future years more of the officer corps might have identified with the Legion, contributing to the leadership at all levels. Field Marshal Lord Methuen, speaking at the Legion's Annual Conference dinner in 1924, was certainly of the view that the Legion needed a greater officer involvement.[14] His remarks were based on the situation in Wiltshire, but no doubt had a wider application. Senior officers such as he, on the other hand, did seem to be playing their part, taking their lead from Earl Haig.

### A priceless heirloom

Despite all of this it must not be forgotten that the Officers had provided the Legion with a priceless heirloom: the Officers' Association Appeals Section was given over lock, stock and barrel to the new body. This section had run the highly successful national appeal to give the Officers financial lift-off. Now it would do the same for the Legion. From that point on the Officers' Department no longer ran any public appeals, although they continued to receive donations.

Nor was this all. Since the Department was no longer a membership organization in its own right it encouraged its 26,000 members to transfer to the Legion, making a cash payment of £10,000 for their administrative support. Some of these former Officers' Association members joined their local Legion branch. For those who did not chose to do so, or had no local Legion branch, a new branch was opened and run by the Department:

St George's, Hanover Square. As an 'officer' branch it might be open to the criticism that it enabled former officers to be in the Legion without making proper use of their leadership qualities; but members were regularly informed of Earl Haig's express wish that ex-officers should join their local Legion branch and take an active interest.[15] In the 1920s St George's was a healthy branch in every sense: it ran an athletic club, using the magnificent facilities of the Legion Club at Mitcham, taking part in competitions with other athletic clubs in the London area and giving its members a chance to keep fit even in the London environment.[16]

Meanwhile it seemed that the Officers might have been too open-handed. As the Department's work became better known and the grip of the recession tightened, so the demands on funds increased. Despite a generous donation in 1922 by Mr H.H. Wills of shares in the Imperial Tobacco Company to the value of some £60,000 and the fact that some six thousand ex-officers were still making annual subscriptions, inroads had to be made into capital and it was necessary to reduce overheads.[17] Again through the generosity of the Duke of Westminster, new offices were made available on a long lease at a token rent and in May 1925 the headquarters moved to 8, Eaton Square.

## A job to do

When the Officers' Association came into the Legion it shed two of its functions, membership and appeals, while a third, housing, was taken over by an associated organization. It was then free to concentrate all of its energies on its benevolent role, which was indeed its sole function within the Legion as the Officers' Benevolent Department. This role encompassed four principal activities: employment, and the problems associated with the lack of it; disablement; assistance to families; and legal and other advice. Those assisted included not only former officers, almost entirely male, and their dependants, together with the widows and their children, but also women who had been members of the nursing services in the war.

Because of the deplorable situation of many former officers after the Great War the Association had been hard worked from the start. But in 1921, the year of its absorption into the British Legion, demand was even greater as the effect of the post-war depression began to take hold. Some 24,000 cases were helped in that year, nearly double the previous year's total. The greatest expenditure was incurred by the Disablement Branch, often in order to eke out the disability pension which proved inadequate. Not far behind was the Families Branch, helping with the payment of doctors' bills, rent demands (the cost of housing had increased sharply because no houses had been built during five years of war) and special treatment for illness. Even clothing was collected and distributed to needy ex-officers and their families and the Annual Report for 1923 noted that stocks of clothing held at the Department's headquarters were inadequate to meet the demand and appealed for more gifts.

The Employment and Relief Branch originally ran an Employment Bureau, but in early 1921 their work had been transferred to the Ministry of Labour since it was felt that money subscribed by the public should not be used to relieve the government of its responsibilities.[18] The employment of disabled officers, however, remained with the Department. But in 1925 the change was reversed: at the request of the Ministry of Labour, the Department took back the placement of able-bodied ex-officers, in return for a lump sum of £10,000. An office was opened at 4, Clement's Inn, in the Strand, with a staff of mainly voluntary workers, ex-regular officers, who interviewed applicants, both able-bodied and disabled, and the office continued to operate until 1932 when its work was transferred to the Department's headquarters office.

The Department's philosophy was to get the former officer back into work in order to make him independent of relief. Hence the new role was accompanied by a reorganization: a Business Branch gave ex-officers start-up loans or grants to help them to start their own enterprises, while the Employment Branch, with 'Relief' dropped from its title to underline the new policy, had two sections: one operated the Employment Bureau at 4, Clement's Inn, while the other relieved distress arising from unemployment, but with the emphasis on loans or grants which would help the recipient back to full employment. Each branch dealt with both the able-bodied and disabled, allowing the former Disablement Branch to lapse.[19]

Assistance was not just given to Great War men. Ex-regular officers were also helped, and they included a category whose plight at that time is sometimes overlooked: those who had intended to make the Navy or Army their career but whose prospects were frustrated by the post-war reductions in the armed forces known as the 'Geddes Axe'.

### 'No man in his senses will employ a disabled man'

There was little doubt that help was needed. Most encouraging could be the outcome of a loan. A former Flying Officer, decorated for gallantry and severely disabled, subsequently qualified as a doctor but was unable to work as a GP because of his injuries: a loan enabled him to buy the equipment to practise as an anaesthetist. A widow whose husband, also decorated, had been discharged with 90 per cent disability was refused a pension when he died as a result of a motor accident. The Business Section helped her to furnish a house to take in boarders. A disabled ex-officer wrote, 'You were courageous enough to advance me the cash to start my business when you could scarcely have known whether it was likely to be a success or not.' Other former officers sent letters in a similar vein: 'a new lease of life when I was absolutely down and out'; 'the day I walked into 48, Grosvenor Square I was in rags and hungry. Now I am faced with much better fortune.'[20]

Loans were interest free and repayment on easy terms. By and large these loans were repaid promptly: it seems to have been a matter of honour for the ex-officers to meet their obligations whatever the circumstances and disabled officers were particularly prompt in paying their debts.[21] Payments in full were received from places as far away as Burma, Nova Scotia, Southern Rhodesia, California and Bermuda, illustrating the enterprise, or perhaps the desperation, of many ex-officers in seeking employment.

Small amounts of money could make all the difference. The Employment Section made grants to provide clothing – some officers had reached the stage where they needed a suit of clothes to be able to present themselves for an interview – and helped with kit for overseas work; it provided the needy with their railway fares to attend job interviews or simply to seek work; it assisted with passages overseas. Ex-officers without means were placed in hostels while on the job search and their bills paid[22] and places provided at a school for training ex-officers as commercial representatives.

Over 5,000 cases were helped each year and wherever possible the Department applied the principle of trying to free the applicant from the need for further relief: a solicitor who had given up his job to join the army in 1914 rose to lieutenant colonel; but on trying to resume the practice after the war he found that he had insufficient capital; with only a little assistance he was able to re-start. A lieutenant commander's widow had three children but no money; with assistance from the Association she started a small school and was able to provide for her family.

Ex-officer or not, it was not easy to place a disabled person at a time of rapidly rising unemployment; as George Bernard Shaw put it in his characteristically forthright way, 'No man in his senses will employ a disabled man when he can find a sound one.'[23] Only 10 per cent of those interviewed actually joined the register.[24] The inference must be that many came along simply to make contact with an organization which was sympathetic to their situation and understood the despair that disabled ex-officers (and any other disabled ex-serviceman for that matter) faced in these bitter times. The feeling that 'someone cared' was a psychological boost to many who might otherwise have abandoned all hope. Nor did this apply only to the disabled; of 27,000 able-bodied ex-officers who called at Clement's Inn in the first year only 8,000 were interviewed and 1,000 placed. The rest simply wanted to talk to someone who understood their situation.

Another group who needed the Department's help were the 'ranker-officers'. These were in the main former NCOs, including many who had finished their original army service and had therefore been pensioned before 1914. Around 7,000 had been commissioned and some found themselves commanding companies and even battalions because of high losses among officers.[25] Yet at the end of the war they resumed their pre-war pensions with only a small recognition of their officer service as is brought out in a letter in the *Legion Journal* of August 1921:

> I am a captain, retired after 29 years' service – two campaigns – five years commissioned service during the late war – severely wounded in France. Pension – hush! – £74 per annum.
>
> In the *Daily Mail* I note that Southwark Borough Council are asking for a retiring allowance of £434 a year for a rate collector . . . and £136 a year for dustman and street sweeper.[26]

If that was insufficient irony, different rules applied in the Navy; the officer would have received £260 in the same circumstances. But the numbers involved were small and government remained indifferent.[27]

Such men might well, however, pursue their war pension entitlements. If so the Department's Claims and Pensions Bureau could advise and in 1925 there were still 1,000 callers a month. Claims and Pensions worked closely with the Legal and Financial Advice Bureau, comprising a number of eminent barristers and solicitors who gave free advice to ex-officers on a recommendation from the department. It would also represent them in appeals before Pensions Tribunals where expert counsel was often needed as time passed and it became more difficult for the claimant to attribute the injury or disability to war service.[28]

One of the chief problems was fraud. A number of officers, some at least of whom were probably conditioned by their background and service to be more trusting than most, were prey to the unscrupulous, losing their savings or inheritance in the process. The members of the Bureau actively helped in such cases: an ex-officer who had sold property was induced to part with the Title Deeds before he had received payment and was then unable either to obtain the money due to him or to recover the property. One of the solicitors on the Bureau's panel took up the case and obtained payment. Another ex-officer fell into the hands of moneylenders and was being pressed for payment; when the Bureau investigated it was found that in fact the officer had overpaid and £50 was recovered.[29]

### Shell shock

The Families Branch helped with the payment of doctors' bills, gave assistance with rent and provided clothing. Education was another responsibility: there were many instances where the death of an officer meant that his widow was unable to continue to pay school fees, or some other war-related misfortune interrupted their schooling. Each case was investigated by the Branch and where the need existed the fees paid either in part or whole depending on the circumstances of the applicant. In addition the Branch sponsored scholarships and bursaries at various schools.[30]

These were the matters in which the Officers' Department could become directly involved. But there was another category which caused deep concern not least because the problems which they endured were not so apparent and only understood by those who had themselves fought in the Great War, and a few specialists. Of those disabled ex-officers known to the Officers' Benevolent Department fully one third were suffering from neurological conditions, a significant statistic indicating the stress inflicted by the war, including the condition then known as 'shell shock'. When, in 1923, the Department was given Rotherfield Court, near Henley-on-Thames, it was decided to use it as a Neurological Hospital for ex-officers and the Ministry of Pensions agreed to take on its administration. About 100 patients were admitted each year with an average six-month stay during which they received psychotherapy and had to undertake an activity ranging from french polishing to poultry farming. The combination enabled patients not only to recover their balance of mind but prepared them for an occupation on discharge or for further training on one of the government courses. In 1936, however, the Ministry decided to make other arrangements for the patients and the building and contents were sold with the proceeds going to the Department, earmarked for educational scholarships.[31]

## 1926 – 1930

### Changes at the top

Having resolved the Charter dispute, in early 1927 Major General Maurice resigned as Vice Chairman of the Department's Executive Committee. He also attempted to withdraw as a co-opted member of the NEC, but the Council would not accept; whatever the rights and wrongs of the dispute it was the NEC's actions that had placed General Maurice in his invidious position and in any case they greatly valued his advice.[32] A few months later Major General Sir Harold Ruggles-Brise, the department's General Secretary, died. Formerly Haig's Military Secretary in the Great War, he was a man of great personal charm as well as genuinely sympathetic towards the problems of the ex-officers. He was succeeded by another Major General, Sir Sydney Crookshank.[33]

The death early the next year of Earl Haig himself made as profound an impact on the Department as it did on the Legion, or indeed on the nation: Haig had been both the Officers' Association founder and its inspiration and his continuing interest as one of the three joint Presidents had been both deep and sincere.[34]

Shortly before his death Haig had set up a committee to establish the Department's financial needs. In the face of the continuing recession the level of demand for help had been high; even ten years after the war well over 1,000 cases were being dealt with each week and in 1928 it was estimated that within five years the capital of the Department would have been wholly used up, an alarming state of affairs considering that on grants

198

for education alone there was a commitment until 1938. The committee calculated that £250,000 further capital was needed, but of course the Department no longer had either the responsibility or the mechanism for its own fundraising; it therefore went to its parent body, the Legion, receiving a grant of £30,000 in addition to the 5 per cent of the Poppy Appeal proceeds due to it under the original agreement. Although the Legion, under pressure itself, had to reduce the amount of the additional grant in 1929 and 1930, there were only minor overspends in the final two years of the decade and the crisis had been passed, aided by a donation from the Naval Prize Fund (although since this derived from the proceeds of the disposal of captured enemy ships its application was limited to former Naval officers) and, to a limited extent but nonetheless heartwarming, by donations from those ex-officers who had, with the Department's help, made good and wished to help their less fortunate fellows.[35]

## Times get even harder

This financial predicament led to major economies in loans to ex-officers, widows and nurses to start their own business or to take up places on training courses. The Business Branch already carefully vetted loan applications as the continuing work of the branch to some extent relied on prompt repayments. The amount lent each year was reduced progressively until 1930 when the expenditure was balanced by income from repaid loans. From then on the strict priority was to assist the more severely disabled to start up in business or receive training for employment.[36]

The responsibilities of Employment Branch included providing relief to those who were not employed and it looked after the disabled as well as the fit. But the financial squeeze was not permitted to affect the disabled category. There was little scope for economy in a case such as that of a three-times wounded major with an MC who had TB in both lungs and then fell ill with acute appendicitis; on a disability pension of £100 a year and a private income of £40 (equivalent to £4,500 in total at today's values) he was unable to pay the surgeon's fees. The Branch needed not only to pay the fees but help with the costs of a nursing home. Nor could it stint on a maintainance grant to a former captain with a DSM and several times mentioned in despatches. As a result of a severe head wound he had lost an eye and suffered from a nervous condition so that he lost his job; the grant enabled him to support his widowed mother while he looked for other work.

In several cases former officers with good qualifications but almost entirely without means and living in the country were brought to London at the Branch's expense to seek employment, making use of the Employment Bureau situated at Clement's Inn. Such officers were, however, only a small part of its custom; it now had over 20,000 callers a year, some 4,000 of whom were interviewed, about half being given letters of introduction to employers. The bureau itself managed to provide work for around 600 ex-officers every year, some getting jobs paying as much as £1,200 annually – a high sum in those days. Nevertheless more than 2,000 remained 'on the books', and the figure began to creep up at the end of the decade, despite all the efforts of the dedicated band of voluntary workers who spent much time calling on business concerns to canvass for vacancies.[37]

## The cost of schooling

Nor did matters get any easier for the Families Branch. The qualification for assistance with school fees, apart from lack of means, was that the child must have been born before 1 September 1921. But the expenditure on education increased as the years passed and more children reached school age, and projections showing that the figure would build up until a peak was reached in 1931-32 were the main reason for the concern over shortage of funds which had to be met by a Legion grant. Already exceeding £25,000 a year in 1926, schooling costs had risen to nearly £30,000 by the end of the decade with around some 1,000 children being assisted at a cost of between £24 and £27 each. Nor did the expenditure cease on leaving school. Many of the boys went on to a service college, such as Sandhurst, which then charged fees, while others entered university and also needed support.

There was also 'general assistance' to families: doctors' bills, removal grants to take up employment elsewhere, meeting the cost of widows' training so that they could become self-supporting, as well as simply keeping a widow and her children going while the outcome of a war pension case was determined.

The clothing store depended on articles being donated. Demand far exceeded supply with something like a thousand ex-officers seeking clothing each year, often in order to present a respectable appearance at a job interview or to take up new work properly clad. But up to 1929 only about a quarter of those making applications could be fitted out – some well-meaning people sent evening clothes, not imagining that the ex-officers were in need of garments to keep out the winter cold – and it was then decided to sell off the more unsuitable clothing and use the money to buy what was really needed. This resulted in raising the level of those who could be suitably clothed to about half the applicants. The rest continued to be not only shabby in appearance and ill-shod but, lacking the proper protection against the elements, prey to ill-health. It was a far cry from the day when they had received the King's commission.

In view of this level of need some might question whether so much should have spent on schooling, particularly as it entailed additional funding from the Legion itself, also hard-pressed. It was, however, a guiding principle from the early days of the Officers' Benevolent Department that the death of a father, or his disablement or financial distress because of the war, should not deprive his children of the standard of education that they would have received but for his military service.[38]

## War Pensions successes

The Department's Legal and Financial Bureau now had a success rate of about 70 per cent in representations before Pensions Tribunals, about thirty to forty officers appealing each year against their war pensions awards through Counsel provided by the bureau, again free of charge. Less successful was a campaign against reductions by the Ministry of Pensions in the amount paid to severely disabled officers, those who had lost a limb, if they had other income. This practice, started in 1927, was based on an inquiry form sent by the ministry to each disabled ex-officer asking about his earnings and the reductions were made by a small committee of civil servants without even seeing the officer. It breached a principle that the Legion itself strongly maintained: that the war pension was not simply to make up for loss of income. But representations to government, even by eminent Counsel, left the Minister unmoved.

The Claims and Pensions Bureau who referred the Tribunal cases were specialists on the intricacies of the pensions regulations. They not only advised on war pensions but on any service pension matter as well as widows' and children's allowances and grants for training or even for emigration, in addition to claims against government departments. It was a very busy office and the work if anything tended to increase towards the end of the decade as a great number of ex-officers took advantage of a small relaxation on the seven-year rule, enabling war pensions claims to be submitted and considered on merit beyond that period.[39]

## 1931 – 1935

### A still grimmer outlook

In the early 1930s the economic depression affected the former officers no less than those they had led into battle. They too were feeling the effects of age which not only intensified the physical and mental effects of the war but meant that once out of work their chances of being re-employed grew slimmer with each passing year. Small wonder that there was much despair as well as deprivation among those who had responded so quickly to their country's call some twenty years before, and that more and more turned to the Legion's Officers' Benevolent Department for help. Many were men whose selflessness in abandoning their employment or professional training at a critical stage had deprived them of a proper start in life, while their colleagues, who had not heeded the call, enhanced their own positions.

The Department's situation was that of a small outpost which, having sustained a series of assaults, had looked forward to a breathing space but now saw once again the hordes massing on the horizon. The anticipation had been that demand on its resources would have reduced so many years after the war; the very opposite was happening. But, despite the renewed pressure, ex-officers in need could no more be refused help than the outpost abandoned. In consequence the financial position of the Officers' Department became increasingly serious, made even worse by a decline in income as the depression affected subscriptions and donations. A committee under Captain Howitt recommended that the Department's 5 per cent of the Poppy Appeal proceeds be augmented by a further $2\frac{1}{2}$ per cent, but, although the Legion's NEC accepted the recommendation, in practice they simply increased the fixed annual grant. As a result of a further recommendation the United Services Fund also made an annual donation from 1932 onwards and the Department's income became more or less assured through these grants. For its own part the Department made severe economies: loans to fund new business ventures ceased and the Business Branch was abolished; the Employment Bureau was merged with the Legion's Employment Department, only a small office being maintained for ex-officer applicants within the London area; and the Disabled Officers' Home and Club was shut. Even so the department showed an annual deficit in these years, forcing it to eat into capital and thereby further reducing income potential. These were difficult times for the officers and crises were only averted by firm management. Nevertheless the work continued and destitute ex-officers and their families got the help they needed.[40]

### Help for the sons and daughters

Following the closure of the Employment Bureau at Clement's Inn in 1932 the Department ran a reduced operation at 20, Grosvenor Gardens, SW1. At first this was solely for London applicants but, in 1934 the new bureau took back from the Legion responsibility for those ex-officers living in the Home Counties. London clearly offered the best opportunities for work and, aided by the contacts established over the years, some 400 of the 500 or so officer placements each year were made by the bureau, the remainder being placed by the Legion's Employment Department. Towards the end of the period it also began to place sons and daughters of ex-officers on the basis that, if they could be found employment, it would not only relieve the parents of their upkeep but the offspring might be able to contribute to the family income. Not surprisingly it proved considerably easier to find openings for the younger generation than their middle-aged, often untrained and sometimes war-weary fathers.

The appointment of an Employment Officer in 1935 in order to liaise with potential employers increased the number of placements that year by over 20 per cent. But the same year a letter to the *Legion Journal* pointed to the degradation of unemployed ex-officers, the majority of whom were not entitled to any unemployment benefit. Such an individual, in order to obtain grocery tickets, had to queue outside the offices of the Public Assistance Committee, 'most probably in a district where he had been well-known and well-respected'. The letter went on to describe the moral and physical deterioration caused by long periods of unemployment, so that even if work was eventually obtained the former officer was unable to do it properly: an ex-officer known to the writer, after months of semi-starvation 'with the accompanying demoralization that want and desperation so rapidly engenders' got a door-to-door canvassing job on commission only for orders for fresh fruit; another was given similar work 'touting for a brush manufacturing firm'. Both failed: they had neither the physical stamina nor the 'cheek' for such work. The writer went on to advocate a system used by the American Legion where the first step was to rehabilitate the ex-officer so that he regained his health and self-respect and was able to tackle work for which he was more suited. There was little chance that the British Legion could adopt such a solution which would involve setting up a network of special institutions, but the letter identified very clearly the hopeless situation of the long-term unemployed ex-officer whose troubles had begun when the war had obliterated that period of his life in which he might have established himself in a proper calling.[41]

The Legal and Financial Bureau was kept busy at this time because of the effect of the recession on employment and attempts by those losing their jobs to obtain some recompense, although this was often no more than an ex-gratia payment, grudgingly conceded. The desperate times increased the hazards to the unwary: businesses in which ex-officers were invited to invest money not infrequently turned out to be dubious propositions if not downright swindles. There was too an increase in the number of former officers seeking help from the Department's Claims and Pensions Bureau over war pensions claims: the passing of the years often aggravated old wartime injuries or illnesses, while those who had previously made light of their condition now found it a serious impairment. But, with the seven-year rule still in force, even with the bureau's expert assistance, it was difficult to satisfy the Ministry. It is sad to record that the majority of such cases had little success because of the great difficulty in establishing an unbroken line of medical evidence to link them indisputably with wartime service.[42]

### Education peaks

Despite the straitened times the Department continued to provide support for the education of officers' children. It regarded this scheme as 'the finest of all War Memorials', pointing out that a properly educated child would be able to get good employment, thus saving the parents futher expense and in time providing them with support. It was the same reasoning that had been applied to the use of the Department's employment facilities to find jobs for officers' sons and daughters.

Some 1,000 children were still helped with school fees each year, accounting for about five-sixths of the Families Branch budget. The high cost meant that an anxious eye was kept on the numbers and there was some relief when it became clear that the peak had been reached, as forecast, in 1932, with nearly 1,300 children being assisted, the numbers thereafter gradually declining. University education and training for the professions continued to be supported, although a number of the children were able to win open scholarships to universities.

As the education corner was turned more attention could be given to the officers' widows who were now getting too old to earn for themselves. Some of course would be supported by their children in the way that the Department had envisaged. But there were many now over the age of sixty who were not eligible for the National Health Insurance Pension and trying to eke out an existence on a few shillings a week from interest on their small savings or from precarious temporary employment; some did not have even these resources. At the end of 1935, despite the shortage of money, steps were being taken to set up a Trust Fund to provide small pensions for these women.

A major activity continued to be the provision of clothing to enable former officers to be presentable at work, or simply to enable them to keep warm; so important was this that in 1935 the branch was re-titled the 'Families and Clothing Branch'. In 1932 the Department's General Secretary had made an appeal through *The Times* and other newspapers and the response had been sufficient to re-stock the clothing store. But such was the demand for boots, shoes, suits, overcoats, even under-clothing and pyjamas, that the shelves were soon depleted again so that of the three thousand ex-officers who applied in 1934 at least half had to be turned away. In the present age where young people spend large amounts of money simply to keep up with the latest fashions, not infrequently out of their state benefits, this need to furnish the ex-officers of the 1914-18 war with the barest of necessities gives some indication of the privation which they and their families endured, to say nothing of the loss of dignity in men who had served their country well.[43]

## 1936 – 1940

### Money problems continue

The improvement in the employment situation in the second half of the 1930s, as re-armament led to an upturn in the economy, came too late for many former officers. They lacked the skills to take advantage of new opportunities and were too old to be trained. As a result relief expenditure continued to climb. With unemployment now often having to be accepted as a permanent condition, the tendency was increasingly to pay regular maintenance.

The effect of all this was still more draining of the reserves, despite the £35,000 annual grant from the Legion and a further £15,000 each year from the United Services Fund. By 1938 the yearly deficit had reached £22,000. Nor was it only due to expenditure on relief: in March 1938, in reviewing the Department's report, the Legion's National Executive Council drew their attention to the 'high level of administrative cost and recommends an examination into this matter with a view to economy'. The review must have had some effect as in 1939 the deficit was reduced to just over half that of the previous year.[44]

## But the work goes on

Despite these financial pressures the Department continued to support the work of the Housing Association for Officers' Families. Housing had long been one of the biggest problems for impoverished officers' families and early in its existence the Officers' Department had set up a Housing Branch to make loans to ex-officers for housing; but it had been closed to avoid duplicating the Housing Association's work. The Association maintained some 200 houses and flats in and around London and made grants and loans to assist disabled officers and widows to obtain and maintain a home.

Nor were the problems allowed to hold back the scheme for a Trust Fund to provide pensions for widows in difficult circumstances. The Fund had been initiated with a transfer of £25,000 from the Reserved Fund, providing an annual income of £750; but the income grew to over £2,000 with legacies and donations, including generous donations from City livery companies. The scheme itself started in 1936 with eleven cases being assisted, but by 1939 there were some sixty annuitants. As with all such schemes, it was a difficult task to decide which of so many deserving cases should benefit.

Although the peak had been passed, expenditure on the education of officers' children did not reduce as quickly as had been hoped because employers were now demanding higher qualifications and there was therefore a greater involvement in post-school training. By 1939, although the number of children being helped with schooling had fallen from the 1932 peak of 1,300 to 300, a further 250 were now being assisted after having completed their formal education. The philosophy continued to apply to both education and employment: provide officers' children with as good a start in life as possible so that they would not be a drain on their parents, adding to their problems.

The Employment Bureau had less difficulty in placing young people than their seniors. Most difficult of all were disabled ex-officers, despite the general upturn in national prosperity. Even those with relatively low levels of disability, and hence very low War Pensions, were becoming less and less fit for work and the condition known as 'latent results of service' or more commonly 'burnt-out veterans' was recognized by the Legion, if not by the government (see page 108). In fact the Department was of the view that the war-disabled had deteriorated to the extent that most of them were either totally unfit for work or, if they found a job, unable to hold it. Such ex-officers found it necessary to seek financial assistance repeatedly and, it seemed, would do so indefinitely. It was yet another of the problems that contributed to the continuing drain on resources. And, with the outbreak of war, those disabled ex-officers who had supplemented their small disability pensions by running a business were in many cases forced to close them, adding to the pressure on the Department.

The general decline in the Great War generation at this time, whether due to the effect of age on an injury of illness in service or to the less recognizable 'burning out', was reflected in the increase in the number of ex-officers assisted in claims for War Pensions, from a little over 1,800 in 1936 to nearly 3,400 in 1939. But even with the assistance of the official known as the 'Officers' Friend' at the Ministry of Pensions only a minority were successful.[45]

It had at one time been assumed that as the years passed so the need to assist ex-officers and their dependants would reduce. This had not been the case; rather the demand had grown, capital had been used and income further reduced in order to meet the urgent needs of a stratum of society which had made the greatest sacrifices of all in the war. Now the country was entering on another war and it seemed that the experience would be repeated. But the coffers had been lowered and there was difficulty in

204

responding to the demands of the current generation of former officers, let alone a new generation. These were daunting times for the Officers' Department; but there were heartening moments, as for instance when an ex-officer who had received £97 in grants came into a small legacy and left £100 to the Department or a deceased officer's sister who had received £48 bequeathed her entire estate of £148.[46]

# 1941 – 1946

## Independence regained

After Haig's death in 1928 his views on unity continued to be respected. The Officers' Department was a recognized element of the Legion, reporting regularly to the NEC. But in 1937 the Annual Report of the 'Officers' Benevolent Department' of the British Legion was re-titled; it became that of 'The Officers' Association', the Legion connection being relegated to a subsidiary line in smaller print.

The gesture seems to have gone unremarked in the Legion itself; in its own Annual Report the relevant entry was was still headed 'Officers' Department'. How matters might have developed had the war not intervened can only be conjecture. But with the outbreak of hostilities in 1939 there was a physical separation. The Legion moved its headquarters out of central London to Richmond in Surrey, remaining there for the rest of the war. The Officers' Department also left the capital, but in their case the absence was only temporary and in May 1940 the Department returned to 8, Eaton Square. Whether as an accidental result of these upheavals, or as part of a planned agenda, the next twelve months would bring a permanent change in the relationship.

After December 1940 the Department ceased to report to the National Executive Council. This had been no mere formality. The Officers' work was regularly reviewed as a part of the Legion's activities, giving rise to discussion and sometimes observations by the Council, and on occasions the Officers' General Secretary was in attendance. But from that time forward no more Officers' Department minutes would be laid before the NEC. The same year, 1940, again perhaps due to wartime circumstances, the Department ceased to contribute to the Legion's Annual Report.*

There is no evidence of any discussion over these changes, either between the Legion and the Officers' Department or within the National Executive Council, and it may be that in the face of pressing wartime problems events were simply allowed to take their course. By 1942, however, the NEC had become concerned over relations with the Officers, appointing a sub-committee headed by the President, General Maurice, who was of course back in familiar territory having brokered the 'Charter' row in 1925, and including Lister. The aim was to discuss 'closer co-operation', but, significantly, the committee would interview representatives of the *Officers' Association*.[47]

The committee may have improved relations, but it could not reverse the tide of events. Legion supervision of officer benevolence had ended. Its former Department had regained its original title and with it its independence. When in late 1945 at a Legion Brains Trust (a popular activity in those years following the wartime BBC programme), there was a question that would not have been asked twenty or even ten years before: 'Is the Officers' Association an integral part of the Legion?' the answer, with both an NEC member and a headquarters staff man on the panel, was even more surprising: 'No, but

---

*From 1964 to 1995 the Officers' Association work was, however, summarized in the Legion Annual Report.

it co-operates closely'. The exchange was published in the *Legion Journal* without comment.[48]

The Officers' Association Report cover would show the Legion connection until 1955; thereafter the role as 'Officers' Benevolent Department of the British Legion' was relegated to the inside pages. In 1998 it was dropped altogether, only the scroll to the badge a reminder of the original unity concept.

## A financial respite

One of the results of the consultations between the Legion and what we will from here on term the Officers' Association over closer co-operation was a more integrated employment service. Already, in the early 1930s, there had been a merger with the Legion's Employment Bureau, with the Officers' responsibilities concentrated on London. The war of course disrupted the normal employment activities. Most employment was subject to the government's direction of labour and the Association's workload had fallen, being mainly concerned with elderly ex-officers, wives and widows and operating since 1940 from Denison House in the Vauxhall Bridge Road. In 1944, with the end of the war in sight, there was a reorganization. New staff were taken on, together with a Legion representative to liaise over employment activities outside London and exchange vacancies. Contacts were established too with the Ministry of Labour, Chambers of Commerce, Rotary Clubs and principal employers, all in anticipation of the demands which would be made when the end of the war would again find thousands of officers seeking jobs.[49]

Better wartime employment opportunities also affected the Association's financial situation. The demand for relief halved, while income was not seriously affected, so that reserves once again began to accumulate. And, as Poppy Day takings rose, the OA reminded the NEC of the 1932 Howitt agreement that the Officers' share of the Appeal should be $7\frac{1}{2}$ per cent. In 1945 therefore the Legion annual grant was increased from £35,000 to £55,000.

The lower level of activity meant that the staff were able to cope, despite being depleted by call-up. They were now led by Colonel A.W. Stokes who had relieved Major General Crookshank as General Secretary in 1941. One of General Crookshank's last decisions had been to move back to 8, Eaton Square in early 1940. He may have regretted it when the blitz struck London later that year. A bomb arriving on the pavement outside failed to explode and for several days the Association's staff had to operate out of the crypt of St Peter's Church nearby.[50]

★　　　★　　　★

The Officers' Association had never been comfortable with the Unity agreement. But, by managing to retain their own organization within the Legion, they had eventually been able to step just far enough aside to reassert their independence while still retaining sufficient links to ensure that the original funding agreement was not jeopardized.

Such manoeuvring should not be allowed to detract from the OA's achievements. It had sustained a sector of society quick to answer the call of duty but vulnerable in the harsh times that followed. It had resolutely maintained that support as the times became even harder. There was much of which to be proud. Now, in the aftermath of another war, there would be new challenges.

# PART II

## 1946-1970

# ARRIVAL OF THE WELFARE STATE

# CHAPTER 9

## THE LEGION AND THE NATION 1946-1970

# *A Time of Change*

### 1946 – 1950

### The fruits of victory

On returning home in early 1946 from serving at Alamein and in Normandy a former Eighth Army lance corporal wrote to the Legion: 'We are very dissatisfied with conditions in this country . . . we are the people who have fought for Britain and we are getting a very shabby deal . . . our food is appalling . . . our wives are exhausted with queueing for hours . . . we cannot even keep warm through lack of fuel . . . we are living in squalor through housing shortage.' He contrasted the situation with that in Holland and Belgium where recovery was much faster: 'We were there and we know it', and asked for 'at least some fruits of our victory'.[1]

The fruits were not to be had, at least not for many years. There was an enormous war debt, mainly to the United States, and one sterling crisis followed another. There were shortages of almost every kind and, to cap it all, the winter of 1947 was particularly severe. Food rationing continued and in 1948 it was even extended to bread and potatoes.

Some of the ex-service community benefited from food parcels organized by the British Empire Services League through veterans' organisations and other well-wishers in the dominions and Kenya which were distributed by Legion branches to war widows and pensioners, and also sent to the Legion's convalescent and country homes. They contained such items as tinned meat, corned beef, jam, marmalade and honey, and even dripping. It is a measure of the time it took for Britain to hoist itself out of this post-war depression that in 1950, five years after the war had ended, Legion branches distributed some 14,000 such parcels to the elderly and incapacitated and that the scheme did not finally end until 1955.[2]

*Post-war food parcels. The Agent General for Victoria hands out parcels sent by the Returned Services League, the Legion's Australian equivalent, at Wandsworth in 1947. Wandsworth was one of fifty-five such distribution centres set up by the Legion.*

Other organizations of course ran similar schemes for the needy, so that the ex-service community was not especially privileged. Indeed, in this period of crisis, one of the most difficult times for Britain in its recent history, the Legion was careful not to promote the cause of the returned servicemen at the expense of the nation as a whole. The *Daily Mirror* noted with approval that the Legion's 1947 Conference had rejected a resolution calling for 'absolute priority' for ex-servicemen in housing, commenting that it was 'a fine gesture. It shows the man who has served and fought for what he is – a fair and reasonable person'.[3]

There was, nonetheless, much to be done for those returning from the war. The shortage of housing caused the greatest concern, but there were also serious delays in training ex-service men and women and many became disheartened and disillusioned, taking inferior jobs as a result. Largely as a result of the Legion's work during the war (see page 29), on which the government had based its demobilization plans, the situation was by no means as bad as that which had followed the 1914-18 war, but an increasing number of ex-service men and women identified with the organization and by 1947 the Legion had over a million members, half of them from the Second World War.

## The Welfare State

For a quarter of a century the Legion had sought fair play for those disadvantaged by service in the armed forces, either the ex-serviceman himself or his family. It had won ex-service priority in employment. It had ensured that government acknowledged that war pensions and war widows' pensions did not just represent an earnings loss; there was an element of compensation for the fact that the injury or death had been sustained in the nation's interest. Its welfare organization covered the entire country and it had pioneered some important medical advances, notably the treatment of TB. As a result, members of the ex-service community were in some ways privileged, but as the Legion would have been quick to point out it was a privilege that had been bought by sacrifice.

Now, however, the state began to extend its own responsibilities towards the community as a whole. The National Health Service Act of 1946 gave free medical treatment to all, beginning the process of creating the 'welfare state' envisaged in the Beveridge Report of 1942. The Health Service itself came into being in 1948 and in the same year, amid gathering momentum, four social security acts, including the abolition of the Poor Law, were passed. The state was now taking charge and, inevitably, the need for a service-related welfare organization began to be questioned, as did the principles on which it operated: why should the Legion need to maintain preference in employment for ex-servicemen if there was to be no unemployment, or at least adequate income for the unemployed, in the new Utopia the government was creating? Why should not an accident in a mineshaft attract the same compensation as a leg blown away by a shell?*

And what was the point of having four or five thousand 'amateur' welfare committees when government departments and their local offices would provide state care? There were suggestions in the press in 1948 that the Legion was now redundant, in part influenced by social theorists, who would anyway like to see ex-service organizations banned. But their views were shared neither by Clement Attlee, the Prime Minister, nor by Lord Beveridge himself, both of whom believed there was a need for the voluntary sector to continue.

The Legion's leaders were in no doubt. The organization's work in fact increased in 1949 (see Chart B1 on page 446) as the local committees, seeking to ensure that ex-service people got their share of the benefits in full, found themselves plugging gaps in the new scheme. Nor could the huge sums now being devoted to Social Security compensate for the personal touch which had for so long been the hallmark of the voluntary bodies. However, they intended to take advantage of the new scheme by switching funds from the relief of immediate distress to the provision of longer term care.

*In fact the miners sought more than the war disability rate for the same injury.

## A political ambush

Meanwhile there was an attack from another quarter. In 1949 the Legion again asked for a Select Committee to investigate the whole matter of war pensions. At this a government minister suggested that the organization was in danger of becoming 'political' and the cry was taken up by others on the government benches, including an ex-service MP, a Lieutenant Commander Pursey, who then embarked on a campaign of vilification of the the Legion, of which he was himself a member, which was duly reported in pro-government newspapers.

All of this was utterly bewildering at first to Legion members; the organization had in the past conducted many parliamentary campaigns on behalf of ex-service interests – that indeed was one reason it existed. So why had this particular approach provoked such a response? The answer was that on this occasion the Legion had walked into a political ambush. The previous year Sir Ian Fraser, blinded in the 1914-18 war and subsequently head of St Dunstan's, had become President. He was also an MP and, acting in both capacities, he naturally put his name to the motion. But Fraser belonged to the opposition party and this gave some on the government side the opportunity to suggest that the case of the war pensioner and the war widow was being exploited for political ends. Legion members of all shades of political opinion were outraged and Commander Pursey, whose campaign had by now reached the stage of demanding that the Legion be disbanded, not only because it had been made redundant by the Welfare State but because of maladministration by 'brass hats' while using women and children to make poppies 'under slave conditions', was, hardly surprisingly, expelled from the Legion.

Equally unsurprising was the outcome: the Commons debate was conducted on party lines and the Legion did not, for the moment at least, achieve its Select Committee. It had learnt a lesson: there may have been advantages in having an MP as President, but there were also pitfalls waiting and Sir Ian's situation would lead to further controversy. And if the episode did not perhaps show the government of the day in the best light there were many among its supporters who genuinely felt upset that the Legion should feel the need to challenge even one aspect of the new social order which was being created. As for the Legion rank-and-file, their view might be summed up by a Conference delegate that year who, noting that Commander Pursey had taken part in the 'Mad Mullah' campaign, wondered on which side he had fought.[4] (See also page 251 for the pensions campaign).

## Silver Jubilee Year

Whatever concerns it may have had for the future the Legion entered the post-war period on a high note. 1946 was its Silver Jubilee and the first full summer of peace was marked by parades and rallies throughout the country, church services, fetes and, despite the shortages, dinners. The Chairman, Brigadier General Fitzpatrick, appeared on television, just re-starting after the war and still very much a novelty. A much wider audience was available to Garrity 'the wonder telephonist' at Legion Headquarters, ex-Galloper of a cavalry regiment and blinded on the Somme, who featured in BBC radio's popular 'In Town Tonight.[5] But there was no national event until early the following year.

The British Legion Exhibition held at the Central Hall, Westminster, in January 1947 not only portrayed the transition from war to peace and the work of the Legion in a series of murals but provided the setting for service reunions. On each of the ten days of the exhibition former members of a different branch of the services met together under one of their wartime leaders. Having exchanged memories and, no doubt, views, on certain matters, admirals and submariners, air marshals and bomber crews, generals and the PBI, were entertained by such current 'hits' as the Beverley Sisters. The gatherings were intended to show that the Legion was an umbrella organization for all ex-servicemen regardless of their service.[6] Certainly this was understood as far as the Royal Air Forces Association was concerned. A series of meetings in early 1947 led to a close partnership between the Legion and the largest of the individual service associations, with the Legion helping RAFA to start up new branches and giving advice with pensions work, while the Association encouraged those leaving the Air Force to join both organisations. RAFA also recognized the Legion's freedom to campaign against government, since, unlike RAFA, it was not inhibited by the presence of serving men and women in its ranks.* In no way put off by the subsequent 'political' storm that marked the Legion's 1948 pensions campaign (see above), RAFA became a strong supporter of the attempts to improve pension rates and was the vanguard of the group of ex-service associations that later joined up with the Legion to form a 'Joint Committee' for this purpose.[7] (See page 266.)

## Remembrance – a compromise

The Legion's publicity arrangements had been thoroughly overhauled for the Silver Jubilee. A Legion film, *Good Neighbours*, was shown on the entire Odeon circuit. A publicity van decorated in shades of blue, equipped with a microphone and powerful loudspeakers, toured the country blasting out rousing marches, bringing cheers from a party of German prisoners of war as it passed through Oxshott. There were Legion displays at the six main demobilization centres and by 1950 a press service was available to branches to provide local publicity.[8]

For all this, in the eyes of the general public the Legion was still largely associated with Remembrance. At the end of the Second World War the government had agreed that the dead of both wars should be observed on the Sunday preceding 11 November, following which the Legion's National Executive Council chose the Saturday immediately before Remembrance Sunday for the all-important Poppy Appeal. Happily for the Legion there was a universal feeling that the poppy, although clearly associated with battlefields of the earlier war, should continue as the symbol of Remembrance. There was some concern that a Saturday would affect poppy sales since most people only worked in the morning and went home in the afternoon, but the subsequent drop from the 1945 record was more likely due to economic circumstances.

By 1948 the Legion's leaders felt able to record that Sunday Remembrance was 'proving satisfactory'. But the rank-and-file took a different view. The 1948 Annual Conference decided unanimously that Remembrance Day ought to be restored to 11 November with the Silence at 11am, in other words a return to the pre-war arrangements. Coupled with this was the feeling that there had been a falling-off in the observance. But the NEC were not prepared to reopen the matter.[9]

The other events connected with Remembrance continued. At the 1946 Festival of Remembrance the accent was on youth, but a group of actors formed from those just out of the forces enacted the story of the poppy and General Maurice uttered the words of Remembrance for the last time as the Legion's President after fourteen years in office. The King looked strained after his wartime concerns, but the following year the newly-married Princess Elizabeth and Duke of Edinburgh were at the Albert Hall and in enthusiasm and emotions the 1947 Festival rivalled that of the pre-war years, all faithfully reported on BBC radio by Richard Dimbleby, with listeners no doubt joining in the

*When, however, the Legion opened its doors to serving men and women many years later it did not feel the same inhibitions.

community singing led by Stanley Holloway.

Nevertheless many in the Legion felt that there should be less spectacle and more remembrance. The solution was a compromise, the producer, former squadron leader Ralph Reader, arranging the programme so that the activity built up to a climax with the Act of Remembrance. But the youthful aspect continued with PT displays and sword dancing by boy soldiers and always a full representation of the women's services, in 1949 showing off their new uniforms against a pageant of female military and nursing dress going back to the time of Florence Nightingale. The Albert Hall was never less than packed for the occasion and some thought was given to moving to a larger venue such as the Empress Hall, but the tradition of over twenty years continued and 1950 saw the first televised broadcast of the event.[10]

# 1951 – 1955

## Austerity ends

Although the 1950 General Election returned the Labour government by a narrow majority a further election the following year saw the wartime leader, Winston Churchill, back as Prime Minister. His return coincided with an upturn in global economy and in Britain the post-war era of austerity at last came to an end, the last vestige, meat rationing, disappearing in 1954. But, while matters improved at home, tensions remained high in Europe and a large British garrison, now part of the NATO alliance, continued to be stationed in Germany, maintained by drafts of National Servicemen from the 160,000 called up each year under the 1948 Act.

By now much of the wartime dereliction was being swept away and a government initiative was producing over 300,000 new houses a year, many in 'new towns' around central shopping areas. There was full employment and even cuts in income tax and at last the path to prosperity seemed clear. There was too a resurgence of national pride symbolized by a young Queen. The much-loved George VI, worn down by wartime cares as much as illness, died in 1952. The previous year he had attended the Legion's 30th Anniversary Review in Hyde Park, inspecting a parade which included four thousand standards and, despite his frailty, standing a full thirty minutes for the march past. The Coronation in 1953 of his daughter, Elizabeth II, was an occasion for much rejoicing. The Legion's National Executive Council rose to their feet to be told that she had agreed to become Patron of the organization and a phalanx of fifty-five Legion standards took part in the Coronation procession, while nearly 40,000 Legionaries paraded for the Royal review of ex-service organizations, marching past the saluting base twenty abreast, followed by a convoy of their disabled comrades in motorized wheelchairs and buses.[11]

## A 'pretty mean' settlement

Taking part in the review, among them some of the wheelchair contingent, was one group of ex-servicemen whose spirits were not perhaps as high as the rest: those who had been brutally treated as prisoners of war by the Japanese. In 1951 their claims for compensation had been debated in Parliament and there were some present who felt that the government had not been as sympathetic as it might have been. Nevertheless the subsequent peace treaty with Japan provided for some £5 million of Japanese overseas assets to be made available, while immediate relief would be provided from similar assets in the United Kingdom, assessed at a figure somewhat below £1 million.

The response by the Far East Prisoners of War (FEPOW) Association was emphatic. They did not consider these amounts adequate, nor did they agree with the method of payment which was intended to reflect the degree of ill-treatment during captivity, something which was extremely difficult to prove a decade later. Above all they wanted a speedy settlement; their US and Australian counterparts had already received their payments based on the number of days they had spent in captivity.

They were, however, told that the Japanese economy would not stand reparations, a view the former prisoners found hard to accept since that economy was already expanding to the extent that it was creating unemployment in parts of the United Kingdom. The only money available was from assets frozen outside Japan, but it would be shared out equally as they wanted and in the end each former prisoner received around £60 between 1952 and 1955 in three instalments, including a bonus of £3 from the sale of the infamous Burma-Siam railway. Parliamentary action by the Legion's President raised the total received by each of the fifty thousand ex-prisoners to £76 10s. At 2000 prices this would be equivalent to just over £1,000.

The Legion had backed the FEPOW claims and the subsequent first instalment of £15 had been described as 'pretty mean' by a Legion spokesman, although one recipient called it 'a marvellous Christmas present'. The 1953 Conference called on the NEC to represent to government the inequity of the British settlements compared with those of America, Canada and Australia and the 1955 Conference resolved that the Legion should press for further compensation. By that stage US former POWs in Jap hands had received £1,000, worth some £13,000-14,000 today.

But there the matter rested. Although much bitterness had been expressed in the debates the Legion did not feel disposed to mount a crusade on the scale of compensation. A later generation might have taken a different view. Meanwhile the former prisoners got on with their lives, assisted by the Legion in war pensions claims whenever their physical condition could be connected to their wartime experiences. Any other trauma went unrecognized. As a postscript, the irony of which was not unnoticed by the FEPOWs, the Japanese Government claimed £5,000 for a fisherman accidentally killed in a nuclear test.[12]

## All change at the Ministry

As with all war disability pensions, the FEPOW claims were handled by the Ministry of Pensions which had been set up for this purpose during the 1914-18 war. In 1922 the government had proposed to merge the Pensions Ministry with another department, but the Legion's strong reaction, seen as against the interests of war pensioners, had stopped it in its tracks (see page 81). Now another merger was planned as part of the development of the state welfare system and this time the Legion was unable to prevent it. A request for a deputation to see the Prime Minister was rejected and a letter to every MP and peer achieved nothing. The merger duly went ahead and in 1953 the Ministry of Pensions and National Insurance was created with the responsibilities now split: while war pensions stayed with the new Ministry, medical treatment of war disabilities went to the Ministry of Health.

Once the Legion realized that it could not stop the merger it offered full co-operation, expressing the hope, somewhat tongue-in-cheek, that any savings would be devoted to increasing war pensions. But there was a real concern that the new arrangement would mean that the special situation of war pensioners would no longer be recognized, particularly as the hospital patients were now the responsibility of another department of state. It was aso a matter of principle: the unique position of the war pensioner should not only exist but should be manifest. A resolution at the 1953 Legion Conference reflected much disquiet.

Many of the fears were removed when, in recognition of the Legion's concern, the Government pledged that war pensioners would receive priority at NHS hospitals for their 'pensionable' injuries or illnesses. But when the 1955 Conference reviewed the situation there were conflicting experiences. Some saw the change as an improvement while others maintained that standards had fallen, with war pensioners having to wait longer for beds since half of those at the old Pensions Ministry hospitals were now taken up by NHS patients. There were complaints too that it took more time to get limbs fitted now that the Ministry of Health was in charge and the Conference sought a return to the previous system. This was plainly out of the question, but the government gave assurances that war pensioners would continue to receive special consideration and that there would be ex-service representation on the management committees of the hospitals concerned.

As far as the pensions side was concerned the change brought few complaints. And it would seem that either the hospital treatment of war pensioners improved or they simply became reconciled to their new circumstances. Nevertheless, some in the Legion felt that the position of the war pensioner had been diminished.[13]

## Another change to Remembrance

Even state welfare could not cope when the East Coast suffered disastrous flooding in the early part of 1953, causing nearly 300 deaths. Following (and no doubt in some cases preceding) the General Secretary's instructions to 'use the Legion machinery to the maximum' Legion halls were opened as reception centres, supplies of food and coal arranged, teams organized to clean and straighten up flooded houses (two coachloads came from Leicester for this purpose), while Women's Section members with washing machines set up laundries. As with similar disasters in the past, Legion help was available to all if it was needed; if, however, there was adequate other assistance then it was concentrated on the ex-service element of the community.[14]

Such practical activity raised the organization's profile. But the Legion anyway attracted more publicity than any other voluntary organization in the post-war period with over 100,000 press cuttings a year and much coverage by the BBC, which, despite the competing claims of the Korean War and the Football League, included highlights of the Annual Report in its Saturday nine o' clock news in January 1951. The BBC gave particularly strong support to the Poppy Appeal, in 1955 broadcasting a dramatized account of how the Legion came to the aid of each of the survivors of a section of infantry hit by a shell in 1944.[15]

The timing of Remembrance Day continued to cause difficulty. The churches had subscribed to the agreement to hold it on the Sunday immediately before 11 November. But that had clashed with important events in the church calendar and it was changed in 1955 to the second Sunday in November. There was some dispute too over the Festival. Television had given it a much wider audience and a number of Legion members, getting Conference support for their views, felt that it had become a showpiece for the armed forces instead of an occasion for ex-service reunion and Remembrance. But the fact of the matter was that the Festival now brought the Legion into the nation's living-rooms and if it was to continue to do so it needed spectacle, which the armed forces could provide. So the spirited hornpipe dancing, the Royal Marine Band sunset ceremonies, the impressive silent drill of the RAF and the leaping gymnasts continued. One story emerged after the death of George VI: the blind Sir Ian Fraser, who as Legion President had sat beside him, told how the King would describe to him the events, with a wealth of detail and a remarkable knowledge of the different forms of military dress.[16]

# 1956 – 1960

### 'You've never had it so good'

1956 was the year of Suez when, despite a successful Anglo-French military action, world reaction forced a withdrawal from the canal zone and Sir Anthony Eden resigned as Prime Minister. He was replaced by Harold Macmillan, the economy settled down and the British people entered a period of increasing prosperity. Wages rose faster than the price of goods and the indications of material wealth began to appear: cars, television sets and other items hitherto regarded as luxuries. The period was to be characterized by the Prime Minister's phase 'You've never had it so good'.

The nuclear deterrent was now in place in Britain's armoury, although duly attended by 'Ban the Bomb' campaigns, and plans were being made for a severe reduction in the strength of the armed forces, heralding the end of National Service. But 1956 also saw the centenary of the inauguration of the Victoria Cross and the Legion was involved by the government in running functions for the three hundred recipients who came from all over the Commonwealth, as well as for their welfare, helping too with the VC exhibition at Marlborough House. Such was the success of the celebrations that the gallant three hundred formed a permanent Association – the Victoria Cross Association – later taking in George Cross holders.[17]

### War pensions lose value

A major social change began at this time with the influx of West Indians and 1958 saw the first race riots in Britain. But the Legion's view had been expressed at the 1956 Annual Conference which not only condemned any antagonism against British ex-servicemen because of colour but regretted all other manifestations of the colour bar. It went on to assure coloured ex-servicemen that they would always be welcome in the Legion. This position was noted in *The Times* following the 1958 disturbances at Notting Hill: ' The British Legion will stand up for their (the coloured ex-servicemen's) right to be treated as equal citizens.'[18]

The Legion's unequivocal stance on such matters contributed to public respect for the organization and to continuing support for the Poppy Appeal. This support was more than ever needed as the continuing increase in the cost of living eroded the positions of war widows and the war-disabled, part of a deepening gulf between those in work and the rest of the community. The Legion's main efforts were now directed at trying to persuade government to restore War Pensions and War Widows' Pensions to their pre-war value, a campaign that was proving to be one of the longest and most frustrating in the organization's history (see Chapter 11). In some ways the better treatment of those returning from the Second World War, which the Legion had helped to ensure, disadvantaged their parents. There was not the same incentive among the younger men to

216

join in the fight, and this was reflected in the membership figures which continued to drift down from the peak which had been attained immediately following the war.[19]

The approaching end of National Service would also in time reduce the size of the pool from which the Legion drew its members. But not only the Legion had a recruiting problem. The Armed Forces were now to be all-regular and in 1958 the War Office sought the Legion's help in finding the men and women to join. It was not too clear what was envisaged, but the National President's interpretation was that the organization should simply try and educate public opinion towards a career in the Forces and the *Legion Journal* carried a series of articles and published rates of pay. The Legion did not, however, miss the opportunity to comment that success in recruiting for the Armed Forces would to some extent rest on what help a man would get when the time came to return to civil life, a field in which it had some hard-won experience.[20]

## Looking forward – and back

The pensions injustices apart, the Legion had now solved many of the problems it had originally faced and the state seemed likely to relieve it of more responsibility in the future, while the change to making regular payments to those in need had taken away some of the pressure at local level. A view was beginning to form that it had spare capacity. In 1958 the *Sunday Times* contributed to the debate by suggesting that the Legion should take on youth work.

The newspaper's proposal was not exactly a new idea. In the inter-war years the organisation had formed a connection with the Boy Scouts Association, largely to try and ensure that young people entertained no false ideas about the realities of war. But many of the boys concerned had found out for themselves in another conflict. The premise now was that the Legion had the character and organization to give youth a lead at a time when social change was creating some restlessness. At the 1960 Annual Conference, noting that most of the 'injustices and anomalies which ex-servicemen had to fight between the war no longer exist', the Chairman introduced a discussion of the relationship between the Legion and the community as a whole. It seemed unlikely to be an invigorating debate until a fluent young Welsh member* took the rostrum and began: 'I belong to the new generation and the new generation looks to the future.' By the time he had ended delegates were experiencing a surge of confidence and hope, while the Chairman, General Bucher, was moved to say, 'That is quite the best speech I have ever heard at any Legion Conference. I agree with every word that he said.' Following the conference a 'Committee of younger men' was assembled to review the whole matter and the Legion seemed set for a new course in the 1960s.[21]

Before this forward momentum began there had been some looking back into the past. *The Official History of The British Legion* was published in 1956. It had been written by an acknowledged historian, Graham Wooton, chosen from outside the Legion in order to provide a vivid and impartial view, and it was well received. Lord Beveridge, whose report had launched the welfare state, considered that the story had been told 'fully and admirably' and the *Manchester Guardian* described it as 'lively and even controversial'. Specially bound copies were presented to the Queen and the Queen Mother and the book was reviewed on radio in a broadcast called 'Service Not Self', which was itself acclaimed. It could certainly not be challenged over accuracy; the proof had been read by T.F. Lister and Colonel Crosfield, both closely involved with the Legion from its beginnings.[22]

This gave the Legion additional publicity, although the President's hope that the press

---

*The speaker, Windsor Spinks, was to become National Chairman in 1984.

would seize on the more controversial parts of the book was not realized. But the organization continued in any case to receive good press coverage, although perhaps rather more selective than in the past. Conference proceedings were reported in most nationals, the pensions campaign had sympathetic support, and there were usually articles of a reflective nature at Remembrance time mentioning the Legion and its work. Television sought spectacle and the pilgrimages to Cassino and Dunkirk to attend the unveiling of memorials in 1957 were well covered by the cameras, with General Horrocks, fast becoming a television 'star', providing a commentary. By 1960, however, press interest seems to have waned a little, the main focus being on controversial matters such as poppy collections in schools, and only one national paper sent a reporter to the Legion's conference that year.[23]

## Something lost?

As the sixties approached there were signs that the grip of Remembrance on the nation was beginning to loosen. One observer noted in 1956 that 'At 11am on last Remembrance Sunday I stood at a busy street corner in Westminster. People were strolling about unconcernedly, cars and taxis were on the move . . . a milkman clattered his racks of bottles.' He went on to suggest that if Remembrance was becoming so inconvenient to people then it should be dropped, or if it was considered worth the cost in pounds, shillings and pence, snarled traffic and frayed tempers then it should be restored to the proper day. It was a view shared by the Legion Conference in 1957: the two-minute silence should be observed at the proper time, the eleventh hour of the eleventh day of the eleventh month. Others outside the Legion felt the same. The headmaster of a church school, addressing a Legion branch on Remembrance Day 1959, said, 'No one over thirty can forget that stillness which made us reflect each November 11th on the sacrifice. . . The transfer of that silence from November 11th to Remembrance Sunday had made us lose something which had a lasting effect on our mind.'[24]

Even so Remembrance continued to be kept in its various ways. In Dublin over 1,000 attended at the Memorial Park. The same number of Legionaries paraded at the Welsh National Memorial in 1958, the first time that the Legion had organized the parade. In Fulford near York the branch members placed a poppy on each ex-serviceman's grave. In Caston in Norfolk the children laid the Legion's wreaths. Each place had its own custom.[25]

Local custom was reflected too in the Festivals of Remembrance around the British Isles that echoed the main event in the Albert Hall. In Dublin, in Heckmondwike, in Felixstowe, at the Ulster Hall in Belfast and in many other places the programmes ranged from the simple to the spectacular. At Abercyon in north-east Glamorgan there was a band, a youth choir and a tableau. At King's Lynn more than 120 performers took part in a programme which included excerpts from 'This Happy Breed' and 'Flarepath'. But all had the same ending – the solemn Act of Remembrance. In London all eyes turned to the Royal party in 1957 when 'Soldiers of the Queen', once again a popular march, roused the audience to sing the words and Her Majesty was seen to be joining in. The Albert Hall ceremony now had the third largest viewing and listening audience in the country, exceeded only by the Queen's Christmas broadcast and the Cup Final. As the *Sunday Dispatch* noted, 'After two hours of this moving ceremony the rest of the evening's programme seemed lacking in spectacle.' Perhaps therefore the country was not, after all, forgetting the sacrifice of earlier generations, simply remembering in a different way.[26]

## 1961 – 1965

### Attempts to join the EEC

The wave of economic prosperity continued into the 1960s, but the government's attempts to secure the trade advantages that might result from Britain joining the European Economic Community were frustrated when, largely due to French influence, entry was blocked on the grounds that Britain's close relationship with the United States would bring too much transatlantic influence into Europe. The American relationship caused difficulties too at home. It had enabled Britain to adopt the Polaris missile as a nuclear deterrent, but this infuriated the anti-nuclear campaigners and the protests intensified.

As far as the Legion was concerned, the possibility of entry into the EEC raised worries over loss of national sovereignty, reflected in a resolution at the 1962 Annual Conference which also sought to preserve the ties with the Commonwealth; it was to be reaffirmed at the 1968 Conference. Such resolutions were simply an expression of feeling and at best thcy would only attract publicity in thc media. But there was also some disquiet among disabled ex-servicemen who felt that they might lose benefits by being put on a par with their continental counterparts. In this case the Legion consulted the government, receiving an assurance that even if Britain entered the Common Market the position of war pensioners or the disabled would be unaffected.[27]

Ties with the Commonwealth were amply demonstrated by the flow of immigrants in these years and the same Conference felt strongly that those who had given war service should have preference when seeking admission to Britain. The following year delegates passed a resolution declaring their abhorrence of the activities of 'certain groups that have arisen' and called for legislation to make it an offence to incite hatred on racial or religious grounds, the resolution being passed to the Home Office. The Legion was merely adding its voice to the many who had expressed the same feelings.[28]

### Clashes with CND

There was no thought, however, of legislating against anti-nuclear marches and the Campaign for Nuclear Disarmament was now in full swing. The Legion certainly supported their right to march; that was one of the freedoms for which two wars had been fought. But it drew the line at the involvement of war memorials in the protests. In Bristol the Legion persuaded the Council to forbid the use of a local Cenotaph as the centre of a CND rally, much to the anger of the CND. In Twickenham CND plans to lay a Hiroshima wreath at the war memorial were strongly opposed by the Legion and a clash was only avoided when the vicar offered the church for the wreath-laying. The CND succeeded in holding a meeting at the war memorial in Kettering but afterwards the memorial was found to be defaced with their symbols. St Ives Legion Branch members formed a shoulder-to-shoulder barrier to prevent the local protesters from meeting at the memorial, but the police interceded and the rally took place elsewhere.

The controversy continued, Legion members being encouraged by Marshal of the Royal Air Force Sir John Slessor to ensure that the memorials to the fallen were not desecrated for political purposes. A resolution at the 1963 Conference asked for pressure on local authorities to this end and the Legion's National Executive Council brought the resolution to the notice of all concerned, from local parish councils to the Home Office.

However, the anti-nuclear campaign had lost impetus by that year, with a decline in public support.

The irony of this episode is that both sides recognized the significance of the memorials as an expression of the hope for peace by acting as reminders of the horrors of war.[29]

## The Legion and youth

There were rallies of a rather different sort in 1961 to celebrate the Legion's 40th anniversary. The accent was on the founders of the movement and in many places the original branches led the march past at County assemblies, while those whose membership dated from 1921 were especially feted whether at a special dinner in Metropolitan Area or at a hot-pot supper and concert as at Ladybarn in Manchester. Brunel Cohen appeared on *This is Your Life*. There were tattoos, carnivals, dinners and dances, services in churches and cathedrals and a London to Nottingham Poppy motor rally, while Legion floral badges were proudly displayed at over 200 parks around the country, Bangor in County Down going one better with a badge in lights.[30] Conference that year was addressed by the Duke of Edinburgh, who, following the line of more Legion involvement with youth, described his Award Scheme. More information was given in the *Legion Journal* and succeeding issues carried articles on youth activities ranging from Boy Scouts to the YMCA, with the suggestion that Legion members should assist these activities in any way that they could – by enrolling as scout or cub masters, by using special skills to help with the Award scheme projects and so on. There was encouragement for Legion branches to form their own youth clubs, but there was to be no central direction: branches were to make their own rules and determine their own activities.*

This drew a limited response. Some branches, mainly in urban areas, formed youth clubs, others assisted existing youth organizations such the Sea Cadets or the Army Cadet Force and a number of members followed the suggestion to become involved as individuals. But it was 'patchy': while fifteen branches in Metropolitan Area ran youth clubs, Cornwall reported in 1962 that 'one branch has formed a youth club and another is being considered'. At the 1963 Conference the Berkshire delegate pointed out that few branches treated the subject seriously and asked for a national policy. But the conference rejected the idea of a Youth Section to stand alongside the Women's Section, the National Chairman stressing that such a step would suggest that the object was to enhance the Legion rather than assist the community. The branches actually involved in youth work were not however satisfied and the 1964 Conference agreed that the NEC should set up a Youth Advisory Council and called for a clear statement on the Legion's youth policy.

The next year the Council set out the policy, and it was clear enough: where a youth activity existed in the branch locality then the branch should try and strengthen it; if it did not exist then the Legion branch should act with others to provide an activity; only where there was no one else to help should the Legion branch go ahead on its own. It went on to emphasize that no special machinery was being set up for youth activities; the existing structure must provide any assistance needed.

It may have seemed a far cry from the heady atmosphere of the 1960 Conference where it had appeared that the Legion was going to make youth a central theme for the 1960s. But the organization was hardly suited to youth work on this scale without affecting its other activities. At any rate the air had been cleared and meanwhile useful assistance had been given to youth organizations. In some branches Legion Youth

---

*Branch Junior Sections had been permitted as far back as 1936; but this had simply been in response to grass roots requests.

Sections had flourished – Newton Aycliffe in Durham attracted 350 young people with 'beat' dances – but the involvement remained small: an article in the Journal in 1965 indicates that there were two youth sections in the East Midland Area and one in Wales.[31]

## 'Stop living in the past'

Assistance to the youth of the community had been only one of the suggestions of the committee which had been set up following the stirring speech at the 1960 Conference. The others were that the Legion should make itself more attractive to the younger generation and become more of a family organization. But whilst the committee was reaching its conclusions a former national serviceman was making his own views known. 'What's wrong with the Legion?' he asked in early 1961. Why is it closing branches and why are Poppy Day organizers in despair? He gave his answer. In order to survive the Legion needed national servicemen; but, lacking the purpose of wartime, many of them had seen their service as a waste of time. For that reason the Legion approach, based on standards, parades and exhortations, drove them away. They lived for today, not yesterday. In the eyes of today's youth, he maintained, a regimental colour was simply a piece of cloth on a pole, not something to die for. If the Legion wanted the national serviceman it should let him see that it was as concerned with the present as it was with the past, interest him in service work and forget the rest. By the same reasoning it was itself to blame for the declining response to the Poppy Appeal: the public saw only parades, standards and bemedalled old soldiers. It must stop living in the past.

Predictably his views provoked a strong reaction and even a former Minister of War, a Legion member, entered the fray to disagree. The matter went straight to the heart of the organization's image problem: was it a charity looking after those who had suffered in the nation's interests or was it simply a social gathering of veterans? In practice it had always been both, but the two aspects did not necessarily sit well together, the latter, as he had pointed out, sometimes obscuring the former.[32]

## A change to the Charter

If it were needed, there was anyway a reminder of the charitable role. Up to 1961 all charities had been governed by a patchwork of acts, some survivors from feudal days, but on the first of January that year, following an eight-year study, the Charities Act 1960 came into force. The Legion was required to register – and so were many of the nearly 5,000 branches – all those with property or investments, an exercise which needed headquarters advice. It was a long process and registration was done geographically, starting in Surrey and Bedfordshire.

Charities got tax relief, but discussion with the Revenue had indicated that the Legion needed to change the Royal Charter to make its charitable aims clear. This was done, but in the process some of the original 1925 wording disappeared – 'to educate public opinion . . . that the welfare of ex-servicemen . . . is a national duty', that 'ex-service men and women . . . are entitled to preferential treatment in employment'. No member of the public would now deny that the nation had a responsibility towards ex-service men and women; if the Legion had achieved nothing else it had at least ensured that. And, in a time of prosperity backed by adequate state relief for the jobless, the concept of 'preference' in employment must have seemed outmoded and perhaps unrealistic. The rewording recorded a significant social change.[33]

Even so enough was left of the old wording for the author of the Legion's Annual

Report to be moved to say of the Charter on its fortieth anniversary '(it) is somewhat forbidding in form and style but it verges on poetry in some of its passages and has the ideals of Lincoln's Gettysburg address in its phraseology'.[34]

## 'A new name and a new look' to Remembrance

The timing of Remembrance was, however, outside the scope of the Charter and the arguments continued. In 1962 the Bishop of Chelmsford deplored the loss of significance by the change of date from 11 November. Furthermore it gave clergy the dilemma of whether to be in church or join in the civic observance in the open air. A newspaper suggested that it was the forces of materialism that had been behind the change, so that prosperity should not be endangered, and other commentators stressed the importance of the 11th. In 1963 the Legion Conference made an attempt at a compromise, suggesting that a two-minute silence be again held on that day. The NEC pointed out that this proposal had been tried before but the government was adamant, a response 'viewed with dismay' by Conference the following year. But the Council was firm: previous approaches to the Home Secretary had not changed the situation and further action was pointless.

Quite another tack was taken by the Archdeacon of Westminster – 'a new name and an entirely dramatic new look'. It brought a deluge of letters to the press but the most emphatic response was by *Daily Mirror* readers – 'no change'. Nevertheless many advocates for change wanted to look forwards rather than backwards and sought a day dedicated to peace, returning to the charge that the Legion's attitude 'glorified war' and showing that its spirited efforts in the 1930s to help keep the peace had soon been forgotten. But the winds from both directions had begun to slacken by 1965 and that year the Legion's National President met with the British Council of Churches who agreed the need to remember past sacrifices. Perhaps the last word on timing lay with the famous cricketer Freddie Trueman who declared that changing the date from 11 November because the weekday traffic might be disrupted 'made his blood boil'.[35]

Even on a Sunday it was difficult to control traffic and delegates at the 1965 Conference called for the nation to honour the dead and stop all people and traffic at 11 a.m. on that day. This caused the NEC some difficulty over implementation but they approached the local authorities and the motoring organizations and instituted a press campaign. Some places had less of a traffic problem, such as the annual service at the top of Great Gable near Keswick in Northumberland, where wreaths and poppies were fixed to the the summit of the mountain. Meanwhile the Legion's branches simply got on with ensuring Remembrance was kept, as they had done year in and year out.[36]

There were small changes in the Festival of Remembrance. In 1962 four poppy collectors who had been out that day were included in the muster to warm applause from the audience and, although an approach by the President, General Leese, to the Archbishop to Canterbury to allow Roman Catholic and Jewish representatives to take part in the service met with the advice that it 'was not yet appropriate', they were able to attend as guests in 1965. The tradition continued for the President to recite Binyon's words 'They shall grow not old . . .'. There had been some dispute over the wording of the second line: 'age shall not weary them' was generally accepted, but in 1960 a signed copy of the poem in Binyon's handwriting, presented to the Legion by a Mr Congreve, read 'age shall not wither them'. It then emerged that another handwritten copy was held by Almondsbury Branch, apparently presented by Binyon to the Branch Chairman when the branch formed and hanging in the local church of St Mary. It contained the line 'Age shall not *weary* them'.[37]

## Churchill's death

Sir Winston Churchill had attended the very first of the Festivals in 1927. The same year he had become associated with Westerham Branch, following his attendance at the ceremony of laying the foundation stone for the new branch headquarters when, as a practised bricklayer, he had exchanged banter with the branch members at their work. At his funeral in 1965 two Legion standards brought up the rear of the cortege as it wended its way through the packed London streets. The only two devices carried in this great procession, apart from Churchill's Banner of the Warden of the Cinque Ports and his Garter banner, were the Legion's National Standard and that of the Westerham Branch, of which Churchill had been President.[38]

# 1966 - 1970

## Material wealth grows

1966 was to some the zenith of the 1960s. England had won the World Cup and London was a centre of modern culture with the accent on youth and ever-receding boundaries for freedom of expression. A new prime minister, Harold Wilson, at the head of a government elected on a modernization platform, spoke of another industrial revolution fired by the latest technology. Rhetoric could not, however, disguise the old problems and there were economic crises as the value of sterling fell and Britain's balance of payments deficit grew, necessitating wage restrictions that led to a wave of industrial disputes. Despite all this, material wealth continued to grow with car and television ownership steadily increasing and more than half of the population becoming home owners, or at least possessing a mortgage. A somewhat surprising end to the decade was therefore the replacement of the Labour government with a Conservative administration.

This period also saw the re-emergence of the troubles in Northern Ireland. Catholic allegations of discrimination developed into civil rights marches, provoking violence which was soon exploited by hard-line Republicans wanting to join the province to Southern Ireland. In 1969 the situation had become so bad that the government sent troops to Belfast and Londonderry. The Legion's immediate concern was for the Northern Irish ex-servicemen and their families caught up in the disorders: one old man who had served in both wars had been burned out of his house, losing all his possessions including his cherished British Empire Medal. Traditionally, the Legion crossed the sectarian divide and a letter to the *Belfast Telegraph* emphasized that any member of the Northern Ireland ex-service community, whether Catholic or Protestant, would get its help. It also moved swiftly to defuse an attempt to organize ex-servicemen along sectarian lines. It was perhaps fortunate at this difficult time that the National Vice Chairman was resident in Northern Ireland.[39]

## Yet more changes in the Ministry

In the more rarified atmosphere of Whitehall further changes were taking place in the organization of the welfare state. In 1966 the Ministry of Pensions and National

Insurance took in the National Assistance Board and became the Ministry of Social Security. But two years later the new ministry was itself absorbed into the Department of Health and Social Security. This meant that the original Pensions Ministry, set up during the Great War to administer war disability and war widows' pensions, had endured its third change of master in fifteen years. But by now both its staff and the Legion were inured to government reorganizations and both changes seem to have been made without difficulty and without any effect on the relationships that had developed and between the Legion and officials.[40]

Nevertheless the Seebohm Report of 1969 into social welfare caused the Legion concern by appearing to suggest that the war disabled were of lesser concern than the chronically ill and arousing fears that the compensatory element of war pensions might disappear in a general levelling up of welfare payments. Moreover, the report argued for more delegation of social welfare to local authorities, a prospect which worried the Legion because of the local authorities' different levels of concern for war pensioners.[41]

## Public relations mobilised

A BBC interview with the National President and the General Secretary on the eve of the 1967 Annual Conference had been carefully prepared: it began with a suggestion that the public image was of parades, ceremonies and poppies, went on to question the need for such an organization in an advanced welfare state and noted that only one in ten ex-servicemen belonged anyway. But the Legion was already well aware that it was undersold – its fundraising was barely able to keep up with the need – and the previous year new PR consultants had been appointed. In an increasingly competitive charity environment the importance of the task meant that the head of the consultancy sat in on National Executive Council meetings.

The public, and particularly the younger generation, needed to be educated in the Legion's work. Not only were their contributions necessary for the Appeal but without their help there would be no Appeal: the loyal band of poppy collectors that had served the Legion so well for so long was now starting to fade away because of age or infirmity. Younger people had to be recruited. There was also a need to get more members into the Legion itself, and this would be an associated campaign.

The immediate aim was to establish a favourable press climate – to be exploited in the period immediately before the Poppy Appeal – launched with a series of press lunches in the provinces. This was followed by national advertising; but the new campaign reached its zenith with young mini-skirted girls photographed with trays of poppies, an image that at once brought the sedate Legion into the 'swinging sixties', and proved an irresistible attraction for the press.

On a more staid note there were Legion articles in national magazines and regimental journals, and also in teachers' publications so that the message could be passed on to pupils; these gave rise to a number of inquiries from schools about the Legion's work and it responded by sending them a new film *In for a Penny, In for a Pound*. Nor was the publicity potential of the Pall Mall headquarters location overlooked: its windows featured articles made by disabled men in the Legion's associated companies, Harrods providing the window dressing free of charge, while a shop inside the building sold the goods and answered inquiries.

By the end of the decade the Legion publicity operation was in full swing. But if the Poppy Appeal still struggled to meet the demands on benevolence and membership had not yet achieved a significant upswing, at least the Legion was holding on to its position at a time when much of the population had never known the effects of war and some held extreme views about the military and any organization connected with it.[42]

## A new distinction

The Fiftieth Anniversary of the Legion was due in 1971 and much thought was given to its celebration as the 1960s drew to a close. Naturally the Sovereign's involvement would be sought; she was the Legion's Patron. But opinions differed over a Royal Review. As a report to the NEC delicately put it: 'a review may not commend itself to the movement as a whole'. This did not in any way imply that the Legion's respect for the monarchy had diminished. It remained fiercely loyal to the crown and any member who failed to stand for the National Anthem faced almost certain loss of membership. The caveat simply recognized that parades were less popular with the new generation of Legionaries than their fathers. In any case the Legion now sought a Royal prefix to its title to mark its Golden Jubilee. This distinction had already been granted to the Canadian Legion but a resolution at the 1966 Annual Conference that the British Legion should seek to follow suit had been precipitate. The time was now ripe, but inquiries to the Home Office indicated that a resolution was needed, so the National Executive Council duly passed one, keeping the matter 'strictly confidential'. It later emerged that the Queen had been only too pleased by the request; the feeling was that, if anything, the distinction was overdue.[43]

## The guardian of Remembrance

The Legion's distinguished service might be about to be recognized but its role as a guardian of Remembrance still put it in the firing line. In 1967 a Sunday magazine cover carried a picture of the Festival of Remembrance across which had been printed 'The annual confidence trick' and the accompanying article saw the occasion as an aspect of 'ritual perversion', exploiting the memory of the dead and encouraging further wars. The same year press and TV reports chose to extract from a Church Assembly debate on the future form of Remembrance only those comments which were derogatory – 'An empty and pathetic formality' – 'glorifies war' – forcing the Legion to issue a statement that it was not a glorification of war but the exact opposite. The Legion was represented on the subsequent committee which revised the Order of Service, aiming to make it more relevant to young people. But the following year there was severe criticism of Remembrance on the BBC's *Any Questions* programme, leading to a confrontation between a panel member and Lord Fraser, who called the remarks 'repugnant'. But the Legion's stand, combined with its campaign to get across the meaning of Remembrance to the new generations, was beginning to make headway. In 1969 it was particularly noticeable that at the Cenotaph service in London and at Remembrance Day gatherings across the country many more young people were taking part than in previous years. The *Daily Express* reported that at the Cenotaph 'There was scarcely a grey head to be seen in the crowd . . . onlookers included students in college scarves and teenagers in 'mod clothes', while the *Daily Sketch* observed that 'Thousands of young people crowded in Whitehall'.[44]

The Festival too remained popular prime-time viewing, broadcast in colour for the first time in 1970, although cut from two to one-and-a-half hours. By now the Legion President's views had been accepted by the established church and both a Roman

Catholic priest and the Moderator of the Free Churches assisted with the service. But the rest remained, the thunderous roar that greeted the arrival of the Chelsea Pensioners, the stirring entry of the massed Legion standards and the drifting cloud of poppies in the silence that followed the Exhortation, awakening deep emotions. Like the Legion itself, it was now part of the fabric of the nation.[45]

★      ★      ★

Much had happened since 1945. The welfare state had been introduced. By fits and starts the nation had grown richer and living standards had risen. There was now little of the grinding poverty that had afflicted the survivors of the Great War and their families. But suffering and deprivation continued to haunt some homes and the Legion still needed to act as the nation's conscience. Remembrance remained the key.

# CHAPTER 10

## STRUCTURE 1946-1970

# *A New Generation Enters*

### 1946 – 1950

**The post-war management**

When he gave up the office in 1947 Major General Sir Frederick Maurice had been Legion President for fifteen of its twenty-six years. They had been momentous times – the grim days of the 1930s, the meetings with Hitler, yet another war and the vital task of preparing the organization for the return of peace. Aged seventy-seven and the Legion's Grand Old Man, he was more than ready to retire.

Maurice suggested Admiral of the Fleet Lord Tovey as his successor, but Lieutenant Colonel Sir Ian Fraser, formerly Legion Vice Chairman, blinded in the first war, head of St Dunstan's and an MP, was also nominated. On the way to Conference in the Isle of Man that year Fraser persuaded the ferry captain to allow him to address delegates over the ship's public address system. Meanwhile the Admiral was detained at a family funeral and Fraser was duly elected. The Chairmanship changed the same year, Brigadier General Fitzpatrick, who had received a knighthood in 1946, handing over to Lieutenant Colonel Gordon Larking, who had been commissioned from the ranks and whose robust approach 'the Legion should not plead . . . it should be strong enough to tell the government what it will accept' – impressed conference delegates. Of a totally different character was his Vice Chairman, Major General Sir Richard Howard-Vyse, who had served with the Household Cavalry, commanded a brigade under Allenby and was to become Chairman in 1950. But both men were destined to give the Legion long and devoted service.[1]

On his departure from office, Brigadier General Fitzpatrick wrote of the Legion staff 'I speak with some experience when I say that I have never been associated with so fine a body of men and women'. The tribute was deserved but some of the staff had been with the Legion from the start and were now getting old. Fourteen retired in 1947, including Captain Willcox, the Appeals Secretary, who was now nearly seventy, and the following two years saw the shedding of many of the additional staff who had been taken on to cope with the extra work arising at the end of the war. Even so, in 1949 there were twice the headquarters staff there had been ten years before.[2]

The working conditions of those who remained were poor. They had occupied the war-damaged building in Pall Mall since October 1946, but building restrictions meant that few repairs could be done until 1949 and in the meantime some departments had to be housed elsewhere. The situation worsened when economies forced some staff back into the main building before renovation was complete. There was not even room for the National Executive Council; from 1946 to 1962 they held their meetings, with a few exceptions, at Church House in Dean's Yard, Westminster.[3]

In 1946 the Legion established an office in Brussels. Its main purpose was to give advice to those wishing to visit war graves and the Legion representative worked closely with the Imperial War Graves Commission, but he was also able to advise the continental branches on a range of matters and this side of his work was to grow.[4]

## Disputed boundaries

The field staff had also been reduced in the immediate post-war years to one office in each Area. By now some Counties were able to help more with administration, but the majority simply lacked the resources and the pattern was irregular. In a few cases there were paid county secretaries whose contribution was recognized in 1948 when the NEC agreed to regard them as Legion staff for pension purposes. County spirit was demonstrated in the bleak winter of 1947: with the trains running behind schedule, if running at all, one seventy-year-old retired colonel cycled one freezing night forty miles to a County meeting in Workington and back. Although Groups remained optional there were moves to get them official recognition and, although a bid at the 1947 Annual Conference failed, a rather more equivocal motion two years later that they 'should have a recognized place' in the Legion was approved.[5] There were no Groups in Metropolitan Area. It was split into eight Districts, but in 1949 they re-formed into four 'Counties' – North East, South East and so on – which, in time, would attract the same loyalties as the shire counties in other Areas. Nevertheless the Metropolitan net cast for fifteen miles around Charing Cross brought controversy as the Legion grew in the post-war years. Some new branches considered themselves part of Surrey or Middlesex, which belonged to another Area, rather than to Metropolitan Area. There was much bickering and even a threat to appeal to the Privy Council before it was agreed that such disputes would be settled by consultation between the Area Chairmen concerned.[6]

## An East African Area?

Boundary disputes would have been unlikely had a 1949 proposal to create an East African Area gone ahead. The Legion was active in Uganda and Tanganyika, and especially so in Kenya where many ex-servicemen had settled, including a former Legion Chairman, Brigadier Sir Francis Fetherston-Godley. There were two sections, African and European, and in the African section, 41,000 strong, there were even some former askaris who had fought at Omdurman. The Legion regularly broadcast from Nairobi, while bulletins were read out at the Legion Welfare Centres that had been established in the Tribal Areas. But, although the Area suggestion did not get NEC approval, the work continued, directed in Kenya by a Kenya Executive Council and only partly distracted by the Mau Mau insurrection in the late 1950s in which many Legion members served with the Police Reserve. In both Kenya and Tanganyika there were headquarters buildings and a club for each section, while much attention was given to education projects for the former askaris. Attending the annual conference in Uganda in 1957, the Legion's National Chairman noted that the African members were just as keen on quizzing the leadership as their counterparts in UK. When independence came the territories formed separate ex-service organizations which affiliated to the British Commonwealth Ex-Services League, the successor to the British Empire Services League. Only Nairobi retained a Legion branch.[7]

## Branches go into property

Back in Britain the immediate post-war years were marked by an enormous growth in Legion branches, reaching a peak of nearly five and a half thousand by 1950, while reflecting the shift from a rural to an urban society. In some cases the existing branch grew too large. Roundhay and Harehills, formed in 1933 with fourteen members, had 2,500 by 1947, having enrolled over a thousand since the war. Unless such branches split into smaller units there was a risk of losing touch with members.[8] Many branches were now investing in property, often as memorials to those lost in the war. The buildings varied enormously, depending on branch circumstances. At Braintree in Essex the local branch acquired a handsome Georgian house, which they renamed Victory Hall; a similarly imposing property was purchased through voluntary donations at Blandford in Dorset, as a memorial to the fallen, while Gorseinon and Loughor in South Wales were the possessors of a mansion set in its own grounds. But Healing near Grimsby knocked two tin huts into one, while Beeston bought buildings on an airfield sixty miles away and re-erected them 'under service conditions', sleeping on site until the work was done.[9]

Headquarters was well aware that a properly housed branch was more effective and kept its membership and a scheme launched in 1948 assisted branches to occupy their own premises. The branch raised 25 per cent of the cost and the Legion arranged a building society loan for the rest, holding the property in trust for the branch. By 1950 it was acting as Trustee for nearly 500 branch properties with others in the process of being conveyed, providing legal advice and arranging mortgages and insurance.[10]

A branch could also get a roof over its head through the activities of its associated club. Indeed most clubs were started by branches on the basis that the profits would finance the purchase of a building to provide a home for both branch and club. But the reverse side of the coin was that running a club brought its own problems and in early 1947 a special committee was set up to deal with their administration, introducing a new set of model rules by which the club had to operate if it wished to include 'British Legion' in its title. A club often handed over its building to the Legion, so that it could not be sequestrated in the event of failure, which was then held in trust for the branch with the club becoming a tenant.[11]

## The membership peaks

The astonishing post-war rise in Legion membership did not happen of its own accord. During the war the Legion had striven to identify with the interests of those serving and as hostilities drew to a close many branches appointed sector wardens who made personal approaches to the returning service men and women. But, even if approached, by no means did all respond: at a strength of one million the Legion represented one in ten of those eligible to wear its badge.[12]

Membership growth continued to be a high priority but nearly as much attention now had to be given to keeping the new members and the 1947 recruiting plan dealt equally with recruiting and retention. Unlike the early days mass meetings were not in favour, although much use was made of cinemas, with displays in foyers and advertising slides. With Army and RAF co-operation pamphlets were distributed to those leaving the services, now mainly national servicemen, and the publicity van toured rural areas. Retention, however, depended on the branch. Well-led, active branches kept up their membership; inanimate ones declined.

It was not easy for headquarters to gauge the size of the membership at any one moment. In theory affiliation fee receipts provided the answer, but in practice the method of payment – branches had to purchase receipts in advance while they sought to get members to pay subscriptions – clouded the picture. But in 1948 it became clear that the membership had reached a peak the previous year and, despite the recruiting campaign, was now starting to drop. The General Secretary was philosophical in 1949, putting the decline down to a loss of the immediate post-war enthusiasm, while others attributed it to expectations not realized or simply the ineffectiveness of some branches. Only in the North West was the membership holding up. Here the Area President and Chairman, General Sir James O'Dowda, had exerted a strong personal influence since 1936. Described as 'the most lovable and modest of Legion leaders', he had visited every branch in his thickly-populated Area and millworkers were proud of his friendship.[13] He finally gave up office in 1949 at the age of seventy-eight, but he left a legacy of active branch membership committees and the Area continued to thrive.[14]

### Second World War men make their voice heard

The Legion's National Chairman in 1946, Brigadier General Fitzpatrick, was a man of stern countenance. But at the Legion's Annual Conference that year he was clearly captivated by the large number of young ex-servicewomen facing him, raising his bushy eyebrows and bowing first to one side and then the other, and receiving curtsies and bobs in return. This, the first post-war conference, coincided with the London Victory Parade. There was much pressure on overnight accommodation, delegates being invited to bed-and-breakfast with London members but, in view of rationing and shortages, instructed to 'bring some food with you'. Nevertheless nearly 1,200 delegates assembled in the

*The 1948 Conference at the Albert Hall with nearly two thousand delegates.*

Dominion Theatre before moving on the second day to a venue large enough to hold them all, the Central Hall, Westminster. Despite these problems it was a lively and optimistic conference. The blind Sir Ian Fraser, then Vice Chairman, conducted the proceedings for an hour, calling for 'Ayes' and 'Noes' in place of the usual show of hands and was rewarded with prolonged applause. Business was brisk. There was much concern with the housing shortage, but the most telling comment came from the South Ealing delegate: 'No resolution has ever built a single house.' Conference was moved when Major Sir Brunel Cohen, giving up office after having been the Legion Treasurer since its formation, said simply at the end of his report, 'I have finished.'[15]

Even more delegates attended the 1947 Conference in the Isle of Man, arriving in the *Lady of Mann* which had taken part in both the Dunkirk evacuation and the D-Day invasion, now with the Legion flag at its masthead, and the *Daily Graphic* devoted three pages of news and pictures to the conference. But the largest attendance was in 1948 when over 1,750 delegates were present at the Albert Hall, representing one third of all branches, the Chairman, Colonel

230

Gordon Larking, controlling them by waving his arms and making use of 'a voice like a bull', as the closing speaker put it. Much feeling was again vented over housing – 'intolerable' – and delegates, the post-war men and women now finding their feet, missed few opportunities to 'ginger up', as they put it, the NEC. There were still over 1,400 present the following year, packed into the Royal Aquarium Theatre in Great Yarmouth, and when the Chairman sought to establish the number of 1939-45 delegates by asking them to raise their agendas, a sea of paper arose. But there were also at least twenty Boer War veterans. When the Duke of Gloucester addressed the 1950 Conference at the Albert Hall it was the first occasion a member of the Royal Family had been present since 1935, when his brother, the then Prince of Wales, had made his 'hand of friendship' speech. By now the Second World War men were taking the lead in many of the debates, especially concerned with the plight of the disabled trying to exist on eroded

*A famous speaker addresses Conference 1950; Jim Prince of Cardiff.*

pensions, giving rise to a *Time*s leader on the subject, while the *Manchester Guardian* commented on the parade at the Cenotaph, 'It's hard to remember that they ever broke the hearts of Sergeant Majors!'[16]

One of the most important matters discussed at Conference was the Legion's financial situation, with the Treasurer often closely questioned by delegates. There was much to discuss in 1947. For the first time receipts did not meet expenditure and the Legion had to draw on reserves. Encouraged by the high income of the war years and conscious of an ageing ex-service community, it had begun to invest in convalescent and retirement homes. But it not only faced increased expenditure on the elderly, it had to meet the needs of a new generation of ex-servicemen and their families. In the meantime Poppy Appeal income had fallen in the bleak post-war years. Nor did the situation improve in succeeding years. In both 1948 and 1949 a quarter of a million pounds had to be taken from reserves, eating into the £2 million accumulated in the war years. Administration too was under-financed, Conference 1950 having refused to raise the Affiliation Fee from 1/6d, set in 1921, to 2/-. [17]

One small financial success was the *Legion Journal* which, although the continuing paper shortage kept it at its war-time pocket-size, now had a circulation of 120,000, nearly twice the pre-war 70,000. Perhaps the concise reporting demanded by the format was popular. The price remained at threepence but in 1950 the easing of restrictions meant that the size could be increased.[18]

## 1951 – 1955

### Tribulations of an MP President

Sir Ian Fraser's presidency continued to be overshadowed by politics. When his party was in opposition there were accusations that he was using the Legion as a weapon against the government. When the situation was reversed he sometimes felt obliged to follow the party whip rather than press the Legion's case. This, hardly surprisingly, led to some criticism within the Legion: in 1950 a Conference motion sought to debar an MP as

President, although it was overwhelmingly defeated, and when Fraser accepted a government decision on war pensions in 1952 a vote of censure was attempted at the Legion's Annual Conference that year. Back in Parliament there was a comment that it would be better 'if the British Legion were to leave politics entirely out of its considerations ... and, in particular, if it were to have as President a non-politician'. Such observations were of course made purely for political ends. But the whole episode would have an effect on the Legion approach to government over the pensions campaign which had provoked these attacks: lobbying ministers under a united ex-service banner would become the preferred tactic.

In any event Sir Ian was held in high regard as a public figure and was made a Companion of Honour in the Coronation Honours List.[19]

### Staff career structure introduced

Another singular honour, although in no way connected with his Legion activities, had been awarded to Major General Howard-Vyse, who had succeeded Colonel Gordon Larking as National Chairman: in 1951 he was appointed Colonel of the the Royal Horse Guards and Gold Stick in Waiting, in effect the Sovereign's protector on ceremonial occasions. He was nonetheless an unostentatious man who worked hard during his three years of office and was well liked by the rank-and-file. His successor as Chairman in 1953 was Captain Hampson, the proprietor of a newpaper in Salford who had served with the Lancashire Fusiliers in the Great War.[20]

Sir Richard Howard-Vyse took a close interest in the Legion staff, holding a party for them at his house after their exertions at the Annual Conference. Nor were they overlooked in the Honours List. The General Secretary, J.R. Griffin, received a well-deserved CBE in 1953, an award which A.G. Webb had been given the previous year for his work as the Legion Pensions Secretary and a high honour for a department head; it recognized an almost unique contribution over thirty years, not only to the Legion but to the ex-service community as a whole. Elsewhere, however, there were problems: a number of long-serving staff had left for better-paid posts and in 1955 a proper career structure was introduced with graded appointments and adequate rewards to take account of long hours and weekend activity,[21] although in 1967 it had to be modified following another batch of staff resignations.[22]

*The Legion's Chairman: Sir Richard Howard-Vyse attending the Queen in his capacity as Gold Stick-in-Waiting.*

In the meantime the completion of an extension to the Pall Mall headquarters building in 1952, at last enabled all departments to be housed together.[23]

### Ceremonial at home and abroad

The duties of the Southern Area staff included the annual Sandhurst parade, started in 1928 and resumed after the war with the 1939-45 men joining their comrades to

*Standards dipped in salute at Sandhurst in 1958, shortly before the break-up of Southern Area cut the size of the parade. The Standard Bearers wear the medals of both World Wars.*

parade with the officer cadets. As many as 5,000 Legionaries were present, together with several bands. It was a colourful event, the cadets in 'blues' and on more than one occasion a Legionary wearing his Boer War uniform or even pre-1914 full dress. When, however, the Area split into two in 1960 the numbers involved fell to 2,000, with only South Eastern Area involved, enabling Lord Mountbatten, the inspecting officer in 1967, to tell the parade to 'break ranks and gather round' for his address. This unusual manoeuvre, recreating Mountbatten's wartime 'pep-talk' technique, left only a bemused Sandhurst Adjutant, mounted on his white horse, in place on the parade ground.[24] But elsewhere Legion rallies had smaller turn-outs than in the 1930s, despite the organization's greater size post-war.

Equally involved in ceremonial were many of the Legion's overseas branches. The Paris

233

branch colour party turned out nearly every week and many other continental branches were regularly involved in local ceremonies. An overseas branch had in many ways a greater responsibility than one at home: their conduct reflected not just on the Legion but on their country and, although some were able to draw support from the Legion's office in Brussels, the great majority had no County or Area to turn to. But national pride was not just reflected by a Legion standard properly borne among a forest of flags from other countries; in 1953 Legion balls and galas were held from Arras to Istanbul to celebrate the coronation, and in many countries outside Europe.[25]

## Membership drift continues

Overseas branches were often a refuge for those living in foreign parts and there was seldom difficulty over recruiting or in finding officers. The situation at home was different and, as the membership continued its slow decline in the 1950s, recruiting efforts were renewed. In 1951 a membership drive had been linked to the house-to-house Poppy Appeal collection, while Bankers' Orders were introduced for subscription payments; for those without bank accounts there were coloured cards for display in local shops: 'British Legion – you may pay your subs here'. Renewed efforts were made to recruit those leaving the services, mainly National Servicemen, with barrack-room posters. But often the old methods proved the most successful: through the efforts of twenty-one wardens Wymondham Branch in Norfolk held on their books every one of a thousand ex-servicemen in six scattered villages.[26]

The numbers still fell. One complaint to a local paper in 1955 was that the branches were in the hands of the 'old guard' who had been 'smugly sitting on their seats' since 1918. It was a long-standing criticism and the riposte was always the same: the younger generation did not want the responsibility. The truth was difficult to determine, but in a branch such as Penrith at this time the Chairman and ten out of the twelve committee members were of the 1939-45 generation.

A Legion survey established that 85 per cent of members had joined for social reasons and the more successful branches were well aware of the importance of membership activities. These ranged from a Saturday 'café continental' at Loughton in Essex to amateur dramatics at Swanage and flower shows at Goole in the East Riding of Yorkshire. While less enterprising branches bought TV sets, Gosforth in Cumberland ran a sports meeting on August Bank Holiday with hound trails and wrestling Cumberland-style, attended by 3,000 people. But although many Legion branches held some activity in the warm summer months, such as a carnival or, in the country towns, a gymkhana, and the august *Observer* newspaper congratulated the Legion on its organizing abilities in the shires, the gradual downwards drift in membership continued.[27]

## Badges and standards

Members who had given outstanding service to their branch were often rewarded with a Legion badge in gold, a practice begun in the 1930s. In 1952 it was decided to regulate the award; it had to be approved by the National Chairman or Vice Chairman and at least ten years' service was required, together with Area and County recommendations. Even so, with branches now able to afford the cost of gold, the number of recommendations continued to grow, attracting criticism that the money could be put to better use by using

234

a cheaper metal; after all VCs lost nothing by being made from scrap metal. Indeed the Legion's highest award, the National Certificate of Appreciation, which had been instituted in 1933, was not represented by a badge until 1960, and then it had no intrinsic value.[28]

Branch Standards also cost money, but more affluence meant that by now nearly every branch had its own standard and County and Area competitions led to the first National Standard Bearer competition in 1952. It was won by a former Grenadier Guardsman, who carried the standard of Ashton-in-Makerfield, near Wigan. The prize, the Ashwanden Cup, was awarded at Conference that year, which also decided that all Legion Standard Bearers should wear black berets with the Legion badge, avoiding the complicated manoeuvre required to remove a bowler hat when lowering the Standard in salute.[29]

## No ban on Communists

Standard bearers were very much in evidence at the opening of the 1951 Annual Conference, on the occasion of the Legion's 50th anniversary celebrations. It was held at the Albert Hall and the national press carried reports on their front pages, although politics still intruded, the *Daily Herald* sourly attacking the President for making what it described as a political speech when he urged the need for adequate pensions for the war-disabled; but the other papers expressed support for the Legion. There was a lively debate over more generous compensation for former prisoners-of-war of the Japanese and delegates themselves were in a liberal mood, at last voting to raise the annual Affiliation Fee from 1/6d, fixed in 1921, to 2/-. There were over 1,300 delegates present in 1951, but the following year the numbers fell by more than half for the meeting in the Isle of Man, although it was unjust to suggest that this was due to the Sunday closure of the island's pubs. At any rate the 1952 Conference made the sensible decision not to ban Communists from the Legion. As the *New Statesman* remarked, the four to one defeat of the motion 'will complicate life for those who have always declared the Legion to be Fascist'. But the *Daily Telegraph* took the organization to task for laying itself open to Communist infiltration.[30]

Numbers built up again for the 1953 Conference at Blackpool which was marked by an innovation, an open debate without resolutions. It dealt with the on-going pensions issue and cleared the air. They were higher still when Conference returned to London in 1954, with a fifteen-minute adjournment to allow members to take part in the D-Day anniversary service which was relayed to the Albert Hall. Those attending the following year's conference at Llandudno might have had difficulty in returning home because of a rail strike, but the General Secretary had prudently booked a fleet of coaches. But before making their way to the buses the 1955 assembly decided that future conferences should be held alternately in the North and South, changing a 1952 decision which included the Midlands.[31]

Throughout this period it was still necessary to draw on reserves to meet benevolent expenditure which now included maintenance of the Legion Homes and a housing loans scheme. Despite apparent small annual increases, in real terms (i.e. in purchasing power) the Appeal income was falling (see Chart C1 on page 447). By 1953 liquid reserves had fallen from the 1947 figure of nearly £3 million to £1.6 million. An economy campaign was launched to restore the reserves to £2 million and this had the effect by 1955 of at least ending further calls on reserves. On the administrative front matters had improved following the increase in the Affiliation Fee charges, but already inflation was gnawing at the gain.[32]

## The *Journal* recovers

The *Legion Journal* too suffered from the effects of inflation and in 1952 it adopted a larger format to attract more advertising, changed to a rotary press to economize on printing costs and raised the price, which had been 3d since the first issue in 1921, to 4d. The moves were successful and in 1953 the magazine made a modest profit of £1,000 compared with a £4,000 loss the previous year. But it still attracted the inevitable criticism, being described at Kent County Conference that year as a 'cross between a parish magazine and Comic Cuts and more of a sedative than a tonic'. This was more than a little unfair. The membership expected the *Journal* to report their doings, but the great issues of the day were also covered, although perhaps to a lesser extent than during the Legion's struggles of the early years. 1954 saw a new editor, Trevor Frowen, an experienced journalist with war service in Burma, who in 1955 introduced two editions, northern and southern, in order to provide more local news. The magazine remained in profit and the same year was able to increase the number of pages. Part of the reason for the recovery was that the Membership and Publicity Committee, which managed the publication, was chaired by Captain Hampson who was not only Legion Chairman but an experienced newpaperman.[33]

# 1956 – 1960

## More changes at the top

Towards the end of his third year in office, Captain Hampson died while travelling back from headquarters to his home in Lancashire. He had been a popular Chairman, friendly and generous, and an outstanding speaker with frequent touches of humour. The Vice Chairman, Major Spinks, a headmaster from Monmouthshire, took over until formally elected to the post at the 1956 Annual Conference, an occasion marked by the Welsh delegates rising to greet the first Welsh Legion Chairman in their native tongue. Although Spinks himself was not a Welsh speaker he had the eloquence of his countrymen, speaking always without notes and making it his special task to inspire younger members to aim for high office in the Legion.[34]

In 1959 the Chairmanship passed to General Sir Roy Bucher. A Scotsman and a distinguished soldier – he had been the last Commander-in-Chief of the Army in India – he was the most senior military officer ever to have held the post. The following year Lord Cromwell, who had been Legion Treasurer since 1946, resigned because of ill-health. Somewhat to delegates' surprise the ovation which followed Lord Cromwell's final address to Conference had hardly died away when his successor and longtime opponent, Major Jackman, was at the microphone. But it was to be Jackman's first and last appearance in the office, the NEC finding it expedient to appoint Sir Alfred Moffat as temporary Treasurer a few months later.[35]

In 1958 Major General Sir Richard Howard-Vyse, an earlier Chairman, had replaced Sir Ian Fraser as President. Fraser had found it difficult at times to reconcile his political loyalties with his Legion responsibilities so that he was bound to be a controversial figure.

*The Legion's leaders: (from left to right) J.R. Griffin, General Secretary, Sir Ian Fraser, President, Lord Cromwell, Honorary Treasurer, Major J.T. Spinks, Chairman, General Sir Roy Bucher, Vice Chairman on parade in Douglas, Isle of Man, during the 1957 Conference.*

Howard-Vyse, a straightforward soldier, was a popular replacement.[36] There were important changes, too, in the staff. Captain Coffer, who had worked for the Legion since 1946, was appointed to the vacant post of Assistant Secretary in 1957 and two years later he became General Secretary on the retirement of J.R. Griffin. Griffin's departure signalled the end of an era. He was the last to leave of a trio of senior staff who had been with the Legion from the outset. T.J. Birrell had retired as Benevolent Secretary in 1957, and A.G. Webb, Pensions Secretary, left the following year. They had dedicated their working lives to the ex-service community. Griffin's administrative talent had enabled Haig and Lister to create the Legion and he had then served it for nearly forty years, adapting it to a new generation. Birrell, like Griffin invalided out of the Army in the Great War and then active with the Federation, had run the Legion's benevolence for six months before the organization itself was formed, going on to earn General Maurice's accolade: 'I cannot think of a more devoted and loyal servant of the Legion.' Of Webb it was said in a parliamentary debate on war pensions: 'He has devoted his life since the First World War to this self-sacrificing task. If any of us go to our deathbeds having done so little harm and so much good we shall rest content.'[37]

With these departures Benevolence and Pensions were merged into a single Service Department. At the same time a new department was set up to take over war graves, pilgrimages, clubs and sports, previously the Secretariat's responsibilities, enabling the Legion's Continental Office in Brussels to be closed in 1960. The changes followed an efficiency review which also recommended that the Midland Area should be divided again into East and West Midland and that Southern Area revert to the original South Eastern and South Western Areas.[38] There was also some merging of committees and a reduction in their sizes.[39]

Wales was unaffected by the review, but its Area Conference in early 1957 felt that Wales should have the same right as Scotland to express its national identity and wanted 'Area' to be dropped from the title. The Legion's Annual Conference that year did not agree, disturbed at the possible effect on the organization's unity and deploring 'the ugliness of nationalism'. But in 1960, by a narrow majority with many delegates still worried that Wales might go the way of Scotland, the proposal was accepted, Conference, however, resisting suggestions that the other Areas should adopt the names of the ancient kingdoms such as Mercia or Wessex.[40]

### Branches 'dig in'

No such strong feelings applied to one of the Legion's oldest branches, the House of Commons Branch, which had ceased to exist in 1955. Legion MPs continued to associate themselves as a 'group', but that too had stopped functioning by 1960 and the Legion no longer had at its disposal an 'insider organization' capable of mustering cross-party support in Parliament on important issues.[41] It was perhaps one closure which would not have been saved by a pamphlet issued in 1950 by Metropolitan Area. So successful was *How to Run a Branch* with its drawings of a determined chairman and his harassed secretary that it was distributed nationally in 1957. But the slow erosion of branch numbers continued and by 1960 there were barely over 5,000. Meanwhile many branches quite literally 'dug in', building their own headquarters now that building restrictions had been lifted and materials were available. Members organized themselves into teams under a branch 'clerk of works' and spent their weekends bricklaying, carpentering and roofing. The building provided a venue for social occasions as well as a headquarters, but 'Old Bill' and trench suppers were now replaced by a 'Hut 29' evening based on the popular US *Sergeant Bilko* TV programme. Meanwhile Odiham Branch in Hampshire held an annual *conversazione* where the guest speakers included Lord Alanbrooke, Churchill's principal wartime military adviser, and members of the British Trans-Antartic Expedition. It was invariably a 'sell-out' with many coming from afar and a long waiting list.[42]

Some continental branches were equally well-established, but by now they faced a new problem: foreign exchange controls and restrictive employment legislation were leading to distress among British subjects, many of whom were ex-service and married to locals, and social welfare systems in these countries lagged behind the United Kingdom. The work of the Legion's Continental Office in Brussels had increasingly turned to assisting branch welfare, but with its impending closure Legion headquarters produced Service Guides based on a study of the social provisions in Belgium, France and the Netherlands.[43]

### Recruiting efforts continue – but how many members?

The continent featured too in the ongoing Legion recruiting campaign. For three years, from 1957 to 1959, General Sir Roy Bucher, then Vice Chairman, made an annual visit to West Germany to talk to large service audiences in the British military garrisons, quite undeterred by his wife's comment that his address of over an hour was 'far too long'. After his elevation to Chairman his successor, Lord Carew, carried out the tour in 1960.[44] Back in the United Kingdom soldiers and airmen were also occasionally targeted, addressed by members of local branches, while the Royal Navy drew attention to the Legion in Fleet Orders.[45]

All this was looking to the future, intended to prepare the serving men and women for the time when they left the service; to those still in uniform only Honorary membership was available. A sample poll showed that some 10 per cent of members were now former national servicemen and the armed forces undertook to distribute a new booklet, 'British Legion Calls', with a detachable reply-paid card, to those being discharged, causing the *Manchester Guardian* to comment on the government's generosity in helping to strengthen the Legion's arm in its campaigns, which were largely directed at government.

But a major difficulty was to establish how many members the Legion actually had. The Chairman therefore ordered a scrutiny of branch accounts and, after deleting the lapsed subscriptions, this revealed that, whereas the Annual Report consistently recorded 'one million members' plus the women's section of around 250,000, the real figure was somewhat under one million with the Women's Section membership *included*. The stage was now set for a major recruiting effort in the 1960s.[46]

## The happy wanderers

It was somewhat easier to record the number of delegates at Annual Conference. There were nearly 900 at the Albert Hall in 1956 to strike a militant note over the nine-year-old pensions campaign: if the war had not been fought and won there would have been no Welfare State. The following year rather less went to the Isle of Man, the special boat drawing into Douglas Harbour to 'The Happy Wanderer' played by the town band. It was just as well as a confusion over booking meant that the Legion had to meet in the Coliseum where delegates sat in their sober suits in tight-packed rows, fingers clutching a pipe bowl or holding a cigarette while listening to the latest government response on the pensions issue. After visiting Southend-on-Sea in 1958, Conference returned to the Albert Hall in 1959 to hear a breezy address from Viscount Montgomery who ended by suggesting that as Field Marshals never left the active list he might not be eligible for Legion membership. The floor left him in no doubt with cries of 'give him a form', adding the warning 'It's gone up a shilling', having shortly before agreed to a rise in the Affiliation Fee. The 1960 Conference at Margate was so briskly managed by the new Chairman, General Bucher, that it ended on the second day, an outcome not appreciated by at least one delegate who felt that it had been an 'undignified scramble' and that the NEC did not obtain from Conference a clear and positive lead on such matters as finance, membership and publicity. But there was no noticeable complaint from the Council.[47]

The 1959 decision to raise the Affiliation Fee solved for the moment the problem of the adminstrative overspend. But the overspend on Benevolence, which included regular donations to other ex-service charities, ranging from the Star and Garter Home to the Gordon Boys School, continued and by 1958 the Legion was spending £1 1s 8d for every £1 received. To avoid selling securities at a loss it was necessary in 1960 to get a bank overdraft of £150,000. With the Poppy Appeal still failing to keep up with inflation the future did not look bright.[48]

Finance was a problem too for the *Legion Journal*. It was distributed mainly through branches. Vigorous efforts might achieve a small profit, whereupon an increase in postal charges put it back into debt. Meanwhile the introduction of commercial television was drawing away some long-standing advertisers. But the crux of the matter was that it was trying to exist in an inflationary world without calling on its readers to pay the true costs and in 1960, after further losses which also reflected increased printing costs, it was forced to raise the price from 4d to 6d.[49]

# 1961 – 1965

## An overdue recognition

In 1961, in the fortieth anniversary year of the organisation he had been instrumental in creating, Lister received a knighthood. The recognition was overdue. Not only the founding Chairman, running the Legion for its first critical years when it strove to get fair play for millions suffering as a result of war service, but a tireless and selfless worker in the ex-service cause ever since, he represented the very soul of the organization. Lister had been in his early thirties when he first led the Legion and he had advice for the younger generation: 'Don't be afraid of opposing older men,' drawing perhaps on the experience of occasions when his view differed from that of Haig.[50]

The current Chairman, General Sir Roy Bucher, entering his third year in office in 1962, had a much more assured position. Even so, he found the pressure unrelenting, with most weekends devoted to the Legion as well as three to four hours a day on weekdays and the need to visit headquarters twice a week and he commented: 'I now think that the post of Chairman of the British Legion must be filled by a person who can devote almost full time to it.' But, as a younger member of the Council pointed out, would the coming generation have the time to fulfill commitments on this scale and hold down a job? It was a question that would never be entirely satisfactorily solved. Older men had more time but found the going hard. Those who held office earlier in life, such as John Brown and Lister himself, had the vigour but needed to make personal and, often, financial, sacrifices.[51]

The office of President was traditionally that of an elder statesman. Few were better-equipped than Sir Richard Howard-Vyse. A distinguished soldier and active in public life, he was the only Legion President also to have held the office of Chairman. When he handed over as President in 1962, having held the post for four years, the farewells were heartfelt: Legion members liked the thought that he was near to 'the seats of the mighty', but they also welcomed his friendly appoachability, for no one was afraid to talk to him. Approaching eighty years of age, he died within the year.[52] His successor was General Sir Oliver Leese, a big bluff man, who had taken over the 8th Army from Montgomery and knew the Legion at every level as a County and branch president and Area patron. Only just installed in the President's chair and forgetting the microphone when telling Annual Conference delegates the amount of a donation just presented to him, he was overheard to respond to cries of 'Mike! Mike!' with a muttered 'Why don't they wash their bloody ears out!'[53]

## Further attacks on Haig

Men such as Howard-Vyse and Bucher epitomized Haig's view that those who had held high rank in the armed forces had a duty to those they had led. There was no greater example than Haig himself. But when the Legion commemorated his centenary in 1961, Haig's reputation had to be defended at the Annual Conference. Since the 1934 publication of Lloyd George's self-justifying memoirs the 'blame Haig' theme had been developed to the point where many of the public now saw him as solely responsible for the enormous casualties of the Great War. A musical play 'Oh What a Lovely War', appearing in 1963, might have been good theatre, but it portrayed Haig as 'a lunatic made to look uncommonly like Hitler' as one critic put it, while a film version in 1967 led to him being called a 'monster' in a BBC programme. Such derision was not appreciated, or even understood, by those who had fought under Haig, nor by reputable historians.

The Legion itself had removed Haig's portrait from the cover of the *Legion Journal* in 1946, but the annual service in his memory at St Columba's church in Pont Street in London was still well-attended (it would continue until 1997), and some Counties held similar services. Nevertheless there was concern that it had now become so fashionable to vilify Haig that the association of his name with the Poppy Appeal might affect public support.

Amid all this controversy Legion members strove to defend Haig's reputation. But the damage had been done and as the century drew to a close there would even be a campaign by a tabloid newspaper to pull down his statue in Whitehall. The irony was that it had been thought unworthy of him in the first place.[54]

## Area 'Organizers'

Among those who had served loyally under Haig both in the Great War and in the Legion were Crosfield and Brunel Cohen. Crosfield, the first Vice Chairman, died in 1962 and Brunel Cohen, the original Treasurer, in 1965. Crosfield was best known as the Legion's 'Foreign Secretary' and had done much to try and promote friendship between former enemies in the inter-war years. Brunel Cohen, seen each year on television in his wheelchair at the Cenotaph parade, became to many people a symbol of the Legion, even though most must have been unaware of all that he had done in the ex-service cause, from fighting the early battles in Parliament to his work for the disabled, the embodiment of the Legion's motto 'Service not Self'.[55]

With their deaths only Sir Frederick Lister remained of the original group of national officers and he, fittingly, was present when NEC meetings were at last able to take place at the Legion's headquarters in Pall Mall in October 1962. He was also present when the Council took a decision two years later to re-designate Area Organizing Secretaries as Area Organizers. The change followed a report by the General Secretary on an organization known as the 'Fellowship', a local ex-service body in the Sheffield area. Some inattention had allowed it to gain ground at the Legion's expense. The Legion always sought to co-operate with other groups but did not like to see them taking over its work. Henceforward more Area staff time was to be devoted to organization and propaganda and less to administration.[56]

## Clubs build membership

The Area Organizers would have been well aware of the sea change taking place in the membership. While the number of branches continued to reduce, those that remained were larger, and in the early 1960s the overall membership began to grow again. It was due to the growing popularity of branch clubs. By 1965 there were over 1,000 Legion clubs; but it was not simply a question of numbers; the clubs were now better housed and better run. The Legion's leadership were not slow to appreciate the effect on recruiting and, if they had needed an excuse to demonstrate more interest in clubs, it was provided by the host of regulations, stemming from new gaming legislation. The rules had to be revised following the 1961 Licencing Act and in the process headquarters won some important concessions which applied to all ex-service clubs. The Gaming Act of 1963, although imposing tighter control, gave clubs more scope for raising money and a national survey of Legion clubs the following year revealed a considerable increase in their profits and reserves, enabling them to improve their facilities still more. By 1964 overall Legion membership had climbed back to over half a million and the Cinderella of the movement was seen in a fresh light, even if one cynical county secretary judged the 'one-arm bandit' to be the Legion's best recruiter. A more elegant definition of the new approach was provided by the National President at the 1965 Conference: 'A social life with a purpose'.[57]

## Looking to the future

While  a 'social life' was mainly, but not entirely, the province of the clubs, the 'purpose' was central to a National Leadership School held at Somerset Legion House in February 1963. Attended by forty-five students over a long weekend, each day began with prayers before the first lecture. But much of the time was devoted to group studies on such matters as the Legion's future or branch/club relations and the students' conclusions were published in the *Journal*. It was the Council's aim to bring on younger leaders and a week-long National Leadership Forum held the following year in a part of London University sought students under the age of fifty. Meanwhile Areas and Counties also got on with their own training schools, generally adopting a more relaxed approach: North Western Area took over Butlin's Metropole Hotel in Blackpool in 1964 and allowed members to bring their wives and children, although they did not attend the lectures.[58]

The Legion's future was also the Duke of Edinburgh's theme when he addressed the Legion's Conference in 1961, on the occasion of its Fortieth Anniversary – he wanted it to make a positive contribution to the life of the country. The vote of thanks to the Duke was seconded by Jim Prince* of Cardiff, introduced by the Chairman as 'Mr Prince of Wales', who had been present at nearly every Conference for those forty years. In a moving speech he stressed the Legion's loyalty to its Patron and her family; nonetheless it was the first time a Royal Prince had been on the Conference platform since 1950 when the Duke of Gloucester had spoken. And the previous occasion to that had been the memorable 'hand of friendship' address by the then Prince of Wales in 1935.[59]

On several occasions a member of the Royal Family had taken the salute at the march-past which followed the Legion's annual Whitsun service at the Cenotaph, the King himself doing so in 1945. Now that parade and service, which in the 1930s had been attended by as many as 12,000 Legionaries with 300 standards, even when Conference took place out of London, was a thing of the past. The Legion might have twice as many members as in those days but they were not 'paraders' and from 1963 onwards a service would be held at the Cenotaph only when the Annual Conference took place in London.[60]

The timing of Conference itself had to be reviewed in 1965 when the government decided to replace the Whitsun holiday with a Spring Bank Holiday. The NEC wanted to keep the customary attachment to Whitsun but Conference delegates determined otherwise and the date was switched to the new holiday weekend.[61]

*See picture at page 231.

## Conference bursts into song

Conferences over this period continued to be firmly handled by General Bucher or his successor as Chairman, Lord Carew, and business was usually completed with time to spare, more resolutions now dealing with domestic matters. But these also could bring Conference to life and, when it was suggested in 1964 that the Soldiers' Chorus from Gounod's Faust should be adopted as the Legion march, the mover's rendition aroused delegates to join in, the resolution being carried in a burst of song. But away from the conference hall old sheets of music were unearthed and when the Epsom Band played the original Legion march composed by Thomas Bidgood in 1921 'imagine our suprise when . . . we discovered a really first class march', and they adopted it forthwith. It seemed that the march, although written specifically for the Legion had never been officially approved. 'Boys of the Old Brigade' had been used but it was felt to be 'too Army' and the Southern Area parade at Sandhurst had marched past to 'Old Comrades', while on radio the popular Billy Cotton Band Show signed off with 'Legion Patrol' written on Armistice Day 1948 and dedicated to the Legion. Much correspondence ensued in the *Journal* and, although other marches by Sam B. Wood and by Greenwood, also entitled 'British Legion', were identified, the general conclusion was that Bidgood's was a 'splendid, happy and lively' march that should never have been allowed to slip into oblivion. On the strength of this the 1965 Conference went back on its previous decision and, forty-four years after it was composed, Bidgood's march was officially adopted.[62]

Possibly the march had lapsed when the national band contest was abandoned in 1935 due to travel problems. The war caused many bandsmen to hang up their instruments but by October 1948 the Legion had some seventy bands, from Guernsey to Catterick, and there were contests at Legion rallies despite difficulties with the Musicians Union. Such difficulties may have been why the Council had decided in 1950 not to resume the national contest, in the past used to identify a 'Legion' band. The band attached to Norbury Branch in the South East Metropolitan County appears to have fulfilled the function of the Legion Military Band in the 1960s; but an approach to the NEC in 1968 to secure recognition as such met with the response that any one of the Legion bands might be equally eligible for the honour. Nonetheless Norbury was an accomplished band with a strength of fifty and a corps of drums. It was put through its paces by an Irish Guards drill instructor and played regularly at West Ham football matches.[63]

## The *Journal's* problems continue

There is no record of Conference bursting into song when it heard the financial reports. But it might have had some excuse in the early 1960s: the increase in the Affiliation Fee in 1959 had led to a marked improvement in the General Account, while a slackening in demand for benevolent assistance, combined with a pegging of administrative costs, had enabled that account to balance, despite the continuing heavy demands of the Homes. However, any glee chorus would have been premature. Inflation was still nibbling away at the balances and by 1965 the Council was again concerned at the financial situation.[64]

A proposal at the 1965 Conference for a Legion lottery based on a number issued with the *Journal* was overwhelmingly defeated – 'Our image will go downhill straight away' the Chairman warned – but if it had been passed it might have also improved the fortunes of the *Journal* itself. The magazine's 1960 price rise from 4d to 6d had resulted in a temporary improvement in its finances, but it had also led to a fall in circulation so that the gain was only temporary and marginal, and the constant rise in costs meant that by 1965 it was again heavily in the red. It sold only 60,000 copies a month to a membership of over half a million and the National Chairman noted in 1962 that the Royal Canadian Legion had solved the problem by making every member a reader, simply including the cost of the magazine in the annual subscription. But similar action here seemed impractical. Members could be unkind – as the Editor himself ruefully admitted: 'The *Journal* has been taken to task more often, and with more righteous indignation, over the years than most other institutions.' But at least one critic shot himself in the foot: making it clear in no uncertain manner that as far as his branch was concerned the *Journal* had no value to the members, he went on to declare that 'not a single copy is taken in this branch', leaving it open as to how he had reached his conclusions.[65]

## 1966 – 1970

### A new generation

The death of Sir Frederick Lister in 1966 marked the end of an era. Enough has been written in these pages to give some idea of his work for ex-servicemen. Lister shares with Haig the credit for the Legion's creation and, like Haig, he was devoted to it. From young Chairman to elder statesman Lister had literally towered over his contemporaries, his tall, stooping figure with its bland countenance unmistakable. In his forty-five years of service to the ex-service community two achievements stand out: the first his performance at the Unity Conference, following which his election as the first Legion Chairman was a foregone conclusion; the second his work during the Second World War to draw up the post-war rehabilitation strategy, the by-product of which was that a new generation would identify with the Legion.[66]

In the same year Lord Carew handed over the Chairmanship to Major J. Ben Davies, visibly moved at the farewell that he got from Conference: as delegates knew he had not spared himself in office. Davies, a former Wales Chairman, was a straighforward and unpretentious man. His successor, Dennis Cadman, who took over in 1969, was the first Englishman to hold office since the death of Captain Hampson in 1955, but he was also only the second former 'other rank' to be Legion Chairman – the first had been Lister himself. Cadman was unmistakably the representative of the Second World War generation and, following the replacement of Colonel Gordon Larking as Treasurer in 1970 by Mr K.C.G. Chambers, he would head a younger team of officers to lead the Legion into its second half-century. The services of the old guard did not, however, go unrecognized; Gordon Larking received a knighthood* for his thirteen years as Chairman and Treasurer.[67]

Having overseen these changes, the President, Sir Oliver Leese, completed the handover to the new generation by giving up his own post in 1970; his successor, General Sir Charles Jones, was the first Legion President not to have served in the Great War. The Governor of the Royal Hospital at Chelsea, General Jones had been introduced to the Legion, and the Legion to him, by addressing Conference as a guest speaker, a sensible arrangement where the prospective President had not previously been involved with the movement.[68]

*Remarkably, it would be the last such honour awarded for services to the Legion in the twentieth century.

## Clubs make money

By now the thousand Legion branches with clubs were furnishing half the total membership, the leadership noting that 'the work of improving the (clubs') control and organization . . . is now paying handsome dividends'. Two pages of the *Journal* were devoted to club news mainly consisting of the opening of smart new premises to replace the old huts, together with extensions and improvements to others. Two hundred delegates attended a clubs conference organized by North Western Area in 1967, declaring that the Legion licencing system, which set a limit on the proportion of non ex-servicemen allowed to use the clubs, was out of date and restricted success. The following year the NEC set up a working party to review the rules and in 1969 the permitted maximum of non ex-service members was increased from 30 to 40 per cent, provided the club accepted

*The clubs prosper: one of many new premises erected in the 1950s and 1960s – the Legion Club at Amble in Northumberland.*

members of the Women's Section. If it did not then the proportion stayed at 30 per cent. The proviso was aimed not so much at breaching male bastions – some clubs were resolutely 'men only' – as to bringing the clubs in line with the concept of the Legion as a family organization.[69]

Opening the doors to more members put many of the clubs in a sounder trading position, although to interpret the mass of legislation emerging from government departments, dealing with such matters as food and drugs, catering wages and redundancy payments, they needed all the help of the Legion's experts. Additional taxation on gaming machines was yet another burden, but even so many clubs were now making healthy profits and by 1970 some £457,000 was being given away by Legion clubs to various causes. Three-quarters of this went to parent branches, mainly to fund building projects in branch-owned premises. Almost all of the rest was donated to charities other than the Legion; only £7,000 – 1½ cent of the total – was donated to the Poppy Appeal.[70]

It was clearly sensible from the club's point of view to assist the branch to develop the branch and club premises and the large donation to charities, many of which were hospital or other local appeals, put the Legion in good standing in the local community. The proportion given directly to the Poppy Appeal suggests that most clubs regarded support for the Legion's benevolent activities as the responsibility of the general public. A number of clubs, however, provided support in kind to the Appeal by making premises available as collection centres and storerooms for poppies and the donations did not include such activities as 'piles of pennies'.

### A new category – Associate Members?

To be admitted to a Legion club it was necessary to be a member of the Legion. If the person was not ex-service it was therefore the practice to award Honorary Membership of the branch. But since this category had been instituted to enable a branch to confer a distinction on someone outside of the organization no subscription was payable. Hence there was no financial gain to the Legion from the 70,000 (out of a total Honorary Membership in 1970 of 75,000) who had acquired membership simply to qualify to enter the clubs. The Privy Council, who oversaw the Legion's Charter, had made it clear that by definition Honorary Members could not be asked for subscriptions and the only solution was to create a new category of membership for non ex-service people, Associate Membership, which could also be seen as giving the Legion a wider stance in the community.

But the proposal created problems. Many in the movement saw it as a threat to its ex-service identity and at the 1970 Conference long queues formed at the floor microphones as the Chairman spoke, always a sign that delegates were disturbed. When they came to have their say it was clear that some saw it as a first step on a slippery downward path – 'the most damaging proposals I have heard' as Jim Prince, the veteran Cardiff delegate, put it. Although slightly more delegates voted for than against the motion, it failed to get the necessary two thirds majority.[71]

### Operation Supercharge

Jim Prince and like-minded delegates might have found the Associate Membership proposals more acceptable if Operation 'Supercharge' had succeeded in driving up the Ordinary Membership. 'Supercharge' had been launched in 1965 on the crest of the gains that had been made in the early 1960s, following the new emphasis on clubs, and was designed to bring the membership strength to a peak by the Legion's anniversary in 1971. It was a five-year plan, described as 'the most sustained, most controlled, most highly organized membership campaign in Legion history'. It had two distinct phases and the first was for branches to 'get their houses in order' by thoroughly overhauling their activities and regaining their lapsed members. When that had been accomplished the second phase would begin – a period of 'intensive' activity to enrol new members.

'Supercharge' immediately sparked debate. There were those who thought that the Legion should open its doors to the Fire Service and Police. Some said the organization only needed a small membership 'as energetic as ants – a commando brigade' of active workers instead of a vast mass without concern as to substance and quality. But the need to be able to show political weight as well as to increase subscription income predominated. 'Supercharge' would be judged on a numerical scale.

Much effort was devoted to the first phase and there were monthly articles in the Journal. To get its house in order a branch needed a Women's Section, a Poppy Appeal Committee, a service committee, an active programme of events, and, if possible a club, well-run of course. Counties set up recruiting organizations, some splitting into zones and appointing zonal officers to advise and assist branches. The headquarters Membership and Publicity Department was reorganized and pamphlets and recruiting aids distributed – all following the theme 'a social life with a purpose'.

Some three years having been devoted to the first phase, the second was launched in 1969. But, as chart A1 shows, overall gains were small. The operation had never really achieved impetus. Membership campaigns, however, enthusiastically driven at higher level, depended on the branches and, for whatever reason, not enough had got 'fired up' or were able to sustain their efforts. The problem remained: how to increase the organization's appeal to a generation that, whether 1939-45 men, national servicemen or regulars, had a fuller and more secure life with far better prospects than their fathers? It would not be easy to solve.[72]

## Conference asserts its authority

Recruiting campaigns, like any activity, needed leadership and at the 1967 Annual Conference the President, General Leese, had made it clear that he believed that one of the Legion's problems was that not enough former officers were prepared to take an active part in its work. The delegates did not disagree, but, when it came to electing their own national officers, were of the view that what counted was the work the candidate had done for the Legion - 'We should not care whether the candidate has been a brigadier or a bombardier' – and at the same conference succeeded in getting the 'cv' restricted accordingly. There was no doubt of Conference's authority when it chose to exercise it and the legal advice was that Conference had the ultimate say. That same year at Blackpool delegates were determined to debate the NEC's action in certain club matters over which, since clubs were not in the Charter, the Council believed they had sole jurisdiction. In the event the debate backed the Council's decisions – but the point had been made.[73]

The next two conferences, at Hastings in 1968 and Scarborough in 1969, produced no challenges to the leadership, debating pensions issues in an orderly but positive way. The only complaint came from one branch chairman – that the small minority of delegates who considered themselves experts on every subject should allow others to speak; but the 1970 Brighton Conference was noticeably well controlled by the new Chairman, Cadman, even when a particularly amiable Irishman tried to take over the microphone to make points that no one else understood.[74]

At three of these five conferences it had been necessary to debate increases in the Affiliation fee. Inflation was now constantly snapping at the heels of the Legion's finances, not only putting the General Account under continuous strain – it had incurred a £70,000 deficit in four years – but negating any rise in the Poppy Appeal so that the annual benevolent shortfall had risen by 1970 to over £200,000. It was always possible to make up this deficiency from legacies and other income, but it meant that reserves, already eroded by inflation, fell. A scheme for branches to deposit money with the Legion had only limited success and the organization was living a hand-to-mouth existence.[75]

The *Journal* too continued to suffer financially, the circulation stuck at 50-60,000 copies a month with advertisement revenue declining. In 1968, with the annual loss now over £4,000, there was a further re-vamp with a front cover in full colour and the aim of increasing the circulation to 100,000. The following year the printing contract was transferred to Preston Hall, something which the membership had long urged. But, although new machines had been installed, there were difficulties in meeting deadlines and higher production costs drove the annual deficit up still further. Nor did adoption of a 'family' format with articles on cooking, fashion and car maintenance and more space for Area, County and branch reports (seventeen out of twenty-one pages in 1969) achieve a better result; despite the involvement of disabled men in the magazine's production less than half of all Legion branches placed regular orders. In 1970 it was therefore necessary to double the price, from 6d to 1s. The immediate result was to lose 5,000 readers and the *Journal* continued to run at a substantial loss. A more radical solution would be needed.[76]

★     ★     ★

The twenty-five years since the war had seen many changes. A new generation was starting to come to the fore. The clubs had become more prominent, arresting the drift in membership but bringing change to the character of the organization. If the Legion was to continue to represent the ex-service community it needed to attract former national servicemen as well as the post-war regulars. And the structure would have to adapt to changing times. The Legion could not afford to stand still.

# CHAPTER 11

## WORK 1946-1970

# *The Need Continues*

### 1946 – 1950

**Emergence from war**

There was a vast increase in the Legion's work-load after the Second World War; not only were perhaps 15 million more people eligible for its help but the original Great War dependency was getting older and therefore more vulnerable. In London and places such as Plymouth Legion Service Offices had been established by local service committees, giving advice on a range of matters including employment. In Blackpool the Legion was joined by SSAFA and the Red Cross and the 'Services Welfare Centre', opened in 1946, dealt with 100 inquiries a day.[1] Many branches actively promoted the Legion's services; based on the wartime scheme where the Air Raid Warden got to know everyone on his 'post', Legion wardens visited those who had recently been demobilised, explaining what help the Legion provided, giving advice and – as a by-line – encouraging membership. Some branches went as far as to set up operations rooms with street maps flagged with the locations of all ex-service people.[2] By 1947, compared with 1939, benevolent expenditure had doubled, pension cases were running at 32,000 as against 4,000, and the amount spent on temporary relief was up by 50 per cent.[3] In 1948 the much-heralded state Welfare Scheme was launched. It clearly would have a great impact on the work of organizations such as the Legion and the same year the Legion issued a Guide to the state scheme to prevent overlap and, equally importantly, to ensure that those in need got their full state benefits, before charitable money was used. As has been noted, some began to question the need for the Legion's activities in the face of all-embracing state welfare But, as they soon discovered, many of the benefits would not be available for some years, while others depended on contributions which ex-servicemen had had no opportunity to make. Nor did the state scheme cover cases such as that of the 69-year-old Boer and Great War veteran who had spent his life in India, finishing up as a cinema commissionaire and, on the eve of independence, was put aboard a troopship to arrive penniless in Liverpool in 1947. The Legion gave him money and sent him to his native town of Hastings where the local branch took charge of him.[4]

**Employment and the unions**

The lesson of the past was that the Legion's welfare was directly influenced by the employment situation. Although there were no signs of large-scale unemployment in 1946, the organization's leaders were becoming worried at the government's lack of progress with training schemes for those being demobilised: 'Many will drift into blind-alley occupations, which means that valuable men are lost to industry because of the unpreparedness of government. This is not good enough,' said the Legion's Chairman that year. But matters got worse rather than better. By 1947 there were still over 30,000 on the waiting list for employment training and even a government minister, Colonel George Wigg, admitted that the scheme had not been well administered.[5]

Colonel Wigg did not, however, believe that ex-servicemen should have preference when it came to filling job vacancies: they were simply one part of the community in which everyone was to be treated equally in the new Britain. The Legion did not agree, and the government itself accepted the organization's view that, qualifications being equal, the ex-serviceman should have preference. But the Northern Ireland government gave former servicemen unqualified preference, a decision that the Legion's rank-and-file applauded as much as they deplored Wigg's views.[6]

Meanwhile the Legion continued to help those seeking work: it ran an employment bureau in London jointly with the Officers' Association and elsewhere in the country found work for former officers as well as men; it fought red tape, of which there was a great deal in the immediate post-war years, over the grant of trading licences and arranged for local trades associations to advise those starting up on their own with their gratuities; it even got the government to change the rules when the nationalization of the transport industry took away the livelihood of many small owners, so that they were found places in the industry.[7]

Until the situation eased in 1950, some thirty-four Legion employment bureaux around the country, working closely with the local Ministry of Labour offices, found jobs for around 17,000 men and women each year. But the Legion did not see eye-to-eye with government in one of its employment practices: the union-influenced policy of 'last in, first out' gave a clear preference to those who had spent the war in industry instead of the armed forces. Nevertheless it made every effort to keep good relations with the unions and on some issues there was a joint Legion/TUC approach and even a suggestion in 1947 that the unions should support the Legion in its war pensions campaign, although this was rejected by Conference with cries of 'no politics'. When the work situation settled down the TUC connection was allowed to lapse, although revived briefly in 1951 to agree that, while it was the Legion's task to ensure that employers gave ex-servicemen and women preference, the unions negotiated over any subsequent redundancy.[8]

The unions were less concerned with another area of Legion employment activity: to assist ex-service candidates, many of whom had been spiritually affected by wartime experiences, to become ordained. The church authorities bore the cost of training but made no financial provision for the families while the training took place. The Legion supported around fifty to sixty candidates' families at any one time during the immediate post-war years and the scheme continued into the early 1960s. In all around 300 were helped, including some ex-servicewomen training for church work. Needless to say the scheme covered all denominations.[9]

## Summer schools

As well its employment activities the Legion was concerned with the wider aspects of resettlement. In 1946 it arranged places for 750 ex-service students at summer schools run by eighteen universities, some organized entirely for Legion students.

The subjects ranged from English Literature to Democratic Government and the idea seems to heve been simply to stimulate minds that had been largely devoted to military matters for five years; one ex-ATS student saw it as a Legion service for the intellect as it might provide billiard tables for recreation. Area Councils helped with selection and the project was run by a Legion Council on Education chaired by Sir Frederick Maurice, a former London University Principal, as well as outgoing Legion President. The success of the first year led to over a thousand places being made available in 1947. This time the Legion decided to capitalize on the project by inviting summer school graduates to conduct discussion groups in branches, a kind of extension of the wartime current affairs discussions held in military units, seeing them also as potential leaders for the Legion. It therefore followed up the summer schools with weekend courses in leading such discussions, which were attended by about a quarter of the students.

Summer schools continued in 1948 but the number of students fell to 650, partly because economic constraints required the Legion to impose a £2 fee. The following year further financial difficulties brought the project to an end. But it had benefited many individuals at a time when brains needed refreshing, even if the Legion itself received only limited gain. [10]

## War Pensions – the first blood is drawn

During the war the Legion had persuaded the government to bring current war disability pension rates into line with those of Great War men. It now managed to get a Select Committee to review the whole war pensions field, taking account of the fact that industrial injury compensation, thanks to trade union pressure, was more generous than that paid for war wounds. But the Committee's deliberations were influenced by the new Social Security scheme and, while there was some relaxation in the rules for war pensions such as the abolition of the seven-year limit for 1939-45 claims, the rate was not changed, the argument being that, like everyone else, war pensioners would have all their needs met by Social Security benefits. [11]

The Legion did not see it that way at all. War pensions and war widows' pensions had been awarded not just to compensate for loss of earning power: they recognized the special circumstances of the injury – the element of sacrifice on the nation's behalf. If war pensions were to be overtaken by some general provision for the needy, that recognition would be lost. Meanwhile their value had been eroded by inflation and in 1948 a campaign was mounted to increase the pension rate, based on approaches to every MP. But there was no opportunity for a debate that year and the Legion had the feeling of being left high and dry: industrial disability rates were now regarded by government as a matter for negotiation between unions and employers, to be passed on to consumers, but where did that leave war pensions? It seemed that those who had ensured the country's survival in two wars, and had paid the price, were of little consequence in the new society they had made possible. Only the press appeared interested in the Legion's case. [12]

The next year, 1949, Sir Ian Fraser MP, the Legion's war-blinded President, put forward a motion for another Select Committee to review war pensions. As has been noted earlier, the government chose to see it as a party political matter since Fraser was a member of the Opposition and the motion was lost amid suggestions that in the new welfare-conscious Britain the organization might have outlived its useful existence.[13]

Somewhat bewildered at the turn of events, the Legion considered what to do next. It remained convinced that the war widows and war pensioners were not receiving justice, but, advised by Lister, who remembered the unsatisfactory outcome of the 1925 Great Petition, the Council rejected that route. Meanwhile the value of the pension further decreased, falling by 1949 to almost half its 1939 worth; chart B3 shows the decline over this period. A year later, in 1950, the government's majority was reduced in a General Election, but it still refused an inquiry into war pensions. Another tactic would be needed, but the Legion was beginning to realize that, under the new culture of universal social welfare, there was less concern for the particular needs of war pensioners and its path began to look increasingly difficult.[14]

There were nevertheless some minor concessions and a long-standing Legion proposal was accepted when the responsibility for peacetime pensions for disablement or death was shifted from the three Service Ministries to the Ministry of Pensions.[15]

## The Legion's Homes – a reprieve

It seemed likely for a time that the welfare state would also embrace the Legion's homes initiative. In 1945 three large houses had been bought and in the following years more were added so that by 1950 there were four 'country homes' and four 'convalescent homes'.

The country homes provided permanent residence for the aged and incapacitated. Maurice House, at Westgate-on-Sea on the north Kent coast was named after the Legion's long-serving President and was opened by him in 1946. Halsey House at Cromer in Norfolk opened in June 1948, Lister House at Ripon, Yorkshire, in 1950 and Crosfield House, formerly Buckland Hall at Bwlch in Wales, the following year. All had been purchased by the Legion, except Buckland Hall which was presented by the Llewellyn family and needed considerable renovation after wartime use by the armed forces. But the handsome facades and sweeping lawns provided the settings for gala openings with dignitaries, bands and massed Legion standards. Each accommodated some fifty to eighty mainly very elderly permanent residents – the first occupant of Maurice House had joined the Lancers in 1876 – in dormitories. Colonel Crosfield well deserved to be remembered in the naming of the Legion's homes; he had scoured the country for suitable properties at the right price and had got some bargains as many property owners had been impoverished by two successive wars and there were, as yet, few new rich to compete.[16]

The first Legion convalescent home was Byng House in Southport, Lancashire, made over in 1946 by the United Services Fund Trustees. The same year a mansion at Sevenoaks in Kent, presented to Mrs Churchill by an admirer of her husband's wartime leadership, was also passed to the Legion. Churchill himself attended the opening ceremony, telling the Legion to 'guard it . . . make sure every hour of the day and every inch of effort does good to those who have the greatest claim on the gratitude of the country' and acknowledging the march past with his famous 'V' sign; it was named Churchill Court.[17] Across the water in Northern Ireland, Bennet House, bought in 1945 and named after the Area Chairman, opened in 1948. Overlooking a busy waterfront, it was the only convalescent home to include some permanent residents. Finally, also opened in 1948, there was Somerset Legion House

*Churchill's famous 'V' sign at the opening of Churchill Court Legion Home in 1946.*

in Weston-Super-Mare. It too was presented to the Legion, but in this case it was the result of a remarkable local initiative by which branches in Somerset had raised £30,000 to purchase the former Norfolk Hotel in memory of dead comrades. It was the brainchild of a Captain Wills, who, passing a war memorial in 1943, had remarked 'No more of that'.[18]

Somerset Legion House was the largest of the convalescent homes, taking about a third of the 3,000 or so patients admitted each year to the four homes. Admissions were based on the recommendations of local branches and they included the chronically ill, providing not only a reinvigorating rest to the sufferers but relief to those who cared for them. A veteran of the Great War with a 100 per cent disablility pension for gunshot wounds breathed his first sea air since 1918, considering it an epoch in his life, while the parents of a totally paralysed 39-year-old got their only break in years when he was admitted.[19]

The Legion's homes had barely begun their work when the National Health Service Act of 1948 implied that they would be taken over by the state. A deputation promptly waited on the Prime Minister and, whatever the act might have intended, all the properties remained in Legion hands. Over the next few years the reprieve might have seemed a mixed blessing as legislation introduced more rules for such institutions, entailing further expenditure and adding to the already substantial maintenance costs. But in 1954 a further act laid a responsibility on local authorities to provide assistance to the elderly and infirm and the Legion was then able to obtain from them annual grants for the country homes.[20] Meanwhile Legion branches played their part, raising funds to provide comforts for patients.

Finances were not the only problems. In 1951 complaints by a Lister House resident led to a story in the *Daily Mirror* that the home 'was run like a barracks'. The Legion's response was to invite the press to an inquiry where it emerged that the

253

main dissatisfaction was that residents had no representation on the House Committee. The inquiry was told that this was against the Legion's practice, but suggestions could be put in the suggestions box. It then transpired that the box was empty since it had been mistaken for the vicar's collection box.[21] The real story of the homes lay in some of the admissions: a 77-year-old former sergeant, a veteran of both the Boer War and the Great War, who had lived with his daughter, but she had to go out to work, leaving him on his own suffering from multiple disabilities; a 75-year-old ex-naval rating who served from 1898 until 1922 but was 'unwanted' by his daughter-in-law. Such individuals no doubt groused from time to time and when someone did not fit in the Legion would try to move him elsewhere, but it seems that the homes were genuinely happy places.[22]

### The 'jewel in the crown' is lost

If the Health Service Act was not applied to the Legion homes, hospitals were another matter. Preston Hall was the Legion's pride: it had pioneered a long-term approach to TB with the aim not just to cure the ex-service patient through the most modern methods but to ensure that both he and his family were then able to live a normal life again, providing the facilities for them to do so. Associated with Preston Hall was treatment for tubercular ex-servicewomen at Nayland Hall on the low Suffolk hills and, for patients of more advanced years, Douglas House, in Bournemouth. Now, however, all of this was to be taken away.[23]

The Act dismembered the entire British Legion TB enterprise: Preston Hall hospital, Nayland and Douglas House were each transferred to their local Regional Hospital Board; but at the same time, in recognition of the Legion's involvement, it was represented on the new Boards. At Preston Hall itself, however, the Industries and the Village settlement remained in Legion hands.[24]

Needless to say there was some concern in the Legion, not only at the loss of the 'jewel in the crown' but over the future treatment of ex-service patients, although this was to some extent allayed by representation on the new management teams and by the assurance that beds would be set aside for ex-service men and women. The Chairman, Colonel Gordon Larking, put a good face on it at the 1948 Conference, assuring delegates that the change would do the ex-service community no harm and that ex-servicemen would still receive separate treatment. Furthermore it would have become increasingly difficult for the Legion to meet the expense of improvements in techniques.[25]

*The birth rate at Preston Hall was as high as elsewhere in 1946, as this picture suggests.*

The Preston Hall hospital management committee in fact continued to consult the Legion's NEC on matters of policy and, as the incidence of turberculosis began to

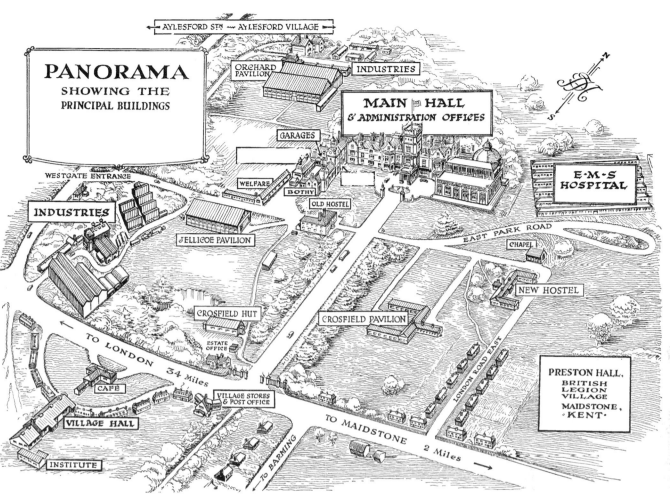

*The Legion Village shortly after the Second World War. It then straddled the main London Road and the 'crescent' at bottom left held the village facilities, including a café, which also catered for passing traffic, while administration was based on the Hall itself. The Crosfield Pavilion, built in 1938 to provide more comfortable accommodation for patients unsuited to the rigours of the open ward system, was now a men's hostel, as was the Jellicoe Pavilion which originally housed the operating theatre. Industries were on two sites: in the north the farm bred pigs and rabbits as well as producing vegetables and fruit in the Orchard Pavilion; the southerly site was used for manufacturing processes. The Emergency Medical Services (EMS) Hospital erected for wartime purposes was now in the hands of the National Health Service, having been reopened as a TB sanatorium.*

decline in the post-war years with improved housing, the Council was involved in the 1956 decision to accept patients with other chest complaints, although they asked that ex-service preference should be maintained.[26]

When, in 1963, the management committee was absorbed into a NHS district committee, there was again some concern in Legion circles, but, following discussions with the Ministry of Health, the Legion was given a strong representation on the new committee, while the hospital's own house committee was predominantly Legion.[27]

All in all the outcome had been satisfactory. The Legion had continued to be involved with its creation without the financial responsibility, which would undoubtedly have strained its resources. But the change in the type of patient being admitted to Preston Hall would raise other problems.

## Other medical concerns

Tuberculosis was not the only medical problem in which the Legion became directly involved. Since the mid-1930s it had been concerned that the remedies for rheumatism and arthritis were largely palliative when it had been advised that hospital treatment might produce positive results. In 1946 the opportunity arose for an experiment and it took over for one year fifty beds at a hospital at Arlesley in Bedfordshire. The Royal Free Hospital, London, helped with the treatment and, of 287 patients admitted over the period, the condition of 236 was improved. So impressed was the Minister of Health, Aneurin Bevan, with these results, that the unit was transferred under the ministry's auspices to a hospital in London at the end of the trial period, leading to units being set up in other hospital regions.[28]

For some patients the experience had been a minor miracle. One ex-serviceman from York had been crippled with rheumatism for sixteen years: when he was admitted to the unit his left leg had contracted with the knee bent almost at right angles; after eight weeks of treatment including manipulation and electro-therapy he was able to walk. Others who had been bedridden for years were able to go back to work. A survey eight years later showed that 25 per cent of patients had continued to improve while 60 per cent still retained their condition at discharge. The experiment had been a striking success, yet the Legion seems to have received little credit.[29]

Less successful were the Legion's attempts to improve the treatment of war-inspired neurosis, often called 'shell shock', with which it had had some experience in the aftermath of the First World War. In 1946 it offered to set up its own rehabilitation centre, but was told that any such institution would simply be taken over by the National Health Service. However, the government itself set up four treatment centres for the reported 130,000 cases, including one for officers.

Still concerned, the Legion decided to augment the government's efforts with a consultancy service in fifteen locations where the official resources were considered inadequate and, after some 1,000 patients had been seen, suggested that a much greater effort was needed. The official response was that matters would improve for both civil and ex-service cases as the Health Service evolved, and with this the Legion had to be content, while giving what help it could to these less-obvious war victims.[30]

## Housing loans scheme – a success story

Housing was not yet, however, part of the welfare state and here there were more opportunities for Legion help. As in the case of the First World War, it was the most widespread post-war problem. Most housing was in the control of local authorities and many gave no preference to returning servicemen, arguing that those who had remained to work in the factories were just as entitled to a roof over their heads. The Legion itself did not demand absolute priority for ex-servicemen, but it wanted due weight given to their claims and a just and consistent policy throughout the country. But all the government felt able to do was to urge the local authorities to give special consideration to the ex-servicemen,[31] which was of little practical use. Private rentals were in short supply, expensive and often unsatisfactory. By 1947 Legion files throughout the country bulged with thousands of cases of former servicemen who were finding it impossible to set up home with, in some cases, their marriage ended as a result. Not all branches were as astute as the one in Barnet which rehoused an evicted family by asking all seven clergy in the area to read from the pulpit Matthew XXV 35: 'For I was a stranger and ye took me in'.[32] Meanwhile new house building was lagging and in any case priority went to miners and agricultural workers.

In this situation the Legion launched a scheme in 1947 to assist ex-service families to buy their own houses. It was restricted to those without proper accommodation who could get a mortgage and was therefore a 'topping up' scheme providing a five-year interest-free loan of around £100 when a house might cost £600 to £1,000. It was strongly supported by the RAF Benevolent Fund who contributed half of the loan to ex-airmen, and by other service associations, and by 1950 over 2,000 families had been helped. It was able to keep going because over 90 per cent of repayments were made promptly, enabling the money to be re-loaned, and in 1954 with the total number of loans now over 8,000, the government began to take note, eventually incorporating many of the ideas in a 'Government Guarantee' house purchase scheme operated through local authorities. This scheme reduced the calls on the Legion, as did the eventual improvement in local housing and by 1960 there were only a few hundred loans being made each year, with the repayments providing a surplus available for other Legion work.[33]

The scheme continued to run down in the 1960s, by then being mainly used to assist ex-regulars who did not have enough service to qualify for a gratuity. But by the early 1970s house prices were increasing at such a rate, especially in the south-east, that the Legion loan, a maximum of £150, made only a small contribution to the cost, and in 1972 it was terminated.[34]

Run by Lister, it was one of the Legion's great success stories, assisting over 20,000 families against two criteria: was the applicant responsible enough to be a house owner? Were his family's housing conditions such that he needed re-housing more than the next man? But much of the credit is due to local service committees for properly 'vetting' the applicants so that the repayment rate, which drove the whole scheme forward, remained high: of a total of over £2 million loaned only £50,000 had to be written-off, a third of which was for compassionate reasons such as the death of the wage earner. The beneficiaries themselves were in no doubt about the value of the scheme: 'the escape from rooms has wrought a change in outlook which surpasses all imagination' was a Yorkshireman's comment in 1950.[35]

## Government pilgrimage scheme

Among the Legion's own properties was Haig House in Ypres, purchased in 1932 in order to provide a base for pilgrims visiting the battlefields of the Great War. Although it had survived the 1939-45 war it was too localized for the scattered cemeteries of that conflict and in 1948 it was sold; in any case the Legion now had an office in Brussels. The same year the government asked the Legion to undertake the care of relatives visiting war graves overseas and over the next few months some 4,000 visits were made to graves in France, the Low Countries and Denmark, Legion headquarters arranging passports, tickets and foreign currency while the Brussels office found the accommodation. Seven-eighths of the cost for two relatives of the

*The first Legion pilgrimage by air: pilgrims about to board a Viking airliner at Bovingdon in 1949 en-route to Italy.*

deceased was met by government, while the Legion paid the rest. There were problems in these early post-war days – the pilgrim sometimes arrived to find that the name on the grave had been changed, a matter which greatly perturbed the Legion as well as distressing the family – but the War Graves Commission faced many difficulties in the aftermath of the war.[36]

These were individual visits and, as the scheme progressed, pilgrims were increasingly helped by a network of local voluntary helpers if the grave lay in a 'liberated' country. The first group visits were made in 1949 to a country not in this category, Italy, and accounted for nearly half of the total of the 7,000 pilgrims assisted by the Legion that year. Since the overland journey would have been too fatiguing for the elderly the visits were made by chartered aircraft in parties of twenty-four. For most of the pilgrims flying was a novel experience and they were highly appreciative, although one group remarked that they would have liked a gramophone aboard to play calming music in bad weather.[37]

In 1950, however, Holy Year meant the suspension of the Italian programme, while delay in the government's annual renewal of the scheme severely reduced the number visiting other parts of Europe, to which, at the time, visits were confined.[38]

Apart from the usual problems with the quality of the tea all had gone well with the pilgrims. None had failed to reach the graveside, however remote – in the Pyrenees, on an island off the Netherlands or at the summit of a solitary Italian hill. Once there, emotions were revealed: a mother, having trudged through the mud to reach her son's grave on the Coriano Ridge in Italy, looked down on it with an expression of bewilderment, grey hair straggling out from a sodden headscarf. No defeat was written on her face, only the eternal question, 'Why?'[39]

# 1951 – 1955

## War pensions – 'How hollow those tributes ring'

With rises in living costs eroding the value of war pensions the Legion continued to press for an increase; a war widow could now receive less than an ordinary widow might get from the National Assistance Board, while a miner would certainly be paid more for a disability than an ex-serviceman.[40] After a five-hour debate in the House of Commons in February 1951 had achieved nothing, a motion of urgency at the Legion's Conference that year sought to double the war pensions rate and the '90 shillings campaign' was launched with a November press briefing, timed to coincide with Remembrance. Indeed much thought had been given to the running of the campaign. There would be no opportunity this time for government (of any colour –

the Labour administration had just been replaced by the Conservatives under Churchill) to accuse the Legion of playing politics: MPs would not be lobbied; instead the plan was to arouse public awareness not only through the press and meetings but also by the Legion's membership acting as propagandists in the workplace or neighbourhood. The message was that war disability pensions and war widows' pensions represented a statutory compensation for war injury, unrelated to need or earning capacity.[41] If their value was allowed to diminish then the nation was turning its back on those on whom it had relied in its hour of need.[42]

The press reacted strongly. *The Daily Mirror* even encapsulated the whole case for increased war pensions in their 'Ruggles' strip cartoon. It featured not only a Poppy Factory employee but the Legion's Chairman, no doubt the only time the Colonel of the Blues would appear in a *Mirror* strip cartoon. In the final 'box' a war widow

Ruggles visits the National Chairman at home . . .

. . . and spends some time at the Poppy Factory

The war widows are not forgotten

*The War Pensions battle – 'Ruggles' of the* Daily Mirror *joins the fray. The cartoon admirably sums up the Legion position.*

spoke: 'The government pledged . . . I'm sure they won't let us down.'[43] And after a Legion deputation had presented the government with 'reasoned and logical arguments' it did relent, to the extent of a 10 shilling rise, well short of the pre-war equity the Legion had sought.[44]

*The Times* thought the government's generosity had been limited by concern that any increase would have to be matched by a corresponding increase in industrial injury compensation – if so it was 'a dubious proposition' – but when, later in 1952, the Legion held a 'Day of Demand' to press the case for 90 shillings, the *Daily Telegraph* described the tactic as 'questionable' and the claims 'a shade exaggerated'. It seemed politics were creeping back in. Nevertheless the Pensions Minister accepted the Legion Chairman's challenge to ride with him on the Big Dipper 'at 90 shillings' during Legion Week at the Festival Gardens in Battersea.[45]

A new phase of the campaign began in the autumn of 1953. Speakers were identified and trained on a special course, subsequently addressing not only Chamber of Commerce dinners but football match crowds at half-time. The activity was designed to lead up to the 1954 budget, but when that budget was announced there was no mention of war pensions and the NEC could only express to the Prime Minister its 'profound dissatisfaction and surprise'. A few months later, however, the government announced another small increase, bringing the 100 per cent war disability pension to 67s 6d, but still far short of the 90 shilling figure. The Legion immediately resumed its efforts, undeterred by comments that it would not succeed because it lacked 'industrial muscle', unlike the firemen whose compensation for injury was now twice that of the war-disabled. That year was the tenth anniversary of the battle of Arnhem and one survivor wrote to the Legion's President that the wounds he had received had left him 100 per cent disabled, unable to take a step without pain, jobless, not even able to endure the strain of running his own business and in some financial difficulty. 'So much,' he wrote, 'for the heroes who fought at Arnhem. How hollow those tributes ring.' The writer was a former lieutenant colonel.[46]

The slogan was now 'A Debt of Honour' and a pamphlet under that title was distributed to every candidate at the 1955 election. As at Arnhem there had been no breakthrough, but the Legion would continue the battle undaunted.

## Starting small businesses

In the world of small businesses breakthroughs were often just as difficult. The Legion's scheme for financial assistance had been re-introduced in 1945, but many ideas were as much hampered by shortages of materials as by shortage of money. As the situation improved, a wide variety of enterprises were started up with Legion help – chimney sweeps, steeplejacks, dentists, cosmetic manufacturers, rug makers and many others. Former ATS were given loans to start seaside boarding houses and the disabled got special consideration. Where ex-RAF were concerned the RAF Benevolent Fund made generous contributions.[47]

As in the past the local Legion service committees were heavily involved in vetting applications. They also helped where they could with another problem of the time – licences. Many business ideas were at the mercy of local bureaucracy still exercising wartime controls: a disabled ex-soldier wishing to extend his tobacconist business into confectionery got up a petition when refused a licence by the local Food Ministry office, but his appeal failed; only after Legion intervention and two months of inquiry into confectionery supply in the area did the Ministry relent and grant a licence. All this was needed to place a row of sweet jars on a shelf.[48]

By 1950 over 4,000 loans had been made and the repayment rate was around 70 per cent, indicating a similar rate of business success. But the scheme took up some £50,000 to £100,000 of Legion funds annually and by 1951 it was deemed to have served its post-war rehabilitation purpose; from thereon it was restricted to those whose need for independent employment was caused by disability or ill-health. In succeeding years it ran down still more, although anyone whose disability was so severe that self-employment was the only option could still get a loan, or even a grant. By 1960 there were only a dozen or so loans and a similar number of grants each year and the following year Conference decided to discontinue the scheme, the Council, however, leaving a loophole for the very severely disabled.[49]

The Legion's job-finding service was also running down. Most of its effort was now concentrated on the older element, although few applicants were as old as the 85-year-old Boer War veteran who was found work as messenger. By 1955 only 3,000 placements were recorded, although not all branches reported their efforts.[50]

## 'Where to, guv'nor?'

Another route to self-employment for those in the London area was provided by the Legion's Taxi School. It had resumed activities in a minor way in 1946. But by 1947 both Ministry and union opposition to expansion had been overcome and around 100 were under instruction, making daytime use of a Boys' Club premises near Kennington Oval. By 1951 nearly 170 were being trained annually and some 20 per cent of London taxis were driven by Legion-trained ex-servicemen. But, in 1952, a new government ruling limited the subsidy to ex-regulars or registered disabled and the numbers fell to around fifty each year. After the forces went all-regular in the early 1960s, the total in training climbed back to 100, the school accounting for around a quarter of all London's taxi drivers by the time it moved to new premises in Brixton Road in the mid-1960s.

Not all the trainees qualified. The London Carriage Office 'Blue Book' listed 450 shortest routes with which candidates had to be familiar, returning each month to the Carriage Office to be tested in a room known as the 'snake pit'. Familiarity entailed bicycling some 5,000 miles during their year's training, although by the early 1960s the push-bike had been replaced by the motor-scooter. For most the 'knowledge' was more difficult even than the stringent police driving test which involved three-point turns in narrow streets. But, under the tuition of former Scotland Yard inspector George Stedman, most did

*The Legion Taxi School resumed after the war; here a trainee practises a three-point turn in a fortunately deserted Thames Embankment in central London. Note the Legion badge over the radiator.*

survive to earn their green badge and the right to say, 'Where to, guv'nor?'[51]

### Concern for the paralysed

The disabled taxi drivers were luckier than the spinal paralysis cases the Legion had 'adopted' in the first year of peace at the Ministry of Pensions hospital at Stoke Mandeville. They were expected to spend the rest of their lives on their backs, but the Legion instead encouraged them to play ball games from wheelchairs and attempt light work, while a shooting brake was provided to take them to football matches.[52]

In 1946, following an investigation led by Brunel Cohen to see to what extent the war-paralysed could live at home, the Legion had acquired a house in Aylesbury where the whole family could learn to live with the disability. The two families at a time in residence did all their own housework, which was the object of their stay, and the Legion was able to learn from their experiences. It was an inspired idea, but after the first nine couples had passed through the difficulty became apparent: the family might learn to cope with the disability, but because of the housing shortage there was nowhere for it to do so. The men returned to their hostels, the Legion turned its attention to housing paraplegics and the Aylesbury venture closed in 1947.[53]

Some 500 men had been permanently paralysed by spinal injury in the war. Of the 400 the Legion was able to contact by 1947, the great majority aspired to home life. Largely through the efforts of local branches, by 1950 around fifty houses had been obtained and the Legion adapted them for occupation based on the Aylesbury experience, widening entrances and installing downstairs bedrooms and baths. Other families were found places in the Haig Homes for the married disabled.[54]

Meanwhile many men had to remain in the hostels, but the Legion's interest in their situation resulted in the formation of a Paraplegic Branch, whose members even managed to produce their own magazine, some copy being produced face down in a hospital bed. Other Legion branches made contact, outings were arranged and help given – tools for work such as clock repairing or, in one case, a typewriter for a patient studying for a Doctorate of Music.[55] By the early 1950s the Legion was making grants to buy and erect garages for specially-adapted cars and starting an annual holiday scheme at Prestatyn. Holiday schemes for the paralysed were not easy to organize: few boarding houses or hotels had the facilities; but the Legion compiled a register and the scheme, which was combined in 1959 with holidays for other categories of severely disabled, provided seaside holidays for around 300 disabled people a year, accompanied by wives and helpers, with Legion members often providing transport to the holiday home. By 1970 the numbers were, however, beginning to fall as age took its toll.[56]

For most it was their only opportunity to holiday and for at least two couples it was their honeymoon, while the local Legion branch organized a party when they heard of a golden wedding anniversary. 'You don't get that on the State,' was the couple's comment.[57]

### War pensions appeals decline

The Legion's success rate in war pensions appeals was very high after the Second World War. But this in itself was disturbing: it meant that the Ministry of Pensions had failed to interpret the rules correctly in the first place, causing delay and hardship. Anyone denied a war pension or wishing to challenge the amount awarded had the right to appeal to a Pensions Tribunal, and on a point of law there could be a final appeal to the High

Court. Some 70 per cent of all such final appeals were represented by the Legion and in 1947 no less than 118 cases out of 151 put before the High Court were allowed, meaning that the Tribunals too were disallowing far too many applications. This was disturbing, but the same year Mr (later Lord) Justice Denning ruled that an Appeal Tribunal could only reject an appeal on a unanimous vote. At the same time the Ministry of Pensions became more sympathetic and by 1955 their better judgement was reflected in a reduced Legion involvement in Tribunal hearings, as is shown at Chart B2 at page 446, while only five cases appeared before a High Court Judge that year. The whole system had become speedier and more efficient, aided by the use of earlier High Court judgements to decide cases.[58]

There was still much work for the Legion in the years that followed. Although the number of cases had declined, many were now complex. First World War problems again emerged in the 1950s as age and increasing disability caused the original condition to deteriorate, while widows sought to establish whether war service had contributed to death; in many cases it undoubtedly had done so, but proof was difficult and time-consuming.[59] But by the 1960s there was much more official sympathy when the Legion sponsored cases such as those of widows whose husbands had died from coronary thrombosis caused by Japanese prison camp privation many years before. Less successful was the case of a post-war Sapper who died of leukemia, the condition having been attributed to his presence on Christmas Island during a nuclear test in 1957. Counsel produced expert evidence on the effects of radiation, but it was disallowed, the Ministry contending that there was no relationship between the nuclear explosions and the disease.[60]

By now the Legion represented over 80 per cent of all appeals, still fighting some First World War cases such as blindness caused by mustard gas and even winning a disability pension sixty-four years later for a gallant old gentleman wounded in the siege of Ladysmith, although, unfortunately for him, it could not be backdated. In 1970, among the cases supported by its five full-time representatives, was that of a widow of a Merchant Navy officer who had lost both legs after his ship had been torpedoed in the Battle of the Atlantic in midwinter and eventually died of a heart attack; after the DHSS had rejected the claim the Legion took it to a Tribunal and she received a pension with arrears of over £1,000.[61]

## Netherlands hospitality

With the ending of government financial help in 1951, visits by the bereaved to overseas war graves declined. However, the Netherlands War Graves Committee continued to assist with pilgrimages to British cemeteries in their country, the Dutch people paying the costs and providing accommodation in their own homes. The pilgrims were much moved by the genuine warmth and sincerity of their hosts, who in 1955 added a children's pilgrimage to the four adult visits; such was its success that a second group came the same year, each child first laying a wreath of poppies and then standing silently before the headstone of a father perhaps never seen. It was almost impossible adequately to acknowledge the Dutch generosity and goodwill, but in 1954 the Legion presented a stained-glass window to the chapel of the student centre 'Ons Erf' near Nijmegen which served as the headquarters of the pilgrimages and in later years there were reciprocal visits, at first by the relatives of Dutch servicemen buried in England and then an annual trip to London for the fundraisers for the Dutch activities.[62]

The feelings of the British pilgrims, are revealed in a letter written in 1963 by a woman whose brother had been shot down some twenty years before, 'Our gratitude is beyond words . . . it would be impossible to relate the many kindnesses that we received, or to tell of the love, sympathy and understanding which surrounded us . . . leaving . . . many were in tears.'[63]

Despite the Netherlands example and a Conference request in 1952, government support for pilgrimages was not renewed. But a Legion visit to Normandy that year was repeated in successive years and 1954 saw several pilgrimages to commemorate the 10th anniversary of the allied landings. The Legion flew ninety relatives of the fallen to El Alamein in 1954, to attend the unveiling of the memorial by Field Marshal Montgomery and the following year, in the most ambitious pilgrimage yet, took seventy-three by air to Italy, visiting nearly all of the British cemeteries in the country. These trips were not without incident: in 1953 the British Rail steamer carrying pilgrims across the Channel was struck by an American vessel and had to be abandoned; but the Legion party showed no sign of panic as they took to the lifeboats and simply carried on with the tour after rescue. And the crew of one of the aircraft en route to North Africa in 1954 were persuaded by the mother of an airman lost in the Mediterranean to fly over the spot so that she could drop roses picked from her garden through the flight deck window. As she did so, they stood and saluted.[64]

# 1956 – 1960

## Benevolent work centralised

In his farewell speech as National President at the 1958 Annual Conference, Sir Ian Fraser commented that there was still room for voluntary bodies: 'For the enterprise, initiative and experiment' which such bodies had provided in the past. Moreover they could 'get very near to the individual's needs, know him personally and fill in the gaps which must inevitably arise in any Whitehall or Town Hall scheme'.[65] Certainly the Legion's own record of initiative and experiment, from Preston Hall in the mid-1920s and the post-war rheumatology scheme to house purchase loans for those lacking proper accommodation, could scarcely be challenged. As to the gaps, there were plenty for the organization's nearly 5,000 service committees to plug. Even more of their attention was now directed to the problems of the elderly: the average age of First World War veterans was sixty-five and not only did they need to be assisted in the established way – food, clothing and bedding in winter – but loneliness was often a problem and the extensive Legion network could help with regular visiting. Caught up in a society increasingly focused on material wealth some entered into hire purchase commitments that they were unable to meet and needed guidance. But in most cases it was simply the struggle to make ends meet on a fixed income. A widow dying of cancer but struggling to see her son through higher education, an unexpected bill for the re-wiring of the house in a dangerous condition, mounting debts, an old soldier with a gallantry award whose pride made him hold out until unpaid bills of £27 compelled him to go to the Legion, all were helped. But it was not only money: a widow crippled with rheumatism was threatened with eviction because her cottage garden was uncultivated; the local branch maintained it from then on.[66]

Each year the amount spent on the relief of such cases steadily rose and, in the interest of economy, most Area benevolent work was centralized at headquarters between 1958 and 1959, the Area involvement from then on being mainly the administration of the local service committees. The change was not achieved without some Area objections, but in this case the NEC seems simply to have decided to act as quickly as possible.[67]

## Hard times in Eire

Times were still hard in the South of Ireland. For every £1 donated in the Republic to the Poppy Appeal £6 was returned for relief work. Unemployment was much greater than in the United Kingdom and state welfare services lagged far behind. An 85-year-old widow of a British ex-serviceman visited by the Legion branch secretary, who was also an *Irish Times* journalist, was found living in a 5s a week room and when she received four bags of coal, a food ticket for £3 and a promise of a 7s 6d a week pension (in fact she was to receive 10s) – help beyond her imagination – her gratitude was embarassing.[68] Others in Dublin had to survive on the subsidized 'twopenny dinners' and a typical problem for the Legion service committees was the large family of perhaps twelve children, left behind when the husband crossed the water to seek work.[69]

Some of the older ex-service people lived in institutions and lodging houses which moved them out during the day and in 1958, with a £1,000 NEC grant, a Legion Day Shelter was opened. 21 Blackhall Street, refurbished by local Legion members and run for a month at a time either by a local Legion branch or one of the Irish regimental Old Comrades Associations, provided thirty men a day with newspapers, wireless and warmth, and a 'Quartermaster's Stores' of second-hand clothing. Many of the men who came lived in unheated tenements and existed on sausages cooked on a biscuit tin lid over a candle; but there would be a picture of King George V on the wall alongside the one of the young private in the Royal Dublin Fusiliers forty years before. On arrival at the shelter at nine o'clock they would be handed a cup of tea and a sandwich, at midday there was bread and soup, and before they left for their doss house or night shelter there would be more tea and sandwiches. There was no alcohol except for the Christmas Dinner, before which there had been a whip-round for a card for the Queen which all the men signed, adding the titles of their old regiments so that she should be reminded of their loyalty.[70] But as the men grew older and too frail to make the journey it was less used, finally closing in 1973.[71] More money became available in 1967 when the Legion won a case in the Dublin High Court. It was successfully argued that a fund established by King Charles II in 1684 for the poor or injured of 'our army in Ireland' should go to the Legion rather than the Irish Defence Forces and a Southern Ireland Trust Fund was established.[72]

## A pensions breakthrough

When a Legion deputation called on the Pensions Minister in 1956 to renew the plea for war pensions to be increased in line with inflation, the members were courteously received. But it was soon made clear that they were wasting their time. Despite the fact that, even after the 1954 rise to 67s 6d, the basic war pension was still barely half its pre-war value (see Chart B3 on page 447), there was to be no further increase: any such concession by government would lead to demands in other areas of social services and in any case individual hardship could always be relieved through the welfare system.

The Minister's response confirmed the Legion's worst fears. Government strategy was to reduce the significance of war disability pensions and war widows' pensions, submerging them in the general welfare provisions that applied to the whole community; any recognition of the country's special debt to the war pensioner or war widow would disappear.[73]

Included in the Legion's deputation had been the Chairman of the Women's Section, Dame Regina Evans, who had pleaded the case of the war widow: the Section's visits to elderly widows had been both saddening and shocking: 'They are not living but subsisting.' RAFA had also been represented on this occasion, but from now on, in order to underline the concern of the whole ex-service community over this issue, the Legion sought the support of the other ex-service organizations. In an unprecedented show of unity representatives of nineteen of them joined a further delegation to the Minister in March 1957 where SSAFA led on the war widows' problems. But once again it was made clear that neither they nor disabled ex-servicemen were acknowledged as a unique group.[74]

The campaign was resumed. Posters were produced depicting a coin with a segment removed to show the pension's reduced value, but, in an echo of the 1948 events, the British Transport Commission decided it was too 'politically controversial' to show on the railways or buses. A meeting at the Albert Hall expressing 'deep concern' was attended by 4,500 members from twenty-one ex-service organizations with over 100 MPs on the platform. The next day a delegation called on the Prime Minister, Harold Macmillan. Somewhat to everyone's surprise after the earlier stonewalling by the Minister concerned, he said that he had something in mind, and two weeks later the 67s 6d was raised to 85 shillings.[75]

So where did the Legion and its comrades-in-arms go from here? The original aim had been 90 shillings, and it had all but been achieved. But in the ten years that had elapsed since the campaign began the pre-war value had sunk even further so that rather more than 100 shillings ($£5$) was needed to regain equity. Opinions were divided: some felt that the campaign had been won and to continue it would be counter-productive, others that it should continue. In the end, with the backing of the 1958 Conference, the Legion decided to press government to fulfil its obligations, particularly towards the war widows, whose situation was still far from satisfactory. A meeting of thirty-one ex-service associations in late 1958 agreed a ten-point plan and a powerful Legion-led delegation went off to the ministry. As a result war widows over seventy received a 10 shilling increase and other measures were agreed to improve the war pensioners' lot. This did not satisfy the 1959 Conference who sought a 'substantial increase' all round and the campaign group of ex-service organizations produced a further list, this time totalling eleven points.

Another visit to the Minister secured more concessions, such as the abolition of the seven-year time limit on claims which still applied to some war widows, and the following year, 1960, the government announced that the rate would go up to 97s 6d. At last, after twelve years' campaigning, the '90 shilling battle' had been won.[76]

At the end of the decade the Legion, and the others, were able to reflect not only on their achievements but how they had come about. The 'special recognition' of the war pensioner and the war widow had been saved, through persistence and argument. A dialogue had been opened with government and it had been maintained. Confrontation had been avoided. And not only had the value of a 'Grand Coalition' of ex-service organizations (which Haig would surely have applauded) been proved but it now existed for future use. The question was, how soon would it be needed? Even 97s 6d did not restore the value of the pre-war 40 shilling pension, as Chart B3 (page 447) shows.

## Service pensions and redundancy

The Legion was less successful when it ventured into a new pensions field. In 1959 the Grigg Committee investigating recruiting for the new all-regular forces expressed disatisfaction at the end-of-service pension rates, particularly over the provisions for widows. A Legion-led deputation went to the Ministry of Defence to find that on the eve of their arrival increases had been announced. However, they only applied to future pensions; those already drawing service pensions would not be helped. As the Ministry might well have admitted, their concern was simply to recruit, hence new pension rates related only to new pay rates.[77]

The deputation saw matters in a different light and sought a two-tier system which would bring everyone on to the existing rate when a new rate was announced. This remained the Legion position, but, although there were some increases, with better provision for widows, it was not accepted by the MOD. The argument was of course that a man was treated according to the contract under which he joined.[78]

These recruiting activities were part of a reorganization of the armed forces on the ending of National Service, which also involved a redundancy programme. The Legion was invited to attend the meetings of the Advisory Board and was able to influence planning for the resettlement of other ranks, especially warrant officers and senior non-commissioned officers. The outcome was that there were few problems for these ranks, but the officers faced a much more difficult situation.[79]

## The debt to the war-disabled

By the late 1950s the total of war-disabled unemployed had been reduced to under 20,000, following the replacement of the King's Roll with a quota system requiring employers to reserve 2 per cent of the workforce for war-disabled, a figure increased to 3 per cent in 1946. It would remain at around that level until the late 1960s when a surge in unemployment generally saw it rise to around 25,000. Despite these relatively low figures – there were about half a million registered as war-disabled – the Legion remained dissatisfied, making a number of attempts to get the quota increased. The real problem was that, despite the legislation, many firms failed to meet the quota.[80]

At the end of the war some 5,000 had been so severely disabled that they could not compete in the ordinary workplace. In subsequent years half had found sheltered employment in the government-controlled Remploy factories.[81] The Remploy scheme had been modelled on the Legion's own work initiatives for the severely disabled[82] and the first Remploy Chairman was Brunel Cohen. Meanwhile the Legion itself continued to employ over 1,000 disabled ex-service people, maintaining its position as the largest employer of the disabled outside government, and its activities included Disabled Men's Industries marketing goods made at home or in small factories. Sales were good in the period after the war and a showroom had been opened again in central London in Victoria Street. Lloyds of London Branch also ran a three-day annual sale, while a resolution at Conference 1961 led to Legion headquarters in Pall Mall providing another outlet. The main sales force was, however, the Women's Section, whose members' efforts were untiring.[83]

The craftsmanship was admired but repeat orders were not always possible, even for the Queen Mother who was a regular DMI customer. It could take a severely disabled man a year to make a tea cosy, but during those long months he was achieving something and, although he might write that 'the extra £3 will make all the difference to my children's Christmas', the real value lay in the benefit to his frame of mind.[84]

The Legion was also involved in transport for the war-disabled. The government accepted responsiblity, but insisted on a single-seat invalid tricycle; the Legion and others wanted a two-seat car so that the man's wife could be present if there was any difficulty. After trials a four-seat mini was accepted by the Ministry, the first specially-adapted car being presented in 1960 to a Poppy Factory worker who had lost a leg on the first day of the Somme offensive. Nonetheless the fact that issue was restricted to the war-disabled led to questions in Parliament from those speaking on behalf of other disabled groups. The government's reply on this occasion was unequivocal: 'It has always been held that the country owes a debt to those who have been disabled in its service'.[85]

## A change of name for the Attendants Company

The appearance of traffic wardens on the streets of Britain in 1960, although welcomed as providing another employment outlet for ex-servicemen, could have threatened another of the Legion's activities for the disabled. But the British Legion Attendants' Company had already seen the need to diversify, having in 1953 changed its title to omit 'Car Park'.[86] The new national company had got into its stride when the end of the war brought cars back on the road and by 1950 there were nearly 300 full-time and 160 part-time mainly disabled employees in over seventy towns, controlled by eight local boards. The post-war uniform which had replaced breeches and boots was frequently to be seen

*By 1960 'Car Park' had been dropped from the title of the Attendants' Company, which now reflected the company's wider role.*

at race meetings, agricultural shows and national events such as the Ideal Home Exhibition, as well as at car parks.[87]

Although the company was financially successful, the welfare of the employees was the first consideration: they were paid good wages, there was a pension scheme and holidays with pay. A Durham man, who had spent eighteen years in hospital after being blown up at Ypres, thoroughly enjoyed his eight-hour day at a busy and tricky market place in the city. He was a widower with a family of six, but when an American visitor, under his wife's instructions, gave him a massive three shilling tip the money was handed in for the benefit of all.[88]

The 1960s saw the redevelopment of many bombed sites, previously used as car parks, and the opening of multi-story parks operated with minimal staff, losing some business for the company.[89] But the earlier diversification paid off and when the company celebrated its silver jubilee in 1968 it was fitting that among other tributes there was one from the Secretary of the All-England Tennis Club which annually employed eighty men at Wimbledon. By then the Attendants Company had on its pay-roll over 900 disabled ex-servicemen, providing commissionaires, school traffic wardens and security guards, while maintaining its reputation as the most widespread and economic car-parking organization in the country. It was, too, a financial success, not only having repaid its £35,000 loan but donating to Legion benevolence.[90]

## Challenges for Pilgrimage staff

Withdrawal of government financial support in 1951 had reduced the numbers visiting war graves overseas, but with more money about in the second half of the decade the Legion's pilgrimage programme built up again. In 1957 the Legion took 1,600 relatives to the unveiling of the Dunkirk Memorial, but shortage of accommodation meant that they had to spend both nights at sea. It was a complicated operation in every way, involving mustering the pilgrims in different parts of the town and bringing each party to the memorial over a footbridge according to a timed programme. But, although the General Secretary and his staff were on duty for thirty-six hours continuously, it all went without a hitch, even the special trains arriving punctually at fifteen-minute intervals to take the disembarking pilgrims to Victoria where a fleet of London Transport buses awaited them.[91]

The staff were put to a further test later that year when 180 relatives were flown to Tunis to attend the unveiling of a memorial some fifty miles into the desert. A violent thunderstorm halted the convoy and the situation became serious as the route ahead disappeared into a rapidly rising lake, while the road behind also flooded. Wading waist-deep, the staff and the accompanying military managed to identify a way out but even so one coachload started to float away until the pilgrims shifted their weight to the back axle, resuming their seats in due course to be led by a 70-year-old widow in 'A Life on the Ocean Wave'. But when they got back to Tunis at one a.m. some were in a state of collapse. The experience did not prevent them from returning the following year, when all went well.[92]

This period also saw the first pilgrimage to the Far East, the Legion taking a party to Rangoon to take part in unveiling a memorial, members of the Rangoon branch putting up the pilgrims.[93] Closer to home was a visit to Norway where there were only a few hundred graves following the ill-fated 1941 expedition, but fifty-two relatives took part.

And there were the annual visits to Normandy, the Netherlands and Germany, as well as a trip to Malta in 1960. It all took a great deal of work, but every pilgrim was able to reach the intended graveside.[94]

## 1961 – 1965

### An ageing ex-service community

By now many of the First World War generation were into their seventies, while some of those who had fought in the Second World War, and their dependants, approached their sixties. Their problems were intensified by a rise in unemployment and even more Legion resources were directed at the elderly. Immediate needs were met by the local Service Committees and often the most pressing of these was fuel; many old people died simply from lack of warmth. By now smokeless zones meant that delivery of a bag of coal was replaced by payment of gas or electricity bills. There were other gaps in the welfare state provisions. An elderly widow suffering from arthritis had to use an outside lavatory in all weathers since the local council refused to modernize the house as the area was scheduled for redevelopment; the branch arranged re-housing. A wife who was unable to afford a telephone to notify the hospital if her husband's life support machine failed had to rely on the public phone until the Legion stepped in.[95]

An ageing population made more use of hospitals and in the 1960s hospital visiting, long undertaken by many branches, became County co-ordinated. Legion funds could be spent, but often branches used their own money to provide comforts. The visits also helped the patients with their problems, ensuring all was well at home, tracing relatives or examining a case for a war pension. Some of the patients had not been visited for many years and their gratitude was touching.[96]

### Help for those unable to work

There was gratitude too from the First World War men and women who had been assisted by the Prince of Wales's Pensions Scheme, started in 1931 to tide over those made unfit for work because of their wartime experiences until they qualified for the Old Age Pension. Despite earlier restrictions on the scheme, by 1960 it was becoming difficult to fill places. In 1963 the Trustees therefore decided to maintain the weekly ten shilling payments until age seventy, re-issuing some pensions already withdrawn. The scheme was finally wound up, as planned, in 1971, with around 500 on the roll, many of whom were then transferred to the Legion's Permanently Incapacitated and Widows scheme.[97]

This scheme dated from 1936, when it had become clear that, among those medically unfit for work, there were some deserving cases who were too young to qualify for a Prince of Wales pension. There were others, equally deserving, who were too old; although they drew the state pension they were still in need. A supplementary scheme was therefore introduced, for the 'permanently incapacitated'. In 1949 it had been extended to widows as more Legion funds became available following the introduction of state welfare benefits. At first there were contributions from Regimental Associations, but by 1962, when the original 800 pre-war beneficiaries had grown to over 8,000 and the previously variable allowance was standardized at a flat rate of ten shillings a week, many associations had been forced to drop out. Since the policy was to transfer an incapacitated man's allowance to his widow, with the passage of time the proportion of widows increased, by

1968 forming the majority of nearly 9,000 beneficiaries. By then it was often simply a supplement to the Old Age Pension, eroded in value but nonetheless providing many with a little extra comfort in their declining years.[98]

Also ageing were many Poles who had fought in the late war and had remained in Britain when their country fell under the Communist yoke. In 1963 the government allocated £50,000 a year for their welfare, asking the Legion to administer the scheme. A British/Polish Advisory Committee was set up, while an Executive Committee under a former Polish major general investigated individual cases, both committees being Legion-staffed. It soon became apparent that more money was needed and the following year the grant was raised to £75,000. Similar sums were disbursed in the years that followed, much of the money being used to provide regular allowances. The scheme gave the Legion staff additional work, but the Poles had been gallant allies in the war and the help was unquestioned.[99]

### The war widows – a unique charge?

There were many elderly people in one particular group who were always of the greatest concern to the Legion, the war widows, and the pensions campaign having, for the time being at any rate, achieved its objective, attention turned to their needs. Despite the war widows' pension increases resulting from the campaign some were still in financial difficulty and the fact that their pensions were taxed caused much indignation. One commentator laid part of the blame on senior officers of the armed forces: they should be less concerned with war memoirs and TV appearances and do more to emulate Haig by fighting the corner of those suffering as a result of war.[100]

Nevertheless several former senior officers were among those representing the forty-three ex-service associations which met under Legion chairmanship in 1961 to plan the strategy. There followed meetings with the Chancellor of the Exchequer and with the Pensions Minister, the point being made that a war widow should not simply be treated like any other widow – she was a unique charge on the nations' resources – and reminding both ministers that as long ago as 1919 a select committee had recommended that the pension should be exempt from tax. But they were unmoved, and doubtless Treasury officials were horrified at even the suggestion.[101]

However, the dialogue had not been entirely in vain: the war disability pension itself was raised to 115s in 1963, with an associated increase in war widows' pensions, accompanied by more concessions to the widows over rights of appeal. If the leaders of the ex-service organizations were disappointed over widows' taxation they seem to have been pleasantly surprised at the amount of the pension increase, attributing the success once again to their joint approach. Nevertheless the discussions continued and in 1965 the basic war disability pension rate became 135s a week. This was a landmark: the pension was now worth more than the pre-war 40s pension (see Chart B3), and again there were rises for the war widows and still further concessions such as financial help for women looking after war pensioners.[102]

Despite the disappointment over the widows' tax issue, much had been achieved since the dark days of the late 1940s and early 1950s when, amid political bickering, it seemed that any special recognition of the sacrifices demanded by war would disappear under the skirts of the welfare state. Not only had the 'special position' been maintained but there was a new and better understanding with government. Yet the bogey of inflation still lurked in the background and war pensions parity had only been maintained by constant reminders to government. Was there not a better way of maintaining its value?

## A new era at the Village

Although the medical side of the TB settlement at Preston Hall had been taken over by the National Health Service, the 'recuperative' element remained under Legion control. It included a 125-bed rehabilitation unit, leading in many cases to the families joining the men in one of the 220 houses in the village. There was accommodation too for single men and the work now included motor car repair and the manufacture of road signs as well as the traditional trades of light building manufacture and printing, while some were employed at the hospital itself. The wives might find work locally or at a village-run restaurant visited by those travelling the increasingly busy route to the channel ports. The elderly were allowed to remain in the village, adopted by the Legion's Women's Section

*The manufacture of wooden buildings was a long-established trade for settlers at the Legion Village. The buildings sold well to local farmers.*

whose members brought gifts and wrote letters.[103]

But the same period saw a decline in the incidence of TB and in 1966 the Legion investigated the admission of those recovering from other disabilities who would benefit from Preston Hall's unique environment, at the same time reviewing the trading situation. It concluded that, in order to re-invigorate the village and gear up the industries, an investment of over £200,000 would be needed, but that the proportion of fit labour would have to be increased from 8 to 15 per cent. Government support was sought for funding, the Legion's Housing Association (see page 274) provided flatlets for widows to release

272

accommodation for newcomers and the NEC made loans to finance new contracts. The Legion's village was about to enter a new era.[104]

### Fortunes vary for Legion enterprises

When Lord Snowdon, Princess Margaret's husband, visited the Legion's Cambrian Factory in 1963, although he admired the quality of the tweed, he took away the mail order leaflet for re-design.[105] It was indicative of the factory's problems. Having prospered in the war years, by 1950 it employed forty men, most of whom lived in a hostel, although six family houses were being built; its high-quality hand-woven tweeds were being exported world-wide and a shop in nearby Llandrindod Wells attracted much custom. But fashion is a fickle mistress and over the following years the demand for tweed slackened so that in 1954 the Legion had to begin annual subsidies.[106] Vigorous marketing, such as

*Cambrian Factory tweed was excellent; but in the fickle world of fashion it needed vigorous marketing. This display formed part of an exhibition in 1965.*

a self-measurement service promoted by the Women's Section, revived sales, but the factory still remained unprofitable and in 1960 an NEC committee recommended disposal.[107] The decision was deferred following a large trade order in 1961, but the order affected supplies for personal customers. The roller-coaster continued. There was good publicity at fashion shows and brighter designs were introduced – one bride even had her wedding dress made of white Cambrian tweed – exports to the United States rose and the factory won the first 'woolmark' in Wales in 1965. But the new fashion for mini-skirts literally lopped the profits of textile manufacturers, while the wool trade was further affected by man-made substitutes, and in 1970 the Legion's National Chairman told the Council that disposal of the factory must be delayed no longer. Then, at the eleventh hour, a new process was introduced which could convert the coarse Welsh wool into lightweight material suitable for modern living. Would this be the factory's salvation?[108]

The Legion found it easier to make a decision in the case of the furniture factory at Warminster. Originally a local initiative and acquired by the Legion in 1945, it employed twenty-five men and did sufficiently well making mainly 'utility' chairs for plans to be made in 1946 for a new workshop. Building restrictions delayed the work until 1951, but it was then able to employ thirty-two, including some disabled, in a modern factory, producing high-quality furniture. But in the early 1960s it ran into trouble and the NEC had to provide an annual subsidy. Even a switch to club furnishings at the height of the Legion club 'boom' could not restore its fortunes and in 1965 it was sold, but with all the employees retained except the office staff, whom the Legion compensated.[109]

### The Housing Association – a new jewel in the crown

The Legion's longstanding involvement with the disabled was now accompanied by a growing concern for the problems of the elderly and in particular their housing difficulties. This led, in 1964, to the launch of one of the Legion's most successful ventures, the British Legion Housing Association. John Rivers, then Head of the Legion's Benevolent Department, had seen the opportunities provided by new legislation; it was now possible to take out Housing Corporation loans to build houses for old people, making repayment from rents subsidized by local authorities. The idea was taken up by Lieutenant Colonel Ralph Grimshaw, the Central Service Committee Chairman. The Legion's role would be to find the sites and manage the scheme and the only financial commitment would be in site purchase and in meeting the loan repayments until the rents started to come in.

It was a sound concept. Even the headquarters funds investment was kept to a minimum by inviting branches, clubs and individuals to buy Legion Housing Bonds at a 5 per cent rate of interest and, of the first £50,000 'pump priming' money, only £15,000 came from the Legion's Benevolent Fund. An active young NEC member, Dennis Cadman, later to be a National Chairman, was put in charge and the pilot scheme was sited in the grounds of the Legion's country home, Maurice House, at Westcliffe-on-Sea. It had teething problems – the Legion bridging fund at first proved insufficient – but the block of seventeen double and four single flats, each with an intercom to a warden and named 'Ralph Grimshaw Court', was opened in 1967.[110]

Despite a sharp rise in interest rates in 1969 the project was pursued with vigour. By 1970 six more schemes had been completed and a further twenty-one were in construction, providing nearly a thousand homes for the old and needy, while ongoing negotiations for future developments involved around a hundred local authorities. Grass roots support was represented by over £200,000 invested in Legion Housing Bonds and by local committees to look after the interests and welfare of the tenants. The Legion had a new jewel in its crown, one that was to grow in size and importance as the elderly ex-service population itself continued to expand.[111]

### In place of desolation

That elderly ex-service population was largely comprised of Great War veterans and in 1964, on the fiftieth anniversary of the outbreak of that war, 350 of them attended a Legion pilgrimage to the battlefields of 1914-18. But few were able to recognize the landscape in which they had fought, such had been the devastation at the time. And when they assembled for a ceremony at the Menin Gate in Ypres it might have been another town: in place of the desolation wrought by war there were beautiful buildings and a bustling community.[112] But so many had wished to go that the pilgrimage was repeated the following year for a further ninety-three, whose memories were stimulated by a dug-out party in the traditional style held by Arras Branch of the Legion.[113]

The Second World War pilgrimages continued – to Greece, to Italy, to North Africa, to Normandy and, of course, to the ever-hospitable Netherlands.[114] Even so, there were many who had been unable to take advantage of the government's post-war scheme to assist widows to visit overseas graves or memorials, which did not anyway extend to the Far East. But there were other ways in which they could be helped. Since 1948 the Legion had run a wreath-laying service, setting up depots overseas, with local volunteers, who sometimes 'adopted' the grave, and placed the wreath on behalf of the relative. Once the scheme was fully operating some 2,000-3,000 wreaths were laid each year, from France to Thailand and, if the relative wished, he or she could have a photograph of the grave. The service, thanks to local generosity, was largely free.[115]

# 1966 – 1970

## Wartime sacrifice forgotten?

In 1966 the Legion's old sparring partner, the Ministry of Pensions, which had already been amalgamated to form the Ministry of Pensions and National Insurance, disappeared entirely when the functions of both departments were absorbed into the Ministry of Social Security. The Legion accepted the change with good grace, being assured that war pensioners and war widows would receive their traditional preferences.[116] Barely had that assurance been given when the government advised local authorities to disregard only the first 40 shillings of a war disability pension when deciding rents; in other words the more the pension paid to a disabled ex-serviceman or war widow the greater the rent. Up to that point the Legion had been working hard to persuade local authorities already operating the scheme to disregard war pensions when assessing income, and about half were prepared to do so.[117] By sanctioning only a partial disregard the government not only indicated that the war pension was not sacrosanct but had pulled the rug from under the Legion's existing efforts. There was even more alarm when the London Boroughs were told by their association to count the whole of the war pension as income when deciding rents and, following Conference 1968, where there was serious concern that wartime sacrifice had been forgotten, a Legion delegation visited the new ministry. The government's response, when it came, was bland: it would of course maintain the principle of ex-service preference, but rents were a matter for local authories, whom it could only advise. The Legion felt that it had been badly let down: it was noted at the 1970 Conference that there were forty-one councils from Hexham in the north to Plymouth in the south which now regarded the whole of the war pension as income when assessing rents; 'What,' it was asked, 'if there had been a (Nazi) Gauleiter acting in their stead?'[118]

The Legion had more success in another battle with the local authorities over housing those leaving the services. Most authorities gave priority to those living in the area, a handicap to servicemen. It persuaded the government to advise that an ex-serviceman who found a job in a particular area should be deemed to have a residential qualification and nearly 90 per cent of the authorities approached by the Legion agreed to this.[119]

## Inflation and war pensions

Although the 1965 war pension rise had given the war-disabled and widows more in real terms than ever before, the cost of living continued to rise throughout 1966; but in the face of the government's obvious economic difficulties the Legion and the other members of the Joint Committee hesitated to press for another increase. In 1967, however, a Legion-led deputation to the Ministry of Social Services resulted in a new rate of 152 shillings, rather above the inflation level and indicative that, despite everything, the government saw war pensioners in a special light; but since their numbers were declining through deaths it could perhaps afford to be generous. And, as has been noted, the other side of the coin was that the pension could be taken into account when entitlement to other benefits such as rent rebate was being considered.[120]

In 1969 there were more increases, although on this occasion they did little more than maintain the value of the pensions. But the stage had now been reached where inflation had become a constant companion rather than a temporary visitor and was reflected in annual wage-bargaining. The 1970 Annual Conference therefore decided on a new yardstick for war pensions: the full rate should be equivalent to half of the average earnings in industry. But the resolution was inopportune: that year Wilson's Labour government was replaced by the Conservatives under Heath and the new administration's first concern was a reduction in expenditure based on facing down union demands.[121]

Nonetheless the deputation's arguments had been acknowledged and there was no doubt that the policy of reasoned discussion with ministers rather than confrontation in Parliament would continue whatever the government's colour. It had already achieved much, winning concessions in the treatment of pensions as well as restoring their value and, even if the 'disregard' issue had still to be resolved, the war pensioner and war widow were once more regarded as a category to which the nation owed a special debt, rather than simply another group in need of welfare support. The Legion, and its close supporters on the Joint Committee, could be proud of what had been achieved. But, could even these relationships maintain that situation in the sea of economic difficulties in which the nation found itself?[122]

## Galanos House is built

There were many war pensioners among the 230 living in the Legion's country homes. They slept five or six to a room in big iron beds, but there were few complaints; at least some had had to endure far worse conditions until a Legion branch found them; one, who had been wounded at Ypres, had lived in a garden shed. But, during the 1960s, there were many improvements to the houses, including curtained beds, with branches in the catchment areas raising money to supplement headquarters funding, already heavily committed as running costs rose and new regulations were imposed. The local branches helped in practical ways too, even stocking the lake at Crosfield House in Wales with trout so that the residents could enjoy their fishing.[123]

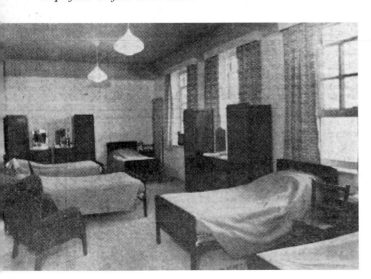

*A Maurice House bedroom following modernization in the early 1960s; but, as the picture shows, residents still slept four or five to a room.*

In 1963 a legacy from a Greek businessman who much admired the British, Christos Galanos, enabled a fifth home to be added. It was to serve the Midlands and to be purpose-built. The Warwickshire county chairman found a site close to the village of Long Itchington with a tree-lined pond and a broad green. 'This is the place,' declared Lieutenant Colonel Grimshaw and the home was opened early in 1967, housing almost all its fifty-six residents in single bedsitting rooms, on one floor for ease of wheelchair mobility. Although it lacked some of the grandeur of the other country homes, such as Crosfield's rich oak panelling, not

*Galanos House (above) was purpose-built – unlike other Legion Homes such as Maurice House (below).*

surprisingly it proved to be much more economic to run.[124]

In addition to the 300 permanent residents of the country homes, around 3,000 people continued to visit the Legion's four convalescent homes each year. But by the late 1960s they tended to be the elderly and chronically sick rather than those in need of a short

277

period of convalescence to help them return to work after an illness and, although the latter category remained the priority, there was a change of name to 'convalescent and rest homes' following an NEC inquiry in 1968.[125]

## Anniversary Pilgrimages

During the late 1960s Legion pilgrimages commemorated anniversaries for both world wars: Great War veterans went to the Somme in 1966 and to Passchendaele the following year, fifty years after those great battles, while in 1969 the next generation remembered the twenty-fifth anniversary of the D-Day landings in Normandy and the Anzio landings in Italy. The men of the Great War had not lost their marching prowess, the parade of the Somme pilgrims through Albert no doubt sustained by the thought that a 'vin d'honneur' as guests of the mayor awaited them at the end.[126]

Some branches still ran their own pilgrimages and Islington North and West's visit to Calais was an annual event, assisted by the Calais branch; in 1966 it remembered the heroic defence twenty-five years before with a service on the quayside, while passing ships lowered their ensigns in salute. But many of the smaller pilgrimages, as well as individuals, were helped by headquarters who planned the route, advised times of boats and trains, booked accommodation and, where possible, arranged for a local Legion branch or an individual member to meet the party at its destination.[127]

But, even as these anniveraries took place, a further generation of British servicemen were dying overseas: in 1967 a Legion member travelled to Aden at the height of the conflict to visit his eighteen-year-old son's grave. There would not be a Legion pilgrimage there for another thirty years.[128]

1966 saw an innovation: a pilgrimage entirely on German soil. There were some misgivings over the reception the party would have, but in the event the ninety-five pilgrims were warmly received and the visits to the graves, mainly airmen shot down in raids on Bremen, were efficiently organized by a local agency. The visit then became an annual event, mainly to north Germany, but in 1970 it included airmen's graves in Bavaria.[129]

★　　　★　　　★

In the years following the Second World War the advent of the Welfare State had relieved the Legion of much responsibility. This provided an opportunity to do more in particular areas of concern such as the care of the elderly, while the organization had been able to exploit the new legislation for activities such as the housing association. And, with the help of others, it had succeeded in maintaining the special position of the war disability pensioners and the war widows, who might otherwise have found themselves reduced to the situation of just another group of state beneficiaries. It had been a watershed in the Legion's history.

278

# CHAPTER 12

## FUNDRAISING 1946-1970

# *The Going Gets Tougher*

## 1946 – 1950

### Inflation wilts the poppy

Captain Willcox, Appeals Secretary since the Legion's formation, retired in 1946. He could look back on his stewardship with some satisfaction. The last two Poppy Appeal collections had been the highest in the organization's history; in real terms, that is inflation-adjusted, they would be unmatched for the rest of the century and the Appeal was at its apogee (see Chart C1 on page 447). In 1947, after an interim replacement, Captain Smith Stewart took over. He too was a long-serving Legion man, having been on the Area staff since 1929, and he faced a daunting task. The Legion had used the proceeds of the wartime collections to purchase properties for homes for the elderly and for convalescent cases. In order to develop and maintain them it needed to sustain the level of income.

The National Executive Council had decided in 1946 that Poppy Day should be on the Saturday before Remembrance Sunday. That year, although there were again good results in some areas, notably the Channel Islands which set the seal on liberation by doubling its 1945 collection record, overall the appeal was a little down on the previous year. Post-war economic conditions were held to be the cause. Nevertheless much effort was put into the 1947 Appeal: posters, window bills and cinema slides were distributed, together with a new 'Guide to Organizers' in which they were told to organize a Remembrance Week, a 'week to be remembered' with whist drives, concerts, auctions, darts and football matches. Local Poppy Queens were crowned amid as much publicity as possible and a broadcast appeal by Earl Wavell stressed the aim: to raise the collection from £1 million to £1½ million. But when the tins were emptied the total was barely that of the previous year.[1]

The Legion's concern over funding its commitments was heightened with the arrival of the Welfare State in 1948. It feared that the public might feel that it no longer needed to contribute to charities and much publicity was devoted to making it plain that state schemes had to be buttressed by organizations such as the Legion. Whether the new state involvement affected the public's attitude to the appeal, or whether it was simply that money was tight because of the combination of high taxation and economic depression, the total again fell, as it did once more the following year when a cold and wet day affected the street collection. The 1950 appeal appeared to reverse the trend with an increase of some £30,000, but creeping inflation meant that in terms of purchasing power it was below the previous total. By now income from the appeal was less than two-thirds of the wartime high, but it would seem that the effects of inflation were not fully recognized at the time, or, if they were, then, perhaps in the interests of the collectors' morale, were not acknowledged.[2]

The decline was certainly not due to lack of effort by those involved. The Football Association was approached for permission to collect at football matches, more effort was devoted to house-to-house collections to insure against bad weather on the day itself and branches told to raise money for the appeal year-round. In 1950 it was noted that the house-to-house collections brought in 40 per cent of the total as against 35 per cent from street collections; the rest came from church congregations or in other collections.[3]

Other forms of fundraising were considered. The 1948 Conference called for a Legion football pool, but the proposal was not implemented by the NEC on the grounds that it would tarnish the organization's reputation and, in a change of mood, the next year's Conference congratulated the NEC on upholding the Legion's prestige and dignity.[4] But, even if propriety was maintained, with the Legion's commitments showing no sign of diminishing, it was a disturbing situation for the organization's leadership.

## 1951 – 1955

### An argument with the BBC

When the Mother Superior of an Irish Catholic Mission in Kenya was asked, 'Would you like some poppies?' she replied, 'No, we've three dogs of our own', but, such local communication difficulties apart, the overseas collections were as high as ever, and even Kenya, in the grip of a terrorist campaign, continued with the appeal.[5] At home, however, there was much leeway to be made up, particularly in

*Sixpence in the tin in 1946. But already there was inflation and in the years that followed the real value of the sixpence would steadily decline; the problem was, how to get people to change their habit of 'sixpence for a poppy'.*

the big towns where, despite the fact that they provided a large proportion of the Legion's membership, now topping one million, there was a shortage of volunteers to organize the appeal, to man the depots and collecting posts, carry out the street and house-to-house, factory and works collections, as well as run poppy stands in cinema foyers. But the press continued to give strong support, the *Daily Mail* publishing case histories of the Legion's work, and publicity in general was good: in 1951 glamorous film stars made the collection in Mayfair, while, somewhat earlier in the day and on the other side of London, the nurses at St Bartholomew's Hospital were out with their poppy trays at six a.m. before going on duty at seven-fifteen.[6]

The BBC had always supported the appeal, but in the post-war years the facilities they offered became restricted, as more charities claimed their attention. Since the war the Legion had been given the Sunday evening 'Week's Good Cause' slot at Remembrance time. In 1952, however, the NEC, consulting the BBC over whether to switch the talk from Remembrance Sunday to the preceding Sunday, were taken aback when the Corporation told them that these times had been given to other charities and the best they could offer was a five-minute talk after the one p.m. news on a Wednesday. Furthermore, under new rules, the Legion would be allowed only one appearance every two years.[7]

In vain the Legion tried to persuade the BBC to change their minds, emphasizing the importance of the Poppy Appeal by indicating that a member of the Royal Family or Mrs

*By 1949 the poppy crosses in the Field of Remembrance were in orderly rows; but the battlefield grave markers remain. Compare this picture with that at page 132.*

Churchill would be asked to speak. The only concession to the Legion was an annual broadcast and the mid-week lunchtime radio talk became part of the pattern, given by a senior service officer, the Legion's President or Chairman, or, in 1955, by the Women's Section Chairman. In any case the Legion could not press the matter too hard; it got enormous publicity each year from the Festival of Remembrance broadcast which since 1950 had also been televised, and there were many other references to the poppy on TV, such as a feature on the making of the Queen's wreath.[8]

TV was, however, in its infancy and for many people entertainment still meant 'the pictures'. In 1954 a five-minute Legion film, 'Where does the money go?', featuring the famous actress Flora Robson as a poppy seller, played to audiences in 400 cinemas.[9] But, although Poppy Day 1952 was encouraging, following a big effort in the house-to-house collections, and it seemed that the downward trend might have ended, in the following years takings were again lower, with inflation further diminishing their value.[10]

1956 – 1960

### No more 'selling' of poppies

A *Times* leader in May 1956 noted that 'Nobody envies those whose job it is to raise money for charity (in the face of) the weight of taxation and the Welfare State. . . it is remarkable that a sum not far short of a million pounds should have been counted as the harvest of the poppy.'[11] But a year later the collection exceeded the magical figure of one million pounds following another flood of publicity. By this time the term 'poppy seller' was being discouraged in favour of 'poppy collector', although there remained a widespread belief that poppies had to be sold at fixed prices. The range had been reduced to two buttonhole poppies, for either of which the public was adjured to 'give generously', and only the car mascot and table decoration had a stated value. But one of the problems was that someone who was accustomed to giving a shilling for a poppy would continue to do so despite the fact that the coin's worth in real terms was constantly falling. This, as much as anything, seems to have been responsible for the failure of the collections to keep pace with inflation. The success of the 1957 collection was not repeated in this period and by the end of the decade the appeal had reached a new low, despite annually renewed publicity drives which included an Exhibition of Remembrance at the Mansion House in London in 1957 and much support on BBC television which showed the Legion film 'Where does the money go?' as well as a feature on the poppy and many references on radio. It seemed that the rules that applied in the case of *The Week's Good Cause* were not so stringently applied to other broadcasts. But BBC television's new rival, Independent TV, showed very little interest in the appeal.[12]

### The Cambridge 'Rag'

One of the brighter features of the appeal at this time was the Cambridge University contribution. In the years following the war the students had 'adopted' the Poppy Appeal and soon people were coming from miles around to see the fun. The colleges competed with each other: in 1950 Fitzwilliam kidnapped the mayor, Clare College towed the Loch Ness monster down the Cam to the accompanyment of bagpipes, while Trinity held a 'bullfight', although the Proctors had to close down a series of Middle Eastern sketches for fear of international repercussions. In 1955, however, they did not prevent 'rugger types' dressed as Arabs kidnapping unsuspecting ladies from the crowd and releasing them only to the highest bidders, husbands' and boy friends' bids being forced up by 'unknowns'.[13] Each year there was a new organizer from a different college and as a result by the late 1950s Cambridge had the highest per capita rate of contribution to the appeal in the country, raising a record £12,000 in 1959. But by now students' attitudes were beginning to change, some suggesting that charities other than the Poppy Appeal should benefit, perhaps influenced by the attacks on Haig and, in the growing anti-war university atmosphere, inclined to associate the Legion with 'militarism'. Although the rags

*'Stand and deliver.' The Cambridge Poppy Day 'rag' was one of the highlights of the Appeal in the years following the Second World War.*

continued to benefit the appeal into the 1960s, they were thereafter increasingly devoted to other charities.[14]

## Concern over poppy collectors

Changing attitudes at universities were reflected in an article in the *Daily Mirror* in 1960 in which it quoted from a students' newspaper in Birmingham: 'Poppy Day helps to preserve the myth of the glory of war.' But the article also drew attention to the fact that there would be no poppy collection in Stepney that year as the Legion could find no one to organize it, in common with a number of other places from Shipley in Yorkshire to the south coast. It was a growing problem as the decade drew to a close. The Legion's 'loyal army' of poppy organizers and collectors were from all walks of life and every level of society and few were members of the organization itself. But one thing they had in common: they were now getting distinctly older and younger people were simply not coming forward to take their places. In Stepney the *Mirror's* article had its effect and the Rector volunteered his services; but elsewhere the gaps in the ranks continued to widen.[15]

A major effort was now needed to recruit new collectors. In the meantime the financial loss had to be mitigated. One solution was to get more support from business houses and the same year more than 6,000 letters were sent out by the National Chairman; they brought in £10,000.[16] Another was to persuade people to make annual covenants which, with the standard rate of income tax at 8s 6d in the pound, meant that a donation each year of a guinea (£1 1s) was increased by a further 15s 5d. But, despite the tax advantage, few seemed prepared to commit themselves, depite a County campaign.[17] A Branch Investment Scheme introduced in 1964 gave Legion branches a return of four per cent, with profits going to the benevolent fund. Some 200 branches took part, but the amounts invested were not enough to generate a significant income.[18] Of more value was a campaign launched the same year to attract legacies by approaches to bank managers, solicitors and others who advised on wills. Yet all such schemes were pygmies compared with the Appeal. The Legion's ability to do its work would continue to rest on the success of Poppy Day itself.[19]


# 1961 – 1965


## A statistical exercise

The problem over poppy collectors had prompted the National Chairman to urge all branch chairmen to get their members out on the streets for the 1960 Poppy Day with trays and collection tins. Inevitably such a general approach upset at least one branch whose members had long done precisely that. But the ensuing correspondence produced some interesting statistics compiled by the Chairman of Hathersage Branch in Derbyshire: the village collected 2s 3d per head of its 1,800 population compared with 7d per head for the 19,000 inhabitants of Buxton and only 2d per head in Sheffield with its population of nearly half a million. In other words the larger the place, the weaker the organization, not perhaps a surprising conclusion, but food for thought when urbanization was steadily increasing. And within the village the biggest return was from the sale of motor car mascots, beating even the house-to-house collection and suggesting that targetting the better-off produced the best results.[20]

The appeal to branches, endorsed by the Annual Conference in 1961, underlined the problem. However much publicity might be generated – and there was continuing support from the press and from television, with the first televised appeal that year, by Lord Fraser, the former National President – the success or otherwise of the appeal depended on having collectors out on the streets on the day, or going around the houses. In 1965 a poppy brooch was introduced to recognize loyalty; even so the gaps in the ranks of the poppy organizers and collectors continued to grow, although many branches, and some clubs, responded to the Chairman's call. But the policy of appealing to the young through the still highly-supportive press now began to make some headway and more of the new generation were coming forward; nevertheless it was too late for 200 areas which had lost organizers over the preceding five years and which had to be added to neighbouring areas so that the overall coverage was even thinner.[21]

A suggestion in 1963 to hold a Poppy Ball at the Dorchester Hotel on 11 November was controversial: the hotel would make no charge and the band fee would be minimal; but was it right to 'party' on such a date? The Queen Mother was consulted and the idea was dropped.[22] Less contentious was an initiative the following year by General Leese, the National President, who secured free use of the Birmingham Bull Ring for a Legion display for a week preceding the appeal. There were dioramas of battle scenes, a weaver from the Cambrian factory, DMI goods, half-hour announcements on the Legion's work, distinguished visitors and television coverage. It was repeated the following year.[23]


## Changes at the Poppy Factory

One of the demonstrations at the Bull Ring was poppy-making. In the 1960s the Poppy Factory employed about 320 disabled ex-servicemen. The figure was a little down on the peak of 380 in 1948 when the demand for poppies had been so great that some of the work had to be sent to Preston Hall and to other ex-service employers. This led to the poppy-making process being partly mechanized, which also enabled the quality to be improved. At the same time the range had been reduced to two designs of buttonhole poppies, although it took time for the collectors and the buying, or 'donating', public to get away from the old notion of paying 1s or 6d according to the size of poppy. Not everyone, however, agreed that the process should be simplified and when Brunel Cohen had suggested at the Women's Section Conference in 1951 that there should be just one style of buttonhole poppy there was vehement opposition from his audience who felt that any more simplification would result in loss of jobs for disabled men. It had taken another sixteen years to make that change.[24]

In fact any spare capacity was used to make other items such as rosettes for the Royal Show or badges for the Legion Conference. Indeed, despite the improved process, there had been at least one further occasion when the factory had been unable to meet the demand: in 1959 a shortage of four million poppies had to be made up by an outside contractor, leading to sharp criticism of the leadership at the Annual Conference that year, although the situation appears to have resulted from over-ordering and hoarding. The same year the poppy with leaf was dropped as being too expensive, the next major change in design being in 1967 when the black bitumen centre and wire stem were replaced by green plastic. Two years later the car poppy was replaced with a sticker, largely because of manpower shortages and production costs.[25]

These improvements in the manufacturing process were accompanied by an upgrading of working conditions. There were changes too on the domestic side. The factory's housing estate accommodated around seventy families, the rest living in council housing nearby, while the upper floors of Cardigan House, reconstructed after acting as the Legion's wartime headquarters, held flats for employees' widows. But in 1968 the widows were rehoused in a new Housing Association block, together with some widowers, and Cardigan House was sold for redevelopment. The sale of another part of the original site provided employees with a new community centre.[26] The factory was still taking on new staff: when the Queen visited in November 1962 she found that the youngest employee was a National Serviceman, disabled after having been shot in Cyprus.[27] Not all the work was done in Richmond; about sixty disabled men worked from home.[28]

Once completed, boxed and labelled – the factory had its own printing press which also produced much of the appeal literature – the poppies were sent to the warehouse close to King's Cross station. In 1970, however, negotiations were begun for the sale of the warehouse, in anticipation of the storeage of poppies at Preston Hall.[29]

## 1966 – 1970

### Public ignorance of the appeal

A public opinion poll on the Legion in 1966 established that, despite the welfare state, 80 per cent of the public believed that it was still necessary to give to charity. Thus far the poll was encouraging. But the rest was less palatable: when asked to name five charities to which they would donate, over 90 per cent did not include the Poppy Appeal; the same proportion had no idea of how the Poppy Day collection was spent; and over half made

*Two faces of the Poppy Appeal in the 1960s; the 92-year old had collected every year since 1921; but now the Legion attempted to modernize the Appeal by enlisting the younger generation and introducing new collecting boxes, plastic-stemmed poppies and carrier bags in place of trays.*

286

no connection between the Legion and the Poppy Appeal, most of them believing that the Legion was only concerned with parades and social life.[30]

The response by the Legion's leaders to this startling public ignorance of an appeal that had been a national institution for nearly fifty years was, hardly suprisingly, to redouble its PR effort. A publicity vehicle was purchased and equipped, a new film made, and poppy collectors' tins and trays revamped. The work of the PR consultants was stepped up, press conferences held and additional TV and radio publicity obtained, while the *News of the World* printed and distributed 10,000 posters free of charge. But, even if the public might be induced to give the appeal greater support if they knew more about it, all would be of no avail if there was no one able to take the money. By now old age had deprived the Legion of the services of more than 50,000 collectors, in addition to the 200 organizers; it was nearly a quarter of the entire appeal organization.[31]

Despite the public's lack of awareness, therefore, as much attention had to be given to recruiting new collectors as to publicizing the purpose of the appeal. 'Ole Bill', the Great War bus, was again hauled out of retirement in Clapham and toured sites in London so that passers-by could be persuaded to volunteer their services as collectors, Legion branches were urged to enrol more young people as well as involve more of their members and their families and villages formed 'flying squads' to help out in adjacent towns. There were approaches to schools and in this way Wimbledon was able to build up a force of nearly seventy youngsters, who, augmented by 'coffee bar cowboys' recruited in a further initiative, succeeded in doubling the house-to-house collection. With the 'swinging sixties' image in mind young girls were recruited from universities and technical colleges, and equipped with the new-style collecting boxes and gaily coloured plastic bags* of poppies, in place of the old trays, their mini-skirted charms provoking the admiring Legion President, General Leese, to coin the phase 'poppy popsies'.[32]

Despite some resistance within the Legion itself, the buttonhole range was reduced to a single style for the 1967 Poppy Day, with the assurance that employment at the Poppy Factory would be unaffected. Not only did this save in manufacturing costs but now there was no question of a 'price' for a poppy; people could give what they wanted for the same poppy and, the Legion hoped, it would be more each year than before, as it was now very conscious of the effects of inflation. But a further problem began to appear as 1970 approached, decimalization. The half-crown (2s 6d) was being phased out and there was some concern that those who had been accustomed to putting this coin in the box would substitute the two shilling piece, or ten pence in the new currency.

The late 1960s were thus busy years for the Poppy Appeal – the need to 're-market' the appeal to a generation for whom many of the newer charities seemed to have more relevance – and at the same time try to restore the 'sales force' to full strength, all the while attempting to compensate for the effects of inflation. If the results were not altogether successful, they could have been a great deal worse. The 1966 Poppy Day produced the best return in real terms; thereafter there was a slow but steady decline so that the 1970 appeal was, in purchasing power, the lowest since 1924. A table published in 1969 confirmed the experience of the Hathersage Chairman in 1961: the amount collected per head of population varied from nearly 16p per head to 3p, the results being directly influenced by the number of organizers and collectors in each area, which in turn reflected the urban or country environment.[33]

A detached observer might express surprise that a body the size of the Legion – over 5,000 branches and more than half a million members if the Women's Section were added – would have difficulty in replacing 50,000 poppy workers; but from the start the appeal

*They were not, however, popular with the collectors, and the tray returned.

organization had been largely independent of the Legion's own structure and, although most of the branches were involved to some extent, the great majority of their members were content to leave the work of the appeal to well-wishers. Nevertheless one Boer War veteran was still selling poppies in London at the age of 96.

Opportunities were still taken to raise money in other ways: sponsored walks became popular in the late 1960s and one such across the North Downs of Kent in 1970 found the Minister of Pensions striding out briskly alongside the chairman of the Legion's Pensions Committee and the General Secretary. But, although good for publicity – and health – such activities produced relatively small amounts.

★      ★      ★

These had been difficult years for the Appeal. If the Legion was to be able to continue its work despite all the other demands on the public's generosity as the century wore on and charities proliferated, then even more work would have to be done on the Poppy Appeal, or another funding source identified, and so far no other source had been found to match the Appeal. In marketing parlance the Legion possessed a unique 'product': it was still considered almost obligatory to wear a poppy at Remembrance; but its value had fallen. How could it be restored?

# CHAPTER 13

## INTERNATIONAL 1946-1970

# *A Changing World*

### 1946 – 1950

**Post-war relationships**

In the troubled years leading up to the Second World War the international spotlight had briefly played on the Legion's efforts to keep the peace through the camaraderie of those who had faced each other in war. All had foundered on the rock of Hitler's ambitions. Now both that ambition and Germany itself lay in ruins, and there was an even stronger determination among the nations who had fought the war that the peace must be preserved.

The old and discredited League of Nations had been replaced by the United Nations and the Legion pledged its support for this new body in a resolution at its first post-war conference in 1946. Later that same year it joined the United Nations Association, its Chairman becoming a Vice President of the association while other officers were members of the UNA Council and Executive Committee.[1] It was, however, already obvious that the key players in post-war international relations would be the United States and the Soviet Union, and that the former would be the champion of what was becoming known as 'the West'.

In the inter-war years the British Legion had maintained a close relationship with its American counterpart and in 1947 the Legion President, Sir Ian Fraser, took up an invitation to visit the American Legion Convention in New York. He found it an unusual experience: there were no debates and the set-piece speeches, including one by General Eisenhower, a candidate for the US Presidency, could scarcely be heard over the buzz of delegates' chatter.[2] Only a few weeks later Fraser hosted a visit to Britain by the American Legion's National Commander's party, some 150-strong. Before the war such visits had met with hospitality of a high order, usually including a reception by the King and a banquet hosted by the Prime Minister. On this occasion the atmosphere was more muted: Britain was in the grip of austerity, partly due to the enormous debts owed to the United States as a result of the war. The visitors found the British inured to hardship: when the party's arrival in London was delayed by a late train, sixty British Legion standard bearers waited patiently, in the end missing their own trains back and walking five miles home without complaint.[3]

**Attempts at a new international body**

The French-dominated ex-service federation, FIDAC, had been one of the casualties of the war. But moves were afoot to replace it. Just prior to the Legion President's visit to New York the Council of the British Empire Services League, meeting in London, had discussed a proposal put forward by the South African representative for a new federation: it would be based on the members of the League and the American Legion, but would eventually take in the other Allied nations and, after five years, the ex-enemies. The British Legion view was, however, that to extend membership to the veterans' organizations of other Allies might result in political entanglements of the sort that had plagued FIDAC in pre-war days, and which would also trouble the Americans. The outcome was a proposal for an American-BESL Association which would maintain close contact with the others. But clearly the first thing to do was to consult the American Legion.[4]

The National Commander's party visit provided the opportunity for discussion. But, although the idea of a transatlantic ex-service body was not new – it had first come up in the 1920s – it soon became clear that, despite the even closer relationships established in the Second World War, the Americans did not want such an alliance;* nor would they under any circumstances join an international federation that even remotely resembled FIDAC. These of course were the views of the American Legion; other minds were at work in the United States which certainly did contemplate an international veterans body, but, as will be shown, on their terms.

Meanwhile veterans' organizations in France were seeking to promote a successor to FIDAC. But the Legion rejected an invitation to attend a 'World Conference of ex-service organizations' in 1948, as did most other national organizations, and the conference was a failure. Again the Legion's concern was with the political aspect; many of those bodies invited to the conference were more political than ex-service in outlook.

Politics had not, however, been a consideration when the Legion accepted an invitation for a party of sixty to visit Czechoslovakia in the summer of 1947; despite the Legion's involvement nine years before in the abortive 'border police' episode there was much conviviality and even a romantic touch with a choir of fifty male voices in a mountain setting, to which the Legion party manfully responded with 'Any Old Iron'.[5]

## Emigration resumes

The British Empire Services League two-yearly conferences resumed in 1947 and, as in pre-war years, apart from airing ex-service problems in the various countries, they were much concerned with emigration. Canada and South Africa wanted new blood but the problem was shortage of housing; India, hardly surprisingly, pointed out that settlement there would raise more questions than it would solve. Australia had already received post-war settlers but there were some problems: the 'ex-imperials' as the UK ex-service immigrants were known, received less in war pensions than their new fellow-countrymen and also felt that the Australian authorities discriminated against them.

Further concern having been expressed at a Legion Conference, the National Chairman paid a visit to Australia in 1948, returning with some suggestions for the Commonwealth Relations Office, although, according to *The Times* correspondent in Canberra, the Legion's misgivings were 'illusory'. But the following year a delegation from the Australian equivalent of the Legion, the Returned Services League, toured Legion branches to explain a scheme whereby RSL members would sponsor immigrants, ensuring that they got living accommodation on arrival as well as a job, if necessary living with their sponsors until another home was found. A ship was chartered by the RSL and duly set sail from Liverpool loaded with emigrants. They no doubt fared much as any other group would in Australia at that time; but at least they had the benefit of support and advice on the spot, although sharing a house with complete strangers must have presented hazards on both sides.[6]

---

*Nevertheless it later transpired that the American Legion had made overtures to the Canadian Legion which had been rejected, the Canadians loyally maintaining that any liaison must be with the BESL as a whole.

## 1951 – 1955

### A new international body – with drawbacks

Both French and British Commonwealth post-war attempts to form international ex-service groupings had failed. But now a new body appeared. In July of 1951 there was a meeting in Rome of the 'International Federation of War Veterans Organizations'. Some individual members of the Legion's National Executive Council had been contacted beforehand by the organizers and had expressed interest. But the Council itself, again scenting politics, approached this new venture with great caution, sending the General Secretary as an observer. His conclusions were that the Legion should keep its distance for the moment, watching developments and consulting with both the American and Canadian Legions as well as BESL. The new body was the result of a US initiative and, it appeared, not short of money. It also began to emerge that an underlying purpose, perhaps even the main purpose, was to establish an ex-service bulwark against communism. This would present the Legion with a dilemma: obviously it supported its own country in opposing the military threat posed by international communism; but within Britain the communist party remained a valid political organization, and there was nothing to prevent a Legion member being a communist (see page 235). Hence membership of an organization taking a political line, even if that line was anti-communist, breached the Legion's strict non-political stance.[7]

Following the GS's advice, the American and Canadian Legions were approached. Their response was somewhat non-committal, but the indications were that they did not intend to support the World Veterans Federation, as the organization was now known. On the other hand the British Foreign Office, pursuing closer relationships with America, saw nothing wrong with the Legion affiliating to the WVF. There were more discussions but, in the end, the National Chairman, having consulted with his predecessors, including Fetherston-Godley, and the National Commander of the American Legion, decided that the Legion would continue to hold back.[8]

The next year the WVF held a further conference – in London. This time the Legion sent two observers and, as well as reporting back to the NEC, their conclusions were briefed to the 1953 BESL Conference. They made it clear that they were still not happy with the WVF. The stated aims included work for peace as well as rehabilitation of disabled ex-servicemen, but it did not appear to be a democratically run organization, policy being largely decided by the organization's Secretary General. The funding source could not be identified, nor was it possible to get access to the accounts. There were also some indications that it was anti-British Commonwealth.[9]

But, in the debate that followed the Legion observers' report, some of the colonial delegates spoke in favour of the WVF; they were interested in the rehabilitation help that was on offer. Although the outcome was an agreement that BESL members should not, at any rate for the moment, join the WVF, the League itself now had a rival claimant for the attentions of some at least of its members.[10]

### Attitudes to communism

Two years later, at its 1955 conference, BESL itself became caught up in the communism debate. Like any other organization an ex-service movement could be infiltrated by communists and those that maintained a strictly non-political stance were all the more vulnerable since no one would be barred from office for political views.

291

Nevertheless the British Legion itself continued to believe that this principle was more important than any risk involved. Not all BESL members agreed; some of their circumstances were quite different and one country, Malaya, was involved in an armed struggle against communist terrorists. But when the National Commander of the American Legion, whose country was in the grip of an anti-communism crusade, wound up his address as guest speaker by saying that the free nations should be united against the 'godless tyranny of Communism', Lord Mountbatten, the League's Grand President, drily remarked, 'Our concern is with welfare. We have no politics.'[11] The words were a direct reflection of the British Legion's view and they underlined a divergence between the American and British Legions at this time: at the 1953 British Legion Annual Conference there had been some criticism of the American Legion following their backing of Senator McCarthy in his pursuit of 'reds under the bed' and a call for more collaboration with the Americans had been rejected.[12]

## 1956 – 1960

### Co-operation with the WVF

Post-imperialism finally caught up with the British Empire Services League in 1958 when its biennial Conference agreed to a change of name to the British Commonwealth Ex-services League, the Legion's NEC registering no objection as long as 'British' remained in the title.[13] Meanwhile attitudes were beginning to change in relation to the World Veteran's Federation. With the NEC's endorsement the General Secretary turned down an invitation to the 1960 WVF conference but at the BCEL conference that same year Lord Mountbatten recommended co-operation with the WVF 'within the bounds of our constitution' and the Legion's National Chairman, acting as conference chairman, backed him, saying, 'The Legion is 100 per cent behind the WVF in its rehabilitation work.' The conference noted that this work was chiefly in countries outside the Commonwealth, but, following its Grand President's advice, it would collaborate with the WVF in any activities which might assist BCEL member countries. However, both the League and the Legion continued to object to the WVF's involvement in the politics of the countries in which it operated.[14]

## 1961 – 1965

### But the WVF encroaches on BCEL

Both the Legion and BCEL sent observers to the 1961 WVF conference in Paris. They noted that it was very well organized – no expense had been spared – and delegates were given a mound of documents as well as a medal to commemorate the tenth anniversary of the WVF. But the debates had a strong flavour of international politics with frequent references to 'peace' and 'freedom', the Yugoslav delegation* putting the communist case, and the observers returned with their views unchanged, despite the fact that by now a number of other British ex-service associations were taking an active part and there was a WVF British Members' Committee.[15] The Legion's position was confirmed by a legal view in 1962 that the Charter did not allow it to spend funds on any activities which might benefit non-British subjects.[16]

*Yugoslavia was at the time a communist state outside the Soviet empire.

292

Nevertheless a number of Commonwealth ex-service organizations were members of the WVF in their own right and there was an uneasy feeling that the BCEL was beginning to be overshadowed in its own constituency. At the 1961 BCEL Ottawa conference there had been a Legion-inspired resolution calling on the League to expand its welfare work in the poorer Commonwealth countries and on the delegation's return this was followed up with the Foreign Office. The difficulty of course lay in matching the WVF's resources and, although the Legion gave a lead to the other 'old' Commonwealth countries in 1963 by increasing its annual grant from £2,000 to £5,000, the following year the League announced that it needed to raise £50,000 a year for welfare and intended to approach business firms and charitable foundations in the United Kingdom. This proposal was not well received by the Legion's NEC; such an appeal could have a direct effect on the Poppy Appeal, already on a downward trend. A compromise was agreed: the BCEL appeal would take place early in 1966, shortly after the Poppy Appeal.[17]

## Other relationships

By now the biennial BCEL conferences had become triennial but, despite the changing nature of relationships within the Commonwealth, emigration was still a principal interest, or perhaps a principal interest as far as the British Legion was concerned. At the 1963 conference in Ottawa the League accepted a Legion proposal that its member countries should continue to assist immigrants, BCEL itself making the contact for each individual with the ex-service organization of the receiving country.[18] There was also some direct Legion contact with the American Legion on the same topic, although there is no record of any similar arrangement being made. That year too the Legion became involved with another American ex-service organization: the Veterans of Foreign Wars. The National Chairman attended its Convention in 1963, the NEC having decided that the size and importance of the VFW should be investigated. But it seems that, although that organization had been in existence since 1919, it had no direct relevance to the Legion's work. Nevertheless the Chairman returned with its Gold Medal of Merit.[19]

With the 'Cold War' still at its height, even the politically-uncommitted Legion was somewhat embarrassed when, in 1961 the Soviet War Veterans asked it to send a delegation to Moscow. The timing – November – made it easy to refuse, and the Foreign Office endorsed the decision. But the Soviets did not give up, sending a message of friendship for Remembrance Day, to which the Legion made only a brief reply. Still they persisted, Marshal Timoshenko issuing a further invitation in 1963; but the NEC considered that the Legion 'could not justifiably commit itself to such heavy expense'.[20] Although there was a continuing concern in these post-war years with maintaining peace – the Legion had sent the Prime Minister a telegram to express the desire of all ex-servicemen for peace when he attended the Geneva Peace conference in 1955 – and there had continued to be Legion Conference resolutions on the subject, any attempt to use contacts between ex-service organizations to avoid war was a thing of the past.[21]

## 1966 – 1970

## WVF gains respectability

In 1966 the British government officially sponsored a WVF conference in London, no doubt in the interest of Anglo-US relationships; but the Legion, as on previous occasions, merely sent an observer.[22]

Meanwhile BCEL's decision to widen its welfare activities, partly at least as a result of the WVF activity in this field, was reinforced at its 1966 Conference, where some of the weaker organizations made it clear that they faced immense problems.[23] Already General Gale, the League's Deputy Grand President, addressing the British Legion Conference that year, had indicated that the BCEL's role was changing in relation to the more under-developed countries, where aged and ailing ex-servicemen and dependants suffered appalling hardship, but funds were inadequate.[24]

In response to this situation BCEL asked some of the 'old' Commonwealth members to investigate the problems of the others at first hand: the Returned Services League of Australia would visit the member countries of South East Asia and the Canadian Legion the Carribean countries, while the British Legion was asked to send a representative to visit India, Pakistan, Ceylon and Nepal.* The Legion's General Secretary was selected for this task and spent five weeks in the Indian sub-continent in late 1967. He found projects in all of these countries which the Legion could assist; they included medical equipment for an ex-service hospital in Pakistan, a rest centre in India and agricultural machinery for ex-servicemen in Ceylon.[25]

If the World Veterans Federation, despite its political motivation, had influenced this shift in emphasis of the BCEL it had perhaps been no bad thing. But it might have happened anyway as the gulf between the rich and poor members of BCEL widened in a changing world. And, despite the wishes of the more conservative members such as the British Legion, politics were now unavoidable: the 1969 BCEL Conference in Jamaica had to be cancelled when the intended hosts could not agree to delegates from the South African and Rhodesian ex-service organizations, because of the political situation in those countries.[26]

★     ★     ★

Between the wars the Legion had frequently taken the lead in international ex-service matters. But the experience had left it with an aversion to anything involving politics. As a result, it was now content to sit on the sidelines. Even the old eagerly-pursued relationship with the American Legion appeared to have lapsed, again partly as the result of politics following the latter's enthusiastic espousal of its country's anti-communist line and there were no more exchange visits. Nor, apart from war grave pilgrimages, was there much direct contact with the veterans' organizations of other countries. Now the Legion's only overseas preoccupation concerned the efforts of the BCEL to assist the situation of the ex-servicemen of the poorer Commonwealth countries.

---

*The situation of the African members of the Commonwealth was said to be already under active review, but the matter was complicated by the South African political situation.

CHAPTER 14

WOMEN'S SECTION 1946-1970

# *A Closer Relationship*

## 1946-1950

### The Section post-war

The Women's Section had emerged from the war with honours, as indeed had the women of the nation, whether serving with the armed forces, in the factories or simply supporting their menfolk. Change seemed to be in the air and the Legion itself had insisted on the same treatment for ex-servicewomen as for the men. Yet some things remained the same. When the Women's Section Chairman, Lady Apsley, wrote to the Legion's NEC in January 1947 asking that the Section be allowed two representatives on the Council, in exchange for two NEC members sitting on the Women's Central Committee, with similar arrangements at Area and County level, she received a discouraging reply: the Charter would not permit the NEC to entertain the idea and, as far as the lower levels were concerned, any such arrangements were up to them.[1] Despite this rebuff the women continued to press the proposal but the Council remained obdurate: they would not allow the women in, even as visitors.[2]

It is possible that these difficulties contributed to Lady Apsley's decision to hand over the chairmanship in 1948, having led the Section for six years following the death of Lady Edward Spencer Churchill early in the war. Although confined to a wheelchair she had carried on undaunted through the exhausting war years despite the death in action of her husband, emerging from that period determined to ensure the Section's future: her policies resulted in keen young ex-servicewomen being selected as Area Organising Secretaries, a complete overhaul of branch officer training, and new branches being opened with the aim of one for every Legion branch. But, as Lady Apsley had made clear, the starting-point was close co-operation with the Legion.[3]

Her successor was a person of no less determination. Dame Regina Evans had been twenty-two years a member of the Women's Section and had been honoured for her war service in the ATS. She took over at a critical time: the Section was now expanding rapidly and needed continued firm leadership. The staff were mainly new, the National Secretary, Mrs Octavia Snow, having been in post since 1946 and there was an element of isolation: since the rebuilding of the Pall Mall headquarters had been hampered by post-war restrictions, the Section was based at 43, Catherine Place, SW1. Moreover the post of Women's Section Chairman tended to be lonelier than that of her Legion opposite number: unlike him she could hardly turn to the President for advice; the Queen, later to be Queen Mother, was a dearly-loved figure, but clearly her involvement was limited.[4]

### Packed Conferences

Each Chairman stamped her authority on the Section at the Annual Conference. It was not an occasion for a shy spirit: in the early post-war years the attendance was huge. At the 1946 conference 1,300 delegates had been present to greet the Queen at the Central Hall in Westminster and the same number attended the following year when, with the Royal Family in South Africa, the Princess Royal presented the trophies. In addition there were the visitors, many of them up from the branches for the fun, and, when the venue was switched to the Albert Hall in 1948, there was a grand total of nearly 6,000 present, only ten of them men, to hear the Queen bid farewell to Lady Apsley. The platform on this occasion was backed by 840 standards, a mass of blue and gold facing over 1,700 delegates. In 1949 and 1950 the attendance was even larger with nearly 1,900 delegates present on each occasion, supported by a gallery-full of visitors. The Section's pride was reflected in the smartness of the standard bearers, enhanced by the National Standard Bearer competition introduced in 1947.

The reports heard by these packed audiences reflected a rapidly expanding organization. By 1950 the number of branches had increased from a figure of just over 2,500 to 3,148, although by the end of the period the growth rate was beginning to slow. Development had been helped by the grouping of branches within Counties, of great help to the small and isolated branches as well as to the new ones, leading to exchanges of views, ideas and information.[5] The younger members were increasingly involved in activities which included looking after the elderly, raising funds for headquarters or, in one case, making a wedding dress out of parachute silk for the use of local ATS girls. Support for the craft activities of the war-disabled men through the Legion's Disabled Men's Industries was redoubled after the war and there were few Section functions which did not have a stall for the sale of DMI goods.[6]

### Care for the war's victims

Towards the end of the war some thought had been given to the creation of a 'Home Service Corps' of ex-servicewomen, a uniformed organization living in hostels and providing domestic services. But, for once, the idea was behind the times and it was finally abandoned in 1947.[7] The money that had been raised was instead applied to another project begun the previous year, a children's home in Richmond, south of London. Lancaster House provided a home for boys and girls of the ex-service community who had either lost both parents or, perhaps the children of broken wartime marriages, could not be brought up by their families. The Section sought to emulate a normal home rather than run a charitable institution; the rooms were brightly painted and the eighteen children aged between five and eight who arrived in August 1946 were greeted with cuddly toys by staff who wore ordinary clothes rather than uniforms.[8] Lancaster House was soon full but the reason for opening a second home in 1949 was that there were some children who needed even more care and attention. Regina House, named after the new Chairman, was also situated in the London area, in Hampstead, where expert advice was close at hand. It took twelve children, all the sad little victims of broken and unhappy homes resulting from the war, emotionally disturbed but of normal intelligence.[9]

The war had also had its effect on the older members of the ex-service community, and in particular the women who had had to bring up families or take care of elderly relatives without a man's support while enduring wartime rationing and conditions – and short of money. Local Legion and Women's Section branches encountered many cases of exhaustion in the post-war years, but there was a shortage of facilities. Queensmead, in Yorkshire, opened during the war, had been augmented by the purchase of a second rest home in Swanage to serve the south. But repairs were frustrated by wartime and post-war

*Lancaster House children's attempted to create a family atmosphere; here the children are at play including running a shop.*

controls and in 1947 the Swanage building was sold, being replaced by Glenthorne, a house overlooking Portland Harbour in Weymouth. Here 220 women could relax each year for a fortnight in fine surroundings and enjoy good food. A third home opened in 1949, Bryntegwel in Aberdovey, serving the Midlands. By 1950 the Section was therefore able to provide convalescent facilities for some 800 women each year, funded by the Lady Edward Spencer Churchill Memorial Fund.[10]

297

## 1951 – 1955

### Still no closer

Despite the earlier discouragement the Women's Section continued to pursue their aim of attendance at National Executive Council meetings. In late 1954, following a meeting of the Section's Central Committee, the Legion's Chairman agreed to thrash the matter out in the Joint Consultative Committee, set up in 1923 to resolve disputes such as this. There was a 'frank exchange of views between the officers of the Legion and those of the Women's Section' over the women's proposition – the same suggestion as that put forward by Lady Apsley in 1947 – that they send observers to NEC meetings with no right to vote or speak and the NEC exercise the same rights at Central Committee meetings. After much discussion it was agreed that the matter should at least be reconsidered by the NEC. But, once again, the Council turned the idea down.[11]

None of this affected the outward relationships. Over 1,000 Women's Section banners had taken part in the Legion's Thirtieth Anniversary parade in Hyde Park and a large Section contingent took part in the Legion's annual parade at the Cenotaph every Whitsun until the custom ended in the 1960s, although, surprisingly, in view of the women's service bands in the war, there was no Section band.[12]

In one respect the Women's Section had achieved equality. Brunel Cohen had presented the accounts for the last time at the Women's Section Conference in 1947. With his retirement the women took charge of their own funds and elected their first Treasurer, Mrs Gilbert Edgar. In 1951 a rising star, Miss Smedley-Crooke, the daughter of an early Legion Council member and MP, took over and, despite the ending of the annual Legion grant for benevolence in 1950, under her firm hand the Section's finances improved, aided by the raising of the Affiliation Fee from 1/- to 1/6d in 1952[13] and by generous donations from branches. In the post-war period branch fundraising had become a significant factor in the Section's finances as Chart D1 on page 448 shows.

It was not the only change at this time. In 1952 Mrs Essie Harris had resigned after nearly thirty years as National Vice Chairman, a remarkable record of service that encompassed the early years of development, the war, during which she briefly acted as Chairman, and the post-war expansion. Earlier the same year the death of King George VI left the Section's President a widow; but, now styled Queen Elizabeth the Queen Mother, she continued in the post she had held for over a quarter of a century. There was, too, a new National Secretary. Mrs Snow, having resigned in 1951, had been replaced by Miss Warren who had been Eastern Area Secretary since the war.[14]

### 'Golden work' – and a dance with the Prince of Wales

In the period following the King's death the Patroness, the Princess Royal, was the royal visitor at the Annual Conference. She accepted 'coronation purses' from delegates in 1953, a total of over £21,000 having been raised for the various funds supporting the Section's work. Attendance remained high, close on 1,800 delegates coming to that conference in the Albert Hall. Numbers fell only slightly when, Conference 1952 having decided to alternate future conferences between London and the provinces, the 1954 venue was Blackpool.

In debate there was much indignation at the problems of war widows at this time. Their pensions had failed to keep pace with inflation (see Chapter 11) so that many had to seek additional allowances to keep themselves and their children fed and clothed, which delegates saw as an undignified outcome of such sacrifice. Yet if a widow went out to work she forfeited those allowances.[15] Such views were represented by the Section's leadership when they accompanied the delegations to Whitehall. But there was also the practical side of Conference: not only were there always stalls for the display of goods made by disabled men, but in 1954, in the course of a talk about the Cambrian Factory, many delegates stood up to display smart two-pieces made from the tweed, no doubt grateful that the conference was held in the spring and not midsummer.[16]

Meanwhile the number of branches continued to increase, reaching a peak of nearly 3,300 in 1955 when Legion branch numbers had been on the decline for five years.[17] But individual membership was starting to fall and in 1954 operation 'Double Up' was launched, members being asked to wear a gold ribbon behind their badge to show the golden work they were doing. Recruiting committees were set up, questionnaires issued and branches motivated, but, a few days before Conference 1955 Lady Apsley, who had organized the campaign, felt that it had fallen a bit flat. To her considerable relief the results suddenly appeared and she was able to tell the conference, to loud applause, that some 16,000 new members had joined.

The 'golden work' had included producing at short notice some 1,500 woollen garments for the troops in Korea for the bitter winter of 1951. The War Office readily took up the offer, but if it was to be of use the garments had to ready in a month and only one pattern book, dating from the previous war, was available. All this limited Operation KK – Knitting for Korea – to the branches in the Metropolitan Area who moved into action at speed. Wool purchased centrally was posted to a branch such as Bexley Heath on Monday and the Balaclavas arrived at headquarters on Thursday. Branch meetings took place to the urgent accompanyment of clicking needles while other knitting circles met in cold halls, but not so cold as their handiwork's destination: the resulting letters of appreciation noted that the wearers had at night to contend with between thirty and forty degrees of frost.[18]

It was not only those in Korea who were in the Section's thoughts; Christmas parcels were sent out to many other places and were as welcome for their thoughtfulness as for their practical value: a Leading Seaman on HMS *Charity* who shared his parcel from Godalming Branch with his messmates wrote that they were amazed that people unknown to them were prepared to send a present at Christmas.[19] Meanwhile all the other activities went on – parties for the elderly, monthly stalls to raise money and to help sell disabled men's goods and the social events. And, as the autumn approached, the section would start to prepare for the Poppy Appeal, as organizers or collectors. But the influence of television was beginning to be felt and attendance at meetings in even the best and most active branches was on the wane.[20]

Occasionally a branch standard had to be replaced and the old one was laid up in the local church with due ceremony. On one such occasion in Melton Mowbray it emerged that the donor of the old standard had been the Prince of Wales. Dancing with a member of the branch at a function in the 1920s he had asked if there was anything he could do for them; told that they would dearly love to have their own standard, in due course one was formally presented by the Duke of Gloucester on his brother's behalf.[21] In the words of the popular song of the time someone had 'danced with the Prince of Wales'.

In early 1953 Women's Section branches were well to the fore in dealing with the flooding of the East Coast. Leigh on Sea had over 350 evacuees staying in their homes, while up and down the coast the women helped turn Legion halls into flood relief centres. At Benfleet the police called out the Section to set up a rest centre in the local school, while branches as far away as the East Riding of Yorkshire collected clothing and bedding for the stricken areas and many more raised funds, with Poppy Day organizers, and doubtless much of their equipment such as collecting tins, in evidence.[22]

## Help for the widows

The Section's Widows Allowance Scheme had been started shortly before the war. At that time it was able to assist only some fifty widows neither capable of work nor entitled to a statutory allowance, providing an allowance of ten shillings per week. By 1947 more than eighty widows were in the scheme and the allowance had increased to fifteen shillings; but, with the introduction in the United Kingdom of state payments in 1950, it was possible to do more for widows in Southern Ireland, many of whom continued to live in dire poverty. Over the next few years the scheme was effectively devoted to widows in that country and expanded so that by 1955 almost all of the 200 widows now drawing the allowance were in the South of Ireland. In the 1960s it was necessary once again to make provision for UK widows, but they were simply added to the total so that by 1970 nearly 500 widows were drawing weekly sums of around ten shillings, which, although the value had diminished with inflation, were gratefully received: 'It makes the winter of my days very happy,' wrote one widow.[23]

Like the other Section schemes, it received no income from the Poppy Appeal. It was entirely supported by the Women's Section branches and only their generosity enabled it to expand when needed The policy to increase the number of beneficiaries rather than to use any additional money to maintain the value of the allowance in the face of inflation was quite deliberate. Although the worth fell each year, it remained a welcome addition to a tight budget, providing as many as possible with little extra comfort each week. And for elderly Irish widows on low state benefits, an additional ten shillings was hardly insignificant.[24]

## The problem of growing up

Tucked away in a quiet warren of streets near the Star and Garter Home, Lancaster House continued to try to provide its sixteen young charges with as normal a life as possible: they went to the local primary or secondary school, joined the Scouts or Guides and brought their friends to tea. In preparation for later life there were cookery lessons for the girls as well as sewing machines provided by the branches, while the boys maintained a vegetable patch in the garden. Life was a little less ordered at Regina House north of the river in Hampstead where the task of looking after twelve boys and girls who had suffered much emotional strain and were now officially described as 'maladjusted' was not easy. The term was not always apt: one nine-year-old arriving in early 1955 after his father had been killed in an accident, and whose mother was unwell, was described as 'a nice little boy, a bit bewildered during his first week at Regina House'.[25]

As the years passed another problem arose. When the young people left to take up work, where would they live? A normal family continued to provide the son or daughter starting in life with a base until he or she became married and set up their own home. But in the case of the Women's Section Homes this would mean that there would be no room for new arrivals. The matter greatly concerned the 1955 Conference who, while reluctant to commit the Section to the cost of a third Home, agreed that something needed to be

300

done. Delegates' views were highly relevant since much of the income for the Homes Fund came from branch voluntary contributions. But in this case there was no consensus.[26]

## 1956 – 1960

### A reunion

In 1959 the Women's Section was at last able to move out of 43, Catherine Place and into Legion headquarters in Pall Mall. The same year Dame Regina Evans resigned after eleven years as Chairman, the diamond and sapphire badge passing to Miss Smedley-Crooke. Dame Regina had seen the Section through an important period of its development and the Childrens' Homes had been one of her great achievements; but still the initiative to find a place for the Section at the NEC table, launched by her predecessor, had not been achieved. Along with the elegant badge of office went that

*The Women's Section have always taken great pride in their Standards: an Area Standard Bearer goes through her movements under the eagle eye of a Guards Drill Sergeant in the 1963 annual competition. Such thoroughness would ensure an impressive display at events like the march-past the Queen at Windsor during the 1977 Silver Jubilee.*

particular objective; but her determined successor would not lack energy for that or any other task.[27]

Dame Regina had been a popular Chairman. At the 1956 Conference in the Isle of Man she drove the Central Committee along the promenade in a horse-drawn tram, while delegates had disembarked from a special boat, gay with bunting of all colours, to 'Has Anybody Here Seen Kelly?' played by the Town Band. Later the same promenade was the setting as 450 Women's Section standards were marched in close array and, despite the location, over 1100 delegates managed to attend. The following year, however, nearly 1,700 were present in the Albert Hall to give their views on the Legion's campaign for an increase in the basic rate of war pensions and once again draw attention to the particular plight of the war widows. As with all the other conferences it had been preceded by similar meetings at County and Area level. Such conferences attracted little publicity except in the local press, but in 1957 Sussex managed to feature in a leader in *The Times*; it was, however, less for the content of the debate as the fact that the delegates had to be called to order as so many of them were knitting.[28]

In 1958 the Queen Mother was present for the first time since her husband's death, coming ashore from the Royal Yacht at Bangor in Northern Ireland where some 750 delegates had met in the Tonic Cinema, the numbers somewhat limited by the size of the hall. It so happened that the Conference coincided with an official royal visit to the Province; now that the location alternated between London and the provinces, there was a tendency for royalty only to attend those in London. But neither the presence of royalty nor the location seemed to affect attendance: in 1960 over 1,300 delegates packed into the Palladium in Brighton to agree an increase in the Affiliation Fee from 1/6 to 2/-, although the Central Commitee had sought 2/6; each member was by then costing the Section 3/- but the delegates' view was that such an increase would affect the donations which supported the Section's work.[29]

## More emphasis on publicity

1956 had been a leap year and it was suggested that where there was still a Legion branch without a Women's Section branch alongside then the women should 'propose' to the men that they should end their bachelor existence. In at least one place the tactic was successful, Wells, described by the County Secretary as 'a male stronghold so long we had practically despaired', at last opening a Section branch. But overall branch numbers continued to decline so that by 1960 the total had fallen below 3,200, due, it was said, to younger people failing to come forward and take office. This led to more emphasis on public relations at local level, although the Section as a whole was often in the news, holding an 'At Home' for editors of women's magazines, which resulted in articles on the Section's work, while the National Officers were interviewed on *Woman's Hour*.

There was more publicity following discussions between the Legion and the Ministry of Pensions which had led to a request in 1956 for the Section to make regular visits to elderly war widows living alone. Many branches became involved in the scheme and in some cases eyes were opened: the plight of the widows was only too apparent and this first-hand knowledge reinforced the Legion's campaign to improve their lot. After Dame Regina Evans had accompanied a Legion delegation to the Ministry of Pensions in 1960 she was interviewed by *The Times* and an article, 'The Widow's Mite', was published.

A novel public relations idea was a series of playlets on the work of the Section. The initial batch was inspired by Lady Apsley, and probably written by her, and the playlets were intended to be performed by branches before members of the public. 'A Cup of Tea' described an afternoon in a Rest Home and 'The Poppy Speaks' was set in a grocer's shop. Some 4,000 copies of the playlets were sold, a few branches wrote their own, and by 1958 some seventy-five branches had actually produced performances. Lady Apsley had also written and produced a pageant 'The Spirit of the Legion' which was performed in Cirencester Park in 1955 to audiences of 1,000 and included scenes such as the burial of Sir John Moore and the death of Nelson, although spirits rose when the Chelsea Pensioners brought down for the occasion enthusiastically embraced Nell Gwyn.[30]

## A problem solved

The problem of a family base for the Lancaster and Regina House leavers was solved in 1957 when a hostel was purchased in Richmond, only a short distance from Lancaster House. Jellicoe House, as it was called, was run by a warden and took eight young people, four of each sex, who had to pay towards their keep. In fact nearly all of them came from Lancaster House as the Regina House inmates tended either to return to their own families in due course or to move on to other institutions.

The advent of Jellicoe House cleared the way for new admissions to the other two homes and they continued with their work. Despite the institutional overtones they seem to have been well run and even happy places. All of the Lancaster House leavers got jobs and one who joined the Grenadier Guards appeared at the Festival of Remembrance. The Women's Section continued to rely heavily on the branches for funding, but the branches did not let them down: as with all of the Section projects they had been involved from the start and knew precisely what the money was needed for.[31]

## 1961 – 1965

## A breakthrough – and a loss

The long struggle to gain the women admission to the Legion's National Executive Council ended on 29 July 1961 when the Chairman, Miss Smedley-Crooke, and the Vice Chairman, Mrs Croft-Faulds, were warmly welcomed to the Council by General Sir Roy Bucher, the Legion's Chairman. It was the result of yet another submission by the women and, although the actual wording of the NEC's response had been that the Women's Section officers would be 'invited to attend as and when required', in practice the women were present at every NEC meeting thereafter, except those held in connection with Legion Conferences. In return the Legion's National Chairman and his deputy had an invitation to attend the Women's Central Committee.[32] At least two of those present on 29 July 1961, Sir Frederick Lister and Colonel Crosfield, had sat on the same Council with Miss Smedley-Crooke's father, as they no doubt reminded her.[33]

The Section's Patroness, the Princess Royal, would no doubt have been delighted. She had held her office since the formation of the Section, almost exactly forty years before, and had watched its progress closely, addressing its Conference on fifteen occasions and taking a particularly keen interest in its activities in her home county of the the West Riding of Yorkshire. If her own position had been overshadowed when the President, the Duchess of York, had become Queen, she nonetheless continued to serve the Section loyally, in effect deputising for the President at the Annual Conference. But in 1965, a month before she was due to address Conference yet again, she died. There was much genuine sadness at the news: she was very popular with the members, in their words 'a giver'. Nor, in any sense, could she be replaced: it would hardly have been possible to have appointed a new Patroness over the head of the Queen Mother.[34]

## Financial problems

Attendance at Annual Conference was a little down from the peaks of the 1950s but it was still necessary to book the Royal Albert Hall for a London Conference which, including visitors and standard bearers, might have well over 3,000 people present. There had in fact been over 5,000 present in the Albert Hall for the 1961 Conference; this, the fortieth anniversary of the Section, was followed by a reception at the Guildhall and a dedication of a new headquarters standard in St Paul's Cathedral, attracting both TV and radio publicity. Away from London in the alternate years the conferences were held in Blackpool or the Isle of Man, but the attendance was then a little less. But, whatever the location or the attendance, finances were always high on the agenda. Since such projects were in the main directly funded through the efforts of individual branches there was a keen and often critical interest in the Children's Homes, the Rest Homes and the Widows' Allowance scheme. If delegates were satisfied with what they heard it would be reflected in the contributions, and the favourable reception given to the announcement of the flatlets scheme at the 1963 Conference resulted in large 'purses' being presented at the 1965 Conference. The debate was not without its lighter moments: at Miss Smedley-Crooke's first Conference in the Palace Ballroom in Douglas in 1964 the delegates became 'rather giggly' when, discussing the Legion's all-male policy in its Country Homes, they were told that it was not in line with modern ideas that males and females should be separated. And they voted for change.[35]

However willing delegates were to support new projects, the general administrative expenses were another matter. With inflation ever increasing costs they were invited in 1963 to raise Affiliation Fees from 2s to 2s 6d; but, even though it now cost over 4s per member to run the organization, the increase was rejected. In 1965, however, the situation had become so serious that they agreed to raise the fee to 3s.[36] Such an increase would normally have put matters right. But the number of branches was continuing to decline and by 1965 there were barely 3,000, and overall membership had fallen by 6,000 in that year alone. This was despite more emphasis on youth with some branches forming their own Youth Sections and, following a 1962 Conference resolution, a decision to admit granddaughters of ex-servicemen and women as Ordinary Members. Meanwhile the need to conform with the Legion meant that the Section's Southern and Midland Areas had to be split into two, adding to overheads.[37]

## Rest Home changes

Conference was always keenly interested in the Rest Homes. There had been three. Queensmead lay in Yorkshire; Glenthorne was in Dorset; and Bryntegwel overlooked Cardigan Bay in Wales. Between them they provided convalescent care for some 800 women a year, many of whom owed at least a part of their condition to the cumulative effect of both pre-war and wartime deprivation, struggling to run a home and provide meals on the slenderest of resources. But in 1952 it had become clear that Queensmead was too small to be efficient and it was sold and replaced with a new property, still in Yorkshire at Skipton, the original name being retained.[38] In the case of Bryntegwel, however, when it became apparent in 1956 that the disadvantages of the remote and hilly setting – long and arduous journeys and staff difficulties – were now outweighing the advantages, it was sold without replacement.[39]

During the 1960s many improvements were made in the two remaining homes: the shared bedrooms were divided up by cubicles, central heating installed, sun parlours constructed and kitchens improved. Ministry of Pensions Welfare Officers and those Section members involved in the war widows visiting scheme now also made recommendations and the guests ranged from a 24-year-old widow to the over eighties. One 75-year-old arriving at Glenthorne in 1966 had never seen the sea; she spent her first day gazing at the waters of Weymouth Bay.

Originally each home was run by its own house committee. But with only two homes to adminster both were directly administered by the central Rest Homes Committee.[40] A few years later, in 1968, the committee came to the conclusion that, as in the case of Bryntegwel some twelve years before, location and staffing problems, accentuated by rail closures, made yet another change of location necessary for Queensmead. The home was therefore sold and in 1970 the third Queensmead was opened on the sea front at Bridlington, still in Yorkshire.

## Closure of Regina House

Change was also in the air for the Children's Homes. Despite the generosity of branches there were financial difficulties as costs went up and Regina House, the home for disturbed children, was not now being used to full capacity since, so long after the war, less families were disrupted as a result of service conditions. In 1963 therefore the decision was taken to sell it and the remaining children were transferred to other homes selected to meet their needs; but the Women's Section continued to keep in touch with each child.

Lancaster House also encountered some difficulties because of too frequent staff changes, which were unsettling to the children, but it continued to carry out its role, providing its young charges with as normal a life as possible before passing them on to Jellicoe House from which they were launched into the world, the process mitigated by the fact that all their cooking, shopping and housekeeping was done for them. In the end of course they found their own homes and two weddings from Jellicoe House particularly delighted Section members.[41]

The closure of Regina House as a home provided an opening for a new venture. Following a decision at the 1962 Conference it was converted into flatlets for widows of ex-servicemen and for elderly ex-servicewomen. Once Conference delegates became enthusiastic over an idea the support was guaranteed. In the case of the flatlets it was overwhelming and the conversions were completed in time for the first tenants to move in in July 1964. They found that the house, built in Hampstead in 1900 as a private residence for William Willett, the originator of daylight saving, had been converted into twelve flatlets, each with a bed-sitting room, a separate kitchen or cupboard kitchen and a shared bathroom. But rents did not meet the upkeep and, although the development costs had been met by donations, the Women's Section would need to provide continuing support.[42]

## 1966 – 1970

### A falling-out with the Legion

Undoubtedly Miss Smedley-Crooke was a spirited character; she had been a rally driver in the Daimler all-female team in the 1930s and her career, as well as service in both the ATS and the WAAF, had included not only management but a spell as a delivery driver.[43] She was determined to ensure the success of the new relationship with the Legion. It was as well that she did so: if the Section's representation at NEC meetings did not prevent a serious clash with the Legion at the end of the decade, it did at least enable the problem to be resolved.

In 1967 Mrs Croft Foulds became Chairman. Having been a regular attender at the NEC as the Section's Vice Chairman she too started with a good understanding with the men. But the Legion omitted to include a Section representative in a delegation to the Secretary of State for Social Services in 1969 which had discussed war widows pensions, a subject in which the Section felt that they had a particular interest, if not responsibility, and the Legion explanation that it was purely a social visit did not impress the women. On the other hand the Section seem to have overlooked an earlier undertaking that they would not embark on capital expenditure without NEC approval when they went ahead with an extension to the flatlets scheme the same year. In this case the matter was a little more serious as the Legion itself was legally liable if the project collapsed through insufficient funding. The Women's Section Chairman's response that, had the Legion taken up the standing invitation to attend Central Committee meetings they would have been aware of the action, made as little impression on the NEC as their own explanation over the pensions delegation had made on the Central Committee.[44]

In this atmosphere sides began to be taken. An explanation of the work of the Legion's Housing Association to the 1970 Legion National Leadership Forum led to a draft Legion Conference resolution critical of the Section's flatlets scheme, implying that it could have been achieved through the Housing Association without cost to the Section. Some spoke of the Legion taking over the Women's Section and a report in the *Surrey Advertiser* even stated that the Legion was planning to close the Section down. Not surprisingly there was much concern among members of the Section as the rumours multiplied, and talk of withdrawal of support for the Poppy Appeal.

The situation was defused at an NEC meeting in October of that year. With the women's leaders now accustomed to sitting at the same table there could be a frank exchange of views and the misunderstandings were resolved: the Legion had no intention of changing the existing relationship and the Housing Association would not take over the Section's flatlets scheme. Nor would fuel be added to the fire by issuing statements of denial; since the leaders were in agreement the rumours would wither away. And so they did.[45]

### More cost-saving

Specific projects such as the flatlets scheme received strong financial support from within the Section. But the Section's own headquarters' finances were hardly buoyant and in 1966 a special annual appeal was launched. As usual the response was good, producing some £15,000 a year to supplement the Affiliation Fee income of £24,000; at the same time the cost of headquarters support for other activities was charged to those activities and the ship restored to an even keel.[46] It might, however, be argued that this method of

306

financing headquarters was a little unfair, since the more active and generous branches subsidised the rest.

Among other cost-saving measures it was decided to stop using the Albert Hall as the London venue for the Annual Conference: at £1,000 a day it was ten times the cost of the Central Hall, Westminster, and with attendance now down to around 1,000 delegates, and tending to fall, there was no need for the extra capacity. The 1967 Conference was therefore the last to be held there, the next London Conference, following a visit to Blackpool in 1968, taking place at the Central Hall. On that occasion there was a new Royal visitor, the Duchess of Kent, whose husband was a serving Army officer. She no doubt admired the delegates' 'dazzling splendour and variety of spring hats', as the *Legion Journal* put it, but in contrast the resolutions were down-to-earth: they dealt not only with the perennial question of the low level of war widows' pensions but sought advances in matters such as the installation of seat baths in the flatlets and the provision of flame-proof materials for the elderly and disabled.[47]

When a Royal visitor could not attend it was the practice for one of the Vice Patrons to be present and the Duchess of Westminster spoke at the 1970 Conference in the Isle of Man. That year it was decided that in the future Conference locations would alternate between North and South rather than between London and the provinces, although it is perhaps unlikely that this decision was solely responsible for the delegates' high spirits on the return steamer when an impromptu sing-song attracted showers of coins from the other passengers. These were duly presented to a worthy cause, the headquarters' fund.[48] Certainly the fund still needed every penny, despite the special appeal. Branches were still closing and by the decade's end the number had fallen to a little over 2,800. Among the closures were a number of overseas branches: Kenya and Bogota, both of which had been generous with food parcels for widows in England after the war, and New York.

At home, while the less enterprising branches failed to overcome their problems of lack of leadership or a suitable meeting place, the active ones continued to thrive with competitions, garden parties, visits and fundraising events while contributing to the community by such activities as running the village play group. Meanwhile, in an effort to counter the downwards drift, headquarters was supplying those leaving the WRAC with information on the Section; if they were lucky enough to encounter the right branch they would no doubt become active members.[49]

## End of the Children's Homes

It was not only membership that was in decline; during the second half of the decade admissions to the Section's Children's Homes also fell and in 1967 both Lancaster House and Jellicoe House were closed, a contributory factor having been the increasing difficulty of getting the right staff. As in the case of Regina House the remaining children were found other homes to suit their needs. Before Jellicoe closed its doors there was a reunion party for the 'old boys and girls'. Many of the young people still wrote to Miss Stumpp, who had been the Warden of both Lancaster House and the Jellicoe hostel, and she was at the party to renew old memories and no doubt admire the two babies accompanying the three married couples.[50]

Enough money having been set aside from the Children's Home Fund to support the remaining children in their new homes and to assist if needed with their education and training, the balance was transferred to the Flatlets Fund. At Regina House all twelve

*The Flatlets Scheme: A retired nurse in her flatlet at Bronwen House, Southport; the kitchen units were behind double doors in the sitting room. Such schemes were supported by purse presentations at Conference with individually worked County purses as shown below.*

flatlets were running smoothly and it was decided to extend the scheme with the purchase of a house in Southport in Lancashire for conversion to eleven flatlets, together with two old people's bungalows. Bronwen House, Southport, named after Bronwen Smedley-Crooke, opened in 1969. Donations were still, however, coming in from branches and in 1970 a conversion at Shore House in Northern Ireland added ten flatlets to the scheme, while the same year work was started on a further twenty-two at Shottermill in Surrey.[51]

Despite all this expenditure on housing the Section's Welfare Fund continued to receive about £10,000 a year in branch donations. It was quite independent of any Legion fund and gave the Section an additional resource in cases where other funds, in particular state funding, could not be used. One such was referred to the Section by the Ministry of Social Security: a wife who had nursed her husband since 1918 when he had been discharged with gunshot wounds to the head lost the television set that had been provided for his use when he died. She had no money of her own and the fund replaced it.[52]

★    ★    ★

Throughout this period the Women's Section had continued to provide the backbone of the Poppy Appeal organization, although the Section itself received no income from the Appeal. To finance its own projects – the Rest Homes, the Children's Homes, the Widows' Allowance scheme – it had to depend on its branches. But this active grass roots involvement was the Section's particular strength, explaining why its level of conference attendance was often two or three times that of the Legion itself.

This interest and involvement had been maintained for a quarter of a century by the generation that had served in the Second World War. Now that generation was itself beginning to age, branches were closing and membership falling. Would an organization that relied so directly on its members for supporting its work be able to maintain the momentum as the war years receded into the distance?

# CHAPTER 15

## OFFICER BENEVOLENCE 1946-1970

# *Still Under Pressure*

## 1946 – 1950

### A new relationship

Amid the upheaval of the early days of the Second World War the relationship between the Legion and its officers' organization had changed. The officers' department had always been a self-contained unit within the parent body, but it had been accountable to the Legion. This was no longer the case. The department's work had ceased to be subject to scrutiny by the Legion's NEC; nor did its activities form part of the Legion's Annual Report. And, although it still acknowledged its function as 'the Officers' Benevolent Department of the British Legion', this was now in the sense of a partnership based on Earl Haig having founded both bodies.[1] Moreover, it had resumed its pre-Unity title – the 'Officers' Association'.

This assertion of an independent status seemed to be generally accepted in the Legion's higher echelons. The Legion's National Officers and five NEC members continued to sit on the eighty-strong Council of the Officers' Association and the Legion was also represented on the OA Executive and Finance Committees; but this was the extent of the involvement. The Legion's rank-and-file, however, continued to maintain that, in accordance with the Unity agreement, officers' benevolence should be adminstered as a direct function of the Legion itself, passing a resolution to this effect at the 1947 Annual Conference.[2] But, as the Legion's leaders recognized, any such attempt would merely reopen the wounds of 1925, when the NEC had unsuccessfully challenged the Officers' separate Charter.

Independent or not, officers' benevolence needed funding. In 1945 the OA had prodded the Legion into fully implementing the 1932 agreement which increased its share of the Poppy Appeal to $7\frac{1}{2}$ per cent; but the increase was subject to a maximum figure which was now invalidated by inflation. A new agreement in 1949 removed the restriction and henceforward the OA would be entitled to the full percentage amount. It was needed: expenditure in the post-war years was unprecedented and the Army Benevolent Fund grant also had to be increased.[3]

Meanwhile the wartime General Secretary of the Association, Colonel Stokes, had been replaced by Brigadier Money whose tenure was cut short by recurrence of a war injury and in turn handed over in 1948 to Major General Grover. Money had nevertheless started to try to restore relationships and Grover continued the work, recognizing the danger of the Legion and the Association taking divergent courses and the importance therefore of restoring mutual understanding. But he also saw that it was principally the Legion's grass roots that had to be convinced of the need for the former officers to have a distinct organization. Speaking at Legion Area and County conferences, as well as at the

Annual Conference, he explained the particular problems faced by ex-officers and the expertise that the Association brought to them. As much as the arguments themselves, it was the fact that he appeared regularly on a Legion platform to explain the Association's work that seemed to reassure Legion members that the Association, even if it now ploughed its own furrow, was still part of the Legion family.[4] Relationships might perhaps have been brought even closer if the Assocation had been able to co-locate with Legion headquarters when it had to vacate the premises at 8, Eaton Square in 1948. But work on Pall Mall was still hampered by building restrictions and the Association took up a lease on 28, Belgrave Square for a nominal sum.[5]

## Looking for jobs

Post-war controls also restricted the activities of former officers trying to start up their own businesses, as did funding: the government assisted the war-disabled to start up but there was no enterprise scheme for the rest. Ideas conceived under the desert stars or in the monotony of a prisoner-of-war camp would not have come to fruition had the Officers' Association not started a Business Grants Scheme under 'three wise men'* of the City of London. But the older officers presented the main employment problem in the post-war years. Employers were reluctant to accept those over the age of fifty or even forty; their working life had been disrupted by two wars and even if they had the right skills they were difficult to place in an organization without prejudicing the promotion of younger men, while ex-regular officers had even less prospects.[6] At a Legion County Chairmen's conference in 1946 one of those attending had come across an ex-RN commander who was now a garage attendant, pushing cars about on the forecourt.[7] But there was also a problem with those young ex-officers who had gone straight into the armed forces without completing their education and had no work training or experience, echoing the situation of so many after the Great War.[8]

The Association's Employment Bureau operated from Denison House in the Vauxhall Bridge Road, trying to match applicants to jobs and informing the successful ones by telegram. But it generally only covered London and the immediate surrounding area. Elsewhere the Legion itself, still very active in employment matters following its great successes of the 1930s, acted on behalf of the OA in assisting former officers to find work, maintaining a Liaison Officer at Denison House. By 1947 the Bureau was placing 100 ex-officers a month, about one in every five who registered, although almost all got interviews with employers. But, once again, it was the ex-ranker officers who found themselves at the bottom of the pile: employers simply did not recognize their abilities[9] and many were forced to take up work as cinema commissionaires, caretakers or storekeepers.[10]

## Benevolence

In a sense, however, these were the lucky ones. Many First World War ex-officers out of work were hard hit by the post-war increase in living costs and had to turn to the Association for relief, as did officers' widows. In Eire the situation was even worse and there was some prejudice against those who had served in the British Forces and even their dependants. With no state pension until age seventy and medical treatment very costly, the Association's Dublin Branch office was a busy place.[11]

In Ireland, as on the mainland, the Association's benevolent work depended heavily on a network of Honorary Representatives whose task was to investigate cases and to make

*who included Colonel Ashwanden, a former Legion Chairman.

310

recommendations. In the immediate post-war period the network needed to be expanded and the Legion's local Service Committees helped by finding former officers to take up this role. The Association also encouraged Legion Service Committees to appoint an officer representative to direct cases to them.[12] Such co-operation was not only of practical benefit; it promoted better relations between the Legion and the OA.

The acute shortage of housing sometimes prejudiced a former officer's ability to take up a job. In such cases the Association was prepared to help with the deposit for a house bought on a mortgage, in much the same way as the Legion scheme. But such was the demand that the initiative was only able to operate for a short time before being restricted to particularly needy cases. Even so nearly 600 ex-officers had been assisted with loans of around £150 to buy their own houses by the time the scheme ran down in the late 1950s.[13]

### A wedding present

The gloom of the post-war years was relieved in November 1947 by the wedding of Princess Elizabeth to Prince Philip. The Belgian people's wedding present was particularly imaginative: it included the funding of holidays for British children and in 1948 the Association organized a visit by two hundred children of ex-officers, most of whom had lost their fathers in the war. They stayed with Belgian families for three weeks and such was the success and the enthusiasm of their Belgian hosts, including at least one wartime Resistance leader, that it became an annual event, only ending in 1961 when a crisis in the Belgian economy prevented any further funding. The Belgian Royal family had even acted as hosts in one case.[14]

## 1951 – 1955

### A new training course

The Legion Annual Report of 1951 referred to the Association as 'our associated body' and the phrase accurately described the situation. The Association's distinguished hierarchy made it in fact difficult to understand how credible had been the original relationship. With its own Patron, the sovereign, military officers of the highest rank in each service as Presidents and scarcely less distinguished Vice Presidents as well as eminent men in the professions serving on the Council, it carried a great deal of heavy artillery. But in any case, largely thanks to the efforts of the General Secretary, General Grover, the relationship worked well even if in the far corners of the Legion there were some who still maintained that such a partnership was not what the Unity conference had intended.

The Legion's Chairman and Vice Chairman were members of the Association's Executive Committee which in 1954 launched an initiative to assist senior retired regular service officers to find employment and to give resettlement advice to all officers about to retire. Senior officers were a particular problem. Many employers, while appreciating their qualities, found it difficult to relate military experience to a civil post. For their part the officers lacked the background to convince employers of their business potential. A Higher Employment Department was set up at 28, Belgrave Square and 'Industrial Appreciation Courses' instituted for such officers at the London Polytechnic. The courses were later extended to include officers down to the equivalent rank of major and proved

311

to be so successful that in 1958 the Ministry of Labour took over their organization.[15] The senior officers had cause to be grateful to the Association. Despite an average age of fifty-four, around half of them were directly placed by the department at salary levels which were twice those of their erstwhile subordinates.

Nevertheless the lower orders also got their money's worth, the same proportion being found jobs largely due to the efforts of the Association's two Job Finders who between them had visited nearly 5,000 firms since 1949. One of their tasks was to try to persuade employers to take on older ex-officers and some were now prepared to set aside jobs specifically for them. Such openings were desperately needed as one half of those registering were over the age of fifty; even so forty-three officers over sixty were found work in 1952. Meanwhile out in the provinces around a hundred former officers each year were placed with the Legion's help.

Those regular officers who had failed to get other jobs or were by now too old for employment were mainly dependent on their service pensions, as were their widows. But in many cases the pensions had been devalued by post-war inflation and shortly after the war the Officers' Association, with Royal Naval and Royal Air Force ex-officer representatives, had formed a committee to put this right. Working with the Officers' Pensions Society the Retired Pay and Pensions Committee took their case to the government in 1952, but, despite the fact that inflation was still remorselessly rising, it was rejected. The time when there would be an annual adjustment to take account of living costs was still far off.[16]

The following year the Association led another campaign on regular officers' pensions. This time it sought justice for those officers pensioned in the inter-war period: for instance a lieutenant colonel who had retired in 1923 with a pension of £546 a year found it worth only half that value in 1953 because of inflation and with no account taken of additional service from 1939 to 1945. Yet an officer of the same rank who had retired in 1945 would receive a much greater pension simply because serving officers were being paid more at that time than in 1923 and a different code therefore applied. It was a glaring anomaly which was the source of real hardship; yet, despite a heated debate in Parliament, the government refused to do anything despite (or perhaps because of) the fact that only 300-400 such officers survived.*[17]

This sort of treatment compounded the other problems that arose from the effect of post-war inflation on small and fixed incomes and made it necessary for the OA to help more than 7,000 former officers or their dependants financially each year, some cases coming to light only through the Officers' Association representatives sitting on the local Legion Service Committees.[18]

## A home for the elderly

The sufferers were mainly the elderly, a category now on the increase and beginning to encounter other problems. One was accommodation for elderly ex-officers who were on their own and, although the Legion had helped by finding some places in their Country Homes, there were not enough vacancies to meet the demand. In 1947 a committee under Colonel Crosfield, who had pioneered the Legion's scheme, acquired Frimley Park at Camberley in Surrey, with support from the Legion and other service charities. But it proved difficult to extend in the face of building restrictions. It was therefore sold and in 1950 the Association bought Huntly, a Georgian house in Devon. Set in large grounds overlooking the Teign estuary, it could accommodate some thirty-five ex-officers who no

---

*Remarkably, despite every effort by the Officers' Pensions Society, similar anomalies in the pay of retired officers exist to this day, although not of the same magnitude. Pensions are, however, now cost-of-living indexed.

*Residents enjoy the sunshine at the Officers' Association Home at Huntly in Devon. Above, a resident in his room at Huntly.*

longer had their own homes. By then the Association had also taken over the former privately-established Disabled Officers' Garden Homes at Leavesden near Watford, comprising twelve bungalows for seriously disabled married men and their families.[19]

The problem of housing the elderly and infirm did not, however, end there. As the numbers seeking accommodation continued to increase the Association had to look elsewhere. It bought nomination rights for places in Homes run by other organisations and set up an office to keep in touch with developments in what was now becoming a national problem and to find further vacancies, in many cases assisting individual ex-officers or their dependants financially.[20]

## 1956 – 1960

### A call unheard

When the Legion gave a new impetus to its recruiting drive in 1959, the Association's General Secretary, Major General Grover, wrote an article in the *Legion Journal* pointing out that, although the OA was not itself a membership organization, it had a strong interest in keeping up Legion membership. Its policy was to encourage ex-officers to join their local Legion branches, especially those currently leaving the services under the defence cuts.[21]

Despite this OA support, not enough ex-officers were coming into the Legion. Since in many cases lack of leadership was the main factor for the closure of branches, a greater involvement by former officers could have strengthened the organization. The OA's well-deserved reputation in the services, particularly for assisting middle-aged officers to get employment, might have aroused officers' interest in the Legion itself. Unfortunately most officers simply did not connect the Officers' Association with the Legion.[22] Nevertheless this was no more than one factor in the general decline in ex-officer involvement in the movement.

## A government task

In 1956 the Employment Department moved to Windsor House in Victoria Street under a new title – 'Resettlement and Employment Department'.[23] It was joined by the former Higher Employment Department and reorganized, one section dealing with junior and short service officers and the other with regular officers at the end of their careers. Placings at this time had fallen a little because of the economic downturn but between one quarter and one third of all those registering were found jobs, while the rest at least had the benefit of sound advice on how to seek employment, as a result of which many of them got their own appointments.[24]

The move was timely. It coincided with the end of National Service and the sharp reduction in the size of the armed forces, as a result of which a large number of regular officers were made redundant – the so-called 'Golden Bowler' scheme. The scheme led to a government approach to the Association in 1957 for help with resettlement. It was accompanied by a Treasury Grant in Aid so that for the first time the government had formally recognized the Association's work. The Resettlement and Employment Department was further reorganized and expanded and a link established with the Ministry of Labour's Regular Officers Resettlement Service with the Association represented on the Advisory Board.[25]

If money was available to help a new generation to cope with life outside the service the government showed less generosity to some of their fathers and mothers. The Legion campaign to restore the value of the war disability and war widows' pensions (see Chapter 11) still had not achieved its object, but the Association had been fully involved, with of course particular concern for the situation of the former officers and their widows. Some of these were among the sixty elderly people for whom the expanded Homes Department was able to find residential places each year, working closely with the Order of St John and the British Red Cross. The OA saw this as a better way of meeting their needs than opening another Home itself, which would anyway have stretched its finances, now showing a deficit each year as the needs of the older generation grew with inflation eroding their savings. Two-thirds of those whom it assisted were now over the age of sixty.[26]

## 1961 – 1965

## Continued pressure

General Grover resigned as General Secretary in 1961 for health reasons. His successor, Major General Carter, also left because of poor health after two years and in 1963 Major General Sir Peter St Clair Ford took over. Two years after his arrival the Association negotiated a new lease for 28, Belgrave Square, together with a complete refurbishment of the premises, allowing the Resettlement and Employment Department to move in and saving on overheads. Since the staff were required to remain in place while all this work went on around them, there were no doubt considerable demands on the GS's leadership. But the Association now had a substantial capital asset with a lease until 2047.[27]

Despite such turmoil, the OA took a step back in the Legion's direction in 1965 when it resumed the practice of including an account of the Association's work in the Legion's Annual Report. Although this was a brief summary rather than a formal report, it served to demonstrate, after a break of 25 years, the links that still existed. In these reports employment and provision for the elderly continued to be the main concerns. Job placement was becoming difficult as the commercial world went through a series of take-overs and mergers, while the regular procession of ex-officers through the doors of the Employment Department had now been joined by those who had entered the Colonial Service after their war service and were now once again out of work. Undaunted, the staff redoubled their efforts, with the job finders making 1,200 visits to employers in a year in the knowledge that threequarters of the offers came from this activity and in 1965 the Department was still able to find jobs for some 650 officers.

By now 75 per cent of applicants for relief were over sixty, mainly of the First World War generation, and many with service in both wars. Residential and Nursing Home placements exceeded 100 in 1965 while the 700 assisted by the Claims and Pensions Branch each year, mainly over a recurring disability, still included cases arising from the battles on the Somme or at Gallipoli; in 1965 the branch even got a war disability pension for a 93-year-old officer who had been wounded in the Boer War, although it appears not to have been backdated. The large stock of first-class garments in the clothing store saved on cash payments in cases of need, and it is worth noting that this scheme was still operating some twenty years after a similar Legion activity operated by the Women's Section had been closed down.[28]

One of the Association's activities had been to provide disabled ex-officers with a car if they needed it for work. In the immediate post-war years cars had been in short supply, but the Association had some connections with the industry and they showed their appreciation of the Legion's help over vacancies in Legion Homes by presenting each new Home with a car as it opened.[29] As well as being of practical help such gestures added to the re-forging of the bonds.

# 1966 – 1970

## Finances under pressure

In 1966 Major General St Clair Ford handed over as General Secretary to Major General Shepheard. The new GS found an organization still hard-worked, with further reductions in the armed forces adding to the load. It was also under some financial strain, with income declining in real terms (see Chart E1 on page 449), while reserves were steadily eroded by annual overspends as it strove to meet its commitments. The Legion, although itself under some pressure, had for some time supplemented the agreed annual share of the Poppy Appeal – $7\frac{1}{2}$ per cent – with special grants. The move of the Resettlement and Employment Department to 28, Belgrave Square made some savings, but the Government grant in aid of officers leaving the services was due to end in 1967, since it only applied to those affected by redundancy. The only bright spot was the decline in education costs; but these had been anticipated. With the elderly needing even more support the outlook was uncertain and wherever possible relief expenditure now also drew on other charities with which the applicant might have a connection, such as professional bodies.[30]

315

This policy of spreading the cost also applied to the widows, based on their husbands' former civil occupations. Spending on widows had gone up by 50 per cent since 1961 and nearly 1,000 were being helped each year. In each case their income, even with the Supplementary Pension, was insufficient to meet their basic needs. Sometimes only a small amount was needed such as a few pounds a week to enable a crippled 83-year-old widow to be nursed at home; but another widow who had lived all her life in India and was penniless needed to have her residential Home fees paid. Many others in such Homes, whether placed by the Legion or existing residents caught up in escalating costs, had to be helped. Huntly, the Association's own Home in Devon, was full and with only thirty-five beds it had a long waiting list. It did not of course take in widows and by 1970 the Association was helping find accommodation for 660 ex-officers and widows, assisting with the fees for 135 of them.

There was particular distress among ex-officers and widows in Eire as medical costs rose while state benefits remained low. The Health Service was far less developed than in the United Kingdom and most people had to pay for their medical treatment and medicines. As elsewhere cases were investigated by Honorary Representatives, but in both Northern and Southern Ireland most decisions were made locally. The same applied to Birmingham, where a local committee of the Association funded by the city's Ex-service Appeal dealt with the cases, and in Kenya where there was a similar arrangement. Scotland operated independently under a Council appointed by the main OA Council, but in all other cases the Representatives' recommendations went to London for approval. So that they could be dealt with promptly, every working day a member of each Relief Committee (one dealt with disabled and one with non-disabled) called at the Association's headquarters to take the decisions.

The combined effect of the credit squeeze and the Selective Employment Tax lengthened the queues at the door of the Resettlement and Employment Department at the end of 1966. There was no let-up in succeeding years as the economic situation remained difficult and increasing numbers of elderly ex-officers sought help after losing their jobs; but even in these bleak conditions the Association managed to assist some 1,400 individuals to get work each year.[31] Some of the jobs were found by the Honorary Representatives who added employment openings to their welfare responsibilities, but the main operation needed funding and in 1968 a Government grant of £10,000 was negotiated. The next year it was accepted that the Association's Resettlement and Employment work should be formally recognized by a grant from Public Funds.[32] This was a considerable breakthrough; hitherto only the redundancy activities had received Treasury Grants. The £35,000 grant enabled the Association to turn the corner financially and, for the first time since 1945, there was no deficit in the accounts.

★      ★      ★

The post-war period had not been easy for the Officers' Association. It had to cope with the problems of the ageing of a substantial part of its constituency, people who, despite their contribution to their country, the new welfare state often bypassed. On shrinking incomes and handicapped by age or lack of experience in the struggle for employment they needed help. Meanwhile fresh cohorts of ex-officers trying to find their way in civil life also claimed attention. But all had been assisted. Moreover relations with the Legion had been restored. Whatever the closing years of the century might hold, the Association could face the future in good heart.

316

# PART III

## 1971–2001

# A NATIONAL INSTITUTION

# CHAPTER 16

## THE LEGION AND THE NATION 1971-2001

# *New Challenges*

### 1971 – 1975

**Troubled times**

The 1970s saw the start of Britain's greater involvement with Europe, stirring some deep feelings. Meanwhile, as the economy worsened and inflation became rampant, unions wage demands added fuel to the fire. After the three-day week and 'winter of discontent' in 1973-4, Heath's Conservative government was replaced by a Labour adminstration under Harold Wilson which negotiated a 'social contract' with the unions, attempting to reverse inflation which in 1975 was 24 per cent.

It was not only inflation which was causing concern. In Northern Ireland the situation deteriorated rapidly in the early 1970s as the Republican element turned their attention against the Army. The first British soldier was killed in 1971 and as the violence spread the Legion had its own first casualty when the Chairman of Belfast Branch was killed in a bomb explosion in October 1972.[1]

Against this turbulent background some in the Legion thought that it should become more involved in the nation's affairs. But the leaders strongly resisted any attempt to give an ex-service view on such matters as entry into Europe, the policy on immigration, or Northern Ireland; only where the issue directly affected the ex-service community would the Legion take a stance, sticking resolutely to the policy which the organization had followed since its inception. It even refused to take part in a BBC radio discussion on Northern Ireland.[2]

Nonetheless one government initiative aroused much disquiet in the organization, particularly among the rank-and-file. The Local Government reorganization of 1974 changed the map of Britain by re-aligning county boundaries. When the Legion's own Boundary Commission recommended that it would be in the Legion's interests to conform, the membership would have none of it and only the Poppy Appeal organization changed.[3]

The Appeal was affected by another new measure: Value Added Tax would add to the cost of poppies, reducing the Legion's benevolent income. A Legion delegation hastened to the Treasury and, after more negotiations, VAT was withdrawn for poppies. Although wreaths had to wait a year longer for the same exemption, it was a notable victory. But the tax still applied to other forms of spending, whether for charitable purposes or not, and it made life more difficult for the clubs, some of which were already struggling to survive.[4]

With inflation at an unprecedented level, devaluing Appeal income while at the same time forcing those on low or fixed incomes to seek even more welfare support, these were not easy times for the Legion.

## A 'Royal' Jubilee

Amid all the difficulties there was one cause for celebration: the Legion's fiftieth anniversary. It was marked with a signal honour: in the familiar setting of the Royal Albert Hall in May 1971 the National President, General Sir Charles Jones, announced to over a thousand Conference delegates and two thousand visitors that the Queen had granted the Legion the prefix 'Royal' in its title. Although the announcement can hardly have been unexpected the applause was tumultuous. The same honour was accorded to the Legion in Scotland. It entailed some changes: the Queen's crown had to be added to the badge, a process involving the monarch's approval to a Royal College of Heralds design and taking over a year; and there was the question of the clubs and the Legion's associated companies. At first it was considered inappropriate to extend the honour to such 'fringe' organizations, but in October the Council reversed their earlier decision, sternly warning the clubs however that they must not bring the title into disrepute.[5]

The 'Royal' announcement gave extra zest to the celebrations. These included a service of rededication at Westminster Abbey where, to the accompaniment of fanfares by the trumpeters of the Coldstream Guards, the Legion's national standards were placed on the altar. After the service thousands of Legionaries marched behind the standards to Horse Guards Parade, on the way giving a smart 'eyes right' at the Cenotaph and, a little further up Whitehall, paying the same compliment to the statue of their founder, Earl Haig. On 1 July, the day of the Legion's foundation, there was a dinner at the Mansion House and a few days later over four thousand members and guests attended a garden party at Buckingham Palace. Each of the Royal hosts, who included the Queen Mother and Earl Mountbatten, as well the Queen and Prince Philip, was accompanied by a Legion 'conductor' – one of the national officers – and two 'finders'. Thus far it was like many another Royal garden party, but it ended with a special Legion touch: as the Queen and the others turned on the terrace to wave their farewells someone in the crowd called out for three cheers. There was a ringing response and, whatever palace officials may have thought at this break with decorum, the Queen acknowledged the gesture with pleasure.[6]

There were of course many other celebrations: services at cathedrals and churches throughout the land, including an ecumenical service at Dublin Cathedral, rallies and Jubilee Balls. Ashby-de-la-Zouch Branch held a week of celebrations – a swimming gala for children, a dance at the Town Hall, a dinner for veterans, a floodlit tattoo, a fete and a concert.[7] Other branches did no less and those which had been in continuous existence from within a year of the Legion's formation proudly attached a special anniversary streamer to their standard.[8]

Over £50,000 was raised within the Legion, not without some effort, to purchase and equip a lifeboat. 'The Royal British Legion Jubilee' was named by the Queen at Henley in July 1972, taking her on a short cruise to the Leander Club before setting off for the Orkneys, the Legion restraining itself from making any comment on the immediate deployment to Scottish waters.[9] There was a commemorative postage stamp and a new book on the Legion, *Red for Remembrance*, by a well-known broadcaster and journalist, Anthony Brown.

For the older members the mood of the 1971 celebrations was stilled the following year when it was announced during the Annual Conference that the Duke of Windsor, the former Prince of Wales, had died. Whatever other judgements might have been made on his life, they remembered him as their comrade-in-arms who had identified with the desperate situation of ex-servicemen after the Great War and who had come among them with compassion and understanding, particularly for the disabled and disfigured. 'We

*The prefix 'Royal' appears on the lifeboat funded by Legion voluntary subscriptions as part of the 1971 Jubilee Celebrations and launched by the Queen at Henley, from which it was sent to Scottish waters.*

have lost a mate,' they said, and they meant it. There were many tributes and a number of branches held services in his memory.[10]

## Publicity – and 'Miss RBL'

The Legion did not shy away from capitalizing on its anniversary. It desperately needed to bolster the Poppy Appeal income which was not competing with inflation. But it was the future that counted and that lay with the younger generation. New films were made: *Aftermath*, with a commentary by Lord Mountbatten, was later selected as one of the top charity films for showing at the National Film Theatre Festival. *One day in November* was targeted at youth and broadcast over the ITV network; this time a young naval officer undergoing helicopter training, the current Prince of Wales, spoke the commentary, the first occasion that he had done so for a charity.[11] Distinguished people, including current 'celebrities', were recruited as Friends of the Poppy Appeal and assisted with its annual launch.[12] And in 1972 the first 'Miss Royal British Legion' was crowned, Eve Holden from

Berkshire. It was not just a matter of looks or personality: Legion judges first grilled the contestants for their knowledge of the Legion's work and the winner was often already involved in some way with the charity. She needed to be knowledgable, her year's 'reign' involved appearances at Legion events and even, on occasion, addressing Conference.[13]

## Remember all who died

The Festival of Remembrance television broadcast also gave the Legion much publicity. But in 1971 the BBC decided that it would no longer be sent out live, but in an edited form. The Legion protested at the loss of audience involvement in what was for many an emotional experience, but the Corporation was adamant. As it turned out the edited version got higher audience ratings.[14]

In 1973 the Legion's Annual Conference resolved that at the annual Cenotaph service, instead of just remembering 'the dead of two world wars', the words 'all who had died in the service of their country' should be substituted. It seemed a sensible change, gathering in conflicts from Korea to Northern Ireland. But the Home Office at this stage simply took note of the proposal, too remote perhaps to understand that those who had served in the armed forces since 1945, and their families, felt no less strongly about their dead than the wartime generations. Conference, however, persisted and in 1979, following a further resolution, the government agreed to the re-wording.[15]

Another Conference resolution had asked that the two-minute silence be re-introduced on 11 November. But in this case the Legion's NEC decided not to press the matter, since it was felt that the government would be unlikely to agree, as turned out to be the case when the Home Secretary's views were sought.[16] And perhaps the timing was indeed wrong. Far from honouring the fallen there seemed to be a prevailing air of cynicism over wartime sacrifice, of concern to many Legion speakers and churchmen, reflected in (and fuelled by) television programmes and the film, *O What a Lovely War* – 'lying, horrid and tendentious' as one sermon put it on Remembrance Sunday in 1972.[17]

## 1976 – 1980

### Hard times persist

By the second half of the decade Britain's economic situation was at last showing signs of improvement. Even so, the Labour government, now under James Callaghan, only hung by a thread and it was no surprise when Margaret Thatcher's Conservatives came to power in 1979. But if the Legion thought that economic recovery or feminine compassion would mean less call on their resources they were mistaken. The new government was determined to cut public spending and looked to charitable organizations to make an even larger contribution to the community's social needs. With the Poppy Appeal still not raising sufficient money to meet current needs and the elderly of the Second World War now starting to reach the age where they needed even more care and attention there was much cause for concern.[18] Once again there were calls for the organization 'to stand up and be counted'. Once again the Legion stuck to its principle of no political involvement, demonstrations or any form of militancy. Even a proposal to form a Parliamentary Liaison Group was rejected on the grounds that such pressure groups could become party political footballs.[19]

## The parade at Windsor

Any gloom over the challenges facing the Legion was, at least for the moment, relieved by one event, the Queen's Silver Jubilee of 1977. The organization joined in the celebrations with enthusiasm. On a Sunday in June of that year a thousand Legion standard bearers assembled at Wellington Barracks in London, marching round the Victoria Memorial and up the Mall to a drumhead service on Horse Guards Parade attended by the Prince of Wales. Then it was straight into buses for the journey to Windsor, a packed lunch on every seat. Still more standards met them at Windsor and 2,700 were dipped in Royal Salute before the Queen on the Great Lawn. There was an inspection by Range Rover, a march-past and two standard bearers from the great throng were brought forward for the Queen to meet. Then the National President handed the Patron an illuminated address conveying to her the Legion's 'loyal and heartfelt congratulations'. All was accomplished with remarkable precision despite the lack of any rehearsal and the orders on the Great Lawn having to compete with the roar of aircraft passing overhead to nearby Heathrow.[20]

## A shift in attitude

Among the standards carried so proudly on parade that day were some from Northern Ireland. Here, despite the difficulties surrounding them, over eighty Legion branches carried on with looking after the frail and needy members of the ex-service community, four of these branches even straddling the so-called Peace Line. And not only did the Poppy Appeal continue to take place each year, but the province had the best results in the United Kingdom. Even the clubs thrived despite the threats of the terrorist bombers; it was said that the IRA were working their way through the telephone directory and were already past 'B'. South of the border, however, the Legion was deprived of one of its strongest supporters, when Earl Mountbatten was brutally murdered in 1979. He had also been President of the branch near his home in Romsey and there were seventy-five standards at his funeral.

Memories were stirred of earlier but equally vicious terrorist activities when an 'In Memoriam' notice was published in the *Daily Telegraph* in 1980. It referred to the Stern Gang, a particularly repugnant Jewish organization which had callously murdered British soldiers, and many others, during the Palestine Mandate. Although the paper's editor apologized to the Legion, it seemed to many to be symptomatic of a shift in public attitudes towards the forces of law and order, particularly the Army, despite bearing the brunt of the peacekeeping in Northern Ireland. Radio and TV programmes now often appeared to go out of their way to denigrate members of the armed forces, so much so that the Legion's President urged members to complain. But the mood also reflected a fear of nuclear war and, following the deployment of cruise missiles in the United Kingdom, white poppies made a reappearance in the late 1980s. Legion members regarded them with no more favour than their fathers fifty years before. They had no place on memorials to the fallen: 'The blood pouring from a soldier is not white'.[21]

Remembrance too remained under attack. A columnist in the *Daily Express* called it a 'hollow sham' in 1976, but of more concern to some Legion members was the absence of maroons in London that year to mark the beginning and end of the two-minute silence. A tradition since 1920, it was now abandoned on grounds of cost: each maroon required two constables on duty and they had to be trained. The decision apparently saved the time of ninety-six policemen, but Shard End No 1 Branch were so angry that they struck the Home Secretary, their local MP, off their list of Vice Presidents. There was some indignation in 1977 when the Romsey Branch Majorettes took part in the local Remembrance Sunday parade, but the ensuing correspondence was more in favour than against; the girls had helped with the Poppy Appeal and they marched with dignity.[22]

Undeterred by the public mood the Legion's Conference again pressed in 1979 for the two-minute silence to be restored on 11 November. But the timing was clearly still not right and the Council again stayed their hand.

## 1981 – 1985

### The Falklands factor

Mrs Thatcher's policies, involving as they did control of the money supply and a cutback in public expenditure, were hardly popular. There was large-scale unemployment, adding to the problems of charities such as the Legion. But inflation was brought under control, and this would help the Legion in its fundraising as well as in its benevolent activities, now much concerned with bricks and mortar in order to make proper provision for the incasing numbers of elderly and infirm.

The Falklands War of 1982 not only restored the government's popularity but had important consequences for the Legion. The NEC had given an immediate donation of £10,000 to the Task Force Commander for welfare, anticipating the South Atlantic Fund launched in response to the public's desire to help. Many Legion branches made their own contributions, but the Legion itself had some concern over such a fund: after immediate needs had been met the residue would go to service charities, but from past experience it knew that the problems would eventually arrive on the Legion's doorstep.

Television brought this far-away war into the family living room and progress was keenly followed. Legion Areas arranged to help families of those on the casualty lists, although the need not to intrude on grief was stressed. Fortunately casualties were relatively low and when the victorious troops returned there was a spirit of euphoria, ensuring the government's re-election the subsequent year. Meanwhile from within the Legion some £30,000 had been raised, of which the donors had earmarked only £2,500 for the South Atlantic Fund, the rest going to the Legion's Benevolent Fund. The message had gone home: in this war, as with previous wars, the long-term need would be the greatest.

But when the cheering had died away, comparisons began to be made between the level of pensions awarded to Falklands veterans and widows and those of earlier campaigns, especially the pre-1973 widows. There was different treatment too over visits to war cemeteries: no one would wish to deny the Falklands widows the opportunity to visit their husbands' graves, but for nearly forty years there had been no government provision for the widows and mothers of those killed in the Far East to make a similar journey and many had died without seeing the last resting-place of a loved one.

The Legion would use both of these factors to pressurize the government into bringing the older generation of the ex-service community in line with their younger counterparts. It would also benefit from a substantial increase in the public response to the Poppy Appeal after the Falklands War.[23]

## The changing face of Remembrance

Representatives of the units that had served in the Falklands received loud acclaim at the Festival of Remembrance that year. The event itself had lost none of its spectacle and was regarded as one the top BBC programmes of the week. Small changes were made from time to time: the Royal British Legion Scotland standard appeared in the muster in 1981 and 1983 saw the first Legion youth band in the programme. But the standard of community singing, at least in the view of some, had declined, despite being led by Ralph Reader personally; it seemed that the audience were less and less familiar with the old tunes. They might perhaps have taken a lead from a choir of thirteen Chelsea Pensioners who in 1976 had brought the house down with their rendition of 'Goodbye Dolly Gray'. Dramas were fortunately few – the Princess of Wales provided well-publicized confusion in 1983 by arriving ten minutes late – but a reminiscence by Raymond Baxter, who had acted as commentator since 1951, could cite only infrequent mishaps: one occasion when the poppies fell early and another when the Legion's distinguished President forgot his lines on giving the Exhortation. However, the Regimental Sergeant Major still worried about the various contingents losing step as they came into the arena.[24]

Across the water there was a change in 1984 when for the first time the Irish Government and Defence Forces attended the Remembrance Day Service in St Patrick's Cathedral in Dublin, still organized by the Legion. Despite some controversy, it raised the profile of Remembrance and Poppy Day in the Republic and the Legion's standard paraded alongside those of the Defence Forces, symbolizing the better relationships that were to be formalized with the Anglo-Irish Accord the following year.[25] But on the other side of the border, in Newry, the wreaths had to be removed from the war memorial on the evening of Remembrance Day as vandals would otherwise have thrown them in the river.[26]

## 'Robbing the poor box'

The Legion itself, along with other charities, would have liked to throw the VAT rulebook in the river. The tax was now 15 per cent and cost the Legion more than £200,000 a year, money which the public had subscribed to assist the needy rather than the Chancellor of the Exchequer. Local authorities were excused VAT on council homes for the elderly. Why could the Legion not be similarly exempt on their residential homes?[27] The irony was that, with government restrictions on public spending accompanied by stress on self-reliance, the charities were being expected to do even more. The Legion's Chairman summed it up: 'Legal robbery from the poor box'.[28]

At this time the Legion was rated sixteenth in a list of charities based on income and headed by Oxfam. It fell below the leading cancer charities (although just above the RSPCA), but like them it had to cope with the by-products of the age, in this case illnesses apparently arising from the Atomic Tests in the 1950s and 60s, foreshadowing future disputes of this sort based on modern forms of warfare. In 1983 the government agreed to set up an inquiry and in the meantime the Legion assisted those who feared their health was damaged.

In another sign of the times, a narrow majority at the 1985 Annual Conference called for the Ministry of Defence to clear the names of those men shot for cowardice in the First World War. They would, it was argued, now be classified as simply suffering from a traumatic stress disorder. But there was by no means a general agreement on the matter. Many in the Legion took the view that the verdicts had been in accord with the law at the time and that it was not right for one generation to sit in judgement on another.[29]

## The Legion's Sixtieth

Celebrations for the sixtieth anniversary of the Legion were centred on the Midlands with a reception in Birmingham followed by a Rededication Service at Coventry Cathedral. Although they followed small but ugly outbursts of rioting in some inner-city areas, including Birmingham, in the event all went well. Nonetheless the Queen heard the Archbishop of Canterbury refer to the 'dangerously combustible state' of the country when she attended the service in Coventry. But outside all was normality when the Legion standards were marched past her to the cheers of the crowd. Appropriately the first Poppy Ball held in London also took place in the Diamond Jubilee year, while Earl Haig's granddaughter named a locomotive after the Legion. The machinery thus honoured may or may not have given ten years useful service but certainly the lifeboat the Legion had presented on an earlier anniversary in 1971 was still going strong, having saved forty-seven lives to date.[30]

# 1986 – 1990

## A Time of change

The closing years of the decade saw the collapse of the Soviet empire in Eastern Europe. For the moment at least tensions were relieved and the mood sat well with the increasing prosperity of most British people. Mrs Thatcher had won her third election victory in 1987 and in a society of house-owning two-car families the opposition parties sought to follow the Conservatives to the middle ground. The political sense of this move became apparent as public opinion began to turn against the government, culminating in the revolt against the 'Poll Tax' and forcing Thatcher's resignation in late 1990.

The new prosperity did not by any means reach down into every corner of society. Amid all the good living there were still the poor, among them the impoverished and elderly victims of two world wars. There were the former prisoners of war of the Japanese, now in their sixties and seventies, many still suffering the effects of their brutal incarceration. The government had not hesitated to subsidize Japanese car investment in Britain to the tune of £200 million.[31] Whatever the economic justification, it seemed bizarre in comparison to Japan's indifference towards these men, some 50,000 in total, but declining. There was a flicker of hope in 1988 when the United Nations' Human Rights Commission agreed to hear compensation claims against Japan by Canadian ex-servicemen, but it led to nothing.[32]

## Veterans Affairs – a new campaign

The Legion and the other ex-service organizations dealt continuously with government departments over a range of matters affecting ex-servicemen and dependants, from war widows pensions to wooden legs. The organization of government meant that some eleven or twelve different departments were involved. Apart from a section of the DSS specializing in war pensions, few of the officials dealing with these matters had any special knowledge of the ex-service community or their problems and, as the war and national service faded into the mists of time, little affinity with the people concerned. Cases might be referred back through ignorance or shuttlecocked between departments in classic bureaucratic style. The outcome was often unnecessary delay, which in human terms meant hardship.

Other countries had long since set up Departments of Veterans Affairs, a solution which the Legion had for some time pondered. There need be no reorganization of existing government departments; the new agency would simply be a focal point to which all ex-service matters could be addressed and which would then co-ordinate the work of the specialist departments involved. It would therefore need only a small staff, but the minister at its head would represent ex-service interests in government.[33]

It seemed a simple and practical solution and the 1987 Legion Conference endorsed it wholeheartedly, noting that the increasing age and frailty of many ex-service people lent a degree of urgency to the proposal. But the government did not agree. Addressing the 1989 conference, a DSS minister told delegates that the suggestion would not result in a better service; it would simply add another layer of administration to the process. The Legion, accustomed to initial rebuffs on matters of this sort, was undismayed. The campaign was clearly not going to be easy, but it would be pursued with vigour. And, with an eye to possible political changes, it secured from the opposition what seemed to be a firm committment to setting up such a department.[34]

## The 'peace dividend'

As the decade drew to a close the sudden and dramatic events in the Soviet Union and the disintegration of the Warsaw Pact meant that NATO no longer seemed to have a role. The politicians were not slow to react and initiated cuts in the armed forces, under the euphemism 'Options for Change'. Many who had intended to follow a service career would now be looking for jobs in a workplace already affected by redundancies resulting from the goverment's tight economic policies. Unless they received proper retraining and help with jobfinding the latest batch of ex-servicemen would simply finish up on state benefits. Their 'redundancy packages' might appear generous, but few servicemen had their own houses and high property costs put such payments in perspective.

The Legion, together with other ex-service organizations, promptly made contact with the Ministry of Defence to express their concern that proper arrangements should be made for the resettlement and rehabilitation of those leaving. In the long run the ex-service charities would be faced with the consequences.[35]

Legion involvement in the resettlement of ex-servicemen and women, particularly in the training field, would develop in the 1990s, but it would need substantial funding at a time when there was increasing competition among charities and PR became even more important. There were now two modern mobile display units travelling the country, while a new video acknowledged by its title that there was still much ignorance about the

Legion's work: it was called *I Didn't Know They Did That*. By 1989 there were eleven buses in Legion livery in public use on the roads and in 1990 the winner of its class in a rally was an Army-crewed car carrying the Legion's name. In every sense the Legion was determined to move with the times.[36]

## 1991 – 1995

### The Gulf War

Following the Iraqi invasion of Kuwait in 1990, an American-led multi-national force, which included a substantial British element, drove out the invaders in a short but decisive battle. Despite fears of high casualties, particularly from Iraqi chemical weapons, there were only seventeen British deaths. But some of the British troops involved already had in their pockets their 'marching orders' as a result of the defence cuts. If they needed

*A Legion Christmas parcel delivery aboard a Royal Fleet Auxiliary vessel.*

*"* THE SPANISH LEGION IN MOSTAR, THE FRENCH FOREIGN LEGION
IN SARAJEVO AND NOW THE BRITISH LEGION HERE!*"*

*This cartoon accompanied a thank-you letter from one of the recipients of a Legion Christmas parcel. Based on a real query from a puzzled local, it was widely circulated among British forces in Croatia and Bosnia-Herzegovina.*

any further blows to their morale, they had only to read the newspapers: at home the recession was deepening with many companies going bankrupt.

Their morale had been very much in the Legion's mind. Such was the media coverage that the forces involved could hardly be called a 'forgotten army', but they were a long way from home and facing an unpredictable foe. With the force deployed and awaiting battle, in the space of three weeks the Legion ensured that each man and woman in the British force, whatever their location, received a parcel by Christmas Day. Much thought was given to the contents: as well as toiletries they included sweatbands and a torch. The Legion also supplied phonecards and sports equipment and the whole operation was supported by an appeal which raised some £500,000.[37]

As with the earlier Falklands conflict a family support network was set up at home, making use of the Legion's structure which extended to every part of the country. Fortunately it was not tested. Nor was it necessary, in view of the light casualties, to organize a collection for a Gulf Fund, a task which the Legion had been asked to undertake.[38]

The parcel distribution proved so popular that it was repeated the following year – there were still forces in place to ensure Iraqi compliance with the Peace Treaty – and later extended to other areas where British forces were serving. By 1993 parcels were being sent to Bosnia, Belize, Cambodia and the Falklands, as well as Saudi Arabia. They continued to be gratefully received; one recipient in the former Yugoslavia wrote: 'It brought me cheer at this time of the year in this land of desperation.'[39]

### The Kohima epitaph

The Legion's Seventieth anniversary in 1991 was marked by a Service of Thanksgiving in Westminster Abbey. The address by the Dean of Windsor, the Right Reverend Michael Mann, was outstanding and moving and he was invited to be the National Chaplain.[40]

The same year saw the origin of a new tradition in Legion services of Remembrance. Following a visit to the Kohima battlefield, the turning point of the war against the Japanese, the Legion's National President suggested that the stirring words on the 2nd Division Memorial *'When you go home, tell them of us and say, for your tomorrow we gave our today'* should be included in the services. And so they were, giving even greater meaning to such occasions.

Thought by many to have had its origins in an ancient Spartan epitaph, the wording was attributed to one of a collection of suggested First World War memorial inscriptions.*[41]

### 'Options for Change'

Following its earlier discussions with the Ministry of Defence, in late 1991 the Legion organized a seminar to thrash out the problems arising from the defence cuts resulting from the disappearance of the Soviet threat. It was attended not only by service chiefs and representatives of ex-service organizations but by leading figures in banking and industry. Thus it was able not only to identify difficulties but come up with realistic solutions. These would form the basis of an ongoing dialogue with the MOD.[42]

The cuts themselves were mainly in the Army, with some 64,000 due to leave by the Spring of 1995. Meanwhile the recession, the longest since 1945, continued and unemployment rose remorselessly. The Legion was now working closely with the other leading organization in its field – the Soldiers' Sailors' and Airmen's Families Association (SSAFA)† and it had been agreed that SSAFA should deal with the housing aspects of the matter while the Legion took on retraining and employment.

The Legion already ran a small training centre in the North West at Ellesmere Port and it now used this expertise to set up a much larger establishment at Tidworth in Wiltshire, which had the advantage of being accessible to many more service units. There was no delay; a start was made in temporary accommodation provided by the military while a permanent site was developed. Tidworth also trained the wives, a hitherto neglected contingent in service redundancy, acknowledging that they might well have to support the family in civil life while their husbands sought employment; moreover it now took two incomes to support a mortgage. In the spirit of the times the Legion obtained part of the funding for the new centre from the European Community, the rest being sought by an appeal.[43]

For their part the MOD appointed a major general to oversee the in-service part of the resettlement process and as a result the operation achieved much impetus. Whether this would have been the case had the Legion and the other ex-service organizations not raised the profile in the way they did can only be a matter for conjecture. At any rate, through the efforts of all those involved, the aim was achieved and thousands of men and their families made a successful transition to civil life.[44]

*By J.M. Edmonds and entitled *Inscriptions Suggested for War Memorials*, published in 1919.

†Retitled the Soldiers, Sailors, Airmen *and* Families Association in 1997, on amalgamation with Forces help.

*The D-Day Commemorations: A Lancaster bomber scatters poppy petals in mid Channel. The Queen and the Duke of Edinburgh review the veterans on the beach at Arromanches; the Legion and other veterans organizations' standards are in the foreground.*

## A time to remember – and a time to celebrate

While one generation was being thus assisted, thoughts were turning back to mighty events in which their fathers and grandfathers had taken part. 1994 and 1995 were significant anniversaries in the nation's life: fifty years before, in June 1944, the allies had landed in Normandy and victory in both Europe and the Far East had been achieved the following year.

At first the government proposed a 'family day out' in Hyde Park to commemorate D-Day; 'spam fritters' was the suggestion of the Department of National Heritage. The Legion and the other ex-service organizations were appalled at this insensitive suggestion. They remembered the invasion chiefly in terms of human sacrifice and the government hastily revised their views. Any celebrations would be carried over until 1995; the 1944 anniversary would be remembered on the beaches where so many died. The Legion chartered the liner *Canberra* as a flagship for the veterans and on 5 June she sailed, part of a vast assembly of ships ranging from yachts to a US aircraft carrier, reviewed by the Queen in the Royal Yacht. There was a poignant moment when a Lancaster bomber scattered poppy petals on the waves and an equally moving service on the beach at Arromanches.[45]

The following year, on the

*Led by the Legion's National Standard and that of The Royal British Legion Scotland, Legion Standards are paraded through Hyde Park in 1995 as part of the VE Day commemorations.*

*The two minutes silence: the campaign for the reintroduction of a silence on November 11th included the 'Pause to Remember' slogan, here used as a title of a Legion yacht which competed in a round England race.*

evening of 8 May, with the Legion's President and the national standard at her side, the Queen lit a beacon in Hyde Park, the signal for a chain of a thousand beacons to flare throughout the land. Two days before, the Legion had organised an open-air concert in Hyde Park; at the close the same Lancaster bomber, escorted by a Spitfire and a Hurricane, flew low overhead, stirring even deeper emotions in the vast audience than the old wartime songs.[46] London might be the centre of attention, but VE and VJ days were celebrated with no less vigour and enthusiasm in the towns and villages: a Legion branch in remote Flintshire organized a street party for 650 children, the largest in Britain it was claimed.[47]

334

In August Second World War veterans marched past Buckingham Palace, the Duke of Edinburgh leaving the Queen's side to join them. The theme was 'Tribute and Promise' – tribute to those who had achieved these two great victories and a promise that they and those who had depended on them would have the nation's care. It was an undertaking that might perhaps have attracted a wry smile from those who had been prisoners of the Japanese. Half a century on their cause was still being fought: the latest government response to a further Legion approach in 1992 was that compensation had been paid under the 1951 Peace Treaty, when each man had received some £76, and 'the Treaty obligations preclude any further approach'. The Prime Minister did however promise to raise the matter on a visit to Japan the following year to promote trade. It was hardly the best platform for an approach and nothing came of it except a rather obscure apology from the Japanese Prime Minister 'to the war's victims' on VJ Day. With whatever they might make of that, the former prisoners-of-war had to be content.[48]

The Legion itself wrote to the Japanese Prime Minister when it was refused permission to lay a VJ day wreath on a war memorial in County Hall, the former home of the Greater London Council, currently being developed by a Japanese company. This time the Japanese gave way and the National Chairman, together with the County Hall Branch Chairman laid their wreath.[49]

### 'The eleventh hour of the eleventh month'

The very success of the Legion's involvement with these commemorative events, however, might have branded it as living in the past. It was important that it should be seen as a contemporary charity and at the beginning of 1995 the 'logo' was changed as part of a re-launch. The new design dispensed with the Legion's badge, instead linking the word 'Legion' to the poppy, which the public did not always associate with the Legion itself. The badge's removal caused some criticism within the organization itself, but the new design won praise in the world at large.[50]

Even so, now that the festivities were over is seemed that the ex-service cause might once again slip from the public mind. It was then that the Legion had an inspired thought. There had long been strong support within the organisation for the reintroduction of the two-minute silence on 11 November at 11 a.m. – 'the eleventh hour of the the eleventh month' – to many a significant and emotive phrase. A resolution at the 1995 Conference came before the Council. Once more there were those who thought that, whatever the merits of the idea, it was simply impossible to bring the nation to a halt each year in the middle of a busy working day; it was trying to put the clock back. But this time the other view prevailed. With only six weeks to prepare, the Legion embarked on a new campaign – 'pause to remember' – and newspaper editors, TV producers, leaders of commerce and industry were canvassed. With the events of VE and VJ Days fresh in their minds, of which a two-minute silence had been a part, there was a surprising level of support. Political leaders were in favour and on 11 November that year more than half of the population observed the silence, according to a later poll which also indicated that well over 90 per cent would like to see it repeated in 1996. After seventy-five years the Legion could still stir the nation's conscience.[51]

The success of the two-minute silence brought Remembrance full circle. In 1919 'even the cynics' had kept the silence. Much had happened since. But, despite all of the changes that had taken place in the world, those that made the sacrifice for their country were still honoured; 'tell them of us' ran the Kohima epitaph. The Legion had not only done so but ensured that their families too were held in special regard.

*A new generation recognizes the sacrifice which war brings: schoolchildren observe the silence on November 11th*

# CHAPTER 17

## STRUCTURE 1971-2001

# *Towards Change*

## 1971 – 1975

**The new generation of Chairmen**

At the 1973 Annual Conference of the Legion the National President invested the Chairman with a chain of office. The recipient of this impressive new adornment, presented by South Eastern Area, was Colonel Hughes. Hughes had taken over the chairmanship from Dennis Cadman the previous year, referring to his predecessor's 'magnificent record of achievement'. It was no exaggeration: the first Second World War man to lead the Legion, Cadman had been an outstanding representative of his generation, young, active and assured. Now, as a still youthful 'elder statesman', he was to add to those achievements with his work on housing (see page 360).[1]

Nor was there any slackening of the pace under Jimmy Hughes, an academic from Belfast, a TA colonel and a man active in many fields. He was certainly one of the most vigorous chairmen the Legion had known, travelling the length and breadth of the country to meet members in branches, clubs and Counties, and his successor would refer to him as 'the nearest thing to perpetual motion that I know'. It was in character that Hughes had signed his Legion application form even before he had finished putting on civilian clothes at the demobilization depot in early 1946; there was simply no time to waste.[2]

Hughes handed over to Charles Busby in 1975. Busby too was of the new generation; he had spent the war flying with the RAF and his election breached a hitherto unbroken line of Army Chairmen lasting back to 1921. Of a quiet and thoughtful disposition, he too had outstanding qualities of leadership and the Legion was highly fortunate at this difficult time to have had three chairmen of such ability in succession. Moreover, all three would go on to enhance the organization's reputation in distinct fields – housing, the Poppy Appeal and at Aylesford.[3]

**Can the staff hold office?**

No matter how competent any Chairman or other elected office-holder might be, he would seldom take a policy decision without staff advice. The reciprocal was that the staff might offer advice but they did not take policy decisions. Nonetheless the staff were also expected to be Legion members. As such they were entitled to play a part in its affairs; the question was – to what extent?

In 1928 Conference had ruled that no staff member could hold an elected Legion office above branch level. In 1973 Counsel's opinion was sought: it was that under the Charter any member was entitled to hold any office. Despite this, after much discussion the Council decided that anyone paid £50 or more a year by the Legion could hold office only below Area. Therefore a staff member could also be a County Chairman, but not Area Chairman. The matter was again raised in 1976; once more Counsel's opinion was that no employee could be banned from any elected office; but the rule remained.[4] It not only prevented an existing staff member from seeking, say, membership of the NEC, but also an existing Council member from taking a post on the staff. Whatever the legal niceties it was felt to be better to have a clear division between staff and elected officers.

The staff's ambitions generally lay with their work. But sometimes a move was in the Legion's interest as, for instance, in 1971 when the highly capable Major Rivers, who had inspired the Legion's Housing Association, left the Service Department to become the Association's Director. With his departure the department again became two: Benevolence; and Pensions and Employment. Rivers had been with the staff for twenty-five years when he moved on, as had Major Tomlins on his appointment as Assistant Secretary when the post was re-instituted in 1973.[5] The same year the General Secretary, Coffer, was made CBE, while there was sorrow at the death of J.R. Griffin, Coffer's predecessor and the architect of the Legion's constitution.[6]

## Boundary – and other – disputes

The Legion was already re-examining its own internal structure when the government plan to change a number of county boundaries was unfolded in 1972 and the working party concerned was tasked to examine the implications. The government announcement had caused much concern in the Legion Counties affected; it was seen as a Whitehall exercise which ignored local character and traditional loyalties, such as those to the county regiment.

It made sense, however, to conform. In both benevolent work and the organization of the Appeal the Legion had to work with the county authorities and plainly to use different boundaries would complicate matters. Somewhat reluctantly therefore the working party recommended that Legion boundaries too should change. But local feelings by now were running high. When the National Chairman addressed Somerset County Conference in early 1974, telling them 'not to get in a tizzie' over changes his advice was ignored: the delegates voted overwhelmingly to keep their present boundaries. By the Legion Conference the following year the opposition had become organized and, although the margin was narrow, the proposals were defeated. Only the Poppy Appeal, which effectively operated its own structure, adopted the new boundaries.[7]

The dispute overshadowed the other activities of the Legion working party, which had sought to reduce the workload at Area level and to strengthen Counties. Indeed at the 1972 Annual Conference Gloucester County had called for the abolition of Areas, calling them little more than expensive post offices. But the main outcome of the study was a pilot scheme to shift some Area benevolent work to headquarters.[8]

None of this affected the Legion in Ireland. There the disagreements were more emphatic. In 1971 the Area office in Dublin had been severely damaged by a bomb, reported as the work of the 'Angry Brigade', and the 1972 Area Conference had to be cancelled, the officers being elected by postal ballot. In Belfast the building which housed the Northern Ireland Area office lost over 100 windows in a bomb attack in 1973; had an unattended suitcase not been spotted by an army corporal there might have been much loss of life. A number of branches and clubs in the Province were also targeted: many routinely entertained groups of troops, while individual members invited soldiers for Christmas; all refused to be intimidated.[9]

338

## Associate Membership

No doubt such hospitality influenced some servicemen towards joining the Legion when they returned to civil life. But, although Legion membership had shown a small increase in 1971, its fiftieth anniversary year, not enough young ex-servicemen were coming into the organization. Meanwhile an increasing number of non ex-service people made use of the clubs through Honorary Legion Membership. A move to introduce a new form of membership for such 'civilians', Associate Membership, had been narrowly defeated in 1970; but discussion continued and by the 1972 Conference opinion had moved just sufficiently to make the change. It meant that over 90,000 more people would pay Legion branch subscriptions; at first these were at half the rate paid by Ordinary Members, but by 1976 Associates were paying the full rate.[10]

Honorary Membership was now for serving members of HM Forces only. A proposal for Family Membership had been dropped, following objections from the Women's Section, who saw it as affecting their membership. But, while most of the new Associate category were interested only in the clubs, some wished to play a part in the life of their branches and their place in the Legion would become an increasingly important issue.

Branch life could still be very active, even in the diminishing rural segment. In Boldon, County Durham, the carnival had been organized by the Legion branch since 1948. Such events remained popular: Charlbury, in Oxfordshire, gymkhana and fete was swamped with entries while for Eardisley Branch's stampede, with heifers loaned by the local Herefordshire farmers, the ground was fortunately soft after rain. Both urban and country branches ran outings for senior citizens, laid on angling competitions or organized their own pilgrimages. But others did nothing except keep an eye open for those in need of help, turn out for the Remembrance service each year and perhaps hold an annual dinner; it all depended on the local leadership.[11]

Some branches were still uneasy about the presence of women. A *Legion Journal* article by Antwerp Branch in Belgium, inadvertently revealing that they did not invite women members to meetings to save them embarrassment, provoked indignation. It was suggested that the Antwerp ladies should follow the example of Birmingham Central: finding it difficult to gain admission to a Legion Branch in 1947 the ex-servicewomen had formed their own all-women branch, the only one in the Legion proper (as opposed to the Women's Section), and at its twenty-fifth anniversary dinner in 1972 there was a silver jubilee message of congratulation from the Queen.[12]

## The clubs flourish

Thanks, in part, to the new Associates, club membership was still rising. Existing clubs were constantly being enlarged to cope with the intakes and new ones were being built in the large housing estates springing up around the country: one such in Gloucester raised the branch strength from thirty-five to 500 in eight months. Morpeth Club was a showpiece: costing £82,000 it had a concert room and games room and a couple of bowling greens. Sheldon in Birmingham owned a three-storey building with parking for 200 cars, a concert room seating 360 with a sprung dance floor and a £3,000 organ; there was even a 'Spanish' lounge with real marble pillars. Sheldon was an 'Ivy Leaf' club, meaning that had its origins in the 'Federation', one of the bodies that had formed the Legion (see page 2).[13]

The clubs were sufficiently close to the Legion to bear the new 'Royal' title. Yet they were still only able to give minimal assistance to the Legion's work: of some £500,000 donated each year two-thirds went to the parent branch, mainly to improve the club premises. Nearly all of the rest went to local charities, leaving under 2 per cent for the Poppy Appeal. The Legion's leaders might tactfully note that 'the clubs are reaching out to the whole community', but, as they well knew, the Appeal was at its lowest ebb.[14]

## A Conference traumatised

Nevertheless a club would often pay for the branch delegates to attend the Annual Conference. For the smaller branch it was sometimes difficult to send a representative. The Legion assisted with the fares, but the cost of accommodation could be a deterrent. In 1972 the veteran Cardiff delegate, Jim Prince, personally endowed a fund to help smaller branches to send a delegate to Conference. It was a generous gesture from a man who strongly believed in the Legion's democratic processes; yet the overall branch representation at Conference remained small, on average about one in every five branches sending a delegate.[15]

Over a thousand delegates were, however, present at the Albert Hall in 1971 to hear the award of the 'Royal' prefix announced by the Legion President, General Sir Charles Jones. It would be the last time that Conference met at the Albert Hall, or indeed anywhere in London, in the twentieth century. The pattern was now to alternate between the North and the South of the country and the following year it took place in the Isle of Man, an old favourite since 1947. But Conference was almost traumatized by the level of security that accompanied the guest speaker, Lieutenant General Sir Harry Tuzo, the military commander in Northern Ireland; the mover and seconder of a vote commending the high standards of behaviour of the troops in the troubled province could hardly get their words out, prompting an exasperated Northern delegate to exclaim, 'What's the matter with them? We should all be very grateful to our troops. Why don't they say so?'[16] Group Captain Leonard Cheshire, the wartime bomber VC and post-war founder of the Cheshire Homes, was guest speaker in 1973, receiving a standing ovation after his rejection of war as a means of solving disputes and his call for the restoration of the two-minute silence on 11 November. The next year's conference saw a fierce confrontation between the Chairman and a delegate who wanted the Charter changed to enable his branch to appeal to Conference against an NEC ruling. Such a provision would have brought the Legion's administration to a standstill, but the delegate persisted until an exasperated Chairman, unanimously supported by the floor, expelled him. Conference was about policy-making, not solving local quarrels, and in 1975 the NEC considered substituting a shorter two-day 'business conference'; but Areas did not support the idea. It would probably not have worked anyway that year, which saw the acrimonious debate over boundaries, attended by 'solid battalions of Legionaries from all over the country'.[17]

## The Journal's problems continue

A 1974 conference motion had sought to close down the *Legion Journal*. The motion was defeated, but the magazine undoubtedly had problems. At a monthly circulation of around 40,000 it lost three pence on each five pence copy, partly due to an earlier decision to use the Legion Press. A big increase in paper costs led in 1974 to a change to tabloid newspaper format and to a price rise the next year to ten pence. But, although the tabloid format was popular – it carried much local Legion news – the price rise lost another 10,000 readers. These could not be recovered and by the end of the decade distribution had sunk to 28,000. In the meantime a re-launch had been planned: from early 1980 a commercial publisher would produce a bi-monthly magazine at new cover price of thirty pence and sold by the Legion, who received copies at a discount. But the editor would be supervised by a Legion board.[18]

In the immediate post-war period circulation had reached 120,000 copies, despite the meagre size and drab layout. The new format, based on brighter copy and more entertainment, sought to recover some at least of those lost readers.

# 1976 – 1980

## Finances and inflation

The magazine's financial problems were insignificant compared with those of the Legion itself. In principle the Appeal maintained the reserves, whose investment income provided the spending money. But inflation and the falling value of collections meant that the investment income could no longer meet benevolent expenditure and part of the Appeal proceeds had to be used to pay the bills, further reducing investment. The General Treasurer's task would have been easier if he had been able to use some of the money that lay in branch coffers, often earning low interest; but any scheme to persuade branches to switch their investments to a Legion fund ran up against innate conservatism.[19]

The General Fund, which paid for the Legion's administration, was meanwhile kept afloat by a series of rises in the affiliation fee subscription. Although such increases were largely driven by inflation, they were invariably contested by Conference, who looked for economies instead. But in the end they had to be accepted and in the ten years from 1976 to 1985 a member's individual contribution rose from fifty pence to £1.50. In real terms these figures were not so dramatic, representing an increase from £2 to £2.50.[20]

In early 1980 the man who had piloted the Legion finances through these difficult times, the General Treasurer, K.C.G. Chambers, died and R.D. Wilson filled the post temporarily, being confirmed at the subsequent conference. By then there was also a new Legion Chairman, Captain Harry Whitehead, who had taken over in 1978. A wartime company commander in Burma, his rallying cry of 'One for Harry' was said to have made North Western Area membership the strongest in the Legion.

## A unionization attempt

A wind of change blew through the headquarters offices in 1978. Not only did David Coffer, the General Secretary, retire, but other senior staff either left or changed jobs. Coffer had completed nineteen years in the post, by coincidence exactly the same length of time as his two predecessors, Heath and Griffin. Over a period of nearly sixty years the Legion had known only three General Secretaries.

The Council chose a high-ranking officer, Air Vice Marshal Charles Maughan, to succeed Coffer. Maughan had wartime service in the Royal Navy prior to joining the RAF, had set a new record for the London-Paris air race in 1959 and held some very clear views on the Legion's role. He was the first, and perhaps the last, General Secretary to spend his lunchtimes jogging in Pall Mall.[21]

As GS, Maughan was responsible for the Legion staff who were, at least in the middle and higher echelons, mainly ex-service and not therefore inclined to be union-minded. Nevertheless a year or two earlier some of the Appeals staff had joined a union – the Association of Scientific, Technical and Managerial Staffs – with the result that the

National Executive Council now found it necessary to set up an Establishment Committee. The ASTMS negotiated an improved pay deal for the lower-paid staff and in 1979 sought to represent the staff in collective bargaining. When the NEC attempted to restrict their activities the union responded by asking that ACAS, the arbitration body, intervene. In the end ASTMS were allowed some rights, but they never gained a proper foothold in the Legion, which was as good an employer as circumstances would permit.[22]

### Some astute property deals

If the staff had any cause for complaint it would have been over the headquarters accommodation; it was now some thirty years since the repairs had been made to the bomb-damaged building the Legion had acquired in 1945 and it badly needed modernizing. In January 1980 work began, the staff moving to Haig House, the original headquarters at 26 Eccleston Square, since occupied by Metropolitan and South Eastern Areas and the Attendants Company. The Legion did well out of the Pall Mall upgrade: the owners of the building paid for the work, which was extensive and which enabled two floors to be sub-let, without any effect on the lease. The alterations took eighteen months, during which the Council met in the Royal Automobile Club opposite the headquarters building, and when the staff moved back in July 1981 they were joined by the Women's Section, the Officers' Association and the British Commonweath Ex-services League. In November of that year the Queen opened the smart new headquarters, to which the name Haig House had now been transferred, receiving from the Legion a nugget of Welsh gold to be used for Royal wedding rings, an imaginative idea, but one which sadly would not lend the marriages any greater stability.

*When the Queen opened the refurbished Legion headquarters in 1981, the Chairman, Mr Ron Buckingham, (left) presented her with a nugget of Welsh gold. The President, General Sir Patrick Howard-Dobson, is next to the Queen.*

As a result of the rebuild the value of the Legion's lease had increased enormously, at no cost and when 26 Eccleston Square was vacated the freehold was acquired and the building then sold. All of this constituted some smart property dealing on the Legion's part.[23]

### Clubs still booming

Legion clubs too were continuing to invest in property, normally held in the name of the branch, as the club boom continued. By 1980 there were over 1,060 clubs with some 630,000 club members; with a total Legion membership of around 740,000 this was a substantial, almost overwhelming, part of the whole. Yet club involvement in Legion activities was still small. The Legion's Housing Association, which had started in 1964, needed investment and offered a fair return; but the amount lent by the clubs never exceeded £40,000 at a time when they donated over £200,000 each year to outside charities. The clubs had their problems: legislation was still increasing by leaps and bounds and they needed help to interpret such provisions as the Control of Pollution Act, so that the headquarters had to expand its advisory services. These included financial advice for clubs in difficulty due to the current high interest rates, if the club was prepared to accept it. But the general mood was upbeat: the premises were well used: 'country and western' dances were all the rage and attracted people of every age and a club such as Herne Bay with 1,800 members had some activity almost every day of the week.[24]

There was continuing concern over the small number of men and women joining the Legion on leaving the services; even the number of serving (ie Honorary) members had halved during the 1970s. The clubs were an obvious draw but the ex-servicemen and women did not always understand the distinction between club and branch: on joining the branch they expected to be allowed to make use of the club. But a locally-popular club would have a full complement of Associate Members and it was difficult to explain why civilians were able to use a Legion club while an ex-serviceman had to wait his turn. Nevertheless recruiting drives in 1977 and 1978 had some success and in 1979 there was a pilot scheme to brief army audiences on the Legion. The 1978 campaign was inaugurated by the new Legion Chairman under the slogan 'Make it another one for Harry'.[25]

*Clubs continued to boom in the 1970s, often providing improved accommodation for their associated branch. In Antrim the Legion began in a hut but by 1981 was housed in the building below.*

## A new approach to youth

Some of the clubs had provided youth club facilities following the Legion's limited involvement in the early 1960s (see page 220). Now the policy was being reviewed[26] and in 1977 a new line was taken: instead of simply helping local youth clubs or, where needed, starting a Legion youth club, the aim was now to interest and involve the young people in the Legion's own work.[27] Some Counties, such as Sussex, sent teams to visit local schools to talk about the Legion and to show the latest Legion film. The impact could be gauged from the question and answer session and it was noticeable that at schools for the backward and deprived there was much more interest, the children identifying with the Legion's work for the disabled.[28] But a questionnaire sent out to all 3,600 branches in 1979 attracted only 100 responses. It established that some thirty branches were still helping local youth organisations like the Scouts while another twenty-

343

five ran their own activities for young people. These included sports teams, such as the 'Young Lions' run by Higher Bebbington in Derbyshire, and bands; the last were particularly popular and there had been three Legion youth bands on parade at a Youth Band salute at Horse Guards in London in 1977.

In 1979 the Legion sponsored a two-year scholarship to one of the United World Colleges and a fifteen-year-old girl, the daughter of an ex-serviceman, took a sixth form course at the Singapore College. It also continued to send young people on Outward Bound courses such as canoeing or rock climbing.[29] The work might be limited but it was still worthwhile.

### 'Not an easy' Conference

Young people had few concerns with the past. But for their elders an address by a German war widow to the 1976 Conference was a sign that the bitterness of the war years had receded. She told delegates that the organization she represented, the VdK, was made up equally of war widows and veterans. The following year the Conference was addressed by General Howard-Dobson, the Quartermaster General, who was to be the next Legion President, although delegates, and perhaps the General himself, were unaware of this at the time; whether the occasion was contrived or not it gave both sides the opportunity to take stock of the other. Although the 1977 Conference was restricted to two days, there was time for a lively debate on the clubs' contribution to the Poppy Appeal – a matter of some contention, as has already been noted – and it was accompanied by boos and cheers. The 1979 Conference was even more noisy: the NEC had taken a decision to sell Churchill Court, one of the convalescent homes, without asking Conference (see pages 362–3), and delegates did not hide their feelings. The Chairman's closing remark: 'It has not been an easy conference', was perhaps a little understated. By contrast the *Legion Journal* was moved to ask, 'Where has all the excitement and imagination gone?' after the 1980 Conference. But both would return in good measure.[30]

# 1981 – 1985

### Keeping on course

At the 1981 Annual Conference General Sir Patrick Howard-Dobson duly replaced General Sir Charles Jones as National President. Sir Patrick, a former cavalryman, had become a Legion member while still serving. He had also at one time been in the Home Guard; perhaps the fact that such a lively individual had been a member helped persuade Conference that year at last to admit Home Guardsmen to the Legion, some thirty years after the issue had first been debated. Towards the end of Conference the new Chairman was piped on to the platform. Ron Buckingham was the first former member of the Royal Navy to hold the office; a London businessman, he had already made his mark on the Legion as Chairman of the Poppy Factory and on handing over it could fairly be said that he had 'piloted the Legion dead on course'.[31]

Air Vice Marshal Maughan resigned as General Secretary in 1983. He had been five years in the post and, as the President told the 1983 Conference, although not everyone had agreed with his forthright style, it was driven by a sincere desire to do his best for the Legion and he had achieved much. He was replaced by the Assistant Secretary, Major

Bob Tomlins, who had been with the Legion for thirty-five years.[32] There was a sad and unexpected change in 1985 when Windsor Spinks, who had taken over from Buckingham as Chairman the previous year, died suddenly after only sixteen months in office. Spinks was part of the Legion 'family': the nephew of Major Tom Spinks, who had become the first Welsh-born National Chairman in 1956, he had made his mark as a young man in an impassioned speech on youth at the 1960 Conference (see page 217). The breach was filled by the Vice Chairman, Robert Scaife, and for the first time the Legion would be led by a former national serviceman. It was hardly an easy situation for the new chairman – under normal circumstances he would have expected a full three years as Vice Chairman as an introduction to high office – but Scaife, as befitted a sturdy Yorkshireman, rose to the occasion. At first a temporary NEC appointment, Scaife was confirmed in office by the 1986 Conference and would serve as Chairman for a total of four years.[33] He led a National Executive Council that now included its first woman; although the Women's Section officers had long attended NEC meetings they were not Council members. Mrs L.E. Gee was elected to the Council in 1984 and would be an outstanding chairman of the Standing Orders Committee; she would, however, tread a solitary path, the only woman member of the NEC in the current century.[34]

Although Captain Jim Prince had never served on the NEC, they had many times had the benefit of his advice at Conference. Disabled in the First World War and the most vigorous of delegates, yet with total loyalty to the organization he loved, Prince died in 1981. The Council stood in silent tribute.[35]

## A new forum – COBSEO

1982 saw the creation of COBSEO, an awkward-sounding acronym for the Confederation of British Service and Ex-service Organizations. An amalgamation of two existing committees, it opened the barrack gate onto civvy street by bringing together all those involved in a serviceman's welfare whether in or out of uniform. One of these committees had been born out of the Legion's War Pensions campaign in the 1950s and, in recognition of the Legion's leadership on ex-service issues, the Legion supplied the chairman. COBSEO continued the tradition and the departing Legion Chairman became its first Chairman.

The new body was large; there were fifty to sixty members. Depending on the viewpoint, it was either a remarkable indication of unity or a clear demonstration of the number of fingers in the service and ex-service pie. Essentially COBSEO was an 'umbrella' organization. Lacking any staff of its own – the Legion contributed the administrative support for its meeings – it mainly co-ordinated the campaign activities of its members, often those initiated by the Legion. But the component bodies retained the right to make direct representation to Government whenever they thought it necessary.[36]

## A plan to 'give Areas the chop'

Internally too, some felt the need for change. A paper in 1982 suggested that at all levels too many Legion officers were elected as a reward for long service rather than on merit. Even the NEC lacked experienced managers; it should co-opt people from outside the organization – a senior officer from each of the three services – as well as civilian professionals.[37] In 1984 a working party on the Legion's future structure presented the fruits of their labours to a special meeting. The most radical of their proposals was to improve efficiency by removing one of the Legion's organizational tiers. But there was more to it than that: the change would give the Counties a much greater role, the NEC itself would be trimmed a little, while Conference would concentrate on policy matters.

The *Legion Journal* nevertheless summed it up as: 'NEC plan gives Areas the chop'. And that was the issue on which the package came apart. Areas were venerable institutions and they attracted much loyalty. When the discussion paper was circulated to the grass roots the fun began. At a meeting with Area and County representatives in late 1984, as the NEC's minute book dryly records, 'considerable misunderstanding' was revealed. Undaunted the NEC pressed on and the matter was duly debated at the 1985 Conference. Several times the Council was accused of not allowing members enough time for prior discussion and, although the leadership retorted 'time is not on our side', nearly two hours of debate ended with a decision to defer the whole matter for three years.[38]

But the process of change had begun.

## The membership battle resumes

Difficulties were emerging too at grass-roots level. Ordinary Members were getting older and their numbers were starting to decline. Associate Members were often young and their numbers increasing, but usually the clubs were the attraction. In a small branch such as Shotley and Erwarton in Suffolk the same half-dozen members did everything, including running the annual jumble sale for Christmas gifts for the elderly, while the young people joined the urban Legion clubs nearby for the cheap beer and the social life.[39]

Nevertheless some Associates were prepared to help and a number had even joined for this reason. In 1982 the first change was made to the rules: at the branch's discretion two Associates might serve on the Committee. But to many long-standing Ordinary Members, especially in branches where the problem had not yet arisen, the idea of civilians playing even a small part in running an ex-serviceman's organization was an anathema. When there was a follow-up proposal the following year to allow Associates to hold branch office it was roundly defeated.[40]

The other solution was to recruit more Ordinary Members and, on the Legion's sixtieth birthday, the 1981 Conference had agreed a major change in the rules: this form of membership would now be open to serving members of the armed forces, hitherto only admitted to Honorary Membership. The service chiefs having given their approval, units were encouraged to appoint Legion liaison officers, while Legion branches and clubs were urged to invite servicemen to their functions.[41]

The response was disappointing. It seemed that many young servicemen identified the Legion with an earlier generation and even the senior service officers invited to address Area Conferences spoke of the 'Dad's Army' image, although, confusingly, this popular TV series concerned the Home Guard. A Legion presentation at Chelsea Barracks indicated that the main interest was in the clubs, but the guardsmen were not always made welcome and there was a low response to a questionnaire sent to servicemen being discharged. In 1983 therefore the National Executive Council decided on a recruiting programme aimed at those serving. A Membership Recruiting Officer was appointed and, in a pilot project, again supported by military commanders, began work among the units in the South West of England. When the Legion's role was properly explained there was more interest, but in the meantime the Ordinary membership continued to decline while the number of Associates increased.[42]

## The clubs in difficulty

The decline in Ordinary Members also affected the clubs. The clubs' contribution to the Legion's overall membership had been enormous, but many clubs were now in crisis, partly because of the effects of the depression, especially in the North and North West, but also due to weak management. The huge extensions of recent years had often been financed by brewery loans which, with bar profits falling, they were unable to repay. Many survived only because of the fruit machines.[43]

The Legion made strenuous efforts to help: there were visits by County teams and seminars, while Area staff devoted much of their time to club problems. In 1983 headquarters appointed a Club Management Advisor, but an expert view was that it would need a team of twenty-one such advisors to solve the problem, and the money could not be found, despite the large profits some clubs were still able to make. In any case by the time some of them woke up to their difficulties it was already too late.[44]

One way of increasing custom was to admit more Associates. Since 1969, the number of Associates had been governed by the '40:60 rule', which meant that 60 per cent of members had to be Ordinary Legion Members. But a motion to raise the percentage of Associates to forty-nine was defeated at the 1984 Conference. Some clubs were driven to ignore the rule, while others broke away from the Legion in order, as they saw it, to remain viable. By 1985 the number of Legion licensed clubs was beginning to fall.[45]

Even so some were still hostile to women. The National President told the 1985 Conference that he knew of one club where the local branch welfare committee had to meet upstairs so that women members of the committee could enter the building via the fire escape.[46]

## A communication gap

As the Legion moved through the 1980s it had become increasingly clear that there had to be some radical changes. The leaders recognized this and developed their plans, but in the Conference hall innovation was unwelcome. At first debate was restrained: 'Seldom were the embers fanned into flame . . . Why have recent conferences become such routine affairs?' asked the *Journal* in 1982. But as the ideas took form and shape there was a widening gulf between the platform and the floor: constructive motions were opposed, seemingly through lack of understanding and, although a sensitive soul would never have aspired to high Legion office, delegates' criticism of their leaders was sometimes wounding. The Llandudno Conference in 1984 appeared to indicate a shift in attitude: 'A gentle breeze has begun to blow' an observer noted, adding that there was a willingness to debate change constructively. But it was a false dawn. Conference's deferment of the important restructuring proposals the following year in Brighton once more put the leadership and the rank-and-file into opposing camps and the problem of communication seemed as intractable as ever.[47]

1986 – 1990

## The mood changes

Undismayed by this adversarial situation, the working party on restructuring re-convened, giving the proposals added credence and authority by setting them in the form of amendments to the Royal Charter as well as improving one of the original sticking points, County financing. This seemed to have some effect; when the matter was reviewed at the 1986 Conference it was decided to advance the decision to 1987. As the seconder to the resolution put it: 'Let's get on with it', but the meaning was not what it seemed to imply.

The following year Conference had the highest attendance for fifteen years, some of the Areas busing in delegates to oppose the motion, which of course provided for their dissolution. As the debate got under way any NEC hopes that their arguments would carry the day were soon dissipated: the queue of delegates at the rostrum microphone to oppose the motion was thirty deep; at the other microphone there were but three delegates. Obloquy was piled on the heads of the NEC and the motion was lost.[48]

The Legion's leaders were now in a dilemma. They knew that change was vital if the organization was to meet the needs of the future; they knew – or they thought they knew – what those changes should be; yet they were not communicating these ideas effectively to those who had put them in office. But while they pondered Communications Forums and the re-introduction of National Leadership Schools other events were astir which would provide that opportunity for change.[49]

The first of these was computerization. Business life was now being revolutionized by computers and neither the Legion nor any other charity could afford to be left behind. In the Legion's case computers offered not only vastly increased efficiency but better communication with the membership. In consultation with experts a plan was made. Although the welfare work and fundraising would ultimately benefit, the first priority was to get the whole of the membership on to a computer: this would enable each member to be sent a *Legion Journal* so that all could be made aware of the issues confronting the organization. In conjunction with modern electronic banking such a database would allow subscriptions to be collected in new ways, easing the task of branches and bringing in the money sooner. Finally it would provide the opportunity to develop marketing schemes to members, offering them the benefits of group discounts while providing the Legion itself with useful additional income.[50]

So much for the plan; but would the Legion accept it? This time no stone would be left unturned in getting the message across: meetings and seminars at branch, County and Area level paved the way and at the vital Area Chairmen's meeting in early 1988 support was unanimous. There was of course some opposition among the rank-and-file: a number of branches indicated that they would not co-operate either on principle or because they felt unable to cope due to age and inflexibility. Nevertheless Conference 1988 was supportive and at the 1989 Conference the proposals were overwhelmingly endorsed, even the doubling of the Affiliation Fee to £3 in order to meet the cost of the change.[51]

The pendulum was now beginning to swing and the following year Conference agreed to instruct a firm of management consultants to carry out a review of the Legion's structure. The decision followed hard on the heels of news of the collapse of the Legion Leasehold Housing (see page 373), an event which not only shocked the Legion and attracted media attention but which led to an inquiry by the Charity Commissioners. There were now therefore two external investigations into the Legion's affairs in progress. If anyone still harboured any doubts as to whether an overhaul was needed they would soon be dispelled.[52]

### A sinister challenge

In these turbulent times the Legion was fortunate to have strong and decisive leadership. In 1987 Sir Patrick Howard-Dobson, who had proved an exceptional

President, handed over to General Sir Edward Burgess, the first post-war soldier to hold the post. 'General Ted' was a 'soldier's soldier', direct, uncompromising and greatly respected. Robert Scaife, whose robust common sense had kept the organization moving forward over an eventful four years, was replaced as Chairman in 1989 by David Knowles, another forceful personality. Meanwhile, Major Tomlins having reached retirement age in 1988, Lieutenant Colonel Philip Creasy had been appointed General Secretary. Outwardly imperturbable, but with an agile mind, he would be the pivot on which great changes would turn.[53]

Challenges to the leadership were not unusual in a robust and democratic organization like the Legion. In early 1989, however, there was a more sinister assault: anonymous broadsheets began to be circulated attacking the National Officers, the NEC and the General Secretary. At the Annual Conference that year they were pushed under delegates' bedroom doors. They purported to be issued by the 'Legion Reform Group' seeking 'to return the Legion to its rightful place as the country's No 1 charity'. Still without revealing who was behind them, the attacks continued into 1990 with threatening telephone calls and vindictive letters. The press began to take notice – the difficulty was that such criticism could now be linked to the Legion Leasehold Housing Association failure – and public support for the Poppy Appeal might have been threatened. But when the instigators resorted to the courts in an unsuccessful attempt to force a motion on to the 1990 Conference agenda, their identity could no longer be concealed. At the conference itself, their leader attempted a further challenge. He met his match in Knowles, a former military policeman; the Chairman stopped him and then ejected him, the delegates showing their support for the firm action. However much the floor might itself criticize the leadership it had no truck with this sort of behaviour.[54]

## Targeting the services

By now membership numbers were in decline, largely because of the closure of clubs: in 1985 there had been 1,033 clubs; five years later the number had sunk to 985. Every effort was still being made to help club management through Legion-sponsored training courses and seminars, but they were independent organizations and some chose simply to pursue their own course even if it led to bankruptcy. Each time a club closed only a minority of the members remained in the Legion with the branch.

There was also a paper loss when the membership record was transferred onto the computer database, the previous system having produced more optimistic figures. The actual process of entering the data entailed much hard work both in branches and at headquarters, and the inevitable mistakes led to some recriminations. But, in proportion to the scale of the exercise, these were relatively minor and the Legion now had accurate statistics as well as members' details.

A national holding branch, St James's Branch, was formed in 1989. It served mainly as a temporary home for serving men and women recruited as a result of the Legion's visits to military units; they could be transferred to a local branch in due course. Two recently-retired army warrant officers were now engaged in direct recruiting from the armed forces, in 1988 taking in the Territorial Army and the other volunteer reserve forces. In 1989 a National Recruiting Officer was appointed and by 1990 a programme agreed between the Legion and the military authorities ensured that each unit in Britain and Germany (with the exception of all-Scottish units) would be visited on a three-year cycle. The briefings were lively and professional, covering all aspects of the Legion's work, and links were retained with the unit by the appointment of a unit Legion representative who was supplied with publicity material.[55]

Whether the new members were recruited from the services or locally, the Legion would only keep them if it was a well-run organization down to the grass roots. The Training Advisory Group, set up in 1986, sponsored a range of weekend courses, from leadership to public relations. Over the years these improved the skills of thousands of members.

*St James's Branch received its Standard from its President, The Duke of York, in 1992, by which time it was already well on the way to becoming the Legion's largest branch. Many of its members were still serving in the armed forces including the Standard Bearer.*
*Graham Downing, to the right of the Duke, was Legion Vice-Chairman and would become Chairman in 1995.*

## Conference makes its views known

The 1987 Conference, dealing with the restructuring proposals, had aroused great passions. But there was a different mood the following year when Major Tomlins, the retiring General Secretary, spoke not only of his forty years' service with the Legion, but of his first association with it: a child of the 1930s depression and gravely ill, his 'basket wheelchair-cum-bed, which was my only way out into fresh air' had been supplied by the Legion. He had recovered to fight as an infantry soldier in the Second World War before joining the Legion staff. The same conference was plainly irritated at not having been consulted over a decision to change the name of the Legion's local 'service' committees to 'welfare'. They changed it back again, although the NEC had strongly felt that the old name confused the public. It was an example of democracy in action but it left a pile of now mis-titled literature, which was perhaps why the NEC was slow to comply with the resolution, earning another reprimand from Conference in 1989 when a further move to introduce 'welfare' was defeated. The 1990 Conference, which had to deal with the Legion Leasehold débâcle, was also memorable for the addresses; both the National President and the Chairman spoke in a measured way, reassuring delegates, many of whom had been deeply disturbed by the event.[56]

Such conferences demonstrated the determination of the delegates to be involved in all aspects of its affairs; yet changes already in train would limit their participation.

## A circulation leap

When Conference 1988 accepted computerization the *Legion Journal's* readership was at an all-time low of just over 20,000. With a style not unlike a parish newsletter it carried few advertisements. The change came with the issue for September/October 1989: now called simply 'Legion' and carrying a goodwill message from the Patron, there was a new look with much more colour and, thanks to a dramatic leap in circulation based on automatic distribution to the 600,000 names and addresses now on the computer database, it not only carried much advertising but also devoted several pages to internal marketing – discounted holidays, insurances and, a sign of the times, a 'Legion' credit card for members.[57] A new era had begun.

Members' marketing schemes were controlled by a new company, RBL Marketing Ltd, which had been set up in 1990. It charged a fee to suppliers, and the company's profits on these ventures, ranging from commemorative medals to funerals, were covenanted to the Legion. The National Service Medal, struck in 1992 and which any former national serviceman could buy, was an instant success, meeting a long-felt need, although it may have contributed to a proliferation of such medals, not all of the same high standard. Other memorabilia, such as a video of 'Songs that Won the War' and even a NAAFI tea caddy, augmented the insurance and credit card earnings and by 1995 the company was contributing over £200,000 annually to Legion funds.[58]

# 1991 – 1995

## The biggest change of all

Despite the 1987 rejection of the NEC Working Party proposals the 1990 Conference, realizing that there had to be some change and conscious of the scrutiny of the Charity Commisioners following the Legion Leasehold affair, had authorized consultants to carry out a wide-ranging study into the Legion. The study had been undertaken by Ernst and Young, leaders in their field, and the findings were briefed to the 1991 Conference, having already been presented at the preliminary Area Conferences. They went some way beyond the original NEC ideas, proposing not only that the Area level be abolished, but also that Counties, which now had a key part to play, should be bolstered by professional staff. There was too a radical change in the management structure at the top: the National Executive Council would lose its executive responsibility, which would be delegated to a Management Board, and the headquarters staff branches would be grouped by functions under a new level of senior management.

Once again the Legion's leaders were at pains to ensure that all would go smoothly. The only decision required of Conference 1991 was to appoint a working party to review the Ernst and Young proposals and report back to delegates the following year; the working party members would have complete independence; there would be no NEC representation.

The Review Working Party duly studied the ideas and later that year it produced its findings. They endorsed the original proposals while refining some of the ideas. As Ernst and Young had suggested, the full-time County Field Officers would assist with welfare and fundraising, while the Area Organizers, to be renamed Regional Organizers after the demise of their Areas, would support membership activities. A new Management Board, found from a severely-trimmed and renamed National Council, would meet monthly, while on the Council itself a past National Chairman would no longer have life membership, serving only for three years after vacating office.*

Interviewed by the *Legion Journal* prior to Conference a member of the Working Party

---

*Apart from those former National Chairmen already on the Council who had a 'reserved right' to life membership.

351

thought the introduction of County Field Officers the key issue, and also the most contentious since they would be paid out of benevolent funds.

In this he was right. At the 1992 Conference the removal of the Area structure, a suggestion which had caused such controversy only five years before, went almost unremarked. But the use of Poppy Appeal money to pay CFOs aroused much passion, although the CFOs themselves would assist with raising the funds. 'The money we volunteers raise by standing on street corners in all weathers will go to paying staff' went the argument. But after some debate, and the defeat of several amendments, the NEC was instructed to proceed. The Legion had embarked on the biggest change in its history.[59]

There was much to do. Caretaker Area Councils were charged with the transition to a County-based structure, a shadow Management Board appointed and the headquarters itself restructured with the appointment of a Controller to oversee each of the principal staff functions: welfare (the term was now accepted as part of the overall change), fundraising and membership. By early 1994 this had been done and all thirty-seven County Field Officers (some of whom supported more than one County) had been recruited, trained and were in place. Meanwhile a 'supplemental' Royal Charter had been drawn up in order to enshrine the changes in the Legion's constitution.[60]

## A duty of trust

Preceding the critical restructuring debate at the 1992 Conference was an address by the National President. It dealt with the Charity Commissioners' investigation into the Legion Leasehold failure and it was delivered in General Burgess's typically straightforward style. The detail of the report is elsewhere (page 374), but if delegates still retained any doubts that change was necessary they were soon dispelled: not only did the Legion's executive machinery need a vigorous shake-up but – and here was the main message – the Legion's officers, at every level, had to exercise a proper duty of trust; in layman's terms this meant that in every matter involving the charity its interests must be paramount. From the National Council's strategic decisions to the often complicated relationships between a branch and a club any other consideration must be ruthlessly excluded.[61]

There was of course nothing new in this. The Commissioners were simply underlining a basic principle that applied to every Legion activity. But, in the changes now about to take place, trusteeship would be an overriding consideration, especially in the National Council whose members would be either 'Trustee Members', those elected and eligible to vote, or 'Non-Trustees', those like the past National Chairmen who simply gave advice. Indeed so deeply did the message penetrate the Legion psyche that it would hover over the Council's deliberations like a guardian spirit.

For the Legion as a whole there was an even more profound effect. Hitherto it had been accepted that, in all matters, sovereignty lay with Conference.* From now on, however, it was made clear that Conference could only advise the Trustees – the elected members of the National Council – whose responsibilities were legally defined and who therefore constituted the ultimate authority.[62]

The ill wind of the Legion Leasehold affair had thus backed to blow from an altogether unexpected direction. If the Ernst and Young report had introduced change, the Charity Commissioners investigation had undoubtedly expedited it.

*Broadly speaking; as Wooton points out in *The Politics of Influence* at p.71, Conference did not control the money supply (although it set the Affiliation Fee rate).

## A machine that works

The effectiveness of the new structure quickly became apparent. From July 1993 the Management Board, meeting monthly, took charge of the Legion's administration. Each of five Trustee members elected from the Council was responsible for a specific subject, supported by a staff Controller, and the board was chaired by the National Chairman, assisted by the other officers, the Secretary General (the new title for the General Secretary) and his immediate staff. Depending on the agenda, outside experts in matters such as finance or publicity, all distinguished in their field, were also present to give advice. The National Council now had a mainly strategic function and the Board's proceedings went to them for approval.[63]

The new system brought about a close working relationship between Management Board Trustees and staff. Freed of routine matters, Controllers could assist the Trustees to develop initiatives within the National Council's corporate plan and the results were soon apparent, especially in the benevolent field (see Chapter 18). Further progress would be aided by the development of information support systems for welfare, fundraising and financial activities, following the establishment of the membership data base, now maintained by inputs from Regional Organizers.[64]

One matter which much exercised the Trustees in their responsibilities was an opportunity to buy the freehold of the headquarters building at 48/49 Pall Mall. It took some deliberation, during which the price rose from £2 million to £3 million, before the purchase was agreed; but the Legion had a good investment – the building was worth some £6 million.[65]

## Key posts

The implementation of such profound change needed a firm hand on the tiller and once again the hour produced the man. In 1992 E.R. 'Ted' Jobson had become National Chairman. Astute and imperturbable, he ensured that the Legion followed the course that had been set, handing over in 1995 to G.G. Downing an organization which, if it it still had some way to go, at least knew where it was headed. In 1993, sixty years after the last naval incumbent, Earl Jellicoe, had reliquished the post, Vice Admiral Sir Geoffrey Dalton became Legion President. Again the Legion was fortunate: Admiral Dalton was greatly experienced in charity work, having become Secretary General of MENCAP on leaving the service. Sadly, however, the appointment of Peter Walsh as General Treasurer in 1995 to replace R.E. Hawkes – this key post was now filled by selection – was short-lived. He died after barely eighteen months in office.[66]

Outside help was also needed from time to time, particularly where government was involved. The Legion's House of Commons Branch was long defunct, but in 1989 two MPs, one Government and one Opposition, had agreed to act as honorary Legion consultants. Now, however, the European Parliament had begun to play an increasing part in everyday life in the United Kingdom. Prudently the Legion made a similar contact in Strasbourg and in 1992 Bryan Cassidy MEP agreed to assist. He was soon advising on European funding of the Legion's Training College project (see page 381).[67]

## Change in the field

The demise of Areas left both the North and the South of Ireland unchanged but in need of new titles and in 1993 the NEC agreed that they should be known as The Royal

British Legion Northern Ireland and The Royal British Legion Republic of Ireland, Wales already holding a similar title. But whereas Wales had three County Field Officers who between them supported all of the principality's counties, CFOs had not been introduced across the Irish Sea, where the existing staff organization continued to function, except that the Area Organizer was now the Regional Organizer.[68]

Despite the misgivings that had been expressed in some quarters, County Field Officers were one of the great successes of the restructuring, as will be apparent from Chapters 18 and 19. The majority came straight from the armed forces following the run-down and all embarked on their new careers with enthusiasm. It was hard work – in order to meet the members a CFO might spend three evenings a week travelling to remote branches on top of his normal activities – and might at first not get the reception he anticipated. But branches and their members soon became strongly supportive of their CFO as he developed a professional expertise in welfare and fundraising that gave new dimensions to their own activities.

Computerization had involved branches in changes that would have been beyond the comprehension of their founders; but the traditional activities continued. The 'trench supper' had no meaning except for the very oldest, but the Second World War was a little closer and at Eaton Socon in Bedfordshire the props were still about – battledress, tin hats and stirrup pumps; the women were even prepared to do their hair in the wartime style before donning the clothes of the time for a 'forties night'. Castle Donnington's Legion shop served as a focal point for coach outings as well as functioning as a charity shop; it also collected subscriptions.[69] Coach outings were popular as motorways enabled parties to traverse the country in a day; but tragedy struck in 1995 when ten members of Christchurch Branch were killed in a crash while returning from just such a trip.

Although St James's Branch, now the Legion's central branch, raised funds for such purposes as a Legion Village minibus, its only social activity was an annual dinner. But its growth was spectacular. In 1991, when the Duke of York accepted the branch presidency, it had barely 2,000 members; by 1995 it had nearly 20,000. Most had been recruited as a result of the Legion's regular visits to armed forces units and were encouraged to transfer to their local branch when they had settled back into civilian life. The recruiting team had been expanded meanwhile and now supported counties as well, training recruiters and supplying aids. But all the effort served merely to stem the decline in the Ordinary membership due to club closure. This was not the only problem; large numbers of members lapsed simply because they did not renew their annual subscriptions. Computerization now provided an answer; the money could be collected by standing order or, preferably, by direct debit; but only a trickle of members were prepared to pay in this way. St James's Branch, where the membership was mainly young, had no objection to direct debit, and used this method exclusively, with the results that we have seen.[70]

## Support for clubs and youth

A single club closure could take 800 members out of the Legion[71] and in 1994, as part of the headquarters staff reorganization, a department was formed solely to support clubs. But it still faced the old problem: insufficient management resources to make any real impact on those clubs needing close supervision, probably about one in every three. Many clubs still made large bar profits but the difficulty, which had been with the Legion since the 1920s, was how to extract even a small proportion of the money; although headquarters-arranged supply deals had been, and still were, attempted, too few clubs made use of them to give the Legion enough 'percentage' to fund a regional management network. They preferred to stick with their own suppliers. Meanwhile total club numbers had fallen to 900 by 1995, despite valiant efforts by the department concerned and the Regional staff.[72]

Some clubs provided meeting rooms for the branch Youth Section to run their activities and Youth Associate membership, introduced in 1990 for those between the ages of fourteen and seventeen, served to recognize young people's involvement in the Legion, although actual membership was small, the majority of young people preferring a less committed approach. The appointment of a National Youth Officer had given impetus to the work but in 1993 the NEC decided that the Leicester Legion Youth Tattoo had only a local impact and should be discontinued. In 1994 the whole youth programme was reviewed by the Management Board who agreed two aims: to help the local community and to make the young aware of the Legion's work. The onus would lie with the Counties and a scheme to train County Youth Advisers was introduced, making use of the Scouts Association facilities at Gilwell Park.[73]

## The bands strike up again

Legion bands once again came into prominence in the 1990s with the appointment of Captain Wheeling as Legion Director of Music. There were some fifty bands in existence and his aim was to ensure that both in standards of performance and appearance all were worthy to represent the Legion. A band festival in the Isle of Wight in 1993 was attended by eight bands and the workshops and rehearsal culminated in a concert where 200 Legion musicians played Tschaikovsky's Fourth Symphony. The next year, at Hayling Island, the number had grown to eleven bands and the aim was to work towards a massed Legion bands concert in 1996, on the 75th anniversary.[74]

Norbury, the most prominent of the Legion bands, had long sought recognition as the Legion's 'Headquarters Band'. At last, in 1987, it had officially become 'The Central Band of the Royal British Legion', able to trace its origins back to the Epsom Home Guard in 1940 and with a Legion connection dating from 1944. Among other claims to fame it had for many years played at West Ham football matches with the cockney actor Warren Mitchell sometimes conducting; 'You'd best stay on, mates' was the half-time cry when West Ham was losing.[75]

## Conferences - the gales subside

The winds blew at gale force around Bournemouth during the 1993 Annual Conference. But, in contrast to the 1987 Bournemouth Conference, they were all outside the hall. In 1987 the reform plans had been angrily defeated; in 1993 there was reasoned debate, and even the presentation of the Supplemental Charter, making clear that Conference only had the power to persuade not to command, and overturning previously accepted practice, was accepted without rancour. With delegates caught up in the momentum of change a new mood seemed to prevail. The previous year at Blackpool Conference had been moved and inspired by an address from Billy Griffiths, who in captivity had been both blinded and maimed, his Japanese captors regarding him as an object of derision rather than pity; yet his speech had been both warm and humorous.

There were minor changes too in the way Conference was run; so that more delegates could express their views the National Chairman introduced an open forum in 1993 with roving microphones and covering topics such as relations between branches and clubs. The following year the controversial subject of more involvement of Associate Members produced some lively comments, subsequently incorporated in a consultation paper. By 1995 open forums were an institution, allowing delegates free expression on the chosen topics, although the Chairman needed to have his wits about him.

At Plymouth that year the traditional parade and service was held to be the best in recent times: one hundred standards led the march to the war memorial on the Hoe and the two-minute silence was marked by the firing of maroons. In a time of change some things remained constant.

\*      \*      \*

The Legion had come through much in these years. Change was necessary but it placed much strain on the rank-and-file membership. For those piloting the ship the process might be exhilarating; for those battened down below decks and buffeted by the changes of course it could be confusing. But in the end all was on an even course again.

*Times change but the bands play on. The Legion's Central Band marches down Whitehall on its way to a service at the Cenotaph.*

# CHAPTER 18

## WORK 1971-2001

# *Manning the Breaches*

## 1971 – 1975

### No let-up

As the Legion entered the 1970s there was no slackening of the pace. The high level of unemployment brought hardship to many ex-service families and heating costs were a problem for the aged, their real income sapped by inflation. Each winter Legion expenditure rose as service committees issued more vouchers for gas and electricity.[1]

In Northern Ireland these problems were exacerbated by community disorder as the IRA stepped up their campaign of violence. Many ex-service families lived in the troubled inner-city areas of Belfast, Londonderry or elsewhere and there were frequent calls on the Legion for financial aid. The Falls and Shankill Road areas accounted for much of the increase in need but their service committees had perforce to operate from the Area office in central Belfast and in some cases the Legion's welfare applications even had to be passed across clandestinely at rendezvous such as the public library. The Legion helped some twenty families in this period to move to England because of intimidation, headquarters liaising with the housing authorities concerned. The work was hardly helped by the IRA's pitiless targeting of the Northern Ireland War Memorial Building which served as a headquarters for many of the ex-service welfare organizations in the province; but the staff, by now experienced in sweeping up broken glass, simply carried on.[2] On both sides of the water the Legion stood ready to come to the aid of the family of a serviceman killed or wounded. When one soldier became a paraplegic there was liaison with the local council to find a house suitable for his family, including two small children, and the Legion paid for the household equipment.[3]

The people in the North of Ireland were highly appreciative of the Legion's work and the Appeal collection went up by nearly 50 per cent in 1971. But in the South spending on benevolence still outstripped collections; although the ratio had begun to reduce as the ex-British service community declined, still £4 was spent for every £1 donated to the Poppy Appeal. If any demonstration of the non-political nature of the Legion was needed it was here; the increased donations in Northern Ireland helped subsidize the work in the Republic.[4]

Unemployment fell sharply in 1973 from a figure just below one million to a little over half that figure. But among those failing to get back to work were a large number of Second World War veterans, now in their fifties. Unlike the 1920s there was adequate state provision for the unemployed; but often they had hire purchase debts, particularly worrying to the widow when a man died, and where possible the Legion helped to clear them. It was one of the gaps in the system and there were others: a widow needing alterations to her house to allow her to look after her crippled daughter; mortgage

357

payments lapsing through illness, so that re-possession of the house was imminent; a new downstairs bathroom for a double amputee widow; urgent re-thatching of an elderly war widow's cottage. There were many such cases the Legion assisted.[5]

### War pensions – a substantial gain

Entitlement to a war disability or war widows pension might also help. Following the Legion's battles of the 1950s and 60s the pensions were now regularly reviewed in order to maintain their value. But the review was biennial and the pensions' value lagged behind inflation. In any case the increases were based on living costs rather than wage levels so that there was no share in the wage earners' gradually growing prosperity. At one time the pension had been equivalent to the national average wage; now it was only one-third of that figure. A resolution at the 1971 Conference reiterated the 1970 demand: that the full war pension rate should be half of the national average wage and that if the pensioner was unemployed he should receive the national wage. This remained the Legion's position, regularly re-stated by delegations to ministers; even so it was somewhat surprised when in 1974 the goverment announced a rise of nearly one-third in the rates for both war disability pensions and war widows' pensions, accompanied by a number of other improvements which the Legion had sought, such as some levelling-up of ex-servicewomen's pensions. Moreover it was stated that future increases would be made annually and would be in proportion to the average increase in national earnings. The effect of the increase can be seen at Chart B3 (page 447); it represented a substantial gain.[6]

The government's action effectively ended the Legion's campaign to maintain the value of war pensions. Although the struggle had lasted nearly thirty years it was a very satisfactory outcome as the chart demonstrates. But there were still other aspects of pensions to be resolved. One of these was the question of 'disregards' – the amount of the war or war widows' pension not reckoned as income when benefits such as family income supplement or local authority rent rebate were assessed. The Legion's long-held view was that the whole pension should be ignored; it represented compensation for a sacrifice made and could not be considered normal income. Government policy, however, was that only the first £2 should be disregarded. The 1974 increases of course intensified the problem: a man who was 100 per cent war-disabled now received £16.40 a week; if only £2 was disregarded £14.40 counted as income, much reducing any benefit entitlement he might seek. In such cases the pensions increase could be nullified.

Conference passed resolutions annually on this vexed topic and Legion delegations continued to convey them to the minister concerned. In 1975 there was a small concession: the 'statutory' disregard was increased to £4; as before the local authorites might disregard a greater amount at their discretion. But this resulted in unequal treatment, depending on where the war pensioner or widow lived. In 1973 the National Chairman had again written to each local authority seeking a 100 per cent disregard; but of the 1,000 councils he approached, under 200 agreed his proposals.[7]

A subject which aroused perhaps even stronger feeling was the taxation of war widows' pensions. Today it might be regarded as the Chancellor taking a slice of the compensation for an injury. At the 1972 Legion Conference a delegate's comment that 'the mother of parliaments is behaving as anything but a mother in this matter' got a resounding 'hear, hear' from the platform as well as the floor. It had been an issue when the Legion was founded and in those days it seemed closer to resolution since the 1919 parliamentary select committee had recommended freeing the pension from tax, but for over fifty years the Treasury had resisted.[8]

Almost no other country taxed war widows payments. Yet all a Legion delegation could get from government in 1972 was an undertaking to consider some form of tax credit. When this was abandoned as unworkable the Legion returned to the attack. But it was not until 1975 that a chink appeared in the government's armour. Ironically the damage was self-inflicted: the previous year's large rise in the pension rates had brought many widows into the tax bracket for the first time and a weekly rise of £2.20 was reduced to 73 pence. In response to protests the government agreed to defer taxation for a year. Meanwhile the Treasury, conscious perhaps of an impending assault, dug in. Their position was that the war widow's pension was simply a substitute for a husband's income; to remove tax would only benefit the better-off and – the real worry – it might trigger other claims for tax exemption. Yet there was no tax on the modest ex-gratia payments to the widows of those killed in Northern Ireland, introduced in 1973.[9]

## Housing progress

Some of the widows might have been consoled by the accommodation increasingly available to them through the Legion's Housing Association, started in 1964 to meet the housing needs of elderly members of the ex-service community. The Association was now moving into top gear. Using government loans, which were repaid from rents subsidized by local authorities, no less than one thousand flatlets had already been built, while twice that number were in the pipeline. The scheme did not benefit just the elderly; by providing the old people with accommodation suited to their needs it released housing for younger people.

When Major Rivers moved from the Legion's Service Department that year to become Director of the Housing Association its activities already stretched from Preston to Folkestone and from Newcastle to Truro. Growth was more rapid than by any other housing association in the country and a feature of the Legion's schemes was the community spirit; built around central courtyards with benches overlooking lawns and flowerbeds, the layout encouraged tenants to get together, while Legion local committees raised money to enhance facilities, ran social events in

*A typical Legion Housing Association development; the interior courtyard encouraged the tenants to get toether.*

the communal rooms and organized outings. When, on a cold day, a Chelsea Pensioner arrived at a Winchester flat to be re-united with his wife, from whom he had for some time been separated by the forced sale of their rented house, he found the central heating on, a meal on the table and food in the refrigerator; all had been done by the local Legion committee. It was small wonder that local authorities welcomed the Legion schemes, and their goodwill helped the expansion.[10]

The Association was run by a Board of Management appointed by the NEC and chaired since its inception by Dennis Cadman. The members were chosen for the expertise they could bring to the work. Despite pressure from some Areas to be represented, the Board stayed small, the operation grew and the Association moved its headquarters from Pall Mall to set up in High Wycombe in 1972.[11]

Efficient management was vital. Changes in legislation in 1973 replaced the local authority rent subsidies with a complicated system of allowances which confused the tenants; a building strike the same year singled out several of the Legion's sites for industrial action, while rocketing land prices forced the Association into higher borrowing, the Legion standing guarantor. But the work went ahead and on the Legion Housing Association's tenth anniversary Cadman was able to point to sixty-eight completed projects providing over 2,500 flats for the elderly, while a professional journal praised the high building standards and excellent landscaping.[12]

### New developments at the Village

One Housing Association development re-housed settlers and widows in the Legion Village at Preston Hall, part of the renewal plan for the village. The decline in the number of TB convalescents in the 1960s had led to a decision to open the village up to those with other disabilities. Central to the plan was the construction of new factory premises which

*The Queen sees a motorway sign being made at the Legion village in 1975. The Legion Chairman, Charles Busby stands alongside the Queen; on reliquishing the chairmanship he would devote himself to the care of the village and its community.*

not only gave the disabled workers better facilities but, in a move away from the old cottage-industry approach, improved production; there was now little room for sentiment for disabled ex-servicemen in the market place. But the products were largely unchanged: a woodworking department produced timber sheds, fencing and their own design of stacking chair, the printing press contracts included the *Legion Journal*, while motorway signs had become an important product.[13]

The development provided a new home for the Poppy Appeal and Disabled Men's Industries also moved into the village at this time, setting up a display of goods for Legion branch 'sales representatives'.

The cost of all this had been reduced by the sale of some of the land, under a plan masterminded by former National Chairman Charles Busby, which included appointing a co-ordinator to oversee both the industries and the community. There was a new spirit abroad and when the Queen visited in December 1975, her planned one hour was extended to two as she talked to employees and visited residents in their houses before being 'farewelled' by the village junior football team in their yellow jerseys.[14]

The village continued to thrive. By 1979 there were some 400 ex-service 'villagers' including ninety severely disabled ex-service men and women working in sheltered conditions. New products were developed such as tubular steel frames for school desks and injection moulding for the burgeoning electronics industry, while the arrival of the Legion's Supplies Department in 1979 gave further employment opportunities to the disabled. The decision to switch the printing of the *Legion Journal* elsewhere was a blow but in a spirit of determined optimism new machinery was installed and other work found. By the end of 1980, however, the renewed recession began to cause problems in all departments with orders for timber pallets falling as the construction industry went into decline, while the cut-back in motorway building forced the signs department to diversify. Despite all these difficulties no employee was made redundant. For a disabled man that would have been a hard blow indeed.[15]

## Netherlands hosting ends

Ex-service widows and their children had long had good friends across the North Sea where the Netherlands War Graves Committee paid for and hosted annual visits by relatives to war graves on their soil. It had started when a former resistance man was impressed by local people placing flowers on the graves shortly after the war. Now, twenty-five years on, it was felt that the scheme should be brought to an end. The last visit was made in 1972 and, in a simple but moving ceremony at Nijmegen, children placed a circle of scarlet carnations around the memorial, watched by seventy pilgrims led by the Legion's Chairman.[16]

The Legion continued to make pilgrimages to the Netherlands under their own arrangements, while there was no lessening of visits to other cemeteries. The anniversary of the Normandy landing in 1974 brought a Legion party of 100 to the beaches, including the Bishop of Norwich who thirty years before had waded ashore from a landing craft. There were new destinations: Berlin in 1972 and Denmark in 1974 where the relatives, taken to the site of an aircraft crash, saw that the farmer himself had placed a memorial and left the place uncultivated. On that trip the pilgrims received much local hospitality, only being required to sing 'Tipperary' in return.[17]

Also in 1974, the Legion's Conference proposed a mass sponsored walk through the battlefields of Europe, alongside European ex-service organizations. The suggestion was

*Netherlands-sponsored war graves pilgrimages in 1972. While school children stand ready to place their flowers, Colonel Hughes, Legion Chairman, lays a wreath at the Nijmegen Memorial.*

put to the European body, CEAC and enthusiastically supported. But they wanted it centred on Verdun, scene of the great French battle of the First World War. This idea 'did not commend itself' to the Legion's Council and the proposal was dropped.[18]

## 1976 – 1980

### An even greater contribution

As the 1970s drew to a close, once again a worsening economic situation placed demands on charities as the government freely admitted that the state could not afford the full range of health and welfare demands, and should not even try. It looked to the voluntary sector to make a larger contribution to the social needs of the community. In the Legion's case the main concern was the need for comprehensive nursing care for elderly First World War veterans, at the same time noting that their Second World War counterparts marched not far behind, their injuries or other disabilities now beginning to make themselves apparent. The columns seemed endless: it was estimated that there would be six-and-a-half million elderly ex-service people around in the year 2000. Meanwhile the government continued to make spending cuts.[19]

### Anger over Churchill Court

The Legion's convalescent homes helped many of those who were growing older. It will be remembered that Legion homes were of two kinds: the five Country Homes, restyled 'Residential' Homes in the late 1970s to reflect their changed emphasis, provided long term care; the four Rest and Convalescent Homes gave short breaks to the weary, particularly those who were recovering from an operation, but did not attempt any form of nursing care.

Three of the convalescent homes were in England, while Bennet House was at Helen's Bay in Northern Ireland. Originally these were male-only, but times were changing and Somerset Legion House, always the pioneer, had for some time accepted married couples. In 1973 the NEC decided that a similar facility should be available in the north of England, sold the original Byng House in Southport which it had inherited from the United Service Trustees, and with the proceeds bought another property in the same area. This was converted behind the original facade, the new 75-bed Byng House opening in 1975.[20]

There was no Residential Home in Northern Ireland, although the convalescent home,

Bennet House, took a few permanent residents. Here the requirement was for a dual-purpose home providing both temporary respite and long-term care. After much investigation it was decided to sell the existing property and buy another on the sea front at Portrush. The new Bennet House opened in 1981, but it would not be the end of the story.[21]

Everywhere costs were rising and the NEC decided in 1978 to close Churchill Court in Kent, given to the Legion in 1946 after it had been presented to Winston Churchill's wife, smallest of the convalescent homes, but with overheads twice as high as elsewhere. The family had been consulted in the decision and had raised no objection, Churchill's grandson remarking that 'The Legion does not want a millstone around its neck.' A sale was duly arranged and by the time the Council took their places on the platform at the 1979 Conference the documents had been signed. Conference, however, had not been consulted in any of this and, with long queues at the microphone, delegate after delegate voiced their anger. It seemed that the NEC might have to reopen the home. In the end, after much debate on alternative courses, the conference accepted the sale, although not before the President had entered the debate: 'We accept the censure,' he said to a strangely quiet audience.[22]

The proceeds of the sale of Kippington Court, the original name, were used to endow a trust to build a rehabilitation and assessment centre for the disabled in the Legion Village. The sale would provide half the money needed; branches and clubs were asked to donate the rest. But the Legion only decided to go ahead after the Health Authority agreed to pay the running costs, on the basis that the general public would be admitted, although ex-servicemen would have priority. There seemed little doubt of the need; only eight such centres existed for a national disabled population of one million, of whom 50,000 were ex-service.[23]

Conference 1980, carefully consulted in all of this, gave their approval to the project, to be called the Churchill Centre; a fundraiser was appointed and planning began. But the path would not be smooth.[24]

### 'You deserved to win this battle'

Conference may have censured the leaderhip over the sale of Churchill Court but it was fully behind their efforts on behalf of the war widows. The 1974 increase in their pensions had resulted in an 'Irishman's rise' for many of the widows, bringing them into the tax bracket for the first time and wiping out much of the gain. It highlighted the unfairness of taxing such pensions and late in 1975 the Legion determined to exploit this small opening: a campaign was mounted, NEC speakers addressed Area conferences, there were press briefings and in early 1976 the National Chairman led a deputation to the Treasury to express the Legion's 'total commitment' to complete exemption of the pension from tax. The response was hardly unexpected: such a concession would open the floodgates to others. But when that year's Finance Bill was debated it was clear that the Legion's campaign had struck home and a backbench amendment secured a government compromise: the Finance Act of 1976 cut the tax on war widows' pensions by 50 per cent. The effect was that those widows whose pension was their only source of income would now pay no tax. The Legion welcomed the concession, but made it clear that it remained determined to secure total tax exemption for the widows.[25]

The campaign was resumed with the Joint Committee of Service and Ex-service Organizations endorsing the Legion's actions and lending their weight to the attack. There were further concessions by government: the rules were relaxed, resulting in pensions being granted to a further 1,500 widows in 1978. But when the Legion's Chairman made yet another visit to press the case for a full exemption, the Chancellor of the Exchequer remained obdurate: he could not agree to an exception being made in favour of war widows. Equally unmoved, Captain Whitehead referred the matter to the Prime Minister.

But Callaghan's administration was now replaced by that of Margaret Thatcher. The new government had a manifesto commitment to remove the tax. Delegates to the 1979 Legion Conference in the Brighton Dome held their own views on pre-election pledges and their debate endorsed the continuance of the campaign. Now, however, the Minister* himself spoke. He proceeded to stun his audience by announcing that the widows' pensions would shortly be made exempt from tax: 'You deserved to win this battle long ago,' he told them; their senses restored, the delegates roared their approval. For sixty years the Treasury had held their position. Yet in the space of a mere five the fortifications had first been breached, and then overrun. It was a mighty victory.[26]

By the end of 1980 two long-standing wrongs had been righted: the value of war pensions had been restored and war widows' pensions freed from tax; but the Legion could not afford to rest on its laurels. There was still the issue of pension disregard when assessing other benefits, and other matters that still needed to be resolved if the ex-service community was to receive fair treatment.[27] One such was the disparity in the treatment of war widows depending on whether they were widowed before or after 1973, arising out of changes in the pension codes which were not retrospective. Some inequity was righted towards the end of 1979 when the widows of servicemen discharged before 1950 were allowed to claim pensions based on their husbands' service, bringing them into line with those discharged in later years; but there was no backdating for the years they had been short-changed.[28]

*By the late 1970s the Attendants' Company had extended its operations into the security sector and disabled employees were in the minority.*

## New skills for the Attendants Company

If there were important changes in the treatment of widows, there were no less significant alterations in the Royal British Legion Attendants Company. By 1977 only some 43 per cent of nearly 900 people employed by the company were registered disabled. Young and fit ex-servicemen had been recruited as wardens for the maximum security lorry park in Preston and for similar duties in other places. Most of those with disabilities were employed in the car-parking division, now manning multi-storey car parks all over the country and although automation was reducing the level of manning many disabled were anyway

* Reg Prentice, Minister of State for Social Services, had transferred his allegiance from the Labour Party to the new government.

approaching retirement. But whether disabled or fully active, 1974 had been a vintage year for both sides of the company: it had seen the winning of contracts for the Houses of Parliament car park as well as the Tower of London entrance security.

The Preston operation was controlled from a central watchtower with floodlights and the wardens had dogs as well as two-way radios. The introduction of sophisticated electronic surveillance and fire-fighting equipment at this and other sites entailed new skills. This posed few problems; the company's greatest asset was the quality of its workforce. Despite intense competition which often undercut contract prices, it had an impressive client list which included the Silver Jubilee exhibitions, the Barbican estate and Spinks, the St James's jewellers. There were no subsidies either from the state or from the Legion; careful management ensured an annual surplus which by 1979 was based on a turnover of £5 million of business. Under an unpaid Board, it was an ongoing success story with which the Legion was proud to be associated.[29]

## A Cambrian factory decision

The Legion was also proud of the Cambrian wool factory in Wales, but its path since the end of the Second World War had been difficult and more than once the Legion had been on the brink of disposing of it. In 1971 discussions were again opened with the Department of Employment and the local authorities, but that year the Poppy Appeal results were good and a more optimistic view prevailed. This was justified by the results over the next few years and a tea room was even opened to cater for the increased visitors to the factory, while suit lengths could be bought at the Legion shop in Pall Mall and taken to Regent Street where Burton's would make them up at a concessionary price. By the factory's fiftieth anniversary in 1977 sales had reached a new record and Group Captain Douglas Bader opened the celebration fete; it rained, but the looms continued to clatter. The clatter was a little less pronounced the following year and by 1980 the renewed depression was taking its toll. That year the ex-service element of the disabled workforce was down to ten out of a total of forty-two and the NEC felt justified in seeking local authority financial involvement on the grounds that it was no longer an ex-service enterprise.

The negotiations were neither short nor easy. But eventually agreement was reached for Powys County Council to assume day-to-day management in 1981, with the Legion name retained and the NEC continuing to provide an annual grant. The factory was now therefore a joint enterprise; the burden on the Legion had been reduced, but it was still financially involved.[30]

# 1981 – 1985

## End of the voucher system

Casualties in the 1982 Falklands War were thankfully small, but the grand total of all the conflicts since 1945 came to 4,000 killed and 16,000 wounded, adding to the Legion's benevolent responsibilities which now also included the families of those still serving, following the decision in 1981 to admit serving members of the armed forces to Ordinary Membership; under the Charter Legion relief was available to all those eligible for such membership, and their dependants. But the effect was marginal on a community of some eight million ex-service people and ten million dependants; the chief concern was the increasing elderly element as life expectancy was prolonged.[31]

It was mainly the elderly who were assisted through the voucher system that dated from the Legion's earliest days (see page 70). In 1981, however, the system changed. Vouchers were withdrawn and branches provided with cheque books to allow them to draw on the Central Benevolent Fund for the direct payment of the tradesmen's bills. This coincided with more calls for help as unemployment rose; in particular there were redundancies among Second World War veterans who were just short of retirement age and therefore vulnerable. By 1984 there was increased benevolent expenditure.[32]

Vulnerable in a different way were former prisoners of war. The Legion had initiated and funded a study into the long-term effects of their captivity. Organized by the British Members Council of the World Veterans Federation, the study found medical evidence that merely being a prisoner of war could lead to a multitude of problems and even early death. In the case of those who had been in Japanese hands tropical diseases and prolonged and deliberate ill-treatment intensified the condition; some of the Legion's Poppy Factory employees had been among them, at the time losing almost half their body weight. Even in Europe aircrew had been severely beaten on their way to the prison camps.

Faced with the report, the government's reaction could only be positive: former POWs were identified and arrangement made for checking them at twelve DHSS hospitals, although it was then found that there was a shortage of tropical disease investigation facilities.[33]

### Officers' war pensions work integrated

As a result of the checks a number of the ex-POWs made successful claims for war pensions, assisted by the Legion, as was a former Irish Guardsman who had been discharged with an anxiety state in 1945. His applications for a war pension had been consistently refused for nearly forty years until the Legion won him a 40 per cent disability pension in 1983, backdated to 1945. Meanwhile other new cases were identified; in 1982 the Legion obtained a 100 per cent pension for a Royal Navy Engine Room Artificer who contracted asbestosis as a result of the use of the material in warship construction and this led to a number of other such claims, although sadly the ERA concerned died before he could receive the pension, but his wife received a widow's pension.[34]

Officers' war pension claims had hitherto been handled by the Officers' Association. In 1984, however, the Legion's Pensions Department took over all new claims for officers and their widows, a rationalization of functions that had been first mooted some sixty years before. The same year saw the start of a rise in the number of claims and appeals generally as Second World War veterans approached retirement age and medical problems connected with their service began to emerge.[35]

The pensions themselves were now subject to annual review. But the Legion was still concerned at the way in which the increases were calculated and applied. The government had said in 1974 that the review would take account of wages as well as living costs, but it soon became clear that the value of the pensions lagged behind not only earnings but also prices; a 9 per cent increase was awarded in 1981 when inflation was running at 12 per cent, so that the pensioners faced a reduction in living standards.[36]

## Frustration at the Churchill Centre

Some war pensioners would benefit from the facilities that were planned for the new Churchill Centre in the grounds of Preston Hall near Maidstone. In the end the total cost of the project had risen from £400,000 to £560,000 but, following an appeal launch by Churchill's daughter, Lady Soames, the money was raised and in November 1982 the centre was made available to the DHSS, the Minister himself attending.

So far all had gone well. Now came a most frustrating time. The local Health Authority was responsible for running the centre, but budget cuts meant that it could not be properly staffed. There was mounting anger in the Legion and when the centre was formally opened by the Duchess of Kent in December 1983 the National President spoke out: 'The Legion feels very strongly that it has been let down.' The Health Authority's reaction was to offer the facilities to adjoining Authorities and this had some effect. But it was not until 1988 that the centre was in full operation, some five years after opening, with patients from outside the local area accommodated in the Mountbatten Pavilion. This was a 25-bedroom warden-care hostel which had been built by the Legion's Housing Association for the elderly and disabled, but which could offer a few rooms to Churchill patients. To some extent it answered the criticism that the rest of the country, and particularly the north, had been overlooked by siting the centre at Maidstone.[37]

The Mountbatten Pavilion provided up-to-date facilities for the frail and elderly and there was much modernization of Legion residential homes at this time; whereas most of the residents had previously shared with up to three others, there was now a programme to give them single bedsitting rooms, while additional medical and nursing facilities were provided,

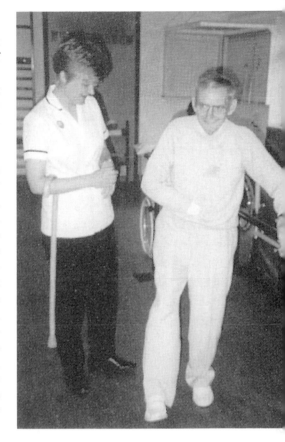

*A patient is help to regain mobility at the Churchill Rehabilitation Centre. The Centre opened in 1982 but DHSS budget cuts meant that it would not become fully operational until 1988.*

together with the accommodation for the extra staff. Two homes, however, were unsuitable for upgrading: Crosfield House in Wales needed a purpose-built replacement and in 1982 a site was found at Rhayader in central Wales; Maurice House at Westcliffe-on-Sea was superseded by a purpose-built residential home at Broadstairs, the residents, including a 95-year-old South African War veteran, all being moved between breakfast and lunch in one day.[38]

Modernization of Halsey House in Cromer took two years but was finished in 1984; the following year the new Crosfield House was completed and work begun on a replacement Lister House in the centre of Ripon. By 1987 four of the Legion's residential homes in England would be new, with the fifth, Halsey House, modernized to a very high standard, while in Northern Ireland Bennet House had been extended by buying an adjoining property. The cost of all this had been some £6 million but the Legion was now able to accommodate nearly 300 residents in total in first class accommodation with up-to-date nursing facilities; nevertheless waiting lists were long and there was pressure to provide even more places.[39]

## A Legion housing celebration

There was pressure too on the Legion's Housing Association, which in 1985 celebrated its coming-of-age. Despite cuts in government funding, difficulties in acquiring land and problems with builders, an average of more than 500 flatlets had been completed each year and the total now stood at over 11,500, with the work still continuing. The 10,000th flat had been handed over to an 88-year-old former Life Guardsman who had been wounded in the First World War, and his wife, and most of the tenants were still of that generation; but an increasing number of Second World War people now applied for flats. In 1982 the authorities had amended the rules to allow non ex-service applicants to be considered for Legion housing, although in practice there were at this time always enough elderly ex-service to fill the vacancies; but it was the first indication of the government tightening its grip since housing association funding had been taken away from the local authorities.[40]

In 1981 steps had been taken to form a sister association. The Legion Leasehold Housing Association sought to help those elderly ex-service people who needed the ease and comfort of sheltered accommodation yet were barred from existing Housing Association tenancies because they were existing houseowners. The concept was straightforward: having sold their own homes they could buy 99-year leases on Legion homes, which in due course could be sold on to those in similar situations. Unlike the original Housing Association the project had to be financed on the open market, although it was regarded as a 'blue-chip' investment. It was therefore at first kept separate from the main operation; but in 1983, following a court ruling on a similar case, it was absorbed within the main Association which oversaw the first development at Sandwich in Kent, consisting of nineteen two-bed and four one-bed houses completed in 1985. More schemes were planned and Legion Leasehold seemed destined to enjoy the same success as the main project.[41]

The Twenty-First Anniversary reception on board HMS *Belfast* in May of that year, hosted by Dennis Cadman and attended by the Secretary of State for Housing had therefore much to celebrate: the Legion ran the second largest association in the country and opened new courts every few months, in many cases Royalty doing the honours; there were generally contented tenants (sometimes rent levels, although not set by the Housing Association itself, caused difficulties) supported by the active local voluntary committees that the Legion organization facilitated; and there was a bright new offspring, the Legion Leasehold, whose future seemed equally rosy.

## The end of the Taxi School

In 1976 the superintendent of the Legion's Taxi School, George Stedman, had retired after 27 years in the job. He remembered that the wives of students often suspected them of having affairs since they were out all hours and came back exhausted. In fact they were learning 'the knowledge'. Two years later the school celebrated its fiftieth anniversary, the Home Secretary, Merlyn Rees, whose father had been one of those gassed in the First World War, unveiling a plaque and presenting the 5,000th licence to a former Irish Guardsman; those present on this occasion included the first woman trainee, the wife of a taxi driver. But despite the celebrations numbers were falling: in the early 1970s the school put as many as 140 new taxi drivers on the streets of London each year; by the 1980s there were barely forty. It was therefore decided to admit sons of ex-servicemen in 1982 and daughters the following year.[42]

Nevertheless in 1982 the Legion still sponsored over 75 per cent of the cabs for the London Taxi Benevolent Association outing for the war disabled; the first stop was Worthing where the Women's Section, who had worked since seven a.m. to prepare a buffet, welcomed guests ranging from First World War veterans to a survivor of HMS *Sheffield*, sunk in the recent Falklands conflict.[43]

Taxi School numbers remained low despite taking in government-sponsored trainees. With the cut-back in government funding in 1990 private individuals were admitted and, following a move in 1992 into newly refurbished premises on the same Brixton site that the school had occupied since 1966, there was a recruitment drive for trainees. But with the reduced numbers of ex-service applications it became pointless to continue. In 1995, sixty-seven years after it had been instituted, the decision was taken to close the school, although the Legion continued to sponsor ex-service taxi driver training at another school.[44]

It was the end of an institution in which the Legion had taken much pride. The heydays had followed the two world wars when the school had helped thousands of ex-servicemen, and some women, to take up lifetime employment. But now it had served its purpose.

## The special status of war-disabled

The Legion was also justifiably proud in 1981 when it won the Manpower Services Commission 'Fit for Work' trophy for its work for the disabled. But still some 20,000 disabled ex-servicemen registered as suitable for employment were out of work, despite the compulsory quota scheme that replaced the King's Roll, which had been wound up, with the Legion's agreement, in 1971. In 1973 the government decided to review the quota scheme itself. This had caused the Legion some anxiety, but the decision was to retain the scheme, passing it to the Manpower Services Commission with instructions to enforce it more strictly, as the Legion had suggested.[45]

Within the overall provisions for the disabled, maintaining the special status of the war pensioner was a constant concern; the Legion suspected that the DHSS would like to regard all disabled as equal, regardless of the circumstances. Mobility was one aspect; if he was in work a disabled ex-serviceman was entitled to a government-supplied car which, from 1976, he could keep if he lost his job. Meanwhile disabled civilians had received a mobility allowance which put them in a better position than the ex-servicemen. From this the Legion inferred that the authorities wanted one scheme for all, with disabled ex-servicemen no longer meriting special status.[46] It was not far wrong. The war pensioners' vehicle scheme was indeed phased out in 1983, but Legion pressure ensured that the war-disabled received a preferential rate of mobility supplement, while non-drivers also got the allowance. But when the Legion had at last persuaded British Rail in 1981 to grant concessionary travel for the war-disabled it found that the Rail Board saw no distinction; all disabled had been included; furthermore the fare reduction was a mere 20 per cent.[47]

Few of those who benefited from the Legion's holiday scheme for the severely disabled had any form of transport. The scheme gave an annual holiday to some 200-300 people of very restricted mobility and, as the years passed, the numbers tended to increase so that by the 1990s over 500 were sometimes involved; Legion members collected them from their homes and took them to guest houses or nursing homes, specially chosen for their facilities and usually at the seaside.

The Legion then turned its attention to another aspect of disability, forming the British

Ex-Servicemen's Wheelchair Sports Association into a Legion branch and organizing the first international ex-service wheelchair games at Stoke Mandeville in 1993, followed by the 1995 games at Gateshead.[48]

### A DMI success story

Even some of the most severely disabled could work from home and Disabled Men's Industries continued to provide an outlet for their skills. The Prime Minister, Margaret Thatcher, bought a number of kitchen items made by ex-service disabled men and women when she visited the display at Preston Hall in 1984. She doubtless had a housewife's eye for serviceability and DMI goods were invariably well-made, the seventy or so homeworkers taking much pride in their craft. DMI head office had moved to the Legion Village in 1971, from which it controlled its country-wide operation, receiving the goods, despatching them to Legion and Women's Section branches for sale at county shows or village fetes, taking back the unsold items and paying the workers the proceeds, while a permanent display in the village enabled branches to make their selections. It was a pity that more of them did not do so; record sales in the late 1970s, especially at the annual sale run by Lloyds of London Branch, had been followed by the effects of the recession and by increased postal charges so that by 1981 the Legion's benevolent fund had to increase its annual grant substantially to enable the company to continue trading. Valiant though the existing branch efforts were, especially those of the Women's Section, they were not enough on their own and, although some Legion Areas ran DMI stalls at their annual conferences, others did not.[49]

*A disabled worker making costume jewellery at home; the problem was to find marketing outlets but great efforts by Disabled Men's Industries in the early 1990s, supported by some Legion branches, enabled the corner to be turned.*

Never at a loss, the DMI management devised new sales schemes: colour pamphlets promoted direct sales while party packs enabled individuals to organize home events. Meanwhile liaison with the DSS War Pensions Welfare Service which visited disabled ex-service people at home had brought more workers into the scheme; but by then the marketing efforts, including a letter to every Legion branch in 1991, had produced some results. Still more workers were taken on and by 1993 the 100 workforce barrier had been broken. The following year the company celebrated its Fiftieth Anniversary, bringing in workers from as far afield as Lancashire and Devon from a total that had now reached 115. D-Day souvenirs helped record sales that year and by now there were 800 live branch accounts compared with 643 the previous year. 1995, with its VE and VJ day highlights, was even better; the sales of memorabilia exceeded all expectations and the 119 workers sitting at home and inundated with orders felt involved and motivated. It was a success story in which DMI and in particular the branch sales organizers, Legion and

Women's Section could take pride, giving new purpose to the lives of many who might otherwise have been aimless.[50]

## Pilgrimages – a new Legion department

A woman reporter accompanying a Legion pilgrimage to Normandy in the summer of 1981 noted that, like Chaucer's pilgrims, each of her fellow travellers had a tale to tell – often the heart-rending loss of a loved one sent off to war with a hurried kiss on a railway station. It had seemed like any other outing until she got to the cemetery, saw the rows of white headstones and observed the emotions of the pilgrims as each placed their wreath carefully on the grave. One was a widow married for only a few months before a telephone call came from the police to her ATS unit to say that he had been killed in the landings. Another was a wartime sweetheart: 'He pleaded with me to get married but I wanted to wait until the war was over.'[51]

Up to 1982 the organization of such pilgrimages was the responsibility of a Legion Benevolent Department staff member. When he died the work was contracted to Holt's, the well-known battlefield tour travel firm, although a Legion courier accompanied each pilgrimage. Holt's seem to have done a good job; at least one pilgrim to the Somme thought that the arrangements were 'superb', ensuring that each of fifty-four pilgrims reached a particular grave in the course of a weekend visit to twenty cemeteries. In 1983, however, the Ministry of Defence took the widows of those killed in the Falklands War to visit their husbands' graves and, although there was obviously compassion for the widows concerned, the trip highlighted the sense of injustice felt by many thousands of other war widows who had never been able to visit their own loved ones' graves in places such as Burma and Singapore. In 1984 the government decided to resume the assisted visit scheme. It began by including the widows in a trip to Normandy that year to commemorate the fortieth anniversary of D-Day and in another to the Far East the following year to commemorate the anniversary of the end of the war.[52]

The Legion was asked to organise the new government scheme as well as to help identify those who should go on the anniversary trips and in 1984 the Council set up a Pilgrimages Department, ending the Holt's involvement but appointing Major Storie-Pugh, who had been the Holt's representative, to head the new department. The scheme attracted a large response, and in 1985 the programme was expanded from ten to twenty-seven destinations including the Far East. In the end the new department arranged pilgrimages for over 750 people that year, including 350 war widows.[53] As one pilgrim wrote on returing from a visit to Tunis: 'We shed tears but we also had much laughter.'[54]

## 1986 – 1990

## SSAFA and Forces Care

The Legion was not the only major organization working for the ex-service community. Amid a host of service and regimental associations and specialist bodies the Soldiers', Sailors' and Airmen's Families Association stood out. Like the Legion it encompassed all three services; but it was essentially different in character. Whereas the Legion relied on its membership to carry out its work, SSAFA trained volunteers as caseworkers and employed professional welfare staff. It preceded the Legion, having been founded in

1885 to care for the families of those in the army and navy and extending that care to the widows and orphans. Latterly SSAFA had expanded its work in the ex-service field, but the two bodies worked alongside each other amicably enough, the Legion acknowledging SSAFA's expertise, while SSAFA recognized the Legion's grass-roots credentials. Indeed some ex-service people, particularly former officers, belonged to both organisations.

In 1987, however, the equilibrium was displaced. A SSAFA initiative sought to improve the co-ordination of ex-service welfare work by gathering the existing agencies into a new network, under the title of 'Forces Care'. The idea undoubtedly had some merit, but in the sensitive charities sector the approach was clumsy. The other ex-service bodies had not been consulted at the beginning and they felt threatened.

The Legion was particularly disturbed. Not only did it feel that its position as the leading ex-service organization was in jeopardy, but, as such, it was annoyed that it had not been taken into SSAFA's confidence when these ideas were being developed. Yet privately it had to acknowledge that its branch service committee system had some shortcomings, especially in comparison to SSAFA's skilled caseworkers; in the now sophisticated welfare environment the committees did not have the same level of knowledge and their approach was sometimes rudimentary. If 'Forces Care' was now to steal the Legion's clothes then to some extent it was itself to blame.[55]

The other organizations, including the Royal British Legion in Scotland, whose existence had not even been acknowledged in the SSAFA plan, looked to the Legion for a lead. There were discussions with SSAFA at high level, but there was never any real possibility of the Legion allowing its welfare activities to be subsumed in another body and in October 1988 the NEC was told that 'Forces Care' was not being pursued. A way out was found: COBSEO, the joint committee on which many of the organizations were represented, set up a study under Sir Greville Spratt, a recent Lord Mayor of London, to improve welfare co-ordination. The resulting report calmed the situation; there were no radical proposals, only suggestions to improve the existing system, and in particular support for the Legion's longstanding suggestion of a Veterans' Department.[56]

Nevertheless the Legion realized that its limitations had contributed to the 'Forces Care' initiative and it determined to put its house in order. Relations with SSAFA were rebuilt and, although a suggestion for a new joint training facility was not realized, Legion members attended SSAFA training courses; in 1990 some 100 were trained. This only showed the scale of the Legion problem: there were perhaps 20,000 who, in theory at any rate, were engaged in welfare. And the conservatism was apparent when Conference 1988 overturned the NEC decision to re-name 'service' committees as 'welfare' committees in an attempt to clarify their role to the public.[57]

Already, in 1987, Advisory Committees had been instituted at County level to raise standards of welfare. But clearly much more was needed and this whole area would be examined in the 1990 Ernst and Young study (see page 351), resulting in changes which would not just restore confidence in the Legion's welfare work but ensure that it achieved a new level of competence.

### The older war widow's plight

The war widows' tax burden had been removed, but the Legion still felt the difference in treatment of those widowed, which depended on when their husband died, to be grossly unfair. However much sympathy there might be for the wife of a soldier killed in Northern Ireland, the unpalatable fact was that her pre-1973 counterpart received only half the younger widow's income. The reason for this was that the present-day widow, in addition to her war widows's pension, received a service widow's pension as well as a 'one-off' compensation payment. Legion or COBSEO deputations repeatedly brought this disparity to the government's notice throughout the 1980s, urging an 'age allowance' for the older widows, but without any apparent effect. In 1988 a £9 million government windfall inspired the Legion to approach 200 MPs in an attempt to use the money to help these war widows. But the government had other ideas for the surplus. Next, the Chancellor was asked to fund increases out of the savings made to the Exchequer as the elderly widows died; but again the response was unhelpful. Nor was it possible to force a debate in the House on the issue. But all this effort had not gone unnoticed and in late 1989 there was at last a breakthrough: the pre-1973 widows were awarded an extra £40 per week which brought their income almost up to the level of the post-1973 widows. Although it is difficult to understand why full parity could not have been granted, it was a satisfying result.[58]

There still remained the question of how much of the pension should be regarded as income when certain other benefits were assessed. The Legion had long campaigned for all of it to be disregarded and was somewhat taken aback in 1988 when the government indicated that they were moving in the opposite direction by suggesting that the whole amount should be treated as income when assessing housing benefit. But Legion protests produced a change of heart and local authority discretionary disregards were allowed to continue. The next year the government actually increased the amount to be disregarded from £4 to £5 and the Legion had some success in persuading local authorities to disregard even more. By 1989 about half of the authorities were disregarding more than the statutory amount, which in 1990 the government increased to £10, and to £50 in the case of the pre-1973 widows. Meanwhile the Legion continued to press for the whole of the war pension to be disregarded when making assessments, reiterating their position that it was not a benefit but compensation for a loss.[59]

## The Legion Leasehold collapse

The amount of their pension disregard was vital to the older war widows living in local authority housing. But for those seeking accommodation it was not just the rent problem; there was a shortage of flats. Legion Housing Association growth began to slow in the late 1980s as government and local authority funding fell and resources tended to be directed towards the inner city areas. By 1988 it had become clear that the environment in which the Association operated had changed. No longer were developments risk-free based on government funding. Private finance was increasingly involved, meaning that building schemes were now commercial ventures demanding new staff skills. That year the Association had to borrow £5 million to finance its programme and, although some 300 properties were completed in 1989, 1990 saw only ninety built. It was a far cry from the heady days of the 1970s when the estate was expanding at the rate of 500 flatlets a year.[60]

Meanwhile the sister organization, the Legion Leasehold Housing Association, which enabled elderly ex-service homeowners to buy leases on sheltered properties, was making strong progress; by 1988 some 140 homes had been completed and the Leasehold operation was once more a separate and self-sufficient entity, looking to expand still further to meet a distinct need. But in 1990 disaster struck. The penal interest rates introduced by the Chancellor the previous year paralysed house sales so that the prospective Leasehold purchasers could not sell their own homes. The result was that

Legion Leasehold was left with empty housing stock on which the loan interest was now £3,000 a day. Leasehold turned to the main Housing Association to bail them out. But now a 'conflict of interest' arose: most of the Housing Association Board members were also Leasehold Board members, and furthermore members of the Legion's National Executive Council. When they had been excluded from voting the decision was taken. It was a regretful but firm 'no thanks'. In some difficulty itself due to the high cost of money, it would hardly be in the Housing Assocation's interests to take on the Leasehold liability as well.[61]

Now it was up to the lenders and by a narrow vote they decided on receivership. This was the end of the road for Leasehold; a liquidator was called in while the Housing Association, having by now completely restructured its Board, helped existing tenants by taking charge of the properties. But it was by no means the end of the story. The Legion itself was among the creditors and was owed over £1 million, of which £380,000 was repayable from sales of assets. A further £100,000 loan was unsecured. Some £700,000 had thus been lost and, since these were charitable funds, a Charity Commission inquiry followed. Meanwhile those engaged in the internal assault on the leadership (see page 349) lost no time in briefing the press, adding to the Legion's difficulties.[62]

When the Charity Commission report appeared it principally criticized the management procedures which had contributed to the failure, noting the conflicts of interest arising out of the same people sitting on different Boards where they had to resolve incompatible aims, while at the same time often lacking housing expertise. But there was no suggestion of fraud and no legal proceedings, although the Legion trustees were admonished. The report was presented to Conference in 1992, the National President noting that the Charity Commissioners were aware that the Legion had since called in experts to review its management structure and using the occasion to remind delegates in no uncertain terms of their own responsibilities in that respect: 'Those of you who came here to rubbish . . . restructuring had better think again.' The subsequent Commissioners' report was placed in the hands of the membership; a committee, composed entirely of members who were lawyers, among them a QC, was appointed to examine the Commissioners' report and ensure the remedial action.[63]

All of this had given a severe shock to the Legion's system. But it also jolted the reform process; few would now argue that change was not needed (see page 352).

### The remarkable Ellesmere Port project

Management had a better record at Ellesmere Port when the Legion took over the local branch employment scheme as a national project in 1988. It dated from 1976 when the branch had decided to employ eight local school leavers on three acres of land behind its headquarters on the south bank of the Mersey opposite Liverpool by converting it into gardens with a bandstand, children's playground and car parking. The branch bore the cost of materials and the Training and Development Commission paid the wages. Similar local projects followed and by 1977 over 100 young people had been found jobs on enterprises such as building a village hall and a Red Cross headquarters, while taking time off to attend vocational training on day release courses. The numbers continued to increase: by 1978 there were 350 youngsters working on similar projects, learning building, painting and decorating skills; by 1981 twelve adults were involved, and by 1985 the scheme operated its own training centre converted from four terraced houses bought by the branch, this  work also having been undertaken by the trainees. By now not only building trades were involved: there were playgroups and sports groups while the administration of the centre needed reception and typing skills; other activities ranged from horticulture to running a magazine. City and Guilds recognition had been obtained and the staff – nearly all ex-service and changed over every two years to give more people a chance to work in this depressed area – had grown to around forty.[64]

By 1988, with National Executive Council representation on the Board to recognize its national status, Ellesmere Port was run as a commercial activity which included advising local businesses on a consultancy basis. In early 1990 there was a move to a purpose-designed building which included facilities for computer technology training and it began to assist with service resettlement: up to 180 ex-servicemen each year could be trained and placed in employment.

It was a remarkable story and, with the 'Options for Change' service redundancies looming, Ellesmere Port seemed destined to be at the forefront of the Legion's efforts to assist those trying to find employment in civil life.[65]

## Small Business scheme resumes

Not only could ex-servicemen be trained at Ellesmere Port, but, if they wanted to open their own businesses, the Legion would help. The Small Business scheme had been re-introduced in 1985, an echo of the early days when the Legion had lent unemployed men £25 to enable them to start up on their own with a horse and cart and avoid the desperate poverty of the 1920s; in the age of the microchip the same principle applied, but it was now an interest-free loan of £2,500 over five years. In the distant past the branch would bring in local experts to enable those starting up to get advice; now Counties established teams of volunteers for the same purpose.[66]

By the late 1980s up to 150 loans were being made each year to assist enterprises as varied as as keep-fit gymnasia, boarding kennels, computer software installation and a market research company. A Legion advisor visited service resettlement courses at home and overseas and 'starter packs' were available to advise those considering self-employment, regardless of whether a loan was sought. When a loan was needed the principle was the same as in the early days; all applications were investigated by the local branch before going to the central committee which approved the loan – or not – depending on whether it was considered to be a viable venture. Age was no bar; applicants varied from the 20s to age 55, raised to 60 in 1988. But if a loan was made then regular progress reports were needed.[67]

Small businesses were as liable to the economic climate as any other activity and in 1990 the number of applications fell sharply.

## The Legion Village revived

The winds of economic fortune blew just as keenly through the revamped Legion Industries site at Preston Hall. The competition was such that profit margins had to be very low to keep the order books full. No allowances were made for disabled men and new customers had to be found and the work diversified: the Signs Department now made factory and industrial signs as well as following social trends by producing 'neighbourhood watch' signs; a new printing press kept up with modern needs; pallet-making was perhaps the most responsive to economic changes, but the woodworking kept going. At the sixtieth anniversary of the Village in 1985, marked by a garden party, despite current concerns there was much to be proud of.[68]

The satisfaction was not confined to long-established activities. A year before, in 1984, Industries had ventured into a new project. In conjunction with the Manpower Services Commission it had set up a Sheltered Industrial Group for disabled ex-service people living in the South East but too far from Maidstone to work in the Legion Village; they were found suitable work in their local area with 'host firms' who were paid by Industries for the value of the work done. It proved to be a success and the following year the scheme, now known as Sheltered Placement, was expanded. In 1988 the government restricted it to 120 employees in the South East, but in 1990 a similar scheme was opened in the Newcastle area. Despite Legion Industries' unfamiliarity with this part of the country, it too was a success and quickly reached the government ceiling, although in both areas the official limitations were disappointing.[69]

As the recession continued into the 1990s so the Industries' problems were unabated; prices were down while the cost of raw materials rose. Yet the workforce remained intact with some 230 disabled people employed of whom 180 were ex-service. But in 1994 and 1995 the situation improved under a new management system with a smaller Board meeting frequently and working to a strategic plan. The plan included a new department called the Special Products Division, set up to provide work for those whose disability was so severe that they could not undertake normal work. It served to emphasize the underlying purpose of the Legion Industries – to provide disabled people with the dignity of useful work.[70]

Meanwhile environmental improvements to the Village, including a community garden scheme, had heralded more development: following the 1986 opening of the Mountbatten Pavilion, there was a new surgery in 1988 while a community centre, incorporating a Legion Club, was added in 1990. The major project was, however, Gavin Astor House, a 33-bed nursing home opened in 1993 to care for the elderly and infirm residents of the Village. Remarkably the whole development had been funded by Industries, mainly from the sale of a plot of land, and it included twelve self-contained flatlets for those who could look after themselves but who might need occasional help from the nursing staff.[71]

Many of the new developments were opened by the Duchess of Kent, who had first visited the Village in 1967 and had subsequently become a deeply interested Patron, bringing her own charm to the occasions. As she would no doubt be aware, much of the credit for its regeneration lay with a former Legion Chairman, Charles Busby, who, as chairman of the Village Committee, had devoted himself to the well-being of this inspiring community.

# 1991 – 1995

## A time of change

An article in the Legion Journal in 1992 summed up the situation facing the Legion and similar charities as the end of the century approached: family support for the individual had largely disappeared, but many were ignorant of their entitlement to state support, which in any case had gaps. Although the Legion's service committees still had their front-line role, they needed more support at County level to provide additional expertise, including a full knowledge of the state benefits system, and to achieve economies by co-operation with other bodies.[72]

It was this need to bring more knowledge to the task, and to make the very best use of money, that led to the introduction of County Field Officers following the 1990-91 Review of the Legion (see pages 351–2). They quickly proved their worth. Having established a rapport with the service committees they liaised with the other charities, usually also represented at county level, to share the financial burden. Not all these charities were ex-service; a man or woman might be entitled to benevolence from a professional or trade association as well as service charities. By 1995 the CFO team was working strongly, enabling the Legion to provide a much more effective service and at the same time saving money. Those who had resisted their introduction now asked for more CFOs and in many counties they became key players in the wider ex-service field.

Now that proper backing had been given, attention turned again to the service committees themselves. Previous attempts to train them had been random and only partly effective. This time, in keeping with the new Legion approach, the job would be done properly. A professional caseworker training team was established and, in a series of courses around the country, it trained some 800 caseworkers in 1995, aiming at a cadre of 2,000 by the end of the following year. Never before had the Legion deployed such a well-trained welfare force.[73]

All that needed to be resolved was the state connection: no less than seventeen government agencies were involved in ex-service welfare and in the Legion's view there should be a single point of entry into the system. The campaign for a Department of Ex-service Affairs – 'veterans' had been dropped from the title since in United Kingdom parlance the word implied old age and war service, neither of which necessarily applied to ex-service welfare – had continued in 1991 with a private member's bill, but time did not permit a second reading. Following the 1993 Conference a campaign group was established and, after taking advice from parliamentary contacts, it re-defined the aim; what was now envisaged was a sub-department under a Minister to co-ordinate all government support for the ex-service community. The argument was that it was more than ever necessary to have such a focal point in a time when few politicians or civil servants had any knowledge of service life and the problems that could result. Media interest in the D-Day anniversary was exploited, there was a presentation to the Defence Standing Committee and Lord Haig, son of the Legion's founder, initiated a debate in the House of Lords. But the government was unresponsive, continuing to maintain that such a department would simply add another layer of bureaucracy. There was, however, a gleam of light, at least for those who believed in the integrity of politicians: the Labour Party, now seen as likely to win office again, pledged that they would implement the Legion's plan.[74]

If evidence were needed that service life held special problems it emerged at the Legion's 1991 Conference. A delegate who had been on Christmas Island during the underwater nuclear tests told Conference during a debate on the effects on those involved: 'I washed in the sea, shaved in the sea, the seawater was distilled for us to drink – how the hell didn't we get radiation into our bodies?' Another contentious issue arose after the 1992 Gulf War when some veterans alleged that their subsequent illnesses were a direct result of their service and the condition became known as the 'Gulf War syndrome'. There was much conflict of opinion on this, since chemical weapons, although present, had not been used. The Legion kept an open mind on the existence of a Gulf War syndrome, but it assisted those who felt that their Gulf service had led to later illness, in the meanwhile supporting the 'syndrome' investigations taking place in the United States.[75]

### Tighter controls

The introduction in 1981 of the system whereby branches had access to central funds for benevolent work had inceased the opportunity for abuse, especially as the cheque limit had been raised to £150 in 1986. One or two high-spending local service committees made regular payments when the need had not really been established. Even where a proper need existed public funds might be available; in one case seven regular Legion beneficiaries were found to be entitled to a state allowance that well exceeded the charity's payments. But a fraud case which came to light in 1992 involved a suspected loss of £70,000 and, with the trustees now very mindful of their responsibilities, the action was drastic: all local committees' cheque books were withdrawn and, although the committees continued to investigate cases, pending the introduction of CFOs, payments were made by Area offices. The change caused a furore; some local service committees felt that their integrity had been impugned and said so. But there was little choice, and, in the context of so much change, it was the sooner accepted. As Chart B1 (page 446) shows, the effect on the overall 'relief of distress' expenditure was marked.[76] Changes in state benefits for the incapacitated also made it possible to phase out the Legion's Permanently Incapacitated and Widows' scheme which had provided regular payments to those in need, and from 1 April 1994 no new applications were accepted.[77]

But the Legion also imposed stricter controls on headquarters activities. Consultants were called in to review costs at the residential homes; their managers then ran budgets more tightly and operating costs were substantially cut. By 1994 there was an annual surplus. Meanwhile the government's 'Care in the Community' programme gave the managers some headaches. Local authorities now supervised the inmates they supported. Since the Legion admitted people from many areas, different authorities were involved and each had their own rules; some even stipulated the number and size of eggs that a resident should eat in a day.[78]

By 1995 there were seven Legion residential homes. A modest investment of £1 had acquired a sixth home in 1989, although the costs of renovation and extension were to prove a little more expensive: St John and the British Red Cross had offered Mais House in Bexhill, provided that the existing twenty-seven residents could remain when the Legion enlarged it to fifty-five beds.[79] Costing £2 million, the work was completed in 1993. The seventh home followed an appeal launched on the fiftieth anniversary of Dunkirk in 1990 to complement a substantial Legion investment. The Dunkirk Memorial House near Taunton in Somerset opened in 1995, although not without some problems on the way: the existing building to which it was anchored was described as 'a jerry-built disaster'.[80]

*The Dunkirk Memorial Home. Such purpose-built residential homes provide a high standard of accommodation.*

All seven homes were now either purpose-built or largely so. A new Crosfield House at Rhayader in Wales had replaced the old mansion at Bwlch in 1986 and a modern Lister House had opened at Ripon in Yorkshire in 1988. They were well-run: the residents, aged from sixty-five to over 100, had 24-hour nursing care, lived in en-suite accommodation and could make use of comfortable public rooms. They received weekly pocket money, entertainers, funded by Lloyds of London Branch, visited and there were regular outings often organized by the local Legion branch who would also adopt residents, remembering their birthdays. Most of the residents' costs were met by income support, with the Poppy Appeal giving some assistance.[81]

All of this had involved the Legion in heavy capital investment, while maintenance of the buildings accounted for some $7\frac{1}{2}$ per cent of the Poppy Appeal. Yet they benefited less than 500 people. Despite the pressing need for more such accommodation, the Council decided in 1991 that no more such homes would be built or acquired.[82]

Accommodation for patients from distant parts was still the difficulty at the Churchill Centre in the Legion Village. Even when the new Gavin Astor House nursing home, sited nearby, took over this task from the Mountbatten Pavilion in 1993, still only four rooms could be provided and the patients often brought wives, husbands or other carers.[83] Nevertheless those who were able to make use of the Churchill facilities were grateful, particularly when they had had to wait years for treatment because of the lack of provision in their part of the country: when a stroke patient got 70 per cent more movement in his limbs, his wife asked, 'Can he come again?' And there was not a dry eye in the room when a member returned to his branch from a visit to the centre and was able to stand for the Exhortation.[84]

There were long waiting lists too for the Legion's three Convalescent Homes ('Rest' having been dropped from the title). But when in 1994 the Council, conscious of their duty to ensure that charitable funds were used only where there was actual need, decided to introduce a charge of £25 a week for those who could afford it, the decision was overturned by Conference, who believed they should have been consulted. Caught between two stools, the Charity Commission and Conference, the trustees consulted the former, and financial assessments were re-introduced in 1996, this time without argument.[85]

Such give-and-take was part of the re-adjustment in the 1990s as the Legion caught up with the times. The new Welfare Division, overseeing all benevolent, pensions, pilgrimages and resettlement activities, provided the expertise, but the Council had to take the decisions. Difficult though they were, there was now much better use of funds.

## A parting of the ways

It was also a time of re-adjustment for the Legion's Housing Association. It had been founded to provide accommodation for the elderly, but in 1991 it raised £10 million to build homes for young service and ex-service people, including those who were leaving as a result of the ending of the Cold War and the subsequent defence cuts. Meanwhile, as Conference 1991 had observed, the Association was now distancing itself from the Legion. This was not merely the consequence of the Leasehold Housing affair; it was now a requirement that such Associations should be independent of all other bodies. And public funding had become conditional on offering half of the tenancies to the local authority, so that in theory 50 per cent could have been filled by non ex-service. In practice the authorities tended to find ex-service people and a bare 7 per cent were 'civilian' occupants.

In 1992 there was a significant change: the Association dropped 'Legion' from its title and became 'Housing 21', a reference to the approaching century, and the following year the Council decided that the Legion should formally disassociate itself from Housing 21, although branches were encouraged to continue to support their local Courts. And at the Association's request the Legion co-opted member was withdrawn from its Board.[86]

Thus ended nearly thirty years of Legion involvement in a successful enterprise which it had launched and nurtured. Another jewel in its crown seemed to have gone, but the judgement had been that for the Association to do its work to best effect it needed not only to be fully independent but to be seen as such. There was some consolation in the fact that the Housing Associations in Northern Ireland and the Isle of Man, which were governed by different rules, kept 'Legion' in their title; although the latter was very small and only maintained one 32-flat development, the former* continued to expand its stock. Nevertheless some in the Legion felt the loss keenly.

## War pensions claims grow

As the century approached its close there was a sharp rise in the number of war pensions claimants (see Chart B2) as the Second World War veterans, now retired, began to relate failing health to their wartime service, encouraged by advances in medical skill which could often establish the link. In keeping with modern belief there was more awareness of entitlement to compensation, combined with a need to supplement an often meagre income in retirement. But there were still First World War cases: a 94-year-old who had been wounded on the Somme and 'paid off' with a lump sum of between £10 and £20 in the 1920s had his case reviewed after he wrote to the Legion in 1991, ultimately receiving a pension of £60 per week. And a 98-year-old who had fought both on the Somme and at Ypres got his first war disability pension in 1995.

The Legion also helped those still serving to exercise their rights. The crown was no longer immune and a serviceman could now sue the Ministry of Defence for compensation in cases of negligence. The Legion assisted such cases and quickly established a good working relationship with the MOD, only pursuing cases in which there seemed to be a genuine entitlement. Added publicity was given to this work through the unit briefings by Legion recruiters (see pages 349-50) and in 1993 over 900 cases were actioned.[87]

Against the general trend, in 1993 the government announced that it would no longer compensate for noise-induced deafness below 20 per cent. Deafness in varying degrees had afflicted many servicemen before ear protection had been introduced and the Legion, which had not been consulted, protested strongly. It believed that it was an indication that the government was once again trying to bring war pensions and industrial injuries into line, and the Legion was no more receptive to this proposition than it had been on previous occasions; the serviceman had suffered on his country's behalf. There was an exchange of letters with the Minister, who was indignant at the Legion's reaction, but the Chairman's measured reply noted that over the years there had been a steady erosion of preferences for war pensioners and that the government had only acted on such issues as the treatment of pre-1973 war widows after much prodding. It all pointed to a need for better understanding between the government and the ex-service community, which was why an Ex-services Affairs Department was needed.[88]

War pension disregards were still an issue. But Hornsey Branch demonstrated in 1991 that local authorities could be convinced: supported by other local branches, they paraded to Haringey Council behind a piper; there the branch chairman addressed the assembled Council, with the result that the disregard was reinstated and war pensioners were saved

*In 1997 the Northern Ireland Housing Association too changed its name – to the Clanmill Housing Association.

up to £50 a week in rents. Legion efforts had by 1994 persuaded some 88 per cent of councils to ignore war and war widows' pensions as income, but a national policy was still needed since councils were apt to change and there were cases such as that of the Burma veteran and former prisoner of war for whom the Legion won a war pension of £46 a week in 1995. The District Council immediately classed £36 as income and cancelled the veteran's benefits, forcing him to repay £800. It was not an isolated case, and in the Legion's view a blatant example of taxation on war injuries.[89]

### The resettlement venture

The Legion and the other ex-service organizations had also been critical of the government's approach to the resettlement of those leaving the forces under the 'Options for Change' programme. Compensation was adequate, even generous by service standards, but it was not just a question of money; the need was for jobs and housing. Acting together under their newly re-established relationship, the Legion and SSAFA split the responsibilites. SSAFA assumed the housing task (somewhat ironic in view of the Legion's long connection prior to the break with Housing 21) while the Legion would deal with training. A Legion-organized seminar in 1991 led to a continuing dialogue between the ex-service organizations and the MOD and, as has been noted, may have influenced some subsequent MOD actions such as the appointment of a Director General of Resettlement and the establishment of a tri-service employment agency.[90]

The Legion's major act was to set up a training centre at Tidworth. At a capital cost of some £6 million, it was a far larger enterprise than the existing centre at Ellesmere Port, but a little over half of the money would come from a European Community grant, while an appeal sought to defray the rest. Time was short and the training began in buildings provided by the Army within Tidworth garrison while funding and construction proceeded. A contract was signed with the MOD for resettlement training in 1992 and renewed in 1994, while the scope of the activities was extended by another contract with the local authority, Wiltshire, and by admitting servicemen's wives for training; there was even a crèche. By 1994 the centre, now housed in impressive new buildings on its own site with the most modern facilities, was running up to ten MOD resettlement courses a week as well as training local people to fill work vacancies in the region and developing commercial training contracts.[91]

Such diversification was important in order to make the

*The Legion Training College at Tidworth trained local civilians as well as running resettlement curses for servicemen. But it encountered serious financial problems.*

enterprise self-sufficient. Not only had the Legion been responsible for half of the capital costs of some £7 million, but it provided an annual subsidy of £750,000 and some members felt that the government should be paying for the retraining; after all they had created the redundancies and in any case those concerned received adequate compensation. But, as the Legion's Chairman pointed out, the organization had been founded to enable ex-servicemen to stand on their own two feet with dignity; moreover 68 per cent of service leavers received no redundancy payments.[92]

Helped by the Leopold Muller Trust* a much-needed sixty-room student accommodation block was added in 1995. Of hotel quality, it enabled the centre not only to meet the MOD's standards but to house other users, who included Legion members attending courses and conferences. Yet in the National Council some of the trustees harboured grave doubts over the viability of the whole enterprise.[93]

There were more doubts over Tidworth's elder sister at Ellesmere Port which had not only provided the inspiration for the new venture but some senior staff. Their departure may have contributed to management weaknesses, leading to an NEC inquiry in 1992; the inquiry revealed no serious problems, but there was some concern at the dependency on government funding through the various subsidized training schemes. Ellesmere Port therefore also made great efforts to diversify through more commercial work; but it was operating in a depressed area and by 1994, following a deferment of the RN and RAF elements of MOD redundancy, combined with a change in government policy which switched funding from training to placement, it was in difficulty. At the end of 1995 the Legion's Council was looking at the options for Ellesmere Port, which included closure.[94]

In attempting to provide the best possible support for those leaving the forces, the Legion might have over-reached itself.

## More help

In 1994 the Legion had appointed a Resettlement Support Officer to liaise with the MOD and to brief those leaving on Legion assistance. Unlike previous eras, the Legion was not directly involved in job placement. Officers made use of the existing Officers' Association service; other ranks were entitled to help from the Regular Forces Employment Association and, although the Legion offered volunteers to assist the forty RFEA local offices, their help was not considered necessary. One person in eight in the country was, however, self-employed and in 1994 the Legion's Small Business Advisory Service, now having to cope with swelling European legislation, had been recognized by the MOD for lecturing and counselling. The Loans Scheme helped over 100 men and women each year and there were many satisfied customers: 'You are the only concern to have given me any assistance despite having approached dozens of organizations from banks to lending institutions,' wrote one ex-RAF man. In 1995 the Small Business offices were moved from the Legion Village to Tidworth.[95]

There were openings with the Attendants Company for those made redundant and the company took advantage of the continuing high quality of intake. When other security companies were being driven to the wall by the recession it increased its business, taking in some of the new shopping malls and, keeping abreast of other new business, winning the important Mercury Communications contract in 1993. By now the workforce had risen to 1,600, but it still included 200 disabled. In 1995 the headquarters moved from Cambridge to Preston where a state-of-the-art control room had been opened two years before. It was not a great distance from Rochdale where the local branch had erected a

*Muller was a Czech refugee whose wife and daughter had died in a concentration camp.

hut to run a car park in 1927 (see pages 88–9); but much had happened since and few businesses could have matched the Royal British Legion Attendants Company for consistent enterprise, based on the sole aim of providing worthwhile employment to ex-servicemen and women.[96]

The Cambrian Factory had been no less enterprising, trying to expand its sales by supplying materials to customers as varied as the Health Service and Burberrys and even taking its stall to the World Trade Fair in Seville. But it still ran at a loss and, although the Legion now shared responsibility with the local council, both sides agreed to sell in 1992 to a new owner. It ended sixty-five years of Legion association with the Factory.[97]

## Surrounded by friends

The green hills among which the Cambrian Factory lay bore perhaps a passing resemblance to those half a world away on the borders of India, where war cemeteries held the graves of thousands, not only from the British Isles but from the Indian sub-continent, all of whom had died in the same cause. Since the mid-1980s the Legion's pilgrimage programme had, with government support, expanded into many parts of the Far East – Thailand, Malaysia, Singapore, even the tiny island of Ambon, a thousand miles off the Australian coast and once a POW camp. But India held a special significance; Kohima was one of the greatest battles of the Second World War. The guards of honour furnished by the Indian Army were immaculate; their buglers sounded the Last Post, the poignant notes echoing over the quiet valleys as the pilgrims stood in silence. Sometimes the emotions overcame them; a widow sank to the ground before her husband's grave and, seeing this, an Indian Army colonel went to sit beside her, putting his arm around her. She grieved because her husband would be alone when she departed. But the colonel comforted her: 'He is surrounded by his friends.'[98]

Such simple humanity often prevailed on these visits. A widow of a soldier killed in Norway made a pilgrimage on her own, but the Norwegians treated her as a VIP. Begonias had been placed on the grave, but when her hosts found that she had also brought begonias they gently replaced the flowers with her own. When a widow visited her husband's grave on Ambon, a fellow pilgrim was the comrade who had first buried him, digging the grave when his own weight was down to four and a half stone. And, in an unconscious echo of the Kohima epitaph, another widow was moved to exclaim: 'Oh just wait till I get back and tell them – tell them that I did it – that I saw my husband's grave, where he fought and died.'[99]

*A pilgrim kneels by her brother's grave at Imphal, having brought with her the medals that he earned but never saw.*

To the government's credit the pilgrimage scheme was extended into the 1990s and a pilgrimage to Poland in 1993 visited the graves of some of those who had taken part in the 'Great Escape' from a POW camp and had been shot on Hitler's personal order. In each of these years around 100 widows undertook the trip, often accompanied by others of their family and in all about 1,000 people travelled annually with the Legion. In 1994 and 1995, amid all the official pomp and ceremony that accompanied the anniversaries of the Normandy landings and the ending of the war, the pilgrims continued quietly to find their way to the graveside and to lay their poppies, guided by the Legion.[100]

★     ★     ★

The Legion's task had not been easy as the old century approached its end. The change of direction had been overdue and it had entailed reshaping the traditional responsibilities of the rank-and-file. But, once the changes had been made, the members had simply got on with it; the Legion's help was still needed, and if it could be done in a better way, then so be it.

# CHAPTER 19

## FUNDRAISING 1971-2001

# *Turning the Corner*

## 1971 – 1975

### The need for change

General Bucher had become Chairman of the Poppy Appeal in 1963, on relinquishing the national chairmanship. In 1964 he established the first Appeals Committee, the work having previously been done by offshoots of other committees. Despite this he then had the misfortune to preside over a period of steady decline in real terms. The public were accustomed to putting the same amount in the collecting box each year when they took their poppies; but, with soaring inflation, each year the coins were worth less. The value of the Appeal could only be maintained by a bigger collection, but, as Bucher pointed out, the organization was simply not up to it; there were not enough collectors and he feared that at some stage professional organizers might have to be introduced, meaning that the whole nature of the Appeal would change.[1]

It had to change anyway. The poppy collectors were mainly women, motivated by the sacrifices of the First World War. They had been reinforced by their younger sisters following a further war. It was a body which had remained largely independent of the Legion itself, with local organizers working directly to the Appeals Secretary. Now the older organizers and collectors were dropping by the wayside and needed to be replaced, and if possible augmented. The Legion's field structure would be involved and every County would have to pull its weight. So would more of the branches. Although some had been actively engaged from the start, others had played little part. The general public would still be asked to assist, but this new approach would affect the structure and perhaps some of the character of the Appeal organization.

At this stage much of the 'intelligence' on the state of the Appeal network came from the Women's Section branches, many of which had been deeply involved in its work. The need for more helpers was greatest in the large cities. When a collector or organizer dropped out the tendency was to amalgamate the area with another, inevitably resulting in a reduced collection. Sometimes the area had to be abandoned altogether and in 1972 there were sixty-six such 'black spots'. Much of the Appeal publicity was therefore directed at finding new helpers, but intakes were barely sufficient to replace the departures and by 1975 there were still around sixty black spots. More Legion branches were now, however, involved and at last the male reluctance to take part in 'women's work' seemed be on the wane.[2]

The new collectors could benefit from the advice of those who had been doing it for years: stand in the middle of the pavement, rattle the tin gently, not agressively and (if a woman, presumably) wear a frivolous hat. Some veteran collectors had a tale to tell: one was handed a baby by a woman who was 'taking the other one to the toilet'; she never returned. The same collector climbed scaffolding on a hotel to collect £1 from the labourers at the top; on descending she was given a hot whisky by the manager.[3] St

George's Hanover Square Branch recalled an urgent summons to No 10 Downing Street; a nineteen year-old typist was sent – it was a busy time – and the Prime Minister, Harold Wilson, took two poppies, positioning her at the foot of the stairs to catch the cabinet leaving. It made an impressive house collection but in the Irish Republic in 1971 the situation in the North meant that house collections had to replace public selling of the poppy. Despite the troubles at least one Dublin lady increased her collection; knowing who bought poppies in the street she called instead at their houses.[4]

The Legion's public relations campaign was now year-round and included urging people, and especially young people, to come forward and help. A dispute over a television appeal in 1971 led to a further initiative. When the broadcaster wanted to introduce anti-war material – US Vietnam veterans throwing away their medals – the NEC instead invited Richard Baker, the well-known television newscaster who had served in the Second World War, to give the appeal. The experience led him to suggest the 'Friends of the Poppy Appeal', consisting of figures from the entertainment world. Formed the following year, it included television stars who would give the Appeal a more up-to-date image and perhaps encourage greater participation by the younger generation.[5]

### Different boundaries do not help

Despite the changes, the Appeal results continued to be disappointing. Although, for the benefit of those who worked so hard each year, each was termed a 'record', in fact they did not keep pace with inflation and, as Chart C1 on page 447 shows, in real terms the five-year total sank even lower than the previous period. More members took part in 1971, stimulated by the Legion's fiftieth anniversary, and the result that year was good. But in the other years inflation was the victor. There was no shortage of new ideas: commando squads of collectors to saturate the large cities and, for safety, teams of four to six to carry out the house-to-house collections. Such initiatives were needed; three-quarters of the total amount collected still came from street and house-to-house activities, the balance being made up of other activities such as bring-and-buy sales, often organized by the Women's Section, wreath sales and church collections.[6]

Although the changes were rejected by the rest of the Legion, the Poppy Appeal adopted the 1972 new local authority boundaries; it would have been difficult to do otherwise since street collections needed the local authority's permission; but there were now double the number of authorities involved. Working to different boundaries did little to help integrate the Appeal into the Legion structure; for one thing it confused individual County results, important in promoting more interest in the Appeal. Happily unaffected by the new boundaries, Armagh and the Isle of Man remained at the top of the league.[7]

### Controversy over rosettes

In 1974 the poppy symbol was used by the right-wing British Movement in anti-immigration propaganda, causing the Legion to threaten the leader of the movement, Colin Jordan, with a High Court injunction. But the Legion's unswerving determination to keep clear of politics had earlier led to difficulties with the Poppy Factory, which had long made badges for political parties; when in 1972 the *Sunday Mirror* disclosed that a group supporting Enoch Powell, the Conservative minister dismissed from the cabinet for his views on immigration, had their badges made at the factory, the National Executive Council decided that in future only rosettes and badges of an uncontroversial nature should be produced; hence it made rosettes saying 'Put the "Great" back into Britain', but

386

refused an order for 'Mother of God, Save Russia'.[8]

Such work was of course taken on to keep the Poppy Factory's workforce fully employed when not meeting their annual order of 30-40 million poppies, as well as wreaths, car stickers and other items. For forty years the poppies and wreaths had been stored at the warehouse at King's Cross, but in 1971 a new warehouse was erected in the Legion Village as part of the redevelopment of the site. At the same time the Appeal staff moved from Pall Mall into a new office block in the Village, like the warehouse purpose-built for a revitalised Appeal.[9]

# 1976 – 1980

## A new vigour

In 1975 General Bucher retired as Chairman of the Appeal. He was replaced by Colonel Hughes. As National Vice Chairman Hughes had already made an impact on the Appeal by introducing league tables to encourage local performance.

Faced with a dwindling and ageing body of collectors, Bucher had sought more involvement in the Appeal by the Legion's own structure. The clubs were also a part of that structure, or at least an offshoot, and raised considerable amounts of money for local charities. Their past record of giving to the Appeal was not impressive but perhaps they had not been properly encouraged and in 1976 Bucher presented a silver salver for the club which donated the greatest sum per member to the Poppy Appeal.

This was a theme which Colonel Hughes took up. At the 1977 Legion Annual Conference he reminded delegates that already he had 'gained a reputation for knocking on club doors' and suggested that they donate a percentage of their profits to the Appeal. This proposal got a mixed reception, some delegates clearly feeling that Legion fundraising had nothing to do with the clubs. Nothing daunted, in 1980 Hughes returned to the theme, challenging branches and clubs to defer support of local community schemes, to which they contributed £600,000 annually, in favour of the Appeal and 'let charity begin at home'. Had they all responded it would have added some 15 per cent to the total. But few did.[10]

Hughes nevertheless believed that the real problem was that the Legion relied too heavily on the annual Remembrance collection. Although it outperformed any other charity in street and house-to-house collections, it lacked the year-round approach of the others, which gave some of them better overall results. He re-launched the scheme for Deeds of Covenant, which in the Legion's case currently raised only £4,000 a year when others had a covenanted income of as much as £1 million a year, one third of the whole Poppy Appeal income. There were other ideas: new collection boxes for use in clubs, 'starter packs' to assist Appeal Organizers to run new fundraising events and a string of articles in the *Journal* on how to organize them. In 1978 the Council formally agreed the year-round policy and considered football competitions and racing sweepstakes; however, they were concerned that branch support for the Appeal might be jeopardised by anything which might affect their own fundraising activities.[11]

The same year the NEC had also agreed to the experimental employment of salaried Appeal co-ordinators in two Areas – Wales and Metropolitan. The decision was taken in the knowledge that some of the other Areas had strong reservations; but at the 1979

Annual Conference the opposition was stronger than had been anticipated – 'an insult to the branch' was Shard End No 1's view – and the pilot scheme was suspended.[12]

Nevertheless the fresh ideas and new vigour were beginning to take effect, while the inflation rate showed signs of slowing, and the 1978 results represented a real gain. Although the two subsequent years were disappointing, perhaps due to the tightening of the economy by the new government, slowly progress was being made. There was still much to do: still more Legion members needed to be involved and that needed greater input at County level; and with 77 per cent of the total coming from the November collections the Appeal could hardly be called year-round.[13]

In 1977 a new Appeals Secretary, Major Tomlins, had been appointed. It was the year of the Queen's Silver Jubilee and the Legion had been invited to assist in the collections for the Jubilee Appeal, as they had done for King George V's Jubilee. But, like the Poppy Appeal, the collection was not all that the organizers had hoped.

## 1981 – 1985

### More competition

In the early 1980s, with the new government looking for greater self-reliance in the community, there was more competition for charitable funds. Nor was inflation yet conquered; the ten pence coin might have replaced the sixpenny piece (equal to 2 pence) in the collecting box but the Legion now sought a fifty pence piece for each poppy. Yet, since the government based its battle against inflation on controlling the money supply,

*Mrs Sara Jones, widow of the Falklands War VC Lieutenant Colonel 'H' Jones, launched the 1983 Poppy Appeal. She later became Chairman of the Poppy Factory.*

the public had little to spare for charities and the 1980 and 1981 appeals were again disappointing. In 1982, however, came the Falklands War, stirring a wave of national patriotic emotion, and the Poppy Appeal that year produced the best result in real terms for ten years. More importantly for the long term, inflation seemed at last under control and the Appeal continued to gain each year, so that by 1985, as Chart C1 (page 447) shows, it was clear that the corner had at last been turned.[14]

Neither the 'Falklands factor' nor control of inflation would have produced these results if the Poppy Appeal organization had not been up to it. In the vanguard was the publicity machine, now very active, arranging exhibitions which toured the country while the membership was provided with synchronized tape/slide shows for local audiences. Much attention was paid to youth: information packs on the Legion's work were sent to every primary school in the country and the Appeal itself was given a youthful image as well as publicity by involving attractive young girls; a group called 'The Poppies', all daughters of ex-servicemen as it happened, toured the major cities in 1983 singing 'The Poppy Song' which included the words 'Wear your poppy with pride for those who have died'. But if anyone thought that this was trivializing the purpose of the Appeal they must surely have been converted when the singers were pictured alongside Mrs Sara Jones, the widow of the Falklands VC, who launched the Appeal that year; it brought home the realities of the sacrifice that war involved.[15]

## County involvement critical

Success, however, depended on the front-line troops, the poppy organizers and their teams of collectors, whose effective deployment was now in the hands of the Legion's own structure. The critical level was County. Although not all had established Appeal Committees, by 1982 the NEC was satisfied that the Counties were playing their part. The results varied greatly; in North Dorset that year the average amount donated was 40 pence per head of population, but elsewhere it could be as low as $1\frac{1}{2}$ pence. Nor could the difference simply be ascribed to varying levels of prosperity; the highest level of unemployment was in Northern Ireland; yet the six counties were consistently among the most generous donors. It all came down to organization and here the great cities and urban areas continued to be the problem; the difficulty of finding collectors in the sprawling suburbs was intensified by rising crime levels, making house-to-house collections an unattractive proposition. Yet this was the most lucrative of the Appeal activities, accounting in 1983 for 36 pence out of every £1 collected, compared with 29 pence raised in street collections. Another statistic bears on the matter: 60 per cent of the Poppy Appeal Organizers were men; 90 per cent of the Collectors, those who would have been required to go and knock on doors in the house-to-house collection as well as sell poppies in the street, were women. Clearly the organization of the Appeal was not yet right.[16]

The 1983 statistic also reveals that by now some 24 pence in every pound collected came from special fundraising events, showing that slowly Colonel Hughes's concept of the Appeal being a year-round activity was gaining ground. There were sponsored walks – members of Ashby-de-la-Zouch Branch walked nearly 300 miles along the Pennine Way to raise £1,500 – and a sponsored canoe trip on the Thames from Abingdon to Blackfriars in 1983 was met by the Lord Mayor of London. A London Poppy Ball,* held in 1981, was a success, although the idea was by no means innovative; Birmingham had run one for many years and the same year a Poppy Ball in the United Arab Emirates raised £7,000. But the London Ball became an annual event, not only raising considerable sums of money, some £24,000 in 1984, but widening interest in the Appeal among influential people. It was invariably organised by the wife of the National President.[17]

Meanwhile the Appeal Chairman explored the business world, now becoming a little more receptive to charity appeals but not yet a major source of income. As in the days of Haig's long-defunct 'Great War Remembrance League', they had their own agendas, as did Legion Clubs; in 1981 the Bucher trophy for club donations to the Appeal attracted only three entries.[18]

## Poppy Factory numbers decline

The Poppy Factory too was a business. The fact that it employed disabled ex-servicemen making perhaps the best-recognized charity symbol in the country, if not the world, and was regularly visited by Royalty did not exempt it from management problems.

---

*Eighteen years before it had been regarded as inappropriate for November 11th; but now another date was used.

Occasionally changes in working practices, brought on by the use of new materials or new machinery for a particular task, led to demands for an increase in the job rate which, if agreed, sparked off resentment among the other employees. Despite efforts to recruit more workers, the numbers slowly declined in the late 1970s and early 1980s to around 120, including ten part-time. A further sixty worked from home, while groups at the Star and Garter Home and two Legion establishments, Maurice House residential home and a housing court in the Legion Village, also assembled poppies. The factory continued to diversify and the 'Miss Royal British Legion' competition led to the production of beauty queen sashes.[19]

When Princess Anne visited the factory in 1983 the longest serving employee, who had been three times wounded in the First World War, was aged ninety and had begun his work on the Old Kent Road site some sixty years before. A fellow worker told the princess he was at the factory as a result of a 'day trip to Normandy'. He had lost an arm on landing on the beach on D-Day.[20]

## 1986 – 1990

### The improvement continues

Those passing along Pall Mall in late 1987 would have seen two plots of soil in the Legion headquarters window display. One was from the Somme and the other from Goose Green in the Falklands. They epitomized the continuing need and Simon Weston, a Falklands veteran whose courageous behaviour in the face of disfigurement had made him a public figure, had planted a Remembrance cross in the soil. He was one of a number of personalities now associated with the Poppy Appeal, including the television comedian Jim Davidson who had made several visits to the men and women now garrisoning the Falklands and who had launched the 1984 appeal. In 1987 Weston toured the provinces with the launch team, while the actor Michael Caine, a Korean War veteran, appealed for collectors. Since the provincial tour was directed at cities where television companies were based there was much media coverage, a 'picture opportunity' provided for each occasion by a young lady presenting a civic dignitary with a flaming torch as a symbol of freedom.[21]

That year an electronic signboard in Piccadilly spelt out 'Wear your poppy with pride' in Remembrance week. It was announced in the *Legion Journal* as 'a scoop for the Legion' to have its message in lights in London's West End, the editor clearly unaware that sixty-five years before, in 1922, a similar message had appeared (see page 125).[22]

Colonel Hughes handed over chairmanship of the Appeal in 1985 to E.R. Jobson, having guided it through perhaps the most crucial period in its history.* Recovery had been partly due to a return to a more stable economic situation, but in order to profit from that situation the Appeal had needed vigorous leadership and as a result there was now a forward momentum. Under Jobson's chairmanship the momentum was maintained and indeed increased: the collections grew substantially each year in the second half of the decade, well exceeding the cost-of-living increases and enabling the Legion to press ahead with its residential homes programme. When Jobson handed over to Ian Cannell in 1989 on becoming National Vice Chairman the Appeal was at its highest

---

*In 1976 the Appeal brought in £2.5 million; in 1986 the total was nearly £8 million. Even after an inflation factor has been applied, converting the figures to £10.2 million and £12.5 million respectively, this was a remarkable achievement in such times.

point in real terms since the early 1950s.[23]

The chairmen might give the direction, but they used a complex machine driven by the Appeals Secretary and his staff. Major Tomlins had left the appointment in 1983 on becoming the Legion's General Secretary and had been replaced by Major Morgan. Much was required of the Appeals Secretary. Although centred on a brief period in November the Appeal was a year-long process and the Secretary spent much time travelling the country addressing Poppy Forums and ensuring that the volunteers were not only trained but motivated. He also presented awards and in 1990 the Poppy Appeal 'For Merit' badge was introduced.[24]

Despite the Appeal's recovery, still greater input was needed if the Legion's income was to be assured. There were now many more charities competing for the public's support and in 1990, ignoring the earlier opposition, the NEC appointed a paid Poppy Appeal Co-ordinator for the Metropolitan Area in a pilot scheme. Although the trial was overtaken by the 1992 decision to introduce County Field Officers, useful lessons were learned, to be turned to good account in the training of CFOs.[25]

## A question of leaves

Meanwhile some of those at the sharp end of the Appeal, the organisers and collectors, were bothered by a rather more down-to-earth issue: the question of leaves. It seemed that the public preferred a poppy with a leaf to a leafless poppy and the 1987 Annual Conference had asked that in future poppies should come with the leaves attached. It seemed a reasonable request but it caused complications at the Poppy Factory: there was no difficulty in making plastic leaves, although there was a of course a cost involved. The problem was the assembly. Not only did it change the established practice but the operation needed two hands. The compromise was that the leaves would be supplied separately, to be attached to the poppy somewhere 'down the line', either at the local branch or even by the collector. To an outsider such detail seems hardly important, but to those involved each year in stripping and re-assembling millions of poppies across the land it was something of an issue. Moreover it touched on an old problem at a time when the factory was due for restructuring: should not the manufacture of poppies now be entirely a machine process, thus saving thousands of man-hours and cutting costs? This was already the case in Scotland.[26]

The answer was the same as before: such a course would be to deprive nearly 200 disabled people, if the home-workers were also taken into account, of their jobs. Not for a moment would it be countenanced by the Legion membership, who would also argue that it was part of the Remembrance ethos that the emblem was assembled in the traditional way by disabled ex-servicemen. And so the restructuring of the Poppy Factory proceeded on this basis, but the working conditions and the machinery were much improved, in the course of which it was discovered that the sewing machines had been so old that they qualified for the Singer museum. New production lines were set up to produce cardboard boxes and plastic bags and a cost-saving programme introduced.[27]

It was not the end of the leaves story. By the 1995 Appeal the factory was able to supply 10 million poppies with leaves, bringing a collective sigh of relief from the volunteers. But by then there had also been another small but significant design change: no longer did 'HF' appear on the centre button. The reference to Haig in 'Haig Fund' was not now, it seemed, considered necessary.[28]

## 1991 – 1995

### Still rising

In November 1991 the BBC's John Simpson placed a poppy in his buttonhole before going off to attempt to interview Saddam Hussein, the Iraqi dictator whose invading armies had been driven out of Kuwait at the beginning of that year. Had the unpredictable Saddam given the interview, Simpson's gesture would have been appreciated by millions of British viewers. They would also have approved of the wearing of poppies in Baghdad that year by the congregation at the British Church. Sixty years on the small flower was still a national symbol of sacrifice in war.[29]

The same year the Poppy Appeal was launched at the Kuwaiti Embassy in the presence of the principal British commanders in the Gulf War, demonstrating its relevance to the present day. Such imaginative acts were needed if the Appeal was to maintain its recovery. Charity giving in general was starting to decline; the average amount donated each year had fallen from a little under £2 to £1.28, while inflation still continued, although at a lower rate than before. Furthermore, there were now 170,000 charities in Britain and they were increasing at the rate of ten a day.[30]

While research showed that more members of the public gave to the Poppy Appeal than to any other charity, the donations themselves followed the overall trend and were getting smaller. In 1990 the public had been urged to put £1 in the box in return for a poppy and the advertising was designed to shock: there were pictures of Nazi troops marching through London, accompanied by the phrase: 'Give Thanks – It could have happened – It very nearly did'. With attitudes to Germany having changed over the intervening years, there was much controversy when the displays appeared on the hoardings and the Legion was involved in forty minutes of live debate on BBC television. But that year, with Cannell as Appeal Chairman, takings were up by nearly a million pounds.[31]

### New sources

In 1991, in order to raise money for the Tidworth Training Centre project, a new Special Appeals department was set up, also raising funds for the new Dunkirk Memorial Home, although this last was low-key since it was judged that the support did not exist to raise the full sum. By 1995, mainly through approaches to the top 500 companies and 300 major foundations, the department had raised nearly £3 million for Tidworth and £250,000 for the Dunkirk Home. This was money which would otherwise have had to come from the Poppy Appeal and it represented a new approach to Legion fundraising, seeking out sources other than the traditional ones.[32]

Meanwhile the traditional source, the general public, continued to be targeted by the main

*There were imaginative ideas to publicise the Appeal in the 1990s; here RAF pilot and rugby international Rory Underwood identifies with the poppy.*

Appeal. The launches remained imaginative with the 1992 Appeal opened at El Alamein on the fiftieth anniversary of the battle, while at the Alamein reunion in Blackpool that year the sons of the two opposing generals, Montgomery and Rommel, exchanged poppies. If this was too much of a trip into the past Flight Lieutenant John Nichol, who had been shot down in the Gulf War and had survived captivity, toured other locations accompanied by the RAF's first woman pilot. It all attracted much media coverage, as did the involvement of Sir John Harvey Jones, the well-known industrialist and former Royal Navy officer, in the 1994 launch aboard HMS *Illustrious*.[33]

## More changes

1993 saw the arrival of County Field Officers. Part of their task was to assist with the organization of the Appeal, but they needed to adopt a diplomatic approach since the volunteers had long been doing the work. Soon there was a map on the wall of every CFO's office. It clearly showed the main problem: the shortage of organizers and collectors, with 'black spots' where there was no coverage. But most CFOs also had an eye to public relations and were able to publicize the Appeal, and the need for more collectors, on local radio and TV. One successful CFO publicity venture was a competition for young children to dress as poppies, in which local schools took part. The winner, a five-year-old, achieved national recognition, appearing in the Festival of Remembrance. But CFOs also took part in the training of organizers and collectors and inspired County events such as sponsored walks.[34]

*New ideas stemming from the creation of a Fundraising Division included the sponsored 'Pedal to Paris' cycle ride.*

The Legion review also led to the setting up of the Fundraising Division in 1993. The Controller oversaw all fundraising activities which now included not only the Poppy Appeal and Special Appeals but a number of other ventures. One such was a legacies campaign, based on advice on will-making and it generated between £1 million and £2 million each year, increasing income by between 10 and 15 per cent. The Legion had been a late starter in actively seeking legacies. On average a charity got one third of its income this way and some received as much as 70 per cent of income in legacies. It revealed how much the new approach had been needed.[35]

A further activity, special events, came into its own with the commemoration of the fiftieth anniversary of the end of the Second World War in 1995. In addition to the main attraction, the concert in Hyde Park already described in Chapter 16, there was a host of other activities: a 'celebrity' cricket match at the Oval, a news gala at the Royal Albert Hall based on old Pathe film clips and patriotic music, beacons, bonfires and street parties at over 2,000 locations, a balloon launch in Portsmouth, a VJ day concert in Holland Park in London and a 'pedal for peace' cycle ride from Arnhem to Dover Castle. Between them these events raised some £750,000 and they gave the Legion invaluable publicity.[36]

An idea that was again examined was a chain of charity shops on the lines of Oxfam or Cancer Research. But the initial investment in terms of fitting out and area management would have been considerable and the Legion was already involved in enough new initiatives. One of these was a scratch card, introduced in 1995. It followed the previous year's launch by the government of the National Lottery which had quickly shown the public's fascination with such activities; within a short time two-thirds of the population were playing the National Lottery regularly and, with a part of the proceeds going to a Charities Board, there was some concern that individual charity fundraising would suffer.[37] For the moment, however, this was most certainly not the case with the Legion. Although a further period of recession in the early 1990s had slowed the Appeal's rate of increase a little, it was still improving in real terms at a time when it could well have been in decline as the wartime years slipped further into the past and the charity field grew even more competitive.

★      ★      ★

The new Legion logo, launched at the beginning of 1995, had brought the poppy symbol into close alignment with the organization's title, enabling the public to recognize the connection between the Appeal and the Legion itself. But it could also be seen as acknowledging the closer involvement of the Legion structure in the Appeal, one of the factors that had enabled the organization's fundraising to turn the corner. Together with the broadening of the sources of support, it meant that the Legion could enter the next century with confidence.

*Queen Elizabeth The Queen Mother has opened the Field of Remembrance almost every year for the past fifty years. She is seen here with Mrs Sara Jones, Poppy Factory Chairman.*

# CHAPTER 20

INTERNATIONAL 1971 - 2001

# *New Relationships*

## 1971 – 1975

### The Legion joins the WVF

Earlier experiences had left the Legion cautious about involvements with international ex-service organizations. In common with many such post-war activities, such groupings tended to polarise, either in the direction of the United States or the Eastern bloc. The Legion clearly supported Britain's position in the western alliance, but it did not wish to be involved in the political debates and the only organization with which it felt completely comfortable was the British Commonwealth Ex-Services League. It was nevertheless keenly aware that changes were afoot in Europe which could affect the situation of ex-servicemen; the question was how to engage with them without venturing into the murky ground of politics.[1]

One of the organizations which the Legion still viewed with some suspicion was the World Veterans Federation. In 1971 the WVF President asked the Legion's Chairman, Dennis Cadman, why the Legion still remained outside the organization, which had been founded some twenty years earlier. The reply was that the Legion was unhappy with its political activities and particularly the fact that it was mainly American-funded. The President, a Dutchman, responded by saying that all that had changed and that the Legion could make a valuable contribution to the WVF now that the United Kingdom was considering joining the European Economic Community. This brought the NEC face to face with the problem. Was it really in the ex-service interest for the Legion to remain on the touchline, especially when it was being beckoned on to the field of play? On the other hand the reference to Britain's possible entry into the EEC indicated a political dimension to the game. Proceeding with caution, the NEC decided that the leadership should explore the ground and in early 1972 there were meetings with WVF officials, followed by the despatching of Legion observers to the WVF's General Assembly in Paris in November 1973. At the subsequent NEC debrief in early 1974 the old political concerns re-surfaced, this time voiced by the Legion's President, and it was eventually decided to refer the matter to Conference. The 1975 Annual Conference felt that the WVF's 20 million members from five continents needed the Legion's leadership and experience, and entry was approved. Within a short time the Legion was a full member of the WVF.[2]

### The BCEL stays British

Unlike the WVF, the British Commonwealth Ex-Services League had little financial backing; its main funding came from the subscriptions of the 'big five' members – the Legion and the ex-service organizations of the 'old' countries. When BCEL encountered some financial difficulties in the early 1970s the Legion offered free office accommodation at its Pall Mall headquarters. But the NEC strongly opposed a 1974 BCEL conference suggestion to drop 'British' from the title, despite New Zealand pointing out that the Queen had used the title Head of the Commonwealth since 1952 and the suggestion was again defeated at the 1977 BCEL conference in Scotland.

However it might style itself the League was now mainly concerned with the situation of ex-servicemen in the former colonies, some of which, in the new parlance, fell into the category of 'third world' countries and, with its new enthusiasm for the WVF, the Legion urged it to establish relations with that organization, despite the Federation having trespassed on BCEL territory in the past by its activities in some of the poorer Commonwealth countries. The Legion nonetheless still felt strongly about the wartime constribution by member countries and it had stayed away from the Australian-hosted world veterans assembly in 1975 because Rhodesia was excluded.[3]

## 1976 – 1980

### Still in a political minefield

As well as being a member of both WVF and the BCEL, the Legion belonged to a body known as CEAC – the *Confederation Européenne des Anciens Combattants* or European Confederation of Ex-servicemen. It had joined in 1973, again only after careful study of the organization and an Annual Conference resolution in favour. But by 1976 it was becoming clear that the CEAC agenda was more concerned with European political issues than ex-service welfare and, after a Legion-inspired internal CEAC review failed to achieve any changes, the Legion decided, in 1979, to withdraw. In future it intended to conduct its European policies solely through the WVF.[4]

As it happened, the Legion was by now deeply involved with WVF European matters. Following the WVF chairman's address to the Legion's 1978 Annual Conference, the Legion's departing National Chairman, Charles Busby, took over as chairman of the British Members Council of the WVF and the following year Colonel Hughes became President of the WVF Permanent Commission on European Affairs, in effect leader of the movement in Europe and the first Briton to hold that post.* The WVF enjoyed high status with both the United Nations and the Council of Europe and was consulted by them in ex-service matters. The Legion now therefore seemed at last to be well placed in Europe. But the political mines were still not far below the surface; Hughes had frequently to abstain from votes and a position the WVF took on disarmament was considered naive by the NEC, likely to be misinterpreted in the UK and embarrassing to the Legion.[5]

### The branches make contact

Grass-roots attitudes were also changing following Britain's entry into the EEC in 1973. The most contact was with German ex-servicemen; possibly the Legion members felt that there was ground to be made up; or perhaps, because many had served with the British Army of the Rhine, they felt more at home with Germans. At any rate Wallingford and Shillingborough Branch invited two members of *Verband deutscher Kriegsbeschadigten* (VdK) to take part in their Remembrance Sunday parade and service in 1973 and in the years that followed Tilehurst exchanged visits with a Schleswig-Holstein branch, a number of other branches established relations with their counterparts in areas of the

*Hughes was awarded the French Legion d'Honneur for his work.

396

Rhine and Ruhr and in 1977 the strains of 'Lili Marlene' rang across Parsons Green when Fulham Branch entertained fifty VdK members from Bochum. The same year a twinning scheme was introduced and branches were urged not only to extend their contacts to other European countries but to cross the Atlantic, making use of the cheap charter flights now possible, for which the Legion obtained credit facilities. By 1978 thirteen branches had twinned with European partners, five with Canadian and one in the United States, while other contacts grew; Poland, still at that time behind the Iron Curtain, even offered rehabilitation and recuperation on the Baltic coast.[6]

In 1978 Conference was addressed by the Head of VdK, exactly forty years after General Reinhard had spoken of 'the common desire for peace', and then given the Nazi salute (see page 64). But it was now the price of that hard-won peace that was the issue; many of the WVF member nations were said to enjoy a higher standard of ex-service benefits than Britain and the feeling continued that the way ahead might lie through the EEC.[7]

### US links renewed

Meanwhile contact had also been renewed with the American Legion. Having attended the Canadian Legion's fiftieth anniversary celebrations in 1976, the National Chairman went on to the United States and was later invited to address the American Legion's 1979 annual convention. Air Vice Marshal Maughan, the General Secretary, who accompanied Captain Whitehead, noted that the American Legion was the largest of that country's ex-service organizations with nearly 3 million members, while the Veterans of Foreign Wars had under 2 million members since entry was restricted to those who had served in combat overseas. Unlike the Legion, however, neither organization provided any benevolence of its own; instead they both acted as pressure groups to ensure that the Government Department of Veterans Affairs met its responsibilities, in the case of the VFW maintaining a highly professional Washington office to lobby congressmen and senators.[8]

## 1981 – 1995

### Europe and its pitfalls

It might well be that British ex-service interests would best be served through the European Community; the Legion would have to see how matters developed. In the meantime the Legion used the WVF to the best effect it could, hosting a Federation international conference on the long-term effects of captivity on prisoners of war in 1981, after which the British Members Council of WVF drew up guidelines for doctors.[9] (See page 366.)

The years that followed, however, saw problems emerge: the attitude of the British public towards greater European unity continued to waver as more and more national authority was lost to the EC; meanwhile the WVF had also become increasingly 'politicized', so that the Legion felt the need to distance itself and in 1994, it ceased to pay its subscription.[10] It needed nevertheless to maintain the European connection, particularly since the European Union was providing substantial funding for the Tidworth project (see pages 381–2) and in 1993 the Legion proposed a new group comprising the ex-service associations within the EC, but on a strictly non-party-political basis.

The proposal had the Community's backing and the new organization was set up at a meeting in Brussels in 1994. It was to be known as the *Partenariat* (partnership) *Anciens Combattants Européen.* But once again the constitution included spectific support for the EC objects. It seemed that the situation was impossible to reconcile; if the Legion wanted to exploit Europe for the benefit of the ex-service community then it could not avoid the political implications.After attempting to set up yet another grouping the Legion rejoined the WVF in 1997.[11]

Political considerations had long dominated the Legion's relations with the Eastern Bloc and particularly the Soviet Union; extreme caution had been the watchword. The end of the Cold War meant that the Legion could respond more positively to Russian overtures and in 1989 the National Chairman and Vice Chairman visited Moscow and Leningrad (St Petersburg), laying wreaths, visiting war veterans hospitals and finding common ground over the problems of military cut-backs, half a million Russian regular servicemen would now be redundant and the Russians sought advice.[12]

The same year there was a pilgrimage to Cassino in Italy, scene of the some of the most bitter fighting of the Second World War. Allied and German veterans were present and when the wreaths came to be laid, at the suggestion of Lieutenant Colonel Bryan Clarke, an NEC member who had fought in the battle, the British and German parties advanced and laid their wreaths together. It seemed to signify that the two great wars that had brought so much suffering to so many, together with all that had followed in their wake, were at last over. A new spirit was abroad.

Elswhere there were still many problems. And in some of the Commonwealth countries the only help was self-help, or the traditional reliance on the family. Yet these ex-soldiers had served the cause of freedom as well as any. Even where a disability pension might have been granted after the Second World War the poverty of the economy, combined with huge distances and poor communications, often meant that it could not be honoured. This was the challenge which continued to face BCEL, in which the Legion had a leading part to play.[13]

⋆      ⋆      ⋆

In the years that followed the Second World War it had been just as difficult for the Legion to conduct its international relationships without touching the political trip-wire as in the inter-war years. Yet it could no more hold back from the new post-war Europe than from its pre-war attempts to maintain the peace so dearly won. For an organization committed to a non party-political approach the path ahead would have to be tackled with care.

# CHAPTER 21

## WOMEN'S SECTION 1971 - 2001

# *Good Housekeeping*

### 1971 – 1975

### 'No richer dividend'

In the Legion's 1972 Annual Report its National Chairman noted that the Women's Section had passed a long way beyond the 'background tea and buns' role it frequently filled in early years; it now raised £90,000 annually for its own benevolent activities and its Poppy Appeal work was outstanding. Colonel Hughes concluded that the Legion's founding fathers showed considerable foresight when providing for a Women's Section in the draft constitution: 'no clause has paid a richer dividend'.[1]

The pace had indeed been high since the end of the Second World War. Rest Homes and Children's Homes had been purchased, fitted out and maintained, the pre-war Widows' Allowance scheme developed and the Flatlets scheme initiated. Since the Section received no income from the Poppy Appeal – it existed to support the Legion rather than use the Legion's resources – all had to be achieved through its own efforts, maintained by a very active and committed generation of women. As Charts D1 and D2 (page 448), show these efforts were both considerable and sustained. The money was raised mainly by the branches and it was this common endeavour which gave the Section its vitality, as well as the involvement expressed by the high representation at its conferences. But, as in the case of the Legion itself, all that it had achieved would be subjected to new situations and fresh challenges as the century drew to a close.

### The women's views

The women were not content simply to get on with these projects; they continued to want to make their views known on certain ex-service issues. When Legion deputations called on government ministries the treatment of war widows was invariably one of the points raised and the Section felt that they should be represented, especially as they were much involved with the widows through their local branches. And, although the Legion was now finding that small groups were often better, the Section's Chairman was included. But the overall role was still supportive and subordinate; when the British Ambassador in Paris suggested that the Section should establish relations with the French War Widows Association the Chairman immediately referred the matter to the NEC. At their suggestion the Women's Section joined the International Committee of European Organizations, hosting a meeting of the Committee in 1974 and attending the Brussels ICEO meeting the next year.[2]

Supportive they might be, but the Section held their own opinions. When the government realigned county boundaries in 1974 and the NEC decided that the Legion should follow suit, the women lined up with the Legion's rank-and-file in rejecting them. A Women's Section conference delegate aptly summed up their view: 'it would put everyone through the mincing machine  and we don't know whether we'll get shepherd's pie or steak and kidney pudding'. But although they might disagree with the Legion's leadership on such matters, they continued to give loyal support in other ways, running a Legion stand at the Ideal Homes Exhibition in 1975 that featured disabled men's work as well as exhibitions of poppy-making which attracted much interest from various royal visitors. There was much royal interest too each year in November when the Section's national officers took the poppies to Buckingham Palace and the other royal houses, and they were often subjected to close questioning on the progress of the Appeal.[3]

In 1971 Miss Warren retired through ill-health after twenty years as National Secretary, one of that generation of Legion and Section staff who had joined on demobilization in 1945 and had given their respective organizations the best years of their lives; in her case she had devoted much time and energy to the Children's Homes. Her place was taken by Miss Sandiforth, Eastern Area Secretary. The following year Mrs Little became National Chairman in place of Mrs Croft-Foulds, who had held the office for four years. At this time the Section tended to longer office-holding than the Legion: since 1948 there had only been three chairmen and Mrs Little would hold the post for six years.[4]

The Fiftieth Anniversary in 1971 was celebrated by a service of thanksiving in St Paul's in the presence of the Queen Mother. It followed the annual Women's Section Conference in the Royal Albert Hall, attended by Princess Margaret and some 1,200 delegates in an array of multi-coloured hats, causing the Legion President, General Sir Charles Jones, to remark that if every member present stuck her hatpin in her nearest male relative the Legion conference some three weeks later might get an equally good turnout. Nearly half of the Section's branches were represented on that occasion, a record never since beaten, but subsequent conferences were no less spirited.[5]

There was a sniff of disapproval when the 1973 membership increase turned out to be largely the result of the expansion in Legion clubs; the Section had little room for purely 'social' members and if that was their reason for joining they should speedily be encouraged to take an active part in the work. The work aspect was also strongly stressed in the official recruiting programme which now included lectures to officers and NCOs at the WRAC College at Camberley. The Section's Chairman made these views very plain to the Legion's NEC in 1974.[6]

## The schemes thrive

The women's conferences were always much interested in the Section's work. The two Rest Homes were inundated with applications and it had been necessary to ensure that the 700 or so women who went each year really needed to rest and were not using the scheme simply for holidays; it was noticeable that applications fell in the winter months. Most of the delegates represented branches that raised funds almost year-round for such schemes and they included the Widows' Allowance Fund, started in 1938 and now assisting some 500 women, the great majority of whom were in Southern Ireland. But they also included a remarkable French woman. One day during the war she was cycling home with food and clothing for an airman whom she was sheltering when she saw an aircraft crash; the pilot was Douglas Bader and in 1972 she was able to present him with a piece of the wreckage. In the meantime she had helped over 200 allied airmen to escape, eventually being interned in Belsen and Buchenwald and widowed when her husband died after arrest by the Gestapo. Now, in her declining years, she was grateful for the 62½ pence a week allowance.[7]

The flatlets scheme, running since 1963, was also supported by branch donations. There were now five locations, both Castle of Mey house at Shottermill in Surrey and Shore House at Whiteabbey in Northern Ireland having been completed in 1971. The Queen Mother opened Castle of Mey the following year, choosing the name herself. Despite the limited size – in effect they were bedsits with a kitchen which could be closed off from the rest – the occupants were contented. There were tenants' associations and social activities, and each woman received a Christmas parcel from the Section. But, as with the Legion, the residents needed greater support at they grew older and in 1975 the Section pressed for more Legion residential care for the elderly, to be told that finances did not permit it.[8]

Funding was of constant concern to both organizations but in the case of the Section it was a matter of taking every opportunity, however small. In 1974 the Marchioness of Cambridge, Patron of the Section's Eastern Area, produced a cookbook. Although the Marchioness had learned to cook in a hospital kitchen in the First World War the book contained recipes given to her by members of the royal family and sold well under the title 'The Royal Blue and Gold Cookbook', American outlets being provided after the Marchioness had given lunch to a US ex-service contingent, demonstrating that she had marketing as well as kitchen skills.[9]

## 1976 – 1980

### A question of autonomy

When the agenda for the 1976 Women's Section conference was published it contained a Central Committee resolution calling on the Legion's NEC to 'legalize the position of the Women's Section; to give it autonomy in the matters of administration, finance and the ownership of property bought by the Women's Section; thus ensuring recognition as a Women's Organization'. But when NEC members sought more information at a Council meeting shortly before the conference the Section's National Chairman firmly declared that her committee thought that there should be no discussion prior to the conference debate. The matter was put to the Legion President who stated, equally firmly, that the Women's Central Committee should be aware of the NEC's views before the matter was debated. These are not recorded, but there is little doubt that Council members were unhappy at any challenge to their ultimate authority in all Legion matters.[10]

The resolution was duly debated by the women. Delegates were told that, as matters stood, the organization had no legal rights: they might raise funds to buy Rest Homes but they did not own them; the property belonged to the Legion. Even their bye-laws had to be approved by the Legion's NEC. 'Women should now be equal partners' they were urged, and the delegates, no doubt also influenced by the prevailing wave of 'women's lib', were in no mood to disagree. The resolution was passed unanimously.[11]

At this stage there might have been a confrontation, with reverberations throughout both organizations and unfortunate media consequences, but wiser counsels prevailed. The Legion's leaders recognized the valuable work the Section did, particularly in the Poppy Appeal. They also appreciated some of the women's frustrations. Yet at the same time it was important that the Legion retained its authority over all activities carried out in its name. The lawyers were called in and talks began, conducted in an atmosphere described as 'cordial'.[12]

The following year the NEC agreed that the Section's Central Committee should be allowed control of its funds and property and could do what it liked with its assets, provided that it was in the Legion's interests and did not contravene its Charter. The Section's conference alone would decide the subscriptions to be paid by members and, a change from a previous ruling, it could now form branches where there was no Legion branch. This did not of course fully meet the terms of the 1976 resolution; the Section might be free to run its own affairs, but only within the Legion, which retained ultimate authority; in no way was the Section an independent body as far as the outside world was concerned. But the 1977 Women's Section conference accepted the compromise.[13]

The affair created friction in only one area: the Legion's Housing Association was now in full operation and it was suggested that, far from being fit to take on more responsibility, the women had wasted their hard-earned money on the flatlets when they could have been paid for out of government-subsidized rents. But the Women's Section chairman would have none of that: without its own legal status the only way the Section could have set up a Housing Association would have been to act through the Legion, once again sacrificing its independence. In other words if they had to pay to run their own show they would do so; it came back to the philosophy that the Section derived its unity and strength from the direct involvement of the members in such activities.[14]

The question of the Women's Section's legal status would recur in 1992 over a staff dispute, when it was confirmed that the Legion was in law the employer of the Section's staff. In the meantime the new relationship worked well and goodwill on both sides ensured that the only disagreements were minor.[15]

## Financial independence

Whether it was connected or not to the independence question, in 1976 the Section did not seek an annual grant from the Legion. The previous year the grant had been £3,000 out of a total income of some £200,000, of which around two-thirds derived from donations, mainly the result of branch fundraising activities. Fifty years before, the NEC's subsidy had accounted for three-quarters of the Section's income and, although there had been previous periods when no grant had been made, the transformation was a measure of the financial independence that had been achieved over the years (see Chart D1 on page 448). Other subsidies would be provided by the Legion, mainly connected with headquarters accommodation, but they were in the nature of a concession; the Section was not dependent on the Legion and from 1978 it published its own report and accounts.[16]

On one thing the women were insistent: administrative costs must be kept to a minimum and now that they had control of their own subscription rates they were all the more determined that there would be good housekeeping. In 1975 the Affilliation Fee had been raised from twenty pence to thirty pence, but it was a period of high inflation and only two years later the leadership sought fifty pence; conference settled for forty pence. With inflation showing no sign of slackening the 1979 conference was asked to double that figure to eighty pence, but fifty pence was all that was allowed; it was, after all, as one delegate remarked, the cost of a packet of tea. When, however, the question of a 1977 silver jubilee present to the Queen arose, there were no objections when the Central Committee, having consulted the President, the Queen Mother, proposed six teak garden seats for Sandringham.[17]

402

Under the terms of the 1977 agreement the Legion still exercised overall control, in 1979 rejecting as 'not in the spirit of the Charter' an attempt by the Section to limit to one year membership of the Central Committee by a departing Women's Section Chairman, currently a lifetime privilege. Yet this time the women were ahead of the men; barely a decade later the Legion itself would apply much the same rule to their past National Chairmen. And so Mrs Little stayed on the Committee for life when she handed over the Chair in 1978 to Mrs Handyside, a doctor's wife from Sunderland. The same year saw the departure of Miss Sandiforth, the National Secretary, who was replaced by Miss Barbara Cooper, a former WRNS officer.[18]

## Welfare help

When the Children's Homes finally closed in 1967, the money had been used to set up a Children's Reserve Fund to help with the education of the children of ex-service parents, particularly widows. For a while it was also used to maintain the children who had formerly lived in the Homes, but by 1973 only one child was still at school, although the rest still kept in touch with the Section who remembered such events as a 21st birthday and sent their congratulations on successes in work or the birth of a baby. By the late 1970s the help was of a more general nature and in 1978 it helped children who had suffered in the flood disasters in the South West that year. The Welfare Fund also helped the victims of the flooding but its remit was much wider: it made grants to enable the elderly and infirm to go on holiday and assisted one young ex-service family where the wife was dying of cancer so that the husband had had to give up work to look after her; it helped a disabled ex-servicewoman who had been turned out of her flat to find other accommodation and gave her a holiday; and it provided aged widows with warm clothing. In such cases the two funds simply did what the Legion's own welfare funds might have done; but the point was that in these instances the Section members were fully involved, raising the money, investigating the cases and making the decisions. It gave an extra dimension to their association with the Legion, and it saved the Legion itself money.[19]

## 1981 – 1985

## Planning for the future

When the Legion's National President told the 1981 Women's Section conference, 'You have a lot to teach the men in the raising of money,' it was not a mere platitude. Despite the series of recessions that had plagued the economy since the war and the burgeoning inflation the Section's investments had reached £1.5 million, all of the money raised by self-help. But it was needed; the Rest Homes required modernization and the staff accomodation had to be upgraded, one of the ongoing problems being the difficulty of retaining good staff. Extensive repairs were needed at some of the flatlets, while the severe winter of 1981 meant that demands on the welfare fund were high.[20]

By 1983, however, one of the flatlet units, Shore House near Belfast, was being under-used and the following year it was put on the market. The move followed the auditors' report the previous year which had suggested that the Section should evaluate its activities; if a scheme had outworn its original purpose then it should be ended, rather than incur high maintenance costs. Their report prompted a discussion paper which was circulated to all branches and which also addressed wider issues. At the 1984 conference, in addition to the decision on Shore House, there were changes in the organization of the Section: the Central Committee was cut and the outgoing Chairman, whose life membership of the Committee the conference had previously attempted to reduce,★ would now serve only for three years. Areas, Counties and branches were urged to follow suit, reflecting a feeling that young blood was needed. There was also a feeling that there was one layer of administration too many, a view that many people took of the Legion's own organization, and in a pilot scheme South West Area prepared to hand over its responsibilities to its counties. Realistic rents were introduced for the flatlets, bearing in mind that the tenants were eligible for benefits, and charges made for the Rest Homes. Not least the finances were combined into one benevolent fund.[21]

## The conferences decide

The 1981 conference at Eastbourne was attended by the Queen Mother who entered, as always, to sustained applause. It was the Section's diamond jubilee year and nearly £100,000 had been raised by branches, in the traditional manner bringing the money in specially-worked purses. Once again the Queen Mother, instead of merely touching the purses, examined each one and made a comment; it might have taken longer but such consideration was much appreciated by the branch representatives concerned. On this occasion the President even stayed to hear some of the debate which, since it dealt with the matter of Affiliation Fees, was vigorous. The Queen Mothers's address received a standing ovation but at the following year's conference in Blackpool the guest speaker also had this rare distinction. She was Baroness Phillips and the delegates appreciated her pithy comments on such matters as the meagre death grant, then £25, and the low level of state pension. In her last conference as Chairman, in 1983, before handing over to Mrs Bigmore, Mrs Handyside was equally scathing about a decision by Islington Borough Council to cut rent and rate rebates to war widows in order to give more help to unmarried mothers, making 200 widows some £4 to £8 a week worse off. It was small consolation for those of the widows who were in the Section's Widows' Allowance scheme that the same conference had raised the allowance by fifty pence to £2.[22]

The 1984 conference was addressed by Princess Anne who impressed delegates with her knowledge of charity matters. But they also agreed to a change to the Widows' Allowance scheme: already amended to include single ex-servicewomen, it became the Widows' and Ex-servicewomen's Scheme taking in former servicewomen who had married, but become widows. Those in the scheme now received a heating grant from the Welfare Fund, as did the tenants of the flatlets, and the fund also assisted war widows to make pilgrimages to their husbands' graves; one widow visiting Bayeux Cemetery was delighted to see that the gravestone bore a poem that she had written in his memory many years before.[23]

The 1985 conference dealt with the effect of inflation on the level of Affiliation Fee in a refreshingly simple way. Having doubled the fee in 1981 from 75 pence to £1.50, it was decided that from then on it would be increased each year by the annual rate of inflation. Since the 1981 rise had more than compensated for current inflation levels, the Treasurer must have slept well that night.[24]

## Year-round help for the Poppy Appeal

The possibility of more war widows was not far from the members' minds when the Falklands crisis occurred in 1982. The Women's Section branches stood ready to assist

---

★ See previous page; on this occasion the NEC were content with the reduction; their own thinking was now moving in a similar direction.

the Legion in its support for the families of servicemen caught up in that war, but fortunately the casualties were few. In the meantime they carried on with their normal activities, still centred on fundraising and support for the work of disabled men. There were bring-and-buy sales, stalls at local village fetes and craft exhibitions. At Kirton in Lincolnshire thirty women and one man knitted their way through sixty balls of wool in two hours to raise funds, while others, equally active, took part in sponsored walks; 169 women tramped the North Downs Way in 1983 in an event organized by Surrey County, raising £4,000 for the Poppy Appeal, although the men marked the route. A sponsored silence by South Norwood and Woodside raised £400; whether the sponsors were their husbands is not recorded.[25]

The Poppy Appeal did well out of this year-round fundraising by the women. In addition to bringing in £142,000 in 1976 for their own funds they had raised an additional £54,000 for the Appeal and in 1981 the Poppy Appeal figure was up to £74,000 on top of the £246,000 already raised for the Section's activities, which, it will be remembered, did not receive any income from the Appeal. It must also be remembered that such fundraising activity was quite apart from the support which the Section's members provided at Remembrance time, when many of them turned out with their collecting boxes and trays of poppies.

Such branch activities were discussed in the National Forums held each year in four major towns around the country, where ideas were exchanged. Yet despite all the activity by some branches, others were in decline, causing an overall fall in membership. Lack of leadership was the main problem; people would not come forward to take office and as a result the officers were those who had rendered the longest service, often lacking the drive to organize activities so that the members simply faded away.[26]

## 1986 – 1990

### No time for computers

The Legion's President's address to the Women's Section annual conference was normally heard in respectful silence. But at one point in his address to the 1989 conference the President got a noisy reaction from delegates. The issue was computerization, which the Legion itself was currently examining and which would be agreed at its Legion Conference that year. The moment, however, the subject was broached with the ladies it was clear that they held strong views. And in the subsequent debate they voted overwhelmingly against it, deploring the high costs involved. They were also deeply suspicious of the scheme itself, not only envisaging mountains of 'junk mail' on their doorsteps but also seeing a unified membership data base as in effect absorbing the Section into the Legion and robbing them of their remaining independence. They would stick resolutely to their decision.[27]

This strong reaction may have had its origins in a rumour, two years earlier, that the Legion was planning an amalgamation of the Legion and the Women's Section. As the women saw it, since the Section was already part of the Legion this could only be a case of the Legion swallowing them up; despite the Legion's National Chairman's assurances at the Section's 1987 conference that no such take-over was planned, the suspicions had persisted. But it was certainly true that the Legion wanted the Section's fullest co-operation; it was the year that the 'Forces Care' row had broken out, challenging the Legion's lead in ex-service welfare (see pages 371–2).

The Section's conferences themselves continued to be lively affairs. In 1986 there had been a major row at the Central Committee's decision to ban those members over the age of sixty from taking part in the standard-bearers' parade through the streets of Blackpool, and at one stage a rival 'pensioners' parade' had been threatened. The Central Committee's ruling, which had been somewhat baldly announced by a note on each Standard Bearers' seat, was overturned in an emergency resolution, an interesting example of democracy in action and of respect for the 'seniors'. Such head-on clashes were unusual, although there was plenty of vigorous debate on such matters as publicity, fundraising and membership and the mood of the moment was reflected in the slogans: in 1986 'Get With It', replaced by 'Hullo There' two years later. Not was there any shortage of fundraising ideas and at Blackpool in 1988 Women's Section sticks of rock made in the traditional way with 'RBLWS' running all the way through were a sell-out. At a more sober level of publicity the conferences dealt with arrangements to train speakers through Speakers' Forums and supply them with speaking notes.[28]

### The Rest Homes closed

Other fundraising ideas included a 'Cuppa for Caring' week and 'Miles of Silver to Seek and Serve', in which the total aggregated mileage represented the distance from John o' Groats to Land's End. The route was actually ridden on a tandem by two WRAC girls who not only had tea with the Queen Mother en route but received a rousing reception when they reached their destination. Both these ideas implied raising money for specific purposes, very much in the tradition of the Women's Section.

The amount raised each year meanwhile rose steadily and by 1990 it exceeded £500,000. The money was needed. Following changes in the Social Security benefits system it was necessary to expand the Widows and Ex-servicewomen's scheme so that by 1990 over 1,200 women were receiving £4 a week, bolstered by cold weather payments, anticipating the government scheme. Money was also used to buy turbo wheelchairs for handicapped children; the scheme had started in 1985 to mark the 'Year of the Child' and the difference they made to the lives of the children concerned, all of course the sons or daughters of ex-service families, encouraged the Section to develop it; one boy who had been 'quiet and reserved' became 'noisy, fast-moving and naughty' on wheels – or in other words, normal.[29]

The fundraising was accompanied by cost-cutting. At the 1988 conference the decision was taken to close the two remaining Rest Homes. They were now out-of-date, no longer

*Rest Homes such as Glenthorne, overlooking the Channel at Weymouth, were well-used up to the 1970s; but by the late 1980s they had become outdated, as the four-bedded room on the right suggests. The Homes were sold and the proceeds funded a scheme which made use of hotels and guest houses.*

meeting modern requirements; people had become used to en-suite bathrooms when away from home and certainly were not prepared to share bedrooms with strangers. The number of visitors had dropped from 850 in 1975 to 550 in 1987 while maintenance costs had remorselessly risen. It was difficult not to be sentimental about the homes; they had been bought with hard-earned Section money during and just after the Second World War in order to give rest to weary women; but now they were outmoded.[30]

Queensmead, in Yorkshire, was sold almost immediately, but Glenthorne in Dorset remained on the market until 1993 when its sale was 'a matter of some relief' the Legion's NEC was told. The proceeds were used to set up a new Rest and Convalescence scheme, using hotels and guest houses, and in the first year, 1989, nearly 300 people benefited; they stayed in over forty different locations and reports were sent back to headquarters so that the best could be listed. Already it was proving to be much more flexible than the previous arrangements.[31]

## Flatlets reduced

There was also a run-down of the flatlets scheme. The house in Belfast, Shore House, under-used since the early 1980s, was sold in 1988. The following year the lease was surrendered on Regina House in north London which had been a Children's Home before being divided into flatlets when the home came to an end. Now only three flatlets schemes remained – Bronwen House at Southport, the two bungalows at Keighley in Yorkshire and Castle of Mey House in Surrey, and all three locations were refurbished in 1990. The Section's property-owning responsibilities had been considerably reduced.[32]

By now there were more frequent changes in the leadership of the Section, the office of Chairman being resticted to three years. Even so much could be achieved; Mrs Raymond, who was elected in 1986, introduced seminars to encourage younger women to take an active part in the Section, over fifty such meetings being held before she handed over to Mrs Nash in 1989. Continuity was provided by the National Secretary and when Miss Cooper handed over to Miss Green in 1990 she had held the post for twelve years. At Area level the staff were being run down following the success of the pilot scheme in the South West where the five Counties now operated on their own and by 1990 the majority of the Section's Areas had followed the same route, dispensing with paid staff as the incumbents either retired or filled headquarters posts, and shifting their tasks to Counties. This to some extent anticipated the Legion's restructuring which would take place a year or two later; but otherwise the Section would not be directly involved in the changes, having, as already noted, rejected the computerization of the membership database which accompanied the exercise.[33]

## 1991 – 1995

### Many events

The 1990s were eventful years for the Section. At the start of the decade it had taken a leading part in the celebrations to mark the ninetieth birthday of the Queen Mother, sixty standards proudly borne across the Horse Guards Parade as the Royal British Legion Women's Section led the civilian organizations in the march past. As if it were a reminder that, despite all this splendour, the purposes for which the Section existed were never far away, a few months later the branches to which the standard bearers returned were forming Gulf support groups to stand alongside those of the Legion as British forces again went to war. Happily their services were not needed.

A month or two after the Gulf War had ended the standards were out again when the 1991 conference celebrated 'Seventy Fan-tastic Years'. It was an inspired moment when, as the trumpets of the WRAC band sounded, more than 700 delegates waved fans to greet the Queen Mother; they had been asked to 'make the walls ring' in welcome and they did not fail. Nor did their President fail them, walking slowly up the hall after giving her address so that she could greet members on her way. The Queen Mother will always be remembered for the support she gave King George VI in the dark days of the Second World War and a few years later, in 1995, celebrations marked the fiftieth anniversary of the end of that war. The Section took its rightful place in the events, the blue and gold standards borne above their immaculate white-gauntleted bearers prominent on a warm day in August 1995 as the parade of men and women who had played their part in the war swung up the Mall in front of Buckingham Palace and the Queen took the salute.[34]

## Spirited Conferences

The spirit of the 1991 conference carried on into later years. In 1992 the theme was 'March-Hareing to Help' and a suitably-costumed 'hare' brought a huge model cake into the hall to receive delegates' cheques. That year Blackpool also saw the National Chairman and her husband riding in an open landau in Edwardian dress to anticipate the civic concert, a traditional music hall for which members were invited to wear the appropriate costume. More importantly, this was the first weekend conference, enabling younger working women to attend. The following year, 1993, the slogan was 'Swing into Action' to increase membership and the standards paraded to the tune of the Dambusters' march to commemorate the RAF raid into Germany fifty years before. There was again a theme to the civic entertainment, a concert and dance in 1950s and

*Imaginative slogans have long given extra vibrancy to Section Conferences. Here on the 70th Anniversary in 1991 the message is clear. At the podium is the Chairman, Mrs Nash; Dame Mary Bridges, who would succeed her, is to the left of the picture; to the right of the Chairman is Miss Green the National Secretary.*

60s costume. If, as someone rather unkindly remarked, it was difficult to tell who was in costume and who was not, there was no doubt that all had a good time. That year fundraising activities were introduced as 'Busy Bees Buzzing for Benevolence' but for the 1994 conference it was 'Do it Any Way You Like'. It produced an astonishing result: the following year the National Chairman, Dame Mary Bridges, who had taken over from Mrs Nash in 1992 and had set a target of £40,000, announced that more than double that figure had been achieved through the efforts of branches.[35] It represented a revival of the kind of top-level leadership which harked back to the days of Lady Edward Spencer Churchill; but such efforts had to be matched at all levels and from 1995 were recognized by the Section's own National Certificate of Appreciation.

## But a slipping membership

Despite all this exuberance at the annual conference, the 'Swing into Action' campaign to revive the membership was needed; numbers had been declining steadily and in 1994 would dip below 100,000, having been as high as a quarter of a million shortly after the Second World War. For some time a Liaison Officer had been visiting the women's services in Germany, working with Legion recruiters and even setting up local branches of the Section in major garrison areas. But with the run-down of the British Army of the Rhine which followed the lessening of tensions in Europe she switched her attentions to the United Kingdom, speaking to Townswomen's Guilds and Mothers' Unions, setting up a Pall Mall holding branch for those women who did not have access to a local branch and encouraging Counties similarly to open their own holding branches. The recruiting campaign itself depended on the Counties and branches with headquarters providing leaflets and posters, but at the end of the planned two years it had, at best, slowed the rate of decline. The current problem of finding younger and more active members to run branches was not unique to the Section and perhaps mirrored a society that had become more self-centred than an earlier generation. But history had been made in 1992 when the Legion's NEC noted that men wanted to join the Kettering branch of the Women's Section, and welcomed it in the absence of a full Legion branch.[36]

The closure of branches and the loss of members made it all the more remarkable that the Section was able to maintain its level of fundraising. But there might have been even better results if some of the branches did not also raise funds for outside bodies. In early 1995 the National Chairman was much concerned that some £50,000 had slipped away down this avenue, especially as the charity rules were now so strict on the matter. It was not a new problem; Brunel Cohen had made the same point in 1943. And it was sometimes difficult for a branch to understand why it should not help the local hospital or other worthy cause, not appreciating that if the money was raised in the Legion's name the donors expected it to go to the Legion.[37]

## The visitor scheme cuts costs

One of the proper fundraising beneficiaries was the Widows' and Ex-servicewomen's Allowance. But like many such payments it reflected the current state of play of DSS benefits; in the late 1980s it had been necessary to increase the payments as state aid was cut; now more state help was available, if people knew how to get it. The Section's welfare visitor scheme had been expanded in recent years and, with the Legion's County Field Officer scheme now in operation, there was more knowledge available. The welfare visitors were a lifeline, giving help, encouragement and advice to women in their own homes or in nursing or residential homes and even ensuring that the Section's birthday scheme remembered each one's anniversary. But they now were increasingly finding that the Allowance could be replaced by a state benefit and they helped their charges to do so, filling in the forms and even taking the applicant to the DSS office. It was thus possible to reduce the number of Section beneficiaries and to increase the amount paid to those that remained in the scheme from £4 per week to £5 per week in 1993. The method of payment also moved with the times, cheques being replaced with Direct Debit transfers. Even if there was no need for a regular payment the welfare visitor might arrange a grant for bedding, clothing, an electric heater or a pair of new spectacles, while the visitor could also arrange for a lifeline unit for use in emergencies. But such visitors could easily be overworked and ten ladies on their list was enough. The need was not just for more money but for more welfare visitors.[38]

The Rest and Convalescence Scheme, which had replaced the Rest Homes, had turned out to be very adaptable, the convalescence being taken as and when needed, with suitable establishments identified for disabled people and generous discounts obtained. Other organisations such as SSAFA and the Royal Naval Association were making use of it but, at around 200 each year the numbers involved were far less than the original scheme, suggesting that the availability of the Homes had perhaps led to over-use in the past with some regarding an annual stay as a holiday.[39]

★     ★     ★

Although the Women's Section had avoided the stress of the parent body's restructuring it had achieved a result not dissimilar. A layer of organization had been cut out and it had become more efficient by disposing of unwanted flatlets and replacing Rest Homes with a more effective system. Despite the erosion of the membership the work continued and the money was raised with no loss of enthusiasm. In 1995 Dame Mary could hand over to her successor, Mrs Arnold, an organization that, like the Legion, was well prepared for the challenges of a new century.

# CHAPTER 22

## OFFICER BENEVOLENCE 1971 - 2001

# *Some Grow Old*

### 1971 – 1975

### Fifty years on

1970 had been the fiftieth anniversary year of the forming of the Officers' Association and part of the commemoration was a special appeal for funds. Money was needed. Since the end of the Second World War the demand for relief had been persistent. No case of real need had been turned away, but each year the Association had overspent. In the anniversary year the budget had at last balanced, largely thanks to the Ministry of Defence making a more substantial contribution to the costs of finding jobs for former officers, at last meeting their moral obligations towards their prior employees. But costs were rising and the appeal to service and regimental charities and private individuals – no public appeal was possible under the original agreement with the Legion – brought in a useful, if not staggering, £16,000. The major service charities, such as King George's Fund for Sailors, of course already made annual contributions to the Association's finances.[1]

The event was also marked by the publication of an Officers' Association history. Written by a founder member of the staff, Squadron Leader Victor Cox, who had spent forty-five years working for the Association, it has proved a most useful source of information, not least for this work.

A financial corner was being turned, but it was not necessarily apparent. At a time of high inflation there was a particular need for prudence. Economies were instituted. Staff who left were not replaced, the Northern Ireland Branch closed in 1974 and the following year the Homes Register, which listed suitable residential and nursing homes, was ended. Such measures continued through the handover of General Secretaries, Major General Janes replacing Major General Shepheard in 1974.

### They fade away

Another turning point was reached in 1971 when the number of widows and dependants assisted by the Association exceeded the ex-officers and by 1975 the ratio was substantially greater: nearly 700 widows to under 500 former officers.[2] The Great War generation of officers was beginning to fade away. Slender as had been the resources of the officers, with meagre pensions and paltry savings eroded by inflation, the widows' resources were often even less. Moreover, financial aid apart, they needed advice and reassurance, an important aspect of the work of the Honorary Representatives. Their workload was increased in an unexpected way when the 1971 postal strike prevented the Association's welfare cheques being delivered and many representatives, knowing how much depended on prompt receipt of the money, acted as couriers and delivered the cheques themselves.[3] The representatives were now also encountering a new category needing help. The economic downturn was costing jobs so that men who had previously had few financial worries now found themselves unable to support even modest commitments due to soaring inflation. The only gleam of light on the horizon at this time was from an unexpected direction. Eire, which had long placed heavy demands on both the Association and the Legion because of inadequate social provisions, was at last beginning to improve its welfare services.

The closure of the Homes Register by no means meant the end of the Association's work in that sphere. If local authorities and other charities could not provide the information then the staff of the Relief section would help. Meanwhile they continued to deal with a steadily increasing rise in demand. Some was for short-term residence, usually in order to give an exhausted wife a break from nursing her permanently sick or disabled husband. But up to a hundred people were placed every year in residential or nursing homes and with costs rising the Association had increasingly to look to other charities to assist with making up the difference between the fees and and individual's own resources, which, even with social service allowances, were often inadequate.[4]

## 1976 – 1980

### Employment problems

As the recession continued the task of the Resettlement and Employment Department became even more difficult. Its title reflected the two principal categories whom it assisted: regular officers leaving the services at the end of their service, which might be a few years or a 'full career' of close on forty years; and those who came to the Officers' Association having been a civilian for perhaps many years but were now out of work and wished to make use of their former service connections, which may have been wartime service or even National Service as well as regular. They were all sorts and conditions of men, and some women, but each received the same painstaking attention.

The regular officers encountering civil life for the first time needed the most counselling. If they were young and had an engineering degree or other qualification there was little difficulty; there were good prospects as a management trainee. At the other end of the scale were the fifty-five-year-olds at the end of a military career and seeking to work for a further ten years. Age was the biggest problem. Employers had been cutting staff in response to the difficult times and the first to go had been the oldest; they were naturally disinclined to take on more in the same category. The main openings were in adminstrative posts such a college bursar, and they were much in demand. Nonetheless the department managed to place many of them.

Between the young officers and their seniors there were those in the middle of their service careers who might have been tempted by offers of voluntary redundancy to seek a new life outside. But the gloomy picture they saw caused many to think again, a decision which helped the department under the circumstances; even civilian firms were now consulting the Officers' Association over making ex-officers in their employ redundant, often those who had been recently placed with them by the Association; it was a case of last in first out.[5]

In all about a thousand officers, former or still serving, sought the department's help

412

each year, some 300 to 400 being placed in work by the staff while most of the others managed to secure their own appointments following counselling. There were some remarkable successes: the situation of a wartime officer who had been unemployed for twenty-two years was seen as a challenge and within ten days he was in a job; a seventy-year-old former officer who was unable to live on a reduced state pension was found a clerical post; and a disabled ex-Army Bomb Disposal Officer got work as a bursar.[6]

### A new generation of elderly

The seventy-year-old had sought work as an alternative to financial aid. But there were many others who could not exercise that option. The surviving veterans of the First World War were now in their eighties and nineties, as were the widows, who now greatly outnumbered them. So far the Association's main work with the elderly had been with this generation. Now those of the Second World War era were beginning to appear on the scene. Moreover costs were escalating. Much of the Association's income came from the Legion grant, which was based on an agreed share of the Poppy Appeal (see Chart E1 on page 449). But between 1977 and 1980 the grant had to be increased in real terms by nearly one third.

The rise in living costs was not confined to the United Kingdom. Many former officers had taken up residence overseas, but with savings declining in value while UK state pensions – despite in some cases exceptional service to their country – were frozen, they or their dependants were often in difficult circumstances. The widow of an officer who had been awarded both a Military Cross and a Distinguished Service Medal in the Great War was penniless in Rhodesia and had to be repatriated and put in a Home. An 83-year-old ex-officer living on Elba had to be given food and shelter until he was paid for the sale of his land to the local council.[7]

The Elba resident might, or might not, have preferred to go to the Association's own Home, Huntly in Devon. Here the average age was eighty and the accomodation, which had recently been modernized was excellent. Even so living in a Home did not agree with everyone: in 1978 six found they did not enjoy communal life and left, while the following year one individual who 'would not conform to normal discipline' had to be asked to go. A happier reason for leaving was the marriage of a 74-year-old in 1977.[8]

## 1981 – 1985

### Co-location at last

In the summer of 1981 the Officers' Association moved into the newly-refurbished Legion headquarters in Pall Mall. It was almost exactly sixty years since they had been associated with what was now the Royal British Legion, but the first time that they had occupied the same building. Had that been possible sixty years before many of the early differences might have been avoided.

The lease on 28, Belgrave Square was sold for a little under half a million pounds and the proceeds invested to provide a useful addition to the income. With the annual share of the Appeal maintained,[9] and with a reducing commitment to Home fees (see below), over the next five years the Association was able to re-build its reserves. As it turned out it was well that it did so.

413

The move was followed by a staff reorganization in which the Resettlement and Employment Department was streamlined, while the Country Homes section disappeared, the task being added to the Assistant General Secretary's duties. Having overseen the move and the staff changes Major General Janes retired in 1984, Brigadier P.D. Johnson taking over as General Secretary.

## Enter the ladies

The Assistant GS had been passed a problem. Despite its situation and amenities Huntly was not full. When a place became vacant, although there was a waiting list it was often not taken up; many elderly officers liked the security of knowing that they had a guaranteed place, but when the vacancy occurred they preferred to stay where they were for the time being; in other cases the family made the application but the ex-officer refused to co-operate, not wishing to leave familiar surroundings and friends, a situation not peculiar to Huntly. In 1983 therefore a bold step was taken, but presumably only after consulting the current residents: ladies were admitted. By 1984 there were four female ex-officers or nursing sisters among the thirty-five people living at Huntly.[10]

The Association's other Homes were the twelve bungalows for disabled officers and their wives at Leavesden. Here too there were problems. Situated to the north of London it was threatened by road improvement schemes. In the event a public inquiry in 1983 decided on other solutions to the traffic demands and, although something of an island in a sea of motorways, it continued to be a well-run and happy place.

*One of the twelve Leavesden bungalows for disabled ex-officers. These are for married couples but, in the event of a death, the surviving spouse is allowed to remain.*

Considerably less happy than the residents of Leavesden were those who had been made redundant as more and more firms cut back on staff. In some cases they had been placed by the Association, perhaps after taking service redundancy. Among them were some who were in need of financial help and there was some increase in the number of applications for relief. There were also more elderly people on the move back to Britain from abroad, while young families were not exempt from problems, especially where the marriage had failed. Another problem was in rural areas where the decline in public transport made people increasingly dependent on cars which they could ill afford to run. Most such problems could be solved with money but it was more usual for the Relief Department to advise on state benefits, reserving the charity's funds for those cases which had no other solution.[11]

There were now more of these funds. In 1983 the government increased payments for those in residential or nursing homes so that the burden on charities was reduced. The effect was dramatic: in 1984 the Association's expenditure in real terms on Home fees fell to less than half of the 1983 total. The following year it reduced still further to a third of that total. But the reprieve would be short-lived.

For those whose income was still marginal the clothing store continued to provide a useful service, although the stock had had to be reduced for the move to Pall Mall. It was maintained by an annual gift from Queen Mary's London Needlework Guild and by widows donating their late husands' wardrobes. As a by-product it had kitted out a number of youth orchestras with gifts of evening dress unlikely to be of use to impoverished ex-officers.[12]

## The computer arrives

There was no let-up in these years for the Resettlement and Employment staff. Jobs were still hard to get and there was now a culture of early retirement in many organizations which was very unsettling for an officer leaving the services at age fifty-five and needing to bolster his savings for final retirement. Others might have received a 'golden handshake' and would welcome five days golf a week in place of the office grind. He could not afford such a luxury but it was now even more difficult to persuade an employer to take him on. But the Association persevered. The best openings for such cases were now in the non-profit making sector and in addition to the hardy stand-by of golf club secretary, no doubt ensuring that the course was fit for the civilian early retirees, other posts had come on the scene in recent years: trade association secretary, charity executive or local government Emergency Planning Officer.[13]

There were now also a small number of women registrants, some of whom secured managerial appointments at worthwhile salaries. And in another new departure there was a formal liaison with the Regular Forces Employment Association to exchange vacancies which could be filled by any kind of background. Most of the traffic was from the RFEA to the OA and the following year, 1985, it could be fed into a computer. The computer enabled procedures to be speeded up, particularly matching jobs with candidates and would be refined over the years.[14]

Some placings did not need computers. An Honorary Representative managed to get a paraplegic former Royal Marine officer a post as an estate administrator, work he could do from his wheelchair. Meanwhile those confined to wheelchairs because of a service disability – and any other ex-officer with a pension claim – were now dealt with by the Legion's Pension's Department. From 1 October 1984 all new claims went to the Legion and twelve months later the OA's Claims and Pensions section closed completely.[15] It was the first integration of functions since the Unity agreement sixty-three years before. Times had changed.

## 1986 – 1990

## More changes

There were other benefits from co-location. Sharing the same building enabled the Legion and Association General Secretaries to consult regularly and in 1990 the Legion GS joined the Legion representation on the OA Council. The Council itself had slimmed down over the years, from around eighty members in 1970 to fifty in 1990. The full Council met, however, only once a year and routine management was in the hands of the Executive Committee; this too had been reduced over the years and was now eleven-strong, including two Legion representatives, one of whom was its General Secretary, and

*Executive Committee Chairmen and General Secretaries are listed at Appendix I Table F.

four ex-officio members representing Scotland and the three service benevolent funds. The relationship between the Chairman of the Executive Committee and the General Secretary was clearly important.*

Other committees ran the various functions and in 1986 working parties were set up to review their activities and those of the departments they supervised. As a result there were further adjustments to the organization which included changing the names of the two principal functions: the Relief Department became the Benevolent Department while Resettlement and Employment became simply Employment. Outside the headquarters the two 'divisional' committees which represented separate areas of the country disappeared, so that in addition to the largely autonomous Scottish Executive Committee – although regulated by the OA Charter it controlled its own funds – there were now only two local committees, Birmingham and Kenya.

## Home fees – the gap widens

The committees performed useful functions. But the effectiveness of the Association's work, particularly its welfare activities, continued to depend on its Honorary Representatives, of whom there were now some 570 at home and overseas. In most areas the work continued at full stretch as increasing numbers of Second World War ex-officers and their wives entered old age. Wheelchairs, home modifications to cope with disability and 'lifeline' emergency help buttons were all in demand, although the bulk of the relief work continued to be the provision of small regular payments to elderly ex-officers or their dependants trying to cope on very small pensions and state benefits and to whom £5 a week, even in these inflationary times, was enough to relieve at least some of the worry in their declining years.

Towards the end of the decade the workload began to level off. The successful campaign by the Officers Pensions Society to improve the pensions of the pre-1973 widows, together with some advances in state benefits, combined with the disappearance from the scene of an impoverished First World War generation. Costs, however, began rise again as the gap between charges raised by residential and nursing homes and state assistance once again widened. In 1985 the Officers' Association's contribution in real terms had been £32,000; by 1989 it had risen to £425,000, despite the fact that it continued to share the costs with other charities. Chart E 2 shows the effect on the OA's expenditure. But not only had reserves been built up, the Legion grant, based on the OA $7\frac{1}{2}$ per cent share of the Appeal, continued to increase, in real terms providing £4.2 million for these five years, compared with £3.3 million over the previous period.[16] In return the OA relinquished its legacy share in 1991, in order to assist the Legion's finances.

All was therefore under control and those such as the retired captain suffering from cancer whose wife had had open heart surgery and whose resources were exhausted, or the army wife who had been interned by the Japanese and emerged physically handicapped, could be helped with Home fees or in other ways.

# 1991 – 1995

## Coming up with the goods

As the century drew to a close the new technology began to make an impact on the

Association's employment service. The computer matching of vacancies to candidates was further refined and procedures were speeded up with a significant improvement in placings. It was also possible to provide a more personal service with the candidate dealt with by the same employment officer throughout. There was now a high quality of applicant, reflecting well on officer selection procedures in the post-war era. Nevertheless the market remained competitive, with the perennial problem of placing the older officer; it meant that some had to take part-time work.

With all these improvements the department was well prepared for the run-down of the armed forces following the end of the Cold War and when the surge came it was able to cope, recording a 42 per cent rise in placings. The high profile of the 1991 Gulf War helped; serving officers came across well in television interviews and employers were impressed, as they were by the subsequent coverage of events in the Balkans. The latter provided more openings; officers leaving the services were recruited for monitoring teams and for other international work in the former Yugoslavia, as well as for field work with charities in Afghanistan and Cambodia. Such appointments were short term, or so it seemed at the time, but they were popular as they could lead to longer appointments with the organizations concerned and in any case filled the gap until the UK job market improved. One officer even took a post to set up a resettlement service for the Ukraine Army.[17]

The MOD, at least in part because of the concern expressed by the ex-service organizations, had set up a Tri-Service Resettlement Organization. This positive approach which included marketing the employment potential of former servicemen led to close co-operation between the TSRO, the OA and the Regular Forces Employment Association. It was helped by the RFEA moving to the Legion headquarters building in Pall Mall which made the exchange of job information much easier.

Service redundancy peaked in 1994, but against the background of a much more buoyant economy employers' interest remained as the armed services stayed in the public eye through media coverage of the continuing events in Bosnia, Kosovo and elsewhere. Although more jobs were now short term or on a consultancy basis placement remained high. So did the opinions of those whom the Association had helped: 'You have a finger on the employment pulse I have not seen elsewhere'; 'I was confident that the Officers' Association would come up with the goods and indeed you have.'[18]

### When the savings run out

As the employment side built up, so did the needs of those for whom productive work was only a distant memory or an impossibility. It was now the elderly of the Second World War who claimed attention but the pattern was as before: advice on benefits – of which there was often a lamentable ignorance – the need for a small regular allowance to make the difference between hardship and a tolerable existence, and help with a sudden and unexpected crisis. Sometimes a lifetime's savings were used up as in the case of an 88-year-old former RNVR lieutenant who had to pay care assistant fees when he had a stroke and his wife also fell ill. A former prisoner of war of the Japanese had exhausted all his money in Nursing Home fees and was threatened with moving out until the Officers' Association moved in and paid the fees.

By now the gap between Home fees and government allowances had closed a little. The Association's outlay was still high but within its resources. Huntly's reputation as a well-run and above all a happy home remained, while on the fiftieth anniversary of the Battle of the Atlantic in 1992 a Leavesden resident with a Distinguished Service Cross and two bars was taken to Liverpool to sit beside the Prince of Wales. That day his battle ensign flew from the mast at Leavesden. It symbolized the spirit of the Officers' Association and those it existed to serve.[19]

★　　★　　★

Since 1921 the Officers' Association and the Legion had been on a long journey together through difficult country. Such circumstances impose strain. One partner might have decided to march alongside the other instead of in file, but they had remained in step. For that many had cause to be grateful – from the destitute ex-officer of the Great War to the young man whose service career had been prematurely ended by the defence cuts.

# CHAPTER 23

## A SUMMARY OF 1996 – 2001

# *Into a New Century*

## 1996 – 2001

### The closing years

This chapter takes the Legion story into the present day. There are difficulties in dealing objectively with contemporary events and it will be for a future historian properly to evaluate the period. The Legion's activities in these years are therefore summarized.

The period has seen the beginnings of attempts to change British society; the new government elected in 1997 was a reforming administration determined to modernize the country and with scant regard for tradition. 'Cool Britannia's' trident drove the hereditary peers from their seats in the Lords and accustomed ways seemed everywhere to be under threat. Nor was the government's course diverted by financial worries; its inheritance included full Treasury coffers and the pound rode high in the currency markets.

### A new image and a new capability

Against this background charities such as the Legion might have expected some reduction in their burdens. But the prevailing concern seemed to be more with appearance than substance. The old in particular were vulnerable and as their numbers grew social provision lagged still further. Old or young, the Legion was prepared. The reorganizations begun in the early 1990s had produced powerful in-house public relations and fundraising capabilities, while at the same time welfare activities were being more efficiently managed. Communications with the outside world were improved: *Legionline* now provided an immediate telephone response to queries about the organization and its work while *Legionbrief* regularly updated MPs and others on its activities. The Legion logo appeared on a British Airways aircraft and on the mainsail of an entry in the Round the World yacht race; the poppy was even projected on to the canopy of the millenium dome at Woolwich, which also saw a vast throng of children in a 'circle of Remembrance' at 11 o'clock on 11 November 2000. Later that day some of them accompanied the Torch of Remembrance in its journey from the Cenotaph to the Royal Albert Hall, reminiscent of the march that had been the climax of the first festival in 1927. Such imaginative ideas not only helped convey the spirit of Remembrance to a generation that had never known war, but underlined the importance of the Legion's work, reflected in the continuing support for the Poppy Appeal.[1]

For most people, however, it was the two-minute silence campaign which brought home the Legion's message. After five years the 'Pause for Remembrance' at eleven o'clock on the eleventh of November was being observed by some 42 million people in Britain, nearly three-quarters of the population. And, following the National Chairman's address to the BCEL conference in 1999, that year the silence began to be observed by the countries of the Commonwealth.[2]

In 1966 a public opinion poll had revealed that over half of the population were ignorant of the Legion's work. A poll in 1999 produced a somewhat different picture: not only were the public in general aware of what the organization stood for, but they identified with it.[3] It was a remarkable transformation. Moreover the government were listening too; the campaign to establish a Department of Ex-service Affairs (see page 327) to ensure that matters affecting the ex-service community were more effectively handled seemed to have succeeded when the Prime Minister announced in early 2001 the appointment of a Minister for Veterans' Affairs.*

Some things went on in the traditional way. The 75th Anniversary was celebrated with a rally and a parade of over 500 standards, as well as a Service of Thanksgiving in Westminster Abbey attended by the Queen. And on the 80th anniversary of the first Armistice Day the local Legion branch laid a wreath on the grave of Laurence Binyon whose lines 'They shall grow not old . . .' have meant so much to so many over the years.[4]

### Into a higher gear

At the heart of this new dynamism were the Legion's key figures. By now it was accepted practice that the National President would come from each of the three services in turn. In 1997 Air Marshal Sir Roger Austin had taken office and the organization responded well to his down-to-earth approach. In 2000 the presidency passed to Lieutenant General Sir Roderick Cordy-Simpson, who had directed NATO operations in Bosnia. Meanwhile Graham Downing had proved an apt Chairman for the times; a former warrant officer in the regular army, he took nothing for granted and his monthly column in the *Legion Journal* often challenged some long-held Legion belief. J.G. Champ took over from Downing in 1998. A bluff and cheerful manner concealed a determined approach and he would set in train further reforms.

In 1996 I.G. Townsend had been appointed Secretary General. He had worked in industry after leaving the army as a brigadier and his clear-sighted approach, backed by modern management expertise, gave a new impetus to change. The field structure was simplified with all staff support centred on Counties, internal communication improved and even Conference itself scrutinized. As will be seen from Table B, such a review was hardly too soon; for many years barely one in five branches had been represented at Conference. As the SG himself told delegates, lack of grass-roots involvement in planning created distrust between members and staff.[5]

The smaller branches would anyway be less likely to send delegates as their membership declined. Some had been forced to close altogether, although new branches also formed, notably the Gulf War Veterans Branch in 1998, which enabled their welfare problems to be dealt with efficiently. But the overall trend was down, club closures, despite every effort by the staff to help, contributing to the decline. Nevertheless there were still the traditional branch activities, to which had been added support for the two-minute silence, with the local Legion giving a lead to the community.[6]

### Living longer

The Gulf Veterans represented some of the younger element turning to the Legion for help and the Legion now sought a public inquiry into their condition. But there were others, particularly the young disabled ex-servicemen; they needed suitable housing,

* The new post will be an additional responsibility for an existing MOD Minister but he will have supporting staff, principally to assist him to co-ordinate ex-service matters across the various government departments. Whether Defence is the right Ministry to deal with ex-service matters and the extent to which this solution will meet the needs of the Legion and the other veterans' bodies has to be seen; but at least the principle has been established.

often a wheelchair, above all training and a job so that they could regain self-respect. All of this the Legion provided. Some of the more recent victims were from the Balkans: a soldier who lost the use of both legs when his water truck overturned while bringing help to refugees; another who lost a leg to a mine.[7]

By contrast there were increasing numbers of elderly ex-service people. Inadequate funding for the Care in the Community scheme meant that charities had to close the gap and in 1999 the Legion reviewed its nursing care strategy. Perversely, new laws were making life more difficult for those running homes and the decision had to be taken to replace Galanos House which could not meet the new standards; yet it had been the Legion's first 'purpose-built' home when it opened in 1967. In the Republic of Ireland, however, there was a new prosperity and donations to the Poppy Appeal began to approach the level of welfare spending in that country.[8]

Meanwhile the Legion had been running an awareness campaign on war pensions, much increasing its own workload. But a government decision had severely reduced entitlement to a pension for noise-induced deafness, a common affliction in the armed forces, and a campaign was begun to restore the entitlement, the Legion working with a specialist charity to obtain the medical evidence. On a brighter note the Legion had by 1999 succeeded in persuading 98 per cent of councils to disregard war pensions when assessing benefits; nevertheless a change of council could bring a change of mind and the Legion goal was to get central government to accept responsibility for a total disregard, as it had been since 1931.[9]

A Legion conference had first supported proper compensation for former prisoners of war of the Japanese in 1953. For over forty years a deaf ear had been turned to their claims and many were now dead, although their widows lived on. Now the 1999 Conference was determined that justice should be done. The outcome was a British government decision to pay £10,000 compensation to each FEPOW. This was somewhat less satisfactory than the Japanese making amends, but at least those concerned had the money.[10]

In addition the Foreign Office had sponsored a 'reconciliation tour' of former British prisoners and Japanese veterans in Burma and Thailand in 1998, which the Legion Pilgrimages Department ran. The scheme to enable war widows to visit their husbands' graves was also extended, but by now the widows were only 10 per cent of those travelling and the department became Remembrance Travel in 1999, taking on battlefield tours for schools.[11]

There were other changes in the interests of efficiency. DMI was merged with Legion Industries at Aylesford, combining with Supplies to form a new body – Supplylines – although the Poppy Factory declined an invitation to join the party. The Attendants Company too had to adapt. As the supply of ex-servicemen and women dwindled it took on non ex-service staff in order to maintain its commercial position, developing a non-charitable 'trading arm' for the purpose. Taking over other enterprises, it continued its remarkable success story and now awarded training bursaries at Tidworth. There the Legion was able to overcome its financial problems by leasing the Training College to a College of Further Education while still providing courses for those leaving the services. Meanwhile it had assisted some 3,000 serving and ex-servicemen and women each year to enter a civil occupation, half of whom passed through the college.[12]

Of some significance was a declaration by the Legion and SSAFA in 2000. It envisaged a joint reorganization, opening the way to mutual working and perhaps suggesting an even closer relationship at some stage. In view of the large number of bodies working independently in the ex-service field the move was a welcome initiative which might in time give a lead to others.[13]

## New ideas

Fundraising continued to be both enlivened and enhanced by a stream of new ideas – the 'Great British Poppy Chain' of sponsored runners along the Norfolk coastline, 'Pedal to Paris' and a similar event to Brussels, veteran car rallies and even monopoly played on the streets of London. The money raised, together with corporate donations and legacies, represented over 40 per cent of fundraising income by 2000. But there was no decline in the Poppy Appeal itself. As Chart C1 on page 447 shows the Appeal increased in real terms up to the end of the century, aided by launches which caught the imagination, such as Vera Lynn, representing the wartime generation, alongside a current, if somewhat more transient, phenomena, the Spice Girls. But the real heroes, and more particularly the heroines, of the Appeal remained the collectors, still out with their trays of poppies in all weathers from dawn to dusk.[14]

Many of these collectors were from the Women's Section which in 1998 had its own launch – the President's Award scheme to mark the Queen Mother's seventy-fifth year in that office. It had two separate strands: to assist people of all ages with service connections with education; and to provide respite breaks for families under pressure.[15]

But the anniversary was also celebrated in the traditional way with a parade of standards at Clarence House. Meanwhile over a hundred women a year benefited from convalescent care under the scheme which had now run successfully for ten years and six hundred in need continued to receive regular payments. And, if the sale of Castle of Mey House in 1998 was greeted with some relief, elsewhere the flatlets scheme continued to provide the elderly not only with a home but companionship.[16]

The Officers' Association too looked after the elderly. Huntly and the Leavesden estate remained full, while nearly 150 ex-officers or their widows were helped each year with nursing home fees. But the bulk of the relief was in regular payments to those who, having given their best years in the service of their country, now had to exist on inadequate pensions. The generations following on had a rather better outlook, largely thanks to the Employment Department, now working with a civilian consulting group under a MOD scheme which had contracted out service resettlement. Nor did the department forget those who had gone before: in 1998 over eighty ex-officers who had been out of work for up to six years were found jobs.[17]

$$\star \qquad \star \qquad \star$$

The dawn of a new century found the Legion, and those associated with it, better equipped, better trained and better prepared than at any time in its history. The task had changed: the acute distress that followed the First World War and the inequities that continued in the wake of the Second had all but disappeared; but even in the new enlightened society the state could not – or would not – meet all needs, particularly those of the old. There was still suffering and deprivation. There was still the danger that sacrifice would be forgotten. There was a still a need for the Legion.

# CHAPTER 24

## POSTSCRIPT 1921 - 2001

# *Some Reflections*

### 1921 – 2001

**The shield**

As the Legion's eighty-year march reaches the crestline of a new century it is tempting to peer over the edge into what lies ahead. But such views are best taken by the organization's current leaders. The historian's task is to look back over the path that has been trodden and reflect on what has been accomplished.

The analogy of a shield and a sword has been used to represent the Legion's functions of protecting the afflicted while attempting to right injustice. That the shield has been held steadily in place is due in equal measure to the Legion's structure and to its ability to raise funds. The work of the branches, especially in the long era of hardship that followed the First World War, has been by any standards remarkable. Motivated by that extraordinary sense of comradeship that emerged from the trenches, they cared for the widows, the orphans, the disabled and the workless. Often there was an inspiring element of selflessness – men who were desperately hanging on to their own jobs, or even unemployed, trying to find work for others. The employment achievements of the early 1930s perhaps constitute the branches' greatest battle honour.

There were some hard times too after the Second World War. But as the welfare state developed the scene changed. In some ways the task became more difficult: the gaps in state provision were not easy to spot and those at risk not always so obvious. The rules too became complex and it was this combination of factors that led to the strengthening of the structure with the introduction of County Field Officers in the closing years of the century. The two elements were interdependent; without the branches the CFO would lack 'eyes and ears'; without the CFO the branch would not have guidance. The shape of the shield may have changed, but it is all the more effective.

However well organized and motivated, all great enterprises need an element of luck. In the Legion's case it came with the poppy. For eighty Novembers the emotional connection with the battlefield has endured, collectors have rallied to its cause in villages and busy urban streets, and the public has supported it. The power of the poppy has kept the shield in place through economic crises and the ravages of inflation. That so many have seen it as a symbol in its own right is an indication of the effect it has.

The Legion has not of course been the sole protector of the ex-service community over this period; apart from all else it did not have the resources. Other charities have played their part, some having done so long before the Legion existed. But the Legion, partly because it was acknowledged as the democratic expression of the views of those who had fought the Great War, took the lead in campaigning. The sword was unsheathed at the outset; it may not be needed so much as in the past, but it has not yet been returned to the scabbard.

## The sword

The Legion began to campaign as soon as it was formed. In the early days it attempted to influence national policy over employment or house-building; not surprisingly it was ignored. Its successes were strictly in its own field and some were remarkable, such as the preservation of the value of the war pension when living costs fell; but it had its failures too. It is worth reviewing these campaigns to establish why some succeeded and others failed.*

The war pensions and war widows measures brought in during the First World War were advanced for their times. But they contained injustices such as the seven-year rule or the system for making final awards. The Legion succeeded in getting changes made because it was deeply involved in the operation of the schemes and could present a compelling case to government. Not all of the changes were reflected by statute; some were administrative. But there were no outright failures and the Legion's by now expert criticism of the 1939 Pensions Warrant was accepted without argument.

The Legion's success in retaining an independent Pensions Ministry in 1922 is the only instance of the government capitulating in order to avoid confrontation with the ex-service segment of the population. But the demobilization disorders were still fresh in the memory, while unrest was rife elsewhere in Europe. Thirty years later, on the same issue, the government simply ignored the Legion's protests. They could afford to do so; by then the movement had long been a responsible and disciplined institution not given to violent protest except at the intellectual level. And in the context of the emerging welfare state the Legion's arguments lacked conviction, while the matter was hardly likely to attract much public sympathy.

Public sentiment was an important factor. The Legion's case in the inter-war years to maintain war pensions at their current values despite deflation had little to sustain it at a time of widespread economic misery. An argument based on sacrifice made for the country did not cut much ice with politicians. But they recognized that the electorate might see war pensions cuts as particularly mean-minded. Nevertheless a few years later, in 1936, the Legion was roundly defeated on the question of an allowance for prematurely aged ex-servicemen; in this instance it did not have the facts to support its case, nor presumably did the government feel that there were any strong feelings about the matter in the country. Both of the key ingredients, either of which might have won the day, were lacking.

On the other hand the two great post-1945 issues of maintaining the value of war pensions against inflation and removing the tax burden from the war widows' pensions did have strong public and press support as well as compelling evidence. But now a new factor entered: dogma. In the view of social reformers war pensions were an irrelevance in the all-embracing welfare state; and Treasury opposition to the war widows' case, on the grounds of setting a precedent, was stubborn. Yet the Legion carried the day in the end by sheer persistence: it took twenty-six years to tie war pensions to the cost of living and twenty-eight to free the widows from tax.

Even more perseverance has been called for in the fight to have war pensions disregarded in the assessment of benefit entitlements. Seventy years have elapsed since the Legion began its campaign in 1931 and for that length of time successive governments have simply held it to be a local authority matter. The force of argument is therefore deflected, while the issue itself is insufficiently emotive to attract any large measure of public support. The case for a Veterans' Affairs Department seemed to suffer from similar difficulties but in the end conviction and persistence prevailed.

* The reader may wish to refer to Table C on page 434, listing the principal Legion campaigns.

424

Thus, over eighty years of Legion campaigning as a responsible institution, success has rested on a number of factors: the strength of the argument, the degree of public support and a determination to overcome political or official dogma. There must also be a willingness to persevere. If some of these are lacking then the battle is unlikely to be won.

## The membership

As we have seen, the Legion discarded at the outset any notion of behaving in the manner of a trade union. A large and widespread membership – well beyond that needed to sustain its welfare work – simply endowed it with the authority to campaign on behalf of the ex-service community. Of course each member was also a voter but the organization as a whole never made any attempt to enlist those votes in support of its objectives; such did not accord with its non-political stance. Nor does that authority appear to have diminished as the membership has declined following the reduction in size of the ex-service population; the proportion of ex-servicemen and women who belong to the Legion has remained more or less constant over the years, at around one in twelve.

A shrinking membership has, however, brought dangers. The closure of branches,* particularly in rural areas, has reduced the Legion's contact with the population, including the ex-service element it exists to serve. But the effect has been mitigated by the better training and support that the remaining branches have received in recent years, especially from the introduction of County Field Officers.

The falling ex-service population has also affected the clubs, although in their case commercial factors are involved as well. The clubs' contribution to the Legion has of course been almost entirely in terms of attracting and sustaining, in perhaps more than one sense, the membership. But, if it is accepted that the Legion needs to demonstrate its grass roots credentials then that contribution has been worthwhile.

One remarkable change over the last quarter of a century or so has been the reduced involvement by former officers in the running of the Legion. In the first fifty years of its existence twelve out of the Legion's fourteen Chairmen were ex-officers, some of very high rank. But since 1971 it has been exceptional for a Legion Chairman to have held commissioned rank. The make-up of the National Council shows a corresponding decline: from 50 per cent in the 1960s to a mere handful in the 1990s. At County level there has been a similar story, suggesting that it reflects the situation in the branches.

The reasons can only be conjecture. But the timing of the change suggests a difference in attitude between the First and Second World War generations of officers. The First World War officers seem to have identified more with those they had led, perhaps because of the particular circumstances of that war, perhaps because of a genuine feeling for the plight of their men in the difficult post-war period, possibly because of Haig's example. They would have ceased to be effective in the Legion after about 1970, which is when the reduced officer involvement becomes apparent. The timing might also suggest a connection with the 1940 loosening of ties between the Officers' Association and the Legion, but this is most unlikely to have been a significant factor; the proportion of wartime officers involved with the OA was relatively small. The split may perhaps have had some effect on post-war ex-officers whose high regard for the OA might otherwise have rested with the Legion. In general, however, they would have taken their lead from those who came before.

Does any of this matter? The Legion has functioned perfectly satisfactorily for the last thirty years and former other ranks have held the highest posts with distinction. Yet few

*See Table B on page 431.

would dispute that the organization as a whole could have benefited from more trained leaders. And it is sad if the Legion does not reflect the bond between the ranks that is at the heart of the armed services.

## The long and the short and the tall

It is fitting to end this account of the Legion's history with the member himself. At one time the high point of the Festival of Remembrance, before the poppies fluttered down and all was still, was the singing of the old familiar songs. Among them, always rendered with great gusto, and perhaps the favourite, 'Bless 'em All, the Long and the Short and the Tall'. It was the private soldier's gentle mockery of his superiors, sung in barrack canteens and on troopships, or muttered in landing craft or glider.

Legion members, too, have come in all shapes and sizes. Some devoted their lives to the organization, and through it to the needs of their former comrades and their families. Others, to use a modern expression, 'were there for the beer'; through the clubs they sought to recapture the companionship of the mess-deck or the barrack room; but many such also took pride in the Legion and its work, even if their contribution was solely to turn out and march with the rest behind the branch standard to the local war memorial once a year. And, in time, some who had come for the beer might reflect on these matters, in due course taking their place with a tray of poppies or bringing cheer to a disabled comrade.

As these pages have shown, Legion members are conservative by nature. They distrust change; but once convinced of its worth there are no more stalwart supporters. They represent common sense and many a National Council, debating the merits of proposition about to be placed before Conference, has been content to set it aside with the conclusion 'Let the delegates decide'.

Such men and women have sustained the Legion for eighty years. In so doing, they have kept faith.

# APPENDIX I

# TABLES

**Notes**

1. The Legion President and Chairman (together with the Vice Chairman) are elected at the Annual Conference in late May/early June. Up to 1993 the General Treasurer was elected, but is now chosen by the National Council, who also appoint the General Secretary (now Secretary General). Similar procedures are followed by the Women's Section. In the case of the Officers' Association the Trustees appoint the Executive and Finance Committee Chairman and the General Secretary on behalf of the Council.

2. The calculations for branch representation at Annual Conferences are not exact. Even where attendance has been accurately recorded the figures are affected by the fact that large branches may send two delegates to Conference. Nevertheless they provided a basis to compare branch involvement in the Legion's government over the years. Table B may be compared with Table E which shows the Women's Section representation.

3. The Legion Campaigns table (Table C) summarizes the major initiatives or policy changes that the Legion has sought from government. There are many other important policy matters with which the Legion has been concerned, but these are those in which it has pursued clearcut objectives.

# TABLE A – LEGION OFFICERS

| Year | National President | National Chairman | General Treasurer | General Secretary |
|------|--------------------|--------------------|--------------------|--------------------|
| 1921 | FM Earl Haig | TF Lister† | Maj JB Brunel Cohen† | Col EC Heath |
| 1922 | » | » | » | » |
| 1923 | » | » | » | » |
| 1924 | » | » | » | » |
| 1925 | » | » | » | » |
| 1926 | » | » | » | » |
| 1927 | » | Lt Col GR Crosfield | » | » |
| 1928 | AF Earl Jellicoe | » | » | » |
| 1929 | » | » | » | » |
| 1930 | » | Col John Brown† | » | » |
| 1931 | » | » | » | » |
| 1932 | » | » | » | » |
| 1933 | Maj Gen Sir Frederick Maurice | » | » | » |
| 1934 | » | Maj FWC Fetherston-Godley† | » | » |
| 1935 | » | » | » | » |
| 1936 | » | » | » | » |
| 1937 | » | » | » | » |
| 1938 | » | » | » | » |
| 1939 | » | » | » | » |
| 1940 | » | Col SWL Ashwanden | » | JR Griffin |
| 1941 | » | » | » | » |
| 1942 | » | » | » | » |
| 1943 | » | Brig Gen ER Fitzpatrick† | » | » |
| 1944 | » | » | » | » |
| 1945 | » | » | » | » |
| 1946 | » | » | Lord Cromwell | » |
| 1947 | Lt Col Sir Ian Fraser | Lt Col C Gordon Larking† | » | » |
| 1948 | » | » | » | » |
| 1949 | » | » | » | » |
| 1950 | » | Maj Gen Sir Richard Howard-Vyse | » | » |

428 †Later knighted.

# TABLE A – LEGION OFFICERS

| Year | National President | National Chairman | General Treasurer | General Secretary |
|------|-------------------|-------------------|-------------------|-------------------|
| 1951 | [Fraser] | [Howard-Vyse] | [Cromwell] | [Griffin] |
| 1952 | » | » | » | » |
| 1953 | » | Capt SH Hampson | » | » |
| 1954 | » | » | » | » |
| 1955 | » | » | » | » |
| 1956 | » | Maj JT Spinks | » | » |
| 1957 | » | » | » | » |
| 1958 | Maj Gen Sir Richard Howard-Vyse | » | » | » |
| 1959 | » | Gen Sir Roy Bucher | » | DE Coffer |
| 1960 | » | » | Col Sir A Moffat (acting) | » |
| 1961 | » | » | Lt Col C Gordon Larking† | » |
| 1962 | Lt Gen Sir Oliver Leese | » | » | » |
| 1963 | » | Lord Carew | » | » |
| 1964 | » | » | » | » |
| 1965 | » | » | » | » |
| 1966 | » | Maj J Ben Davies | » | » |
| 1967 | » | » | » | » |
| 1968 | » | » | » | » |
| 1969 | » | DI Cadman | » | » |
| 1970 | Gen Sir Charles Jones | » | KCG Chambers | » |
| 1971 | » | » | » | » |
| 1972 | » | Col J Hughes | » | » |
| 1973 | » | » | » | » |
| 1974 | » | » | » | » |
| 1975 | » | TSC Busby | » | » |
| 1976 | » | » | » | » |
| 1977 | » | » | » | » |
| 1978 | » | Capt HB Whitehead | » | AVM CG Maughan |
| 1979 | » | » | » | » |
| 1980 | » | » | RD Wilson | » |

†Later knighted.

429

# TABLE A – LEGION OFFICERS

| Year | National President | National Chairman | General Treasurer | General Secretary‡ |
|------|-------------------|-------------------|-------------------|-------------------|
| 1981 | Gen Sir Patrick Howard Dobson | RW Buckingham | [Wilson] | [Maughan] |
| 1982 | ″ | ″ | ″ | ″ |
| 1983 | ″ | ″ | ″ | Maj R Tomlins |
| 1984 | ″ | WS Spinks | ″ | ″ |
| 1985 | ″ | CF Scaife (acting) | ″ | ″ |
| 1986 | ″ | CF Scaife | ″ | ″ |
| 1987 | Gen Sir Edward Burgess | ″ | ″ | ″ |
| 1988 | ″ | ″ | ″ | Lt Col PCE Creasy |
| 1989 | ″ | DT Knowles | ″ | ″ |
| 1990 | ″ | ″ | ″ | ″ |
| 1991 | ″ | ″ | RE Hawkes | ″ |
| 1992 | ″ | ER Jobson | ″ | ″ |
| 1993 | VAdm Sir Geoffrey Dalton | ″ | ″ | ″ |
| 1994 | ″ | ″ | ″ | ″ |
| 1995 | ″ | GG Downing | PB Walsh | ″ |
| 1996 | ″ | ″ | ″ | Brig IG Townsend |
| 1997 | AM Sir Roger Austin | ″ | J Holloway JA Tedder | ″ |
| 1998 | ″ | JGH Champ | ″ | ″ |
| 1999 | ″ | ″ | ″ | ″ |
| 2000 | Lt Gen Sir Roderick Cordy-Simpson | ″ | ″ | ″ |
| 2001 | ″ | IP Cannell | ″ | ″ |

‡In 1992 post retitled Secretary General.

430

# TABLE B – ANNUAL CONFERENCES

| Year | Place | Venue | Branch Delegates | Branches | Branch Rep % |
|------|-------|-------|------------------|----------|--------------|
| 1921 ‡ | London | Queen's Hall | 718 | | |
| 1922 | » | Cannon St Hotel | 340 | 2,089 | 16 |
| 1923 | » | Queen's Hall | 656 | 2,259 | 29 |
| 1924 | » | » | 428 | 2,503 | 17 |
| 1925 | » | » | 505 | 2,662 | 19 |
| 1926 | » | » | 572 | 2,774 | 21 |
| 1927 | » | » | 605 | 2,940 | 21 |
| 1928 | Scarborough | Futurist Cinema | 584 | 3,109 | 19 |
| 1929 | London | Queen's Hall | 759 | 3,330 | 23 |
| 1930 | Cardiff | Empire Theatre | 626 | 3,532 | 18 |
| 1931 | London | Queen's Hall | 820 | 3,715 | 22 |
| 1932 | Portsmouth | Guildhall | 801 | 3,865 | 21 |
| 1933 | London | Queen's Hall | 992 | 3,994 | 25 |
| 1934 | Weston-Super-Mare | Knightstone Pavilion | 1206 | 4,075 | 30 |
| 1935 | London | Queen's Hall | 959 | 4,130 | 23 |
| 1936 | Buxton | Garden Pavilion | 805 | 4,207 | 19 |
| 1937 | London | Queen's Hall | 874 | 4,305 | 20 |
| 1938 | Newcastle-on-Tyne | Palace Theatre | 838 | 4,367 | 19 |
| 1939 | London | Queen's Hall | 911 | 4,412 | 21 |
| 1940 | » | » | 531 | 4,358 | 12 |
| 1941 | » | Cambridge Theatre | 463 | 4,318 | 11 |
| 1942 | » | Wigmore Hall | 548 | 4,266 | 13 |
| 1943 | » | Porchester Hall | 463 | 4,318 | 11 |
| 1944 | [No Conference due to travel restrictions] | | 4,338 | | |
| 1945 | London | Dominion Theatre | 1,110 | 4,458 | 25 |
| 1946 | London | Dominion Theatre /Central Hall, West'r | 1,208 | 4,759 | 25 |
| 1947 | Douglas, Isle of Man | Villa Marine | 1,257 | 5,053 | 25 |
| 1948 | London | Royal Albert Hall | 1,759 | 5,280 | 33 |
| 1949 | Great Yarmouth | Royal Aquarium Theatre | 1,371 | 5,364 | 26 |
| 1950 | London | Royal Albert Hall | 1,233 | 5,408 | 23 |

‡The 'Unity' Conference founding the Legion.

# TABLE B – ANNUAL CONFERENCES

| Year | Place | Venue | Branch Delegates | Branches | Branch Rep % |
|------|-------|-------|------------------|----------|--------------|
| **1951** | London | Royal Albert Hall | 1,434 | 5,399 | 27 |
| **1952** | La Piette, Guernsey | St George's Hall | 601 | 5,371 | 11 |
| **1953** | Blackpool | Winter Gardens | 877 | 5,352 | 16 |
| **1954** | London | Royal Albert Hall | 954 | 5,277 | 18 |
| **1955** | Llandudno | Pier Pavilion | 696 | 5,261 | 13 |
| **1956** | London | Royal Albert Hall | 861 | 5,234 | 16 |
| **1957** | Douglas, Isle of Man | Coliseum | 681 | 5197 | 13 |
| **1958** | Southend-on-Sea | Kursaal Ballroom | 704 | 5163 | 14 |
| **1959** | London | Royal Albert Hall | 838 | 5,078 | 17 |
| **1960** | Margate | Winter Gardens | 693 | 5,027 | 14 |
| **1961** | London | Royal Albert Hall | 882 | 4,936 | 18 |
| **1962** | Scarborough | Spa Grand Hall | 726 | 4,861 | 15 |
| **1962** | London | Queen's Hall | 759 | 3,330 | 23 |
| **1963** | Torquay | Town Hall | 676 | 4,819 | 18 |
| **1964** | Douglas, Isle of Man | Villa Marina | 611 | 4,744 | 22 |
| **1965** | London | Guildhall | 801 | 3,865 | 21 |
| **1966** | Margate | Winter Gardens | 671 | 4,632 | 14 |
| **1967** | Blackpool | Winter Gardens | 741 | 4,555 | 16 |
| **1968** | Hastings | White Rock Pavilion | 658 | 4,482 | 15 |
| **1969** | Scarborough | Spa Grand Hall | 696 | 4,404 | 16 |
| **1970** | Brighton | The Dome | 709 | 4,283 | 17 |
| **1971** | London | Royal Albert Hall | 1,073 | 4,225 | 25 |
| **1972** | Douglas, Isle of Man | Villa Marina | 693 | 4,135 | 17 |
| **1973** | Torquay | Pavilion Theatre | 760 | 4,066 | 19 |
| **1974** | Harrogate | Winter Gardens | 710 | 3,984 | 18 |
| **1975** | Margate | Winter Gardens | 916 | 3,931 | 23 |
| **1976** | Llandudno | Pier Pavilion | 828 | 3,835 | 22 |
| **1977** | Bristol | Colston Hall | 674 | 3,775 | 18 |
| **1978** | Blackpool | Winter Gardens | 814 | 3,733 | 22 |
| **1979** | Brighton | The Dome | 792 | 3,610 | 22 |
| **1980** | Blackpool | Winter Gardens | 830 | 3,574 | 23 |

432

# TABLE B – ANNUAL CONFERENCES

| Year | Place | Venue | Branch Delegates | Branches | Branch Rep % |
|------|-------|-------|-----------------|----------|--------------|
| 1981 | Brighton | Conference Centre | 793 | 3,607 | 22 |
| 1982 | Scarborough | Spa Grand Hall | 735 | 3,518 | 21 |
| 1983 | Portsmouth | Guildhall | 708 | 3,451 | 21 |
| 1984 | Llandudno | Aberconwy Centre | 753 | 3,407 | 22 |
| 1985 | Brighton | Brighton Centre | 786 | 3,435 | 23 |
| 1986 | Blackpool | Winter Gardens | 810 | 3,335 | 24 |
| 1987 | Bournemouth | International Centre | 945 | 3,371 | 28 |
| 1988 | Douglas, Isle of Man | Villa Marina | 565 | 3,322 | 17 |
| 1989 | Bournemouth | International Centre | 921 | 3,315 | 28 |
| 1990 | Scarborough | Spa Grand Hall | 795 | 3,294 | 24 |
| 1991 | Brighton | Brighton Centre | 833 | 3,268 | 25 |
| 1992 | Blackpool | Winter Gardens | 891 | 3,232 | 28 |
| 1993 | Bournemouth | International Centre | 791 | 3,217 | 25 |
| 1994 | Blackpool | Winter Gardens | 752 | 3,209 | 23 |
| 1995 | Plymouth | Arena Pavilion | 614 | 3,211 | 19 |
| 1996 | Scarborough | Spa Grand Hall | 635 | 3,181 | 20 |
| 1997 | Bournemouth | International Centre | 671 | 3,180 | 20 |
| 1998 | Blackpool | Winter Gardens | 660 | 3,153 | 21 |
| 1999 | Bournemouth | International Centre | 619 | 3,126 | 20 |
| 2000 | Blackpool | Winter Gardens | 655 | 3,098 | 21 |
| 2001 | Bournemouth | International Centre | 621 | 3,006 | 21 |

433

# TABLE C – LEGION CAMPAIGNS

| Year started | Objective | Text pages | Outcome | Assessment<br>S = success<br>(s) = partial success<br>F = failure |
|---|---|---|---|---|
| 1921 | Employment preferences for ex-servicemen<br>    -75% of govt-aided schemes<br>    -priority in job-filling | 73 | Govt agreed | **S** |
| 1922 | Retain separate Min of Pensions | 81 | Govt agreed | **S** |
| 1923 | Set up a National Work Scheme | 73, 85 | Govt refused | F |
| 1923 | Remove pensions 7-year time limit | 78 – 9,<br>103 – 4 | Rule stayed but claims allowed | (s) |
| 1923 | Right of appeal against war disability pension 'final award' | 79 – 80 | No appeal but cases reconsidered | (s) |
| 1923 | Maintain war pensions rate despite fall in living costs | 80 – 1 | Govt agreed | **S** |
| 1924 | Compel employers to accept quota of disabled ex-servicemen | 76 – 7,<br>117 | 1944 Disabled Persons Act | **S** |
| 1924 | Village settlements for TB ex-service men | 81 – 2 | Govt refused but supported Legion settlement | (s) |
| 1931 | Disregard war disability pension in assessing benefits | 103, 358,<br>373, 381 | Partial disregard only (by statute) | (Ongoing) |
| 1936 | Financial help for prematurely aged ex-servicemen | 108 – 9 | Govt refused | F |
| 1939 | Rectify 1939 Royal Warrant shortcomings, as compared with 1919 Warrant<br>    - lower pensions scale<br>    - retained 7-yr time-limit on claims<br>    - burden of proof on appellant<br>    - no provision for appeal | 110 – 11 | <br><br>Level by 1943<br>Lifted in 1947<br>Shifted in 1943<br>Granted in 1943 | <br><br>**S**<br>(s)<br>**S**<br>**S** |

| Year started | Objective | Text pages | Outcome | Assessment |
|---|---|---|---|---|
| | | | | S = success<br>(s) = partial success<br>F = failure |
| 1948 | Double war disability pension, hit by inflation, to 90/- | 251 – 2, 258 – 60 | Raised to 85/- in 1957 | S |
| | Thereafter to equate pension to half average earnings | 275 – 6, 358 | Tied to cost of living in 1974 | (s) |
| 1953 | Retain separate Min of Pensions | 214 – 15 | Govt ignored | F |
| 1961 | Free widows' pensions from tax | 271 – 2, 359, 363 – 4 | 50% tax relief in 1976<br>100% relief in 1979 | (s)<br>S |
| 1973 | Raise pre-1973 widows' pensions to level of post-1973 | 364, 372 – 3 | Raised in 1989 | S |
| 1987 | Dept of Ex-Service Affairs | 327, 377, 420 | Govt appointed Minister in 2001 | S |
| 1996 | Restore low-level deafness war pension | 380, 421 | Govt so far refused | (Ongoing) |
| 1998 | Public inquiry into Gulf War illness | 377 – 8, 420 | Govt so far refused | (Ongoing) |
| 1999 | Millenium gratuity for FEPOWs | 421 | Govt agreed to pay each FEPOW £10,000 | S |

| ANALYSIS | | | | | |
|---|---|---|---|---|---|
| Years initiated | Success | Part success | Failure | Ongoing | Total |
| *1921-1945* | 7 | 4 | 2 | 1 | 14 |
| *1946-1970* | 2 | 2 | 1 | | 5 |
| *1971-2001* | 3 | | | 2 | 5 |
| Totals | 12 | 6 | 3 | 3 | 24 |

# TABLE D – WOMEN'S SECTION OFFICERS

| Year | President | Chairman | Hon Treasurer | National Secretary |
|---|---|---|---|---|
| 1921 | Countess Haig | Lady Robertson | Brunel Cohen | Miss Miller |
| 1922 | [Women's Section under Legion NEC control] | | | |
| 1923 | Princess Alice | Lady Edward Spencer Churchill | » | Miss Niven Gerds |
| 1924 | Duchess of York | » | » | » |
| 1925 | » | » | » | » |
| 1926 | » | » | » | » |
| 1927 | » | » | » | » |
| 1928 | » | » | » | » |
| 1929 | » | » | » | » |
| 1930 | » | » | » | » |
| 1931 | » | » | » | » |
| 1932 | » | » | » | » |
| 1933 | » | » | » | » |
| 1934 | » | » | » | » |
| 1935 | » | » | » | » |
| 1936 | » | » | » | » |
| 1937 | » [Now The Queen] | » | » | » |
| 1938 | » | » | » | » |
| 1939 | » | » | » | » |
| 1940 | » | » | » | » |
| 1941 | » | » [Mrs Harris*] | » | » |
| 1942 | » | Lady Apsley | » | » |
| 1943 | » | » | » | » |
| 1944 | » | » | » | » |
| 1945 | » | » | » | Miss Owen |
| 1946 | » | » | » | Mrs Snow |
| 1947 | » | » | Mrs Edgar | » |
| 1948 | » | Dame Regina Evans | » | » |
| 1949 | » | » | » | » |
| 1950 | » | » | » | » |

436      *Acting Chairman following Lady Edward Spencer Churchill's death.

# TABLE D – WOMEN'S SECTION OFFICERS

| Year | President | Chairman | Hon Treasurer | National Secretary |
|------|-----------|----------|---------------|--------------------|
| 1951 | [The Queen ] | [Dame Regina Evans] | Miss Smedley-Crooke | Miss Warren |
| 1952 | [Now The Queen Mother] | » | » | » |
| 1953 | » | » | » | » |
| 1954 | » | » | » | » |
| 1955 | » | » | Mrs Orme | » |
| 1956 | » | » | » | » |
| 1957 | » | » | » | » |
| 1958 | » | » | » | » |
| 1959 | » | Miss Smedley-Crooke | » | » |
| 1960 | » | » | » | » |
| 1961 | » | » | » | » |
| 1962 | » | » | » | » |
| 1963 | » | » | » | » |
| 1964 | » | » | » | » |
| 1965 | » | » | » | » |
| 1966 | » | » | » | » |
| 1967 | » | » | Mrs Waters | » |
| 1968 | » | Mrs Croft Foulds | » | » |
| 1969 | » | » | Mrs Bigmore | » |
| 1970 | » | » | » | » |
| 1971 | » | » | » | » |
| 1972 | » | Mrs Little | » | Miss Sandiforth |
| 1973 | » | » | » | » |
| 1974 | » | » | » | » |
| 1975 | » | » | » | » |
| 1976 | » | » | » | » |
| 1977 | » | » | » | » |
| 1978 | » | Mrs Handyside | Mrs Maxwell | Miss Cooper |
| 1979 | » | » | » | » |
| 1980 | » | » | » | » |

# TABLE D – WOMEN'S SECTION OFFICERS

| Year | President | Chairman | Hon Treasurer | National Secretary |
|------|-----------|----------|---------------|--------------------|
| 1981 | {The Queen Mother] | [Mrs Handyside] | [Mrs Maxwell] | [Miss Cooper] |
| 1982 | »» | »» | »» | »» |
| 1983 | »» | Mrs Bigmore | »» | »» |
| 1984 | »» | »» | Mrs Nash | »» |
| 1985 | »» | »» | »» | »» |
| 1986 | »» | Mrs Raymond | Mrs Dyer | »» |
| 1987 | »» | »» | »» | »» |
| 1988 | »» | »» | »» | »» |
| 1989 | »» | Mrs Nash | Mrs Ingram | »» |
| 1990 | »» | »» | »» | Mrs Green |
| 1991 | »» | »» | »» | »» |
| 1992 | »» | Dame Mary Bridges | »» | »» |
| 1993 | »» | »» | »» | »» |
| 1994 | »» | »» | »» | »» |
| 1995 | »» | Mrs Arnold | Mrs Cole | »» |
| 1996 | »» | »» | »» | Miss Simpson |
| 1997 | »» | »» | »» | Mrs Wood |
| 1998 | »» | Mrs Ingham | Miss Sprackland | »» |
| 1999 | »» | »» | »» | Mrs Myers |
| 2000 | »» | »» | »» | »» |
| 2001 | »» | Mrs Cole | »» | »» |

# TABLE E – WOMEN'S SECTION CONFERENCES

| Year | Place | Venue | Branch Delegates | Branches | Branch Rep % |
|------|-------|-------|------------------|----------|--------------|
| 1921 | | No Conference | | | |
| 1922 | | No Conference | | 126 | |
| 1923 | London | Caxton Hall, Westminster | ? | 175 | |
| 1924 | London | Adelphi | ? | 270 | |
| 1925 | London | Holborn Restuarant | ? | 419 | |
| 1926 | » | » | 175 | 511 | 34 |
| 1927 | » | King George's Hall, Carlisle St | 226 | 700 | 32 |
| 1928 | » | Central Hall, Westminster | 287 | 860 | 33 |
| 1929 | » | » | 363 | 1,029 | 35 |
| 1930 | » | The Kingsway Hall, Strand | 453 | 1,147 | 39 |
| 1931 | » | » | 455 | 1,220 | 37 |
| 1932 | » | » | 479 | 1,283 | 37 |
| 1933 | » | » | 535 | 1,390 | 38 |
| 1934 | » | Queen's Hall | 562 | 1,476 | 38 |
| 1935 | » | » | 598 | 1,552 | 39 |
| 1936 | » | » | 671 | 1,637 | 41 |
| 1937 | » | » | 697 | 1,667 | 42 |
| 1938 | » | » | 966 | 1,735 | 56 |
| 1939 | » | » | 767 | 1,790 | 43 |
| 1940 | » | » | 604 | 1,819 | 33 |
| 1941 | » | » | 355 | 1,822 | 19 |
| 1942 | » | Central Hall, Westminster | 632 | 1,855 | 34 |
| 1943 | » | » | 784 | 1,933 | 41 |
| 1944 | » | » | 675 | 2032 | 33 |
| 1945 | » | » | 917 | 2,161 | 42 |
| 1946 | » | » | 1,275 | 2,386 | 53 |
| 1947 | » | » | 1,322 | 2,619 | 50 |
| 1948 | » | Royal Albert Hall | 1,717 | 2,864 | 60 |
| 1949 | » | » | 1,862 | 3,042 | 61 |
| 1950 | London | Royal Albert Hall | 1,856 | 3,148 | 59 |

# TABLE E – WOMEN'S SECTION CONFERENCES

| Year | Place | Venue | Branch Delegates | Branches | Branch Rep % |
|------|-------|-------|-----------------:|---------:|-------------:|
| 1951 | London | Royal Albert Hall | 1,723 | 3,206 | 54 |
| 1952 | » | » | 1,662 | 3,260 | 51 |
| 1953 | » | » | 1,755 | 3,274 | 54 |
| 1954 | Blackpool | Winter Gardens | 1,495 | 3,278 | 46 |
| 1955 | London | Royal Albert Hall | 1,642 | 3,291 | 50 |
| 1956 | Douglas, Isle of Man | Palace Ballroom | 1,079 | 3,273 | 33 |
| 1957 | London | Royal Albert Hall | 1,667 | 3,242 | 51 |
| 1958 | Bangor, Northern Ireland | Tonic Cinema | 719 | 3,238 | 22 |
| 1959 | London | Royal Albert Hall | 1.509 | 3,217 | 47 |
| 1960 | Brighton | Palladium | 1,301 | 3,183 | 41 |
| 1961 | London | Royal Albert Hall | 1,458 | 3,167 | 46 |
| 1962 | Blackpool | Winter Gardens | 1,120 | 3,139 | 36 |
| 1963 | London | Royal Albert Hall | 1,192 | 3,131 | 23 |
| 1964 | Douglas, Isle of Man | Palace Ballroom | 864 | 3,080 | 28 |
| 1965 | London | Royal Albert Hall | 1,216 | 3,015 | 40 |
| 1966 | London | Royal Albert Hall | 1.094 | 2,963 | 37 |
| 1967 | London | Royal Albert Hall | 1.087 | 2,920 | 37 |
| 1968 | Blackpool | Empress Ballroom | 974 | 2,876 | 34 |
| 1969 | London | Central Hall, Westminster | 984 | 2,836 | 35 |
| 1970 | Douglas, Isle of Man | Palace Ballroom | 806 | 2,808 | 29 |
| 1971 | London | Royal Albert Hall | 1,254 | 2,764 | 45 |
| 1972 | Blackpool | Empress Ballroom | 894 | 2,711 | 33 |
| 1973 | Eastbourne | Congress Theatre | 745 | 2,706 | 28 |
| 1974 | Blackpool | Empress Ballroom | 757 | 2,641 | 29 |
| 1975 | Eastbourne | Congress Theatre | 655 | 2,625 | 25 |
| 1976 | Blackpool | Empress Ballroom | 744 | 2,609 | 29 |
| 1977 | Eastbourne | Congress Theatre | 614 | 2,576 | 24 |
| 1978 | Blackpool | Winter Gardens | 734 | 2,541 | 29 |
| 1979 | Eastbourne | Congress Theatre | 629 | 2,469 | 25 |
| 1980 | Blackpool | Winter Gardens | 651 | 2,413 | 27 |

440

# TABLE E – WOMEN'S SECTION CONFERENCES

| Year | Place | Venue | Branch Delegates | Branches | Branch Rep % |
|------|-------|-------|-----------------|----------|--------------|
| 1981 | Eastbourne | Congress Theatre | 691 | 2,349 | 29 |
| 1982 | Blackpool | Winter Gardens | 627 | 2,317 | 27 |
| 1983 | Eastbourne | Congress Theatre | 596 | 2,266 | 26 |
| 1984 | Blackpool | Opera House | 714 | 2,196 | 33 |
| 1985 | Brighton | Brighton Centre | 665 | 2,150 | 31 |
| 1986 | Blackpool | Winter Gardens | 701 | 2,099 | 33 |
| 1987 | Brighton | Brighton Centre | 591 | 2,065 | 29 |
| 1988 | Blackpool | Opera House | 665 | 2,027 | 33 |
| 1989 | Bournemouth | International Centre | 749 | 2,002 | 37 |
| 1990 | Douglas, Isle of Man | Villa Marina | 468 | 1,970 | 24 |
| 1991 | Bournemouth | International Centre | 754 | 1,927 | 39 |
| 1992 | Blackpool | Winter Gardens | 604 | 1,821 | 33 |
| 1993 | Brighton | Brighton Centre | 553 | 1,818 | 30 |
| 1994 | Blackpool | Winter Gardens | 564 | 1,757 | 32 |
| 1995 | Bournemouth | International Centre | 540 | 1,715 | 31 |
| 1996 | Blackpool | Winter Gardens | 538 | 1,712 | 31 |
| 1997 | Bournemouth | International Centre | 474 | 1,610 | 29 |
| 1998 | Blackpool | Winter Gardens | 455 | 1,567 | 29 |
| 1999 | Bournemouth | International Centre | 540 | 1,539 | 35 |
| 2000 | Blackpool | Winter Gardens | 429 | 1,462 | 29 |
| 2001 | Bournemouth | International Centre | 376 | 1,448 | 26 |

# TABLE F – OFFICERS' ASSOCIATION OFFICERS

| Year | Chairman of Executive Committee | General Secretary |
|------|--------------------------------|-------------------|
| 1921 | Gen The Hon. Sir HA Lawrence | Maj Gen Sir HG Ruggles-Brise |
| 1922 | » | » |
| 1923 | » | » |
| 1924 | » | » |
| 1925 | » | » |
| 1926 | » | » |
| 1927 | » | Maj Gen Sir Sidney D'A Crookshank |
| 1928 | » | » |
| 1929 | Col Frank D Watney | » |
| 1930 | » | » |
| 1931 | » | » |
| 1932 | » | » |
| 1933 | | » |
| 1934 | » | » |
| 1935 | » | » |
| 1936 | Col Frank D Watney | » |
| 1937 | » | » |
| 1938 | » | » |
| 1939 | » | » |
| 1940 | » | » |
| 1941 | » | Col AW Stokes |
| 1942 | » | » |
| 1943 | » | |
| 1944 | » | » |
| 1945 | » | » |
| 1946 | Brig The Hon HKM Kindersley | Brig HDK Money |
| 1947 | » | » |
| 1948 | » | Maj Gen JML Grover |
| 1949 | » | » |
| 1950 | » | » |
| 1951 | » | » |
| 1952 | » | » |
| 1953 | » | » |
| 1954 | Brig The Lord Kindersley | » |
| 1955 | Brig TMJ Babington Smith | » |
| 1956 | » | » |
| 1957 | » | » |
| 1958 | » | » |
| 1959 | » | » |
| 1960 | » | » |
| 1961 | » | Maj Gen JN Carter |
| 1962 | » | » |
| 1963 | » | Maj Gen Sir Peter St Clair-Ford |
| 1964 | » | » |
| 1965 | » | » |
| 1966 | Maj Sir John Hogg | Maj Gen JK Shepheard |
| 1967 | » | » |

442

# TABLE F – OFFICERS' ASSOCIATION OFFICERS

| Year | Chairman of Executive Committee | General Secretary |
|------|--------------------------------|-------------------|
| 1968 | (Maj Sir John Hogg) | (Maj Gen JK Shepheard) |
| 1969 | » | » |
| 1970* | » | » |
| 1971 | » | » |
| 1972 | » | » |
| 1973 | » | » |
| 1974 | » | Maj Gen M Janes |
| 1975 | » | » |
| 1976 | Lt Col R Marriott | » |
| 1977 | » | » |
| 1978 | » | » |
| 1979 | » | » |
| 1980 | » | » |
| 1981 | » | » |
| 1982 | » | » |
| 1983 | » | » |
| 1984 | » | Brig PD Johnson |
| 1985 | Capt PB Mitford-Slade | » |
| 1986 | » | » |
| 1987 | » | » |
| 1988 | » | » |
| 1989 | » | » |
| 1990 | » | » |
| 1991 | » | » |
| 1992 | » | » |
| 1993 | » | » |
| 1994 | » | » |
| 1995 | » | » |
| 1996 | » | » |
| 1997 | » | » |
| 1998 | » | Brig JMA Nurton |
| 1999 | » | » |
| 2000 | Lt Col RAH Nunnerley | » |
| 2001 | » | » |

*From 1970 onwards the Executive and Finance Committees were combined.

443

# APPENDIX II

# CHARTS

**Notes**

1. All of the data used in the charts are extracted from the Legion's Annual Reports and Accounts or the Women's Section or Officers' Association equivalent. Where there is the occasional omission in otherwise consistent reporting an average figure has been inserted.

2. Financial data have been converted to 2000 values in order to provide true comparisons of activity over the years. I am indebted to Miss J Webb of Nuffield College, Oxford, for advice on the conversion.★

3. The 5-year 'time-base' for each chart matches the chapter layout in Parts 1-3.

★ Which was based on calculations for similar entries in: Halsey, A.H. with Webb, J. (eds) (2000) *Twentieth-Century British Social Trends*, Macmillan, Basingstoke. These derived from the RPI figures published by the Office of National Statistics.

---

## CHART A1    Membership

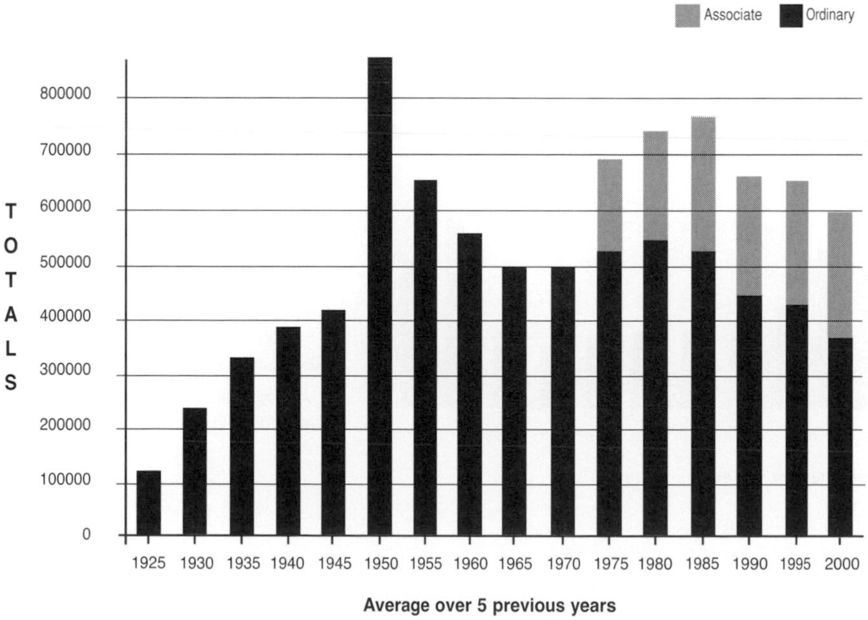

**Average over 5 previous years**

Legend: Associate, Ordinary

**Commentary**

1. The chart reflects

    - the high intakes immediately following the Second World War

    - the impetus given to membership by the 'clubs boom' in the period 1965-1980

    - the introduction of Associate Membership in 1973, when existing Honorary Members were granted Associate status

    - the increasing proportion of Associates to Ordinary Members as the Ordinary Membership declines.

2. Figures up to 1991 are calculated from Affiliation Fee receipts; beyond that date they are computer-derived. Women's Section members are not included.

# CHART B1    Legion Benevolence

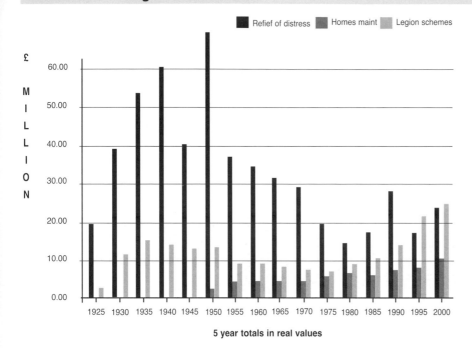

**Legend:** ■ Relief of distress  ■ Homes maint  ▨ Legion schemes

£ MILLION

5 year totals in real values

## Commentary

1. The chart represents the principal components [of] Legion welfare spending and shows how the patt[ern] has changed: high expenditure on Relief in the ea[rly] years has given way to more spending on Homes and Legion Schemes (see below). But no capital costs are included.

2. Spending on the relief of distress was high in t[he] 1930s and 1940s (although it reduced during the 1939-45 war) but thereafter fell as the Welfare St[ate] developed. A fall in state relief led to an upsurge [in] the 1980s; but the subsequent reduction was in p[art] due to stricter control of local relief spending.

3. Legion Homes were introduced in the late 194[0s] and the amount spent on their maintenance has steadily increased. By the 1990s it equated to ha[lf] of spending to relieve distress.

4. 'Legion Schemes' include such items as gran[ts to] the Poppy Factory and Legion Industries and to t[he] Officers' Association. Spending rose in the 1930s and 1940s, when activities included the Prince of Wales's Pension Scheme, and again in the 199[0s] when there was major expenditure on training schemes, principally Tidworth.

# CHART B2    Pensions Work

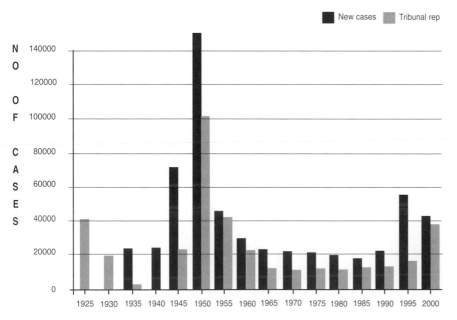

**Legend:** ■ New cases  ▨ Tribunal rep

NO OF CASES

Average over 5 previous years

## Commentary

1. The chart shows the totals of new pensions cases in which the Legion assisted and Legion representation at Pensions Appeal Tribunals. Three 'surges' are apparent
   - post First World War, for Tribunals (no new case records kept)
   - post Second World War when, in addition to those cases, First World War veterans were reaching retirement age
   - in the 1990s, when the Second World War generation reached retirement age. The effec[t] was increased by the Legion's pensions awareness campaign.

2. The ratio of Tribunal work to new cases reflect[s] the readiness of the Pensions authorities to acce[pt] claims: if there is a high rejection rate then more cases go to Appeal; greater acceptance reduces the Appeals. The Legion has always represented 70-80% of all Appeals.

3. Appeal Tribunals ceased in 1934. They were reintroduced in 1943 following Legion pressure.

## CHART B3    War Disability Pension Rates

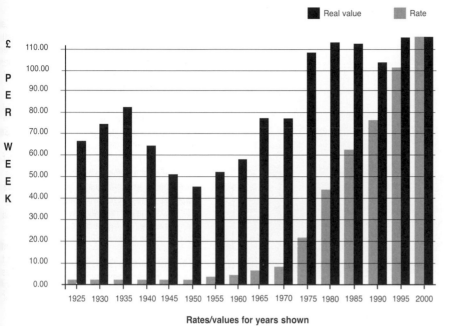

**Real value** ■    **Rate** ▨

£ PER WEEK

Rates/values for years shown

**Commentary**

1. Although the rate remained constant from 1921 to 1945 the value of the pension rose and fell according to changes in the cost of living: shortly after the rate was set in 1920 (when £2.00 was roughly equivalent to £48 today) living costs fell and by 1935 its real value was over £75. But the Legion was able to persuade the government not to cut the rate.

2. After the Second World War, however, inflation severely reduced the value of the pension and it took a fierce and prolonged Legion-led campaign to restore its purchasing power. After a substantial increase in 1974 the value was maintained by annual reviews (although they lagged a little in the early 1990s).

3. The rates shown are for a private or equivalent, with a 100% disability.

4. War widows' pensions are a little less than the rates shown, but follow the same trends.

## CHART C1    Appeal Income

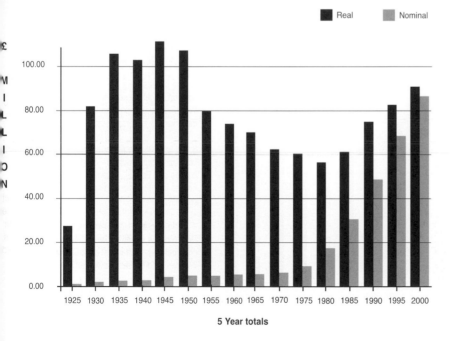

**Real** ■    **Nominal** ▨

£ MILLION

5 Year totals

**Commentary**

1. The chart shows collections at their face value at the time (the 'nominal' value) and at their subsequent inflation-adjusted or 'real' value.

2. In real terms the Appeal built up quickly to produce its best results in the 1930s and 1940s, with record donations during the Second World War. It then had to contend with inflation and fell away until a reduced inflation rate combined with better results post-1980 to restore the situation.

3. The increasingly steep climb in the nominal values between 1950 and 1980, when compared with falling real values, demonstrates the extent of inflation at this time and its effect on the Appeal.

4. For most of the period the Appeal has provided over 90% of the Legion's income for benevolent activities.

5. Figures shown are gross and include wreath sales and all-year-round fundraising as well as the Poppy Day collection. The Appeal in Scotland is not included.

6. In constructing the chart each individual year's collection has been adjusted for inflation. Hence the 2000 five-year totals for nominal and real values differ.

447

## CHART D1  Women's Section Income

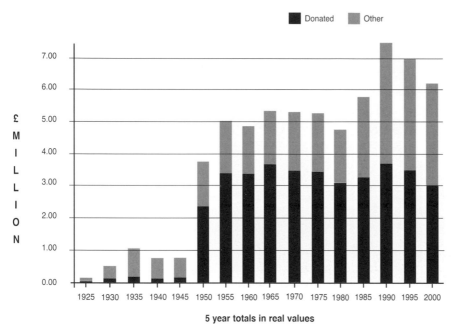

**5 year totals in real values**

### Commentary

1. The chart shows the influence of donations (mainly branch fundraising) on the Women's Section income.

2. Up to the end of the Second World War the income was only sufficient to administer the Section. Post-war intensive fundraising enabled a number of welfare activities to be undertaken without recourse to any Legion funds - see Chart D2.

3. The level of fundraising has been more or less maintained in real terms since. But over the years surpluses have built up investments so that the total income has increased. Between 1980 and 1995, in real terms, investments grew from just over £1 million to nearly £3 million.

4. In most years the Section has received a Legion grant. In the very early days it formed a substantial part of the income; but latterly it was less than 1% of the total.

## CHART D2  Women's Section Benevolence

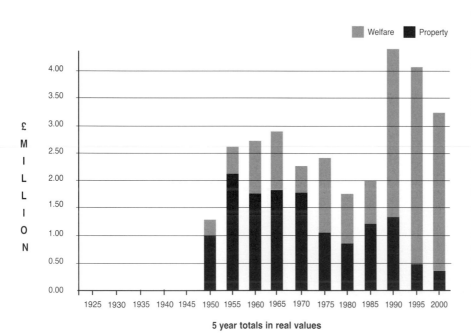

**5 year totals in real values**

### Commentary

1. Women's Section benevolence is entirely financed out of the Section's own funds, including donations by branches - see Chart D1.

2. The chart shows the introduction of the Section's welfare schemes after the Second World War and, by comparison with Chart D1, the dependency on branch donations.

3. Up to 1985 the major spending was on property connected with welfare - children's homes, rest homes and flatlets. Disposal of the children's homes in 1968 reduced some of the property costs.

4. Following the 1988 decision to dispose of the Rest Homes spending on welfare increased considerably, the largest beneficiary being the Widows' and Ex-servicewomen's Allowance scheme.

448

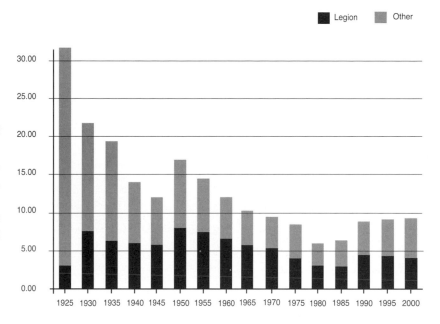

**Commentary**

1. The chart shows the income to the Officers' Benevolent Department/Officers' Association, split between Legion grants, representing the Officers' share of the Poppy Appeal, and other income. Originally 5%, by 1950 the Officers' entitlement had risen to $7\frac{1}{2}$%.

2. In the early days the Department had considerable income from other sources, mainly donations by the public, often in securities and invested. But high relief demands in the mid-1930s (see Chart E2) forced it to draw on reserves and it subsequently became increasingly dependent on Legion and other grants, the amount of Legion grant reflecting the fortunes of the Poppy Appeal (Chart C1). Latterly the other income has built up again.

3. For consistency it has been necessary to exclude some income components arising out of the 1994 revised accounting procedures.

---

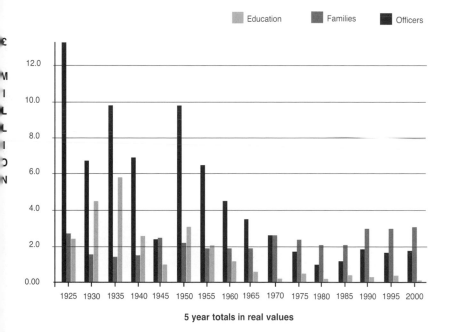

5 year totals in real values

**Commentary**

1. The chart shows the components of Officers' Benevolent Department/Officers' Association benevolent spending.

2. Education grants were made for children whose schooling or further training would have been affected by the war (eg death of the father). Spending was therefore high in the period following each war. There was particular concern over the size of the commitment in the mid-1930s.

3. Families relief has grown over the years, due in the main to assistance with Nursing or Residential Home fees.

4. Officers relief refers to assistance in the employment field as well as direct financial aid. It was high in both immediate post-war periods, but particularly so after the First World War. Latterly government grants have reduced job-finding costs.

449

# SOURCES AND CHAPTER NOTES

## PRINCIPAL SOURCES

AR — Annual Reports/Reviews of the British Legion/Royal British Legion.

AA — Annual accounts of the Royal British Legion, published separately since 1997

MB — Minute Books of the Legion's National Executive Committee/National Committee.

LJ — *Legion Journal*, under various titles including *Legion, Legion Magazine*.

WSAR — Annual Reports of the Legion Women's Section.

OAAR — Annual Reports of the Officers Benevolent Department/Officers' Association.

OAH — The Officers' Association: *The Story of the First Fifty Years*.

Wooton — Graham Wooton: *The Official History of the British Legion*, Macdonald & Evans, 1956.

## OTHER WORKS CONSULTED

John Stevenson: *British Society 1914-1945*, Allen Lane, 1984

Arthur Marwick: *British Society Since 1945*, Allen Lane, 1982

Graham Wooton: *The Politics of Influence*, Routledge and Kegan Paul, 1963

Anthony Brown: *Red For Remembrance*, Heinemann, 1971

JM Winter: *The Great War and the British People*

Adrian Gregory: *The Silence of Memory - Armistice Day 1919-1946*

Dianne Graves: *A Crown for Life - The World of John McRae*, Spellmount, 1997

The Countess Haig: *The Man I Knew*, Moray Press, 1936

Peter Reese: *Homecoming Heroes*, Leo Cooper, 1992

AJP Taylor: *From Potsdam to Sarajevo*, Thames and Hudson, 1966

Winston S Churchill: *The Second World War Volume I - The Gathering Storm*, Cassell, *1948*

James Hale: *Branching Out - The Story of The Royal Canadian Legion*, published by the RCL, 1995

Philip Ziegler: *King Edward VIII the Official Biography*, Collins, 1990

Richard Garrett: *The Final Betrayal*, Buchan and Enright, 1989

BH Liddell Hart: *History of the First World War*, originally published by Cassell in 1930 as *The Real War*

James H Sephton: *Preston Hall Aylesford*, privately published 1997

Lt Col George Malcolm of Poltalloch: *We Will Remember - a historical record of the British Legion Scotland*, published by BL Scotland, 1959

## CHAPTER NOTES

Abbreviations are shown above under 'Principal Sources'. For the Annual Reports and *Legion Journals* the year refers to the closing date eg AR 47 refers to the 1946-47 report and LJ 56 to the 1955-56 volume; but the LJ filing system is not consistent. The page number follows the oblique (/) stroke.

### Chapter 1

1. This account is based on the following sources:

   An article by Lister at LJ 46/77

   Graham Wooton's *The Official History of the British Legion* chapters I to IV, the draft of which was seen by some of the participants, including Lister. Most other accounts use the same source.

   An article at LJ 81/Jan/6 which deals in particular with Haig's role; but there are some errors, not least of which is to state that he was present at the Cenotaph on 15 May 1921. Haig's involvement is also mentioned by Gen Howard-Vyse, then Legion Chairman, in a speech reported at LJ 51/Apr/50.

   A memoir by Crosfield at LJ 46/Feb/33 referring to Lister's role.

   Richard Garrett's *The Final Betrayal*, chapter XI of which deals very clearly with the events surrounding the Legion's formation.

   I am also grateful to John Hussey for his notes on Haig's work in the ex-service field prior to the Legion's formation.

2. Reese: *Homecoming Heroes* p 106

### Chapter 2

1. Stevenson: *British Society 1914-45* p 44
2. JM Winter: *The Great War and the British People* p 73.
3. MB 21-4/2
4. A copy is bound into LJ II between pp 104 and 105
5. LJ II/111
6. LJ IV/49
7. LJ V/137
8. MB 24-6/83
9. AP Cartright: *The First South African*; Notes by Paul Kilmartin of the South African Military History Society, in possession of the author. Claims that a letter to the *London Evening Standard* in May 1919 prompted the Silence [see LJ 96/Mar/30] may be discounted; the Cabinet reacted to Fitzpatrick's letter.
10. *The Times* 12 Nov 1919
11. MB 21-24/22; LJ I/28
12. LJ I/101
13. MB 21-4/10, 22, 32
14. *The Times* 12 Nov 21; LJ I/26
15. LJ I/126

16. LJ IV/13
17. AR 23/38
18. LJ I/157-8
19. Wooton/89-91 and Appx 18. Neither the Annual Report nor the *Legion Journal* make any mention of this episode, although the Metropolitan Area 'activity report' in the June 1926 Journal notes that the branches of the Area were as solid as a rock behind the NEC in their declared policy of neutrality (p368). The GS was at the time still editor of the *Journal*.
20. Home Office memorandum of 22 February 1984 p 5
21. MB 26-30/66; LJ VII/117,145,147,149; AR 28/54
22. AR 29/54; LJ VIII/144,180
23. LJ VII/278, 285
24. LJ VII/279 - a speech to Metropolitan Area confererence
25. LJ VII/295-7 - from branch reports
26. AR 30/48; MB 30-5/12; LJ VIII/151, 156
27. LJ 30-3/140, 173, 175-6, 178
28. LJ 32-3/389
29. AR 30/9; MB 26-30/177, MB 30-35/8; LJ IX/329, 334-5. Wooton devotes a chapter to the episode - Chapter XX.
30. AR 33/17,18; MB 30-5/113; LJs 32-3/243, 248, 338, 414, June 33 Met sup i,xii, 33-4/28
31. LJ 33-4/130, Met sup Mar vi, x, 414-422
32. LJ 34-5/483 - and John Brown took successful legal action - LJ 35-6/10 clm 1
33. LJ 34-5/238, 336, Irish sup Mar 35 ii
34. Home Office memorandum of 22 February 1984 p 20; LJ VII/170
35. LJs 33-4/Nov 33 sup Irish iii and xi, 201,210, 34-5/206,255,285, 35-6/28
36. AR 34/7, 43; LJs 31-2/146, 216-220, 32-3/196, 221, 34-5/398
37. LJs 32-3/379, 413, 33-4/ Oct Met sup xiv, Jan 34 Met sup iv, 34-5/ Feb Met sup iii
38. AR 35/5; LJs 36-7/243, 283, 37-8/217, 352 38-9/55
39. LJ 50/134
40. AR 39/5, MBs 35-8/89, 38-45/9,LJs 37-8/307, 38-9/113, 353-4, 413, 39-40/113, 118
41. LJ 40-1/236
42. ARs 41/54-9, 42/42 MB 38-45/73,117,176,183 LJs 40-1/180, 40-1/87, 180, 233, 320, 42/148-9, 324, 43/204, 223, 44/73, 85 and 89, 45/17. An article in the Sussex *Daily News* in September 1939 by Capt CH Madden reflected the fear that a new generation of ex-servicemen might see the Legion as outdated and form their own organization.
43. LJ 43/144
44. MBs 38-45/48-9, 54, 101 LJs 39-40/182, 254, 42/206, 115, 45/237
45. MB 39-45/63; LJ 39-40/340
46. AR 42/5-6
47. MB 38-45/128
48. LJ 42/113
49. LJ 43/5
50. LJ 44/105, 183, 223
51. MBs 38-45/209, 45-52/2; Gregory: *The Silence of Memory*, pp 188 and 191
52. LJ 45/231
53. MB 38-45/135,177, LJs 43/224, 44/225, 45/224
54. AR 45/5-7; LJs 44/137, 45/2, 237

**Chapter 3**

1. Wooton p 28
2. LJ I/32-33
3. Wooton p 29
4. LJ VIII/261
5. Wooton pp 28-9; MB 21-4/186; LJ I/32-3
6. LJ I/9
7. MB 21-4/2; LJ I/4]
8. MB 21-4/46 and LJ II/8
9. LJ I/84
10. MB 21-4/72
11. AR 23; MB 21-24/30, 46,60
12. MB 24-6/55-56
13. Malcolm of Poltalloch: *We Will Remember* pp 3-5
14. MB 21-24/24,31
15. LJ I/103
16. LJ II/123
17. MB 21-4/124, 24-6/42
18. LJ II/201
19. LJ I/197
20. LJ I/257
21. LJ I/270
22. AR 25/8
23. LJs III/261, 393, IV/355, V/23
24. AR 23/41; MB 21-24/8, 20, 98, 104; LJ III/115
25. MB 21-24/32-34
26. LJ III/217
27. AR 25/43; MBs 21-4/189, 24-6/8,48 and 58; LJ IV/225 (advert)
28. LJ I/158-9
29. LJ I/134 and 141
30. LJ IV/64
31. LJ IV/9
32. LJ I/85, 231
33. MB 21-4/27, 24-6/83,110
34. LJ 46/105
35. Wooton/63; LJs III/6, IV/13, 51, VIII/180
36. LJ I/124
37. AR 23/6; LJ II/244
38. LJ II/5-13
39. LJ IV/6,7

40. LJ II/291: he refers to 'a visit to those terrible but magnificent cemeteries out on the other side (which) . . . brings home the spirit of comradeship'.

41. AR 26/11 and 14; LJs V/346,342, VI/5

42. LJ IV/11,12

43. AR 38/4; MBs 21-4/86,93,121,134,150, 24-6/64,106; LJ V/5

44. MB 26-30/71; LJ VII/301,307,VIII/113,146, 35-6/286-296

45. MB 26-30/27

46. MB 24-6/136,149, 26-30/32,64, 127,145,154; AR 29/7, 30/13. But Lt Col George Malcolm of Poltalloch in *We Will Remember* at page 17 states that the idea was dropped after Scotland's branches had rejected it in a referendum. He gives no date for the referendum but implies that it was in 1928 or earlier. If so, it is surprising that the negotiations continued into 1929.

47. MB 26-30/19,28,29,87,92; AR28/7, 29/8; LJ VI/302

48. LJ V/297

49. LJ IX/92: 'County Organisation'

50. LJ V/161, VI/107,195

51. LJ VIII/121, 30-1/78,102,145

52. AR 26/8; LJ VI/45,65

53. AR 28/7,29/830/9

54. AR 26/6,10; 27/5 LJ IX/13; March 1926 Special Circular

55. LJ VII/366

56. LJ IX/124,182

57. LJ VIII/150

58. LJ VIII/215

59. AR 26/45; MB 26-30/87; LJ V/297,348

60. MB 26-30/118,128,164

61. AR 26/6, LJ VI/6

62. LJ VI/171,172

63. ARs 27/10,12,35, 28/8; MB 26-30/20,29; LJs VI/286,302, VII/6, 206, 284

64. LJ VIII/311

65. AR 28/9; LJ VII/330,331; VIII/3,9,11,13

66. AR 30/9; MB 26-30/177; LJ 30-31/2,9

67. ARs 26/35, 27/38, 28/53 30/49; MBs 26-30/136, 30-35/7; LJ V/198, 225, VII/311, VIII/309, IX/332, 30-1/65

68. MB 26-30/16, LJs VI/274, 317, VII/98, 107, 210

69. AR 31/7; LJ 31-2/283, 314, 448, 35-6/216

70. AR33/7; LJ 30-1/ 432, 31-2/214, 281, 450, 33-4/237, 238, 270, 305

71. MBs 30-5/61, 68 74, 134,188,198, 35-8/4, 6, 7, 50, 56, 64]30-31/2,9

72. LJ 32-3/12

73. ARs 31/8, 33/8, 34/9, 35/10; MB 30-5/122; LJs 30-1/366, 459, 31-2/458, 33-4/318, Apr 34 SE sup, 34-5/ Dec34 HC sup

74. ARs 32/10, 11, 51, 33/9; MB 30-5/173; LJs 30-1/220, 299, 366, 31-2/81-90, 114, 250, 257, 334, 32-3/53, 138, 195, Dec 32 Met

sup vii, 34-5/313, Mar 35 Met sup, 537, 35-6/58

75. ARs 32/14, 33/7; MBs 30-5/87, 110, 138, 166, 173, 201; LJs 30-1/325, 443, 445, 31-2/120, 327, 32-3/56, 80, 113, 162, 179, 270, 337, 33-4/Jul 33 Met sup, 273-4, 432, 34-5/213, 296, 301, 302, 35-6/94

76. AR 33/6; MB 30-5/87, 103; LJs 32-3/16, 126, 177, 246, 280, 34-5/102, 153

77. ARs 31/9, 32/11, 33/10, 34/12, 35/12; LJs 30-1/436, 441, 447, 31-2/401, 442, 32-3/62, 422, 434; 33-4/14, 346, 414; 34-5/519; 35-6/9

78. MB 30-5/85; LJ 32-3/ 202,248 and Jan 33 sup vii; Lawrence article LJ 33-4/160; 'Old Bill' LJ 33-4/273

79. ARs 31/53, 32/51, 33/50, 34/45, 35/45; LJs 31-2/281, 304, 315, 324, 347, 446, 32-3/ 195

80. MB 30-5/ 148, 113, 123; LJs 33-4/ Jan 34 Met sup, 378, 398

81. MB 30-5/196; LJs 30-1/447, 33-4/420-2, 34-5/5, Aug 34, 287

82. MB 30-5/174; LJs 31-2/68, 34-5/449, 35-6/112, 39-40/294, 41/298, 322

83. AR34/6, 44; MB 30-5/130,140; LJ 34-5/205, 396

84. AR 37/6; MB 35-6/67, 38-45/8; LJ 37-8/189, 283

85. MB 38-45/35,40, 85; LJ 38-9/318, 39-40/223, 338

86. LJs 39-40/208, 259, 337, 42/130-1, 184

87. MB 38-45/35, 69, 74; LJ 40-1/8, 91, 181

88. ARs 36/10, 37/8, 38/9, 39/9; MB 35-8/20, 58, 63, 365; LJ 39-40/85

89. LJ 36-7/51-4, 402, 38-9/43, 39-40/41-6

90. AR AR 38/8, 39/7; MB 35-7/71, 80, 38-45/11, 39; LJ 39-40/10, 52

91. LJs 35-6/42136-7/62, 103, 145

92. LJ 36-7/104, 145178, 298

93. LJs 36-7/5-15, 424, 38-9/4-12, 39-40/335

94. LJs 39-40/223, 43/105, 107, 38-9/315, 43/28, 46

95. MB 38-45/154; LJ 43/122, 144, 168

96. AR 45/10, 12; LJ 45/43, 64, 68, 75 with picture

97. ARs 41/9, 43/8, 44/8, 45/8,9

98. MB 38-45/186

99. AR 39/9, 40/9-10; LJ 40-1/41

100. ARs 39/9, 40/9, 42/8, 43/8, 44/8, 45/9; LJ 40-1/41,228, 43/128

101. AR 41/13; LJ 40-1/211, 267, 43/93

102. LJ 44/100

103. MBs 35-8/106, 38-45/18, 23; LJs 42/100, 115, 43/17, 44/160

104. AR 43/21, LJs 42/186, 43/116, 44/183

105. ARs 41/11, 42/10, 43/9,44/8; MB 38-45/165-171, 177; LJs 44/123, 168

106. AR 45/8; MB 38-45/188; LJ 45/103-4,129, 132

107. ARs 42/22, 45/10; LJs 40-1/258, 42/232, 45/147

## Chapter 4

1. LJ I/13
2. LJ I/13
3. LJ II/62
4. AR 23/61
5. AR 23/60
6. LJ IV/33
7. LJ V/71
8. AR 23/62-64
9. AR 23/63
10. MB 21-24/84
11. AR 25/8
12. LJ I/124,171, II/58, III/307, IV/299; ARs 23/17, 25/18
13. LJ II/62
14. LJ III/269
15. LJ I/64
16. LJ III/196
17. AR 25/22; LJ IV/210
18. LJ II/81
19. MB 21-4/185, 24-6/7,17-18
20. AR 25/45-47
21. LJ I/100
22. LJ I/275
23. LJ II/14
24. LJ II/86
25. LJ II/79
26. LJ II/296
27. MB 21-4/183, 24-6/31; LJs III/338,373, IV/8
28. LJ III/257
29. AR 24/28; LJ II/55
30. LJ I/137,138
31. LJ II/104
32. LJ IV/217
33. AR 25/29, LJ III/9, IV/265. I am grateful to Helen Bettinson for her help with this passage.
34. This is a very brief summary of several articles by AG Webb, Head of the Legion's Pensions Department, dealing with the provisions of the War Pensions Act 1921, including LJ I/66,186
35. LJ I/62
36. LJ II/167
37. LJ II/193
38. AR 23/24 and LJ III/8,247
39. MB 21-24/183, AR 23/24, LJ IV/19
40. MB 24-6/47; LJ IV/389,393
41. LJ IV/214,227,393
42. LJ V/74
43. LJ V/141,174; Wooton/80-82
44. LJ II/112
45. LJ II/110
46. LJ III/271
47. MB 24-6/99
48. LJ II/296, IV/288-290
49. AR 23/18
50. LJ III/303
51. MB 24-6/45,59-61; AR 25/19-21; Wooton/84-5; LJ IV/286,361
52. AR 25/19-22; LJ IV/360-1
53. LJ V/140
54. LJ I/75-76
55. MB 21-24/182
56. LJ IV/252
57. AR 23/26
58. LJ I/60
59. LJs I/60, II/229
60. LJ IV/12
61. AR 26/13
62. ARs 26/13,27/18; LJs V/ 221,253,255, VI/ 30,142, VIII/200, IX/2,32,265
63. ARs 26/12,42,51, 27/68, 28/81; MB 26-30/3-5,17, LJ VI/114
64. ARs 26/48, 27/64, 28/79, 29/60, 30/53; MB 26-30/26; LJs VII/222, VIII/206
65. LJ VIII/96
66. ARs 26/32, 27/28, 29/37, 30/39; LJ VII/184, 216, VIII/184
67. LJ VI/210
68. ARs 26/14,21, 29/17,18, 30/12,21; MB 26-30/115, 126,181
69. ARs 26/55, 27/73, 28/22, 29/20, 30/25
70. ARs 26/60, 27/76, 28/24,29/27, 30/27
71. AR 27/22, 29/23, 35/9; MBs 26-30/26, 30-5/89; LJs VI/302, VII/92
72. LJ VII/ 213, VIII/340
73. ARs 29/20, 30/24;LJ IX/91,340
74. ARs 28/25, 29/24, 30/27; LJs VII/169, 322, VIII/76, 134
75. AR 26/22; LJ V/222,254,VII/201
76. AR29/47; LJ VIII/127
77. AR 26/23
78. ARs 26/23, 58, 27/13, 19, 28/30; LJI/229, 257, 287, 316, 331,VII/19,66,102,342
79. ARs 29/27-31,30/30;MB26-30/152,160; LJ VIII/178,287, IX/69, 30-1/107
80. LJ IX/212
81. ARs 27/75, 28/31
82. AR 28/30, LJ VII/154,VIII/91
83. ARs 28/28, 29/48, 30/43; MB26-30/77,118; LJ VIII/118
84. LJ VII/101
85. LJ VI/218
86. ARs 26/25-7, 27/30, 28/41, 29/39, 30/41; MB 26-30/35,61,115; LJs V/256,VI/91, 218, 235, VII/73, 156, 30-1/96
87. LJ VI/329
88. ARs 28/33, 29/44, 30/47
89. AR 28/49; LJs VII/375, VIII/128, 293; MB 26-30/71-2, 78
90. LJ V/273, VI/109, VII/42, 51, 99, 127
91. AR 27/37; MB 26-30/12, 50, 58, 60; LJs VI/218, 229, 265, 299, VII/42, 51, 99, 127
92. ARs 28/50, 94; MB 26-30/96,118; LJs VII/128, 155, 169, 180, 203, 211, 306, 334, 360, VIII/31-7, 57,60-8

93. AR 29/12; MB 30-5/24; LJs VIII/265, IX/66, 30-1/68
94. AR 30-1/11, 28; LJs 30-1/231, 390, 32-3/11, 56, 58, 126, 33-4/89, 159
95. ARs 31/ 58-61,96, 32/ 56, 33/ 55, 34/6, 51; 35/48; MBs 30-5/48, 165, LJs 31-2/214, 33-4/89
96. ARs 34/56, 35/60
97. ARs 32/7, 33/31, 34/ 35; MB 30-5/95; LJs 32-3/235, Jan 33 Met sup i, 278, 304, 344
98. ARs 31/11, 27, 32/15, 24, 33/7, 23, 34/13, 19, 35/20; MB 30-5/48, LJs 31-2/214, 295, 32-3/112, Apr 34 Met sup, 33-4/322, 34-5/149, 261, 35-6 Nov 35 Irish sup
99. AR 35/59; MB 30-5/167; LJs 31-2/255, 415, 32-3/315, 33-4 Oct Met sup vi, 34-5/395, 491, 35-6/ Sep 35 Met sup iv
100. ARs 31/29, 32/26, 33/25, 34/22; LJs 30-1/227, 33-4/ 354, Apr 34 Irish sup xiv, 34-5/ 73, 228, Nov 34 SE sup, 309, 396
101. LJ 31-2/372
102. ARs 33/6, 34/ 31, 35/25; LJs 33-4/119, Oct 33 Met sup Sep vii, 204
103. AR 34/26-7; LJ 32-3/205
104. AR 34/6; MB 30-5/137; LJs 31-2/256, 323, 368, 32-3/198, 246, 33-4/ 304
105. ARs 31/39, 32/33-4, 33/32, 34/28, 35/25; LJs 30-1/298, 351, 392, 31-2/72, 110, 293, 33-4/239, 340
106. ARs31/6, 19-20, 42, 32/38, 33/16, 36. 34/35, 35/32; MB 30-5/39; LJs 31-2/32, 71, 251, 293, 394
107. ARs 31/43, 32/35, 39, 33/37, 34/36, 35/33; MB 30-5/152/ LJs 30-1/434, 31-2/360, 32-3/245, 33-4/23, 349, 34-5/ 262
108. ARs 31/40, 32/37, 34/30, 35/26; LJ 30-1/273
109. ARs 32/6, 51, 80, 33/47, 49, 34/45-6; MB 30-5/88, 107; LJs 30-1/231, 238, 240, 466, 31-2/102, 138, 393, 32-3/390, 33-4/ Sep 33 Met sup, 181, 441, 34-5/105, 136
110. ARs 36/70, 37/38; LJs 35-6/328, 377, 36-7/327
111. ARs 36/70, 38/40
112. ARs 36/16, 37/18, 39/16; LJs 35-6/379, 37-8/212, 326
113. ARs 37/21, 38/20 ; MB 35-8/89; LJs 35-6/446, 37-8/244, 308, 344, 381, 38-9/40, 41, 112
114. AR 39/37-42; MB 38-45/38
115. MB 38-45/73; LJ 40-1/145
116. LJ 39-40/204
117. AR 40/16; LJ 39-40/233
118. AR 40/17-18
119. ARs 36/45, 39/16, 40/19, 42/25
120. ARs 36/16, 37/14, 38/14, 39/13, 40/18; LJs 35-6/375, 38-9/316
121. AR 37/15, 38/15, 39/14; MB 35-8/81; LJs 35-6 Apr Met sup iii, 38-9/15, Met sup Sep 39
122. AR 40/20; MB 38-45/28; LJ 36-7/363
123. ARs 38/24, 39/22; LJ 39-40/56
124. AR 38/21
125. AR 39/18; LJ 40-1/32
126. AR 36/23
127. AR 38/25; LJ 36-7/135,256. Orwell's brother-in-law was Laurence O'Shaughnessy who had much improved the equipment at Preston Hall,  but who was to be killed on active service with the RAMC in Flanders in 1940. I am indebted to Mark Presland for this information.
128. ARs 39/23, 40/30
129. LJ 38-9/424, 428
130. ARs 39/33, 40/35; LJ 40-1/10
131. LJ 40/312
132. ARs 42/24, 43/25, 45/27
133. LJ 43/196
134. LJ 43/178
135. LJs 43/6, 44/214
136. LJ 44/179
137. LJs 44/179, 45/3
138. MBs 38-45/184, 45-52/4; LJs 44/167, 45/6, 188, 190
139. MB 38-45/186, 189, 192 (insert), 211; LJ 45/87
140. AR 41/12, 42/12, 45/15-16
141. ARs 42/25, 43/23, 45/31
142. ARs 41/15-17, 43/11, 44/15; 45/15-16; MB 38-45/69; LJ 72/Mar/14
143. AR 44/14; LJ 45/145
144. LJ 45/192
145. LJ 45/112
146. ARs 44/16, 45/18; MB 38-45/105, 122, 135, 156, 212; LJs 44/74, 83, 45/138
147. ARs 41/17, 42/18, 43/12, 43/148, 44/16, 45/18; LJ 43/148
148. ARs 44/13, 45/113-5; MB 38-45/139; LJs 43/26, 44/30, 44 45/112, 114
149. ARs 41/21-5, 42/15-18; LJ 40-1/256
150. AR 43/15; LJ 43/149
151. LJ 42/65, 89, 107, 45/27
152. ARs 41/26, 42/18, 43/19, 44/24, 45/25; MB 38-45/132; LJs 43/83, 45/197

**Chapter 5**

1. Wooton/30-31
2. Wooton/33. Both Wooton and the OA History describe it as a share of the Poppy Appeal, but the PA was not launched until after unity had been achieved.
3. OA H/18
4. AR 23/101;MB 21-4/5
5. MB 21-24/125, 24-6/5,79,99,113-4; LJ I/107
6. Poppy Appeal Report 23/50; MB 21-24/125
7. Wooton/38
8. *Graves: A Crown for Life* pp 201-202
9. *Graves: A Crown for Life* p 250
10. *Graves: A Crown for Life* p 267-268
11. LJ 42/187

12. LJ I/101
13. LJ I/107. Lord Ismay in his *Memoirs*, published in 1960, states at p 61 that Haig told him that he had personally underwritten the cost of the first Poppy Appeal. However, the entry is inaccurate over another aspect of the Appeal and should not, therefore, be relied upon.
14. LJ I/142
15. LJ 37-8/108
16. MB 21-24/82
17. LJ I/8
18. LJ II/7
19. LJ I/252
20. MB 21-24/51; LJ II/16,33,82; Wooton/40
21. LJ II/82
22. MB 21-24/175
23. AR 23/20
24. ARs 23/33, 25/24,35; MB 24-6/8,48, 21-24/110, 24-6/8; LJ IV/403. Further information on the objects of the Poppy Factory supplied by Colonel Hughes.
25. Hale: *Branching Out* p 26
26. LJ II/82
27. LJ II/173
28. LJ III/85
29. Poppy Appeal Report 23/5-10
30. AR 23/36
31. *The Times* 12 Nov 23 p7; AR32/37; LJ III/147, 175
32. Poppy Appeal Report 23/10
33. LJ IV/189,203
34. LJ IV/221,294
35. LJ IV/137
36. LJ I/131
37. AR 25/38-39;MB 21-24/114, 24-6/16,100
38. AR 25/36; MB 24-6/67; LJ IV/251, 290 V/136, 36-7/121
39. AR 25/36
40. ARs 26/8, 39, 27/91, 28/98, 29/97, 30/11, 84; MB 26-30/71;LJ V/282, VI/181, VII/153, 165-6, 30-1/101
41. LJ 46/106
42. GS salary raised to £1,000 from 1 July 27; the Appeal Sec earned £2,000 – MB 26-30/34
43. MBs 24-6/125, 129, 136, 26-30/86, 136
44. AR 30/87; MB 26-30/113, 136, 180; LJs IX/196, 266-7, 280-1, 30-1/13
45. ARs 29/101, 30/ 49, 31/42; LJs VIII/318, IX/6, 224, 237
46. ARs 26/28, 27/20, 28/26, 29/50, 30/44; MB 26-30/110; LJs VIII/175, IX/246
47. *The Story of the Field of Remembrance*, published by the British Legion Poppy Factory in 1937 and revised in 1949
48. ARs 31/91, 103, 32/91, 33/87, 34/80, 89, 35/85; MB 35-8/9; LJs 32-3/379, 33-4/136-8, 34-5/152
49. MBs 30-5/179,199, 35-8/2; LJs 31-2/144, 33-

4/Dec 33 WS sup 8
50. MB 30-5/201. Special Circular March 1926.
51. ARs 31/46, 32/43, 33/41, 34/39, 35/36; MB 30-5/199; LJs 31-2/432 35-6/29
52. ARs 36/66, 37/67, 38/66, 39/7, 59; LJ 35-6/333, 36-7/170; 37-8/53
53. LJ 39-40/251
54. LJ 40-1/13
55. AR 36/28-30,32; LJ 36-7/258, 37-8/220
56. AR 38/27; LJ 39-40/128
57. MB 38-45/72; LJ 40-1/175]
58. AR 41/50; LJ 40-1/116, 155
59. AR 42/38 MB 38-45/102; LJ 42/95
60. LJ 43/185, 44/10, 232, 45/225
61. AR 45/41
62. ARs 41/18, 42/15; LJs 42/30, 130, 196
63. ARs 43/14, 44/18, 45/19; MB 38-45/164. The scouts wore scarves in Legion colours and carried the Legion title on their shirts.

**Chapter 6**

1. MB 21-24/4
2. LJ III/205. Crosfield gives the figure of 500,000, and if correct it was an extraordinary achievement.
3. LJ II/136
4. MB 21-24/108
5. LJ II/161
6. LJ II/213
7. LJII/294
8. LJ III/109-110
9. LJ III/111-112
10. MB 24-6/15
11. LJ IV/78,113,121
12. AR 25/13; LJ V/103
13. AR 25/12; LJ V/72; James Hale:*Branching Out*. pp 12-13. Note that Lister's account in the *Legion Journal* refers to the new Canadian organization as the 'British Legion in Canada' but this was the press title.
14. ARs 26/15, 27/13, 28/16, 63-4, 29/13, 30/17; MB 24-6/29; LJs VI/262, 316, VII/17, 260, IX/38, 59
15. AR 28/2; LJs VI/13, VII/120
16. AR 27/19; MB 24-6/178; LJs VI/36, 85, 122, 178, VII/35
17. AR 28/16; LJ VIII/87
18. ARs 26/15, 27/15, 28/18, 29/15, 30/19; MB 24-6/165; LJs VIII/115, 30-1/150
19. LJ VI/144
20. ARs 32/23, 33/14, 43; MB 30-5/105, 154; LJs 32-3/342, 33-4/169, 425, 34-5/8, 185
21. ARs 31/23, 32/21, 33/21, 34/16, 35/18; MB 30-5/38, 49; LJs 32-3/152, 200, 33-4/170, Mar 34 Met sup i, 34-5/201, 35-6/134
22. AR 35/42; LJ 35-6/9-17; Wooton pp169-182: note that Wooton appears to have consulted, among others, the Duke of

456

Windsor, who presumably is the 'highest authority' that he cites; Philip Ziegler *King Edward VIII* the official biography p 209; Bloch, Michael, *Operation Willi*, Wiedenfeld & Nicolson 1984 (background). Foreign Office papers since released show that Maurice's letter to Vansittart outlining the Legion's policy was intended to avoid the government just this sort of embarrassment; but he, too, had not reckoned on the Prince of Wales's personal involvement. There was subsequently some Foreign Office pressure on the Legion to ensure that they pursued relations with ex-service organisations of other former enemy countries and not just Germany. [Public Record Office FO 371, file 18882].

23. AR 35/42; MBs 30-5/198, 35-8/2; LJs 34-5/349, 391, 35-6/49, Aug 35 Met sup iii, SE sup iii, 35-6/93, 130, 179, 187, 195

24. ARs 31/20, 33/19; MB 30-5/143; LJs 31-2/185, 33-4/64

25. LJ 35-6/325-6

26. AR 36/7, 12, 27; MB 35-8/53; LJ 36-7/167,211

27. LJ 35-6/485

28. AR 38/16,32; LJ 36-7/87, 115-6, 37-8/47,83, 90

29. AR 37/30; LJ 36-7/398, 38-9/15,76

30. LJ 35-6/365, 401, 409, 36-7/405, 38-9/81, Met Area sup Sep 38i

31. Public Record Office FO 371 file 21783. Duff Cooper's letter to Halifax on the Legion involvement and Halifax's comments are at page 139.

32. No 10 sent a copy of Maurice's report to the Foreign Office. It is held at the Public Record Office on FO 371 file 21782 at page 351. No 10's covering letter, which also makes it clear that the original approach came from the Legion, is at p 359.

33. AR 38/32; MBs 35-8/108, 38-45/2; LJs 38-9/111, 353, 155-162, Met sup Nov 38 i, 167, 247, 356, 39-40/86

34. ARs 36/7,13, 37/11, 29, 38/32, 33, 39/27, 30; MBs 38-45/17, 47, 201, 287, 298; LJs 36-7/126, 205, 319, 401, 399, 37-8/213, 281, 38-9/14

35. AR 39/29; LJ 39-40/149, 40-1/230

36. AR 39/28; MB 38-45/3,10; LJ 39-40/76-84

37. MB 38-45/137, 142; LJ 40-1/203

**Chapter 7**

1. LJ I/46
2. LJ I/116
3. LJ I/142 and 165
4. LJ I/46
5. MB 21-24/67, 24-6/84,105; LJ II/8,170
6. AR 23/47; MB 24-6/72; LJs I/142, III/357
7. LJ I/142
8. LJ IV/159
9. MB 21-24/36
10. MB 21-24/84, 94 and 109
11. LJ II/265
12. MB24-6/29; LJ V/179
13. AR 25/76-9; LJ IV/21,93
14. LJ III/319,357,377
15. AR 25/80; LJ IV/397
16. AR 23/48; LJ IV/398
17. LJ I/46
18. LJs III/156,191,319,339, IV/371
19. LJ III/285, IV/339, V/19,49,110
20. MB 24-6/38; LJ IV/12
21. LJ IV/21,93
22. LJ IV/57 ,229, V/83
23. LJs III/319,38, LJ IV/303
24. AR 26/14, 63-4; MB 24-6/140; LJ V/179, 211, 265, 295
25. AR 30/76; MB 26-30/88; LJ IX/164
26. ARs 30/76, 31/81; MB 30-5/23
27. LJ 30-1/114, 185
28. ARs 26/66, 27/79, 28/ 88, 29/88, 30/13, 76; LJs V/355, VI/313, 324, VII/367, VIII/294, IX/342,
29. ARs 26/70, 27/84, 29/88, 92; LJs VIII/212,269, IX/164
30. LJ VI/243
31. ARs 26/75, 27/98, 28/105, 29/92, 104, 30/93; LJs VII/81, 107, 154, 215, VIII/122, IX/70, 165
32. ARs 31/81, 32/80, 33/78, 34/69, 35/76; MB 30-5/179; LJs 30-1/270, 31-2/39, 224, 33-4/WS sup Dec 33, 34-5/159, 35-6/199
33. ARs 31/88, 32/88, 33/83, 34/76, 35/83; LJs 30-1/400, 455, 31-2/408, 32-3/478, 33-4/435 June 34 WS sup, 34-5/523, June 35 WS sup
34. ARs 32/7, 33/81, 34/71, 35/78; MB 30-5/69; LJs 32-3/358, 33-4/60, Dec 34 WS sup
35. ARs 31/13, 86-7, 32/82-6, 33/81-3, 34/72-4, 35/78-80; LJs 31-2/151, 124, 34-5/ Oct 34 WS sup 3,
36. AR 34/70MB 30-5/98; LJs 32-3/252, 317, 354
37. ARs 31/98, 32/98, 33/95, 34/87, 35/93
38. ARs 36/63,37/61,72. 38/59, 65, 72, 39/51; MBs 35-8/98, 38-45/98, 38-45/49; LJs 35-6/604,36-7/265, 38-9/381, 39-40/99,129, 308
39. ARs 37/62, 40/47; LJs 35-6/605, 36-7/444, 37-8/394, 38-9/419, 423
40. ARs 36/59, 37/64, 38/61, 39/56, 40/ 48; MB 38-45/161; LJs 35-6/303
41. ARs 35/58-61, 37/58-65, 38/61, 39/54-8, 40/48- 50; LJs 35-6/343, 467, 40-1/126
42. AR 41/29; LJ 42/82
43. ARs 42/30-5, 43/30 ; LJ 42/139
44. AR 45/33-5
45. MB 38-45/151, 166
46. MB 38-45/177; LJ 43/66

457

47. AR 43/30; LJ 43/217
48. MB 38-45/167; LJ 44/88
49. LJ 45/31, 89
50. ARs 41/42, 42/35, 43/36, 44/36, 45/37; LJs 40-1/317, 42/88, 43/109, 43/62, 112, 45/90,94
51. AR 43/33-5, 44/39, 45/37
52. ARs 41/47, 43/45, 44/36, 45/37
53. LJ 45/46

## Chapter 8

1. JM Winter: *The Great War and The British People* p 281
2. OAH/8
3. Anthony Brown: *Red for Remembrance* p 10 and Reese: *Homecoming Heroes* p 106
4. Countess Haig: *The Man I Knew* p 136
5. CH/136-7; OAH/9, Wooton/14
6. OAH/11-12
7. OAH/16
8. AR 23/71
9. Wooton/23
10. LJ I/10
11. MB 24-6/80,96
12. MB 24-6/134
13. Wooton/97
14. LJ IV/15
15. OAH/15; LJ IV/51
16. LJ IV/138
17. AR 25/68
18. OAH/19
19. AR 25/58
20. AR 25/71-2
21. AR 25/62
22. LJ II/59
23. LJ II/189
24. AR 23/81
25. LJ I/71
26. LJ I/45
27. LJ I/47; IV/4, 6, 88
28. AR 23/85, 25/68
29. AR 23/93, 25/74
30. LJ II/59
31. AR 25/61
32. MB 26-30/255
33. MB 26-30/45; LJ VII/2, 78
34. Countess Haig: *The Man I Knew* p 136; AR 28/60
35. ARs 28/30, 103, 29/70, 103, 30/62, 91; MB 26-30/76
36. ARs 27/49, 28/68, 29/77, 30/66
37. ARs 27/50, 28/68, 29/77, 30/66
38. ARs 27/53, 28/70, 29/79, 30/68; OAH/14
39. ARs 27/55, 28/72, 29/82, 30/70
40. ARs 31/67, 97, 32/68, 97, 33/64, 93, 34/59, 86, 35/64, 91
41. ARs 31/72, 32/73, 33/70, 34/63, 35/68; LJ 35-6/147
42. ARs 31/75, 32/76, 35/73

43. ARs 31/74, 32/75, 33/73, 34/65, 35/71
44. ARs 36/49, 37/48, 38/51; MB 35-8/88; LJs 35-6/497, 38-9/273
45. ARs 36/49, 37/48, 38/51, 39/45; LJs 38-9/273, 39-40/253, 316
46. LJ 35-6/497
47. MB 38-45/117-8
48. MB 38-45/118; LJ 45/427
49. ARs 42/12, 44/14
50. OAH/25-7

## Chapter 9

1. LJ 46/32
2. ARs 47/15, 48/13, 49/13, 50/12, 51/11, 53/12, 54/11; LJ 47/293
3. AR 47/6,8; LJ 47/153
4. LJs 49/155, 50/3
5. LJ 46/5,134, 172
6. AR 47/13; LJs 46/197, 47/2, 77
7. MB 46-52/44; LJs 47/77, 107, 198, 275, 48/69, 173
8. ARs 47/13, 48/12, 50/11; MB 45-52/28; LJs 46/94, 99, 201, 237, 47/22, 239
9. ARs 47/14, 48/7; LJs 46/147, 185, 47/153, 251, 48/113.
10. MB 45-52/159; LJs 46/154, 272, 276, 47/270, 282, 48/238, 49/232, 50/282
11. AR 53/5; MB 52-7/5; LJ 53-4/May/20, Aug/1214
12. LJs 52/June/3, Oct/4, Dec/19, 53/Jan/19, 52-3/Feb/18, 53-4/Jul/6, 54-5/Sep/12, Nov 4, Feb/21, 55-6/Jul/8
13. ARs 53/6, 26, 54/20; MB 52-7/33; LJs 53-4/Apr/2, /Jul/3, /Sep/6, 55-6/Jul/9, /Sep/4
14. AR 53/32; LJ 53-4/Mar/7
15. ARs 54/10, 55/11; LJs 51/17, 55-6/Dec/4,11
16. MB 52-7/70, 89; LJs 52/Mar/1, 54-5/Dec/12-13, 55-6/1
17. LJs 56-7/2, 57-8/Mar/13
18. LJs 56-7/June/13, 58-9/Oct4, 59-60/June/6
19. AR 57/5,7
20. AR 57/7; MB 58-62/198; LJ 58-9/Mar/9
21. AR 60/8; MB 58-62/284; LJs 60-1/Jul/4, Sep/6, 9
22. AR 57/22; MB 52-7/88; LJs 56-7/Feb/16, Sep/6, Nov/4,16, Dec/3, 57-8/Feb/26, Mar/4
23. ARs 56/19, 57/21, 58/16-18, 59/16, 60/16; MB 58-62/230; LJ 58-9/Dec/5
24. LJs 56-7/June/5, Jul/11, 24, 57-8/Jul/9, 60-1/Jul/14,30
25. LJ 58-9/Dec/14
26. AR 60/11; LJs 56-7/Dec/6, Jan/13, 57-8/Dec/16
27. MB 58-62/367; LJ 62-3/Mar/21
28. MBs 58-62/373, 62-6/75; LJs 62-3/July/18, 63-4/July/12
29. MB 62-6/74; LJs 62-3/Sep/20, Oct/13, 63-4/May/12
30. LJ 61-2/July/23-5, Sep/16-18, Oct/3, 12-14
31. ARs 61/9, 63/9, 65/55; MBs 58-62/333, 62-6/135; LJs 61-2/Oct/4, Dec/4, June/16,

Feb/4, Mar/4, Apr/4, 62-3/Apr/8, May/4, June/4, July/4, 63-4/July/14, Sep/4, 65-6/Apr/4, May/28

32. LJ 60-1/Jan/5, Feb/8,11, 15, Mar/19, 25, Apr/11
33. MB 58-62/235, 323; LJ 61-2/July/6
34. AR 64/14
35. AR 64/53, 65/53; MB 62-6/74; LJs 62-3/Dec/18, 63-4/Dec/16, 64-5/Dec/16; the *Daily Telegraph*, however, reported on 1 Jan 99 that recently released official papers indicated that the Legion and others supported some reform but that the Queen objected.
36. MB 62-6/204
37. LJs 60-1/Feb/3, 61-2/Apr/17
38. LJ 65-6/Mar 22
39. LJ 69-70/Oct/12
40. ARs 66/13, 67/9/ 68/10
41. LJ 69-70/May/3
42. ARs 66/59-61, 67/56, 68/7, 58, 70/61; MB 66-9/78, 139; LJ 67-8/Aug/20
43. MB 66-9/37, 107, 137H, 69-73/38, 54, 68, 80; LJ 65-6/Feb/20. Additional information supplied by DI Cadman.
44. AR 68/7,8-9, 59; LJ 67-8/Nov/17
45. LJ 65-6/Jan/8, 67-8/Dec/17, 70-1/Oct/12

**Chapter 10**

1. MB 45-52/7,20,53; LJs 47/126,49/2, 50-2/105. Additional information supplied by DI Cadman.
2. LJs 47/117,169 50/52
3. ARs 47/14, 48/12, 49/12, 50/9; LJs 46/238, 251, 49/152, 212, 50/43
4. AR 50/14; MB 46-52/45; LJs 47/119, 48/117
5. AR 48/8; MB 45-52/75; LJs 47/151, 280, 49/132
6. AR 47/10; MB 45-52/135, 159, 161-7; LJs 47/101, 49/146, 170, 49/211
7. MBs 45-52/140, 52-7/122; LJs 48/124, 49/73,144, 52/Nov/7, 53-4/Nov/16, 57-8/Apr/5, Jun/16
8. ARs 48/9, 49/9;LJs 47/35, 54, 49/39, 83-4,165, 166, 207, 219
9. LJs 46/209, 20, 48/11, 33, 86,141
10. AR 49/12, 50/10; LJ 48/43
11. ARs 48/10, 49/10, 50/10; MB 45-52/102;LJ 46/267
12. LJs 46/273, 292, 50/41
13. LJ 49/45
14. AR 50/12; MB 45-52/73; LJs 46/243, 292, 48/19,24, 49/212, 50/41, 85, 183
15. LJ 46/74, 148
16. ARs 48/8, 50/8; MB 45-52/116; LJs 46/74, 47/140, 48/102, 113, 49/122, 50/117, 119, 129
17. LJs 47/244, 48/191, 209, 211, 49/3, 82, 50/131,165
18. AR 47/14, 48/11, 49/11; LJs 47/197, 50/82, 197
19. MB 52-7/32; LJs 52/Mar/5, Jun/1,2, Jul/1.

Additional information supplied by DI Cadman.
20. MB 45-52/209; LJs 51/129, 53-4/Jun/7
21. MB 52-7/106, 111, 223
22. MB 66-9/76E
23. AR 52/6
24. LJs 54-5/Oct/4, 56-7/Oct/5, 60-1/Nov/8, 60-1/Oct/5, 63-4/Nov/19, 69-70/Mar/3
25. ARs 51/16-23, 53/13; LJs 51/3, 52/3
26. MB 52-7/54, 64; LJs 51/12, 56, 54-5/Jan/15, 55-6/Apr/19, May/3, June/4, Jul/11
27. LJs 51/140, 54-5/Apr/21, Sep/19, Oct/15, 55-6/Apr/19
28. MBs 45-52/212, 52-7/9,13, 69-73/31, 58-62/290, 331, 361, 368, 369, 62-6/28; LJs 54-5/Nov/5, LJ 55-6/Apr/67-8/Nov/8. The Certificate of Appreciation was introduced following a 1932 Conference Resolution and announced in the 31 March 1933 General Circular.
29. AR 50/6; MB 45-52/231; LJs 52/June/1-2, July/6, 53-4/Nov/19, 55-6/Mar/11
30. LJs 51/84, 85-9, 52/Oct/19, 53-4/Apr/13, 52/July/4-5
31. MB 52-7/2,101; LJs 53-4/Jul/4, 55-6/June/3, Jul/4
32. ARs 51/5, 53/6, 52; LJs 52/5, 53-4/Jul/8, Sep/2, 55-6/Jul/7
33. AR 53/10; LJs 52/2, 53-4/Aug/7, 55-6/Nov/4
34. LJ 69-70/Jan/4
35. MB 58-62/302; LJ 59-60/June/10, 60-1/Jul/9,15
36. MB 58-62/213. Additional information supplied by DI Cadman.
37. MB 58-62/151, 212, 253; LJs 58-9/Aug/8, 59-60/Oct/16
38. AR 60/10; MB 58-62/192 insert, 194 insert
39. MB 58-62/269
40. MB 58-62/298, LJ 57-8/Mar/7, Apr/14, Jul/12, 60-1/July/14
41. MB 58-62/290
42. LJs 56-7/Oct/18, 57-8/Nov/9, 58-9/Nov/14, 59-60/June/25
43. ARs 57/9, 58/10 59/12, 60/13
44. MBs 52-7/165, 58-62/263; LJs 57-8/Oct/3, Nov/8, 58-9/Dec/5, Jan/4, 60-1/Aug/6
45. AR 58/6; LJ 56-7/ June/9, Jan/2
46. AR 60/8-9l; LJ 59-60/Aug/7
47. LJs 56-7/June/19, 57-8/Jul/7, 58-9/Apr/13, 59-60/June/10, 60-1/Jul/3, Sep/18
48. AR 60/10; MB 58-62/304; LJs 56-7/June/11, 57-8/Jul/5, 58-9/June/17, 59-60/June/8, 60-1/Jul/9
49. AR 56/20, 58/18, 59/18, 60/17; LJ 60-1/Sep/5
50. MB 58-62/309; LJ 60-1/Feb/1,2
51. LJ 62-3/Dec/16, Jan/8
52. AR 69/9; LJ 62-3/Jan/16
53. LJ 62-3/July/11
54. MBs 58-62/263, 66-9/148; LJs 48/59, 56-7/Jul/15, Aug/4, 58-9/Apr/6, 60-1/Jan /3,

May/12, 61-2/June/26, July/19, 63-4/Sep/20

55. LJs 62-3/Oct/16, 65-6/June/16
56. MB 62-6/16, 158, 171, 183
57. ARs 61/14, 62/12, 63/13, 48, 64/12, 51, 65/9,10; LJs 62-3/July/19, 63-4/Dec/20, 64-5/Mar/12, June/23, Sep/10, 65-6/July/19
58. AR 63/13, 64/14; LJs 63-4/May/17, 64-5/Mar/7, Apr/22
59. AR 61/12; LJ 61-2/June/5
60. AR 62/45; MB 62-6/7,38; LJs 30/9,33-4/14, 63-4/Mar/11
61. MB 62-6/186, 206, 21
62. LJs 60-1/Oct/3, 64-5/June/25, Sep/12, 64-5/Nov/8, Jan 8, 65-6/July/18, Aug/9
63. AR 36/43; MB 45-52/182, 66-6/130; LJ 46/39, 48/7, 33, 59, 75, 147, 201, 50/126, 65-6/Oct/18, 66-7/Feb/21
64. ARs 62/11, 65/10; LJs 61-2/June/16-17, 29, 62-3/July/17
65. ARs 61/17, 62/12, 63/51, 64/55, 65/55; MBs 58-62/357, 62-6/17; LJs 61-2/July/4, 62-3/Sep/8
66. MB 62-6/234; LJ 66-7/Apr/4
67. LJs 66-7/Jul/3, 13, 69-70/June/3, 70-1/July/6, Jan/3,4
68. MB 69-73/24; LJ 70-1/July/8
69. ARs 66/10, 69/8; MB 66-9/88; LJs 65-6/Jan/10, 67-8/Oct/10, Nov/10, 68-9/Apr/10, 69-70/July/10
70. AR 70/58
71. AR 70/9; MB 69-73/35, 40A, 44, 6570; LJ 70-1/July/10-12
72. AR 66/10
73. MB 62-6/236;LJs 66-7/Oct/3, 67-8/July /13-14, 68-9, July/14
74. LJs 68-9/ May/13, 70-1/July/4
75. AR 67/31, 68/33, 69/33, 70/7-8, 33; MB 62-6/235
76. ARs 66/61, 67/57, 68/61, 69/61, 70/64; LJs 69-70/Feb/3

## Chapter 11

1. LJ 46/4, 19,24
2. LJs 46/27, 96, 49/83
3. LJ 48/10
4. LJs 47/ 231, 48/30, 32, 49/174
5. LJs 46/4, 52, 88, 155, 47/17, 35
6. LJs 46/14,44,57,81
7. LJs 47/36,139
8. AR 48/6, 50/18; MB 45-52/11, 38, 196; LJs 46/177, 194, 274, 47/230, 289, 291, 48/17, 79,118
9. ARs 47/32, 52/34, 53/34; LJ 58-9/Feb/3
10. ARs 47/16, 48/14, 49/125; LJs 46/8, 214, 233, 286, 47/228, 278, 48/117
11. AR 47/ 26, 27; LJ 46/29, 99, 123, 47/108
12. AR 48/6, 22; LJ 48/170-2

13. LJs 48/237, 49/7, 45, 103
14. AR 50/20; MB 45-52/123
15. AR 49/23
16. LJs 46/48,52, 75, 221, 270, 48/131
17. LJ 46/50, 52, 244
18. LJs 46/87, 48/181, 59-60/Sep/6
19. AR 57/29-30
20. AR 54/14, 18
21. LJ 52/8
22. AR 57/29
23. LJ 47/224
24. AR 48/7
25. LJ 48/116
26. MB 52-7/128, 139
27. MB 62-6/46, 79
28. AR 53/32; LJs 53-4/Oct/15, 54-5/Oct/12
29. LJs 47/41, 56-7/Jul/17, 66-7/Jan/12
30. ARs 47/29, 48/24; LJs 6/195, 48/125
31. LJs 46/83, 271, 47/16
32. LJ 47/30
33. ARs 48/33, 50/28, 51/38, 52/36, 53/35, 54/6,15, 55/18, 56/28, 57/28, 58/23, 29, 59/24; MB 45-52/73; LJs 47/30, 51/66, 54-5/Jul/4, Sep/4
34. ARs 61/24, 62/21, 63/23, 65/18, 66/23, 70/20, 72/17
35. AR 60/24; LJ 51/66
36. LJ 48/22, 48
37. LJ 49/125
38. ARs 48/6, 14, 87, 49/14; LJs 48/87, 225
39. AR 50/14; LJ 50/155
40. LJs 51/35, 36, 65
41. LJ 51/180
42. AR 51/6, 28; MB 45-52/201; LJs 51/129, 162, 178-180
43. LJ 52/Feb/cover
44. AR 52/6, 27
45. LJ 52/Apr/1, May/2, Sep/4, 53-4/July/10
46. MB 52-7/46, 81; LJs 53-4/Oct/4, Dec/6, 9, Feb/3-4, 54-5/Mar 12, 15, May/6, Oct/3, Jan/4-5, Apr/7
47. AR 48/31; LJs 47/210, 48/195, 199, 216
48. LJ 50/189]
49. ARs 49/31, 50/27, 51/37, 52/35, 54/18, 55/19, 59/24, 60/24, 61/25, 64/23
50. AR 51/6, 52/6, 24, 53/23, 54/25, 55/28
51. ARs 47/20, 48/17, 50/12, 52/25, 53/24, 59/31, 64/12, 70/30; LJs 46/142, 293, 47/12, 52/Mar/12, 55-6/Jun/6, 64-5/Sep/29, 66-7/Aug/20
52. LJ 54-5/Oct/12
53. AR 47/29; LJ 46/11, 75, 46/108-9, 211, 47/37, 286, 48/2
54. ARs 48/25, 49/24
55. LJ 47/229, 50/90
56. AR 53/28, 59/22
57. ARs 56/26, 70/17
58. ARs 47/6, 48/22, 49/24, 50/21
59. ARs 50/28, 52/28, 54/22, 55/25

60. ARs 56/34, 57/35, 59/9, 60/27, 61/28, 62/26, 63/26, 64/28; LJs 61-2/Jan/17, 62-3/Dec/4
61. ARs 65/26, 66/27, 67/26, 68/25, 69/24, 70/27
62. AR 51/14; LJs 51/148, 53-4/Mar/2, Oct/8, 54-5/Nov/7, 55-6/May/4
63. LJ 63-4/July/8
64. ARs 52/15, 54/29; LJs 52-3/July/5, 53-4/June/1, 54-5/Sep/8, Nov/19, Dec/10
65. LJ 58-9/June/6
66. ARs 57/27, 58/22
67. AR 59/8; MBs 58-62/23A, 216
68. LJ 59/60/Feb/4
69. LJs 50/142, 53-4/Mar/11, Aug/3
70. AR 58/24; LJ 58-9/Mar/121, 63-4/June/16
71. LJ 73-4/May/8
72. MB 66-9/61; LJ 66-7/May/20
73. LJ 56-7/June/25
74. AR 57/32; LJ 57-8/June/9
75. LJ 57-8/Mar/6, Nov/16, Dec/5
76. ARs 58/5, 59/26, 60/26; MB 58-62/308;LJs 59-60/May/7, June/12, 60-1/Dec/9
77. AR 59/9; LJs 59-60/Apr/2, 60-1/Apr/12
78. AR 59/26; LJ 59-60/Oct/6
79. ARs 57/37, 58/30, 59/31, 60/31; LJ 59-60/Nov/9
80. ARs 47/20, 48/18, 49/18, 50/17, 52/24, 55/27, 59/30, 60/30, 66/33, 67/29, 70/29; LJ 46/54, 224
81. ARs 60/30, 68/26
82. LJ 70-1/May/7
83. ARs 47/22, 48/19, 49/19
84. LJs 52/Mar/9, 55-6/Aug/5
85. AR 60/27; MB 58-62/290; LJs 59-60/May 5, 60-1/Aug/4, Sep/10
86. LJ 56-7/June/27
87. AR 47/23, 48/20, 49/20; LJs 46/34, 64, 48/29, 50/190
88. LJs 52/Apr/5, 54-5/Oct/10, 55-6/Nov/2
89. LJ 65-6/Mar/12
90. LJs 68-9/Jan/5, 70-1/Apr/4
91. LJ 57-8/Aug/12
92. AR 58/32; LJ 57-8/Dec/7
93. LJ 58-9/Mar/6
94. ARs 56/5, 43, 57/39, 58/32, 60/33
95. ARs 62/17, 21, 63/18, 65/15
96. ARs 64/23, 65/19,68/19, 70/21
97. ARs 50/31, 56/37, 62/18, 63/19, 70/16
98. ARs 49/31, 54/14, 55/17, 64/18, 65/20, 70/16, 18; LJs 62-3/Apr/3, Jan/3
99. ARs 63/24, 64/25, 65/21, 70/23
100. AR 61/27LJ 61-2/Aug/13
101. AR 62/10,24; LJ 61-2/Jan/5, Feb/9, 62-3/Jan/5,15
102. AR 63/12, 26, 64/14, 26, 65/22; MB 62-6/34; LJ 63-4/Jan/18, Mar/18
103. LJs 61-2/June/16, 62-3/July/25, 27, 63-4/Jan/8, 64-5/Apr/16
104. MBs 66-9/24, 51D, 53, 80; LJ 70-1/Sep/5
105. LJ63/4/July 27
106. MBs 45-52/224, 52-7/62, 105; LJs 50/190, 51/149, 52/2
107. MB 58-62/301
108. AR 66/60; MB 69-73/83; LJs 65-6/Feb/16, 68-9/May/12, 70-1/Sep/16
109. ARs 47/25, 48/21, 49/22, 64/12; MBs 45-52/194, 62-6/20, 70, 148; LJs 50/190, 56-7/June/27, 57-8/Jan/3, 58-9/Jul/17, 61-2/June/17, 63-4/Apr/10
110. AR 64/11, 26, 65/22; MB 62-6/94, 215; LJs 64-5/Feb/17, 66-7/May/19, 67-8/July/16
111. ARs 69/12, 70/11; LJs 68-9/Mar/14, 69-70/Mar/17, May/4, Feb/8
112. LJ 64-5/Nov/22
113. AR 65/60
114. ARs 62/53, 63/56, 64/60, 65/60
115. AR 50/14, 51/14, 61/35
116. AR 66/33; LJ 66-7/Aug/3
117. ARs 56/62, 58/31, 59/31, 60/32, 63/30
118. AR 68/9; MB 66-9/102, 135; LJs 68-9/June/3, 69-70/Mar/6, LJ 70/July/15
119. AR 55/30
120. ARs 66/13, 26, 67/12, 23; LJs 66-7/Sep/4, 67-8/Oct/8, 68-9/Sep/6
121. ARs 69/20, 70/11, 24; LJ 70-1/July/14, Oct/4
122. LJ 69-70/Sep/4, Dec/6
123. ARs 61/22, 62/20, 63/21; LJ 62-3/Feb/16
124. ARs 66/12, 67/18, 69/15; MB 62-6/33; LJs 65-6/Nov/10, 67-8/June/16
125. ARs 65/16, 68/17
126. AR 66/65
127. LJs 66/7/June/15, 68-9/Sep/21; 65-6/June/4
128. LJ 67-8/Aug/16
129. ARs 67/60, 68/29, 69/29, 70/32

**Chapter 12**

1. AR 48/7; LJ 47/18, 195, 226, 255, 277
2. LJs 48/171
3. LJ 50/43, 149
4. LJs 48/146, 49/130
5. LJs 51/23, 52-3/16
6. LJ 51/145
7. MBs 45-52/235, 52-7/4, 15; LJ 53-4/Jul/5
8. LJs 54-5/Dec/7, 55-6/Nov/5
9. LJ 54-5/Jun/12
10. AR 54/7
11. LJ 56-7/Jul/16
12. AR 58/16,17; LJ 56-7/Mar/14, Oct/3, Dec/5,6
13. LJs 52/12, 55-6/Jan/17
14. MB 62-6/202; LJ 59-60/Jan/2
15. AR 59/7; LJ 60-1/Dec/16
16. MB 58-62/305
17. LJ 61-2/Feb/3
18. AR 64/11
19. LJ 57-8/Oct/16
20. LJ 60-1/Jan/2
21. ARs 64/52, 65/10; MB 62-6/214; LJ 63-4/Apr/25
22. MB 62-6/40, 42
23. MB 62-6/99, 157; LJs 64-5/Dec/17, 65-6/Dec/16
24. ARs 47/24, 48/20, 49/21; LJ 51/93

25. MB 58-62/259; LJs 59-60/June/14, 67-
    8/Oct/16, 69-70/July/12
26. AR 67/38
27. LJ 62-3/Dec/3
28. LJ 62-3/Nov/16
29. MB 69-73/69
30. AR 67/63
31. AR 66/69; MB 66-9/25
32. ARs 66/11, 67/30; MB 66-9/68; LJs 66-
    7/Feb/18 68-9/Dec/3
33. AR 70/53

## Chapter 13

1. MB 45-52/11, 32
2. LJ 47/249
3. LJs 47/215, 48/47
4. LJ 47/175, 177
5. MB 45-52/97; LJ 47/192
6. ARs 47/10, 247 48/9; MB 46-52/6; LJs 47/175-
    6, 48/64, 138
7. MB 45-52/219
8. MB 45-52/222, 242, 52-7/4
9. MB 52-7/13, 37; LJ 53-4/Jul/12
10. LJ 53-4/Jul/12
11. LJ 55-6/18
12. LJ 53-4/Jul/6
13. MB 58-62/192, 204
14. MB 58-62/217; LJ 60-1/Aug/13
15. MB 58-62/321, 338, 348
16. MB 62-6/24
17. AR 63/12; MB 62-6/56, 57, 90, 170, 178. DI
    Cadman provided additional information
    on the Ottawa BCEL Conference.
18. AR 63/11; MB 62-6/90
19. AR 63/11; MB 62-6/37, 52
20. MBs 58-62/359, 365, 62-6/98
21. MBs 52-7/98, 58-62/216
22. MB 66-9/35
23. LJ 66-7/July/15
24. AR 68/11; MB 66-9/40; LJ 68-9/Sep/20
25. MB 66-9/123

## Chapter 14

1. MB 45-52/37
2. MB 46-52/ 52, 53, 110
3. LJ 47/9
4. ARs 47/41-3, 48/39; LJ 48/57
5. LJs 47/48, 50/32
6. LJs 47/50, 189, 48/18, 39
7. AR 47/41; LJ 46/42, 104
8. LJ 46/52, 128, 179, 227, 47/92
9. ARs 48/41, 49/41; LJ 49/46
10. AR 49/40, 41; LJs 46/42, 49/35
11. MB 52-7/75, 86, 89
12. AR 51/42
13. AR 54/41; MB 52-/3
14. AR 52/40
15. LJ 51/117

16. LJ 54-5/June/16
17. AR 55/44
18. LJs 51/23, 52/June/14
19. LJ 54-5/May/18
20. LJ 54-5/Dec/17
21. LJ 54-5/17
22. LJ 53-4/Mar/3
23. ARs 1947-1970
24. AR 60/53
25. ARs 51/43, 52/43; LJ 55-6/Mar/16
26. LJs 52/Aug/12, June/20, Nov/21
27. ARs 59/10, 52; MB 58-62/266
28. LJs 56-7/June/19, Jan/18
29. ARs 58/40, 59/49, 60/52; LJ 58-9/June/20
30. ARs 54/38, 56/58; LJs 54-5/Oct/16, 55-
    6/Aug/16, 56/7/Nov/22
31. ARs 56/60, 57/53-4, 59/52, 60/54; LJs 57-
    8/Sep/15, 59-60/Dec/23
32. AR 61/57; MB 58-62/330, 339
33. LJ 62-3/June/3
34. AR 65/66; LJ 65-6/May/4
35. LJ 64-5/June/36
36. LJs 63-4/June/27, 65-6/June/29
37. ARs 61/52, 62/57-8, 63/61, 65/67; MB 58-62/283
38. AR 53/40; LJ 52/Nov/14
39. AR 56/59
40. AR 62/20, 63/64, 65/69
41. AR 62/61
42. AR 62/62, 63/66, 64/70, 65/71; LJ 64-5/Sep/16
43. LJ 67-8/Sep/28, Nov/29
44. MBs 66-9/143, 69-73/17, 24
45. MB 69-73/81
46. ARs 66/81, 67/73
47. AR 69/72; LJs 67-8/June/27, 69-70/June/15
48. AR 70/72; LJ 70-1/June/12
49. ARs 66/77, 67/68, 68/71; LJs 68-9/Nov/25, 68-
    9/Oct/23
50. AR 67/71-2; LJ 67-8/July/28
51. ARs 67/72, 68/75, 69/75, 70/75
52. LJ 70-1/Aug/23

## Chapter 15

1. OAAR 46/6 and 'historical note' at OAAR 50/6
    and subsequent reports
2. LJ 47/161
3. MB 45-52/136; LJ 49/170. Additional material
    supplied by Officers' Association.
4. OAH/30; OAARs 1946-50; also references in
    many LJ reports to Gen Glover's talks at
    Legion conferences
5. OAAR 46/15
6. OAH/26
7. LJ 46/266
8. OAH/29
9. LJ 46/138, 48/89
10. LJ 49/252
11. OAH/32
12. OAAR 50/14

| | |
|---|---|
| 13. | OAH/30; OAAR 59/8 |
| 14. | OAH/31 and OAARs of the period |
| 15. | OAAR 58/12 |
| 16. | OAH/27 and 34 |
| 17. | LJ 53-4/Jan/3 |
| 18. | LJ 51/42 |
| 19. | OAH/28 |
| 20. | OAH/33 |
| 21. | LJ 59-60/Jan/13 |
| 22. | Between 1989 and 1993 the author discussed Legion activities with over 100 senior officers of all three services; in nearly every case they were familiar with the OA and its work but did not in any way associate it with the Legion. |
| 23. | OAH/38 and OAAR 56/11 |
| 24. | LJ 51/42 |
| 25. | AR 57/38; OAH/35 |
| 26. | OAAR 59/5 |
| 27. | OAH/37 |
| 28. | AR 65/63 |
| 29. | OAH/28 |
| 30. | ARs 66/16, 67/15, 67/75, 70/15; OAAR 66/17 |
| 31. | ARs 66/72, 67/65, 68/25, 69/65, 70/67 |
| 32. | OAAR 69/7 |

| | |
|---|---|
| 30. | MB 77-81/302; LJs 81/Sep/6, 82/Jan/10,14 |
| 31. | MB 77-81/297 |
| 32. | LJ 88/Mar/2 |
| 33. | LJ 87/July/2 |
| 34. | MB 90/8; LJs 87/July/27, 90/July/9 |
| 35. | AR 90/12; LJ 90/July/3 |
| 36. | ARs 86/16, 87/16, 88/18, 89/19, 90/19 |
| 37. | AR 91/5; MB 91/12, 19; LJ 91/Jan/3 |
| 38. | LJs 91/Mar/5, 92/Mar/26 |
| 39. | LJs 92/Jan/20, 93/25 |
| 40. | MB 92/17; LJ 91/Nov/20 |
| 41. | Letter from Maj Gen JML Grover to the Secretary of The Burma Star Association dated 9 Feb 1969 |
| 42. | AR 91/7 |
| 43. | AR 92/14; LJ 91/May/3 |
| 44. | AR 91/7 |
| 45. | AR 94/8; LJ 94/July/7, 14-16 |
| 46. | LJ 95/April/13, July/23 |
| 47. | LJ 95/July/20 |
| 48. | MB 93/73 and papers attached to 25 Feb 93 meeting; LJ 95/Sep/6 |
| 49. | AR 95/3 |
| 50. | MB 95/11; LJ 95/Jul/13 |
| 51. | AR 95/6, 96/13; MB 95/54; LJ 95/Sep/3 |

## Chapter 16

| | |
|---|---|
| 1. | LJ 72-3/Nov/12 |
| 2. | MB 69-73/149; LJ 73-4/Mar/1 |
| 3. | AR 73/9; MB 73-5/5 |
| 4. | AR 73/9 |
| 5. | MB 69-73/147 |
| 6. | MB 69-73/116; LJ 71-2/Aug/4 |
| 7. | LJ 71-2/Aug/10 |
| 8. | MB 69-73/103 |
| 9. | AR 72/8; MB 69-73/90, 183; LJ 72-3/Aug/16 |
| 10. | AR 72/9-10; LJs 72-3/July/3, Sep/12 & 17, Oct/6, 13 |
| 11. | AR 74/41; LJs 72-3/Oct/16, 75/Nov/1 |
| 12. | AR 73/41 |
| 13. | MB 69-73/144; LJ 72-3/Dec/16, Jan/6, 73-5/Nov/12 |
| 14. | LJ 72-3/July/20 |
| 15. | MB 73-5/43, 95; LJ 80/May/30 |
| 16. | MB 73-5/55 |
| 17. | LJ 73-4/Nov/5 |
| 18. | ARs 79/6, 90/5 |
| 19. | MB 77-81/201 |
| 20. | AR 77/5; LJ 77/July/1 |
| 21. | LJ 80/Jan/16 |
| 22. | LJs 76/Dec/16, 77/Jan/16, July/9, 78/June/7 |
| 23. | AR 82/5; MB 82/24, 43 |
| 24. | AR 83/6; LJ 83/Jan/21 |
| 25. | LJ 84/Mar/12 |
| 26. | LJ 85/Mar/20 |
| 27. | LJ 84/Jan/2 |
| 28. | LJ 85/July/28 |
| 29. | LJ 85/July/31 |

## Chapter 17

| | |
|---|---|
| 1. | AR 72/10; MB 73-5/15 |
| 2. | AR 74/8; LJ 75/Sep/1 |
| 3. | LJ 75/Sep/16 |
| 4. | MB 75-7/282 MB 69-73/179, 217, 231 |
| 5. | AR 71/13; MBs 69-73/140A, 73-5/16, 61; LJ 73-4/Jan/12 |
| 6. | LJ 73-4/Oct/13 |
| 7. | ARs 71/14, 73/9-10; MB 69-73/163, 73-5/49, 75-7/207A |
| 8. | MB 69-73/163, 207, 212B; LJ 72-3/July/19 |
| 9. | AR 71/12; MB 69-73/130, 165; LJs 73-4/Aug/16, Sep/23 |
| 10. | AR 71/11; MB 69-73/135, 201; LJs 71-2/Nov/13, 72-3/July/17, Feb/5 |
| 11. | LJ 73-4/Aug/8, 21 |
| 12. | LJ 72-3/June/7, Feb/5, Aug/12 |
| 13. | LJs 73-4/May/10 |
| 14. | ARs 71/54-7, 72/54, 73/38, 74/28 |
| 15. | AR 72/11; MB 69-73/193 |
| 16. | LJs 72-3/July |
| 17. | LJ 73-4/July/4, 74/July/1, 75/July/1 |
| 18. | AR 76/16; LJ 79/Nov/1 |
| 19. | AR 78/6; LJ 84/July/26 |
| 20. | MB 77-81/39; LJ 84/Nov/3 |
| 21. | LJ 81/Nov/31 |
| 22. | MBs 75-7/230, 267, 317, 77-81/17, 187, 196, 207, 227 |
| 23. | ARs 79/8, 81/15; MB 77-81/98, 175, 81A/21 |
| 24. | ARs 78/7, 80/8; LJs 79/Aug/2,5. 76/Aug/13 |
| 25. | ARs 79/6, 80/6; LJ 78/Apr/4, May/4 |
| 26. | AR 75/5; LJ 74/Mar/1 |

27. AR 77/5
28. LJ 78/Apr/4
29. MB 77-81/113; LJ 78/Dec/8
30. LJs 76/July/1-4, 77/July/16, 79/July/1, 80/July/3
31. Conf 81 Jubilee issue/1,3, LJ 84/July /29
32. MB 83/2, 16; LJ 83/Jan/6, July /22
33. MB 85/43; LJ 85/Nov/2
34. MB 84/29
35. MB 82/2: LJ 82/Mar/1
36. ARs 82/10, 83/6, 8, 84/6,10; MB 86/45
37. MB 82/48, 49
38. AR 85/5; MB 84/41, 48, 49, 53; LJ 84/Nov/9, 85/July/29
39. LJ 82/Nov/28
40. MB 82/40; LJ 83/July/28
41. AR 81/10
42. ARs 82/12, 83/12, 84/13; MB 77-81/276, 81/A/33-4; LJ 81/May/15
43. AR 81/10; LJ 83/Mar/18
44. AR 82/13; LJs 83/Mar/18, 84/Sep/ 22
45. LJs 84/Sep/36, 85/12
46. LJ 85/July/24
47. MB 81/A2, 83/46, 84/5; LJs 81/July/3, 82/July/8, 84/July/2
48. MB 86/47,68; LJs 86/July/30, 87/July/22
49. AR 87/5-6; MB 87/47
50. LJ 88/May/12
51. AR 88/5; MB 88/15,42, 43,47; LJs 88/May/12, 89/July/22
52. AR 90/7; LJ 90/July/23
53. MB 88/2; LJ 88/Jan/12
54. MB 89/34; LJs 89/July/12, 22, 26
55. AR 88/17, 89/18, 90/18; MB 88/51; LJs 88/May/16
56. LJs 88/May/14, July/21-7, 89/July/30, 90/July/8-16
57. AR 86/19, 87/17, 88/18; LJs 88/May/12
58. ARs 91/23, 92/28, 93/30, 94/32, 95/27
59. AR 91/6; MB 91/55, 92/51; LJs 91/Mar/3, July/8, Nov/34, 92/May/11, 19
60. AR 92/6
61. AR 92/6; LJ 92/July/3, 19
62. MB 92/92-7; LJ 93/July/14
63. AR 94/6; MB 93/21
64. AR 94/27
65. MB 94/110 and Healy & Baker letter 6 Oct 94
66. LJs 93/July/18, 95/July/11
67. MB 89/13,92/43
68. MB 93/48,72
69. LJs 85/Mar/22, 92/July/15
70. AR 95/15; MB 91/61
71. MB 91/8
72. ARs 91/18, 93/21, 94/25, 95/15; MBM 29 July 94
73. ARs 91/18, 92/20, 93/38, 95/14; MB 93/10; MBM 16 Jul 94
74. Paper att to NC 16 Jul 94; LJs 91/May/16, 94/Jan/23, Nov/19
75. MB 87/5; LJs 80/May/26, 90/July/6

**Chapter 18**

1. ARs 71/11-12, 72/9, 14, 73/14
2. LJs 71-2/Dec/7, 72-3/Dec/9
3. AR 73/17
4. LJs 71-2/Mar/9, 72-3/Dec/9
5. ARs 71/9, 72/16, 73/17
6. AR 74/13; MB 69-73/94; LJ 72-3/July/18
7. ARs 72/22, 74/14, 75/9-10; MB 69-73/160, 168; LJ 71-2/July/20, 73-4/July/10
8. AR 72/21; LJ 72/Jan/13
9. MB 73-5/157; LJs 75/Oct/1, Dec/4, 76/Mar/1
10. AR 71/13; LJ 71-2/July/39
11. MB 69-73/163, 168, 177; LJs 72-3/Feb/12, Apr/15, May/16
12. MB 73-5/82; LJs 73-4/Sep/16, 75/Nov/12
13. AR 71/12: MB 69-73/97, 214; LJ 75/June/3
14. AR 75/5; LJs 73-4/June/6, 76/Jan/1
15. ARs 79/10, 80/10; MB 77-81/160
16. LJ 72-3/ Aug/25
17. LJs 73-4/Jan /10, 74/Aug/1
18. MB 73-5/152
19. ARs 79/6, 79/7, 80/5
20. MB 73-5/6, 22
21. MB 75-7/220, 231, 77-81/85, 255
22. AR 80/8; MB 77-81/38, 85, 93, 104, 148, 161, 195
23. MB 77-81/148,195
24. MB 77-81/250
25. AR 76/9; MB 75-7/233, 266; LJ 76/Aug/16
26. ARs 77/9, 78/6, 79/7; LJs 77/July/4, 78/June/1, 79/June/16, Jul/1
27. AR 77/9
28. AR 80/6, LJ 79/Dec/9
29. ARs 79/11, 80/11; LJs 73-4/May/17, Feb/2, 74/Jul/11, 77/May/9, 78/May/1,Dec/9
30. ARs 79/10, 80/10; MB 69-73/98, 161,209, 75-7/211, 77-81/62, 113, 258; LJ 74/June/1
31. AR 83/5; LJ Conf 81/5
32. AR 82/11, 84/11; MB 82/47
33. LJ 82/Sep/24
34. ARs 82/9, 11, 83/9; MB 83/13; LJs 83/Mar/15, July/5
35. AR 84/10
36. AR 81/8
37. AR 83/5; MBs 81/A24,31, 82/44, 83/6, 49, 84/11, 86/13, 87/56; LJs 81/Mar/10, 84/Mar/10, 86/May/28
38. AR 81/10, 82/11, 83/10; MB 83/9; LJs 81/Sep/16, Jan/22
39. ARs 81/10, 84/11, 88/14; MB 83/22, 32; LJs 81/Sep/16, 86/May/9
40. ARs 81/13, 82/16, 83/15,85/16
41. ARs 81/13, 83/15, 85/16
42. ARs 82/10, 83/10; LJ 75/May/9, 78/Nov/8
43. LJ 82/Sep/10
44. ARs 87/11, 90/11, 91/9, 92/13, 93/16, 94/21, 95/10; MB 94/10; LJ 94/Sep/6
45. ARs 73/22, 75/10, 76/9, 79/7; LJ 71-2/Apr/28, 75/Apr

46. AR 76/9, 80/7; LJ 80/Nov/15
47. ARs 72/11, 81/8, 83/8, 84/9; MB 73-5/151; LJ 83/Sep/33
48. LJs 81/Jan/12, 95/July/6
49. ARs 79/10, 80/10, 81/15, 83/18; MB 69-73/104; LJ 84/Mar /14
50. ARs 86/22, 93/36, 94/38, 95/30
51. LJ 81/Sep/21
52. ARs 82/11, 83/10; MB 82/26;LJs 82/Mar/15, July/18
53. AR 85/11; LJ 85/Mar/10
54. LJ 85/July/6
55. AR 90/14; MB 87/11,16
56. MB 87/56; LJ 88/July/22
57. MB 89/65, 90/22
58. AR 88/9; LJ 90/Jan/3
59. ARs 86/9, 87/9, 88/11, 89/9, 90/10
60. ARs 86/18, 87/21-1, 88/24, 89/24, 90/7 and 24
61. MB 90/13
62. MB 90/23, 81; LJ 90/May/16, July/8
63. LJ 92/July/3,19; report attached to NEC meeting 28 May 93
64. LJs Apr/78/1, 77/May/2, 78/Nov/10, 81/Jan/1, 85/May/31
65. AR 88/5, 90/25; MBs 88/15, 22, 46, 90/65
66. AR 85/6; LJ 85/July/25
67. ARs 86/5, 13, 87/11, 88/12, 89/11, 90/12; MB 87/4; LJs 88/Mar/30, July/27
68. ARs 81/14, 82/17, 83/17, 84/18,85/19
69. ARs 84/18, 85/19, 87/11, 90/26
70. ARs 93/35, 94/37, 95/28
71. ARs 83/17, 86/21, 89/27, 60, 90/27 92/33, 93/35, 95/29; MBs 89/60, 92/86; LJs 86/Sep/32
72. LJ 92/Nov/17
73. ARs 94/5, 95/17
74. ARs 91/10, 93/7; MB 94/62, 123; LJ 91/Sep/26
75. Report attached to Nat Council meeting 16 Jul 95; LJ 91/July/10
76. ARs 91/14, 92/15; MB/92/80
77. LJ 94/May/6
78. AR 93/18, 94/16; MB 94/86
79. MB 89/28
80. AR s 86/12, 87/13, 91/13,93/17; MB 86/43, 51, 89/28, 90/74, briefing paper attached to Nat Council meeting of 26 Feb 94; LJ 86/July/23, 88/Sep/22, 90/Jan/10
81. LJ 91/Jan/16
82. AR 92/16; MB 91/9, 93/12
83. ARs 92/17, 95/29
84. AR 92/17; LJ 90/Nov/9
85. AR 95/18; MB 94/26; LJs 94/July/10, Sep/7
86. ARs 91/26, 92/30-1; MB 92/78, 93/22; LJs 91/July/10
87. ARs 92/12, 93/14
88. AR 93/14; MB 93/14-15; LJ 93/Sep/34
89. LJs 91/Sep/9, 95/Sep/7
90. AR 91/7
91. ARs 91/7, 93/7, 94/33
92. LJ 94/Mar/7
93. MB 94/11, 38, 125, 95/91; LJ 95/Nov/7
94. ARs 91/28, 92/12, 93/34, 95/32; MB 95/83
95. AR 95/22; MB 92/44-8
96. ARs 91/27, 92/32, 93/33, 94/35, 95/31; LJ 93/Mar/9
97. ARs 91/28, 92/33
98. AR 89/15; LJ 89/Sep/6
99. AR 89/15; LJs 87/Jan/12, 89/Jan/20
100. ARs 93/19, 94/20, 95/19

**Chapter 19**

1. LJ 71-2/Aug/8
2. MB 69-73/224
3. LJ 72-3/Oct/26
4. LJs 72/Jan/16, 75/Mar/1
5. AR 72/11; MB 69-73/132, 142
6. ARs 72/7, 9, 73/8, 74/18
7. AR 75/11
8. LJ 74/July/2
9. AR 71/2; MBs 69-73/236B, 73-5/11, 77; LJ 74/Oct/6
10. LJs 76/July/1, 77/July/5, 80/Sep/27
11. AR 77/12; MB 77-81/51, 97; LJs 77/Apr/2, 79/Apr/8
12. MB 77-81/102, 146
13. LJ 80/Nov/16
14. LJ 80/Nov /16
15. ARs 81/11, 82/13, 83/13; LJ 83/Sep/16, Nov/19
16. ARs 83/7, 84/8; MB 82/12; LJ 85/July/24
17. AR 84/8; MB 81 A/30, 82/43, 84/2, 85/2; LJs 82/May/18, 83/Jan/11, 17, 81/Mar/13,15
18. MB 82/14; LJ 80/Nov/16
19. ARs 81/15,83/19, 85/20; MB 69-73/210A, 77-81/102
20. ARs 83/19; LJ 83/May/24
21. AR 85/7; LJ 87/Nov/15
22. LJ 87/Nov/21
23. AR 90/8
24. LJ 90/Jul/19
25. MB 89/57
26. AR 87/26; LJ 88/Mar/26
27. ARs 89/28, 90/29; LJ 88/Mar/26
28. MB 94/8,16
29. LJ 91/Nov/5
30. AR 91/6,8, 10
31. AR 91/8
32. ARs 91/11, 95/11
33. ARs 93/11, 94/12
34. LJ 95/Jan/5
35. ARs 91/11, 93/13, 95/11
36. AR 95/11
37. Paper attached to Nat Council mtg 16 Jul 95; MB 94/30; LJ 95/Nov/6

**Chapter 20**

1. MB 69-73/204
2. AR 75/5; MB 69-73/150, 236, 73-5/97; LJ

75/July/2

3.    AR 80/7; MB 73-5/45, 63, 65, 129, 139, 147, 75-7/307; LJ 77/Jul/4
4.    ARs 73/10, 79/7; MB 73-5/11, 17B, 77-81/84, 105; LJs 76/Feb/8, July/7
5.    AR 79/7; MB 77-81/106, 166; LJ 79/Sep/16. Additional information from Col J Hughes.
6.    AR 79/7; MB 73-5/45, 75-7/226; LJs 75/Dec/8, 76/Aug/7, 80/May/3
7.    LJ 80/May/11
8.    AR 76/5; MB 77-81/25; LJs 76/Aug/13, Nov/9, 78/Sep/1, 79/Aug/4
9.    ARs 81/8, 85/8
10.   MB 94/7
11.   AR 93/7; MB 94/7, 36, paper attached to Nat Council meeting of 8 Apr 95. Additional information from Col J Hughes.
12.   MB 89/62
13.   LJs 84/July/24, 92/May/29

## Chapter 21

1.    AR 72/10
2.    AR 75/27; MB 69-73/158,167
3.    AR 75/6LJ 75/June/1
4.    LJ 71-2/Nov/23
5.    AR 71/17; LJ 71-2/June/16
6.    ARs 73/50, 74/36; MB 73-5/148; LJ 74/Nov/14
7.    ARs; LJ 72/25, 72-3/Oct/23
8.    ARs 72/71, 74/41-2; LJs 72/24, 72-3/Aug/23, 75/June/16
9.    ARs 74/36, 75/27; LJ 74/June/1
10.   MB 75-7/230
11.   LJ 76/June/1
12.   MB 75-7/244, 262, 286
13.   MB 75-7/305; LJ 77/June/5
14.   LJs 76/Sep/16, Oct/4
15.   MB 92/36
16.   MB 77-81/30
17.   AR 77/30
18.   ARs 77/30; LJs 78/June/1, 79/June/1
19.   ARs 76/31, 77/30, 78/8
20.   WSARs 82-3; LJ Conf 81/25, LJ 82/July/25, 83/July/32
21.   WSARs 83-4, 84-5
22.   AR 81/12, LJs 81/July/26, 82/July/22, 83/July/32
23.   WSAR 84-5; LJ 84/July/30
24.   LJ 85/July/35
25.   LJs 73-4/Dec/24, 83/Nov/29, 84/Nov/26
26.   LJ 84/May/30
27.   LJ 89/July/31
28.   WSARs 1986-90
29.   WSARs 1986-90
30.   WSAR 87-88; LJ 88/July/30-33
31.   WSAR 89-90
32.   WSAR 89-90
33.   AR 93; WSARs 85-86 to 89-90
34.   WSAR 1991-2; LJ 91/Sep/9
35.   WSARs 1991-95
36.   AR 93/27; MB 92/27; WSARs 1992-3 to 1994-5
37.   MB 95/6; WSARs 1993-4 to 94-5
38.   WSAR 1992-3 - 1994-5
39.   WSAR 1999-2 to 1994-5

## Chapter 22

1.    OAAR 70/8
2.    OAAR 75/7
3.    OAAR 71/8
4.    AR 71/65
5.    OAAR 75/13
6.    OAAR 78/18
7.    OAAR 78/18
8.    OAAR 77/11
9.    MB 81/A20
10.   OAAR 83/10
11.   OAAR 84/11
12.   OAAR 72/7
13.   AR 83/14
14.   AR 84/15; OAAR 84/13
15.   AR 84/15
16.   See ARs 1986 - 90 'Service Benevolent Funds'
17.   OAAR 90/10, 95/10
18.   OAAR 93/11
19.   OAAR 93/11

## Chapter 23

1.    ARs 96/13, 97/6; LJs 96/Nov/26, 00/Aug/5
2.    AR 99/16; LJ 99/Aug/5
3.    AR 99/3
4.    AR 96/9; LJ 99/Feb/8
5.    LJ 00/June/14
6.    AAccounts 97/7
7.    AR 99/5
8.    AR 99/6-9; Eire figures supplied by Head of Poppy Appeal and by Welfare Division at Legion HQ.
9.    AR 99/6-9
10.   LJ 99/Apr/5
11.   ARs 98/5, 99/8
12.   ARs 97/9, 98/16, 99/8, 14
13.   LJ 00/Oct/6
14.   AR 97/3-4, 5; LJ 98/Aug/12
15.   AR 98/6
16.   AR 98/6; WSAR 97
17.   OARs 98/7, 11, 99/9

# LIST OF ILLUSTRATIONS

# Acknowledgements

Imperial War Museum - pictures at pages 82, 96, 187.
Tophams - pictures at pages 100, 104, 158, 162, 233, 286, 332-333.
Hulton Getty - pictures at pages 90, 97.
The picture on the jacket of a Royal Marine was kindly supplied by Peter Holgate.

I am most grateful to all of those who helped to find the illustrations, particularly Alan Wakefield of the Imperial War Museum, Mrs Wendy Bromwich of the Women's Section of the Legion, Wing Commander Malcolm Caird of the Officers' Association, Alan Purdie of the Legion staff, Dave Burton of the Poppy Factory, Mark Presland of Royal British Legion Industries, Captain Ted Whealing, Legion Director of Music and David Evans, Managing Director of the Attendants' Company. If, however, the quality of any of the pictures is lower than it should be, it is my own judgement that is at fault.